THE LAST STAND OF THE TIN CAN SAILORS

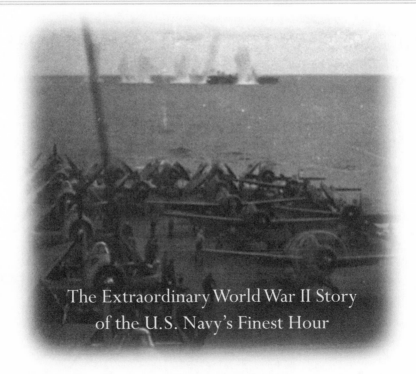

The Extraordinary World War II Story
of the U.S. Navy's Finest Hour

THE LAST STAND

of the

TIN CAN SAILORS

James D. Hornfischer

BANTAM BOOKS

THE LAST STAND OF THE TIN CAN SAILORS
A Bantam Book / February 2004

Published by
Bantam Dell
A Division of Random House, Inc.
New York, New York

See pages 485–486 for credits pertaining to photographs and art throughout.

Book design by Glen M. Edelstein

Maps and Order of Battle Illustrations by Hadel Studio inc.

Library of Congress Cataloging in Publication Data
Hornfischer, James D.
The last stand of the tin can sailors : the extraordinary World War II story of the U.S. Navy's finest hour / James D. Hornfischer.
p.   cm.
Includes bibliographical references and index.
ISBN 0-553-80257-7
1. Leyte Gulf, Battle of, Philippines, 1944.   2. World War, 1939–1945—Naval operations, American.   I. Title.
D774.L48H67 2004
940.54'25995—dc22   2003062792

Manufactured in the United States of America
Published simultaneously in Canada

10 9 8 7 6 5 4 3 2 1
BVG

To those in peril on the sea

Contents

Part I
Tin Cans   15

Part II
Last Stand   143

Part III
A Vanishing Graveyard   357

Part IV
Highest Traditions   403

Acknowledgments   429

Men of Task Unit 77.4.3
  Killed in Action,
  October 25–28, 1944   431

Bibliography   445

Source Notes   467

Photo and Art Credits   485

Index   489

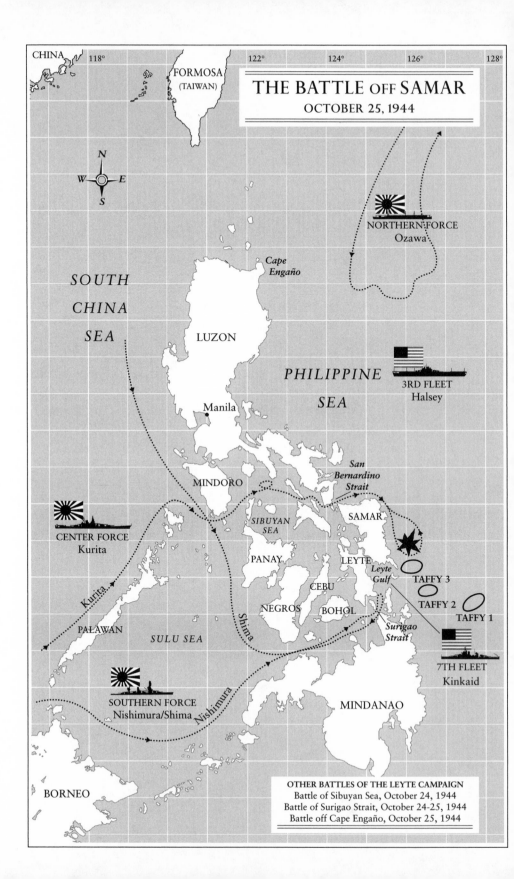

THE BATTLE OFF SAMAR
OCTOBER 25, 1944

CHINA

FORMOSA (TAIWAN)

118°   122°   124°   126°   128°

N
W E
S

NORTHERN FORCE
Ozawa

Cape Engaño

SOUTH CHINA SEA

LUZON

PHILIPPINE SEA

3RD FLEET
Halsey

Manila

San Bernardino Strait

MINDORO

SAMAR

CENTER FORCE
Kurita

SIBUYAN SEA

PANAY

LEYTE

Leyte Gulf

TAFFY 3

Kurita

CEBU

TAFFY 2

TAFFY 1

NEGROS

BOHOL

PALAWAN

SULU SEA

Shima

Surigao Strait

7TH FLEET
Kinkaid

SOUTHERN FORCE
Nishimura/Shima

Nishimura

MINDANAO

BORNEO

OTHER BATTLES OF THE LEYTE CAMPAIGN
Battle of Sibuyan Sea, October 24, 1944
Battle of Surigao Strait, October 24-25, 1944
Battle off Cape Engaño, October 25, 1944

THE INVASION OF LEYTE, PHILIPPINE ISLANDS
October 17–25, 1944

DRAMATIS PERSONAE

General Douglas MacArthur
Supreme Commander, Allied Forces, Southwest Pacific Area

U.S. Seventh Fleet ("MacArthur's Navy") and Leyte Invasion Force

Vice Adm. Thomas C. Kinkaid
Commander, Seventh Fleet and Task Force 77

> **Rear Adm. Daniel E. Barbey**
> Commander, Task Force 78

> **Vice Adm. Thomas S. Wilkinson**
> Commander, Task Force 79
> Invasion force, embarking Lt. Gen. Walter Krueger's Sixth Army

> **Rear Adm. Jesse B. Oldendorf**
> Commander, Seventh Fleet Bombardment and Fire Support Group
> Battleships and heavy cruisers

> **Rear Adm. Thomas L. Sprague**
> Commander, Task Group 77.4
> Escort Carrier Group
> "Taffy 1," **Rear Adm. Thomas L. Sprague**
> "Taffy 2," **Rear Adm. Felix B. Stump**
> "Taffy 3," **Rear Adm. Clifton A. F. Sprague**

Taffy 3 (Task Unit 77.4.3)

Northernmost escort carrier task unit of the Seventh Fleet, operating off the Philippine island of Samar

Rear Adm. Clifton A. F. ("Ziggy") Sprague

Escort Carriers (CVE)

Fanshaw Bay (flagship), **Capt. Douglass P. Johnson**
St. Lo, **Capt. Francis J. McKenna**
White Plains, **Capt. D. J. Sullivan**
Kalinin Bay, **Capt. T. B. Williamson**
Gambier Bay, **Capt. Walter V. R. Vieweg**
Kitkun Bay, **Capt. J. P. Whitney**

Screening Ships

Cdr. William D. Thomas

Destroyers (DD)

Hoel, **Cdr. Leon S. Kintberger**
Johnston, **Cdr. Ernest E. Evans**
Heermann, **Cdr. Amos T. Hathaway**

Destroyer Escorts (DE)

Samuel B. Roberts, **Lt. Cdr. Robert W. Copeland**
Dennis, **Lt. Cdr. Sig Hansen**
Raymond, **Lt. Cdr. A. F. Beyer**
John C. Butler, **Lt. Cdr. John E. Pace**

U.S. Navy

Fleet Adm. Chester W. Nimitz
Commander in Chief, Pacific Fleet

Adm. William F. Halsey, Jr.
Commander, Third Fleet

> **Vice Adm. Marc A. Mitscher**
> Commander, Task Force 38
> Fast Carrier Force

> **Vice Adm. John S. McCain**
> Commander, Task Group 38.1

> **Rear Adm. Gerald F. Bogan**
> Commander, Task Group 38.2

> **Rear Adm. Frederick C. Sherman**
> Commander, Task Group 38.3

> **Rear Adm. Ralph E. Davison**
> Commander, Task Group 38.4

Imperial Japanese Navy

Adm. Soemu Toyoda
Commander in Chief, Combined Fleet

The Sho-1 Plan (for the defense of the Philippines)

> **Vice Adm. Jisaburo Ozawa**
> Commander, Northern Force (decoy force)

> **Vice Adm. Takeo Kurita**
> Commander, Center Force

> **Vice Adm. Shoji Nishimura**
> Commander, Southern Force

> **Vice Adm. Kiyohide Shima**
> Commander, Southern Force (Second Striking Force)

October 25, 1944
San Bernardino Strait, the Philippines

A giant stalked through the darkness. In the moonless calm after midnight, the great fleet seemed not so much to navigate the narrow strait as to fill it with armor and steel. Barely visible even to a night-trained eye, the long silhouettes of twenty-three warships passed in a column ten miles long, guided by the dim glow of the channel lights in the passage threading between the headlands of Luzon and Samar.

That such a majestic procession should move without challenge was surprising, inexplicable even, in light of the vicious reception the Americans had already given it on its journey from Borneo to this critical point. Having weathered submarine ambush the night before, and assault by wave after wave of angry blue aircraft the previous afternoon, Vice Adm. Takeo Kurita, steward of the last hopes of the Japanese empire, would have been right to expect the worst. But then Kurita knew that heavenly influences could be counted upon to trump human planning. In war, events seldom cooperate with expectation. Given the dependable cruelty of the divine hand, most unexpected of all, perhaps, was this fact: unfolding at last after more than two years of retreat, Japan's ornate plan to defend the Philippines appeared to be working perfectly.

For its complexity, for its scale, for its extravagantly optimistic overelegance, the Sho plan represented the very best and also the very worst tendencies of the Imperial Navy. The Japanese military's fondness for bold strokes had been evident from the earliest days of the war: the sudden strike on Pearl Harbor, the sprawling offensive into the Malay Peninsula, the lightning thrust into the Philippines, and the smaller but no less swift raids on Wake Island, Guam, Hong Kong, and northern Borneo. Allied commanders believed the Japanese could not tackle more than one objective at a time. The sudden spasm of advances of December 1941, in which Japan struck with overwhelming force in eight directions at once, refuted that fallacy.

In the war's early days, Japan had overwhelmed enemies stretched thin by the need to defend their scattered colonies throughout the hemisphere. But as the war continued, the geographical breadth of its conquests saddled Japan in turn with the necessity of piecemeal defense. America rallied, the home front's spirits boosted by the gallant if doomed defense of Wake Island and by Jimmy Doolittle's raid on Tokyo. As heavier blows landed—the Battle of the Coral Sea, the triumph at Midway, the landings on Guadalcanal and the leapfrogging campaign through the Solomons and up the northern coast of New Guinea—Japan's overstretched domain was in turn overrun by the resurgent Americans. The hard charge of U.S. Marines up the bloody path of Tarawa, the Marshalls, and the Marianas Islands had put American forces, by the middle of 1944, in position to sever the vital artery connecting the Japanese home islands to their resource-rich domain in East Asia. The Philippines were that pressure point. Their seizure by the Americans would push the entire Japanese empire toward collapse.

The strength America wielded in its counteroffensive was the nightmare prophecy foretold by Adm. Isoroku Yamamoto and other far-sighted Japanese commanders who had long dreaded war with an industrial giant. As two great American fleets closed in on the Philippines in October, with Gen. Douglas MacArthur's troops spearheading the ground assault on the Philippine island of Leyte, Japan activated its own last-ditch plan to forestall the inevitable defeat. It was unfolding now. Admiral Kurita was its linchpin.

The Sho plan's audacity—orchestrating the movements of four fleets spread across thousands of miles of ocean and the land-based aircraft necessary to protect them—was both its genius and its potentially disastrous weakness. Adm. Jisaburo Ozawa, leading the remnants of Japan's once glorious naval air arm, would steam south from Japan with his aircraft carriers and try to lure the American fast carrier groups north, away from Leyte. With the U.S. flattops busy pursuing the decoy, two Japanese battleship groups would close on Leyte from the north and south and deal MacArthur a surprise, killing blow.

Admiral Kurita had departed Brunei on October 22 with his powerful Center Force, led by the *Yamato* and the *Musashi,* the two largest warships afloat, aiming to slip across the South China Sea, pass through San Bernardino Strait above Samar Island, and close on the Leyte beachhead from the north. Meanwhile, the Southern Force, led by Vice Adm. Shoji Nishimura and supported by Vice Adm. Kiyohide Shima, would cross the Sulu Sea and approach Leyte from the south, through Surigao Strait.

On the morning of October 25, after their thousand-mile journeys through perilous waters, Kurita's and Nishimura's battleship groups would rendezvous at 9:00 A.M. off Leyte Island's eastern shore, encircling the islands like hands around a throat. Then they would turn their massive guns on MacArthur's invasion force. Japan would at last win the decisive battle that had eluded it in the twenty-eight months since the debacle at Midway.

Kurita's grandfather had been a great scholar of early Meiji literature. His father too had been a distinguished man of learning, author of a magisterial history of his native land. In the morning Takeo Kurita, who preferred action to words, would make his own contribution.

Off Samar

Gathered around the radio set in the combat information center of the destroyer escort USS *Samuel B. Roberts,* they listened as a hundred miles to their south, their heavier counterparts in the Seventh Fleet encountered the first signs that the Japanese defense of the Philippines was under way. There was no telling precisely what their countrymen faced. It was something big—that much was for sure. And yet, until the scale of the far-off battle became too apparent to ignore, they would pretend it was just another midwatch. By the routine indications, it was. They watched the radar scopes and the scopes watched back, bathing the darkened compartment in cathode-green fluorescence but revealing no enemy nearby. The southwest Pacific slept. But something was on the radio, and it put the lie to the silent night.

The tactical circuit they were using to eavesdrop was meant for sending and receiving short-range messages from ship to ship. Officers used it to trade scuttlebutt with other vessels about what their radar was showing, about their course changes, about the targets they were tracking. By day, the high-frequency Talk Between Ships signal reached only to the line of sight. But tonight, the earth's atmosphere was working its magic and the TBS broadcasts from faraway ships were propagating wildly, bouncing over the horizon to the small warship's vigilant antennae.

They had come from small places to accomplish big things. As the American liberation of the Philippines unfolded, the greenhorn enlistees who made up the majority of the *Samuel B. Roberts*'s 224-man complement could scarcely have guessed at the scope of the drama to come. On the midnight-to-four-A.M. midwatch, the *Roberts*'s skipper, Lt. Cdr. Robert W. Copeland, his executive officer, Lt. Everett E. "Bob" Roberts, his communications officer, Lt. Tom Stevenson, and the young men under them in the little ship's combat information center (CIC) had little else to do than while away the night as the destroyer escort zigzagged lazily off the eastern coast of Samar with the twelve other ships of its task unit, the small, northernmost contingent of the sprawling Seventh Fleet. When morning warmed the eastern horizon, the daily routine would begin anew: run through morning general quarters, then edge closer to shore with the six light aircraft carriers that were the purpose of the flotilla's existence and launch air strikes in support of the American troops advancing into Leyte Island.

With a mixture of pride and resignation, the men of the Seventh Fleet called themselves "MacArthur's Navy." The unusual arrangement that placed the powerful armada under Army command was the product of the long-standing interservice rivalry. The two service branches, each wildly successful, were beating divergent paths to Tokyo. From June 1943 to August 1944, MacArthur's forces had leapfrogged across the southern Pacific, staging eighty-seven successful amphibious landings in a drive from Dutch New Guinea and west-by-northwestward across a thousand-mile swath of islanded sea to the foot of the Philippine archipelago. Simultaneously, Adm. Chester W. Nimitz's fast carrier groups, accompanied by battle-hardened Marine divisions, had driven across the Central Pacific.

The perpetual motion of the American industrial machine had built a naval and amphibious arsenal of such staggering size, range, and striking power that the vast sea seemed to shrink around it. "Our naval power in the western Pacific was such that we could have challenged the combined fleets of the world," Adm. William F. Halsey, Jr., would write in his memoirs. The rival commanders had used it so well that the Pacific Ocean was no longer large enough to hold their conflicting ambitions. There was little of the Pacific left to liberate. Behind them lay conquered ground. Ahead, looking westward to the Philippines and beyond, was a short watery vista bounded by the shores of Manchuria, China, and Indonesia. Once the Far East had seemed a world away. Allied soldiers, Marines, sailors, and airmen operating along the far Pacific rim early in the war—the Flying Tigers in China, the U.S. Asiatic Fleet in Java, the Marines on Wake Island, the defenders of Bataan and Corregidor—were consigned to oblivion, so desperately far from home. Now that U.S. forces had crossed that world, the greatest challenge was to agree on how to deliver the inevitable victory as quickly as possible.

For most of the summer of 1944 a debate had raged between Army and Navy planners about where to attack next. On July 21 Franklin Delano Roosevelt, newly nominated at the Chicago Democratic Convention for a fourth presidential term, boarded the heavy cruiser *Baltimore* at San Diego and sailed to Oahu for a summit meeting of his Army and Navy leaders. In a sober discussion after dinner at the presidential residence in Honolulu, Nimitz and MacArthur repeated to their commander in chief the same arguments they had been espousing to the Joint Chiefs of Staff these many weeks. The Navy preferred an assault on Formosa (now Taiwan). MacArthur had other priorities. On a large map FDR pointed to Mindanao Island, southernmost in the Philippine archipelago, and asked, "Douglas, where do we go from here?"

Without hesitation, MacArthur replied, "Leyte, Mr. President, and then Luzon!"

It had been nearly three years since Bataan fell and the American Caesar fled that haunted peninsula by night aboard a PT boat, arrived in Mindanao, and boarded a B-17 bomber for Australia to endure the exile of the defeated. On March 20, 1942, at a press conference at the Adelaide train station, he declared, "The President of the United States ordered me to break through the Japanese lines . . . for the purpose, as I understand it, of organizing the American offensive against Japan, a primary object of which is the relief of the Philippines. I came through and I shall return." Torn from context and conflated to a national commitment, "I shall return" became MacArthur's calling card and his albatross.

For the general, fulfilling his famous promise to the Philippine people was not solely a question of military strategy but also a point of personal and national honor. He told his president of the backlash in public opinion that might arise if the United States abandoned seventeen million loyal Filipinos to their Japanese conquerors. And the lives of some 3,700 American prisoners—the ravaged survivors of Bataan and Corregidor—would fall in immediate peril if the archipelago were bypassed and its occupying garrison starved out, a strategy many U.S. planners favored after seeing it succeed against other Japanese strongholds.

Nimitz reiterated the Navy's preference for driving further westward to seize Formosa. Such a move would land a more decisive blow against the long communications and supply lines that linked Tokyo to its bases and fuel supplies in Sumatra and Borneo. MacArthur and Nimitz made their best arguments, and after extended discussion FDR sided with his general. MacArthur had flown in with virtually no time to prepare. Such was the force of his personality and persuasive gifts that even Admiral Nimitz was ultimately won over. The Philippines—Leyte—would be next.

And so it began. Two great fleets gathered at staging areas at Manus in the Admiralty Islands and at Ulithi in the Carolines for the final assault on the Philippines. Under MacArthur, as it had been since March 1943, was Vice Adm. Thomas C. Kinkaid's Seventh Fleet. Nimitz retained the Third Fleet, which sailed under the flag of Admiral Halsey.

The Seventh Fleet had a wide variety of ships to ferry and supply the invasion force itself. In addition to an alphabet soup of troop-, tank-, and equipment-carrying landing craft—APAs, LSTs, LSDs, LSMs, LCTs, LCIs and LVTs—it had amphibious command ships, ammunition ships, cargo ships, oilers, seaplane tenders, motor torpedo boats, patrol craft, coast guard frigates, minesweepers, mine-layers, repair and salvage ships, water tankers, floating drydocks, and hospital ships. Standing guard over this wide assortment of hulls were the combatant vessels of the Seventh Fleet: Jesse Oldendorf's bombardment group, composed of battleships and cruisers, and, farther offshore, Task Group 77.4, a force of sixteen escort carriers under Rear Adm. Thomas L. Sprague, divided into three task units and screened by destroyers and destroyer escorts.

On October 20, 1944, two and a half years after retreating from the strategic archipelago, Douglas MacArthur, Supreme Commander, Allied Forces, Southwest Pacific Area, made good on his grand promise. At seven A.M. sharp, the Seventh Fleet battleships *Maryland, West Virginia,* and *Mississippi* trained their main batteries on Leyte Island's beaches and hills and opened fire on the conquerors and murderers of Bataan. The American liberation of the Philippines was under way. For exactly two hours the massive rifles roared. Then, precisely on schedule, the shelling stopped and Higgins boats began spilling out of the larger ships that housed them. Lt. Gen. Walter Krueger's troops clambered down rope ladders thrown over the sides, the landing craft circling until their full number had gathered. Then the invasion force spiraled out into a series of waves that surged across San Pedro Bay and broke on Leyte's eastern shore.

As two corps of Sixth Army soldiers pushed inland from the coastal towns of Dulag and Tacloban, newspapers back home captivated the public with reports of the ongoing offensive. MACARTHUR RETURNS TO PHILIPPINES IN PERSONAL COMMAND OF AMERICANS. FDR VOICES GRATITUDE FOR NATION. The drama had been stage-managed from the beginning. On Leyte's Red Beach the cameras were ready for the general's star turn, carefully positioned to capture the liberator coming ashore. He obliged them with a flourish, wading from a landing craft ramp to inspect the damage inflicted by the Navy's bombardment. Then, with Philippine president Sergio Osmeña at his side, General MacArthur, resplendent in pressed khakis, sunglasses, and marshal's cap, corncob pipe in hand, leaned into a microphone held by an Army Signal Corps volunteer and spoke to history:

This is the voice of freedom, General MacArthur speaking. People of the Philippines! I have returned. By the grace of Almighty God, our forces stand again on Philippine soil—soil conse-

crated in the blood of our two peoples. . . . Rally to me. Let the indomitable spirit of Bataan and Corregidor lead on. As the lines of battle roll forward to bring you within the zone of operations, rise and strike. . . . The guidance of divine God points the way. Follow in His Name to the Holy Grail of righteous victory!

If anyone aboard the *Samuel B. Roberts* fancied that his ship would be spearheading something so grand as a God-inspired drive to righteous victory, he was probably wise to keep it to himself. The destroyer escort was but a tiny cog in this unimaginably large and capable engine of war, its men smaller still, though collectively they were the long arm and clenched fist of an enraged democracy at war. Their flotilla, Task Unit 77.4.3, with the radio call sign Taffy 3, was far from center stage. One of three escort carrier task units positioned off Samar to watch MacArthur's back, Taffy 3 had a supporting role, vital in its way if unlikely to generate for its leaders headlines to match those of its theater commander. Its six squadrons of FM-2 Wildcat fighters and TBM Avenger torpedo bombers flew air cover for, and struck ahead of, the American troops advancing ashore. As the planes came and went from their oceangoing hives, seven small warships—destroyers and destroyer escorts, including the *"Sammy B."*—steamed in a protective ring that encircled Taffy 3's escort carriers.

Like the twelve other skippers in Taffy 3, Captain Copeland well knew that his task unit was far from being the most formidable American force operating in the Leyte Gulf area. As the happenstance transmissions coming to him via the TBS circuit now reminded him, that honor belonged to Admiral Oldendorf's battle line. Steaming a hundred miles to Taffy 3's south, the six battleships of Oldendorf's Bombardment and Fire Support Group were the Seventh Fleet's heavy hitters. Five of them—the *California,* the *Maryland,* the *Pennsylvania,* the *Tennessee,* and the *West Virginia*—were scarred veterans of Pearl Harbor. Each had absorbed the enemy's treacherous blow on that Sunday morning nearly three years before. Now, lifted from the harbor mud, refloated, refitted, and sent to rejoin the Pacific Fleet, they were together again. They had set a trap in the deadly gauntlet of Surigao Strait, and tonight that trap was closing on one of several Japanese fleets sailing to challenge MacArthur's invasion.

Dawn was still hours away as Copeland's officers and the rest of the crew in the *Sammy B.*'s CIC gathered to listen to an accidental play-by-play broadcast of an era in naval warfare thundering to a close. They did not immediately grasp the significance of the rogue bursts of radiation that skittered off the nighttime ionosphere and into their shipboard radio receiver. The signal—now crisp and clear, bringing the voices to them as if over an intercom, now cut through with static, incomplete—gave them only hints of what was happening in waters far to the south. They were American voices, Navy voices: upright, impersonal, but girded with the confidence that comes from long hours of drill and training. Their tenor and cadence had a practiced nonchalance, but there was no escaping the sense that down in Surigao Strait, big things were happening.

"Skunk 184 degrees, 18 miles."

"Captain of McDermut *is taking first target, you take one farthest north."*

"Proceed to attack. Follow down west shoreline. Follow other groups in. Then retire to north. Make smoke."

On most nights, Bob Copeland and the others in the CIC gladly hit the sack when the midwatch ended at four A.M. But tonight the escalating drama of the events in Surigao Strait had moved them past the point of needing or wanting sleep. They were camped out for the long haul. Sleep could wait. As the men of the morning watch began to rouse themselves to relieve the midwatch, the voices on the radio were joined in chorus by the sound of something else: gunfire.

"Fish are away."

"This is going to be quick."

"I have a group of small ones followed by a group of large ones. When the large ones reach twenty-six thousand yards, I will open fire."

Twenty-six thousand yards. Fourteen and three-quarter statute miles. To a sailor aboard a destroyer escort, the reach of a battleship's big guns inspired awe. When they fired, sending their armor-piercing bullet trains shrieking out over the horizon, shooting out of a thunderhead of cordite smoke, the shock wave flattened the seas around them. The full sonic experience of the shelling could not be appreciated over the radio. Indeed, it could seldom be fully appreciated by anyone other than its target. But the sudden sharp cracks of the great guns now and again obliterated the voices coming over the speaker.

The sound and the fury stirred the men's imagination and their curiosity.

If they switched off the TBS radio, it would all have gone away. The echoes of the American battle line loosing hell to their south would have vanished, leaving them contemplating their blank radar scopes. Since its defeat in the Marianas Islands in June, the Japanese Navy had stayed out of sight, gathering its strength for a final showdown. Now it was increasingly apparent that MacArthur's move against the Philippines had at last stirred it to action.

In the radio shack next to the CIC, the *Roberts*'s communications department—Tom Stevenson's group—had been picking up an unusual amount of radio traffic. It was all in code, its meaning mysterious until the inscrutable five-character sequences could be transcribed and decrypted by radiomen using decoding wheels. The only unfiltered real-time information they got came via the Talk Between Ships radio. They sat around the plotting table, studying charts, building a visual picture from the clues coming over the TBS frequency. As the fragmentary broadcasts began to resolve into a notion of what was happening in the narrow straits south of Leyte Gulf, no level of drill or training could quite suppress their jubilation.

They felt no concern for their own safety. The flanks of Taffy 3—and of their sibling task units Taffy 1 and Taffy 2—were guarded by the Seventh and Third Fleets, the greatest gathering of naval strength the world had yet seen. Let the Imperial Japanese Navy come to challenge the invasion. The contest had begun, and the men aboard the *Samuel B. Roberts* had it right there on the radio.

*　　*　　*

OUTSIDE, FROM HIS WATCH station in the starboard twenty-millimeter gun tub just forward of the bridge, seaman second class George Bray, an enlistee from Montgomery, Alabama, saw quick flashes of light illuminating the southern horizon and figured them for a storm. Most of the enlisteds had no particular love for the ocean, and the rainy season in the southwestern Pacific seemed to do its level best to keep things that way. A few days before, en route to their station off the island of Samar, the *Roberts* and her consorts had been swallowed by an unexpected typhoon. The ship had rolled so sharply—to fifty-nine degrees on the inclinometer—that at terrifying intervals it was easier to walk on bulkheads than stand on deck. The rolling lasted for three full days. Most of the crew who had not been to sea before lay in their bunks, paralyzed by nausea. But the pitching hull permitted that luxury only to the resourceful. After a few hard falls out of the sack to the deck, a bluejacket learned to sleep—or suffer—with a leg hooked around the chain that suspended his bunk from the ceiling.

As ever, sailors learned to get by. In the mess, they could press a slice of wet bread under their supper tray to keep their meal on the table—when nausea permitted them to stomach a meal, that is. Some retched so badly they thought they might die. When landlubbing enlistees from plains states felt the ship heel over to starboard—thirty-five, forty, forty-five degrees—then make the long, creaking roll back to port, it was natural for them to fear the ship would sink. After suffering through a days-long spell of the cork-in-a-washtub gyrations, it was just as natural to worry that the ship might remain afloat. When the three-day ordeal was over, the feeling that the poor troops ashore were getting a raw deal had abated if not entirely disappeared.

With memories of the typhoon fresh in his mind, Bray turned and shouted up to the wing of the bridge, where Bob Copeland had come for a breath of fresh air and a look at the action on the horizon. "Hey, Captain, look at that storm."

"That's not a storm, son," Copeland said. "It's a battle. We've got it on the radio in here."

A battle. George Bray hadn't been a shellback long enough to weigh knowledgeably the risks of possible combat against the perils of another hungry typhoon. For now, the Alabaman was glad simply to have something to look at, because nine nights out of ten the lone benefit of the midwatch was relief from the stale heat of the poorly ventilated sleeping quarters belowdecks. Navy men went to great lengths to find breathable air in the torrid latitudes of the South Pacific. You slept on deck if you could; under a blower or an air duct failing that. When no officer was looking, radioman third class Dick Rohde would stretch his standard-issue hammock from the bridge wing to a superstructure sponson and sack out, dangling from the starboard side of the ship. Whenever the ship went over to starboard, his makeshift aerie, with Rohde in it, would swing out over the open ocean. If it rained, the cool, fresh water rolling off the roof of the pilothouse would cascade down over him. He wouldn't have had it any other way.

If fresh air was the reward of the midnight deck watch, boredom was its potentially steep price. Snoozing on duty was a sure route to Captain's Mast, a disciplinary proceeding where an enlisted man who was found guilty as charged could get busted down a rating or win himself eight hours of extra duty, possibly in that hell-on-earth known as the engine room. Though life in the wartime Navy was full of potentially catastrophic risk, mostly it was isolated and monotonous, broken only by the regimented pleasures of watching movies and opening mail from home. As the ship made its way, steaming, always steaming, yet never seeming to arrive at an actual destination, Bray and the three others in his gun mount took turns standing and sitting in pairs. While two of the men sat down and shot the breeze, the other two would stand, one with binoculars, the other donning headphones with a ready link to the officer of the deck on the bridge.

Now the sudden spectacle of the distant pyrotechnics—the blooming and vanishing oases of light beneath the Pacific's vast vaulting darkness—concentrated Bray's attention. As he watched the gunfire backlight the southern horizon, a thought began pecking in the corner of his mind:

If that's a battle, well, God Almighty, what might we be getting into?

San Bernardino Strait

Sunrise would come at 6:27 A.M. on the day that might well settle the endgame, if not the outcome, of the long struggle in the Pacific. As the mightiest ships of the Imperial Japanese Navy boomed through the northern strait toward the wide waters of the Philippine Sea and the slumbering dawn, Admiral Kurita dared hope that the Sho plan might succeed. He had suffered losses severe enough to deter most commanders—the great battleship *Musashi,* victim of five waves of air strikes the afternoon before; three heavy cruisers, sunk or forced home by submarine attack. But battle was not new to him, nor loss.

Kurita's tenure with the fleet was deep. During the invasion of Java in March 1942, he had led the Japanese cruiser force that sank the USS *Houston* and HMAS *Perth* in Sunda Strait. He had commanded the heavy cruiser *Mikuma,* sunk at Midway, the battleship

Kongo during the audacious Japanese bombardment of Guadal-canal's Henderson Field, and the aircraft carriers that had covered the Tokyo Express, as the daring Japanese effort to resupply the be-sieged Solomon Islands became known. In the disastrous battle in the Marianas Islands in June, he had the distinction of being the only es-cort commander not to lose any of the carriers he was shepherding. The losses he had suffered on the present mission were but the latest chapter in a career scarred smooth by battle. According to an Ameri-can historian, Kurita "had been bombed and torpedoed more often than almost any other Japanese admiral."

So much lay behind him; what lay ahead? Though the night was yet clear as he exited San Bernardino Strait after midnight on Octo-ber 25, events were moving through the thickest of fogs. Of his coun-trymen—Admiral Ozawa and his decoy force, Nishimura in the south—he had had no word. Poor radio communications meant that he would not learn of their success or failure until it was far too late for the news to matter.

There was no telling what would greet Takeo Kurita in the rain-squalls to the east, beyond Samar Island. At the moment, American eyes were looking elsewhere. Soon the whole world would be watch-ing. For now, all that was watching him were the sharks.

Part I

TIN CANS

"Captain, how often does a little ship like this sink?"
"Usually just once."

—*The Gismo,* newsletter of the USS *Samuel B. Roberts,* September 30, 1944

One

On January 20, 1944, three months prior to the commissioning ceremony that would make it a U.S. Navy warship, the welded hull of DE-413, its prow festively draped in red, white, and blue bunting, slid off the ways at the Brown Shipbuilding Company and entered the Houston Ship Channel with a roaring sidelong splash. At the launching ceremony, administered by the employees of Brown's pipe department, a prayer was said to be in the hearts of all who watched: "May she be a sound ship, capable of rising to the heights when her supreme moment comes."

The hull that would become the USS *Samuel B. Roberts* had been laid down alongside the hull that would become her sister ship, the *Walter C. Wann,* on December 6, 1943. Two weeks later the twins were moved from their initial production stations, and work began on the *Le Ray Wilson* and the *Lawrence C. Taylor.* From July 1942 to March 1944 the shipwrights, marine electricians, pipefitters, machinists, and welders at Brownship would turn out sixty-one destroyer escorts, one pair following the next with punch-clock efficiency.

As the shipyard workers continued making the *Roberts* ready for sea, installing gun mounts, laying ducts and wiring, and testing the ship's many internal systems, a group of newly minted seamen left the naval training center at Norfolk, Virginia, and boarded a train to

Houston to fill out the ship's complement of seamen and rated petty officers. The weathered World War I–era passenger train took five days to make the trip. The recruits' place in the world was reflected not only in the nineteenth-century decor of their accommodations— a potbellied stove warmed one end of the car; gas lamps lit their card games—but in the unceremonious manner by which their train got shunted aside whenever a line of boxcars had to get through. During wartime, and decades before America would develop a culture of personal convenience, there was no denying that cargo could be as important as men.

Once, interminably delayed while a long freight train squealed by ahead of them, the enlistees, accompanied by the two youngest ensigns assigned to the *Samuel B. Roberts,* John LeClercq and Dudley Moylan, piled out of their passenger car and passed the time riding cows bareback in a pasture. Another time, stuck in a mountain railyard with nowhere to go, they got off the train, took over a rural diner, and helped cook their own dinner. Three railcars full of young sailors and no drill-field exercises to burden their days—it was a memory that would grow dearer with time, and it bonded them as only the great adventures of youth can.

What the kids had gone through in basic training was meant to adjust their perspective on their relative individual worth in this new world. For teenagers entering military service during wartime, the shock of boot camp was bracing, equalizing. It leveled the little hills and valleys of socioeconomic differences, broke down egos, and made new recruits glad to end up wherever the Navy Department's Bureau of Personnel might send them. When Dick Rohde, son of a New York City ship chandler who went broke in the Depression, arrived at boot camp in Newport, Rhode Island, he first encountered the well-calibrated cruelty that would ensure his smooth entry into the wartime fleet.

Sharply dressed in his neatly pressed uniform, the boot camp company commander, as World War II–era Navy drill instructors were known, lined his men up at first muster and addressed them gently. "I know what it's like for you guys. A couple days ago you were home with your mothers and fathers. Now all of a sudden here you are. You're up in this strange part of the country. You've been rooted out of your homes. You're homesick. You've got your hair all shaved off and you got those shots. I just want to tell you that for the next six weeks, I'm going to be your mother and your father. I'm going to make sure things go just as nicely for you as possible. That's the reason I'm here. If there's any way I can accomplish these things I'm gonna do it. I want you to know that."

Well, this I can handle, Rohde thought. Maybe it wasn't so bad that the Marines had turned him away, the big sergeant behind the desk saying something alluringly dismissive like, "Go home and grow up and then come back and we'll talk to you." Rohde didn't go home. He went around the corner to the Navy recruiter, who had ready good use for an eager seventeen-year-old. Let the Marines slog through mud—Dick Rohde from Staten Island was going to sea.

"Now, I'm going to call the roll," the company commander said. "I don't know how to pronounce some of your names, so if I make a mistake, please correct me." He got down to Rohde on the list and called out, *"Road?"*

"Uh, sir, that's *Rohde,*" his young charge offered, emphasizing the long *e.*

The company commander walked up to the freshly cropped boot, and it was then that Rohde discovered the true nature of the instructor he had dared to admire. "No, that's *Shithead!*" he roared. "Your name from now on is *Shithead!*"

Thus began a six-week program of drill-field marching, obstacle-course running, weapon maintenance, latrine cleaning, and more. Each morning when Rohde's name came up at muster, the company commander called out *"Shithead?"* When Rohde's mother heard about the treatment her son was getting at the hands of the U.S. Navy, she vowed to blow the lid off the scandal through the good offices of Mr. Walter Winchell and his little newspaper column. Her son put an end to that plan. Perhaps mothers were poorly equipped to appreciate the educational value of scrubbing a concrete courtyard with a medium-bristled toothbrush. Dick Rohde survived boot camp. He became a sailor.

Rohde had skills the Navy prized. As a one-time page to a Wall Street investment banker, he was a proficient typist. That, combined with the rudimentary Morse code he had learned in radio club at Staten Island's Curtis High School, set him up to strike for a radioman's rating. With new ships launching daily from shipyards all around the country, bodies were needed—and minds too. There was a shortage of trained radiomen to man the sets. In March 1944 Dick

Rohde went to the U.S. Naval Training School in Boston, where radiomen were made.

The genius of the Navy's personnel system was that it sorted young men by their talents, trained them for specialized duty, and funneled them to places where their knowledge would benefit the nation most. A recruit with promise in a particular technical area could go to a service school to study a specialty. Someone with a keen ear for pitch recognition would be encouraged to attend sound school in Key West, Florida, where he learned to operate sonar equipment. An enlistee with an engineering background might be a candidate for radar school at MIT in Cambridge. Most recruits went straight to sea, where they got about the sweaty business of scraping paint, loading supplies, maintaining equipment, and doing anything else the petty officers said needed doing. Seamen who discovered their callings aboard ship could affiliate themselves with a particular department and "strike for a rating" in that area. A sailor with the designation "seaman first class (radioman striker)" would be the gofer of the radio department. As long as he didn't slip too often with the coffeepot, he would in time get promoted to radioman third class, a petty officer rating that signified his expertise in the chosen field.

After completing basic training at Newport and graduating from radio school in Boston, Rohde went to the receiving station at Norfolk, Virginia, where like scores of men he awaited assignment to a ship and got further training. The training never quite ended, for there was always something else to learn. At Norfolk Rohde's training went beyond drill-field rote and began to reflect the realities of life under fire. One day he entered a large room enclosing an indoor swimming pool. Into one end of the pool was poured fuel oil, which was summarily set alight. He and his fellow seaman recruits were directed to jump into the smoking, flaming water, to splash the burning fuel away from them, and to make their way to the clean end of the pool. Nary an eyelash was singed, but their minds were seared indelibly with a glimpse of what might lie ahead.

Like many others in the mob that had boarded that train in Norfolk, George Bray had not joined the Navy looking for a fight. Like most enlisted men, he was a pragmatist. The calculus was simple: a war was on. If you were eighteen or older, the thing to do was join the service. If you were seventeen, you could get a parent to sign your enlistment papers. Or you could just lie about your age. Ends justified means: if you wanted to impress a girl, your best bet was to get yourself in uniform as quickly as possible. The only question was what service you preferred.

When the Japanese hit Pearl Harbor and the war started, Bray had been as eager to sign on as the next kid. But he tempered idealism with practicality. He looked at the options available to him and chose the Navy for reasons that recruiters surely exploited in the 1940s: he would get three meals a day, clean bed linens, and none of the trench-humping that was the daily lot of the infantryman.

Not that Bray was a shrinking violet. Back in Alabama he had made the high school varsity football team as a seventh grader. He was a hard-nosed halfback, adept at catching passes out of a Notre Dame–style T formation, which had come into fashion in 1943 when Fighting Irish quarterback Angelo Bertelli brought it to South Bend and won the national championship and the Heisman Trophy along the way. Halfway through his senior year Bertelli had joined the Marines. If military service was good enough for one magician of the T formation, it was good enough for another. And so Bray found himself aboard the U.S. Navy's smallest man-of-war, a destroyer escort.

In Houston the men came aboard the *Roberts* as it was undergoing a final fitting out prior to the commissioning ceremony that would convert it from the private property of the Brown Shipbuilding Company to a public asset as a United States Ship. Those who came by train found that their Spartan accommodations had been good preparation for shipboard life. Their bunks on the *Roberts* were three-high, with forty or fifty men to a compartment. There was little venting, let alone air-conditioning. But comfort is an afterthought for a teenager on the cusp of adventure. Dick Rohde swooned at the thought of what was in store for him in the Pacific. "There was always something new, always something exciting," he said. "We weren't homesick at all. It was just 'Wow, what's going to happen next?' "

Two

What happened next would be up to Bob Copeland. It was his world—the enlisted men just lived in it. The commander of three previous ships, Captain Copeland, a naval reservist from Tacoma who had left behind a budding legal career to assume his fourth command, arrived in Houston on March 4, 1944, and instantly liked what he saw in the *Roberts*. Holed up at the Rice Hotel while the ship neared completion, he and his officers spent each day at the shipyard, watching the nondescript slab of metal become a warship.

Fair-minded, firm, and shrewd, Copeland, at the advanced age of thirty-three years, had a rare gift: the ability to assert his authority and make his men like it, both at the same time. No one on the *Samuel B. Roberts* was ever heard bellyaching that they had gotten a raw deal from Bob Copeland. He wasn't above turning to an enlisted man and asking, "So, how's your family?" If he saw a picture of a sailor's girlfriend on a desk, he would be likely to ask, "You still hearing from her?" He led his crew from a position of trust. And they trusted him for his ability to lead.

The skipper of the *Roberts* had been a lawyer exactly as long as he had been an officer. Commissioned as an ensign the same day he was admitted to the Washington State Bar Association, he had maintained a trial law practice in Tacoma while fulfilling his commitment to the naval reserve, with meetings one night a week. The fact that Bob Copeland was not "regular Navy"—an Annapolis graduate with a full commission and a full-time job in the fleet—owed more to his sense of family duty than to a lack of devotion to naval service.

Like the rest of his generation who grew up amid the patriotism and Wilsonian high-mindedness of World War I, Copeland had come of age aspiring to be a warrior. Eight years old when the Great War ended, he had spent his childhood infused with enthusiasm for playtime war, prancing around in doughboy getup, tin hat cocked over his forehead, stockings pulled up over his calves, wooden rifle at the ready. In his teenage years, when his peers had moved on to playing sports, Bob Copeland was up in his room running his own private navy. He kept his fleet on paper, order of battle formed up, a command hierarchy drawn. Though his devotion to naval strategy might have led him to neglect certain skills that would be useful at sea— such as the ability to swim—it filled his imagination and prepared him for the managerial reality of command.

At a critical juncture in his young life, he had been offered the chance to attend Annapolis. Every Fourth of July young Bob Copeland watched the fleet weigh anchor in Tacoma's Commencement Bay to help the city celebrate Independence Day. Destroyers, cruisers, and battleships, and the Admiral. The Admiral was there. The opportunity was not lost on Bob Copeland. He aimed to see the Admiral, if only he could buck up his courage to make the trip. Every day he went down to the docks where small boats ferried townsfolk out to see the ships. But each day Copeland's nerve failed him. Finally, on the last day the fleet was to be there in July 1927, he mustered the will to amble aboard the small harbor ferry and go see the Admiral. Tucked in his pocket was a letter of introduction from the mayor of Tacoma. He approached the flagship, climbed aboard, and handed the envelope to the officer of the deck. The letter was passed to the executive officer, then to the Admiral himself.

Before Copeland could grasp what was happening, an invitation was extended to him. He would see the Admiral in his flag quarters. A kid who commanded a world-beating fleet on paper was permitted to sit down and talk to a man who earned his living doing the real thing. They talked for hours. Copeland's knowledge of naval history, his appreciation for fleet organization and command, won him an unexpected prize: the Admiral told him he should go to Annapolis.

Better than that, the Admiral wrote a letter. To Copeland's congressional representative. Who wrote a letter. To the commandant of Annapolis. An appointment to the Naval Academy was there for the taking.

But his mother, who had an extreme, unreasoning fear of water, could not abide the idea of her only child going to sea. So the family doctor was summoned. He mustered his most ominous tone of voice and said to the seventeen-year-old something like this: "Robert, your mother's health concerns me deeply. She might very well have a heart attack if you decide to enter the service. Please don't cause her this stress." Born to his parents ten years into their marriage, Copeland knew that he was a long-wished-for and only child. He decided that he could not inflict such pain on his mother. Bob Copeland, the dutiful only son, declined his appointment to the breeding ground of admirals.

He would settle for living in smaller worlds. In 1929, Copeland enlisted in the naval reserve and, six years later, was commissioned as a naval reserve officer, coincident with his completion of law school. Having fulfilled his commitment to the service, he returned to civilian life in 1935 to practice law in Tacoma until 1940. Ordered back to active duty during the Navy's prewar expansion, he commanded two auxiliary ships and the destroyer escort USS *Wyman* before reporting to Houston as skipper of DE-413. He liked the men he found there. In Houston, standing on the bridge of the protean warship, watching the workers of the day shift scramble down the gangway and into the safety of their civilian lives, Copeland noticed two officers looking up at him from the dock. His instinct told him he would come to know them well. He ambled down and asked them if they belonged to his ship. They did. One was Lt. William S. Burton. The other was Lt. Lloyd Gurnett.

In Burton, Copeland found a kindred soul, for Burton had previously been a lawyer too. But the attorney from Cleveland had the edge on his captain in family prominence: Burton's father, Harold Burton, a World War I Army captain and the former mayor of Cleveland, was a member of the U.S. Senate. (He would become, after the war, a justice of the U.S. Supreme Court.) Copeland was relieved to find that Burton did not let it go to his head. "He stood on his own and successfully lived down his family fame. Bill by his own abilities and his own personality won his way completely with both the officers and the enlisted men."

Lieutenant Gurnett was a mustang, a sailor who had climbed the enlisted ratings—in Gurnett's case, to chief quartermaster—and finally achieved a commission at sea. "Lloyd knew his navy, knew his job, and didn't know when to quit working. No man on board worked harder or loved the ship more than he," Copeland would write. Because Gurnett's dedication was so readily apparent, Copeland gave him the post of first lieutenant, making him responsible for the construction department, which handled damage control, shipkeeping, messing, berthing, and repairs. The officers were joined by their so-called nucleus crew: thirty-odd chief and first-class petty officers who had the experience to whip a green crew into shape, as well as other key officers, including Tom Stevenson, the communications department boss, and Bob Roberts, the ship's executive officer.

The *Samuel B. Roberts* was christened in posthumous honor of a twenty-one-year-old naval reservist from Portland, Oregon, Samuel Booker Roberts, Jr., killed on Guadalcanal when, at the height of fighting on September 28, 1942, he took the landing craft he commanded and motored in to draw fire away from ships trying to rescue Marines trapped in a Japanese crossfire. When the secretary of the Navy informed Roberts's bereaved mother that DE-413 would be named in her late son's honor, she planned to come down from St. Louis to attend the ceremony. Her husband was an engineer working for Mississippi River Flood Control, but even he couldn't stop the great river from rampaging as the big day, April 28, 1944, approached. Floodwaters washed out the southbound rail lines, and travel became impossible. The wife of the flood controller had no choice but to yield to high water. She wrote Bob Copeland with her regrets and enclosed a photo of coxswain Roberts, which the captain placed in the wardroom.

She also made a request: would he find a place on his crew roster for Jack Roberts, her youngest son, who was finishing basic training at Great Lakes Naval Training Station? The younger Roberts badly wanted the assignment. From Galveston, Copeland wrote the Navy Department with a request to bring Jack Roberts aboard.

Commissioning is a signature moment in the life of a warship. An authority on naval history has observed, "If launching may be likened to birth, and christening the endowment of individuality, then at commissioning the ship is at the threshold of a productive and rewarding maturity." It constitutes its formal transfer to the care of its commanding officer. Its officers and crew assemble on the quarterdeck as the fleet's district commandant or his representative reads the directive that assigns the vessel to the fleet. The Navy band plays the national anthem, the ensign is hoisted, and the commissioning pennant is broken out. The new commanding officer reads his orders and assumes command, and the first watch is set.

A productive and rewarding maturity—close though it was for the *Samuel B. Roberts*—lay far in the future for Bob Copeland's two small children. His wife of four and a half years, Harriet, had been there when all three of his previous ships had been commissioned, from his first command aboard the coal-burning tug, the *Pawtucket*, to his most recent tour aboard an older destroyer escort, the *Wyman*. He wanted her there in Houston for the commissioning of the *Roberts,* and he let her know it, cajoling her in letter after letter to make the long trip from Tacoma. But his efforts at persuasion could not overcome the imperatives of new motherhood. Though she wanted to be there for her husband, Harriet Copeland had an infant daughter and toddler son to care for. And so on the day the *Samuel B. Roberts* became a Navy warship, Bob Copeland took command of her without the comfort of family. Copeland would continue to chide his wife for missing the commissioning. "I think I overdid it," he later acknowledged. He finally relented when Harriet wrote him, saying, "There's an old saying that one picture is worth ten thousand words, and the enclosed picture will perhaps explain why I wasn't there." Tucked inside the envelope was the front cover of the *Saturday Evening Post*. It depicted the inside of a firehouse, firemen clambering aboard an engine as it raced out of the station. Their mascot, a Dalmatian, was left sitting on a large red pillow, suckling a litter of puppies as the pumper zoomed off to battle the flames. As Copeland raced off to his own four-alarm fire in the Pacific, he could not be sure he would ever see Harriet and their children again.

After the commissioning ceremony on April 28, the *Roberts* departed for Bermuda with a group of other destroyer escorts for an extended shakedown cruise to test and break in the ship's physical plant. But as an experienced commander like Bob Copeland well knew, the successful operation of a warship would depend as much on his ability to forge the character of the ship's crew as on the Texans' skill in forging the curve of the ship's keel.

After shakedown was complete, the *Roberts* escorted a paddle steamer up the East Coast to Norfolk, then continued northward to Boston for a final fitting out and inspection prior to going to war. In Boston seaman second class Jack Roberts reported for duty. The only people on the ship who knew his connection to *the* Mr. Samuel B. Roberts were the skipper and his executive officer, Lt. Bob Roberts. No one suspected a thing, for the surname Roberts didn't stand out: the ship already had two of them. By the time the fact of young Jack Roberts's relation to the heroic landing craft skipper of Guadalcanal slipped out a few months later, his captain wrote, "Jack Roberts had made his own way, and his place in the ship's company was secure for him in his own right."

When he finished boot camp, Jack Yusen was ordered to join the *Samuel B. Roberts* at Charlestown Navy Yard in Boston. On June 7, 1944, as the U.S. Army was consolidating its hold on the Normandy beachhead, Yusen loaded his seabag aboard a truck with eleven other recruits and was driven to the docks to meet his new ship. When he saw the big turrets and bristling guns, his first thought was, *What a ship!* Then a petty officer approached the New Yorker and his buddies and asked, "What are you guys looking at?" The petty officer told them that the object of their admiration was in fact a British heavy cruiser. He then pointed to the dry dock on the other side of the pier. "You're going on that one over there."

The large waterless enclosure appeared to be empty, save for a single mast that stuck up out of it, a radar antenna affixed to its top. "That's your ship," the petty officer said. Yusen and his friends were crestfallen. "We looked down the dock at the little ship—306 feet long—and then looked at the big cruiser, and said, 'Oh my God!' "

How quickly disappointment turned to pride. Destroyer escort sailors tended toward an intensity of pride that was out of all proportion to their undersized ships. Four days into his new life as a *Samuel B. Roberts* sailor, Yusen walked with his buddies on liberty into a Boston pub. When Navy men meet in barrooms or dance halls, or wherever women are nearby, they seldom pass up the opportunity to boast about their ship. Yusen said, "They'd ask you what ship you were on. We'd say, 'We're from the *Samuel B. Roberts*—the USS *Samuel B. Roberts*, DE-413.' You'd say that with pride. You might be talking to someone on a heavy cruiser. So you're just telling him that we're as good as you. We had that pride already. We had been on the ship for four days. So much pride, and it had been only four days."

The feeling that destroyer escorts were special manifested itself in surprising places. In a stained-glass window that adorned the Norfolk yard's nondenominational chapel, someone had glued an image of a destroyer escort, cradled like a baby in the arms of Jesus Christ. The image struck somebody as sacrilegious and was removed. But the sentiment was surely genuine enough.

Pride would take the *Sammy B.* far. But the fact remained that the destroyers that the *Roberts* would join in Taffy 3's screen—the *Hoel,* the *Heermann,* and the *Johnston*—carried two and a half times the gun power and more than three times as many torpedoes as their smaller cousins. Sailors who possessed the detachment of distance— for instance, the men on the escort carriers who relied on the tin cans for protection—grasped the practical significance of entrusting their well-being to the more diminutive ships. When they looked out and saw DEs skirting the perimeter of the formation in lieu of destroyers, they would just shake their heads. Could they be trusted to protect them?

Bob Copeland of the *Samuel B. Roberts* readily validated their concern: "We were short of destroyers—we were always short of destroyers—and actually this was a destroyer's job. So they used a lot of DEs to finish out the screens. In all we had three destroyers and four DEs that made up the screen ships. We actually should have had eight or ten in the screen. We were overextended and trying to carry on a big operation."

Destroyer escorts were not built to ride high in the battle line and trade salvos with an enemy fleet. The *Roberts*'s designed displacement—the weight of the seawater that her hull displaced—was 1,250 tons. Fully loaded for battle, she displaced about 2,000 tons. She went to war with 228 men: 217 enlisted and eleven officers. But by the standards of the fleet she was a pipsqueak. The battleship *Missouri,* with a complement of 1,921, was nearly three times the *Roberts*'s length and almost thirty times her weight. Unlike the Mighty Mo, the *Roberts* had not been built for engaging armored dreadnoughts at 28,000 yards. Destroyer escorts were runabouts. In port, they delivered mail to the larger ships. At sea, they rode the outer edge of a formation, keeping watchful eyes, sonar stacks, and radar scopes to the ocean and the sky.

Whereas the big ships' bulk was their best insurance against heavy seas, destroyer escorts lived at nature's fickle mercy. As the seas went, so went the DEs. In an unpublished 1945 dispatch sent shortly before he was killed by machine-gun fire on Okinawa, Ernie Pyle evoked the precarious seaworthiness of the tiny vessels: "They are rough and tumble little ships. They roll and they plunge. They buck and they twist. They shudder and they fall through space. They are in the air half the time, under water half the time. Their sailors say they should have flight pay and submarine pay both."

The *Roberts* was rated for twenty-four knots but could make nearly thirty when her two twelve-thousand-horsepower boilers were spinning her Westinghouse turbines at full steam. Her armament was light. A destroyer escort's main battery consisted of two single-barreled five-inch/38-caliber naval rifles, one fore and one aft. A triple torpedo mount amidships was her most powerful weapon against enemy surface ships. A well-located torpedo blast could cripple a large capital ship. But with a range of not more than ten thousand yards, the torpedo's effective use required that the ship maneuver to virtual point-blank range—and survive that approach despite her complete lack of armor or other self-protection beyond the whims of luck.

Destroyer escorts were every bit the equal of destroyers (DDs) in antisubmarine operations. They used the same sonar equipment, but DEs were more maneuverable, able to turn a circle less than half the diameter of what a destroyer circumscribed. Still, the pilots and crew on the escort carriers (CVEs) would have preferred to see full-fledged *Fletcher*-class destroyers riding shotgun on the task unit. But it was 1944, the ocean was vast, and the same American heavy industry that raced to fill the oceans with aircraft carriers was hard pressed to turn out enough destroyers to protect the flattops. Destroyer escorts, cheaper and faster to build, filled the bill of necessity. And they did it well.

*   *   *

THROUGH SOME OLD-FASHIONED SHIPYARD horse trading in Boston, Copeland secured certain mechanical improvements—a pair of gyro repeaters for the bridge wing foremost among them. With the new compasses his quartermasters and watch officers would be able to take more accurate bearings. To help turn his mostly teenage crew into a team ready to fight a desperate and savage enemy, Copeland brought aboard key noncommissioned officers and technical specialists through the Navy's personnel lottery.

As the *Samuel B. Roberts* left Boston Harbor and broke into the wide waters off Cape Cod, Captain Copeland set course for Norfolk. Provincetown was coming into view on the starboard bow. Ens. John LeClercq, the officer of the deck, and his captain, seated in his bridge chair, scanned the morning sea and listened to the slow cadence of the sonar system's echo-ranging machine as it sent its sharp falsetto calls into the deep in search of enemy submarines. Suddenly Copeland noticed that the outbound ping was getting a hard echo in return. "Before I could fully believe my ears, the sonar operator called out, 'Good contact! Four hundred yards—up Doppler!'" referring to the acoustic signature a bogey made while closing with the ship. Copeland thought to himself, *Barely out of port, and a submarine is already stalking us?*

Recognizing the possibility of collision, Copeland leaped from his chair and grabbed the engine order telegraph to ring a stop bell. Before the skipper could send down the order, there came a deep, hollow-toned *boom* and a reverberating crash that shook the ship. It felt as if a torpedo had hit. Copeland rang a "back full" order to the engine room, but the impact continued to grind along. A few seconds later a second violent seaquake shook the ship.

"I was belowdecks when there was a great shock, then a grinding sensation along the keel, and finally the stern shook violently," chief yeoman Gene Wallace recalled. "I rushed to the deck, and there on the sea was evidence that the *Roberts* had made her first kill. There was blood on the water and bits of flesh—positive evidence of a kill—*of a whale.*"

The *Roberts*'s first underwater kill was a magnificent sixty-foot-long specimen whose backbone had been severed by the ship's slender bow. The stricken animal spouted a geyser of blood as the officers and crew raced topside, ran to the rail, and looked on aghast. The whale's immense bulk rolled alongside the starboard side of the ship as a growing blood slick stained the water. The destroyer escort's churning starboard screw sawed at the whale, cutting clean through its backbone again. The crew watched transfixed as the ruined beast surfaced behind the ship.

No captain ever wants to report that he has run his ship aground—certainly no captain with hopes for a bigger command. But what other conclusion should be drawn from the dented bow, the bent keel, and the broken screw? Captains customarily made up stories to cover for their negligence. "It is legendary in the Navy," Bob Copeland later wrote, "that unless she sticks fast, no ship admittedly runs aground, all groundings being laid to collisions with submerged logs and the like." But this was no phony sea story, and Copeland didn't want a stench of suspicion hanging around him or his ship. The exec, Lt. Bob Roberts, took a fix on the ship's position, documenting its location well clear of shallow waters where a grounding could take place. Meanwhile, Captain Copeland, ever the lawyer, ordered his crew to gather up the exonerating physical evidence. Several chunks of whale hide and flesh were recovered from the ship's hull and preserved in medicinal alcohol by Dr. Erwin, the division medical officer.

Copeland continued on to Norfolk to have the broken propeller repaired in dry dock. No question ever arose as to the origins of the *Samuel B. Roberts*'s inaugural bruising. It was an incident that grew in comic magnitude as time went by. But just as surely could it be said that the *Sammy B.*'s voyage to the Philippine Sea had begun with a very poor omen. Such dramatics—and the small vessel had yet to enter a combat zone.

*   *   *

WHILE THEIR SHIP WAS convalescing in Norfolk, Lieutenant Roberts and Captain Copeland made final adjustments to the crew roster, weeding out a few ne'er-do-wells from the ship's complement of 219. Among the 217 keepers, Copeland could sense a coming together that boded well for the upcoming journey to the Pacific. The skipper gave his crew leave and instructed them to report back to the ship in time for its departure a few days later.

Bud Comet, a nineteen-year-old seaman, took the opportunity to visit his family in their coal-mining settlement on the Guyandot River in northern West Virginia, where they lived in a home owned by the coal company. So long as Mr. Comet showed up reliably at the mine and obeyed his superiors and called his boss "Mister," he would have a place to live and get the hours he needed to bring home a living wage to his family. Mostly he fed his family out of his vegetable garden—after he gave the best produce to neighbors. "My dad figured there were people there poorer than us, he gave the best stuff to them, and we got what was left. If he killed a hog, he gave most of the hog away," Comet said. When the visit was over and Bud was due to rejoin the *Samuel B. Roberts,* he saw his father off to work, then left to catch the train to Norfolk. He found a seat aboard the train and looked up to see a familiar face sitting across from him. "I want to talk to you," his father said.

Bud knew that the foreman at the coal mine didn't grant time off lightly. From the look in his father's eye, he could see that what his father was about to say was likely going to be important.

Mr. Comet was concerned for his son's future. It was 1944. The world was at war. He told the teenager he was worried that he would get out to the front and be overwhelmed or afraid and wouldn't do his job. If he screwed up and went over the hill and if the MPs had to track him down and haul him to the brig, he would bring upon his family the worst of sins: dishonor. If there was one thing he needed to avoid, his dad said, it was dishonoring his mother.

He reminded his son of his own beginnings. Born in Italy, the senior Comet was raised under the worst of political systems. He had come to this country and managed to make a living and provide for his family. What this meant, he said, was that America was worth dying for. Death would be acceptable, so long as it was honorable. "An honorable man dies once," he told Bud. "A coward dies a thousand times." Comet thought he had heard that line somewhere before, maybe from Shakespeare. His father didn't mention anything about the Bard. Bud Comet was pretty sure his father had never read Shakespeare. He said, "I think he got that out of his heart."

But Bud Comet's heart was already spoken for. He had fallen hard in love. The object of his affection was the *Samuel B. Roberts.* "I had confidence in the ship. I had confidence in the people who I had met on the ship. I had confidence in the officers who I saw on that ship. Mr. Roberts, our executive officer, was Annapolis—very strict, strictly Navy. I felt that he would be more strict than anybody else. There was Stevenson and Moylan. I had a lot of respect for them."

Comet grew to like Dudley Moylan. The ship's junior officer, with an English degree from Duke and a "ninety-day wonder" commission from Notre Dame's officer candidate program, was prone to spontaneous kindness. On late watches, once in a while, Ensign Moylan would bring by a pot of coffee and some cups, toss them around, fill them, and sit down in the gun tub with the men and visit and just talk, one man to the next. Junior officers could be that way. John LeClercq was like that too. There was an unshakable goodness to him, with his blond hair and easy, boyish smile. He had a natural empathy for even the greenest sailor. LeClercq and Moylan were the only officers with the group that made the five-day train journey from Norfolk to Houston.

Enlisted men who talked with Johnny LeClercq weren't put off by his gold bars. He didn't put up any of the barriers that other officers did. "I remember LeClercq," Bud Comet said. "He looked at you always and smiled—like he was in love with the ship too and the people that he was serving with and was very proud." Somehow the *Samuel B. Roberts* just seemed to foster that kind of pride. It tended to trickle down from the top.

Of course, anybody caught up in the fantasy that the *Samuel B. Roberts* was the Good Ship Lollipop always had Bob Roberts to reckon with. He could be arch and domineering. But in that sense his personality meshed well with the job description for an executive officer. He was remote even from his own officers. Enlisted men lived in another universe altogether.

Like Lloyd Gurnett, he was a mustang, an officer who had entered the Navy as an enlisted man and performed well enough to win a field appointment to Annapolis. Coming out of high school in Ridgefield, Connecticut, he had been beaten to his congressional district's Naval Academy appointment by an ambitious Yale University sophomore. So he made his Navy career the old-fashioned way. He jumped into the enlisted ranks with both feet and within two years won entrance to Annapolis by taking competitive examinations at sea.

He and Copeland were among the few experienced officers on the *Samuel B. Roberts*. Most of the others were so-called "ninety-day wonders." There was no small amount of sarcasm behind the title, for veteran petty officers seldom acquiesced to the authority of the young men who swaggered aboard as newly minted ensigns in the naval reserve. In theory a ninety-day wonder was superior even to the seniormost chief. But if a young officer planned to have a long and thriving career in the naval service, he was wise to defer to his chiefs' experience.

At the top of the chain of command of enlisted men, the warrants, the chiefs, and the first-class petty officers were the ones who had the experience to get things done at sea, from tying lines to launching boats to bringing on stores to organizing work parties. On the *Roberts,* Red Harrington, the first-class boatswain's mate, was the catalyst for most of what the deck force accomplished. The radio department relied on the leadership of Tullio Serafini, a grizzled but popular chief whose naval service dated back to World War I. Chiefs did not wear golden-barred epaulets or cap brims laden with braided "scrambled eggs." They did not dine with fine silver in the officers' ward. But they were capable men who had spent their best years at sea. By virtue of seniority, a forty- or fifty-year-old warrant officer, whose half-inch gold stripe gave him the actual privileges of an ensign, earned more money than many an admiral.

In his two years as an enlisted man, Bob Roberts had painted enough bulkheads and tugged enough lines to acquire a certain saltiness to his personality. But as the only Annapolis graduate aboard the ship—class of 1940—he comported himself with the assured professionalism that only Bancroft Hall and Tecumseh Square could breed. His blend of experience and pedigree made him a respected leader. Beyond those emotional nuances, the exec's job was intellectually demanding as well. To handle the considerable responsibility of supervising the CIC, the executive officer of a destroyer or destroyer escort had to have a quick mind. During a torpedo run it fell to him to perform the exacting work of selecting the ship's course to put it in optimum position to fire its torpedoes. A computer was available to help with the mathematical chore. But computers, even simple durable mechanical-analog devices like the first-generation Mark 1A fire-control computer, could fail. In those cases, the human mind had to step into the void and determine the target's speed and course, his own best firing course, the torpedo's optimum speed, and all the difficult geometry that that work involved. Bob Roberts's mind was among the best. Copeland called him "as fast as a slide rule and as accurate as a micrometer . . . an A-1 crackerjack boy, as sharp as a phonograph needle."

Bob Roberts probably looked at a young officer like John LeClercq, so full of niceness and interpersonal engagement, and saw a greenhorn who needed a little toughening. The exec knew how to focus impressionable minds by hitting them where they were strong. Once he pulled LeClercq aside and told him he didn't like his attitude toward the Navy and thought he didn't take enough interest in his men. LeClercq rated himself highly on both counts and seethed at the remark for weeks. Later, he exacted an underling's brand of revenge. When he was scheduled to take the ship's whaleboat to retrieve the punctilious exec from liberty, LeClercq found a defensible reason to be three and a half hours late. He and his buddy, the juniormost officer on the ship, Dudley Moylan, got a laugh out of the passive insurrection. But LeClercq was dead serious about avenging his honor as a friend of the crew. "As long as I have the confidence and trust of the enlisted men," Johnny wrote his mother, "Mr. Roberts can go to blazes."

*　　*　　*

IN NORFOLK, LLOYD GURNETT pulled some strings (or just as likely, picked some locks) and requisitioned for the crew its very own ice cream maker. The luxury of carrying such a machine typically belonged to aircraft carriers and other larger ships. Usually escort vessels contended for the privilege of rescuing a downed pilot, knowing that their reward in exchange would be five gallons of the frozen treat. Now the *Roberts* could tend to its own needs in the realm of iced confectionery.

Before leaving Norfolk, Bob Copeland decided to add one last recruit to the ship's complement. How the dog first came aboard had less to do with the captain's preferences than with the drunken enterprise of some *Roberts* sailors on shore leave. The small black mutt was found on the dock, smuggled aboard, and hidden someplace where officers seldom went. Before too long, in a fit of candor, one of the sailors went to Captain Copeland and asked permission to keep the dog on the ship.

Copeland and Gurnett took the dog into the wardroom, sat down over coffee and cigarettes, and decided that greater expertise than theirs was required if the dog was to be made a crew member in good standing. It was well after midnight, but they summoned Doc Erwin.

The sleep-ruffled physician arrived as ordered, standing on the cold floor of the wardroom in slippers, a skivvy shirt, and cotton khaki trousers. As the doctor rubbed his eyes, Copeland said, "We have a new recruit on board, and I want you to give him a physical and make out a health record for him so that we can properly take him up in the ship's company." Erwin stared at him. Had he really been called at three A.M. to perform a routine physical exam on a new crew member?

Gurnett brought Erwin some coffee. "Come on, Doc, sit down," he said. The physician looked around for his patient. Copeland gestured beneath the large table. Erwin looked down at his feet, saw the puppy, and erupted in anger. He told the captain what he thought of his and the first lieutenant's little joke. On the verge of stomping off to his bunk, he was stopped in his tracks when Copeland said, "Oh, this dog is going to be the ship's mascot, and everything has to be just so." Grudgingly, the doctor pulled out his stethoscope and got to work.

His skipper was impressed. "He really gave the puppy a thorough going-over. He took the stethoscope and checked the dog's heart and lungs, and he got the blood pressure thing out and wrapped him up. I don't think he had any more idea how to take a dog's blood pressure than I did. He made out a complete medical report on the puppy. He put on a good show for just the two of us, Gurnett and me. Then he sent for the chief yeoman. I think he was as put out as Dr. Erwin had been at being broken out of his bunk. However, he entered into the spirit of it too and made up a service record for the puppy. We forthwith named the mascot Sammy."

Given the rating seaman second class, Sammy received a rapid promotion to petty officer during a tour of the boiler room initiated by an obliging fireman who found him peering down a hatch toward the black gang's wonderland. The noise of the boilers threw the animal into a fit. As he relieved himself onto the hot steel deck, he earned his rating of water tender first class.

A sailor adept at tailoring, Sam Blue, took a kapok life jacket and, with a few cuts and stitches, fashioned a miniature life jacket for the dog. Sammy made a splash. Speculation flew in *The Gismo,* the ship newsletter, that he had a canine paramour in Tokyo and saw the DE-413 as his quickest way across the Pacific.

The teenagers and young men aboard the *Samuel B. Roberts* acquired a certain degree of affection for the mammals that touched their lives, both the one they had accidentally killed and the one they now saved. With their official mascot now on board, the boys joined by their dog, the ship's journey to the Pacific was delayed no further.

Three

From Pearl Harbor, transferred from the Third to the Seventh Fleet, the *Samuel B. Roberts* escorted convoys to the naval base at Eniwetok, a huge coral atoll whose massive lagoon, a circular landscape of coral heads filled with white sand and bright blue water, was cut through with sleek gray warships. The *Roberts* made the Oahu-to-Eniwetok run twice before continuing south with a convoy toward Manus, at two degrees south latitude, in the Admiralty Islands, where part of the Philippines invasion force was gathering.

Getting there required that the *Roberts* cross the equator, an event that is of some significance in Navy tradition. When a ship crosses the equator, it is common for one with a significant complement of newcomers to hold a crossing-the-line ceremony. Apart from usual divisions of rating and rank, men aboard warships fall into two classifications: so-called "shellbacks" have crossed the equator before; "pollywogs" have not. The distinction is treated as important enough to push aside the meritocracy of rank that separates the men. A pollywog lieutenant is still merely a pollywog, and a shellback seaman a shellback.

On a ship full of reservists and new recruits like the *Roberts,* the pollywogs vastly outnumbered the shellbacks. Bob Roberts was the senior shellback. Only two other officers, Lt. Herbert W. ("Bill")

Trowbridge and Lt. Lloyd Gurnett, had crossed the equator before. They were joined by twenty-five or thirty enlisted initiates of the "charmed circle," as Bob Copeland called them. The rest of the officers and crew, nearly two hundred men, were pollywogs, Lt. Cdr. Robert Witcher Copeland among them.

Their initiation was as much theater as ceremony and as much hazing ritual as theater. In preparation, the shellbacks broke out old swabs, manila line, canvas, and bunting from the ship's stores and fashioned costumes for King Neptune and his "royal family" to wear. The screen commander's signalman, a man named Price, played Davy Jones, Neptune's messenger. Bill Trowbridge, garbed in a long-tailed coat, a silk top hat, a golden wig, and a big white mustache, was the royal judge. To Copeland, he "looked like a country circuit judge of Abe Lincoln's time." A carpenter's mate, Dari Schafer, "painted and powdered . . . until he actually looked pretty delicious," was Neptune's wife, dolled up in hula skirt and a brassiere. The royal dentist was there, and the royal barber too. But the best-of-show prize went to Tullio Serafini. The old chief radioman, all 240 pounds of him, made an ideal royal baby. He showed up wearing a big diaper fashioned from a mattress cover or a large sack and held with a big safety pin. Aside from that, he didn't wear a stitch.

The initiation began when Davy Jones, dressed in a pirate suit made from black bunting, declared that the ship was about to enter the domain of Neptunus Rex and demanded that all shellbacks ensure that the pollywogs pay their due respects. Copeland had his yeoman pass a special order that all crewmen were to wear their undress whites, and officers to wear their dress whites.

It began with minor indignities. An officer who was particularly unpopular with the crew was forced, in the highest heat of the equatorial day, to sit on the steel deck over the sound hut, above the pilothouse, and don a complete suit of foul-weather clothing, which included multiple layers suitable for the arctic and a rubberized topcoat. Over it they strapped a kapok life jacket and perched a sou'wester hat on his head. As the officer baked from within, he stayed topside as ordered for an hour and a half, keeping the watch with a large pair of binoculars. Pollywog Copeland was sent forward to stand by the jack staff and keep a lookout on the horizon, using a portable foghorn as a long glass. He played along gamely, calling to the bridge a steady stream of lookout's reports: seahorses drawing carriages, and all manner of other fanciful trappings of Neptune's realm.

After the shellbacks lingered over steaks and a rich variety of side dishes, while the pollywogs watched and waited, the pollywogs were given beans, bread, water, and coffee. Then the initiates were ordered to hear the charges against them. The less memorable or colorful crewmen were accused of "being a pollywog." Most, however, had additional charges to defend. When Bob Copeland's turn came,

> *I found myself charged by King Neptune with the most heinous of crimes. I had killed a whale. A protected whale, of all things, served in Neptune's royal hunting grounds for Neptune's exclusive sport and game. . . . On the face of it I was guilty. The whale was certainly dead. My ship had killed it. And of course, as everyone knows, the captain is responsible for what the ship does, good or bad. It appeared that I was as guilty as Robin Hood for invading Sherwood Forest and shooting the bloody king's deer.*

Around eight P.M. all hands were ordered to stand down for the night. The following morning the initiation resumed. The crews aboard the five other ships in the convoy's screen were holding their own crossing-the-line ceremonies. To ensure that at least a few of the ships had a full watch at any given time—this was, after all, wartime and Japanese submarines were about—the ships started their ceremonies thirty minutes apart.

On the *Roberts* the pollywogs were ordered to the fantail, stripped down to their shorts, and faced prosecution for their offenses. Fire hoses were turned on them—all warships had firefighting gear that would make most municipalities proud. Bob Copeland was duly soaked; then the royal devil, wielding a pitchfork whose copper tines were wired to a high-voltage, low-amp electricity source, stuck him a few times, delivering a bracing jolt. Ushered before the King, charged by Lieutenant Trowbridge, the royal judge, Copeland produced the soaked piece of paper containing a poem he had written in his defense. His alibi went, in part:

> *I hit the whale, that much is true*
> *But I pray, my Lord, what could I do?*

My ship was on a mission bound
When the royal whale did choose to sound.

My ship, it never had a chance.
Your whale came rushing like a lance,
Straight up at us from depths below
We were attacked by an unseen foe.

The whale we hit, death was his fate;
But not in malice, rage or hate.
No other course was left to me
So self defense is now my plea.

After considering the plea, the court handed down a verdict requiring the skipper to visit the royal dentist and the royal barber, kiss the royal baby, then run the royal gauntlet. By the time the captain, now a shellback, returned to his cabin to clean up, he had had his hair smeared with fuel oil paste and his mouth washed by a valve sprayer filled with diesel oil, vinegar, paprika, and other imponderable ingredients; he had planted a kiss on royal baby Serafini's grease-loaded navel, and he had run the gauntlet, crawling through a fifteen-foot canvas ventilation tunnel filled with a two-day-old compost of eggshells, coffee grounds, potato peels, and other unmentionables, while shellbacks pounded him through the canvas with large wooden paddles.

Copeland cleaned up as best he could, then returned to the fantail in time to see the four mess stewards, Washington, First, Butler, and Lillard—the only black men on the ship—get theirs. "Those mess men were good fellows and they took the initiation in stride. If I ever had any race prejudice in me, the war knocked it out of me." The system of segregation that kept the black sailors in the mess could not withstand the bonding effects of the crossing-the-line ceremony.

The only thing worse than participating in the ceremony was sitting it out. Watching his shipmates run the gauntlet, one crewman became squeamish and asked to quit. Lieutenant Roberts didn't miss a beat: "We'll dismiss him; he's out of it." Indeed, the ceremony was purely voluntary. This sailor was free to go. About two hours later, once it sank in that he was now the only pollywog aboard the ship, he returned and begged to be "given the works."

According to Copeland, "I suppose we were mean, but we wouldn't let him have it. . . . He had had his chance and he flubbed the dub. I still can't help but feel sorry for the poor boy. I know what he missed. He really missed the feeling of something you can't put into words, a feeling of belonging."

*   *   *

COPELAND'S CREW BELONGED. There was no more practical preparation for war than the fraternal coming together of the young men who gave the *Samuel B. Roberts* life. At Manus, the ship itself found new associations too. On October 12, after Bob Copeland and the other skippers had been briefed on the planning for Operation King Musketeer II, as the Philippines invasion was known, the destroyer escort joined her cousins in the Seventh Fleet: the old battleships of Admiral Oldendorf's Task Group 77.2, the escort carriers of Task Group 77.4, and most of the other tin cans that would join her under the call sign Taffy 3 for the long journey to Leyte.

Four

The three destroyers of Taffy 3—the *Hoel,* the *Heermann,* and the *Johnston*—were the only ships in the Seventh Fleet task unit that were not conceived as lesser versions of a more capable vessel. Escort carriers were bargain-basement aircraft carriers. Destroyer escorts did the work of destroyers with less than half the main weaponry and one-third less speed. But the trio of *Fletcher*-class tin cans were deep-sea thoroughbreds, members of the finest class of U.S. destroyers produced during World War II.

Tin cans. Destroyers wore the nickname proudly, for none better suited these ships whose three-eighths-inch steel decks creaked and bent in wave troughs but rode out storms like corks. The destroyers' forerunners were the torpedo boats that had shown their offensive value as early as the Civil War. Their successes spurred U.S. naval planners to carry their design forward as the industrializing nation mobilized to defend the far reaches of the hemisphere as required by the Monroe Doctrine. Assistant Secretary of the Navy Theodore Roosevelt championed the construction of "torpedo boat destroyers" seaworthy enough to sail with the oceangoing battle line and protect it from an enemy's torpedo boats. In the years leading up to World War II, as the Navy experimented within the strict zero-sum environment bounded by the variables of size, speed, offensive power, survivability, and cost, the modern concept of the destroyer evolved.

By 1944 the *Fletcher*-class destroyers that rode with Taffy 3 represented the state of the art. They were the first class of U.S. warship to be designed free of treaty limitations. Because their design coincided with the massive ramp-up in production during the early years of the war, more *Fletchers* were produced than any other class of combatant vessel. From the February 1942 launching of the *Nicholas* at Bath Iron Works in Maine to the June 1944 launching of the *Rooks* at Seattle-Tacoma, 175 *Fletcher*-class destroyers would be built by the time World War II ended. Most of them served in the Pacific. Because the absence of treaty restraint enabled the Navy's General Board to tailor the new destroyers to their mission rather than to the requirements of diplomats, the *Fletchers* were large ships. Overstretching a football field at 376 ½ feet in length, they were far more imposing than the nickname "tin cans" might have suggested. It would have taken Ted Williams's best swing to hit a baseball from a *Fletcher*'s fantail all the way to its graceful bow. With a displacement of 2,050 tons (2,700 with a full fuel load), they were swift, seaworthy, and stout, with considerable firepower. Though rated at a top speed of thirty-six knots, the *Fletchers* carried enough weaponry to make the biggest enemy feel their punch—ten Mark 15 torpedoes, five single-mounted five-inch/38-caliber guns, a formidable thicket of twenty- and forty-millimeter machine guns, two roller racks of depth charges, and the sophisticated sensing equipment to land them on their targets. That ships so swift could span the distance from home plate in Fenway Park to the Green Monster in deep left-center field was impressive testament to the power of the Navy's industry and technology. Yet in the taxonomy of U.S. warships of the 1940s, destroyers were mere dust mites compared with the new battleships named for states and roaming the seas on behalf of their federal union.

Individual warships draw much of their personality from two sources: their mission, and the personalities of their most prominent officers and chiefs. With destroyers, a certain tension existed between their mission and their mind-set. Their mission had long been defined by the Navy's expectation that any war against Japan would involve refighting World War I's Battle of Jutland: heavy ships trading salvos at long range; destroyers standing faithfully by the battle line, interposing—screening—as needed to protect the higher-value ships. The destroyers' offensive value was largely an afterthought.

Destroyer commanders tended to have a more expansive view of their combat potential. Recognizing the power of their principal armament—torpedoes—to turn the tide of a battle, they chafed at their role as auxiliaries. But even as the Japanese were ravaging American fleets in the Solomon Islands with torpedoes and aggressive tactical doctrine that made their destroyers giant-killers, and even as carrier aircraft were proving decisive at Midway and elsewhere, American tacticians insisted on the supremacy of the heavy gun and refused to free destroyers to operate in an offensive role.

As the war proceeded, the big ships won followings back home with front-page headlines and photos. But the less glamorous grunt work performed by the destroyers helped make their larger cousins' iconic status possible. They worked the outer perimeter of their task forces, pinging the deep for submarines and watching the skies for planes. "Tin cans" may have been the moniker that stuck to them, but a *Heermann* sailor appreciated their true nature: "the hunting dogs of the fleet." Their vigilant work allowed their more regal principals to maintain the illusion of invulnerability. Though battleship guns were often decisive wherever they engaged, as often as not the bigger ships asserted themselves by their mere presence. Destroyers and destroyer escorts asserted themselves with their weapons or did not assert themselves at all.

If battleships and carriers were corporations, with payrolls of thousands managed by a bevy of mid-level managers who wore the gold stripes of lieutenants and lieutenant commanders, destroyers and destroyer escorts were mom-and-pop shops. Where the capital ships carried themselves with a certain institutional hubris that existed apart from the men who ran them, the DDs and DEs were steel-plated extensions of their most prominent individual officers and chiefs. In this respect, the standard persona of a fleet destroyer was made unique by the shaping and molding of human hands. Bob Copeland shaped the identity of the *Samuel B. Roberts*. But in that respect, among the skippers of Taffy 3's screen, he was not unique.

The leader of the seven ships that screened the six escort carriers of Taffy 3 was the USS *Hoel*. Commissioned on July 29, 1943, at the Bethlehem Steel shipyard in San Francisco, the *Hoel* had the luxury of two competent, popular skippers: the current boss, Cdr. Leon

Kintberger, and the former captain in whose shadow he worked: his predecessor, Cdr. William Dow Thomas, who stayed aboard as Taffy 3's screen commander.

Barrel-chested and good-humored, Thomas had been a popular captain. His popularity and knack for command earned him the just desserts of the skipper who does his job a bit too well—he got promoted straight out of it. Newly promoted and awaiting reassignment, he was not able to get off the *Hoel* before the Leyte operation began. So he chose to remain aboard his old ship as commander of Taffy 3's seven-ship screen. He could be found in the wardroom every night, playing cribbage over coffee. Kintberger, cheerful and pleasant, handled the inevitable benign pressure of Thomas's continued presence with aplomb and grace. Alfred Thayer Mahan had written of the "Nelson touch," a personal style of command favoring cordial social relations with officers, professional appreciation, and confidence. The Nelson touch was "rarely the result of careful calculation, but bespeaks rather the inner graciousness of the heart that [Nelson] abundantly possessed." The *Hoel's* wardroom seemed to operate by Nelson's principle. Not every ship was so fortunate.

Cdr. Amos T. Hathaway, age thirty, had once been the *Hoel's* executive officer. As exec, he was effectively the ship's general manager, Commander Thomas's right hand in all matters. He imposed discipline. He maintained the good order of the crew, the upkeep of equipment, set the daily schedule, and oversaw its fulfillment by the senior petty officers. As boss of the CIC, he was the ship's eyes and ears. But the way he interpreted and acted upon the things he saw and heard was seldom to the liking of the *Hoel's* crew.

Hathaway was a martinet, as disliked by his men as Thomas was admired. As martinets are wont to do, he disposed of his duties with an exacting severity. That trait served him well, for executive officers seldom advance by gaining the affections of underlings. Shortly before the *Hoel* joined Taffy 3, Hathaway got a promotion and command of his own ship.

The men of the *Hoel* who had the closest acquaintance with his predations and mind games quietly cheered his departure. But that departure took him only as far as the other side of the formation. When Amos T. Hathaway took command of the *Heermann,* one destroyer's relief became another one's pain.

As the new skipper of the *Heermann,* Hathaway made his mark quickly enough. The day before he was to inspect his crew at a full muster, he asked his chief yeoman and captain's talker, Harold Whitney, to bring him the service records of the full crew. He spent the night with the records and the next day demonstrated the power of his photographic memory by walking down the ranks, stopping at every fifth or sixth man, and asking about his wife, family, and hometown, by name and with nary a mistake.

Though he stood six foot four, he weighed around 130 pounds. With sunken cheeks, protruding ears, and eyes that naturally bugged, he was wiry not only in physical bearing but in voice and attitude too. He was reflexively peevish and relished keeping his officers off balance and on their guard. His memory made him a marvelous stickler for "Rocks and Shoals," as the Navy regulations, *Articles for the Government of the Navy,* were known. He would reject written reports without comment—"This is wrong. Fix it." But he was just as likely to upbraid someone for slavishly following the rules when they didn't suit him.

The patrician collegiality that marked many Navy wardrooms was altogether missing from the *Heermann.* The native Coloradoan's shrill voice could often be heard chastising someone over one or another point of order. "He was a son of a bitch," said a former *Heermann* officer fifty-six years after the fact. "He made Captain Queeg look like a sissy." That officer wasn't alone in his ill sentiments. The *Heermann*'s physician, Dr. Edwin Bebb, was required to keep a monthly medical record on each of the ship's officers. Though he knew he was shielded by his medical credentials, Bebb feared his skipper would resent his adverse assessment of his psychology and seek a pretext to court-martial him.

When Hathaway had been the *Hoel*'s exec, his underlings could take refuge in the kindness of their skipper, William Thomas. But on the *Heermann,* where he stood atop the chain of command, Hathaway's will was law, and officers who flouted it by coddling persecuted crew members risked drawing his fury. The *Heermann*'s wardroom buzzed with half-cocked fantasies about doing the skipper in. *Something* had to be done, the thinking went. This was not His Majesty's Navy circa 1835. This was America. Someone suggested that it might be arranged for Captain Hathaway tragically to lose his footing out on deck during a storm. But regicide was beyond them. Ultimately they settled on less capital forms of aggression.

One day when Hathaway was gone from his quarters, someone found a way to insert a handful of marbles into the compartment above his sea cabin. Every time the *Heermann* rolled—and like any destroyer it rolled often and deeply—the captain was serenaded by the clangorous lullaby of the little spheres rolling across the thin steel plating over his bunk.

Such petty conspiracy-mongering bound the *Heermann*'s crew together against a common enemy. At least Hathaway served in that role until a real foe could be engaged. Perhaps when the shooting started, the crew would see their skipper's malign will as a weapon in its own right. What force might it have when joined with theirs and turned upon an actual enemy?

The *Hoel* was run by the popular duo of Kintberger and Thomas, the *Heermann* by the white-knuckled autocracy of Amos Hathaway. The fighting culture of Taffy 3's third destroyer, the *Johnston,* was the product of one man's inspired leadership: that of its first and only captain, Cdr. Ernest E. Evans.

When Evans arrived at the Seattle-Tacoma shipyard to oversee the fitting out of the brand-new USS *Johnston,* DD-557, he impressed his crew immediately with the substance of his will. At the ship's commissioning ceremony on Navy Day, October 27, 1943, he informed his raptly attentive audience: "This is going to be a fighting ship. I intend to go in harm's way, and anyone who doesn't want to go along had better get off right now." As if to underscore the invitation, he added, "Now that I have a fighting ship, I will never retreat from an enemy force." Something in the tone of his voice told his listeners that he was deadly serious. Not one of them accepted his offer to leave the ship ahead of whatever trouble he had in store for them.

Indeed he *was* serious. As an officer aboard the World War I–era four-piper destroyer *Alden,* Evans had witnessed the disaster of the Battle of the Java Sea in February 1942, in which a Japanese heavy cruiser force made short work of an Allied fleet. Two weeks after the battle Evans assumed command of the *Alden.* But he never expunged from his mind the sting of having to flee from the Japanese. In that sense, he came to the *Johnston* with a cross to bear.

Evans had initially pursued military service with the dream of becoming a Marine officer, but an appointment to Annapolis escaped him. So in May 1926, at the age of nineteen, he said farewell to Muskogee, Oklahoma, and enlisted in the Navy. Thirteen months after his enlistment he won entrance to the Naval Academy class of 1931 via fleet competition. His Annapolis midshipman's moniker, "the Chief," would prove to be apt for at least two reasons. First, he was by nature always in charge. Anyone who met him could feel the way his charisma naturally filled a room. Then there was the matter of his proud Cherokee heritage. His ancestry was not overwhelmingly evident in his appearance. The set of his dark-browed gaze, the large chest, and the subtle smirk of his lips accented by a neat black mustache made him look like a somewhat stouter incarnation of Clark Gable. It was clear to all who met him that Ernest E. Evans was not a man to trifle with. He bestrode his narrow bridge like a colossus. The fighting spirit of his forebears animated him.

Evans appreciated the hidden nature of things, the power of the unseen over the tangible. In matters of discipline, he generally preferred to let the idea of his wrath do the work of the actual thing. He never exploded in anger as Hathaway did. He seldom if ever upbraided a subordinate openly for poor performance. But then he seldom smiled either. "He expected every man to do his job without any psychological ploys," Lt. (jg) Ellsworth Welch, Evans's antisubmarine warfare officer, remembered. Evans trusted people to do their work. If they failed, he let them—he knew instinctively, as they did, that they wouldn't fail him twice. He never quite had to spell out the consequences; the very thought that the skipper might become disappointed was enough. The *Johnston*'s gunnery officer, Lt. Robert C. Hagen, said, "He had great faith in all of us, unbelievably so. I don't recall him saying a mean word to me the whole time. . . . The captain was a true, instinctive fighter. . . . We were on a high-class ship because the captain was high-class."

If Ernest Evans was not destined to be a Marine, he would settle, seventeen years after his enlistment, for running a warship like one. That meant simply that he would take care of his men. He would also, soon enough, take care of Marines. In February 1944, during the invasion of the Marshall Islands, the *Johnston* drew shore bombardment duty to support Marines advancing against stiff enemy opposition on the islands of Kwajalein and Eniwetok. For Evans, it was not just another assignment. Beyond his generalized desire to grapple with an enemy, he had empathy for the mud-slogging grunts moving into the Japanese killing fields ashore. He knew this: he could well have been one of them. The *Johnston* got in close, sometimes so close as to pierce the veil of distance that usually stood between Navy men and conditions ashore.

For many of the crew it was their first sight of blood. According to Edward Block, a coxswain, "a landing craft came alongside with young kids who had been wounded on the islands. They were brought to our ship because we were close in to the beach and we had a doctor on board. To see those young kids lying there all shot up brought tears to my eyes and I cried. There but for the grace of God . . ."

The crew of the *Johnston* witnessed more of it during the Marianas campaign, during the bombardment of Guam. Broadside to the beach, pounding the caves in the cliffs above with a full battery of five-inch fire, the *Johnston* fired so furiously that the guns glowed red. Bob Hagen had to take the occasional break, just to let the barrels cool. During a lull boatswain's mate first class Bob Hollenbaugh went below to check on Gun 54's handling room, when he encountered a young Marine in the care of the *Johnston*'s medical division. Hollenbaugh approached the Marine, who held fast to consciousness despite the gruesome fact that he had had an arm shot off, and asked him how he felt. "I'm fine, sir." The kid told the boatswain's mate that he had entered the Marines just nine weeks ago. "That kid looked like he was about fourteen years old," Hollenbaugh said. "My God. What is this world coming to? I'll never forget the expression on that kid's face. And he still had the presence of mind to look up at me and call me sir."

Evans cared about the kids fighting ashore. Time after time he took the *Johnston* closer to shore than the Navy's bombardment plan specified. When his allotted number of shells were fired into the island—such quantifiables being carefully managed by higher command—he beseeched his superiors for more. "Damn it, they need fire support, and we're going to give it to them," he said. Twice during the shelling of Guam, Evans boarded his wooden captain's gig, was lowered into the water, and motored over to the task group's flagship to ask for more ammunition. He got it.

"We would pull away from our positions near the shore and reload with ammo and then pull back in to resume firing," fireman third class Milt Pehl said. "At times we were so close to shore that we were actually hit by small arms fire." In the first year since her commissioning, through six invasions, the *Johnston* never suffered a hit worse than that.

The full-court-press gunnery duty placed a lot of pressure on the men directing the shooting. In Bob Hagen, one of the destroyer's senior lieutenants, Evans had the kind of gunnery officer the skipper of a fighting ship had to have. Of the seventy men in his gunnery department—which included not only the men who manned and loaded the guns but also the fire-controlmen in the gun director and the radar-men in the combat information center, the crews on the two quintuple torpedo mounts, and the "ping jockeys" on the sonar stack—only seven had ever been to sea before coming aboard the *Johnston*.

Hagen had pushed them hard in training, teaching them the job by rote and repetition. Training a green deck force, never a small task, was made more difficult still when the man responsible for that job on the *Johnston*, the chief boatswain's mate, went "over the hill" the day before the *Johnston* was scheduled to go to sea. A ship had to have a chief bosun. If Captain Evans did nothing else to impress his crew, he would still have ensured their eternal gratitude for securing as a replacement chief boatswain's mate Clyde Burnett.

Burnett was a child of the fleet. An orphan reared in south Texas by four different families, the *Johnston*'s chief boatswain's mate began his life of service in the Civilian Conservation Corps before enlisting in the Navy more than two years before the Pearl Harbor attack. Burnett had just returned from a tour of duty in the Pacific when Evans found him ashore at a Navy receiving station in San Diego. "The captain put the make on him," Bob Hagen said. "The guy didn't have a chance."

As a superior chief bosun should be, Burnett was right hand to the captain. Ernest Evans relied on him as a liaison to his enlisted force. In turn, Burnett delegated their supervision and discipline to his capable first-class boatswain's mates. Harry Longacre ran the First Division, the hundred-odd sailors who comprised the deck force on the forward half of the ship. His counterpart aft, boss of the Second Division, was Bob Hollenbaugh, a sharp, no-nonsense Indianan whose father, a machinist's mate in the Dantesque boiler rooms of a World War I–era battleship, had counseled Bob to get a topside rating at all costs. Hollenbaugh performed his duties cleanly and professionally and with not a little relish. On a crew made up mostly of first-time seagoers, his, Longacre's, and Burnett's most vital contribution was their experience.

Burnett proved to be a popular chief. The boyish twenty-four-year-old with the lantern jaw and quiet manner watched over the kids on the *Johnston*'s deck force like a father. The kids who swabbed and painted and scraped and loaded supplies and took on fuel loved him like one.

But forging a crew into a hardened fighting unit mostly required, not love, but discipline and ruthless, repetitive drill. In that respect Evans prized Lieutenant Hagen's tough, stickler's nature. He let his gun boss draw up the general quarters or battle stations assignments and gave him the discretion to call the crew to GQ most anytime he liked. Hagen used that freedom liberally, so much so that the *Johnston* acquired its own inevitable nickname, long before it reached a combat zone, "GQ Johnny." When the claxon sounded, the men raced to their guns and searched for targets. For antiaircraft gunners, there were long nylon target sleeves towed by pilots—very brave pilots—from the nearby air station. Crews on the five-inch mounts fired on sleds pulled behind tugboats—very brave tugboats—at varying ranges on the surface.

It took a lot of drill for the crew's proficiency to live up to the precision of their equipment. Each of the *Johnston*'s five-inch gun mounts was engineered with the precision of an outsize Swiss watch. The turret assemblies were three stories tall, running deep into the bowels of the ship. Each gun mount sat atop an ammunition handling room, where crew loaded shells onto hydraulic hoists—dumbwaiters—that whisked the shells upward. Below the handling room was a magazine that fed all the handling rooms.

Among the greatest innovations of the 1940s-era Navy were the radar fire-control systems with which all new surface combatants were equipped. Unlike the weapons on the smaller destroyer escorts, the guns of a *Fletcher*-class destroyer were controlled centrally by its gunnery officer. Seated in the enclosed gun director platform high above the bridge, Hagen operated a two-handled steering mechanism that controlled the aiming of the *Johnston*'s five main gun mounts. When Hagen ordered the gun crews in the mounts to "match pointers," the guns came into alignment with the director, and the gun captains relinquished control of their mounts to Hagen. At that point the two men beside him in the gun director, the pointer and trainer—teenage enlisted men named George Himelright and James Buzbee—took over. They kept whatever they were shooting at fixed in the crosshairs of their telescopes, one for gauging bearing (or direction), the other gauging elevation (or distance).

In heavy seas, the sight of a destroyer's five director-controlled guns swaying in unison to stay on target as the ship pitched, yawed, and rolled could be unsettling. This synchro-gyroscopic wizardry relegated the men manning the guns to auxiliary backups whose duties went beyond simple loading only if the system broke down. As long as range and target data kept feeding the fire-control computer, they had no aiming to do and little discretion to exercise. Gun crews had only to pull rounds off the hydraulic shell hoist and lay them in front of the powder canisters in the sliding breech tray. Their most immediate challenge was to keep their fingers and hands from getting crushed between a heavy shell and the breech mechanism.

In another day, eyesight was essential to gunnery. Optical rangefinders were useful to a point, but the critical work of spotting shell splashes and correcting aim belonged to those with the sharpest eyes. By 1944, even in its first generation, American fire-control technology was so good that it could make a top performer out of a man who would probably have been unsuited to the job not long before.

At age seventeen, having beaten out sixty applicants in competition for the honor, Bob Hagen arrived at Annapolis as an aspiring plebe—only to get sent home that same day for flunking a routine eye exam. He opted for the enlisted route, scraped paint for two years aboard the battleship *Texas,* then returned to the States to attend junior college and finish his bachelor's degree at the University of Texas. In his second bid for an officer's commission, Hagen attended the reserve officer "ninety-day wonder" program at Northwestern University. In September 1941 in Chicago, Bob Hagen at last got his ensign's gold stripe.

Hagen saw action almost immediately off Guadalcanal, as assistant communications officer and radar officer aboard the destroyer *Aaron Ward.* In a ferocious nighttime surface engagement against superior Japanese forces in November 1942, he took shrapnel to his left biceps, nearly bled to death from his wounds, and won a Silver Star for gallantry. Returning to the States to convalesce, he decided that he would rather pursue his career in gunnery than in communications. "The gun boss could fire a hundred shots and hit once and he's a hero," he said. "In communications, if you screw up [in transcribing] one letter, all hell breaks loose, and you've committed a mortal sin. I said to myself, 'I'd rather be a hero.'"

*   *   *

HAGEN FINISHED GUNNERY and fire-control school in Washington, D.C., learning to use the gyroscopes and servo motors that ensured that imperfect eyesight would not impede his advancement. For certain specialized purposes, the *Johnston*'s Mark 1A fire-control computer and Mark 37 radar were better than any pair of spectacles, if rather more expensive to clean.

Following her commissioning at Seattle-Tacoma, during the *Johnston*'s shakedown cruise off San Diego, Hagen tackled the challenge of training his crew of inexperienced pollywogs to operate the sophisticated gunnery system. "We were all so green. The gun crews didn't know what they were doing, and I wasn't so sure what I was doing either," he said. In the first days of shakedown, when drills were going poorly, Hagen wrote a friend aboard another ship, "Stay out of our gun range—anything can happen." He was in Captain Evans's thrall, eager to please his charismatic skipper. But the captain made it plain that Hagen was on his own in bringing his gunners to proficiency. This freedom to hang himself with his own hawser was nearly as bad as suffering under an ill-tempered micromanager. The pressure began to get to him.

Bob Hagen was "a nervous wreck" during shakedown. Well groomed and intense, a compulsive smoker, disdainful of repose, Hagen had an intellect as sharp as his personality. Intelligence and initiative were de rigueur for a destroyer officer. On a small ship the performance of a few key individuals could make or break her. Hagen had little patience for those who struck him as slow or stupid. In drawing up general quarters station assignments, he distinguished the thinking men from rote operators, installing the latter in the sweaty jobs in the handling rooms and magazines and the former in sonar, CIC, and fire control, where human discretion could make a decisive difference.

Unlike his captain, Lieutenant Hagen didn't hesitate to dress down an underperformer in front of his shipmates. Aware of their growing resentment, he became cautious among the crew. When possible, he avoided walking the decks alone at night, for fear an embittered sailor might "accidentally" knock him overboard.

But many men were firmly convinced that Bob Hagen, like Clyde Burnett, was one of the best things that could have happened to the *Johnston*. In six weeks of drill his program of training turned the gunnery department into a competent working team. Boatswain's mate first class Bob Hollenbaugh was especially sharp. The captain of Gun 54, mounted on the stern of the ship, had the initiative and savoir faire to lead young enlisted men effectively. Hagen also had confidence in Lt. Jack Bechdel, his torpedo officer, and in Julian Owen, a resourceful gunner's mate with a knack for repairing broken machinery.

The crews in the five main gun mounts—numbered 51, 52, 53, 54, and 55 from bow to stern—competed for bragging rights as the ship's fastest gun gang. An average rate of fire for a five-inch/38-caliber crew was fifteen rounds per minute. Gun 55, the rearwardmost turret on the ship, got off eighty-four rounds in one four-minute firing drill, an average of twenty-one per minute. With results like that, Hagen dared to begin feeling his oats. Writing again to the same friend he had warned several weeks before to stay clear of his scattershot batteries, the lieutenant discarded all modesty: "You may now bring on the Japanese fleet." Before an opposing fleet appeared in his sighting telescope, however, the apprentice gun boss would first have to prove his proficiency in action against enemy shore targets.

During the bombardment of Kwajalein in the Marshall Islands, Hagen wielded the hammer that Evans used to support the Marines. There the strict training regimen and the engineered precision of the radar-controlled gunnery system came together at last. Captain Evans took the ship in close to the beach, dropping anchor to stabilize her as a gun platform on the northern edge of the landing zone, which frogmen from the Navy's Underwater Demolition Teams had marked with navigation lights visible only from the open sea. Hagen was "nervous as a cat," gripping his slewing handles with white knuckles as the destroyer closed with enemy shore gunners. "They could have machine-gunned us to death, and we were trying to figure out how to defend ourselves," he said. "All of a sudden over the

loudspeaker came this song, and the lyrics, 'A *sleepy lagoon* . . .' "
Hagen found that well-trained crewmen could bring humor to any
situation. Call it the product of confidence.

*   *   *

AT CLOSE RANGE the *Johnston*'s entire chorus of weaponry came to
bear on the island. There was the sharp, ear-ringing bark of the five-
inchers, the rhythmic thumping of the twin-mounted forty-millimeter
machine guns, and the faster metallic chatter of the single-barreled
twenties. Men from a damage-control party broke out rifles and
made like Davy Crockett from the main deck. Lt. (jg) Ellsworth
Welch took out his .45-caliber revolver, outstretched his arm, and en-
filaded the distant enemy with the handgun.

From his perch in the gun director, Hagen spied a Japanese officer
on the beach, waving a saber, rallying his troops to the fight, and
thought, *Why not?* He put the officer in the sights of his slewing device. The fire-control computer clicked and whirred and zipped coordinates to the *Johnston*'s five main gun turrets. When Hagen closed
the firing key, they all barked as one. The technology lived up to its
brutal promise. The five-shell salvo obliterated the man.

"Mr. Hagen, that was very good shooting," called Captain Evans
from the bridge. "But in the future, try not to waste so much ammunition on one individual."

Five

The thirteen warships that were gathered under the code name Taffy 3, their crews totaling about 7,200 men, sailed under the command of Rear Adm. Clifton Albert Frederick Sprague. He was one of the new generation of naval officers who had made their careers in naval aviation. A graduate of the Annapolis class of 1920, he had been tagged with the nickname "Ziggy" for the kinetic style of his gait—limbs agangle, "tousled hair swinging fore and aft"—as he shuffled off to class. Though just five feet nine inches tall, he was sturdily built, a skilled and enthusiastic baseball player, and according to a Naval Academy classmate, "clever in nearly every sport."

Sprague had heard the call of the sea at an early age, from his family's oceanfront cottage in Rockport, Massachusetts, thirty-five miles up the coast from Boston. There he had spent his childhood summers fishing from the jetties of the picturesque Headlands with Buster, his Irish setter, and prowling the rocky shoreline of Sandy Bay with his younger sister, Dora, hunting for crabs to use as bait. His attraction to the ocean became so strong as to be physical; he had to be near the sea. To Clif Sprague, traveling even a few miles inland was like entering a vast, arid desert: tolerable for short stretches but leaving him eager to reimmerse himself in the ion-charged salt air.

For the newly minted ensigns pouring out of Annapolis, naval aviation offered fresh career paths to be blazed, unprecedented opportunities to learn and to lead.

In 1919, as Sprague was nearing the end of the Annapolis curriculum, the General Board of the Navy declared that "fleet aviation must be developed to its fullest extent." The board, a committee of admirals who counseled the secretary of the Navy, predicted that in future naval battles "the advantage will lie with the fleet which wins in the air." Embracing the dangers and uncertainty of the field at a time when its preeminence was anything but assured, Ziggy Sprague and the Pensacola class of 1921 were pioneers. When he finished Pensacola's fledgling aviation program after nine months of flight training, he joined a small cadre of naval officers who were qualified to fly. Sprague knew change was coming, and he positioned himself to contribute to it. His assignments throughout the 1920s exposed him to the latest thinking in carrier operations. Assigned to Philadelphia's naval aircraft factory in 1923, he helped engineers work out the wrinkles in the catapult systems that launched the heavy aircraft from their carriers. Later, Sprague worked as a test pilot at Hampton Roads Naval Air Station in Virginia, assisting the inventor Carl Norden in devising safe ways to land planes on a carrier deck.

If Sprague helped create this world, it in turn placed its mark upon him. It was evident in the physical structure of his countenance. Early in his naval career Sprague acquired what people in the aviation trade called an "instrument face," the pug-nosed look of the test pilot. When the arrester hook on the tail of his plane snagged the wires stretched across the experimental flight decks upon which he practiced, as often as not the jerk caused his plane to stop with considerably greater suddenness than his face did. His frequent collisions with the cockpit instrument panel literally reshaped the contours of his appearance. His nose was slightly flatter than it should have been, his teeth looser. Aviation was a dangerous business, to be sure. By the time the war was over, nearly a quarter of Sprague's Pensacola class—eight out of thirty-four—had been killed in mishaps on the flight line.

Despite this revolution's stark dangers, Sprague was thrilled to be part of it. He loved airplanes, cherished the very idea of flight. But like any revolution, naval aviation came up against a reactionary old guard, many of them at the highest levels of Navy command. The battleship officers, whose traditional "gun club" culture had long dominated the fleet, wanted nothing to do with these flaky flying futurists who seemed blind to the beauty and breathtaking power of an eight-gun main-battery broadside. Sure, battleships carried airplanes. Parked on catapults mounted on their sterns and after turrets, floatplanes were useful for scouting and gunnery spotting. But by and large they were considered bothersome contraptions notorious for soiling the handsome teak of the dreadnoughts' quarterdecks with oil and grease.

As for the men who flew them, the old guard didn't see commissioned aviators as special or different. They were simply regular officers with a peculiar specialty. Naval aviation was a sideshow. This conceit revealed itself in the fact that in 1923 eighty-eight out of the hundred pilots trained that year were transferred back to duty in surface ships so that they could sharpen their talents as line officers. Advocates of airpower resisted this chauvinism, stating that "aviation is essentially and fundamentally a different profession. . . . Practically every country in the world . . . has accepted the assignment of personnel to aviation as a permanent life work." But the old guard at Annapolis would hear none of it. Chief of Naval Operations William S. Benson listened to the proponents of the brave new wild blue world and dismissed it all as "just a lot of noise." The officer he appointed to supervise the Navy's air arm held the lofty rank of lieutenant junior grade.

By the mid-1920s, however, while Ziggy Sprague was trying out catapults and putting arrester systems through their paces at the Anacostia Naval Air Station near Washington, D.C., neither rhetoric nor administrative gamesmanship could trump the arrival of an idea whose time had come. The U.S. Navy was on its way to becoming a carrier-based fleet. The *Lexington* and the *Saratoga* were operational, converted in midconstruction from battlecruisers to aircraft carriers. The move was in part motivated by the need to satisfy the new limitations on large warship construction that the Washington Naval Treaty imposed upon the United States, Britain, and Japan. But their transformation was also a clear sign of the shape of wars to come. Their eight-inch main batteries were shunted aside to starboard, making room for spacious flight decks that stretched from stem to stern. Beneath those 888-foot expanses of wood, the hydraulic catapults

Sprague had tested would launch aircraft into the sky. On landing, they would be brought safely to a stop by the arrester wire systems he had helped Carl Norden to refine.

In 1925 Sprague married Annabel Fitzgerald, whom he had met at a naval officers' party on Christmas Day, 1924. Their wedding was notable for the absence of her brother, a wanderer whose migrations seemed to intensify whenever important family occasions loomed. She was not close to F. Scott Fitzgerald; she did not approve of the author's fast lifestyle. Annabel must have been dismayed at some level too by the life her husband had chosen. He was away on assignment when their first daughter was born and was routinely called to service at times when his family needed him. Courtney, his first daughter, would one day explain, "The Navy was his life, and it came first. It never entered our minds that the Navy didn't come first."

In March 1928, assigned to the *Lexington*, Sprague moved from the laboratory to the front line. He was given a plum, highly visible job as its flight deck officer and assistant air officer. Like a cello virtuoso appointed to conduct a symphony, the veteran test pilot relished the intricacies of command. Orchestrating the movements of planes and the tempo of flight operations aboard ship drew on all of the knowledge he had gained, all of the instincts he had developed in previous assignments. He learned how to coordinate the flight deck crews as they moved planes for launch and recovery operations and how to anticipate what weapons and equipment would be needed and when, the sequence in which they were to be used, and the order in which the planes would fly off the ship. He rehearsed the choreography that would make the *Lexington*, home to two thousand sailors and seventy-two airplanes, an efficient fighting ship.

Though distrust of the Japanese was widespread in the Navy, Sprague was among the first to appreciate exactly what the Japanese might do. In June 1928 the *Lexington* participated in a mock surprise attack on Pearl Harbor. By night the ship crept to within 250 miles of the great Pacific base and launched its planes at dawn. As the American planes flew close overhead, interrupting innumerable breakfasts with the rattling reverberations of their piston-driven engines and an onslaught of flour-filled sacks dropped from their bomb bays, the defenders on Oahu received a bracing glimpse of the future. To Sprague and others in naval aviation, it was proof enough of the hitting power of their new weapon. The following year the *Lexington* took part in a successful air raid drill on the Panama Canal. Slowly but steadily aircraft carriers were breaking the battleship's monopoly in the business of projecting offensive power at sea. Sprague spent fourteen months aboard the *Lexington* before doing a tour on shore duty in May 1929. He was in the vanguard of the new wave. But if any lessons were distilled from those early mock assaults on the Pacific Fleet Headquarters, the Navy had all but forgotten them come December 7, 1941.

That day, as captain of the seaplane tender *Tangier,* Sprague watched every ship tied up to Ford Island except his get hit during the Japanese attack. Loaded with torpedoes, an inferno awaiting its spark, the *Tangier* early in the battle became shrouded in smoke from the burning wrecks around her. The previous day, December 6, Sprague had upbraided his crew for their sloppy performance during an intensive series of drills. He broke with his nature and let them have it. Gathering his officers in the *Tangier*'s wardroom, Sprague said, "We're not prepared. We can't trust the Japanese. How do you know the Japanese won't attack tomorrow?" The next morning the Combined Fleet struck. The *Tangier*'s gunners were by many accounts the first in the harbor to fire on the Japanese. They brought down three enemy planes, and their ship was never hit.

Among his classmates in the Annapolis class of 1920, however, Sprague was among the last to lead an aircraft carrier into action. Forrest Sherman was captain of the *Wasp* as early as 1942. J. J. "Jocko" Clark commanded the *Yorktown.* Thomas Sprague—no relation to Clif—began skippering the *Intrepid* in June 1943. When Sprague was ashore at Annapolis serving as a flight instructor ten years out of the academy, one of his students was a man who would become the most publicly acclaimed naval officer since Dewey. Capt. William F. Halsey decided early on to stake his professional fortunes on the wings of the naval air service. "I was eating, drinking, and breathing aviation," Halsey wrote in his memoirs. "I flew as often as . . . Ziggy Sprague would give me a ride."

While Sherman, Clark, and Tommy Sprague were living on the sharp edge of the naval air war against Japan, Ziggy Sprague was ashore, first supervising air defenses along the Atlantic and Gulf coastlines of Florida, then commanding Seattle's Sand Point Naval

Air Station. But soon enough Sprague would have a new seagoing command. It would only strengthen his appreciation for what carrier-based airpower could do.

In October 1943 Sprague took command of the newly minted *Essex*-class fleet carrier *Wasp,* the seventh Navy ship since the Revolution to carry that storied name. The *Wasp*'s most recent namesake, captained by Forrest Sherman, had been sunk by a Japanese submarine off Guadalcanal the year before. But American industry saw to it that *Wasp* number six was replaced by an even more formidable ship. Built to house nearly 3,500 officers and crew, the *Wasp*'s seventh incarnation was launched at Quincy's Fore River Shipyard on August 17, 1943.

Ziggy Sprague was slow to make his mark on the new ship, slow even to be noticed. The ship's newsletter reported that Captain Sprague, true to modest form, "came in quietly and took over with so little fanfare that it was several days before the word got around." But there was no doubting his effectiveness. One of Sprague's officers aboard the *Wasp* was Lt. John Roosevelt, the youngest son of the president who would shortly make Sprague an admiral. Lieutenant Roosevelt wrote that Sprague "took a very green crew and molded us together into a unit that each and every one of us had a personal pride in."

At the *Wasp*'s commissioning ceremony in Boston, Sprague had told the assembled crew, "The air group is the only reason for the carrier's existence. Remember that. . . . Their comfort and efficiency is our major concern. . . . A carrier, offensively, you know, is no better than the air group it supports." They were the words of a true flyboy.

Sprague's appreciation for his air groups was shared at the highest level of carrier command. The Navy's leading maestro of carrier operations, Vice Adm. Marc A. Mitscher, knew that a pilot's value went beyond economic calculation. "You can train a pilot for $50,000. But never, ever tell a pilot that," Mitscher would tell his biographer. "We can't buy pilots with money. . . . The whole striking force of this carrier, all we spend in preparation and operation up to this point, finally is spearheaded by a hundred young pilots. Each of these boys is captain of his own ship. What he thinks, his confidence in what he is doing, how hard he presses home the attack, is exactly how effective we are. . . . We don't hypnotize them. These kids aren't crazy."

As important as pilots were, good old-fashioned seamanship remained essential in carrier operations too. On this score Sprague performed admirably. At the helm of the *Wasp* under air attack during the Battle of the Philippine Sea in June 1944, he maneuvered the ship so skillfully that he dodged three bombs dropped by Japanese planes and won the Navy's Legion of Merit for the engagement.

About three weeks later, on July 9, 1944, Captain Sprague was appointed to the temporary wartime rank of rear admiral by order of President Franklin Roosevelt. The president's son, Lieutenant Roosevelt, observed, "When he was promoted from Captain to Admiral, we were all happy that his fine quality of leadership had been recognized but, at the same time, we felt a personal loss when he left the ship."

Sprague, at age forty-eight, was one of the youngest flag officers in the fleet. But admirals did not command individual ships. He would leave the *Wasp* and graduate to bigger things—though in his case bigger things meant smaller ships. In August he found himself assigned to command Carrier Division 25, which consisted of the escort carriers *Fanshaw Bay, Midway, White Plains,* and *Kalinin Bay.* When the Seventh Fleet's escort carriers were divvied up into three task units for the Leyte operation, Carrier Divisions 25 and 26 were joined under the rubric of Taffy 3. Sprague commanded the combined unit from his flag quarters on the *Fanshaw Bay.*

The *Fanshaw Bay*'s skipper, Capt. Douglass P. Johnson, was a gentlemanly Cincinnatian who like Sprague had graduated in the Annapolis class of 1920 and earned his wings during the genesis of naval aviation. Johnson had endeared himself to his crew on the *Fanny B.*'s maiden voyage, ferrying aircraft to Australia. Fleeing an enemy sub, Johnson was informed that the carrier's boilers were reaching their temperature limit. In the fine rhetorical tradition of Farragut, Dewey, and Nelson, Captain Johnson shouted into the voice tube, "Piss on them then. We need more speed."

Ziggy Sprague was not ambitious in the outwardly grasping manner of some of his colleagues at the flag rank. His predecessor in command of Carrier Division 25 was Rear Adm. Gerald F. Bogan, who was promoted to command one of Halsey's Third Fleet carrier groups. During his tenure aboard the *Fanny B.*, Bogan could not seem to bear the perceived indignity of flying his flag from the cramped quarters of an escort carrier. He made sure his officers and crew participated in his misery. Though most were new enlistees and reservists who had never before been to sea, Bogan demanded perfection of them, or at least perfect compliance with "Rocks and Shoals," which began with the declaration: "The commanders of all fleets, squadrons, naval stations, and vessels belonging to the Navy are required to show in themselves a good example of virtue, honor, patriotism, and subordination."

The indelicate assessment of one senior *Fanshaw Bay* enlisted man was that Bogan was a "first-class horse's rear end." And the disdain was decidedly mutual. With only one officer excepted, Bogan later wrote, "the entire crew [of the *Fanshaw Bay*] was incompetent." Years after the war he would harbor bitterness toward the carrier, decrying it as "the worst ship I'd ever seen in any Navy." If Bogan's attitude toward the *Fanshaw Bay* was determined by the drag he thought it exerted on his professional ascent, perhaps an ambitious officer was bound to hope that his assignment to command an escort carrier division was a short one. Climbing the flag ranks required heading to the front lines with the big fleet carriers, not sitting in a rear area aboard a dawdling Kaiser coffin. Quiet, gently ironic, professorial in bearing, Sprague never let his ego interfere with his work.

As flag commander, Sprague was no stranger to the well-being of the *Fanshaw Bay*'s crew. He made it his business to walk the decks of the *Fanny B.* and stay mindful of the predicaments of the enlisted man. His style had long been one of good humor and egalitarian informality. He knew how to put nerves at ease with offhand storytelling and easy good humor, a habit of character that was evinced in the wrinkled laugh-lines around his mouth. He was the kind of officer who stopped by the radio room after midnight in his robe and slippers to chat over coffee with whomever he found on duty. At sea he allayed homesickness by easing the enforcement of certain regulations: the galley and mess hall stayed open at all hours, and gambling, while never encouraged, was quietly tolerated. As it was on more than a few Navy ships, gambling was a cottage industry aboard the *Fanshaw Bay*. Marathon craps and poker games were run on the sly in the ship's metal shop and other hideaways belowdecks. The sharp sound of dice ricocheting off metal bulkheads could keep a light sleeper awake through the night. But Ziggy Sprague turned a deaf ear to it, considering it a harmless vice. At best it was a dependable morale-builder for enlisted men, far from home and at sea for the first time.

A *Fanshaw Bay* crewman recalled, "For the first time we had a man in charge of the task unit who made us feel like we were on his team. A man who wasn't mad because he hadn't received an *Essex*-class command."

Ziggy Sprague was wise to use a light hand with the reservists and greenhorn enlistees who manned the *Fanshaw Bay*. Coming from the factories and high schools and cornfields of America, many had received aboard the *Fanshaw Bay* their first sight of the open sea. With several exceptions among the small core of career officers and petty officers on the ship, they were the very definition of a motley crew, in the words of one, "a conglomeration of farmers, ranchers, mechanics, scholars, carpenters and about everything there is *but* actual sailors."

Harold Kight enlisted in January 1944 at age twenty, joining fifteen of his buddies on a train from Holdenville, Oklahoma, to San Diego for boot camp. The oldest of five children from a 250-acre farm in Gum Springs, Oklahoma, south of Tulsa, he had grown up helping his father cultivate corn, peanuts, cotton, pecans, and cattle—whatever would sell in the uncertain economy of the post-Depression plains. Working the fields with his three brothers and sister gave him an appreciation for nature's bounty. Assigned to the *Fanshaw Bay* as a seaman, he struck for a ship's cook rating, working as a mess cook in S Division, which comprised the galley staff and the ship's supply department.

The quality of food at sea was a crapshoot whose odds tended to vary with the length of time the ship had been away from port, despite the blandishments of the 1944 edition of the *Cook Book of the United States Navy:* "Active men need large amounts of energy, 3,000 to 4,500 calories per day. . . . Planning the menu, therefore, should be of primary importance to the commissary personnel, for upon it depends, to a great extent, the health and morale of the men in the general mess." The *Cook Book* suggested that menus be prepared a week in advance. A chart offered seasonal pattern menus for the three daily meals—breakfast, dinner, and supper. In autumn, a

Tuesday breakfast should feature orange juice, hot wheat cereal, scrambled eggs and ham, coffee cake, butter, milk, and coffee. Main supper dishes included pork sausage links and sauerkraut pie, smothered ham slices, tomato rarebit on toast, and spareribs with barbecue sauce. "While the emphasis in menu planning is placed on the nutritive value of the food," the *Cook Book* said, "attention must also be given to providing meals which are interesting, attractive, varied, and satisfying. This is helpful in maintaining good morale."

The ubiquity of meat products on the template menus suggests a degree of optimism on the part of War Department nutritionists. CVEs were short on refrigerated storage space, and so meat and other perishables never lasted long. The Army guys who came aboard from time to time professed to love the food. Coming from their jungle hellholes where they subsisted on lizards, frogs, worms, and who knew what else, they must have seen a plate of mutton garnished with the ever-present navy beans as an exotic and flavorful indulgence. "Hey, we had good chow; they bragged on it," Kight said. "You couldn't find any better bakers than the Navy had aboard those ships," he said. The bread was fine, so long as weevils didn't infest the flour.

If the cooks of S Division could not hope to please all comers, at least they could serve them efficiently. Like the victory gardens and scrap metal drives back home, the *Cook Book* reflected the nation's preoccupation with using limited assets efficiently.

> [A] large mess serving 1,000 men will use less food than ten messes each serving 100 men. To conserve food and avoid great amounts of leftovers, the following reductions are recommended: For messes of 500 to 1,000 men, reduce the ingredients in the recipe by 5 per cent. For messes of 1,000 men or more, reduce the amounts of the ingredients in the recipe by 10 per cent.

The imperative to avoid waste was contagious. Inside the front cover of his Navy cookbook, Harold Kight scrawled a recipe for making cottage cheese out of sour milk: "*Pour milk into double boiler, heat over warm water until soft curd has formed, pour into thin cloth bag and drain. Remove curd from bag, break into fine pieces and moisten with cream and season to taste.*" In the wartime Navy, you learned to make do. You made food out of waste. You took shortcuts to get the job done. Indeed, the very same notion of efficiency and making more out of less was at the very core of the small carriers that Ziggy Sprague would take into harm's way.

*　　*　　*

ESCORT CARRIERS HAD MANY nicknames, only a few tinged with anything resembling affection: jeep carriers, Woolworth flattops, Kaiser coffins, one-torpedo ships. Wags in the fleet deadpanned that the acronym CVE stood for the escort carrier's three most salient characteristics: combustible, vulnerable, expendable. That most everyone seemed to get the joke—laughing in that grim, nervous way—was probably the surest sign that it was rooted in truth.

When the *Fanshaw Bay,* the *Samuel B. Roberts,* and the rest of Taffy 3 took up positions off the Philippines, painful memories of the escort carrier *Liscome Bay* were still fresh in their minds. The disaster that befell her became an indelible memory for all who served on CVEs. Before dawn on November 24, 1943, Capt. Irving D. Wiltsie was turning his ship into the wind to launch the morning antisubmarine patrol off Makin Island in the Gilberts chain when an explosion shook the ship and a tall column of water rose from the starboard side. Faster than the human mind could register fear, the collapsing column of seawater was turned to vapor by a massive, flaming secondary explosion triggered deep within the bowels of the ship. A torpedo from a Japanese sub that had slipped past the screening ships hit the escort carrier on her starboard quarter, bursting in the aircraft bomb stowage compartment below the waterline.

The explosion blasted skyward a storm of oil, molten metal, splinters of burning decking, and shredded human flesh, a grisly potpourri that rained down on ships of the task group for miles around. The Taffy 3 destroyer *Hoel* was bombarding Makin at the time. "It didn't look like any ship at all," wrote Lt. John C. W. Dix, the *Hoel*'s communications officer. "We thought it was an ammunition dump. . . . She just went *whoom*—an orange ball of flame."

Fourteen pilots and aircrew from the *Liscome Bay*'s squadron, VC-39, sitting in their planes awaiting launch, met fiery deaths at the controls of their aircraft. Hundreds of men belowdecks were incinerated by fire, slain by force of shock, or cooked by superheated steam released from broken boilers. Flames that would have overwhelmed four alarms' worth of firefighters in a major city formed an inferno whose roar drowned out all but the loudest shouts. But they were quenched altogether just twenty-three minutes later when the *Liscome Bay*'s eviscerated hull slipped hissing and groaning beneath the waves. Lost with her were 644 men, including both Captain Wiltsie and Rear Adm. Henry M. Mullenix, the commander of the escort carrier group.

The *Liscome Bay*, a product of the shipyard at Vancouver, Washington, had survived just 109 days from her commissioning. But for the rest of the war the memory of her hellish end lurked in the consciousness of anyone aboard an escort carrier.

In 1944 a journalist traveling with the Taffy 3 escort carrier *White Plains* wrote, "A jeep carrier bears the same relation to a normal naval vessel that is borne to a district of fine homes by a respectable, but struggling, working-class suburb. There is a desperate effort to keep up appearances with somewhat inadequate materials and not wholly successful results." Nonetheless, in important ways the *Fanshaw Bay* and her five sister ships in Sprague's Taffy 3 task unit—the *Gambier Bay*, the *Kalinin Bay*, the *Kitkun Bay*, the *St. Lo*, and the *White Plains*—were the very emblem of American power. The way they were built and deployed signified both the Navy's unparalleled mastery of the vital business of carrier warfare and America's coming-of-age as a nation of shipbuilders.

Like her larger cousins the *Lexington* and the *Saratoga*, the *Fanshaw Bay* and her sisters in the *Casablanca* class of escort carriers were adapted from blueprints for a vessel with an altogether different nature and mission. An escort carrier was built on a cargo ship's hull. Shipbuilding magnate Henry J. Kaiser was the Lee Iacocca of his day, a visionary industrialist whose name was a household word. Among his innovations was the Liberty ship, a cargo vessel that could be mass-produced virtually like an oceangoing Model T. Using a breakthrough welding technique, submerged arc welding, that could stitch steel plate with molten rivets up to twenty times faster than existing methods, Kaiser's shipbuilders produced a Liberty ship in an average of only forty-two days.

Seeing that he was in a position to bolster not only America's merchant marine but also the Navy's offensive capability, Kaiser's next brainstorm was to reconfigure his merchantmen as aircraft carriers. However brilliant their means of construction, Kaiser took shortcuts on components and materials. Escort carriers did not have many watertight compartments, a standard damage-control feature on American combatants. The ships were driven by inexpensive, idiosyncratic Skinner Uniflow steam turbines, peculiar in design and nonconforming with Navy specs for cylinder lubrication, filtering, and quality of fittings, and foreign to the young mechanics coming out of America's wartime technical schools. In combat conditions breakdowns were common. The hull of a CVE was no better than its engines. High in sulfur and phosphorus content, the thin steel was brittle, a deficiency that worsened when all the hatches, vents, and other structural discontinuities were accounted for.

Though compromise had its costs, it was necessary if the ships were to be built in time and the Navy was to pursue the war using naval airpower. The escort carrier's most essential variation from the design of the Liberty ship was the addition of a 477-foot flight deck. It was made of wood, inlaid with steel fittings for tying down planes. The expense of the cross-deck wood planking could not be avoided. A carrier spent much of its day enveloped in an invisible cloud of aviation-fuel vapors. A dropped wrench, a bomb dolly unloaded too hard onto a metal flight deck, could create a spark that could well be disastrous. A wooden flight deck reduced the frequency of sparks that could ignite a carrier's tinder. If fire was a concern, heat wasn't. Temperatures belowdecks on warships cruising the equatorial latitudes were sweltering. In his campaign to cut costs, Kaiser did not install blower systems to ventilate the lower compartments. Crews sweated miserably.

Accompanying Atlantic convoys in 1943, the CVEs and their air groups were deployed to defend merchant convoys against submarine attack. Soon other missions came their way. There was certainly no shortage of new CVEs looking for work. In a one-year sprint of production from July 8, 1943, to July 8, 1944, Kaiser's shipyards launched fifty *Casablanca*-class escort carriers. Ferrying new aircraft to the front was one such job, unglamorous but essential to maintaining a high-tempo air war against Japan. The *Fanshaw Bay*'s first mission was to take a load of P-38 Lightnings to Australia in 1944. If some belittled them as "buckets," escort carriers formed a highly effective bucket brigade, carrying urgently needed planes to the far reaches of the Pacific. And the Marines soon learned to love them as well. Sailing with invasion fleets to give air support to American troops. CVE pilots became expert in placing bombs into hard-to-hit caves and crevices. The learning curve was steep, but so was the cost to Japanese defenders.

Significantly too, the low cost of the CVEs was its own form of defense. With the escort carriers' aerial striking force spread over a larger number of small flight decks, the loss of any one ship did little to reduce the group's overall strength. With its six escort carriers, Taffy 3 fielded the same number of aircraft—about 165—as two large fleet carriers. But if a Japanese plane got lucky, penetrated Sprague's defenses, and scored a bomb hit that sank one of their number with most of its planes aboard, the group's collective striking power would drop by only one-sixth, not one-half. This simple arithmetic was itself a powerful military virtue. With so many wooden-planked flight decks arrayed against them, be they the 477-footers of the CVEs or the 872-footers of the *Essex*-class fleet carriers, Japan had little hope of whittling away America's control of the skies.

The *Fanshaw Bay*'s baptism by fire was rather less calamitous than the *Liscome Bay*'s. It came in June, during the invasion of Saipan, two months before Sprague came aboard as commander of Carrier Division 25 and the other ships of Taffy 3. Launched by catapult in his fully loaded TBM Avenger, Lt. (jg) Joseph W. Oberlin, one of Composite Squadron 68's outstanding pilots, lost power on takeoff for a predawn mission. The plane hit the sea ahead of the ship. With the carrier bearing down on the sinking plane, Captain Johnson ordered a stop bell. As engineers in the firerooms worked furiously to slow the steam, the ship narrowly avoided running over the pilot and his two crewmen. But a few minutes later, after the VC-68 plane had slipped beneath the surface, several deep explosions shook the water and rattled the ship's brittle hull. It was the Avenger's depth charges, exploding at their preassigned depth. "Boy, I thought we'd bought the farm, and so did everyone else!" recalled crewman Vernon Miller. "The pipes rattled, and the dust about choked us. But when all settled down and we got the full-speed bell again, we were still afloat." Lieutenant Oberlin and his two enlisted crewmen, gunner Don Yoakum and radioman George Koepp, were less fortunate. The shock from the undersea blast killed them in the water.

Two days later the American invasion force came under attack by some seventy Japanese bombers and torpedo planes. Leonard Moser, an aviation machinist's mate first class, was standing on a catwalk near the after elevator. Leaning on the rag mop he had forgotten he was holding, he watched the Japanese planes bear down on the *Fanshaw Bay*. Intense fire from her gunners and the surrounding destroyers knocked three Japanese planes into the sea. A sleek Tony fighter plane survived the barrage, flew over the ship, puffs of smoke reaching back from its fuselage into its slipstream as the shells struck home. Moser thought the plane would explode in midair, right above the ship. But then he saw the bomb. It fell from the plane's wing, arced downward, and struck the *Fanshaw Bay* smack on the after elevator. The bomb penetrated the elevator and exploded in midair above the hangar deck below, where plane handlers were fueling and arming their aircraft for battle.

The bomb's detonation burst Leonard Moser's eardrums and set aflame the business end of his mop. But the most serious damage was belowdecks. When the bomb exploded, Lt. (jg) Tommy Lupo, a TBM Avenger pilot from New Orleans, and his roommate were running across the hangar deck to the ladder that led up to the flight deck. Lupo and his buddy were talking as they ran, and when Lupo turned to say something to him, his roommate was headless. The pilot ran at least five steps without his head.

Fire consumed the aft part of the hangar deck. Fourteen men died there; twenty-three more were wounded. The blast burst a saltwater main, and as water raced through open compartments, the ship began to founder. With water rushing in faster than the submersible pumps could send it back out, the ship began to list and settle. Asbestos insulation shook loose from the pipes and ducts overhead and choked the pumps with its detritus.

Members of a repair party dove beneath the surface of the chest-deep water, scooping handfuls of asbestos from the intakes of the pumps. Augmented by bucket brigades manned by all available hands, the pumps needed four hours to bring the water level down to the kneecaps. The ship would survive.

The *Fanshaw Bay* was lucky. The bomb's blast had shredded a thick braid of intertwined electrical cables, which began to burn, dropping molten chunks of the conductive alloy onto a rack of aerial torpedoes stacked on the hangar deck. "Whatever kept them from exploding I'll never know," Leonard Moser wrote. "Had they exploded, I'm sure it would have sunk the ship. God was with us."

Offshore of the sprawling deathscapes of Makin and Tarawa

atolls, the bomb blast left fourteen men dead aboard CVE-70. They were duly buried at sea en route to Pearl Harbor for repairs. The *Fanny B.* was still a lucky ship: she had been one live igniter switch away from becoming a full-scale reenactment of the calamity of the *Liscome Bay.*

Rear Adm. Clifton A. F. Sprague had not grown up religious. Formal worship had played no role in his upbringing in Massachusetts. When he made the *Fanshaw Bay* his flagship on August 28, just ten weeks after its near catastrophe off Saipan, he came aboard a ship that had already once tested the extent of its blessings. Sprague would soon have his own opportunity to try the fickle mercy of King Neptune, or God.

Six

Warships have two names: the one they are christened with and the letters and numbers that designate them in the fleet's inventory. Ziggy Sprague's flagship the *Fanshaw Bay* was named for a scenic bay in Alaska, a name that conferred upon the ship an identity by which the crew, the public, and history might remember her. But she was known to the fleet's record keepers as CVE-70, the letters indicating her type, and the number giving her just enough individuality to set her apart on the Bureau of Ships' ledgers.

The aviators who made their home aboard the *Fanshaw Bay* during the Philippine operation had no name to give them a collective identity. Under the command of Lt. Cdr. Richard Spalding Rogers from Berkeley, California, who had finished a tour in the Atlantic flying antisubmarine patrols against German U-boats, they were known simply as VC-68. The letter V indicated that the squadron flew heavier-than-air vehicles. This designation was a relic of naval aviation's early days when helium-filled dirigibles appeared to be permanent fixtures in the fleet. The C indicated the squadron's type: a *composite* squadron, one composed of a mix of aircraft types. Larger carriers had two or three distinct squadrons, each specialized by their mission: VT for torpedo bombers, VB for dive-bombers, and VF for fighters. Escort carriers had no such luxury. One group was all they had.

VC-68's complement of aircraft and personnel varied. It typically had at its disposal twelve to sixteen FM-2 Wildcat fighters, eight to twelve TBM-1C Avenger torpedo bombers, and four pilots for every three aircraft. It was a versatile mix. Although Wildcats no longer flew from the frontline fleet carriers—those ships fielded the F6F Hellcat fighter, superior in every way—the FM-2s were sturdy and dependable. When flown well, especially at lower altitudes, Wildcats could hold their own against the nimble Japanese A6M Zeros. The Wildcat pilots learned to depend on their plane's native advantages: its armored cockpit, self-sealing fuel tanks, and heavy armament of four .50-caliber wing-mounted machine guns. On these inherent strengths squadron tacticians developed and refined team-oriented tactics that could defeat the faster, more maneuverable Zeros. Though their primary mission was air-to-air combat—shooting down enemy aircraft while protecting American ships and attack aircraft—the Wildcats could carry a light bomb load too. Their pilots, however, found to their dismay that the bombs could be difficult to drop: a pilot had not only to pull the bomb release but also to jerk the plane's rudder back and forth, shaking the plane in midflight to dislodge the bombs from their notoriously sticky mountings.

The TBM Avenger torpedo bomber was a marvel of aviation engineering, faster, longer-ranged, and more powerful than the death trap that was its predecessor, the Douglas Aircraft Company's TBD Devastator. Designed by Grumman but manufactured later in the war on the more capacious assembly lines of the General Motors Eastern Aircraft Division, the Avenger packed a tremendous punch. Its massive bomb bay could carry either a single 2,000-pound Mark 13 aerial torpedo—devastating against enemy shipping—or four 500-pound bombs. The plane's big weapons bay could hold a still larger number of 100-pound antipersonnel bombs for attacking troops on the ground. Or the planes could be outfitted with depth charges for antisubmarine patrols. The plane's wings were fitted with rails—four on each side—for firing air-to-surface rockets five inches in circumference, useful for blasting targets ashore or at sea. Finally, the Avengers had a pair of wing-mounted .50-caliber machine guns, a third housed in a rotating, flat-sided glass-domed turret behind the plane's long greenhouse canopy, and a smaller .30-caliber machine gun, the "stinger," behind the weapons bay and below the fuselage. It took three men to fly the Avenger: a pilot, who was usually an officer, and two enlisted men—a gunner to operate the turret and a radioman below.

The potential mix of weaponry made the Avengers marvelously versatile. Tactics evolved to maximize the value of all of these weapons types. Avenger pilots could put their aircraft into a shallow dive, fire their wing-mounted machine guns to zero in on a target with phosphorus-tailed tracer bullets, then let loose with the rockets, which were aligned to follow the path of the bullets. Avengers carrying bombs could place them on target in any number of ways. They could be dropped from higher altitudes or placed with greater accuracy from a shallow dive. Since the Avengers were primarily designed to attack ships with torpedoes, flying level as they approached their targets, they were not optimally equipped for steep dives. They had no air brakes, the flaps of perforated metal that swung down from the trailing edge of the wings to slow and control the plummeting plane. Some Avenger pilots treated their lumbering aircraft like dive-bombers nonetheless, plunging from the clouds to lay bombs on enemy targets with pinpoint precision. They were as likely to die from impact with the top of a palm tree as from the inevitably withering enemy antiaircraft fire.

A torpedo attack, uniquely dangerous, required a pilot to fly low, slow, and perfectly straight. The mantra, drummed into every torpedo bomber pilot during flight training, was "needle-ball and airspeed." The challenge was to keep his eyes focused on two instruments, the needle-ball, which indicated the plane's orientation on the horizontal plane, and the airspeed indicator. If the pilot could keep both instruments within the narrow parameters needed for a successful drop, the torpedo would enter the water like a free-style swimmer hitting the water from a racing podium: flat, straight, and true. A pilot who flew too fast, or with any degree of pitch, yaw, or bounce, or at an altitude that caused the torpedo to enter the ocean with excessive force, was likely to see his torpedo veer off course or "porpoise."

The cruelty of the torpedo pilot's trade was that the greater his proficiency at straight, slow, and exquisitely stable flight, the greater his chances of being blown from the sky. By reputation, fighter pilots were the wilder breed of aviator—daring individualists who itched to match reflexes with an enemy counterpart in the skies. In less sober moments fighter jocks were prone to razz the Avenger guys as "pickle luggers," their bulky aircraft as "turkeys." Yet when the Wildcat drivers paused to consider what their buddies at the stick of an Avenger might be called upon to do—bore in on a hostile warship, one eye focused on needle-ball and airspeed, the other on the target, alight from stem to stern with guns aimed their way—few were eager to trade places with them. A TBM pilot from the escort carrier *St. Lo,* Ens. William C. Brooks, said, "They looked at us and said, 'Good God, I wouldn't get into that thing and do what you do for all the tea in China.' "

*   *   *

THE OLDEST SALTS ABOARD the USS *St. Lo,* its chief petty officers, knew a thing or two about ship names. They knew at least this: that according to tradition, it was plain bad luck to have your ship's name changed when under way during wartime. The blessings of the Navy's christening ceremony were many and manifold. You just didn't throw that away. If you did, disaster was sure to follow.

Although the Navy secretary's custom had been to name Henry Kaiser's new *Casablanca*-class escort carriers after bays, when CVE-63 came off the ways at Vancouver, Washington, on August 17, 1943, the triumph at the Battle of Midway in June 1942 was still deliciously fresh in mind. And so in a rush of bureaucratic exuberance, perhaps, the ship was christened two months later in honor of the battle that had turned the war's tide. The USS *Midway* was born.

But someone in the Navy Department soon thought better of giving such an outsize name to the decidedly in-size ship. The honor of carrying the name Midway should belong to a carrier more majestic than a Kaiser coffin. Midway, the battle, had turned the course of the war. *Midway,* the ship, should reflect the glory of its namesake victory just as proudly as the *Saratoga* and the *Lexington* did theirs. With the Navy's next big carrier, a 45,000-ton thoroughbred designated CVB-41, under construction at Newport News, Virginia, the name was summarily wrested from CVE-63 and given to the new leviathan.

On October 10, 1944, as the *Midway* lay at anchor in Seeadler Harbor, at Manus in the Admiralty Islands, news arrived that the jeep carrier would be renamed the *St. Lo* in honor of the Army's recent triumph in France after the D-Day landings. Few of the veteran crew aboard CVE-63 seemed disposed to appreciate the honor, however. When the news came down of the name change, the groans of the chief petty officers reverberated through the ship's brittle hull so loudly as to defy the rumpus of the Uniflow turbines. "Damn Navy," said an old chief boatswain's mate. "You don't change the name of a ship. It's an ill-fated ship. It'll be at the bottom of the ocean in two weeks."

As career sailors—many were in their forties—they had served in the U.S. Navy since the Depression, had lived and breathed the legends and superstitions that formed the core of Navy tradition. Stories circulated of newly renamed ships taking to sea, never to be seen again. In some divisions on the *St. Lo,* as many as ninety percent of the men requested transfers. Still, many younger members of the ship's company—the teenage seamen, the twentysomething ninety-day wonder ensigns and lieutenants junior grade—brushed off the superstitions of their elders. "We didn't shudder and shake about it," said Ensign Brooks, the junior ensign in the *St. Lo's* resident squadron, VC-65. "We respected their view, but we didn't get all uptight about it. We were too busy doing something else."

Ever since the *St. Lo* had taken position off Samar with the *Fanshaw Bay* and the other ships of Taffy 3 on October 18, there was indeed no shortage of things for pilots to do. Fliers assigned to morning patrol were roused from their quarters at four A.M. After reveille the Filipino stewards served them a quick breakfast of coffee, eggs, and navy beans. Then, chart boards in hand and parachute harnesses strapped to their backs, they climbed to the flight deck before the sun was up, vaulted into the cockpits of their planes, and ignited their big radial engines to life. Running through the preflight checklist as plane handlers muscled the aircraft into their harnesses on the catapult track, the pilots pressed back against their headrests as the big steam pistons under the flight deck slung the planes from zero to seventy knots in just sixty feet of space. Spitting flames from their exhaust stacks under their cowlings, the heavily laden torpedo bombers dropped from the flight deck toward the water before their big propellers grabbed enough air to carry them away into the predawn darkness ahead of the ship.

Flying at three or four thousand feet, with their fourteen-cylinder, nineteen-hundred-horsepower Wright radial engines throttled back to minimum RPMs and the manifold pressure set for efficient fuel consumption, the TBM-1C Avengers could remain on station for up to six or seven hours on a single mission. Their extended vigilance—patrols were more customarily four or four and a half hours—put tremendous pressure on any Japanese submarines aiming to take a shot at Taffy 3. The enemy often stalked American ships by dawn, hoping to catch a carrier silhouetted against the sunrise for an easy torpedo attack. But when the morning light was just right and the wind was in check and if the sub was not too deep, a pilot looking down at the proper angle to the ocean's reflective sheen could actually see the silhouette of the underwater predator, like the dim form of a trout in a shaded pool. If friendly surface ships were close, the pilot would radio the contact to the fleet, summoning a destroyer to hunt it down. Then he would dive down and drop his depth charges on the target.

The urgent tempo of wartime operations always put a little guesswork in the difficult business of distinguishing friendly subs from foe. It was a lesson that the *St. Lo*'s aviators had learned the hard way three weeks before taking up station off Samar, during the invasion of Morotai. On October 3 a spread of torpedoes had appeared from the deep, narrowly missing the *St. Lo* and the *Fanshaw Bay*, and struck the USS *Shelton* in the stern, leaving the destroyer escort dead in the water. At eleven A.M. that morning Bill Brooks, launched to conduct a "hunter-killer" search, spotted a suspicious contact close to the enemy sub's expected location, and radioman Ray Travers blinkered that day's Morse code signal to the submarine.

The sub, running with her decks awash but her conning tower still clearly visible, not only failed to return the correct signal but did not respond at all. It continued to dive. By the time Brooks swung around again and winged over to strike, the submarine was under water. He dropped a stick of depth charges some fifty to seventy-five yards ahead of where he guessed it had submerged, then released a canister of fluorescent green dye to pinpoint the vessel's last known location. Brooks reported his attack and remained on station until relief arrived in the form of the destroyer escort USS *Rowell*.

The *Rowell*'s ping jockeys heard through their headsets the telltale *ping-woo-woo-oo* that signaled contact with an undersea target and began dropping depth charges. Shortly after the foam of the last detonation settled, the *Rowell*'s crew watched as iridescent bubbles of oil surfaced near their ship. Floating up with the mess was an assortment of flotsam and debris that signaled the end for the target and all hands aboard her—the American submarine USS *Seawolf.*

After investigation by a board of inquiry, no discipline was taken against Brooks or his crew. But the lesson of the Morotai incident was clear: when bad luck strikes, it is usually the function of a cause far simpler and more readily determinable than crossed stars or a changed ship name.

*   *   *

LIKE THE REST OF the pilots of the fleet, Taffy 3's fliers were the product of a carefully structured, multilayered training system that did for the Navy's raw human assets what the great coastal and riverine shipyards were doing for its steel. The Navy's aviation program had ballooned in scope since the early 1920s, when Ziggy Sprague joined Pensacola's inaugural class of cadet fliers. By 1943 pilot training had been standardized and systematized. With some thirty thousand aircraft rolling out of America's factories each year and Detroit's automotive production lines ramped up and recalibrated to the close tolerances needed to build airplanes, the Navy scrambled to find enough pilots to fly them.

Mostly the service looked to college students to swell its naval aviator ranks, although a college degree was not required if one had the strength and smarts to complete the rigorous training. At first the Navy restricted the privilege of flight to newly commissioned ensigns and other officers. Then grudgingly the Navy relented in the face of war's demands, allowing senior enlisted men to enter pilot training. In 1943 the Navy announced its goal to train 25,000 student naval aviators that year in order to keep pace with combat and operational losses and fill the flight decks of carriers under construction. A network of preflight and primary flight training schools sprung up all across the country, from Long Island to San Diego, from Corpus Christi to the Great Lakes.

Bill Brooks did his preflight training at Chapel Hill, North Carolina, learning the basics of aerodynamics, meteorology, mathematics, survival swimming, naval etiquette, and other subjects that did not require strapping oneself into a cockpit. Emerging from Chapel Hill as a cadet, he first flew solo during primary flight training at Independence, Indiana. There he became acquainted with the N3N

Yellow Peril, a two-seater biplane trainer that was forgiving to green hands practicing stalls, rolls, loops, and S turns but that had a dangerous tendency to ground-loop—to cartwheel on landing from the torque created by the engine and the narrowly set landing gear. A pilot could be killed on impact, or a hard shock could rupture a fuel line in the exposed, air-cooled engine, causing a catastrophic fire.

Certified proficient at the entry level, Brooks and his thirty-five classmates moved on to intermediate training at Pensacola, where they flew increasingly powerful single-wing planes: the Vultee Valiant, better known to its trainees as the Vultee Vibrator, and the North American SNJ Texan. Now that the trainees had more or less proven their physical and psychological resilience, their reward was to fly planes that were actually armed. Training at Whiting Field included low-level bombing, strafing, night flying, aerobics, and combat tactics. When they finished the syllabus, the pilots had a choice to make: would they go on to fly fighters, torpedo bombers, or dive-bombers? For Brooks—six foot one, 185 pounds, a former member of the Southern Cal football team—sitting down in a fighter plane's cramped cockpit was "like getting into a shoebox." His knees were jammed up under his chin, the controls too close for his long arms. So he chose the more spacious cockpit setup of torpedo bombers.

To train as a torpedo bomber pilot, Brooks went to Baron Field Naval Air Station near Mobile, Alabama—nicknamed "Bloody Baron" owing to the occasional crashes that resulted when the airfield's swirling red dust gummed up the planes' air-cooled engines. There Brooks rehearsed higher-risk operations like night missions, tactical flying, and field carrier landings. Nearly one-third of the trainees washed out before they completed intermediate training. It was the final hurdle before Cadet Brooks returned to Pensacola to get a set of wings pinned to his chest and the single gold stripe of a commissioned Navy ensign sewn into his sleeve.

At advanced flight training at Opalaca, Florida, the discipline and danger of attacking a ship while flying with fixed needle-ball and airspeed was drummed into Brooks day and night. He spent several days there flying the accursed Douglas TBD Devastators. "They flew like a bus," Brooks said of the sluggish old death traps of the Battle of Midway. Brooks did not relish the thought of riding the misnamed Devastator into battle. But soon enough the next-generation Grumman Avengers arrived. Flying the faster, more powerful plane—dropping torpedoes, both dummy and live, into hundred-foot-long target sleds towed by tugboats—pilots experimented with higher altitudes and faster airspeeds for dropping a torpedo and speeding to the escape. The Avenger could successfully drop while flying at 280 knots at an altitude of 500 feet. That was more than double the optimum attack altitude for the Devastator and twice its rated speed. At the same time the pilots went to ground school to refine their knowledge of emergency procedures, hydraulics, and cockpit layout. They drilled until they could operate all systems blindfolded—an exercise that could save the life of a pilot whose windscreen was blown out during combat and who became blinded by a hot spray of engine oil.

After he finished advanced training, a young man aspiring to become a certified naval aviator had to pass one last test: mastering the difficult art of landing on a moving redwood flight deck and catching an arrester wire with the tail hook. Before entering the pool for a squadron assignment, a trainee pilot had to land six successful touch-and-go's at the Navy's Carrier Qualification Training Unit, which operated two makeshift aircraft carriers on Lake Michigan, converted paddlewheel excursion boats named the *Wolverine* and the *Sable*. Completing this task required the instincts, courage, and feel that separated a carrier pilot from his land-based brethren. Those traits had to be second nature, because a pilot returning from combat might well have to perform this feat while fatigued after a long afternoon in the air, or while slowly bleeding to death from wounds suffered in battle. Sometimes a pilot had to do it at night, when the cues from the landing signal officer—who for an aviator is the most important individual on the ship after the captain—were but two red fireflies darting to and fro in the darkness.

The final air strike of the Marianas campaign was a case in point showing the dangers of nighttime carrier landings. Vice Admiral Mitscher's decision to launch late in the day—too late for a daylight return—was a calculated gamble. When the pilots returned after dark, locating their carriers in the void of the nighttime sea was nearly impossible.

As his fliers felt their way home through the night, their fuel tanks nearly empty, Mitscher broke the strict nighttime blackout rule, designed to hide the fleet from enemy submarines. He had won the lifelong love of his aviators by following through on his own affection for them. With his pilots desperately searching for a place to land, Mitscher ordered all ships of his task group to switch on their lights.

Jittery about possible exposure to submarine attack, some of his carrier skippers were restrained in their pyrotechnics. But Capt. Clifton A. F. Sprague of the *Wasp* complied with gusto. Sprague lit up his ship like an oceangoing Christmas tree, impaling the night with the probing white fingers of his giant arc spotlights. He switched on the red flight deck lights. Sailors pointed aloft hand-held flashlights. Destroyers fired star shells to illuminate the storm-threatened night. The light show was glorious, like "a Hollywood premiere, Chinese New Year's, and Fourth of July rolled into one," according to the historian Samuel Eliot Morison. With exhausted American aviators bouncing down onto any flight deck that presented itself, losses were kept to a minimum.

Mitscher's gallant risk deeply impressed his aviators. A dive-bomber pilot from the *Enterprise* wrote, "I heard pilots express the opinion that the admirals looked upon the fliers as expendable, and I suppose they must to a certain extent, but I shall never again feel that they wouldn't do everything conceivable in their power to bring a pilot back. . . . It was a demonstration I shall never forget."

*   *   *

WHEN BROOKS COMPLETED HIS training at Glenview, Illinois, he flew to the Grumman factory near Floyd Bennett Field on Long Island to pick up a TBF Avenger, then ferried himself cross-country to San Diego to await a squadron assignment. With none immediately forthcoming, Brooks was ordered to the ordnance depot at Whidbey Island, Washington, where he and other pilots worked with engineers from all around the country—Caltech, Harvard, Columbia, General Electric—to solve the problem of the dud torpedoes, which for the first two years of the war had submarine skippers and torpedo pilots alike risking life and limb in a potentially fruitless effort. A simple engineering miscalculation had resulted in firing pins that failed to ignite.

Completing the syllabus at Whidbey in June 1944, Ensign Brooks boarded a Pan Am China Clipper from San Francisco to Oahu, gathering with hundreds of other newly minted pilots at Ford Island Naval Air Station to await assignment to the fleet. From there he hopped toward the front, from island to exotic island. At Eniwetok, the Navy's forwardmost base at the time, Brooks joined VC-65, the squadron assigned to the escort carrier then known as the USS *Midway*.

The pilots of VC-65 were older than their ship's company. Averaging twenty-three to twenty-four years of age, they had wives and kids. The thirty-year-old squadron commander, Lt. Cdr. Ralph M. Jones, well liked for his fairness and seasonable temperament, knew his business and minded it so long as his pilots knew theirs. If one of them screwed up, he didn't need to raise his voice to register his displeasure. He just glowered—gave them the "big glom." With a graduate engineering degree from MIT, he was a skilled TBM pilot with a Navy Cross to his name. Jones's plane was always first in line for the catapult whenever a combat mission was scheduled.

Although the imaginary bulkheads that separated the air group from the ship's company were thinner and more permeable aboard CVEs than aboard the larger carriers, fliers on both generally considered themselves a breed apart from their deck-bound counterparts. They were concerned with different things, their world uncircumscribed by the boundary of their ship's hull. From high altitudes they were accustomed to seeing their carrier for the rectangular mote that it actually was, traversing a watery plain that reduced it to but fleeting consequence. Flying on a combat mission, they watched their carrier vanish into the vast expanse of ocean. Returning to it was like a homecoming. Befitting these differences, pilots lived in quarters separate from the ship's company. They ate separately, slept separately, socialized separately. They made the ready room their home, gathering there to learn what was new in the world, to read *Time* magazine and listen to Tokyo Rose. Her tauntings, exquisitely delivered in a singsong Nipponese accent, were seldom irritating enough to defeat the bliss of hearing the Glenn Miller Orchestra six thousand miles from home. Pilots listened to her while playing Acey Deucy and Red Dog, while shooting dice. As often as not, Tokyo Rose's broadcast was rooted in just enough truth to be informative and just enough falsehood to be entertaining.

Jones seemed to understand the value of a little sporting rivalry in the squadron. Like his task unit commander, Admiral Sprague, he tolerated gambling in the wardroom. And whenever the Avenger and Wildcat pilots started trading jabs about their aviation pedigree, he just smiled. Larry Budnick, a Wildcat jockey, said, "We razzed the torpedo pilots a lot. We were the guys who were winning the war, you know. It was a friendly rivalry." Just as the Avengers were dubbed "turkeys" or "pickle luggers," the FM-2 Wildcats, with their noisy nine-cylinder, fourteen-hundred-horsepower Wright engines, were "Maytag Messerschmitts." For all the horseplay, mostly they were a serious group, soft-spoken and focused on their mission. Lt. (jg) Leonard "Tex" Waldrop, an Avenger pilot who sported a red beard in mute defiance of squadron guidelines, was affable and agreeable, expansive in a way that befitted the stereotype of his native state. Lt. Tom Van Brunt from Tallahassee was a widely respected TBM pilot too. Though he was among the senior pilots in the squadron, having served stateside as a primary training instructor, Van Brunt had made fewer carrier landings than anyone else on the *St. Lo.* Most of VC-65's pilots had four months of combat experience already. Van Brunt would have been a section leader but for the fact that he was nearly as green as a freshly commissioned ensign when it came to touching down on a flight deck. He had made just five of them—and not one since his wheels last touched the deck of the training ship *Wolverine* during carrier qualifications.

*   *   *

BILL BROOKS'S GREAT-GRANDFATHER HAD been a whaling captain who sailed from ports all along coastal Massachusetts during the mid-1800s, doing his part in the ravenous harvest of the Atlantic coast whale population. When the onset of the Civil War boosted demand for oil, he and other whalers decamped from New England's overpicked seas and took their ships south, around Cape Horn to San Francisco, where they continued to hunt blubber, ranging out to the waters off Maui, then "uphill" against currents and winds to the bounteous waters off Alaska.

A hunter like his great-granddad, Brooks pursued an altogether different sort of Pacific Ocean quarry: the steam-powered gargantuans that flew the pennant of the Imperial Japanese Navy. The twenty-four-year-old pilot was positioned to continue in his great-grandfather's footsteps, if only the U.S. Navy would let him. The sole complication was the fact that the Avenger pilots who flew from CVEs had been, by and large, stripped of their harpoons, their Mark 13 torpedoes. They were not meant to attack enemy surface warships. That job fell to the fliers aboard Admiral Halsey's carriers. Charged with antisubmarine patrol and striking at ground targets in support of Army troops, the Avenger crews of Taffy 3 watched as the war moved beyond them with respect to their primary mode of attack.

Taffy 3's aviators contented themselves with perfecting a type of warfare that was in its infancy and critical to the retaking of the Philippines: the close support mission. The pilots of VC-65 had been pressed into this vital work from the first day of the Leyte invasion. Before the troops went ashore on October 20, Navy special-operations frogmen swam to the beach to clear away obstacles that might impede the progress of the landing force. When their work was finished, Brooks and his squadronmates buzzed the beach at daybreak, cruising low over the wave tops, guns, bombs, and rockets primed and ready as motorboats below zoomed in with big hoops hung overboard to scoop the frogmen out of the water before the enemy could find the range with their shore batteries. With Brooks and his buddies overhead, a Japanese gunner would have been a fool to open fire.

Other times the payload in Brooks's bomb bay was of the nonexplosive variety: bundles of printed leaflets exhorting the Philippine people to support their American liberators. As Brooks took his plane down to 250 feet, treetops zipping by below, his radioman, Ray Travers, opened the bomb bay doors and released a paper storm over the scattered Filipino villages. Though the brutality of the Japanese occupation had all but ensured their wholehearted support in any event, the propaganda boosted their hopes and secured MacArthur's legacy as their savior.

Like the rest of the Avenger crews, Brooks, Travers, and turret gunner Joe Downs preferred more direct forms of engagement with the enemy. Barges, truck convoys, ammo dumps—all were suitable and rewarding targets for a weapons-laden Avenger on a ground support strike. Every day since the landings began on October 20, planes from all three Taffies ranged up and down the Philippine archipelago knocking out enemy infrastructure, interrupting troop movements, playing havoc with communications. Hugging the jungle canopy a hundred feet off the ground, Brooks would hunch forward, looking through his dashboard-mounted gun sight, hunting for quarry. A pilot flying ground support was wise to mind the danger of lingering too long over a target. Those who came in too flat often paid with their lives. Wildcat fighter planes had enough agility for their pilots to fly in steeply. Plummeting at a sixty-degree incline, nearly perpendicular to the ground, they presented the smallest possible target, forced the antiaircraft gunners into a difficult high-angle shot, and built up maximum speed to flee a target area that was sure to be popping with hot lead. Brooks in his Avenger couldn't manage such a steep dive, but he knew the value of maintaining his airspeed for a fast escape. Rather than pull up sharply and make a high-altitude exit, as some instructors had taught him, Brooks liked to stay low and fly away at treetop level. That technique kept him moving fast and shrank the breadth of terrain from which enemy gunners could hit him. Another way pilots minimized the amount of shrapnel lodged in their tails was to approach the target in a curving pattern. That enabled them to stay out of the path of fire directed at the plane ahead. Boring in straight, close behind another pilot, was a sure way to get eaten up by the inevitable fusillade of wayward ordnance that missed the lead aircraft.

On the inland strike missions, pilots risked exposure to any number of unseen enemy gun positions hidden beneath the trees. And they took a lot of fire from panicked gunners on American ships too. A few barrages of forty-millimeter tracer fire from a friendly ship was all it took to convince many pilots of the ineluctable stupidity of the average gun crew. It was downright harrowing to be airborne while battleships offshore were bombarding targets ashore. Pilots flying gunnery spotting missions became sandwiched in an invisible corridor between salvos from the big ships offshore. While they spotted shell bursts and called in corrections, fourteen-hundred-pound battleship shells flew overhead in trios, plainly visible to the eye. Below, the smaller warheads of the cruisers whizzed past.

Close support of troops was a new job for naval aviators, and the CVE pilots were the first to master it. On a close support mission Brooks would fly to an assigned station and report to an Army air coordinator skimming the trees in a Piper Cub, keeping tabs on his men on the ground. The coordinator would radio instructions: *"Proceed to point Able. Make pass to 000 down to 180, along that ridge."* Usually directed to fly parallel to the line of battle, Brooks would wing over to the attack, when possible dropping out of the clouds to mask his plane from Japanese antiaircraft gunners.

With a payload ranging from ten hundred-pound fragmentation bombs for attacking troops and vehicles to a pair of five-hundred-pound semi-armor-piercing bombs for hitting reinforced targets, a fully laden Avenger was a veritable flying ammunition depot. And if he banked the plane sharply, turning it up on a wing, Joe Downs could swing the sphere of his turret out to the side and cut loose on targets of opportunity with his single-mount fifty. Swooping down in elements of three or four planes at a time, the Avenger pilots tended to get the attention of the Japanese. "Stuff would be coming up all around you," Brooks said. "You'd think, *How come I'm not being hit?* You'd thank the dear Lord that you weren't. You'd come through it. You'd join up with your buddies. When you made your exit, you felt like you had conquered the world."

Brooks became proficient in the art of skipping bombs into caves. He would start the attack at four thousand feet, then go into a dive, juking to dodge flak. But rather than drop his bombs at the customary altitude of two thousand feet, he would fly right down to the deck. By lifting the nose of his plane at the last minute, he could skip his delayed-fuse bombs off the ground and right into the mouth of the cave. More than once he felt the sickening thud of the concussion and shrapnel from his own payload ravaging the tail section of his plane. About as often as not he would discover, on his return to the carrier, fronds of coconut trees stuck in the creases of the wings and fuselage.

Seven years Brooks's junior, just seventeen, aviation ordnanceman third class Joe Downs regarded his pilot with no small measure of awe. "He seemed fearful of nothing. And he had this burly manner. If you tried to lie to him or something, he would just look at you as if to say, 'Do you want me to beat you into the ground now or just throw you overboard?' But he had a great sense of humor."

Of their various missions, aviators enjoyed antisubmarine patrols the least. They offered none of the kinetic thrill of pursuing an enemy truck across a bouncing jungle trail, bullets and rockets tearing down and converging at the point of attack. On A/S duty, a pilot stuck to his quadrant and flew slowly, watching the glittering sea for hour after hour. "It's all sea and sky, sea and sky, for hours," said Tom Van Brunt. Spotting a periscope from four thousand feet required eagle-sharp eyesight and tremendous sustained concentration. Though no pilot was ever documented to have crashed his plane by falling asleep at the stick, drowsiness was a constant threat. Perhaps this was why Avengers carried three men: they could keep each other awake.

"It used to get so hot at night aboard ship," Joe Downs said. "The sleeping situation was miserable. You'd have fifty, sixty guys in the bunkroom, with poor ventilation, no A/C. You'd get up early for morning general quarters, have chow, then go out on submarine patrol around five A.M. You'd hit this nice cool air, and it was the darnedest thing to stay awake. By six or seven o'clock, your eyes just didn't want to stay open anymore."

From his cramped position in the ball turret, Downs could spread his knees and look down at Ray Travers on the radio set. The drone of the piston-driven engine drowned out all attempts at speech, and the intercom was used sparingly, to avoid bothering Ensign Brooks in the cockpit. But every now and then Downs would get suspicious of the inert form below him. He'd give Travers a hard poke with his foot, just to make sure he was conscious. With a sharp slap on the ankle, Travers would return the favor.

*   *   *

NINETY PERCENT OF A pilot's life was standing by and waiting. Pilots waited in the ready room to get called to their planes, playing cards, talking aviation (always talking aviation), and boasting of their victories, confirmed and otherwise. One thing pilots never talked about was death.

A memorial for a fallen member of the air group was unfailingly a requiem of silence. Since June, in action over the Marianas and Morotai, VC-65 had lost six pilots and ten crewmen. The men were not mourned, at least not openly. "The skipper would assign someone to gather his things and clean out his stuff. We'd get to port and ship it home. There were no eulogies or comments," Bill Brooks said. "This was an unwritten law. And there was dignity in it, because everybody knew that at any given moment it could be us. You just didn't want to dwell on it. You had a job to do, and if you dwelled on it too deeply, it impeded your own proficiency. The fellow would be replaced, and you'd feel damn lucky it wasn't your turn."

If a body was recovered, there would be a burial at sea, a solemn ceremony led by the chaplain and attended by all hands; the body was wrapped in canvas sheeting and dropped over the side weighted with a five-inch shell. But his squadronmates did not talk about him, did not discuss the circumstances of his end. "You might get upset if someone got drunk and got hit by a truck. But combat was another matter," Brooks said. With so much time spent waiting, mourning could not be allowed to ferment into despair. For the faithful, there was ample opportunity to pray.

On the *St. Lo* those who sought other forms of salve could join the group of enlisteds who gathered on the flight deck three nights a week to hear ordnanceman John Getas sing. The quality of the diversions available aboard a ship at sea depended on the talents of its citizens. In Getas the *St. Lo* happened to boast one of the better operatic baritones in the fleet. Though the boys from Kentucky and Alabama and other points south preferred their hillbilly music, Getas could count on a turnout of ten, fifteen, twenty guys who would enjoy his renditions of "On the Road to Mandalay," or any of three hundred-odd other numbers he had memorized. Joe Downs kept a hand-cranked Victrola record player in the enlisted sleeping quarters, sandwiched between the hangar and the flight deck amidships, suspended from the bottom of the flight deck.

Life in the war zone permitted quieter diversions as well. At Seeadler Harbor on Manus, the staging ground for the Leyte invasion, Tom Van Brunt discovered that his younger brother Bernard was on a cargo ship, the *Luna,* that happened to be in port too. They were seven years apart but good friends. Van Brunt got permission from his skipper to go ashore and seek out his brother's ship. The dock foreman told him that the *Luna* was anchored at the far side of the harbor. The foreman said he could get Van Brunt to the ship, but wasn't sure he could get him back in time for the *Midway*'s scheduled departure the next morning. As Van Brunt was trying to figure out what to do, a motor whaleboat gurgled up to the dock and tied up to the other side. The boat was making the *Midway*'s mail call. Its coxswain was Bernard Van Brunt.

Tom summoned his best officer's *vox Dei* and called down to his brother, "Hey, coxswain, don't come alongside until I *tell you* to come alongside. Okay: come alongside." The surprise of their reunion was proportionate to their distance from home in Tallahassee. The brothers went aboard the *Luna* for dinner, which was fine except that their brotherly bond could not withstand the curiosity of the cargo ship officers captivated by the novelty of entertaining a combat pilot. Tom ate in the wardroom with them while Bernard went belowdecks with the crew. That night, though, the two men returned to the *Midway,* and Bernard got a tour of a CVE.

Courtesy of the wardroom steward's mates, they enjoyed a feast worthy of officers' country. Then they retired to the flight deck. "It was a glorious, beautiful, tropical evening," Tom Van Brunt recalled. All night long they watched the ships in the harbor flash their big searchlights off the clouds overhead, blinking messages to each other via Morse. They spent the night talking, and from the conversation Tom Van Brunt learned something surprising: that his kid brother had become a man. The next morning news came down that the name of the *Midway* would be changed to *St. Lo.* His brother was the only person in his family who knew.

The men of the *St. Lo* stole fun where they could find it. But mostly the crew diverted themselves with endless, repetitive work. The nine-hundred-man complement of a CVE was like a one-company town working perpetual overtime. That they were a coherent community was obvious to all. A jeep carrier's thin hull enclosed all the trappings of small-town life: the barber shop, the doctor's office, the post office, the power plant, the waterworks, the church, the soda fountain, the boxing ring, the sweatshop factories, and the tenement-style housing. Its residents, loosely grouped into three classes—the pilots, the airedales (as the flight deck crews, aviation mechanics, and technicians were known), and the ship's company who operated the ship—worked around the clock. Aviation machinist's mates labored through the night tuning aircraft engines for their morning missions. Ordnancemen and armorers bore-sighted machine guns, snapped rounds into ammo belts, pulled dollies laden with bombs, and hoisted rockets onto launch rails. Parachute riggers packed chutes. Aviation metalsmiths repaired damaged wings and fuselages. Deckhands swept down the hangar deck and swabbed the redwood flight deck, cleaning up oil and grease. And there was always paint to chip. That was an all-purpose time-filler, but crucially important. The Navy had learned the hard way, at Pearl Harbor and elsewhere, that handsomely painted surfaces burned furiously, producing clouds of poisonous smoke. The monotony of the remedy had at least one immediate benefit: most every sailor in the fleet soon acquired the thick wrists and forearms that came from repetitive scraping.

The pilots and aircrewmen were the exclusive practitioners of the razor's-edge lifestyle that the shipbound men could only shake their heads at and admire. The life of a flier was never in more immediate peril than while landing a plane. Bringing an aircraft down through shifting crosswinds to land on a pitching flight deck was an experience that Ernie Pyle likened to "landing on half a block of Main Street while a combined hurricane and earthquake is going on."

At night, pilots could enjoy the daily ounce-and-a-half ration of brandy authorized by Navy regulations. But it was rotgut, and enterprising pilots found better use for it hidden inside their pillows, where the steward's mates would find it and be induced to perform a more thorough cleaning of the quarters. The squadron medical officer could be counted on to keep a secret stash of medicinal alcohol. Sweetened with iodine and burnished with caramel coloring, it could pass, after the third or fourth shot perhaps, for actual sour mash. The enlisted men distilled their own liquor from raisins and yeast. Empty five-inch shell canisters made useful brewing vats for the raisinjack. Ten days of fermentation in the South Pacific sun turned it into palatable moonshine.

Like the squadrons aboard the five other carriers of Taffy 3, VC-65 had twelve to fourteen Wildcat fighters and roughly the same number of Avengers. Its human complement averaged eighteen fighter pilots and twelve torpedo bomber pilots. The war was turning against the Japanese in part for their inability to replace trained aviators killed in battle. Experienced Japanese "sea eagles" stayed with the squadrons until they were shot down and captured or killed. American pilots, on the other hand, were supported by a massive training and logistics apparatus that ensured a steady rotation of talent and matériel to and from the combat zone.

Aircraft continued to roll out of American factory assembly lines to reinforce squadrons on the war's many fronts. "They came out like sausages there for a while," said one former Navy planner. The Navy's production of human assets was no less impressive. At naval air stations all over the American mainland, veteran pilots were returning from the fleet to train new fliers to fill squadron vacancies caused by combat or operational deaths. That VC-65 fielded pilots as skilled as Ralph Jones and Tex Waldrop to begin with was one thing. That it could replace its losses along the way with pilots as good as Tom Van Brunt and Bill Brooks was quite another.

Seven

The war was going badly for Japan. In June 1944, during the invasion of the Marianas Islands—which contained the important bases at Guam, Saipan, and Tinian—the Japanese Imperial Combined Fleet had sailed with its remaining carrier force to challenge the American colossus. Like the battles of Midway and the Coral Sea before it, the Battle of the Philippine Sea was fought almost entirely in the air. U.S. Navy fliers shot down so many Japanese planes, killed so many of their seasoned pilots, that the Japanese aircraft carriers were effectively detoothed as offensive weapons. A fair number of the American pilots knew their way around the hunting fields back home, and clearly they had benefited from the practice. They took to calling the battle the Great Marianas Turkey Shoot. Afterward, with the Japanese in retreat, the subsequent invasions of Morotai and Peleliu—critical preparation for the move on the Philippines—had gone unchallenged by the Imperial fleet. Already B-29 bombers were raining fire on the empire's industrial centers. Only one of the aircraft carriers that had struck Pearl Harbor remained afloat, and it, the lucky *Zuikaku,* had been by October bled of most of its aircraft and experienced pilots. Nursing its strength since its defeat in the Marianas, the Japanese military awaited America's next move before committing itself to what might well be its final major fight.

Although the Combined Fleet could not sustain a general offensive in the face of America's overwhelming superiority, and though its airpower had been whittled down to a paltry force of land-based planes operating from the Philippines and Formosa, its commanders held on to the slim hope that if they could choose the time, place, and circumstances, they might yet land a staggering blow against the oncoming U.S. juggernaut. They would gather their strength and take their best shot. The only question remaining was how to commit limited forces so as to best disrupt America's next move.

Would the Americans invade Formosa and Japan's southern home islands? Hokkaido to the north? Would the Philippines be the next target? Could Nimitz and MacArthur be so audacious as to attack Honshu itself and the central Japanese home islands? Designated the Sho-Go (Victory Operation) plan, a strategy was drawn up by the Supreme War Direction Council to defend against the inevitable offensive. Prepared in late July, as MacArthur was wooing Roosevelt in Hawaii, and debated, revised, and approved by the emperor on August 19, the Sho-Go plan was conceived in four variations depending on the geographical region America targeted for its next major thrust. The Sho-1 plan was aimed at deflecting an American assault of the Philippines; Sho-2 would defend Formosa and the southern Japanese home islands; Sho-3 would be used to counter an invasion of Honshu and Kyushu, the central home islands; and Sho-4 was designed to defend Hokkaido and the Kuriles in the north.

Though the Japanese had hints of the American decision to invade the Philippines almost as soon as MacArthur, Nimitz, and President Roosevelt had adjourned their conference at Pearl Harbor, they got their first solid markers of American intentions on October 12, when, just before dawn, four fast carrier groups of Mitscher's Task Force 38—the backbone, muscle, and fist of Halsey's Third Fleet—closed to within fifty miles of the Formosan coast and began launching air strikes intended to neutralize Japanese airpower in the theater as preparation for an invasion of the Philippines.

By seven A.M. the first echelons of Grumman F6F Hellcat fighters were sweeping over Japanese airfields on Formosa, interrupting the breakfast of the ground crews scattered along their runways. Resistance was futile. Those few of Vice Adm. Shigeru Fukudome's 230 fighter pilots who managed to get aloft, Fukudome wrote, "were nothing but so many eggs thrown at the stone wall of the indomitable enemy formation." Three days of carrier strikes, consisting of 1,378 sorties, left Formosa in ruins.

The Third Fleet's savaging of Formosa and nearby islands forced an unnerved Japanese high command—both Admirals Fukudome and Toyoda were caught on Formosa during the attack—to prepare both the Sho-1 and Sho-2 plans for activation. In fact, Rear Adm. Ryunosuke Kusaka, who as Toyoda's chief of staff was effectively in command of the Combined Fleet while his superior was hunkered down on Formosa, ordered Sho-2 activated on the morning of the first attack. But a few days later, on the morning of October 17, Japanese lookouts spotted an advance force of U.S. Army Rangers coming ashore on Suluan Island in Leyte Gulf. It was then they knew that the Philippines was America's real objective. On the evening of October 18 Admiral Kusaka ordered Sho-1, the Philippines variation, into effect.

The Sho-1 plan was massive in scale, Byzantine in complexity, and exacting in its requirement that four fleets separated by thousands of miles of ocean time their movements with near-impossible precision. From the far-flung imperial anchorages in Japan's Inland Sea, from Borneo in Malaysia, and from Singapore's Lingga Roads, the fleets would sortie to the attack. If they could execute the Sho-Go plan as written, land-based aircraft would assault the American carrier groups while a decoy force of aircraft carriers under Vice Adm. Jisaburo Ozawa lured Halsey's Third Fleet north. Exploiting the gap created by the diversion, two battleship forces, one under Vice Adm. Takeo Kurita, the other under Vice Adm. Shoji Nishimura, with Vice Adm. Kiyohide Shima's Third Section in support, would then slip through the waters north of Samar and south of Leyte respectively.

The plan played to Japan's strength, for the Imperial Navy still fielded a formidable force of big-gunned surface ships. Two of its 71,659-ton battleships, the *Yamato* and the *Musashi,* were the largest warships in the world. The *Nagato,* the *Fuso,* and the *Yamashiro,* aged though they were, had displacements in the neighborhood of 40,000 tons. The imperial fleet had two fast 36,601-ton battleships in the *Kongo* and the *Haruna.* And its dozen-odd 13,000-to-15,000-ton heavy cruisers and several squadrons of hard-hitting destroyers were capable combatants that had drawn their share of American blood earlier in the war.

Converging from north and south on MacArthur's landing beach, the two battleship forces would catch the U.S. troops in a pincers movement. The heavy ships would sink at their leisure any transports or supply ships off Leyte, then turn the guns inland and blast the American armies from the rear while imperial troops rallied ashore. If they worked quickly enough, the Japanese fleet might rout MacArthur and make good its escape before Halsey recovered and inflicted an overwhelming air attack upon them. The challenge, of course, would be to move the big ships that formed the two pincers through long stretches of American-patrolled seas, intact and on time, and hope that Admiral Halsey would act as they suspected he might when presented with Ozawa's bait.

There was good reason for Japan to expect Admiral Halsey, whose Third Fleet guarded MacArthur's northern flank, to take the bait and chase Ozawa north. Japan's carriers had long been his obsession. And indeed, recent history proved the necessity of knowing where the carriers were. Japan had attacked Pearl Harbor on a day when the *Enterprise* and the *Lexington* were at sea. This cost her the chance to destroy, rather than merely wound, the U.S. Pacific Fleet. The carriers, having dodged the treacherous blow, went on to spearhead the Allied counteroffensive in the Pacific. At Midway six months later a U.S. scout pilot's fortuitous peek through a break in the clouds enabled the American carrier planes to strike the Japanese flattops first and turn the tide of the war.

The Navy did not fully appreciate it at the time, but with Japanese naval airpower virtually wiped away in the Marianas Turkey Shoot, it really no longer mattered where the Japanese carriers were. Japan didn't have enough trained pilots to make them a threat. That the hopes of the Sho-1 plan were vested in battleships was a sure sign that Japan knew its tenure as a carrier power was at an end.

That hard truth was not lost on Jisaburo Ozawa, the most talented of Japan's carrier admirals. His seniority in the Combined Fleet lagged behind only that of its commander in chief, Adm. Soemu Toyoda. But for the distinguished vice admiral, widely thought the most capable commander in the Japanese Navy, reality could not have been more bracing: in the age of the aircraft carrier, the Sho-1 plan relegated him to leading Japan's remaining carrier strength on a mere decoy mission. It was likely a suicide mission as well. Steaming from Japan's Inland Sea with the fleet carrier *Zuikaku,* the light carriers *Chitose, Chiyoda,* and *Zuiho,* two hybrid battleship-carriers *Ise* and *Hyuga,* and a force of light cruisers and destroyers, Ozawa fielded the last of Japan's paltry naval air strength.

Ozawa's carriers were like dragons whose fiery breath had been quenched. At the controls of their 116 combat aircraft were rookie pilots whose training barely sufficed to land them safely aboard their carrier after a mission. His screen was composed not of fast fleet destroyers but of coastal defense vessels prone to crippling mechanical breakdowns.

But prevailing in battle was not Ozawa's mission. If he could just get Halsey's attention, chances were good that the Bull's predilections would get the better of him. If Ozawa could entice the Third Fleet commander to chase him, it might open for Kurita the northern path around Samar, through San Bernardino Strait, and into Leyte Gulf, where the Center Force's big ships, rendezvousing with Nishimura's Southern Force, could devastate MacArthur's landing beach. Like an aikido master, Ozawa would turn Halsey's aggressiveness against him. All of it hinged on Ozawa's allure as bait.

On October 24 Ozawa steamed down from the north, making radio noise and planning to launch an air strike on any American ships it might find. Steaming off Cape Engaño, a peninsula jutting out from the northeastern shore of Luzon, Ozawa did everything he could to be noticed. It was oddly appropriate: *engañar* is the Spanish verb "to deceive."

If Ozawa's deception worked, battleships would do the rest. The Southern Force, with elements under Admirals Shoji Nishimura and Kiyohide Shima, would approach MacArthur through Surigao Strait, south of Leyte. The more powerful group, the Center Force under Takeo Kurita, would trace the coast of Palawan—a long slash of an island that separated the South China and Sulu Seas—maneuver through the ramble of islands in the Sibuyan Sea, and then exploit the gap created by Ozawa's diversion, moving through an unprotected San Bernardino Strait before turning southward around Samar Island and attacking Leyte Gulf as the Sho-1 plan's northern pincer.

With the superbattleships *Yamato* and *Musashi,* the battleships *Nagato, Kongo,* and *Haruna,* ten heavy cruisers, and several squadrons of destroyers, Kurita had more than enough muscle for the job. His challenge would be to survive the inevitable onslaught from American planes and submarines on his approach to San

Bernardino Strait. If he could, he might yet hope to meet the Southern Force in Leyte Gulf.

*   *   *

GUARDING THE LEYTE INVASION beach's northern flank was Admiral Halsey's Third Fleet. Its primary strength lay in the seventeen fast aircraft carriers of Task Force 38, nominally led by the legendary carrier boss, Admiral Mitscher. The carriers, supported by a powerful surface force that included six new battleships, had greater speed and a much longer reach than the Seventh Fleet did. But Halsey's fleet had a somewhat less clearly established mission. His orders, drawn up by Chester Nimitz in line with the agreement brokered by President Roosevelt in Hawaii, required the Third Fleet to "cover and support" MacArthur's troops "in order to assist in the seizure and occupation of all objectives in the Central Philippines" and to "destroy enemy naval and air forces in or threatening the Philippines area." But an amendment to the operations order, added by Nimitz a few days later, stated, "In case opportunity for destruction of major portion of the enemy fleet is offered or can be created, such destruction becomes the primary task."

Whether it was offered by the Japanese or created by the Americans, that opportunity began to materialize on the morning of October 24, when Third Fleet pilots made multiple sightings of Japanese warships. At 8:22 A.M. Halsey received a report from an *Intrepid* flier that a Japanese fleet was in the Sibuyan Sea, in the waters west of Samar. Less than an hour later, at 9:18, planes from the *Enterprise* patrolling the Sulu Sea to the south spotted and attacked another Japanese flotilla containing two battleships evidently headed east toward Surigao Strait. The sightings themselves were more important than the minor damage the planes inflicted. All of the reports coming in from the Navy's interlocking web of search planes and picket submarines were telling the Americans the same thing: the enemy had been stirred to action.

Because the Imperial Combined Fleet faced serious fuel shortages, U.S. naval intelligence had learned to predict its maneuvers by tracking the advance movements of its fleet oilers. To divine the intentions of the Imperial Navy, one had only to follow the trail of oil.

The Joint Intelligence Center, Pacific Ocean Area (JICPOA), had reported more than a month earlier, on September 18, that "large scale logistic preparations are in the making." On October 2 JICPOA reported that Japanese tankers had left Sumatra for the fleet anchorage at Lingga and were rehearsing underway-refueling operations. Two weeks later the Combined Fleet was reported to have placed seven fleet oilers at Admiral Kurita's disposal and ordered two freighters to yield their fuel to the Center Force's warships if Kurita needed it. On October 20 Navy intelligence discovered that two tankers awaiting Kurita's orders in the Tonkin Gulf had been directed to rendezvous with the admiral in the western Philippines and refuel the Center Force, also known as the First Diversion Attack Force.

So the tea leaves were there to be read. The only remaining question was exactly when and how the Japanese would strike. On October 23 two U.S. submarines operating west of the Philippines had ambushed a large northbound surface force steaming through the Palawan Passage. The *Darter* and the *Dace* sunk two heavy cruisers, the *Atago* and *Maya,* and forced a third, the *Takao,* back to Singapore for repairs. With the morning sighting on October 24 of this same enemy flotilla in the Sibuyan Sea west of Samar, and of the battleship force headed toward Surigao Strait in the south, the full picture was beginning to emerge. From his Seventh Fleet flag quarters aboard the USS *Wasatch* in Leyte Gulf, Vice Adm. Thomas Kinkaid could at last see the Japanese plan unfolding: a Japanese task group would navigate Surigao Strait and challenge Leyte Gulf from the south. Another threat loomed to the north, in the Sibuyan Sea. But it was accounted for—Halsey's carrier pilots were all over it, striking hard on the afternoon of October 24 and sinking the superbattleship *Musashi.* Now Kinkaid had his own welcoming party to prepare.

At 2:45 P.M. that afternoon he ordered Jesse Oldendorf to ready his big ships for a night battle. If the Imperial Navy was going to break through Surigao Strait and reach Leyte Gulf, they would have to defeat the multilayered trap that Oldendorf would set for them. Having seen MacArthur's Sixth Army to the beach on the twentieth without incident, Oldendorf's Pearl Harbor battleships, those resurrected old souls of the U.S. Navy, prepared to return to doing what they had been built to do. A challenge was coming. The challenge would be met.

Eight

Steaming by night toward Surigao Strait aboard his Southern Force flagship, the battleship *Yamashiro,* Admiral Nishimura knew what awaited him and held no illusions about his chances for victory. At 12:35 P.M. the previous day a float plane catapulted from the heavy cruiser *Mogami* had radioed the fifty-nine-year-old admiral with word that a powerful American battleship force was gathering at the far end of Surigao Strait. The pilot may have been prescient. It was not until mid-afternoon on the twenty-fourth that Admiral Kinkaid, having anticipated that Nishimura was headed his way, ordered Jesse Oldendorf to move his heavies down to the strait and prepare for a night action.

What drove the Japanese admiral to sail to nearly certain death is between his ghost and his Maker. A close friend of the Japanese admiral had seen in him a death wish ever since Nishimura's only son, Teiji, a top student at the naval academy at Etajima, had died when his float plane exploded during operations in the Philippines in 1942. That Nishimura did not now withdraw from Surigao Strait, that he did not pause and regroup with Admiral Shima's cruisers and destroyers, trailing him by some forty miles, suggested bravery more than foolhardiness, for bravery is motivated by purpose, and Shoji Nishimura's purpose had been established not by his own personal loss but by the strategic designs of the Japanese naval command. With the Imperial Japanese Navy's far-flung forces committed to the attack, the Sho-1 plan was beyond the point of no return.

From his flag bridge on the *Yamashiro,* Nishimura evaluated the odds facing him and knew that the success of the Sho-1 plan depended on his commitment to it. Even if executing it meant his own death, his effort was likely to lock down a sizable American fleet committed to his destruction and spare Admiral Kurita's Center Force that many more opponents in its own bid for Leyte Gulf.

Nishimura rested his fortunes on the strong keels of the *Fuso* and the *Yamashiro.* The battleships had spent most of the war in Japan's Inland Sea on training missions, because, like Oldendorf's old battlewagons, time was passing them by. They were no longer fast enough for the demands of the carrier war. But now heavy-gunned ships such as the *Fuso* and the *Yamashiro* were the best Japan had left. The late Admiral Yamamoto, who had first championed naval airpower in 1915, had once derided the big ships as "like elaborate religious scrolls which old people hang up in their homes." "These battleships," he once said, "will be as useful to Japan in modern warfare as a samurai sword." Perhaps. But perhaps too the stark reality that no alternative remained would allow the old swords to be unsheathed to fight as their designers had intended. Under Kurita and Nishimura, they might flash in the air once again.

The Japanese high command had debated the merits of employing the last of Japan's naval strength on what many commanders saw as a useless sacrifice. Kurita's chief of staff, Rear Adm. Tomiji Koyanagi, thought it beneath the navy's ancient dignity to send its proudest ships gunning for transports in a harbor. He considered it preferable from a military standpoint, and infinitely better from the standpoint of pride, to seek a decisive battle with the enemy's carrier forces. Koyanagi argued that a successful disruption of MacArthur's invasion force would only delay the inevitable. The invasion would regroup, supported by the powerful American carrier force. On the other hand, if Halsey's carrier groups could be somehow destroyed, the Americans would be unable to sustain their drive toward the shores of Japan. Some officers felt that if the navy was going to risk its existence on the Sho-1 plan, at the very least it should be led personally by the Combined Fleet commander in chief himself, Admiral Toyoda.

It was clear to all that with the outcome of the war hanging in the balance, reserving the empire's strength was no longer feasible. A decisive battle was needed. This was not a sudden realization. The doctrine of Decisive Battle had driven the Japanese Navy's strategy and planning since at least 1930. Shaped by the inevitability of fighting a larger American fleet—a situation imposed upon Japan by the 1922 Washington Naval Treaty—the doctrine rested on ensuring local superiority in the western Pacific. It envisioned fighting a war of attrition against the westward-bound foe. In home waters a powerful Japanese battleship force would finish off an American fleet that had been worn out and whittled down by the need to sustain the fight across long distances in the Pacific. Decisive Battle depended upon seizing America's forward bases and forcing the U.S. Navy to pick its way across the Pacific, where it would be susceptible to attrition by hit-and-run attacks from a mobile advance force comprised of submarines and torpedo-armed destroyers and cruisers.

On August 1, 1944, Combined Fleet Top Secret Operations Order Number 83 directed Japanese forces "to intercept and destroy the invading enemy at sea in a Decisive Battle." Land-based aircraft would sink the American aircraft carriers while the battleships concentrated on penetrating Leyte Gulf and attacking MacArthur. That mission would be pursued at any cost. At a combined meeting in Tokyo of Japan's army and navy staffs, Adm. Tasuku Nakazawa, chief of the navy's operations section, observed tearfully that the defense of the Philippines could be the Japanese Navy's final opportunity to meet with an honorable end. "Please give the Combined Fleet the chance to bloom as flowers of death," he told his compatriots. "This is the navy's earnest request." It was a request that Shoji Nishimura was fully prepared to honor. Jesse Oldendorf was ready to indulge it too.

*   *   *

LIKE THE OTHER JAPANESE admirals who sailed in fuel-hogging battleships, Nishimura was forced to operate far from the comfortable embrace of the Japanese home islands, out of Borneo and Singapore, closer to what remained of his empire's meager fuel reserves. Notwithstanding that logistical handicap, the mission was going well thus far. He had been remarkably lucky since leaving Brunei Bay, in

Borneo, on October 22, his two battleships accompanied by the heavy cruiser *Mogami* and four destroyers. First, though the harbor was closely watched by U.S. search planes, he slipped past the web of reconnaissance patrols that Seventh Fleet intelligence had cast all around the Brunei port.

Next, Nishimura passed unseen and unheard through the tripwire of American submarines cruising the Sulu Sea between Borneo and the Philippines to the east. Finally, on the morning of October 24, southwest of the island of Negros, he came under attack by twenty-eight planes from the *Enterprise* and the *Franklin* of Halsey's Third Fleet. A bomb struck the quarterdeck of the *Fuso,* causing a raging fire that destroyed her complement of float planes. The destroyer *Shigure* was hit too, losing her forward gun turret. But Nishimura's striking power, modest though it was in comparison to what the Seventh Fleet was marshaling to meet him in Surigao Strait, was intact.

*   *   *

TIPPED TO THE JAPANESE approach that morning, Admiral Oldendorf used the late afternoon of October 24 to plan his welcoming party for Nishimura's force. He had more than enough firepower to handle whatever the enemy might send at him.

Entering the bramble of the Philippine archipelago from the west, through the Sulu Sea and into the crease of ocean between the islands of Negros and Mindanao, Nishimura would first face successive swarms of American PT boats, charging him three by three, thirteen waves in all, firing their deck-mounted torpedoes, then withdrawing under cover of darkness and lurking nearby to report his position to Oldendorf throughout the engagement.

As he took a northeasterly course and headed for the confines of Surigao Strait itself, he would next face Oldendorf's hard-hitting destroyers. The "tin cans"—a name that belied the destroyers' potent offensive hitting power—would come at him in three squadrons, ranging down both the eastern and western sides of the narrow strait to launch torpedoes at him from the flanks. Each destroyer carried ten of them; the crossfire, Oldendorf and his commanders hoped, would be devastating.

Oldendorf's six battleships, under the tactical command of Rear

Adm. George L. Weyler, would cruise single file across a fifteen-nautical-mile stretch of water at the northern outlet of the strait. Steaming parallel to them, five miles to their south, would be eight cruisers under Rear Adm. Russell S. Berkey, three to Weyler's right flank and five to his left. Straddling the exit of the strait, the battle line would be poised to finish off any of Nishimura's ships that survived the smaller ships' onslaught.

Oldendorf's five wounded veterans of Pearl Harbor were joined by the battleship *Mississippi,* which had escaped the treacherous enemy blow on December 7. It had taken nearly three years for the damaged ships to recover and return to a place where they might do their builders' terrible bidding. Civilian engineers and Navy technicians came from the West Coast to join Pearl Harbor's yard workers. The army of gathered electricians, mechanics, burners, divers, and pumpers worked around the clock, as often laboring under water in diving suits as under the scintillant Pacific sun. They were the seed of a salvage organization that would boast 27,000 civilian workers in addition to 3,000 Pearl Harbor Navy Yard personnel.

The great ships were patched, pumped, and lifted from the muck, righted with winches, and set upon by the yardbirds at Pearl before being taken to shipyards along the West Coast for repairs and refitting. Shipyard craftsmen replaced their torn hull plates, burst bulkheads, silted boilers, and melted electrical wiring. Naval architects and engineers took down their great cage masts and installed more prosaic-looking structures that housed the latest fire-control radars.

Admiral Yamamoto had morosely foreseen that the sneak attack would provoke America to just the sort of industrial and human mobilization that returned the old battleships to the line. They had taken varied paths to the waters of Leyte Gulf, climbing the curve of the earth across the Pacific, their massive steam-powered screws pushing them along at the speed of a swift bicycle rider. They had visited a series of islands en route, supporting American troops as they went ashore on island after island, from Peleliu to Morotai to the current operation in the Philippines. They escorted convoys along lengthening supply lines across the southern and central Pacific. Their gun turrets, housing rifles that fired shells fourteen to sixteen inches wide and as tall as a man, had been built a generation ago to fight other battleships. But that battle had thus far eluded them. Enemy dreadnoughts had yet to fall within their reach.

Late in the war, as the Navy employed them in shore-bombard-ment roles, America's aging thirty-thousand-ton monsters had be-come little more than massive seagoing artillery platforms. Perhaps it was only appropriate that such machinery, too slow to keep up with the carriers, be placed under the Army's command.

But now, at Surigao Strait, thanks to the desperation of a Japa-nese Navy sailing to stop MacArthur at any cost, the world would learn that the pronouncements of the old ships' obsolescence were a bit premature, if not wholly exaggerated. Pearl Harbor's ghost ships were not yet ready to fade into history or legend. The dashing new breed of carrier admirals, smug aboard their graceless floating bird farms, might well have declared the battle line obsolete. The presence of Oldendorf's six battleships in the strait was a declaration of a dif-ferent sort, one that should have sent a message to the warlords in Tokyo who had ignored Admiral Yamamoto's prophecy: if America could raise its old dreadnoughts from the dead, what chance could the U.S. Navy's enemies possibly have?

Oldendorf would take no chances throwing the dice in the fog of war. Here, in the narrow waters of Surigao Strait, there would be no pitched battle. Nishimura would have no room to maneuver. Olden-dorf's fleet would hold its position astride the northern end of the strait and devour Nishimura's column like a log thrust into the busi-ness end of a U.S. Navy wood chipper.

At 2:40 A.M. on the morning of October 25, 1944, the destroyer *McGowan* radioed Oldendorf, *"Skunk 184 degrees, 18 miles."* The beams from the tin can's radar set had found the enemy in the dark-ness. All that remained for Oldendorf's fleet was to close the trap and destroy it.

Nine

Blocking Surigao Strait's twelve-mile-wide opening into Leyte Gulf, the American battle line spanned nearly three miles of ocean. The six ships that formed it plowed the strait's waters at a leisurely five-knot speed. When the battle line was headed to the east, the *West Virginia* led the way, followed in half-mile intervals by the *Maryland*, the *Mississippi*, the *Tennessee*, the *California*, and the *Pennsylvania*. When on Admiral Weyler's command the ships turned to the right, they did so in majestic unison, plowing a 180-degree arc and falling back into line on a reversed course and sequence, with the *Pennsylvania* in the lead and the *West Virginia* at the rear.

The battle line, the preferred formation of admirals since 1655, when James, Duke of York, had routed the Dutch at the Battle of Lowestoft, endured for nearly three hundred years on the strength of its irreducible merits: it offered naval commanders both command unity and concentrated firepower. For any naval officer, the dreamed-of scenario was to "cross the T" of his opponent, concentrating their full broadsides on approaching ships that could respond only with their forward batteries. In the narrow waters of Surigao Strait, geography made doing so a much easier proposition. All Jesse Oldendorf had to do was hold his position astride the restricted waters and let the enemy column walk into his crossbar.

But his battleships would not start the fighting. That honor would fall to the smallest combat vessels the U.S. Navy had ever sent into battle. Lt. Cdr. Robert A. Leeson's thirty-nine PT boats had come off the assembly line at the Higgins Industries plant in New Orleans built to deliver high-speed hit-and-run torpedo attacks. Lurking like schools of barracuda along the islands of Bohol, Leyte, and Panaon in the eastern Mindanao Sea, they had a twofold mission: to harass, and to track, the approaching Japanese force. The small boats with their fifteen-man crews were well equipped for both jobs. Their three twelve-cylinder Packard gasoline engines gave them top speeds of forty-one knots. At that clip they could close range quickly with a target, launch four stubby Mark 13 torpedoes, turn on a dime, and escape. They were adept at patrol, and their offensive potential was considerable. But Leeson's crews hadn't fired a torpedo in anger since the Guadalcanal campaign in August 1943. And attacking an enemy battleship was not something they had ever done before.

The weather was so clear as to be threatening—"too beautiful to serve our purpose," one destroyer commander would write. The quarter moon shone a luminescent path across the sea to its viewer. Wind was soft and the seas were light, with visibility to a good eight thousand yards, about four and a half miles. But as the Japanese approached, the night darkened. The moon fell toward the western horizon, and rainsqualls walked through, laying black clouds across the sky and making the night, here and there, opaque to all light. Flashes of lightning offered fleeting glimpses of what was about to happen in the strait.

At 10:50 P.M., under a setting moon, Leeson's first section of PT boats ventured out from the dark corners of the shoreline to attack Nishimura's force. The ships up the strait heard a tremendous racket as the Packard V-12s roared to life and the torpedo boats raced to the attack. The Japanese ships opened the shutters of their searchlights, illuminated the PT boats, and opened fire. The PTs slashed in in successive trios, loosing torpedoes at the enemy. All missed. The Japanese returned fire, repelling the nuisance but inflicting little real damage. A PT boat skipper grabbed the mike on his TBS radio and exclaimed, "I've got a big one in sight. . . . My God, there are two more big ones, and maybe another." On Allied ships far to the north, men watched star shells glow like miniature suns and searchlight beams sweep the seas.

The noisy dance lasted three and a half hours. Ten of the PT boats were hit, but only one of them severely. PT-493 took three hits from the 4.7-inch guns of the destroyer *Shigure*. The shells blew away her charthouse, holed her wooden bottom, killed two sailors, wounded five, and forced the boat to ground on the rocky shore of Panaon Island. Bravely led by their skipper, Lt. (jg) R. W. Brown, the crew jumped off the stricken boat and formed a defensive perimeter, rifles and machine guns at the ready in case the Japanese came for them. But Admiral Nishimura's goals were far larger than finishing off a few scrappy PT boat sailors. The Americans were left alone, and when high tide came, the splintered hull of their boat rose from the rocks and disappeared into the sea.

Shortly before 12:30 A.M. Oldendorf received a dispatch from his PT boats, duly relayed to him by the PT boats' tender, the USS *Wachapreague*. It was the first report he had gotten on Nishimura's exact disposition and location since ten o'clock the previous morning. Oldendorf evaluated it, found no surprises, and had the satisfaction of knowing that his Japanese counterpart would arrive right on time for the fiery reception that the rest of the Seventh Fleet was planning for him.

*   *   *

THE TWENTY-TWO DESTROYERS THAT filled Admiral Oldendorf's screen carried a total of 111 five-inch guns and 214 torpedoes. Even without the battleships, a destroyer force like that might well have been able to destroy the bulk of Nishimura's and Shima's fleets all by itself. Very nearly it did.

At about 2:30 A.M. Capt. Jesse G. Coward led three ships of Destroyer Squadron 54, the *Remey*, the *McGowan*, and the *Melvin*, down the eastern side of the strait while two more, the *McDermut* and the *Monssen*, hugged the western shore. Behind Coward followed six destroyers from Capt. K. M. McManes's Destroyer Squadron 24, steaming south in two sections: the *Hutchins*, the *Daly*, and the *Bache* were closest to the Leyte Island shore; the HMAS *Arunta*, an Australian destroyer assigned to the squadron, followed by the *Killen* and the *Beale*, cruised off their port quarter. Finally, Capt. Roland Smoot's nine-ship Destroyer Squadron 56 would attack in three columns: the *Robinson*, the *Halford*, and the *Bryant* ranging down the eastern side; the *Newcomb*, the *Richard P. Leary*, and the *Albert W. Grant* down the middle of the strait, head-on, firing, then looping back; and the *Heywood L. Edwards*, the *Leutze*, and the *Bennion* on the west side of the strait.

At 2:56 lookouts aboard the *Shigure* reported three ships at a range of eight kilometers. The large searchlights aboard the battleship *Yamashiro* switched on, bathing the *Remey*, at the head of the American line, in hot white light and making her crew feel like "animals in a cage." She endured the spotlight for three minutes before coming close enough to the enemy to fire her torpedoes. It took little more than a minute for the *Remey*, the *McGowan*, and the *Melvin* to loose their torpex-loaded fish at the enemy. Leaping from their tubes set at an intermediate speed of thirty-three and a half knots, the torpedoes would need eight minutes to reach their targets. Captain Coward turned to port and withdrew to the northeast at flank speed of thirty-five knots. Eight minutes went by, and precisely on cue several large explosions flashed as the battleship *Fuso* was hit amidships by two torpedoes from the *Melvin*. With boilers likely shattered, the *Fuso* slowed from twenty to twelve knots as her skipper, Rear Adm. Masami Ban, swung her out of formation to the right to avoid collisions with the ships cruising in column astern.

At 3:10, barely ten minutes after Coward's three tin cans launched their torpedoes and just a few minutes after the *Fuso* was hit, the *McDermut* and the *Monssen* fired their own spreads, wheeled around, and made good their escape. The wait for the torpedoes to reach their targets ended in pyrotechnics at 3:20, when torpedoes from the *McDermut* hit no fewer than three of Nishimura's four destroyers. The *Yamagumo* disappeared in a succession of great explosions, sinking with a sizzling noise like a "huge, red-hot iron plunged into the water." The *Michishio*, shattered at the waterline, was left behind, crippled and burning. The *Asagumo*, her bow blown off by the blast, controlled her flooding well enough to retire to the south.

The *Monssen*'s shooting was almost as good as the *McDermut*'s. A torpedo from that ship struck the hull of the *Yamashiro* on the port side to the rear. The blast forced the big battleship to slow to ten knots as damage-control parties flooded two magazines as a precaution against a massive secondary explosion. But the *Yamashiro*'s captain, Katsukiyo Shinoda, soon returned his ship to eighteen knots.

Nishimura and Shinoda were unaware that the *Fuso* had fallen out of line. At 3:52 the Japanese admiral radioed the *Fuso* stating, "Notify your maximum speed." Clearly he thought the *Fuso* was behind him as he rushed toward the American fleet. Little did he know that unimaginable catastrophe had befallen his most formidable ally.

After taking the torpedo hit from the *Melvin* at about 3:08 A.M., Admiral Ban had sheered the *Fuso* to the right so as to prevent the cruiser *Mogami* behind him from colliding with his rapidly decelerating battleship. As the *Mogami* steamed past on her port quarter at 3:13, the *Fuso* began listing to starboard. True to the Japanese Navy's stubborn form, she continued for a few minutes to advance, at a north-by-northeasterly course, toward the American battle line. But at 3:18 the ship reversed course back to the south, the advancing deterioration of the *Fuso*'s starboard list likely having tempered Admiral Ban's fortitude. Shadowed by two PT boats, the *Fuso* retired to the south as damage-control parties struggled to stanch the inrush of seawater into her starboard-side torpedo wounds. Twenty minutes later, at 3:44, all hands topside on the destroyer *Daly* observed three large blasts. "Each explosion was a round ball of dull orange flame which subsided and disappeared almost immediately," the ship's skipper wrote. They took these for their own ship's torpedoes. "The ship which was hit by these torpedoes immediately opened fire with major and minor caliber guns, frantically throwing steel through 360 degrees, and initiating general gun action between both forces," wrote the commander of the *Daly*.

But within seconds the nighttime heavens flashed into daylight as a great explosion shook the *Fuso*. The *Hutchins*, eight miles away, reported "two faint [explosions] and a loud snap." The *Fuso*'s immolation could be seen as far away as Oldendorf's battle line some twenty-five nautical miles to the north. Lookouts aboard the *Mississippi* reported "flames reaching above the mastheads." It must have been a magazine explosion, for nothing else could explain its terrifying power—or its lurid result. American radar operators watched their scopes in wonderment as the *Fuso*'s single large radar signature split apart. Her keel and armored hull shattered by the force of the blast, the great 39,154-ton ship broke in two.

Consumed by flames as hot as a steel mill's forge and bright enough to illuminate warships nearby, the *Fuso*'s innards were revealed in cross-section. The pieces refused to sink. Burning and smoking furiously but seemingly animated by defiant spirits, they remained stubbornly afloat. The bow and the stern of the *Fuso* had acquired separate lives. Each piece clung bizarrely to life, populated by crewmen who refused to concede their ship's destruction by doing the prudent thing and abandoning her. The lazy two-and-a-half-knot current carried them back down the strait, to the south whence they had come.

Nishimura was reeling, and the U.S. battleships had yet to open fire on the faltering Japanese fleet.

* * *

THE FIRE-CONTROL OFFICERS IN the combat information center of the *West Virginia*, their big turrets rotated out to starboard, had been chafing for an opportunity to open fire ever since they had first spotted the enemy column on their scopes. Admiral Weyler had ordered them to open fire when the range to the approaching Japanese targets had closed to 26,000 yards (14 ¾ statute miles). At 3:53 A.M. the "Wee Vee" opened the major gunfire phase of the battle, the onetime gunnery champ of the fleet unleashing the power of her sixteen-inch guns for the first time at an enemy ship. Two minutes later the *Tennessee* and the *California* joined the barrage with their fourteen-inch rifles.

The *West Virginia*'s gunnery officer laughed aloud as he announced a first-salvo hit to his captain. The older ships in the battle line, equipped with the older Mark 3 fire-control set, were still blind to the enemy at this extended range. But the enterprising gunnery department aboard the *Maryland* managed to defeat the inadequacy of its radar by locking in on the towering columns of water raised by her three sisters' falling shells. By ranging on the big splashes, which registered momentarily on the antiquated Mark 3, the *Maryland*'s gunners fired four dozen sixteen-inch rounds at the enemy. The *Yamashiro*, struck all around her towering pagoda mast, was quickly enveloped in flames.

Meanwhile, Admiral Berkey's cruisers had found the range themselves. The light cruisers *Denver*, *Columbia*, *Boise*, and *Phoenix* made up for their thin skin with offensive firepower that was simply vicious. The *Boise*'s gunnery officer, Lt. Cdr. William F. Cassidy, wasn't even pausing to spot the fall of his six-inch salvos on radar. He had them locked in continuous rapid fire.

Captain Smoot, commanding Destroyer Squadron 56 farther down the strait, had a front-row seat:

The devastating accuracy of this gunfire was the most beautiful sight I have ever witnessed. The arched line of tracers in the darkness looked like a continual stream of lighted railroad cars going over a hill. No target could be observed at first; then shortly there would be fires and explosions, and another ship would be accounted for.

In just eighteen minutes of shooting, Oldendorf's left-flank cruisers fired 3,100 rounds at the Japanese column: "It seemed as if every ship on the flank forces of the battle line opened at once, and there was a semicircle of fire which landed squarely on one point, the leading battleship."

That hapless ship was the *Yamashiro*. From the bridge of the besieged dreadnought, Nishimura looked for help. He radioed in vain to the *Fuso,* which he believed to be to his rear, encouraging Admiral Ban to make full speed in his support. The destroyer *Shigure* hailed the battleship repeatedly as well. It seems that the *Shigure*'s skipper mistook Nishimura's own ship for the *Fuso*. Nishimura probably heard the *Shigure*'s misdirected broadcasts to *"Fuso"* and falsely took heart, thinking the battlewagon was in line behind him, accompanied by the destroyer.

In reality the *Fuso* was drifting with the current away from Nishimura's onrushing force, its two halves ghoulishly still afloat. Nishimura's southern pincer of the Sho-1 plan was all but destroyed, his largest ships foundering, his destroyers either sunk or sinking, consumed with the imperatives of their own survival. Nishimura did not bother to radio a status report to his compatriot Shima, following behind. He would be left to discover the extent of the catastrophe for himself.

At 4:08 A.M. Shima arrived on the scene. Nishimura's flagship *Yamashiro,* steaming northward at twelve knots, was firing blindly into the darkness with her two forward turrets. Silhouetted by her own fires raging amidships, the *Yamashiro* straddled the light cruiser *Denver* and hit the destroyer *Albert W. Grant* with her 5.5-inch secondary battery. But Oldendorf's ships were too powerful and too numerous, as the cold eyes of their radar gazed through the darkness upon the dying ship. The American gunners were on their game now, their adrenaline overflowing as the pneumatic hoists whisked shells from the magazines up to the gun crews, who placed them onto loading trays, slid the trays into breech blocks, discharged the shells at the enemy, and ejected the empty casings through the bottoms of the turrets to the decks below as the cycle began again and again. A projectileman in one of the *Boise*'s forward turrets broke his left hand while laying shells in the breech tray but missed hardly a beat loading his gun.

Flames appeared to consume the *Yamashiro*'s entire length. At 4:11, having swung out to the west in an effort to unmask and fire her amidships gun turret, the battleship absorbed two more destroyer torpedoes. Listing heavily to port, the *Yamashiro* capsized and sank at 4:19, taking with her Admiral Nishimura, Captain Shinoda, and the vast majority of her fourteen hundred men. As the *Yamashiro* was in her death throes, turning over onto her side, Shima blandly radioed Nishimura, *"We have arrived at battle site."*

Shima's force too should have been eaten alive, except that at 4:09, ten minutes before Shima radioed his counterpart aboard the foundering *Yamashiro*, Admiral Oldendorf gave him a reprieve, ordering all American ships to cease fire. It was a necessary decision, to be sure. A minute before, Oldendorf had received an emergency message from Captain Smoot's Destroyer Squadron 56 saying that his valiant tin cans were taking fire from friendly ships. The *Grant* was hit by seven rounds from the *Yamashiro* and the *Mogami*. But eleven more came from the merciless barrage of the American light cruisers, whose errant salvos contributed to the carnage that killed thirty-four men and wounded ninety-four more. The destroyer captains who had so courageously pressed the attack when the enemy was at full strength were now caught in a terrible crossfire.

The ten-minute pause in shooting brought an eerie silence to the strait. The smoke-shrouded surface of the water was still lit by the white glare of star shells overhead, drifting downward on parachutes. Occasionally through the smoke, wrecks of warships smoldered. The cruiser *Mogami*, brightest of them all, could be seen from the bridge of the cruiser *Louisville*, "burning like a city block."

The captain of the cruiser *Nachi*, under Shima, spotted the *Mogami* and, believing the ship dead in the water, attempted to move ahead of her to make a torpedo attack. But the *Mogami* was still making eight knots, which meant that the *Nachi*'s navigator had miscalculated badly. At 4:30 the two ships collided, the *Nachi*'s sharp stem glancing heavily off the *Mogami*'s starboard bow.

Shima had gotten no direct report on what had befallen his Etajima classmate's force. On entering the strait, the retreating *Shigure* blinkered to Shima, "I HAVE RUDDER DIFFICULTIES." But the *Shigure*'s skipper offered Shima nothing further regarding Nishimura's fate. He would later explain, "I had no connection with [Shima] and was not under his command." The blazing Japanese wrecks that lit the waters told Shima all he needed to know. "If we continued dashing further north," Shima wrote later, "it was quite clear that we should only fall into a ready trap."

At 4:32, having spied a trio of fleeing Japanese ships on the radar fourteen miles away, Admiral Oldendorf took his cruiser the *Louisville*, the *Portland*, the *Denver*, and several destroyers to pursue Shima's retreating force. "In the pale pre-dawn twilight the scene in Surigao Strait was appalling," Lt. James L. Holloway III, gunnery officer on the destroyer *Bennion*, later wrote. "I counted eight distinct fires, and the oily surface of the gulf was littered with debris and groups of Japanese sailors who were clinging to bits of wreckage and calling out to us as we raced past."

After forty-five minutes of pursuit Oldendorf had the Japanese in gun range again. In one of the most bizarre gunnery engagements of any naval war, the *Louisville* closed with the forward half of the battleship *Fuso* and opened fire at a range of nearly eleven statute miles (18,900 yards). Into that hulk the flag cruiser fired eighteen rounds of eight-inch armor-piercing ammunition. Within minutes whatever spirits were keeping the blackened, smoking wreck afloat were dispelled. At 5:36 it disappeared from the American radar screens.

About a mile away, in waters steadily burning from a long slick of bunker oil, the *Fuso*'s stern section remained miraculously afloat, drifting southward at the speed of a slow walk. Sometime before 6:30, as the sun began to warm the eastern horizon, the destroyer *Asagumo,* her own bow blown off during Captain Coward's torpedo attack, had pulled close to the floating pyre to take on survivors. It was only then that the *Fuso*'s after-section crew decided to abandon ship.

As survivors of the *Fuso*'s nightmarish ordeal quit the burning hulk and swam for the safety of the *Asagumo*'s decks, an American

PT boat was watching them. At 6:30 Lt. (jg) H. Stadler, commanding PT-323, saw opportunity and sped to the attack. While the stern section of the *Fuso* went bubbling into the depths of Surigao Strait, Stadler pounced on her would-be rescuer like a cat on a wounded pigeon. He closed range and fired his torpedoes. One of them struck the *Asagumo*, wounding her mortally. Then at 7:07 the Japanese destroyer was caught by the light cruisers *Denver* and *Columbia* and three U.S. destroyers. The *Asagumo* returned fire, her after turret barking long after her bow was awash. By 7:21 the ship was gone.

At dawn the remainder of Oldendorf's task group formed into a circular antiaircraft disposition and steamed southward down the strait. According to the skipper of the *Daly*,

> *At daylight seven heavy pillars of billowing black smoke could be seen on the horizon ahead. One by one these pillars of smoke disappeared as the ships from which they originated sank under the gunfire of our ships. Hundreds of survivors were reported in the water, almost all of whom refused to be rescued and were left to their fate.*

The wounded and the healthy alike turned away their American rescuers. A flustered destroyer commander radioed to Oldendorf, *"All survivors in water are Nips and refuse a line. What do you want done with them?"* Seconds later came the task group commander's cold reply: *"Let them sink."* Some of the defiant Japanese, those with sufficient muscle or will to survive, managed to swim ashore on Leyte or Dinagat Island, only to be set upon by Filipino guerrillas who relished the spectacle of their sinking and welcomed the opportunity to hack them to pieces with their bolo blades.

Ten

Naval combat is nothing like ground war, but that does not make it any less terrifying. Death comes suddenly, shrieking down with little warning from the sky. If a two-thousand-pound projectile fired from long range has your number—if the lazy, decaying parabola of its trajectory terminates on or near your ship—you are finished, no matter how fine your reflexes or how assiduous your training. In size and explosive power, naval gunfire in this war dwarfed anything in the Army's arsenal. The biggest howitzer that MacArthur's troops used fired a 155-millimeter shell, about the same size as the six-inch rounds of light cruisers. Battleship shells were several orders of magnitude heavier. When they struck, they shredded armor, burned steel, and vaporized flesh. They killed any number of ways: by flame, by shock, or by storm of flying shrapnel.

As in ground combat, chance is often decisive to the outcome. Eight of the nine ships of Captain Smoot's DesRon 56 made daring sorties against Nishimura's battleships and executed a clean escape. But the *Albert W. Grant* was in the wrong place at the wrong time. Blasted by friendly fire, she steamed away with thirty-four dead, thirty-four families soon to receive dreaded telegrams from the Navy. And even when the order of battle appeared to doom a ship to destruction, death was no foregone conclusion. The Japanese destroyer

Shigure, lucky to the end, had escaped destruction not only at Surigao Strait but earlier in the war as well. One of her skippers, Tameichi Hara, grandson of a samurai, would write a widely acclaimed memoir and become celebrated worldwide as the "unsinkable captain." But even he admitted, "The fact that I survived was entirely a matter of luck."

The night was illuminated by two sources of light: the flash of American guns and the flames consuming Japanese ships. The crewmen of the *Samuel B. Roberts,* cruising off Samar about a hundred miles north of the action, were not alone in watching the distant pyrotechnics. The men aboard the invasion ships in San Pedro Bay lay awake all night watching the fireworks, though the sounds did not reach them. Only combatant vessels with TBS sets tuned to the right frequency enjoyed the full experience.

"Large target has disappeared from sight. Target referred to bearing 205 distance 11."

"Keep track of enemy and make reports on course and speed—we are going to make chase for them."

"We have one dead in the water—we are going to present him with five fish."

"We have quite a few survivors in the water. Do you desire we pick them up?"

"Pick them up. Do not overload your ships with survivors. Search each man well to see that he does not have any weapons. Anyone offering resistance—shoot him."

"Take three destroyers, polish off cripples."

The men standing the midwatch in the *Samuel B. Roberts*'s combat information center had begun celebrating as soon as they determined that a rout was on. They pumped their fists, clapped, and cheered. The exec, Bob Roberts, was uncharacteristically ebullient. Hearing the sounds of victory coming over the radio from Surigao Strait moved the tough twenty-eight-year-old to pink-cheeked reverie. He turned to his skipper and said, "By God, I think we finally got 'em."

Proximity to combat was what a warship commander, or a litigator, lived for. Listening to rogue transmissions of the fighting in Surigao Strait, Captain Copeland and the other men in the *Roberts* CIC knew that the stakes of their innocuous support operation had been dramatically raised. The enemy had been spotted, met, and routed.

Suddenly the work of baby-sitting a bunch of escort carriers was getting a whole lot more interesting.

*   *   *

AS THE SOUTHERN FORCE was meeting its end in Surigao Strait—the *Fuso* shattered, the *Yamashiro* capsized, Oldendorf's battle line sending salvo after salvo after the stragglers—Kurita's massive Center Force had an entirely different reception in waters far to the north. Plunging by night through the darkened narrows of San Bernardino Strait, his Center Force was the most powerful gathering of surface combatants the imperial fleet had ever sent into battle. That fact alone should have ensured it a vigorous greeting by American naval forces in the strait.

Standing on the flag bridge of the *Yamato*, Kurita expected at any moment to see the flash of enemy battleship guns in the distance, to feel the deep reverberations of submarine torpedoes tearing into his battle line as they had in the Palawan Passage the night before. He could not believe the Americans were not there to challenge him. Astonishingly, the night remained quiet. It appeared that luck was on his side.

Eleven

Admiral Kurita's Center Force was far more powerful than the weaponry Nishimura had brought to Surigao Strait. In addition to two squadrons of heavy cruisers, he had the *Yamato* and the *Musashi,* the biggest battleships anywhere on the high seas. For the Japanese sailors aboard the cruisers and destroyers escorting them, the sight of the two gargantuan 863-foot vessels in the battle line stirred the heart. Together with the old *Nagato* and the fast battleships *Haruna* and *Kongo,* it was a gathering of heavies such as Japan had never before assembled.

The decision to commit the *Yamato* and the *Musashi* to the gamble to penetrate Leyte Gulf had been controversial. Kurita's chief of staff, Tomiji Koyanagi, was not alone in his preference for going after America's carrier groups to slaughtering transports in a harbor. As journalist Masanori Ito summarized the dissent's position, "We do not mind death, but we are very concerned for the honor of the Japanese Navy. If the final effort of our great Navy should be spent in engaging a group of empty cargo ships, surely Admirals Togo and Gonnohyoe Yamamoto would weep in their graves."

Kurita had committed himself to the Sho-1 plan with a resigned fatalism. Like the rest of the Imperial Navy's high command, he saw that the plan placed him in a desperate position. It was aimed at setting up the Decisive Battle, but so far the only side suffering the attrition upon which the Decisive Battle doctrine depended was the Combined Fleet. The strain was evident in the fuel shortages that had forced Kurita to operate far from home in Brunei, where refined bunker oil was more readily available; in the lack of aircraft to protect his ships; in the perpetual infighting between the army and the navy that arose as much from natural interservice enmity as from the shortages. Prior to departing Brunei, Kurita gathered his demoralized commanders aboard his flagship, the heavy cruiser *Atago,* and addressed the growing dissent about the wisdom of pressing the attack.

"I know that many of you are strongly opposed to this assignment," he said. "But the war situation is far more critical than any of you could possibly know. Would it not be a shame to have the fleet remain intact while the nation perishes?" Though dashing into Leyte Gulf was risky, Kurita deemed it "a glorious opportunity. . . . You must remember that there are such things as miracles. What man can say that there is no chance for our fleet to turn the tide of war in a decisive battle?"

The Sho-1 plan's weaknesses were plain enough to see. It relied on the optimistic notion that Japan could fight a complex sequence of battles on its own precise timetable, at places of its choosing, against an enemy that would acquiesce to every ambush and feint and refrain from the discourtesy of overwhelming it with superior force. The Decisive Battle strategy envisioned Japan holding the Philippines, Guam, and other forward bases but did not reckon with an enemy whose fleet nourished itself at great anchorages such as Ulithi, Manus, and Hollandia. Nor did it account for a flexible, thinking enemy that broke imperial codes and exploited technical breakthroughs such as fire-control sensors and search radar. And it certainly did not allow for an enemy equipped with the audacity of a Bill Halsey, the prudence of a Raymond Spruance, the methodicalness of a Jesse Oldendorf, or the resourcefulness of a Ziggy Sprague.

After departing Brunei on the morning of October 22, Kurita had walked into one disaster after another. First came the devastating submarine attack in the Palawan Passage. Shortly after dawn on October 23, nearly a full day into his sortie, sailing along the island of Palawan west of the Philippines en route to San Bernardino Strait, Kurita's group was ambushed by two U.S. submarines. Japanese radio intelligence had traced American sub transmissions that originated near Kurita's location. But the subs did not announce their presence until they were ready to deliver the crushing blow.

At 6:34 A.M. Kurita's own flagship, the *Atago*, sailing at the head of a column of five cruisers and two battleships, was struck by four torpedoes. Sixty seconds later two more torpedoes blasted the *Takao*, following the *Atago* directly astern. These six hits came courtesy of the submarine *Darter*, captained by Cdr. David H. McClintock. About twenty minutes later four more torpedoes, fired by Cdr. Bladen D. Claggett's *Dace*, hit the heavy cruiser *Maya*, third in line in the Center Force's eastern column, sailing about five hundred yards ahead of the *Yamato*. A shattering explosion filled the night as the *Maya*'s magazine exploded. "After the spray and smoke had disappeared nothing of her remained to be seen," wrote Rear Admiral Ugaki aboard the *Yamato*.

The end had come fast for the three stricken cruisers. The *Atago* sank in eighteen minutes; the *Maya* died in four. The *Takao*, her rudder blown away together with two of her four screws, limped back to Brunei under destroyer escort for repairs. As the rest of his destroyer screen scoured nearby waters for their undersea assailants, Kurita was fished from the sea and that afternoon moved his flag to the more expansive quarters of the battleship *Yamato*.

Having weathered the onslaught of submarines, Kurita had pressed on northeastward, entering the Sibuyan Sea on the morning of the twenty-fourth. That body of water was some two hundred nautical miles wide, a rabble of islands and passages that provided a haven for enemy submarines and restricted a large formation's ability to maneuver while under attack. On the eastern side of the Sibuyan Sea was San Bernardino Strait, the bottleneck that separated the Sibuyan from the Philippine Sea. Beyond the strait were the waters where Halsey's Third Fleet lurked between the Center Force and its Leyte objective.

*   *   *

JAPAN'S FAITH IN MIRACLES was rooted in its history, replete with the apparent results of godly intervention, from the typhoon-assisted triumph over Kublai Khan in the thirteenth century to the rout of the Russians at Tsushima Straits in 1905. But if Kurita was counting on Heaven's blessings to fall upon the *Yamato* and the *Musashi*, there would first have to be a reckoning with the treachery of their very existence.

At least one Japanese commentator implied the existence of a dark curse in their extralegal origins. "The giants of Japan's Navy were good ships," Masanori Ito wrote, "but they were built in bad conscience." When secret plans to build them began in earnest in October 1934, Japan violated in spirit the Washington Naval Treaty. Negotiated in 1922, the arms-limitation agreement held Japanese, American, and British battleship forces to a 3-5-5 tonnage ratio. At the time none of the three major seagoing powers had built a new battleship in fifteen years. That suited Japan's proponents of the treaty very well. The Combined Fleet's ten prewar battleships maintained the sixty percent proportion. When more militant voices on the general staff prevailed and Japan defiantly withdrew from the treaty in 1936, the *Yamato* was already nearly two years into construction, her keel rapidly growing into a hull at Kure Harbor. Work on her sister ship the *Musashi* was just a year behind at Nagasaki. The omens of their construction almost immediately began to reverberate in the larger culture. The rope netting that screened the *Yamato*'s construction site from view was so expansive that for months Japanese fishermen had suffered a shortage of hemp.

Even with the 3-5-5 treaty ratio in place, Japanese planners had figured they could maintain at least a regional advantage over the Americans. With the United States saddled with two oceans to defend, Japan could gain superiority in the Pacific. And because American ships had to have beams small enough to fit between the locks of the Panama Canal, the Japanese, free from constraints of intercontinental geography, would hold a size advantage as well. The addition of the two giants increased the ratio of Japanese to American battleship tonnage to 4-to-5. Displacing 72,000 tons each, they were more than twice the size of any warship Japan had ever built.

But as Japan had already proven at America's expense, the age of the battleship was passing. At about ten A.M. on the morning of October 24, the radar operators on the *Musashi* reported enemy aircraft approaching: the harbingers of Marc Mitscher's Task Force 38. And now the second catastrophe fell upon Kurita en route to San Bernardino Strait.

A scout plane from the *Intrepid* had brought the good news of the sighting to Admiral Halsey. The admiral spent fifteen minutes querying the pilot and conferring with his staff. Then he sent a terse but catalyzing order over the TBS circuit to his task force commanders: *"Strike! Repeat: Strike! Good luck!"*

When the American aviators arrived over Kurita's fleet, the spectacle of the Center Force steaming eastward was a commanding one. The wide circle of distinct white wakes was visible from as far as thirty miles away. The first wave struck at 10:26 A.M., with four dozen planes from the *Intrepid* and the *Cabot* air groups winging over to the attack. The former occupant of the *Fanshaw Bay*'s flag quarters commanded those carriers, and it was he, Admiral Bogan, who sent the first of four waves of planes against Kurita. During the course of the afternoon as Admiral Oldendorf was preparing to fight the Southern Force in Surigao Strait, Halsey would launch 259 planes against the Center Force.

The heavy cruiser *Myoko* and the *Yamato* were hit, but the *Musashi* took the brunt of the assault. Her skipper, Adm. Toshihira Inoguchi, sailed with 769 survivors of the heavy cruiser *Maya*, sunk by the *Dace* in the Palawan Passage. Manning whatever battle stations their cruiser training suited them for, supplementing the efforts of the *Musashi*'s own crew, they fought bravely. SB2C Helldiver dive-bomber pilots drew first blood, landing four near misses near the bow and opening minor leaks in the hull. A direct hit atop a heavily armored 18.1-inch turret was closely followed by a torpedo hit forward. Inrushing water caused a five-degree list to starboard.

The agony of the ship's destruction was only prolonged by her efficient damage control. Belowdecks a network of pumps emptied and filled compartments on both sides of the ship to avoid capsizing. Directing three teams of sailors in control rooms spread throughout the ship, the *Musashi*'s damage-control officer, Lt. Masanao Naito, orchestrated the pumping and counterflooding to ensure that the wounded ship remained upright. About an hour later, around 11:45, Avengers placed three more torpedoes into the ship's port side. The flooding was so great that emergency pumping could not keep pace. Naito filled every compartment on the ship's starboard side but could not stop the list. Admiral Inoguchi slowed his ship to twenty-two knots to reduce the water pressure on the fractured bulkheads.

The last wave of Third Fleet planes arrived over the Center Force at about two P.M. Lt. Cdr. Joseph T. Lawler, leading a group of sixteen Hellcat fighter planes from the *Enterprise,* had spotted the long white wakes trailing from the ships of Kurita's Center Force as they maneuvered in the Sibuyan Sea. The spectacle of such a huge fleet was familiar to any pilot who had flown over one of Halsey's sprawling task groups. But still a lump rose in Lawler's throat. He led his flight beyond the enemy ships to the west, then circled back at twelve thousand feet in order to attack with the sun to their backs. Spreading out into three groups, they chose up targets and dove down in an attack that converged on the stricken *Musashi.*

Fires were already raging in one of her engine rooms. The blaze had severed a main steam pipe, stopping one of her propeller shafts. Near misses and torpedo strikes had pierced some lower compartments and filled others with lethal carbon monoxide. A bomb exploded on the large tower that housed the bridge, ruining Admiral Inoguchi's left arm and killing several other officers. Then four more torpedoes burst into the forward part of the ship. The battleship's heavy armored bow plates were torn outward. One of them jutted out like a cataract, carving into the sea like an armored plowshare. Now the inrushing torrents of seawater were too great even for the *Musashi* to endure.

Though the imperial crest fixed to her prow stood proudly above the water, her bow was nearly submerged. The ship settled until water lapped over the forecastle. Her two forward turrets, each one heavier than a large destroyer, appeared to float atop the surface of the ocean, just offshore of what appeared to be a small steel isle: her superstructure. It occurred to Admiral Inoguchi to beach his ship and fight her as a shore battery, but her bow was tilling so deeply beneath the waves that a course change would likely have capsized her. As her crew shifted all movable objects to the port side to keep the ship from turning turtle, Inoguchi gave the order to abandon ship. His final report that he handed to his executive officer, Capt. Kenkichi Kato, included an apology to the emperor for his failure to carry his ship to its assigned destiny. His executive officer asked to join him in the ship's final plunge. "Damn fool!" the captain replied to Kato. "My responsibility is so great it can't even be compensated by death and I must share the ship's fate, but the executive officer is responsible for taking the crew to safety and getting them aboard a second and third *Musashi* to avenge today's battle."

Kurita had appealed for air support from the army's Second Air Fleet on Luzon and from Ozawa's decoy carrier group. But just ten fighters were available to cover Center Force. The four unlucky pilots who happened to be patrolling over the fleet when the Americans attacked were downed immediately. There was little point sending the rest of them. They wouldn't stand a chance against the fighters from the Third Fleet.

Kurita was calm amid the chaos, assessing the damage and weighing his prospects for fulfilling his part of the Sho-1 plan mission. The *Musashi* was gone. The *Nagato* had taken two torpedo hits but was seaworthy except for a reduced twenty-knot maximum speed. The light cruiser *Yahagi* had been hit, limiting the fast ship to just twenty-two knots. As worrisome to Kurita as his lack of air cover was the shorthanded status of his destroyer screen. Two of the escorts had broken formation to stay behind with the stricken *Musashi*. The day before, two more had accompanied the heavy cruiser *Takao*, torpedoed off Palawan, back to Lingga Roads. Held by their slowest member to an eighteen-knot cruising speed, his ships would be sitting ducks for any enterprising U.S. sub commander lurking in the area. His eleven remaining destroyers would be hard pressed to cover him. Aggravating his concerns, a dispatch from Combined Fleet Headquarters brought this warning: "PROBABILITY IS GREAT THAT ENEMY WILL EMPLOY SUBMARINES IN THE APPROACHES TO SAN BERNARDINO STRAIT. BE ALERT."

Kurita's staff informed him that American carriers, wherever they were, had enough daylight left to launch as many as two additional waves of air attacks against him before night fell. He had not yet heard from Ozawa, who was supposed to be maneuvering northeast of Luzon and drawing this devastating offensive power to himself. If Kurita continued eastward toward San Bernardino Strait in these last hours of daylight on the twenty-fourth, it would only make the trip shorter for his attackers.

Kurita feared that the air attack had put him hopelessly behind schedule to meet Nishimura in Leyte Gulf. Was Nishimura still even alive? Kurita had not heard from him since the previous night, at 10:10 P.M., when the Southern Force commander had radioed him that he was on schedule to penetrate Leyte Gulf with the *Fuso* and the *Yamashiro* at four A.M. on the twenty-fifth. If he turned away now, Kurita knew he would be hard pressed to meet him.

Twelve

At 3:30 P.M., seeing little point in continuing to sail into the American meat grinder and despairing of his ability to adhere to the Sho-1 plan's timetable while under constant air attack, Kurita ordered his remaining ships to withdraw westward. He transmitted a message to Combined Fleet Headquarters: "IF WE CONTINUE WITH OUR PRESENT COURSE OUR LOSSES WILL INCREASE INCALCULABLY, WITH LITTLE HOPE OF SUCCESS FOR OUR MISSION. THEREFORE, HAVE DECIDED TO WITHDRAW OUTSIDE THE RANGE OF ENEMY AIR ATTACK FOR THE TIME BEING, AND TO RESUME OUR SORTIE IN COORDINATION WITH SUCCESSFUL ATTACKS ON THE ENEMY BY OUR AIR FORCES."

The turn westward brought the fleet back to the *Musashi*, dead in the water and settling. Adm. Matome Ugaki, the commander of the First Battleship Division, hoped the crew would do their best to save the ship but could not muster the words to cheer them on.

Steaming away from the Americans gave Kurita a change of heart. Emboldened by a lack of further air strikes and feeling he should at least attempt a rendezvous with Nishimura—he still did not know the fate of the Southern Force—Kurita decided at 5:14 to resume heading east. The *Yamato*, the *Nagato*, the *Haruna*, the *Kongo*, and their heavy cruiser and destroyer accompaniment heeled around toward San Bernardino Strait again. An hour later the response to

Kurita's four P.M. dispatch to headquarters arrived. Toyoda's order—his exhortation—was classically fatalistic, steeped in the Japanese propensity for invoking destiny: "WITH CONFIDENCE IN HEAVENLY GUIDANCE, THE ENTIRE FORCE WILL ATTACK!" As grim as the message's implications were, at least it removed from Kurita's weary shoulders the burden of discretion. The Sho-1 plan had come too far to turn back. The decision to commit the Imperial Japanese Navy's most powerful squadron had been made by its supreme commander.

Back on its way toward San Bernardino Strait, the Center Force passed the *Musashi* once more at sunset, around six P.M. on the evening of October 24. An hour and a half later the great battleship, left behind by her comrades, rolled suddenly to port and vanished beneath the sea. Admiral Inoguchi remained aboard to the end, to perish along with half the ship's crew.

A plume of steam and smoke rising above the point of her sinking was the *Musashi*'s farewell to her task force, and to the wider world to whom her existence had been a lurking mystery. Built to conquer leviathans, the *Musashi* was done in by swarms of tiny flying machines. The rules of war had changed. Now the survivors of the *Musashi* understood it as surely as did their counterparts from the USS *Arizona*.

*   *   *

WITH THEIR SINKING OF the *Musashi,* Halsey's Third Fleet carrier pilots had dealt the most concentrated and crushing aerial assault on a warship in recorded history. The battleship had absorbed seventeen bomb hits and nineteen torpedo hits before going under. At Pearl Harbor a single bomb had caused the catastrophic magazine explosion that destroyed the *Arizona;* two torpedo hits had capsized the *Oklahoma.* The *Musashi*'s torturous end showed how far naval aviation had come. The sinking of the *Musashi* was the first time a Japanese battleship had been sunk solely by air attack. That the ship had been the largest one afloat only underscored the point.

But the *Musashi* was not a carrier, and so Halsey was not satisfied. All his career he had dreamed of bringing an enemy carrier force within range of his planes. His every instinct told him that they were nearby, moving toward some objective that could only as yet be guessed at. His gut told him that the Japanese would not commit their fleet to battle without carriers to support them.

Intelligence reports brought him tantalizing hints of their whereabouts, yet for days the imperial flattops eluded him. He dreaded the thought that the enemy carriers might sit out this campaign altogether, as they had done during the Gilberts and Marshalls campaigns in 1943. Worse, he worried that the Navy might repeat its timid performance in the Marianas, letting Japanese carriers slip away in the night. If the Japanese would not come to him, he resolved, he would go to them.

He had more than enough strength to make a complete rout of it, if he could find them. Among the ninety-four combatant vessels of the Third Fleet were six powerful battleships—the fast new breed, with sixteen-inch guns and the very latest fire-control systems, ably commanded by Vice Adm. Willis "Ching" Lee, an expert in every gun from a .45-caliber to a sixteen-inch, a member of the 1920 U.S. Olympic rifle team, and the hero of the naval battle for Guadalcanal, where his flagship *Washington* had sunk the battleship *Kirishima*. But carriers were the Third Fleet's centerpiece. Halsey had sixteen of them, eight heavy and eight light, packed with planes and divided into four task groups commanded by the best aviation minds the Navy had yet produced. Admiral Mitscher, the most aggressive carrier commander of the war next to Halsey, flew his flag aboard the *Lexington* in command of the Third Fleet's carrier element, named Task Force 38. Under Mitscher were Vice Adm. John S. McCain aboard the *Wasp,* Rear Adm. Frederick C. Sherman aboard the *Essex,* Rear Adm. Gerald F. Bogan aboard the *Intrepid,* and Rear Adm. Ralph E. Davison aboard the *Franklin.* Between them they had nearly twelve hundred aircraft, with battle-hardened fighter pilots— twenty-nine of them aces—flying the marvelous new F6F Hellcat, as well as torpedo-bomber and dive-bomber pilots flying Avengers and Helldivers. Six heavy cruisers, nine light cruisers, and no fewer than fifty-seven destroyers rounded out Halsey's force.

He would crush the Japanese—if only he could get out of babysitting MacArthur. The general and his Army planners expected the Third Fleet to guard their northern flank, protecting the troop transports and the beachhead at Leyte. Nimitz and the Navy, on the other hand, felt pressure to let Halsey go hunting. In the Leyte battle plan, these two prerogatives collided in a way that allowed the second to defeat the first. On one hand, the Third Fleet was charged to "COVER AND SUPPORT FORCES OF THE [SEVENTH FLEET] IN ORDER TO ASSIST IN

THE SEIZURE AND OCCUPATION IN THE CENTRAL PHILIPPINES." It was to "DESTROY ENEMY NAVAL AND AIR FORCES IN OR THREATENING THE PHILIPPINE AREA." So far so good: Halsey would attack only if a Japanese fleet threatened the Philippines. But at the final hour Nimitz had given Halsey the wiggle room the aggressive commander craved, permitting his standing orders to be modified by means of Operations Plan 8–44. It read: "IN CASE OPPORTUNITY FOR DESTRUCTION OF A MAJOR PORTION OF THE ENEMY FLEET IS OFFERED OR CAN BE CREATED, SUCH DESTRUCTION BECOMES THE PRIMARY TASK."

This new mandate was broad enough to erase Halsey's duty to MacArthur and Kinkaid. He was free to abandon guard duty. He had the discretion to chase the Japanese Navy regardless of the Seventh Fleet's needs or expectations. Indeed, Halsey now enjoyed not only the liberty to pursue an enemy fleet, his "primary task," but the operational flexibility to "create" such an opportunity in the first place. If his degree of creative license was open to interpretation, Halsey, whose ears were tuned to hear what they wanted to hear, could be counted upon to make the most of it. Suddenly offensive operations sounded like Halsey's primary objective, whether the beachhead was safeguarded or not. As for protecting MacArthur, Halsey figured, wasn't that what the Seventh Fleet was for?

At 3:12 on the afternoon of the twenty-fourth, Halsey had sent to his commanders a contingency plan providing for the formation of Task Force 34, to be composed of four fast battleships, the *Iowa, New Jersey, Washington,* and *Alabama,* five cruisers, and eighteen destroyers. Under Willis Lee's command, they would stand ready to guard San Bernardino Strait against a possible about-face by the Japanese Center Force. Admiral Kinkaid overheard the message and assumed his Seventh Fleet's northern flank was protected. Monitoring the radio traffic from his headquarters at Pearl Harbor, Nimitz too believed that Task Force 34 had been detached to stand watch over a possible reversal of course by Kurita's wounded but still-dangerous Center Force.

At 3:40 P.M., less than thirty minutes after Halsey circulated his battle plan, Third Fleet fliers spotted one of Ozawa's task groups. Halsey's moment had arrived: he had found enemy carriers. Confronted with two enemy fleets—a mysterious carrier force lurking to his north and a ravaged and retreating Center Force several hundred miles to his west—and thinking it "childish" to stand idle sentry over

San Bernardino Strait when such plentiful game had been flushed, Halsey planned to attack the carriers at dawn's first light. At 8:22 P.M. on October 24 Halsey ordered Admirals Bogan, Davison, Sherman, and Lee to sail north after Ozawa's force. As Samuel Eliot Morison memorably observed, "Halsey was no man to watch a rathole from which the rat might never emerge." Halsey retired early, leaving it to his chief of staff, Rear Adm. Robert B. "Mick" Carney, to put his orders into effect during the night.

Halsey's subordinate admirals had doubts about his decision. Bogan, having reviewed pilot reports saying that Kurita's Center Force had turned around and resumed its course toward San Bernardino Strait, drafted a message to Halsey, then called his fleet admiral over the TBS radio and read it to Halsey's staff himself. *"Yes, yes, we have that information,"* replied the staffer. The abruptness of the response deterred Bogan from explicitly recommending that Willis Lee's battle line, together with Bogan's carriers *Intrepid, Cabot,* and *Independence* and the other ships of Task Group 38.2, turn south and cover the strait.

Willis Lee was similarly put off. The battleship admiral notified Halsey via signal flags that the Japanese carriers dangling to the north were a decoy and that Kurita's retreat had been temporary. In response Lee received only a pro forma *"Roger."* Lee later called via the TBS radio to make the same point again. He was sure, he said, that Kurita was headed for the strait. No further reply came. He let the matter rest.

Shortly after Halsey's second in command, Admiral Mitscher, went to sleep for the night, Mitscher's chief of staff, Cdr. Arleigh Burke, received the sighting report from the night fliers from the *Independence* and confirmed its essential facts at 11:05. Kurita was in San Bernardino Strait. Burke and another officer woke Mitscher and told him they considered it urgent to send Lee south. Mitscher asked them whether Halsey had gotten the report. They said yes—to which the vice admiral replied, "If he wants my advice, he'll ask for it." With that Mitscher went back to sleep.

*   *   *

ONCE THIRD FLEET SEARCH planes had discovered Ozawa's Northern Force on the afternoon of October 24, the Americans at last had a full picture of the Japanese naval presence around the Philippines: Nishimura's Southern Force was marching toward destruction in Surigao Strait to the south; Kurita's big Center Force, hit hard by Halsey's aviators that afternoon, had lost the superbattleship *Musashi* and the heavy cruiser *Myoko* and was in the Sibuyan Sea; and now came Ozawa, tantalizingly on the edge of the search perimeter to the north.

Without the benefit of hindsight, who in October 1944 could have known for sure exactly what Ozawa had? An intelligence report received by Willis Lee suggested that two new fleet carriers, the *Amagi* and *Katsuragi*, had recently joined the Combined Fleet. If the two new ships sailed with the veteran *Zuikaku*, such a carrier force could pose a powerful threat to Halsey and MacArthur both, assuming it had enough planes and pilots. The day before, a lucky Japanese bomb had sunk the Third Fleet light carrier *Princeton*, with a secondary explosion that inflicted even heavier loss of life aboard the light cruiser *Birmingham*, alongside to assist her. Halsey incorrectly surmised that Ozawa's planes had been responsible for the attack. And like every other graduate of the Naval War College, he had been schooled never to divide his strength in a combat zone.

Among the Third Fleet's operational brain trust, everyone except Halsey himself seemed to know what was coming. As far as he was concerned, he was right where he belonged: patrolling Poseidon's Pacific precincts, running down enemy aircraft carriers wherever he might find them. Other considerations had seldom waylaid him from that pursuit. As commander of the *Enterprise* carrier task group on December 7, Halsey had cursed his luck for missing the chance to intercept the Japanese Pearl Harbor strike force. (In reality, he would not likely have survived the encounter.) Reportedly his first words upon seeing the destruction at Pearl were "Before we're through with 'em, the Japanese language will be spoken only in hell!" That fighting spirit animated his every move. The public had embraced his feisty public persona. They didn't call him the Bull because he sat around babysitting troop transports when larger quarry was just over the horizon.

He hated the nickname. "Bull" was the creation of a press corps eager to give the public a larger-than-life figure in whom to place their hopes against an implacable enemy. He disdained it as artifice, a fictitious character whose phony, flamboyant persona was one of the petty humiliations a man suffers when swallowed by fame.

But if Halsey had not already been known as the Bull, the papers would have had little choice but to so name him now, if only for the snorting manner in which he lowered his horns and took the entire Third Fleet—carriers, battleships, everything—in pursuit of Admiral Ozawa, the matador of Cape Engaño, and his dangling red cape.

Meanwhile, Kurita's powerful squadron raced through San Bernardino Strait by night, fighting a treacherous eight-knot current but aided by the glow of navigation lights arrayed on either side of the channel. The fact that the lights had been switched on had been duly noted by Third Fleet fliers. Night reconnaissance pilots from the light carrier *Independence* had spotted the beacons and reported the illuminated channel as a suspicious sign, even as Halsey was steaming north in preparation for a morning strike on Ozawa. The night fliers' inconvenient report was not enough to pull the Bull away from his northward course. He would not divide his force in the face of the enemy. Nor would he stand idly by while an enemy carrier force—white whale to his Ahab—taunted him to his north.

* * *

AT THREE A.M. ON Wednesday, October 25, Takeo Kurita led his Center Force out of San Bernardino Strait north of Samar, heartened, delighted, and above all surprised by the absence of an American welcoming committee. Kurita had expected American battleships to greet him. If dreadnoughts were not waiting, then surely he would tangle again with submarines. The trauma of the ambush in the Palawan Passage was fresh in his mind. But there were no submarines; at least there were no torpedo wakes. Since it was dark, there were no new swarms of planes like the ones that had struck down the *Musashi* the afternoon before.

At 5:30 A.M., in preparation for daylight, Kurita ordered his fleet out of its multicolumned night-search disposition and into a circular antiaircraft formation. Owing to the wide, thirteen-mile front that his squadron spanned, the reorientation would take more than an hour to complete. When morning dawned, they would take their chances against whatever the U.S. Navy might hit them with, then steam south and do their emperor's bidding with MacArthur's invasion force in Leyte Gulf.

Thirteen

It was 5:45 A.M. on October 25, a half hour before dawn, when a TBM Avenger piloted by Bill Brooks, with Joe Downs squeezed into the gun turret and Ray Travers at the radio set below, slingshotted from the deck of the USS *St. Lo* and climbed toward the dark eastern horizon. At the same time Oldendorf was leading his cruisers in pursuit of the remnants of the late Admiral Nishimura's Southern Force, planes from Halsey's Third Fleet were taking wing to strike Ozawa's carriers. For Brooks and the other pilots flying from Taffy 3's CVEs, it was time to hunt submarines.

The previous afternoon Brooks and his squadronmates had returned from patrol to hear reports that a great victory had been won by the better-publicized harpoonists flying from the big carriers of Halsey's Third Fleet. When word came down that Halsey's planes had struck Kurita's Center Force—had actually sunk the *Musashi*, the sister of the *Yamato*, the world's biggest battleship, and forced the rest of the task force into retreat—it appeared there was little possibility of getting into the thick of the action.

Aboard the *Fanshaw Bay*, Rear Adm. Clifton Sprague had been keeping close tabs on Taffy 3's air activities, monitoring their radio reports and, when necessary, directing their movements. The night before, Admiral Kinkaid had ordered the commander of all three

Taffies, Rear Adm. Thomas Sprague, to prepare for a busy morning. One group would fly down into the Sulu Sea to help Oldendorf track down any stragglers from the night action at Surigao Strait. The Seventh Fleet commander also instructed Sprague to send a dawn patrol to the north, over San Bernardino Strait.

Every morning the thirteen ships of Taffy 3 were abustle with activity long before sunup. Aboard the six CVEs, crews were busy in the hangar deck and on the flight deck readying planes for the morning launch. From the bridge of the *Fanshaw Bay,* turned eastward into the wind, Ziggy Sprague watched his planes take flight. A dozen Wildcat fighters went up to fly patrol over Leyte Island, protecting troops there from Japanese air attacks. It had taken just eight minutes for the plane spotters and catapult team on the *Gambier Bay* to put eight Wildcats aloft. The *St. Lo* launched four more. Fifteen minutes later another group of Wildcats went up to cover Taffy 3. They were followed by a mixed group of Wildcats and Avengers armed to strike at Japanese ground positions on Leyte.

The antisubmarine patrol from the *St. Lo,* consisting of four Avengers and two Wildcats, were the last Taffy 3 planes to take off on routine morning missions. Bill Brooks, Tom Van Brunt, and two other Avenger pilots—Lt. (jg) George H. MacBride and Lt. (jg) Gerald E. Fields—fanned out to all four points of the compass centered on their task unit. With the planes aloft and morning general quarters over, the crews of the thirteen ships returned to their bunks or went to the mess to grab a little breakfast.

Chewing an unlit cigar—smoking in the cockpit was forbidden—Brooks took his Avenger to four thousand feet, searching for a suitable aerie from which to monitor the waters below. Though sunrise was at 6:27 A.M., the cloudy morning meant full daylight would be late in coming. Wherever a rainsquall lay, the gray clouds fell to the sea like drapes. Brooks climbed their layers, seeking a higher ceiling where he might watch a wider stretch of ocean. The CVE pilots were not instrument rated. As a saying in the ready room went, "If the birds don't fly, neither do we." On the morning of October 25 the birds flew. They just didn't see especially well.

One never knew where a submarine might lurk. As for the rest of the Japanese fleet, it seemed that threat was well in hand. Overnight incomplete accounts of Oldendorf's victory at Surigao Strait had reached the ships of Taffy 3. The TBS circuits burned with the news.

Aboard the *Samuel B. Roberts,* Captain Copeland, giddy from his impromptu all-night eavesdropping session in the CIC, celebrated with his staff. The victory meant that Sprague's group had little to fear from the Japanese. Certainly nothing could get at them from the south. And the idea of a threat coming down from the north was less worrisome still. The Third Fleet was there, its striking power dwarfing even that of Oldendorf's formidable group. An enemy fleet aiming to reach MacArthur on the beachhead at Leyte would have to get through Halsey first. His Third Fleet had already proven its mettle against the most powerful ships Japan could muster. The Japanese had nothing that could touch it.

Seventh Fleet operations plans were explicit that "any major enemy naval force approaching from the north will be intercepted and attacked by Third Fleet covering force." Admiral Kinkaid had been secure in the knowledge that Willis Lee's Task Force 34 was blocking the strait with its four battleships. He knew the task force was likely to be short on air cover—not that there was any pressing need for it. Certainly he wasn't expecting any surprises.

Some twenty miles northwest of Taffy 3, Bill Brooks, at the stick of his Avenger, continued searching for openings in the layers of cumulus. The weather did not cooperate. As he finished an eastbound leg of his improvised search pattern and turned to the left heading north, another Avenger came into view. The pilot, probably Ens. Hans Jensen from the Taffy 2 carrier *Kadashan Bay,* who was investigating a strange blip on his radioman's radar display, waved at him and went on his way. A few minutes later Brooks swung his plane clear of a big squall and found what he was looking for: a large hole in the floor of the clouds.

Then Ensign Brooks found what he was not looking for: there, spanning the visible slice of ocean below, were ships, lots of them. Against the blue-black dawning sea, their darkened shapes appeared, a majestic assortment of battleships, cruisers, and destroyers trailing white wakes that betrayed their southeasterly course and considerable speed. Brooks flipped on the intercom and told Downs and Travers, "Hey, look at that. Halsey must have come down from the north." It had to be Halsey, the heavy units of the Third Fleet, in all their armor-clad glory.

Downs pressed the intercom button and said, "Thank God they're on our side."

Brooks felt a tinge of doubt. There were no carriers among them. *If this was Halsey, where were his carriers?* And the ships: to the extent that their contours could be distinguished from his perch in the clouds, they didn't look like American ships. In ship identification training, Brooks, Downs, and Travers had been shown, over and over, the silhouettes of ships flashed for a fraction of a second on a projection screen. The men of VC-65 drilled constantly in the *St. Lo's* darkened ready room, training to recognize in an instant not only the silhouettes but their telltale wakes as well.

Were these American ships? Looking down as the armada filed by below him, Brooks made out the tall pagoda towers of Japanese battleships and cruisers. The doubt evaporated into a stunning realization: *they are Japanese.*

As if to punctuate the thought, black clouds of cordite smoke began to appear around his plane as the Japanese gunners drew a bead on the lone Avenger. "The sky just turned black," Downs said. "They had our course and altitude. They were really popping them in there." The enveloping drone of the Avenger's Wright engine behind the firewall at Brooks's leather-booted feet drowned out the bark of their blasts. But he could feel them. The detonations buffeted the heavy torpedo bomber in violent staccato. Every so often a spectacular blossom of pyrotechnics would bloom in their immediate vicinity. The air burst would leave behind a smokeless, shimmering circle, some hundred feet in diameter. It looked to Downs like a burning ring of white tinfoil. It sparked and burned for twenty, thirty seconds, then dissipated. As mysterious and hypnotically beautiful as it was, Downs wanted no part of it. Brooks was less concerned for his own aircraft than for his task unit. The Japanese battleships were no more than twenty miles away from Taffy 3—already in long-gun range. Their wakes trailed behind them like long white tails. These ships were hauling ass.

We're never going to see daylight, Brooks thought. *These guys will blow all our ships out of the water.* He pulled his plane up out of the thicket of flak bursts and took inventory of the mass of warships arrayed beneath him.

It was 6:43 A.M. Brooks tuned his transmitter to the frequency used by the *St. Lo,* code-named Derby Base for purposes of radio communication, and delivered the news: *"Enemy surface force of four battleships, four heavy cruisers, two light cruisers, and ten to twelve destroyers sighted twenty miles northwest of your task group and closing in on you at thirty knots."*

Though the pilot had estimated the makeup of the enemy fleet nearly to a T, Ziggy Sprague, overhearing the report, was incredulous and not a little bit annoyed. *Now there's some screwy young aviator reporting part of our own forces,* the admiral thought. Sprague considered the report preposterous, if not flatly irresponsible: Brooks had spotted nothing other than Task Force 34, the battleship group under Admiral Lee that Halsey had left behind to guard San Bernardino Strait while he took his carriers north. The excitable ensign had only magnified his error by breaking radio silence, potentially revealing the presence of U.S. carriers to Japanese radio snoopers. And this to report his stunning discovery of an American surface force.

Sprague hailed the *Fanshaw Bay*'s executive officer in the CIC, where the movements of nearby aircraft were tracked: "Air plot, tell him to check his identification." Though evidence of the unthinkable was continuing to mount—radiomen were starting to get some strange transmissions: a chatter of Japanese voices as Bill Brooks's Avenger came under fire—Sprague wanted proof. Brooks would have to convince him.

An angry voice on the other end of the frequency laced into Brooks with some choice Navy language. Whether it was Sprague or a controller in the CIC was impossible for the pilot to know. He didn't much care whether the abuse came from a rear admiral or a mere ensign. He didn't enjoy being doubted. Brooks knew a thing or two about his mission. In advanced flight training he had paid close attention when instructors discussed the way the sea looks under different wind conditions, when they trained him to judge a ship's speed from the size and shape of its wake, and when they repeated, time and again, the flash-card drill for ship recognition. Seated in the Avenger's gun turret, Joe Downs heard his pilot vent a few epithets of his own. If confirmation was what the admiral needed, that's what he would get. Ensign Brooks would go down and verify his report.

Suitably awed by the heavy if inaccurate volume of antiaircraft fire rising up to them from the Japanese fleet, Downs was less sure it was necessary to prove anything. But he was not flying the plane. As VC-65's junior pilot rogered the order to confirm and pushed his stick forward, putting the Avenger into a thirty-degree dive, Downs, seated facing to the rear, watched the plane of the sea pivot down out of sight and the clouds above him swing into view. The plane dropped down to two thousand feet, back into the bramble of flak.

Brooks lingered over the Japanese fleet for a few long minutes as Ray Travers snapped some pictures with the big K-20 camera mounted in the bomb bay. Brooks slid a metal-framed plotting board out of his control panel and checked his briefing and navigation notes. It didn't take long to confirm his location. And from this altitude there was no mistaking the distinctive architecture of the battleships and cruisers below. He radioed the Taffy 3 flagship with the bad news: *"I can see the pagoda masts, and I see the biggest red meatball flag I ever saw flying on the biggest battleship I ever saw."*

The pagoda masts were unmistakably Japanese. Though the *Kongo* happened to be the creation of a British shipyard and British ship designers, the ubiquitous xenophobia of the day credited its ungainly profile to the imagined idiocy of the bucktoothed, bespectacled Japanese. The ships had once been the laughingstock of the U.S. Navy. The belief circulated among American officers that they would capsize in heavy seas, toppled by their lofty centers of gravity. But chauvinism about Japanese engineering and naval architecture had been as ill-founded as chauvinism about Japanese tactical skill and bravery. Early battles in the Java Sea and off Savo Island, among others—disasters all for Allied fleets—had revealed both Japan's deadly mastery of surface combat and the lethal design of her warships. The contours of these seagoing towers of Pisa—impossible to confuse with the sleeker lines of America's new fighting ships—had become a dreaded sight.

Dread. It was precisely what Ziggy Sprague now felt. Brooks's report of the pagoda masts was the clincher. And he grasped fully its meaning: against battleships and heavy cruisers, Taffy 3 didn't have a prayer. Among his thirteen ships there wasn't a gun heavier than a five-incher. The fifty-four-pound shells they fired, readily loadable by hand, could not penetrate cruiser or battleship armor. They had a surface range of about seven miles. Even the smallest of the four Japanese battleships facing him fired shells that were fourteen inches in diameter and some fourteen hundred pounds in weight. Each armed with an eight- or nine-gun main battery with a range of more than twenty miles, and with speeds approaching thirty knots, the Japanese battlewagons could easily run down and destroy Sprague's plodding escort carriers. There were four battleships. And the heavy cruisers were arguably even more dangerous. Each one of them—with a treaty-busting displacement of thirteen to fifteen thousand tons fully loaded—carried not only an eight-inch main battery but torpedo tubes as well. And they were swift, capable of thirty-five knots. The Japanese destroyers themselves—eleven of them to Sprague's three—were together probably more than a match for his entire force.

What chance did Sprague have? His destroyers carried torpedoes. But using them required charging into a range that would be suicidal against capital ships in broad daylight—ten thousand yards at most. They would never make it. The Avengers aboard the CVEs carried some ship-killing weapons: torpedoes and semi-armor-piercing bombs. But there were precious few of them, and most of the bombs were of the light antipersonnel variety, useful for killing troops on the ground and overturning jeeps but useless for stopping a large warship.

Sprague tried to think like his enemy. His first thought was that the Japanese would detach a few heavy cruisers to deal with Taffy 3's ships and send the rest of the force straight down the coast to Leyte Gulf. With or without the help of the *Yamato* and the other battleships, the heavy cruisers, Sprague figured, would mop up and wring out most of Taffy 3 in fifteen minutes.

*   *   *

IT WAS 6:47 A.M. when Ensign Brooks confirmed his sighting of the Japanese fleet and relayed it to Ziggy Sprague. At precisely the same moment, Admiral Halsey, on the flag bridge of the battleship *New Jersey*, received a radio message from Admiral Kinkaid:

"Question: Is TF 34 guarding San Bernardino Strait?"

What the hell was this? Halsey wondered. Why was Kinkaid bothering him now? Sent by the Seventh Fleet commander at 4:12 A.M., two and a half hours before Halsey got it, Kinkaid's inquiry had traveled from Leyte Gulf two thousand miles east to Manus, languished for a few hours amid a pile of other communiqués, then been routed to the Third Fleet commander. At MacArthur's insistence, all messages between the Third and Seventh Fleets were routed through his Admiralty Islands headquarters. The communications staff there was deluged with transmissions, the urgent ones all but indistinguishable from the merely important.

Halsey read the late-arriving message from his Seventh Fleet counterpart and thought him out of touch, if not entirely delinquent. Task Force 34, the heart of Willis Lee's battle line, sailed with him. In the earlier dispatch Halsey had meant that Task Force 34 "will be formed" only on his further command. He was shocked that Kinkaid had assumed the actuality of a mere contingency. Wasn't it plain enough that Halsey had not detached the four battleships? And why was the Seventh Fleet relying on him in any event? Conceived as a defensive force, it had more than enough firepower. With Oldendorf's heavies at his disposal, Kinkaid could watch his own back. As Halsey's assumptions began colliding with Kinkaid's in the unforgiving light of day, Kurita curled around Samar with his whole Center Force.

The black puffs of flak grasping at Bill Brooks's Avenger were now visible to the crews on the decks of the thirteen ships of Taffy 3. Above a gray rainsquall to their northwest, they could see the dense pattern of black clouds hanging like layers of charcoal in the sky. Then came their first view of something more frightening still: from below the northwestern horizon, beyond the curve of the earth, rose dark gray towers: the fighting tops of Japanese men-of-war.

As it was dawning on Taffy 3's commanders that something had gone inexplicably, disastrously wrong, the big triple turrets of the *Yamato,* and the only slightly smaller guns of her brutal consorts, were drawing a bead on the Kaiser coffins of General MacArthur's Navy.

*   *   *

BILL BROOKS WAS SOBER with fear. Against the drone of his plane's radial engine in front of him, he, Ray Travers, and Joe Downs were as quiet as mice. "My gut feeling was we were never going to see the afternoon," Brooks said. It was of course academic whether death arrived in the form of a shard of shrapnel from an exploding antiaircraft round or from a hard landing in the sea with his carrier sunk. There was nothing to be done against such a powerful Japanese force. Brooks figured the best thing he could do now was use what few tools were at the ready to take some of the bastards down with him.

What tools did he have? He was armed for antisub patrol, not an air strike. In the weapons bay down in the belly of Brooks's Avenger—behind him, below Downs in the ball turret, and forward of Travers in the radio compartment—sat four 250-pound depth charges. They couldn't do much to a surface warship. With fuses sensitive to water pressure, not impact, they wouldn't explode even with a direct hit. Dropped like bombs on the deck of an enemy ship, the best that could happen was that their metal cases might shatter and give crewmen standing in the open a few splinters and cuts. Or he might get really lucky and hit an officer in the head. But it was hardly the kind of attack that had given American naval aviation its world-beating reputation.

Feeling more than a little useless, Brooks looked down at a column of four heavy cruisers below and had a desperate brainstorm. Perhaps he could improvise a new use for his submarine-killing ordnance. With their hydrostatic fuses set to detonate at a certain depth, the depth charges might be useful after all. Perhaps if he dropped them not *onto* a ship but *forward* of it, into the water directly in its path, the underwater explosion might rupture it from below. He might shake it up, slow it down, create a leak or something. Who knew?

Brooks swung around and lined up on the tail of the cruiser column. When attacking a submarine, doctrine called for a pilot to dive and drop his weapons at an altitude of 300 feet. Brooks thought better of it here. He didn't want to get that close to the bristling heavy cruiser. Nor did Downs: 1,500 feet was much too close for his liking. He would have preferred an altitude about ten times that high. Flying directly over the ship at 1,500 feet, black puffs of flak jarring his plane and vibrating his rib cage, Brooks ran down the last heavy cruiser in line from the rear. At 180 knots, the Avenger rapidly overtook the thirty-three-knot ship. As he passed ahead of the target, Brooks jerked his ordnance release lever, letting go his four depth bombs. As they dropped down and behind his plane, the Avenger lurched as if cut from a tether.

He harbored no lofty expectations. He didn't linger to see the result. His mind was occupied with the imperative of escape. Brooks was an avid quail hunter back home. He knew that the hardest bird to shoot was the one that was flying straight away from you, dipping and veering over the brush. So he followed the game bird's example. He pushed his Avenger down to the water, building speed for his exit, just fifty feet above the wave tops. Downs, facing to the rear, watched the four depth charges plunge down toward the ship. He saw two of them strike the forward deck of the ship, and two land in the water forward of the bow. Very likely no damage was done. But at least the *St. Lo* and VC-65 had delivered a little calling card to the Japanese fleet. Ensign Jensen from the *Kadashan Bay* had done just the same.

Pulling away from the cruiser column, Brooks tapped the intercom button and checked in with Downs and Travers. "Anybody hurt back there? What's going on?" They chatted gamely, trying to settle their nerves. Aside from a piece of shrapnel that had caught Downs in the hand, the crew was fine. Brooks tried to raise Bendix Base—the *Fanshaw Bay*—but the radio gave him only silence. Either Admiral Sprague was no longer speaking to him or a chunk of flak had knocked out his transmitter. From the deadness on his headphones he knew it was the latter. Brooks thought over his options. He knew that the *St. Lo* and the other Taffy 3 escort carriers would not be landing planes. They would be fleeing under fire, probably to the south, zigzagging to dodge shells, out of the wind. Possibly their flight decks had already been shredded by shellfire. Many of them might already be sinking.

From his briefings Brooks knew that a second group of jeep carriers, Taffy 2, was operating south of his task unit. He knew their general direction and was confident he could find them in the open ocean. With fuel running low, he cut back his RPMs and reduced his engine manifold pressure to a minimum. Preferring to be "a live pilot rather than a dead hero," he ruled out further futile heroics against the Japanese fleet. He decided that his best contribution to the coming one-sided slaughter would be to get himself to a place where he could load a torpedo or a rack of heavy bombs and return to the Japanese fleet, this time meaning business. He set his course for Taffy 2. He would find a friendly carrier, land, rearm, and get back in the air just as soon as he could.

It was 7:15 and shaping up to be a very long morning.

Part II

LAST STAND

In no engagement in its entire history has the United States Navy shown more gallantry, guts and gumption than in those two morning hours between 0730 and 0930 off Samar.

—Samuel Eliot Morison

Fourteen

The seas rolled calmly, stirred by a gentle easterly wind, when the early risers of the morning watch rose for breakfast at three A.M. to relieve the midwatch at four. Aboard the destroyer *Johnston,* washrooms filled with boisterous morning energy, lockers slammed, and the galley came alive with the hissing of steam, the banter of cooks, the sizzle of eggs and bacon. Quartermaster striker Robert Billie went to the mess, poured himself a cup of coffee, and decided to forget going back to bed. There were only two hours until morning general quarters would be called at six. Any teasing hints of sleep he might get would only deepen his fatigue. Until he could sleep in earnest, he might as well fill the remaining time with useful work. He went to the chart room to update his charts.

In previous campaigns, from the Marshalls to the Solomons to the Carolines, the *Johnston*'s crew had long ago proven their ability to function on a fractured sleep pattern. At six, per the daily routine, the claxons sounded, setting the steel decks and ladders vibrating with the concussion of quick footsteps. The dawn-dusk call to battle stations was part of the daily regimen of structure and discipline designed to keep minds sharp and equipment ready. The *Johnston* stood down after a few minutes on alert.

Then, unexpectedly, the general quarters claxon sounded again.

After a midwatch in the *Johnston*'s laundry, seaman first class Bill Mercer was fast asleep in his bunk when the GQ alarm began shrieking for a second time. He was at first slow to rise. But word that enemy ships were near shot life into him. Mercer sprang to his feet and sprinted toward his battle station on the port side forward forty-millimeter mount. He ran past Lee Burton, a ship's cook who was busy setting up the breakfast chow line, and said, "How about some bacon? It may be the last I ever get." Burton told Mercer to help himself, and he did, gladly and generously. Then Mercer saw the tall shell splashes straddling the escort carrier *Gambier Bay* off the *Johnston*'s port bow and immediately lost his appetite.

Ellsworth Welch, the *Johnston*'s junior officer of the deck, was leaning over the rail on the port side of the bridge taking in the warm aromas of breakfast when he first saw the columns of water towering over the decks of an escort carrier. Instinctively he looked skyward, expecting to see enemy bombers overhead. But then he realized that their air-search radar would have long since spotted any planes.

Torpedoman first class Thomas Sullivan mistook the sound of splashing water for dolphins at play. When he turned and saw the geysers, Sullivan knew that what he was seeing was the handiwork of a more warlike species of mammal.

In the chief's quarters, chief boatswain's mate Clyde Burnett was lying in his bunk awaiting breakfast when a ship's talker came on the PA and announced that a Japanese fleet was some fifteen miles away. "I thought someone was joking until I got topside and looked aft. The whole horizon seemed to light up from the gunfire," he said.

*   *   *

ABOARD THE *HOEL*, LT. John C. W. Dix knew something peculiar was in the air when he went belowdecks, cup of coffee and cigarette in hand, and ducked into the low-ceilinged compartment that housed the destroyer's combat information center. The *Hoel*'s executive officer, Lt. Fred Green, was at the plotting board, listening intently to voices on his headset and transcribing numbers with a grease pencil on the Plexiglas: 4, 6, 10. "Our Combat Air Patrol reports strange ships," Green said, "four battleships, six cruisers, ten tin cans. Listen, the pilot's coming in again."

A burst of static washed through the speakers, bringing a distant voice: *"I'm drawing fire."* Another wave of noise: *"The bastards have pagoda masts."* Dix checked the radar scope. In the upper left corner was a cluster of small green blips. Dix counted seventeen of them. Their range was less than forty thousand yards—about twenty-two miles.

Waiting in line for breakfast near the starboard hatch leading to his general quarters station in the forward fire room, water tender second class Chuck Sampson saw Dix come running down the ladder from the CIC shouting something about enemy ships closing with them. Sampson abandoned his place in line and dropped through the hatch and down the ladder to his battle station. Standing on the grating that divided the cavernous chamber into a split-level power station, Sampson shouted above the boilers' din, telling his fellows on the black gang what was happening.

Lt. Cdr. John Plumb, the engineering officer, arrived from the bridge to make sure the *Hoel*'s four boilers were lit. His snipes had already turned the wheels and thrown the switches that cut the boilers onto the main steam line. In the engine room someone threw open the main steam stop. Within minutes the ship had full power, its exhaust stacks unfurling large black clouds of boiler smoke.

As quartermaster Clarence Hood took the helm with Herbert Doubrava, the fighting tops of foreign warships became visible on the horizon, a scattered but growing forest of angry steel. An alarmed voice was heard coming over the TBS: *"Where the hell is Halsey?"*

The *Hoel*'s general quarters alarm began ringing now, a pulsing, synthesized minor-key gonging "designed to jar the brain, to wake you, speed the senses, make you feel the pitch of keen excitement in the air, the urge to reach your battle station fast," as Lieutenant Dix put it. For the second time that morning the ship came alive with the percussion of soles on steel decks. The galley emptied. Earlier risers gulped down the last of their scrambled eggs, navy beans, and cinnamon rolls, then sprinted through narrow passageways, ducked through hatches, raced up and down ladders.

When GQ sounded, there was never any question where to go or what to do. But when the alert was unscheduled, a degree of mystery surrounded why exactly you were doing it. According to Lieutenant Dix:

Maybe it's just a false alarm. You run. You don't know what it's for, and so you run. Torpedoes could be heading for the ship or bombers diving in. You never know. Nobody tells you what it's for. You run. You take your station first and then you ask. Nobody seems to know. The bell still rings. It's hardest on the guys who stay below. You've reached your station—forward magazine. The other fellow's there. He grabs the phone and calls up to the handling room to ask what's up. They're telling him the word. You watch his face, and now he's telling you and watching yours. You hear him say, "The Japs have opened fire." He's talking numbers. Twenty ships! A fleet! You don't believe it's true because you can't get out on deck and see it for yourself.

Aboard the *Samuel B. Roberts,* Bob Copeland and everyone else who had spent the night listening to the Surigao Strait fighting on the TBS frequency knew that somewhere a Japanese fleet was in fast retreat. They had heard it with their own ears: the sighting reports, the heavy blasts, the satisfied chuckling of gunnery officers, and the plain-language chatter of Oldendorf's skippers, exuberant as they ran down the stragglers of the Southern Force. The Japanese were fleeing, but in which direction? The question was of more than academic significance, for Taffy 3 steamed about a hundred miles north of where the Seventh Fleet's big boys had routed Nishimura the night before. If the Japanese were fleeing north, there might be something to see.

Copeland was leaving the bridge to get a cup of coffee in the officers' mess when Ens. Dudley Moylan, the officer of the deck on the morning watch, said, "Surface radar reports that they have a contact, sir, bearing three-three-zero approximately thirty or forty miles away." Edward Wheaton, a radar technician second class, said the image was kind of fuzzy, but yes, there was a dense pattern of echoes on the surface radar's A-scope. Like the radar returns observed by monitors on the island of Oahu on December 7, 1941, they were easy to dismiss. Just as likely they were echoes of rainsqualls or nearby land masses.

Peering out of a porthole from the pilothouse, Copeland spied a mass of gray clouds looming on the horizon. He told Wheaton, "Well, there's a storm over there, but there could be something inside of it, so keep an eye on it." Copeland was halfway down the ladder

Fleet Adm. William F. Halsey: Third Fleet commander, home front hero, scapegoat off Samar.

HARD!

"We Have Returned" On October 20, 1944, America began the liberation of the Philippines, led by Gen. Douglas MacArthur (foreground right) and Seventh Fleet commander Vice Adm. Thomas C. Kinkaid (foreground left).

Vice Adm. Takeo Kurita, commander of the Center Force, linchpin of the Sho plan.

The Center Force battleship *Kongo*.

The Center Force flagship *Yamato*.

The Center Force departs Brunei on October 22, 1944, as Japan activates the Sho-1 plan for the defense of the Philippines. The battleship *Nagato* leads, followed by superbattleships *Musashi* and *Yamato* and two divisions of heavy cruisers.

Rear Adm. Clifton A. F. ("Ziggy") Sprague, commander of Task Unit 77.4.3 (Taffy 3).

(Top row, left to right) **Robert M. Billie, Edward Block, Roy Lozano, Clint Carter, Bobby J. Chastain, Joseph M. Check;** (second row) **Jesse D. Cochran;** (third row) **Edward M. DiGardi;** (fourth row) **Robert Hollenbaugh.**

Escort carriers riding heavy seas.

Ens. John S. LeClercq, assistant gunnery officer, *Samuel B. Roberts*.

Burton L. Hoover

Ernest Evans's U.S. Naval Academy yearbook photo.

Idle time aboard the USS *Johnston*, DD-557, shortly after her commissioning.

Cdr. Ernest E. Evans, skipper of the *Johnston*.

Cdr. Ernest E. Evans (at microphone), addressing the crew of the *Johnston* at its commissioning ceremony in Seattle, October 27, 1943.

Allen Johnson

Charles R. Landreth

Cdr. Leon Kintberger, skipper of the *Hoel*.

Leon Kintberger's U.S. Naval Academy yearbook photo.

(Left to right) **William E. Mercer, John Mostowy, Harold E. "Dusty" Rhodes, John Schindele, Robert J. Sochor, Sr., Clarence Trader.**

aul Henry Carr grade
chool photograph and
ith a friend enjoying
alf roping and riding.

GM2 Paul Henry Carr,
gun captain,
Samuel B. Roberts.

The USS *Hoel*,
DD-533, departs
San Francisco,
August 7, 1943.

(Top row) **Ellsworth Welch, Willard Frenn, Bob DeSpain, Jack Creamer;**
(second row) **Chester Fay, Glen Foster, Walter Gammon;**
(third row) **Francis Hostrander, Everett Lindorff, Lynn Lowry.**

The USS *Samuel B. Roberts,*
DE-413.

Sailors run the gauntlet
during the *Fanshaw Bay*'s
crossing-the-line ceremony.

Lt. Cdr. Robert W. Copeland, skipper of the USS *Samuel B. Roberts*.

(Left to right) **Clyde Burnett, Sam Lucas, Paul Miranda, John Oracz.**

Ens. William C. Brooks.

Ens. William C. Brooks, an Avenger pilot from the *St. Lo*, spots the Japanese fleet.

Jack Yusen (left)
and Dick Rohde (right).

Lt. (jg) Tom Stevenson, the *Samuel B. Roberts*'s communications officer.

Amos Hathaway's, U.S. Naval Academy yearbook photo.

Cdr. Amos T. Hathaway, captain of the USS *Heermann*.

Lt. Robert C. Hagen, the *Johnston*'s gunnery officer.

(Left to right) Glenn Parkin, Charles Sampson, Fred Green, Donald "Tiny" Heinritz, Clarence Hood.

VY SHIP SINKIN

A native San Franciscan is Lieutenant Bob Hagen and glad was he to see home after sinking of his destroyer, U. S. S. Johnston, in Philippine Sea battle. He was gunnery officer on the ship.

Gun captain Clint Carter aboard the USS *Johnston*.

The USS *Heermann* makes smoke during the Battle off Samar, photographed from escort carrier USS *Kalinin Bay*.

(Left to right) **Richard Santos, L.E. "Bud" Walton, Bob Wilson.**

The *Gambier Bay* under fire from a Japanese
heavy cruiser, probably the *Chikuma,* visible on
the horizon.

to the mess when a lookout called to Moylan, "Object on the horizon. Looks like the mast of a ship."

With dozens of others George Bray thought he'd go out on deck and get himself an eyeful. He heard a voice come over the ship's loudspeaker. It was the executive officer, Bob Roberts: "If you're interested, come up on deck. Remnants of the Japanese fleet are fleeing over the horizon." Here was something out of the routine. Bray, who was belowdecks turning in his laundry at the time, ran topside in time to see a white phosphorescent fireball illuminate the predawn morning with a phony brilliance, its smoky fingers falling in shallow arcs into the sea. The realization sickened him: somebody was taking a range on them. Sight-seeing hell, they had gone and gotten themselves into a fight. As the general quarters alarm sounded, Bray ran to his battle station in the after living quarters, grabbed the steel helmet out of his footlocker, and hustled to the stairwell where repair party number two was supposed to report.

Gunnery officer Lt. Bill Burton, who had an especially sharp eye for ship silhouettes, confirmed for his captain that the mystery ships on the horizon belonged to Imperial Japan. Battleships. Heavy cruisers. They were big ones. Bob Copeland never got his coffee. He got on the TBS radio and raised Admiral Sprague aboard the *Fanshaw Bay*. Copeland didn't tell Sprague anything the admiral hadn't already heard from Ensign Brooks, whose Avenger was at that moment being buffeted by flak from Kurita's ships.

The revelation that the enemy was not fleeing but advancing had the surreal quality of a dream. In everyone's mind the far-fetched possibility of disaster had hitherto been shouted down by the certainty that any Japanese force approaching from the north would have to confront the thoroughbreds of the Third Fleet. Just the day before, the crews of Taffy 3's ships had lined the decks to watch the carriers *Franklin* and *Enterprise,* accompanied by the fast battleships *Alabama* and *Washington* and an assortment of lesser ships, steam northward to join the rest of Halsey's huge force. In the wake of that parade of dreadnoughts, reports that Japanese fleets were on the move inspired little fear. Oldendorf was to their south, Halsey to their north. There was nothing to fear from Japanese surface raiders.

On the bridge of the *Samuel B. Roberts* Lt. Tom Stevenson, in his slippers, chinos, and a T-shirt, and the assistant gunnery officer, Lt.

(jg) John LeClercq, watched the towering mainmasts of Japanese battleships rise on the horizon and felt their sense of safety dissolve. Now and then the distant silhouettes were obscured by silent flashes of light from their cannonade. Although neither acknowledged as much to the other, Stevenson and LeClercq both knew they had little chance to survive. Heavy shells were inbound, and their own tiny ship was much too far away to strike back. As they prepared to head for their battle stations—Stevenson below to the CIC, LeClercq to supervise the aft forty-millimeter gun mount—the two officers shook hands and wished each other luck.

Captain Copeland picked up the intercom mike and addressed the *Roberts*'s crew. That he was speaking for himself struck Ens. Jack Moore as unusual and urgent. Normally seaman Jack Roberts was the public address voice of his namesake warship. His southern drawl was all but unintelligible to anyone not acquainted with Dixie's rhythms and diphthongs. But the skipper's diction was as crisp as a litigator's. He was talking fast and sounding more than a little nervous.

"A large Japanese fleet has been contacted. They are fifteen miles away and headed in our direction. They are believed to have four battleships, eight cruisers, and a number of destroyers.

"This will be a fight against overwhelming odds from which survival cannot be expected. We will do what damage we can."

Jack Moore was already at his GQ station in *Sammy B.*'s decoding room. The ensign had been late getting there, having stayed awake till the close of midwatch reading a novel in his bunk. When Moore arrived in the small windowless compartment containing the coding machine, the chief radioman, Tullio Serafini, was already at work. Moore offered a sleepy "good morning" and Serafini acknowledged it. The portly Italian chief never talked much. Though he had played the royal baby at the crossing-the-line ceremony, he was the oldest man on the ship at forty-three and had little in common with boys twenty and more years his junior. Serafini was an immigrant from the Old Country whose Navy service dated to World War I. When Pearl Harbor was attacked, he had left a well-paying job in the Philadelphia Navy Yard and reenlisted despite both exceeding the age limit and his status as father of two. Serafini felt that he owed a debt of gratitude to the United States. Moore sensed that Tullio Serafini was the sort of guy who always made good on his debts. Captain Copeland was only too glad to accept payment on behalf of the nation. Recognizing Serafini's talents, he waived the time requirements to make chief.

As a mail censor, Moore had gleaned some of Serafini's personal history from a birthday letter the chief had written to his son. "Be a good, stout boy and mind your mommy all of the time, even when you think she might be wrong, so that your daddy can be proud of his eight-year-old man when he comes home again. [Signed] Your loving Daddy. P.S. Keep up the good grades in school." The way Moore saw it, "Serafini's entrance into the war was analogous to our country's entrance. . . . They had worked and developed what they had until now it was worth protecting, even if it meant sacrificing their very being."

A pronounced *click* on the intercom punctuated the end of Copeland's announcement to his crew and left the young ensign and the old chief sitting in disbelieving silence. Serafini turned to Moore, cocked his head to the side, and puckered his lips in comic sadness. The communicator had nothing to say.

Through the *Samuel B. Roberts*'s tour of the Pacific, Moore had learned to calm his men's fears by reciting the betting odds that stood in their favor. En route to the Philippines, he had posted odds of ninety to one favoring their safe return. During the big typhoon at Leyte, he put them at fifty to one. "What are the odds, Mr. Moore?" The question from an enlisted man took him aback. For the first time Moore could remember, the odds were not with them. He figured them at more like one to one—a fifty-fifty chance. Not fifty-fifty the *Roberts* and her band would win the battle, but fifty-fifty that any given man would live to see the next day's sunrise. The enemy was too close, too big, too fast. One to one; that was about right.

Some other numbers helped tell that story. If the Japanese cruisers and destroyers could make thirty knots, they would gain about a mile on the fleeing eighteen-knot American carriers every five minutes. Any group of ships, no matter how swift, was effectively hostage to its slowest member. Moore avoided dwelling on where this arithmetic would put them in an hour or so. He occupied himself with the decoding machine, numbly punching in the five-character sequences he got from the radiomen.

The five-character code blocks came from the radio department next door, where a row of enlisted men were busily transcribing encrypted radio traffic transmitted in Morse code over their ear-phones. The six exchangeable wheels inside the coding machine took Moore's keyed input and spun and lined up and printed a thin white ribbon of plain-English prose. One of the messages that spooled out onto the ticker tape was important but brief. It was from Admiral Nimitz, addressed to all ships. According to Moore, "It read something like this: DUE TO THE SPLENDID AIRMANSHIP SHOWN IN YESTER-DAY'S ENGAGEMENTS, AND WITH A CONTINUING OF SUCH COORDINATED ACTION, I CAN ASSURE A DEFEAT OF THE JAPANESE NAVY FROM WHICH IT WILL NEVER RECOVER." Ensign Moore threw the message to the floor in disgust. He didn't know much about Kurita's Center Force. Nor, as it happened, did Admirals Halsey and Nimitz. Whatever might be said of Admiral Kurita's group, it had surely recovered from its beating by Third Fleet aviators the previous afternoon. It was bearing down now on Taffy 3, aiming to prove it.

THE BATTLE OFF SAMAR, OCTOBER 25, 1944

JAPANESE FORCES

Center Force, Vice Admiral Takeo Kurita

BATTLESHIPS

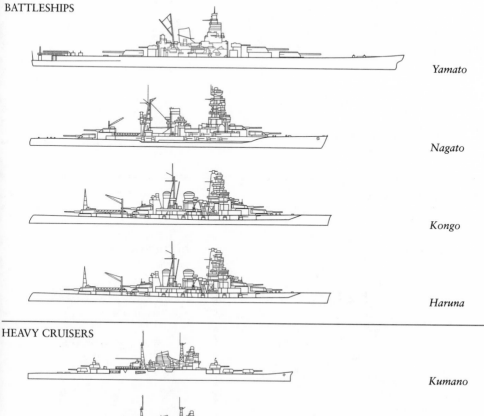

Yamato

Nagato

Kongo

Haruna

HEAVY CRUISERS

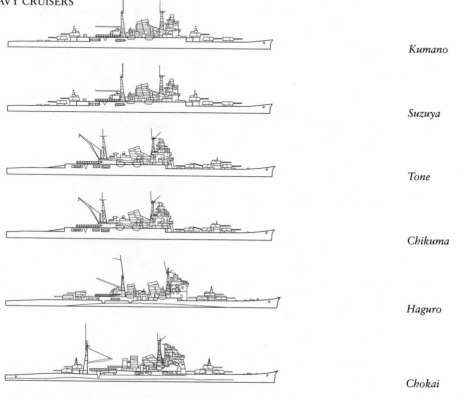

Kumano

Suzuya

Tone

Chikuma

Haguro

Chokai

LIGHT CRUISERS

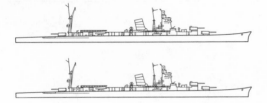

Yahagi

Noshiro

DESTROYERS (11 total, formed into 2 squadrons, Desron 2 and Desron 10)

Asashio-Kaguro class

AMERICAN FORCES
Taffy 3 (Task Unit 77.4.3), *Rear Admiral Clifton A. F. Sprague*

ESCORT CARRIERS

Fanshaw Bay (CVE-70) VC-68

St. Lo (CVE-63) VC-65

White Plains (CVE-66) VC-4

Kalinin Bay (CVE-68) VC-3

Gambier Bay (CVE-73) VC-10

Kitkun Bay (CVE-71) VC-5

DESTROYERS

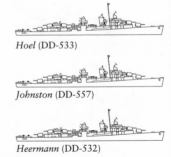

Hoel (DD-533)

Johnston (DD-557)

Heermann (DD-532)

DESTROYER ESCORTS

Dennis (DE-405)

Samuel B. Roberts (DE-413)

John C. Butler (DE-339)

Raymond (DE-341)

Fifteen

At 6:35 A.M., as sunrise revealed a grayed-out and hazy dawn, the most powerful concentration of naval gun power the Japanese empire had ever assembled reordered its geometry in preparation for daylight operations. Twenty-five miles to Taffy 3's north, lookouts on the heavy cruiser *Chokai* and light cruiser *Noshiro* reported aircraft approaching. So Halsey's planes were coming after all, Takeo Kurita must have thought. Almost simultaneously, cat-eyed lookouts on the battleship *Nagato* spied masts on the horizon visible here and there through the rainsqualls that dropped down from the heavens like gauzy shrouds. An eight-knot easterly wind roused low swells from the sea. From the *Yamato*'s gunnery platform high above the bridge, Cdr. Tonosuke Otani, Kurita's operations officer, squinted through a range-finding telescope and spotted the flat-topped silhouettes of American aircraft carriers.

The presence of carriers meant this was not Nishimura's squadron. Kurita could not believe his luck. Here, within gun range at last, were the fast, first-line *Essex*-class fleet carriers that constituted the heart of the American fleet. There looked to be six or seven of them, accompanied by what lookouts took for *Baltimore*-class heavy cruisers, powerful combatants only six feet shorter than *South Dakota*–class battleships. The imagination of Admiral Koyanagi,

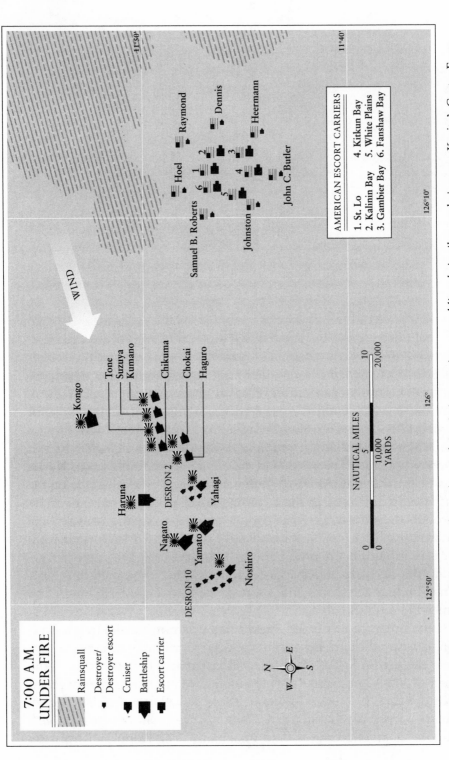

As Ziggy Sprague's task unit flees eastward into the wind, its six jeep carriers scrambling their pilots and aircrews, Kurita's Center Force begins its high-speed pursuit, its battleships firing heavy salvos at extended range.

Kurita's chief of staff, ran wild. He believed they faced not an escort carrier group, but four or five big carriers escorted by one or two battleships and ten or more heavy cruisers.

At 6:59, loaded with rounds designed to penetrate heavy armor, the great 18.1-inch rifles of the battleship *Yamato* trained to starboard and opened fire on Taffy 3 at a range of nearly twenty miles. One minute later Kurita issued a fleet-wide order for a "general attack." The *Kongo* turned out to the east, in fast but independent pursuit. Ahead of the *Yamato* to port, the six heavy cruisers of Cruiser Divisions 5 and 7 formed into a single column, trying to take the lead in the chase. Angling to the southwest, the *Nagato* turned her sixteen-inch rifles twenty-five degrees to port and opened fire at a range of more than twenty miles. The swift *Haruna* loosed fourteen-inch salvos using its crude radar set.

Apparently unaware of the speed advantage his ships held over their American prey, Kurita seemed eager for his heavy cruisers to press the fight before the Americans could escape. A more disciplined (or better-informed) commander might have drawn his ships into a single line of battle, with destroyers in the forward van to scout the enemy and maneuver for a deadly torpedo attack.

For all the strength the Japanese Center Force brought into play, its commanders were unsettled about the manner in which the battle began. In the midst of the shift to a daytime antiaircraft formation, with each captain operating at his own freewheeling discretion, confusion took command of the Center Force. Vice Adm. Matome Ugaki, commanding Kurita's First Battleship Division, composed of the *Yamato* and the *Nagato,* observed, "each unit seemed very slow in starting actions due to uncertainty about the enemy condition." "I feared the spirit of all-out attack at short range was lacking," Admiral Ugaki would write.

The heavy cruisers led the Japanese charge on Taffy 3. Cruiser Division 7's commander, Vice Adm. Kazutaka Shiraishi, was a fifty-two-year-old Nagasaki native who had not had a seagoing command since 1940. Shiraishi received Kurita's order, *"Cruiser divisions attack!"* and turned his ships to the southeast, steaming at their maximum speed of thirty-five knots. Aiming to flank the American ships from the east, he radioed each of his captains in succession: *"We are closing the enemy. Intend to engage to starboard."* Then—bizarrely— though a general attack had been ordered, the vanguard of any such attack, the Center Force's two divisions of hard-hitting destroyers, led by the light cruisers *Noshiro* and *Yahagi,* were ordered to the rear.

Though there were doubters in his midst, Kurita was overjoyed by his perceived good fortune in encountering American carriers. At seven o'clock the Center Force commander dispatched a message that delighted Combined Fleet Headquarters: "WE ARE ENGAGING ENEMY IN GUN BATTLE" . . . and then "BY HEAVEN-SENT OPPORTUNITY WE ARE DASHING TO ATTACK THE ENEMY CARRIERS." The emperor's fleet had been handed a dreamed-for chance. Carriers were queens of the seas, mobile and lethally armed with ship-killing planes. Now it was the Imperial Japanese Navy's turn to move on the Philippine chessboard. Its rooks had America's queens, so Kurita thought, lined up for slaughter.

Sixteen

As flecks of antiaircraft fire dotted the northern horizon around Bill Brooks's Avenger, Ernest Evans emerged from his sea cabin on the destroyer *Johnston* and sized up Taffy 3's predicament in an instant. Situated closest to the advancing enemy fleet, he could not have missed his ship's consignment to quick destruction. Faced with it, Evans evidently saw no need to await orders from Commander Thomas aboard the *Hoel* or from Admiral Sprague. If carrier commanders traditionally saw the destroyers' primary battle role as laying smoke screens to cover the flattops' escape, Evans had other ideas about what he was supposed to do. Destroyers sortied. They interposed. They sacrificed themselves for the ships they were assigned to protect. Evans would do his duty for the *Fanshaw Bay*, the *St. Lo*, the *Gambier Bay*, the *White Plains*, the *Kalinin Bay*, and the *Kitkun Bay*. If that meant closing with an enemy whose guns were big enough to sink him with a single hit, so be it. He would make good on his commissioning-day promise—his warning—to his crew: the *Johnston* was a fighting ship. He would not back down.

Recalling his skipper's speech in the context of the present situation, Bob Hagen, the *Johnston*'s gunnery officer, grew ill. As the ship's senior lieutenant, he knew his skipper. The certainty that Evans would turn the ship into the teeth of the Japanese fleet saddled him with dread. *This is an impossible situation with this skipper,* Hagen thought. *He's not going to run. He doesn't know how.*

Hagen practically heard the orders before his skipper delivered them. His rapid-fire sequence suggested he had rehearsed all his Navy life for a moment such as this.

All hands to general quarters.
Prepare to attack major portion of the Japanese fleet.
All engines ahead flank.
Commence making smoke and stand by for a torpedo attack.
Left full rudder.

Lt. (jg) Ellsworth Welch couldn't help but be impressed with his skipper's brio, his calm, his directness of action, and clarity of thought. *Why didn't I think of that?* he found himself wondering. *Nothing like having a pro in charge.*

Left full rudder meant that the ship would peel off to the north-northwest, away from the illusory sanctuary of the formation and charging toward the enemy fleet. The order made Robert Billie, a Minnesotan, want to go to ground like a gopher. "That was the only time I ever wanted to dig a trench."

Bob Hagen ran his numbers—the fire-control computer could not help him here—and drew the same conclusion Jack Moore had on the *Samuel B. Roberts*: there was probably a fifty-fifty chance of survival. The long odds notwithstanding, he was in no hurry to climb up to the gun director. Though the situation seemed to demand urgent action—and indeed, he could count on his men being inside each of the five main gun mounts within about ninety seconds of going to general quarters—what was the point of hurry-up-and-wait? The gunners would have nothing to shoot at until the range to the enemy had closed from 35,000 yards to 18,000 yards, about six miles. Until then, the gunnery officer felt no immediate need to gaze upon the enemy ships through his binoculars.

The shellfire put out by the Japanese force was overwhelming. Battleship main battery rounds plunged down at the *Johnston*, shrieking like locomotives, smacking the sea with a slap and roar and sending up towers of dye-stained seawater. At that moment Hagen had as good a view of the Japanese dreadnoughts as he cared to have.

The *Johnston*'s gun boss contemplated the audacious path his captain had chosen and said quietly, "Please, sir, let us not go down before we fire our damn torpedoes."

He did not doubt that Ernest Evans would do his best. Like the other officers on the *Johnston*, Hagen had come to see him as "a captain who could strike fighting spirit from his men the way steel strikes spark from a flint." Evans's conduct impressed him indelibly. "I can see him now," Hagen would write, "short, barrel-chested, standing on the bridge with his hands on his hips, giving out with a running fire of orders in a bull voice."

That Evans acted on instinct, ahead of actual orders, was elemental to his constitution and his experience. The crew in turn vested their faith in the all-encompassing will of the Cherokee warrior who had sworn that he would never withdraw. And who knew, perhaps promises as portentous as his carried with them some kind of implicit magic that assured their survival. The laws of probability and the lessons of recent combat history, however, heralded a different outcome. At the Battle of Savo Island, Japanese cruisers and destroyers had needed only six minutes to annihilate an Allied cruiser column. At Midway, American dive-bombers had wiped out most of a Japanese carrier task force in four decisive minutes. Alone against heavy cruisers and battleships—cruising through shell splashes fired by vessels up to thirty-five times her size—the *Johnston* would have no business surviving even that long. As the Army troops at Bataan or the Marines on Wake Island could attest, Americans had been overwhelmed in battle before. The Pacific had afforded them several occasions to refight the Alamo. Now, it seemed, it was the Navy's turn.

As his ship sped to the northwest, alone against the Japanese fleet, Ernest Evans had no illusions that the *Johnston*'s five-inch main battery would do much damage. He knew that his only chance to send Japanese iron to the bottom of the Philippine Trench was to get close enough to fire his ten torpedoes, mounted in two quintuple mounts amidships, and plant a little torpex into their underbellies. Until then, all he could do was make his best speed and blow out as much smoke as his boilers were capable of making.

When the firemen received Captain Evans's order to make smoke, they misinterpreted it as a reprimand. "But we are not making smoke," came the defensive reply. Boiler room personnel trained hard to do anything *but* make smoke, lest the ship betray its location or foul its boiler tubes and require a painstaking cleaning. Evans grabbed the sound-powered phones and yelled, *"I want a smoke screen, and I want it now!"*

On the fantail, Lt. Jesse Cochran, the assistant engineering officer and head of a repair party, had trouble getting the chemical smoke generator going. Its valves were stuck fast from saltwater corrosion. Torpedoman first class Jim O'Gorek used a big adjustable wrench and vise grips to jog them loose, while Cochran and his party set depth charges on safe and dogged down all hatches and doors on the aft part of the ship. After a minute or so of urgent wrenching, the gray concoction was billowing in the ship's wake, hanging close to the sea in the humid monsoon-season air. As the Japanese star shells burned overhead like miniature midday suns, advancing the light of the early morning, black smoke flowed from the ship's two stacks, turning dawn back into night.

Smoke making was an act of sacrifice: the smoke flowed *behind* the ship that made it, shrouding everything in its wake. It gave its maker no protection. If Taffy 3 had a prayer to survive, it would depend on confusing Kurita and shielding the retreating escort carriers from view. "We were making smoke, zig-zagging and heading for the Jap fleet," seaman John Mostowy would write, "at flank speed and alone."

As the *Johnston* came around to port on Captain Evans's order, taking a northwesterly course toward the Japanese fleet, seaman first class Bill Mercer pulled on a kapok life jacket. He was fastening it tight when a seaman named Gorman asked him if he was scared. Mercer, a Texan, said hell yeah, he was scared. In fact, his heart was thumping so hard beneath his ribs that he feared the Japanese might hear it. The only words Gorman could find in reply were a strange non sequitur: "This is fun."

To quartermaster Neil Dethlefs, the situation seemed like the work of a cruel and uncaring universe. He had been on the *Johnston* for only three weeks. Not long ago he had been working aboard the hull repair ship *Prometheus* at Tulagi when the *Johnston* entered the harbor flashing signal lights requesting a replacement for a quartermaster who had trouble with seasickness. Dethlefs and another quartermaster on the *Prometheus* fit the job description, so they cut a deck of cards to determine who had to go. Dethlefs pulled an eight to his colleague's king and dutifully reported to his yeoman for transfer to the destroyer. The bitter thought seized him now: he had arrived aboard the *Johnston* just in time to get himself killed.

As Captain Evans rang up flank speed, officer of the deck Lt. Ed DiGardi knew the *Johnston* wasn't ready for an extended high-speed engagement. The fuel report indicated that the ship had only 12,000 gallons of fuel oil. At standard cruising speed, the ship burned 500 gallons an hour. But at a flank speed of thirty-six knots, the rate jumped to 5,000 gallons an hour. In just over two hours the tanks would be bone dry. The ship would go dead in the water, whether it was hit or not. Lieutenant DiGardi told the engineering officer, Lt. Joe Worling, to do what the engineer already knew had to be done: mix the oil with the 10,000 gallons of diesel fuel the ship carried in separate tanks. Though engineers hated the way the dirty-burning grog fouled the delicate boiler tubes and required a painstaking cleanout, there was no alternative in these desperate circumstances.

Not everyone was entirely despondent. Looking down to the bridge from the gun director, Bob Hagen swore that he could see Captain Evans's "heart grinning" as he led his ship into the fight.

Seventeen

From the bridge of the *Fanshaw Bay*, Ziggy Sprague took in the vicious columns of water rising around the *White Plains* and the other CVEs on the edge of the formation nearest the enemy and saw a terrible beauty. The splashes from the salvos rose in a rainbow of colors: red, pink, purple, green, yellow—each so dyed in order to help the enemy gunners correct the fall of their shots.

In the whole horrible course of the war in four wide oceans, not once had an American aircraft carrier come within gun range of an enemy surface ship. The historic nature of Sprague's plight was not lost on him. In the triumphant closing phase of the war against Japan, Admiral Sprague, an emissary of the world's greatest sea power, was going to see all six of his flattops sunk by gunfire. It was certain to happen. It wouldn't take more than fifteen minutes. There was no other possible outcome.

For the kid from Rockport, the situation was beyond imagining. "I wouldn't say it was like a bad dream, for my mind had never experienced anything from which such a nightmare could have been spun." Once Clifton Sprague had dreamed of going to West Point, of parading on horseback before cheering crowds down his hometown thoroughfare. He had become a Navy admiral instead. Now he would have his appointment with notoriety, leading thirteen ships whose pending destruction would go down in history just as surely as they would go down to the bottomless deep of the Philippine Trench: "Neither could such dream stuff have been recalled from my reading in some history book, because nothing like this had ever happened in history."

By any measure the mathematics of the engagement were preposterously against them. The *Yamato* displaced nearly seventy thousand tons. She alone matched almost exactly in weight all thirteen ships of Taffy 3. Each of her three main gun turrets weighed more than an entire *Fletcher*-class destroyer. Her armor belts—sixteen inches thick at the waterline and more than two feet thick on her gun turrets—were impenetrable to an American destroyer's guns. Her nine 18.1-inch rifles were the biggest guns that ever went to sea, firing 3,200-pound shells more than twenty-six miles. Their development was so secret that even Admiral Kurita did not know their true size. The superbattleship's secondary battery of six six-inch guns packed twice the hitting power of anything Ziggy Sprague's largest escorts had. The ship was a great gray beast whose bulk pressed down into the ocean and possessed it, displacing enough water to raise measurably the level of a small lake. At flank speed of twenty-seven knots, the *Yamato* sliced the sea and drew it back around her in a roiling maelstrom, leaving a wake that capsized small boats.

The *Yamato* was not the only ship that completely outgunned Sprague's task unit. The *Nagato,* displacing 42,850 tons, fielded eight sixteen-inch guns, and the *Kongo* and her sister ship the *Haruna* (36,600 tons) were fast frontline battleships armed with eight-gun fourteen-inch batteries. Kurita's six heavy cruisers were thirty-five-knot killers that had a cumulative displacement equal to that of the *Yamato*. Finally, Kurita had two flotillas of destroyers, eleven in all, each led by a light cruiser, the *Yahagi* and the *Noshiro* (8,543 tons), with six-inch batteries. On paper each of the destroyers matched the *Johnston*, the *Hoel*, or the *Heermann* in speed and torpedo power if not quite in gunnery. The only weapon in Sprague's modest arsenal that Kurita could not match was aircraft. Each of the six American jeeps carried about thirty planes. But loaded with depth charges, antipersonnel bombs, rockets, and the machine guns in their wings—not to mention the propaganda leaflets they sometimes carried in lieu of more kinetic payloads—they were not armed for attacking heavy surface ships.

A fighting force cannot be reduced to its order of battle any more than a ship's value can be reduced to the number of guns she carries or the shaft horsepower her turbines can generate. A vessel draws life from the spirit of her crew, which derives in large part from the leadership qualities of her chiefs and officers. Morale defies quantification—and yet it weighs significantly on the ultimate lethality of the tools of war. A ship's effectiveness is the product of thousands of bonds that develop between individual officers and crew. The bonds form and break in a chain reaction, the power of which is determined by drill, by relationships, by fortitude, faith, and values. Task force commanders can be only abstractly aware of these uncountable qualities as they exist on the particular ships under their command. The officers of the ships themselves see these qualities more clearly but still can only guess how the chemical reactions will coalesce when the real shooting starts and men begin to die. And so orders of battle are drawn up to focus on the tangibles: speed, displacement, armament, and sensors. On that score Taffy 3 scarcely even registered on the scale of force that Takeo Kurita brought against them.

Thanks to Ensign Brooks's diligent sighting report, Admiral Sprague knew precisely what he faced. "I thought, we might as well give them all we've got before we go down," he later recalled. That meant getting into position to launch planes and putting as much distance as possible between his ships and the faster Japanese. Both of those goals could be met by heading east, into the wind.

Ziggy Sprague coolly measured what would become a steadily shifting matrix of variables—enemy course headings, patterns of wind and squalls, the effectiveness of his own ships' evasions and protective smoke laying and the effect of the enemy fire—and instinctively planned his escape. He ordered his ships to turn from their northerly course to an eastward one, on heading 090. Three factors recommended that course: first, it was directly away from the Japanese fleet; second, it brought a strong wind rushing from bow to stern over his carrier decks—an apparent headwind of twenty-two knots was necessary to get a fully loaded Avenger airborne, even with catapult assistance; and third, it took him toward open ocean, where he could hope for the intervention not only of rainsqualls but perhaps also of other American ships. "I wanted to pull the enemy out where somebody could smack him," he would write; either Oldendorf or

Halsey, wherever they were, could handle that job. "If we were going to expend ourselves I wanted to make it count."

At 6:50 Sprague flipped on the TBS radio and ordered the skippers of his command, *"Signal execute on receipt. Shackle baker uncle easy unshackle turn."* Between the words *shackle* and *unshackle* was the coded numerical heading Sprague intended to follow. *Baker Uncle Easy* were the encoded integers for a heading of 090. All as one, the helmsmen on twelve of Taffy 3's thirteen ships turned to the right, bringing their ships on an eastward heading. Sprague also passed the order to begin making smoke for concealment. Aboard the jeep carriers, flight deck crews raced to ready their planes for launch.

It took only five minutes to turn the six nimble carriers onto a windward course. Sprague ordered, *"Launch all planes as soon as possible,"* then hedged against the long-shot possibility that the fleet opposing him might yet be friendly: *"Caution all pilots to identify all ships before attacking."* The roar and colorful splashes of incoming shells, however, all but removed that distant possibility.

Many of Sprague's planes had been airborne since first light, flying off before daybreak to strike targets on Leyte. Now, needing the bombs they carried, he ordered them to abort and return. He also needed help from the other two Taffies to his south. On the TBS circuit he raised the commander of Taffy 2, Rear Adm. Felix Stump, *"Come in please. Come in please. . . . To any or all: We have enemy fleet consisting of BBs and cruisers fifteen miles astern closing us. We are being fired on."*

Admiral Stump got on the line, already briefed by intercepted radio transmissions, and said, *"Don't be alarmed, Ziggy, remember we're back of you. Don't get excited! Don't do anything rash!"* Since Stump's Taffy 2 was the only of the three Taffies not under direct attack—Taffy 1 would be fighting off land-based Japanese aircraft most of the morning—he was best positioned to help Sprague. Still, something about his tone tended to undercut his advice.

Thomas Sprague, in simultaneous command of Taffy 1 and all three Taffies, recognized that in the coming fight Ziggy Sprague should be free to decide how to conduct it. All that Thomas Sprague could do for him was cover bureaucratic bases and ask the Seventh Fleet's commander of support aircraft for permission to launch all available torpedo bombers and "go after them." The request was duly granted, and thereafter, according to Admiral Stump, "no orders were received from anyone during the entire day, nor were any necessary." It was Ziggy Sprague's battle to win or lose, "using the initiative that was required under the prevailing circumstances."

Ziggy Sprague knew that help was a long way off. What he didn't know was that Jesse Oldendorf's battleships, idling in Leyte Gulf after their historic victory in Surigao Strait, would be kept from coming to his assistance because Admiral Kinkaid feared the Southern Force might turn around and attack again through Surigao Strait. Though one might question the wisdom of ensuring against a contingent disaster when a very real one was already at hand, the cold fact of October 25 was that Admiral Sprague, the ships and men of Taffy 3, and their brothers to their south, would have no help from the overwhelming naval power marshaled to their north and south. They were on their own.

Sprague's moves in the crucible of imminent combat were swift but not rash. One trait of good commanders is that they make simple decisions at the right times and without delay. Sprague was an instinctive and forceful decision maker. He played golf in a hurry. He didn't line up his putts. He just walked up to the ball and hit it. When he met his future wife, Annabel, he knew immediately he would marry her. At Pearl Harbor he knew right away what to do with the few weapons he had on the *Tangier*. On the morning of October 25, with an overwhelming Japanese task force pressing down on him, he saw instantly the surest route to his slim hope of survival. If he did not completely resign himself to dying, he at least accepted the reasonable certainty of an imminent swim. If no assistance came from other ships, Sprague would settle for the intervention of a heavenly being of whom during quieter periods of his life he had asked, and to whom he had given, relatively little.

Eighteen

In the ready room of the *St. Lo,* VC-65's skipper, Ralph Jones, pulled on his Mae West, a parachute harness, helmet, and goggles as fast as he could. The pilots and aircrews of VC-65 followed suit, the *boom boom rummp* of the enemy ships' near misses urging them on as they scrambled to the flight deck and climbed into their planes. Kurita had found their range. Pink, red, and blue columns of water rose up around them. Something crazy was happening—they were under attack, but by whom? There was no cause to question it, but how the hell was this possible? Takeoff would have to be quick, or it might not be done at all.

Ens. Ed Breeding had been up half the night, listening on the combat frequency to the fractured transmissions of the fighting down in Surigao Strait. Strapped into the cockpit of his FM-2 Wildcat fighter, engine started and idling, in queue for takeoff, the twenty-three-year-old watched as colorful spouts of water climbed into the air to starboard and port, then collapsed in rings of sea foam. A teenage plane handler jumped onto his wing, gestured toward the maelstrom, and asked, "Sir, what's that?" The other pilots had nicknamed Breeding, a farmer's son from Hill County, Texas, "Speedy" for the pace of his Texas drawl. He said, "Well, it looks like somebody's shooting at us. You better put me on that catapult so I can go shoot back."

Until he saw with his own eyes the big shells inbound from the battleships and heard with his own ears the crackling whistle of their descent, Holly Crawforth, a *St. Lo* radio technician, thought it was all some kind of sick joke. Confronted with a sudden vision of his capture and torture at Japanese hands, he took his dog tags and threw them away. On the sound-powered phones he could hear the guys in the engine room getting panicky. Belowdecks men fretted about the possibility of a torpedo hit swallowing them from below. "Tell us what the hell is happening!" they shouted.

The *St. Lo*'s skipper, Capt. Francis J. McKenna, called course changes to his helmsman, zigzagging hard, trying to throw off the aim of the Japanese gunners. As vital as his evasive maneuvering was, it complicated matters for pilots aiming to get airborne. With the flow of wind over the deck shifting with each turn, aviators never quite knew how crosswinds and engine torque would affect their takeoff. The catapult crews preferred to fire when the ship was facing the wind, so the rhythm of the launch was disrupted and the planes started their missions widely separated.

As ever, Lt. Cdr. Ralph Jones was first in line for takeoff. The catapult whipped him airborne, and the catapult crews raced to gather the harness and string it to the next plane rolling forward. Jones turned sharply to the left, fifty feet off the water, and headed for the Japanese fleet. Inching ahead in his Wildcat, Breeding's squadron-mate, Lt. (jg) Larry Budnick, far from his Superior, Wisconsin, home, thought to himself, *Let me the hell off this thing.* Smoke from the carrier's exhaust stacks, which rose barely above the flight deck, stung his nose with its acridity. One by one the planes ahead of him whipped aloft—Avengers using the catapult, Wildcats making deck runs. At last it was Budnick's turn. He opened his throttle, rolled down the deck, and roared aloft after his commander.

The usual strike plan called for the Wildcats to escort the Avengers to the target and coordinate their attacks. En route the pilots of the swift Wildcats kept their throttles back, weaving and circling to stay with the lumbering torpedo bombers. At the target the fighters winged over to strafe while the Avengers lined up their excruciating low-altitude runs. That kind of teamwork was impossible now. There was no time to fly by the book. Larry Budnick had a hard time finding other fighter pilots to form up with. He found his radio frequency congested with confused transmissions: *"I'm over here, where are you?"* *"If you can't find me, go in by yourself."* There was no rhyme to the babel, and no structure to the minuet. In the rush to get airborne, Commander Jones had had no time to give his pilots rendezvous instructions. It was going to be every pilot for himself.

*　　*　　*

ON THE *FANSHAW BAY*, Royce Hall rose early, ready for another day's dull routine. The aviation ordnanceman first class from Emanuel County, Georgia, was the turret gunner on the TBM flown by Lt. Harvey Lively. Their aircraft, last in line for takeoff, was perched on the aft end of the flight deck. Hall climbed into the torpedo bomber through the small radio compartment hatch in the belly, twisted his torso around, stepped up, and squeezed into the flat-sided sphere of the Avenger's ball turret. Hall sat down in the turret's metal bucket seat, fingered his trigger, and peered through his illuminated gun sight. When he saw the great towering splashes around the ship, he craned his neck and looked skyward through the Plexiglas, expecting to spot enemy bombers. But Hall could not see above the low ceiling of clouds. Then he noticed the yellow-orange flashes of light breaking through the curtain of squalls on the northwestern horizon. The light bloomed and faded but never seemed completely to disappear. At first he took it for something burning—maybe a ship in its death throes. But when large splashes began bracketing the *Fanshaw Bay,* walking the water around her in tight three- and four-shell patterns and dousing the flight deck with dye-stained seawater, Hall knew that what he was looking at were blasts from the muzzles of some very large ships.

"Hey, Guns, what's going on?" asked radioman Willie Haskins, seated below in the radio compartment, looking up at the soles of Hall's leather-booted feet. "Oh hell, some SOB is shooting at us from way over yonder somewhere," the Georgian replied. As the plane handlers muscled the Avenger forward toward the catapult, Lively, Hall, and Haskins, as the last crew to leave Sprague's flagship, never thought they would make it airborne. The *Fanshaw Bay* was bracketed by at least fifteen shells before their TBM ever got into launch position. Finally the plane handlers hooked the catapult cable to hooks underneath the wings and looped it around the hook buried in the flight deck's catapult track.

Without ceremony, the catapult fired. Hall reflexively tucked his chin between his knees to keep inertia from jamming his face back into his gun sight, and suddenly they were airborne—or nearly so. As the heavy plane clawed its way heavenward, Hall was treated to the turret gunner's backseat view of the flight deck rising up above him as the aircraft dropped toward the water, the towering bow of the ship cutting the sea in pursuit of the plane until the Avenger's fourteen cylinders finally caught air, gained the sky, and outraced its host vessel. Looking back at the thirteen ships of Taffy 3, Hall said a quiet good-bye. "My first thought," he later recalled, "was that I would never see any of the task force above the water again."

On the flight decks of the five other escort carriers of Taffy 3, a similar dance was taking place: pilots jogging to their aircraft, radial engines turning over, a queue to the catapult forming up, and planes flinging skyward. They left their ships carrying whatever ordnance they happened to have. The aviation ordnancemen, meanwhile, pushed their wheelbarrows to the edge of the deck and dumped overboard all bombs, rockets, and other armaments that were not already loaded onto an aircraft. From the *Fanshaw Bay*'s plane captain's shack, VC-68 aviation machinist's mate Dave Lewis awoke to the sound of commotion, looked up, and saw an ordnanceman named Bob Kenny running down the flight deck shoving a two-wheeled bomb cart loaded with a hundred-pound bomb that hadn't found a taker. Kenny was a big man, built like a football player, but Lewis had never seen him move so fast. "He was not inclined to exert himself. If he was running, I knew this was really serious." Lt. Verling Pierson, watching the bombs going overboard, was impressed with the crew's initiative if not entirely hopeful about its benefits. "A futile gesture, but it gave them something to do."

As the pilots readily appreciated, it was probably more dangerous to remain aboard the fuel- and explosive-laden jeep carrier than to take off and glide-bomb a Japanese capital ship. As Leonard Moser, a plane captain on the *Fanshaw Bay*, was changing a carburetor on a VC-68 aircraft, half a dozen pilots hovered nearby, coveting a chance to climb into that cockpit and get their tails off the ship. The aviation machinist's mate finished the job, then climbed up into the cockpit. "What are you doing?" one of the pilots asked.

"I'm going to check this damn engine out," Moser said, "and then go find a hole to hide in." The pilot said that he would do his own engine check this time, thank you very much. Moser stepped aside. "He got in, started it up, and took off with a cold motor. My helper didn't even have all of the cowling on. That pilot was glad to leave."

*   *   *

SEATED IN HIS TBM Avenger on the deck of the *Kalinin Bay,* his engine idling as he awaited launch, Lt. (jg) Earl Archer was soaked like a cat in a storm. The crash and splash of the near misses landing near the carrier had drenched him thoroughly. For the first time in his life, he really prayed: *Lord, please don't let me die sitting here on deck.* He was number three for takeoff, behind VC-3's skipper, Lt. Cdr. Bill "Pops" Keighley, and Lt. Patsy Capano. He was among the few TBM pilots with a full weapons load: four five-hundred-pound bombs, eight rockets, and two magazines full of .50-caliber ammo. Finally his turn on the catapult came, and his prayer was answered: he was airborne and outbound.

On the day Pearl Harbor burned, Earl Archer had driven his Buick from Hope, Arkansas, to Little Rock aiming to enlist in the Army Air Corps. When Archer, a junior at the University of Arkansas, arrived in Little Rock, he had a spiking fever. It might have been pneumonia. "When you get well, we'll sign you up," the recruiter said. Archer got home and talked to a friend who told him that naval aviation was where the action was. For a daredevil who came home from college on Friday nights so he could race cars at the fairground on the weekend, action was important. Archer went to New Orleans with his friend and signed on to be a Navy pilot.

In flight training at the naval air station at Lake Pontchartrain, Archer never missed a chance to go into town for a little nightlife. Tall and thin, eyes hooded by drooping lids that made him look sleepy all the time, he was improbably adept at getting girls. He told them his eyes looked that way because of an injury from shrapnel.

The line worked so well on the girls at New Orleans's Copa Cabana Review that Archer became a semiregular patron of the Roosevelt Hotel, convenient for high-style rendezvous. So notorious was he among his fellow cadets for his stays in that hotel's Blue Room that "Blue Room" became his nickname. Soon it was shortened to just "Blue."

Blue Archer was still in training when the Battle of Midway was fought. At the officers' club one day, an officer told him the Navy needed volunteers for torpedo bomber duty. Archer had heard about the catastrophe of Torpedo 8, the torpedo bomber squadron from the *Hornet,* butchered nearly to a man on June 4, 1942. But his concerns about danger—"Torpedo training? Are you crazy?"—were nothing that two martinis and the worldview of a race-car driver could not overcome.

From sinking a cargo ship with depth charges on an antisub patrol to retrieving an American flier from an airfield on Saipan still partially controlled by the enemy, there wasn't much Blue Archer hadn't done in his time as a VC-3 Avenger pilot. He was given to crazy stunts and inappropriate exuberance. When he snatched the flier from the airfield, he had landed under fire, stopped just long enough for the stranded aviator to clamber aboard the Avenger, then, gunning the engine, spun his plane around and started back down the runway, strafing the Japanese at the far end of the airstrip, swerving to spread his fire like a scythe as his plane gained the sky. Returning to the *Kalinin Bay,* Archer felt the urge to celebrate a little. He was already a well-known hot-rodder. Fully trained as a landing signal officer as well as a pilot, he felt that he knew how far to stretch the safety rules. So in he came, low over the waves—and lower still over his carrier's flight deck. He buzzed his ship, sending flight deck crew ducking from the roar of his big Wright radial engine. When the jeep carrier's air officer dialed his radio frequency and warned him not to try any such foolishness again, Archer circled back as if to land, flipped his plane over on its back, and buzzed the five-hundred-foot length of his carrier once more. His reward was restriction to the ship during shore leave—lubricated by an ample supply of beer provided by his delighted squadronmates. As far as torpedo pilots went, Blue Archer had seen and done it all—all, that is, except attack the main body of the Imperial Japanese Navy.

About fifteen minutes had passed since the Japanese had been sighted. The six jeep carriers of Taffy 3 had most of their available planes in the air. The pilots and their aircrew were on their own. They would see what they could do against Kurita's onrushing leviathans.

Nineteen

It took just minutes for the Japanese gunners to demonstrate the horrible potential of their broadsides. At 7:04 the *White Plains* was straddled on a diagonal. "This salvo measured the carrier as calipers," the action report noted, with a four-shell salvo from a battleship missing narrowly, two off the port quarter and two off the starboard bow. Even though the shells missed, their underwater blasts twisted and shook the CVE hard enough to throw men from their feet, send loose deck gratings hurtling across the engine room, and knock heavy equipment from its stowages. The ship lost steering, its radar failed, and when a circuit breaker was thrown open by the shock of the blast, its compartments went dark.

The damaging effects of shells that missed left to the imagination what might happen if others were actually to find their mark. Moments later they did. At 7:10 an eight-inch round from a heavy cruiser hit the *White Plains*. But because it was an armor-piercing round, fused to penetrate hardened armor plate and ignore lesser impediments such as mere metal sheet, it passed straight through without exploding, like a bullet holing a shoebox.

To the Japanese gunners, the thick funnel smoke flowing from the stacks of their targets presented the illusion of ships burning fiercely.

The *Yamato*'s great guns roared until about 7:05, when the carriers vanished momentarily into a wash of rainsqualls. Even when they had a clear line of sight, the Japanese still did not know what they faced. From the elegant proportions of their superstructures to their twin stacks to the graceful rise of their forecastles, *Fletcher*-class destroyers had silhouettes similar to those of *Baltimore*-class heavy cruisers. Japan recognition books did not include Henry Kaiser's hybrid freighter/flattops. At 7:16 lookouts on the *Kumano* spotted an aircraft carrier afire. Satisfied with the presumed kill, they changed targets two minutes later and threw their next salvos at the *St. Lo*. By this time Vice Adm. Kazutaka Shiraishi had realized something vital: his quarry were not *Essex*-class fleet carriers after all but light carriers. But the cruiser commander apparently never relayed that information up the line. About that essential fact, Kurita would remain thoroughly in the dark.

Ziggy Sprague had no idea what the Japanese knew or did not know about his force. Armed with his own good reconnaissance, he could assume only that the Japanese knew what they faced. "At this point," Sprague would later write, "it did not appear that any of our ships could survive another five minutes. The task unit was surrounded by the ultimate of desperate circumstances." He knew that the sluggish exertions of his carriers' Uniflow engines, the copious smoke, and the dauntless efforts of his carrier pilots would not be enough to save his carriers from annihilation.

At some point Sprague's screen, as a unit, would have to form up and engage. As soldiers must occupy ground in order to win a land battle, control of the sea is best asserted by ships, not planes. Admiral Kurita had demonstrated that eloquently the previous afternoon when most of his Center Force survived five heavy air strikes from the Third Fleet and continued through San Bernardino Strait. If ever there was a time for America to bring its naval airpower to bear, this was it. Meanwhile, Sprague might yet forestall the onslaught of the Japanese fleet by throwing his destroyers into the breach.

With salvos from the pursuing Japanese battleships and cruisers landing close around Taffy 3's carriers in all directions, Sprague got on the TBS circuit at 7:16 A.M. and ordered the screen commander, William Thomas, aboard the *Hoel*, *"Stand by to form two torpedo groups, big boys in one group and little fellas in another group."*

There was little anguish in the decision to send the small ships to almost certain destruction. Under the impossible circumstances, there was nothing else for them to do.

*   *   *

WHEN CLINT CARTER REACHED the *Johnston*'s fantail and climbed into position in the left rear corner of Gun 55, assuming his general quarters post as its captain, he dryly informed the other men crowded into the steel enclosure, "Admiral Halsey is shooting at us." Once the telltale pagodas rose into view on the horizon, they all knew otherwise. But until reality settled in, Carter's gun crew shared the disbelief of everyone else in Taffy 3: *This can't be the Japs. We've got Halsey watching our back.* Linked to Bob Hagen in the gun director via headset and sound-powered phones, Carter reported that Gun 55 was manned and ready. As the *Johnston* ran solo through a forest of shell splashes, swerving through rainsqualls and the backdrafts of her own smoke, all the gun crews could do was wait as the range closed, then feed the gun as rapidly as possible and hang on for the ride as Lieutenant Hagen slewed them from target to target.

Up in the gun director over the pilothouse, Bob Hagen felt powerless. "All this time I had been completely, sickeningly impotent. I had checked my gun stations, seen that everything was in order, but after that there was nothing I could do but wait." Evans had ordered him to fire on any enemy target that came into range. At a range of 25,000 yards, the ship still had not been hit. Was someone looking out for them?

At 7:10 the distance from the *Johnston* to the nearest Japanese heavy cruiser closed to the five-inch/38-caliber's maximum range of eighteen thousand yards, or about ten statute miles. Evans directed Hagen to target the leading heavy cruiser in the column to starboard. Hagen's fire-controlmen, George Himelright and James Buzbee, fixed the ship in the director's sights and fire-controlman Tony Gringheri entered ranges using his stereoscopic rangefinder on the mainmast. The data passed down into the ship's Mark 1A fire-control computer. Developed by the Ford Instrument Company in the 1930s, the intricate but sturdy array of gears, cams, shafts, and dials was an analog device with no memory as we understand it today. Rather, it was designed only to predict the position of its target and align each of the

five turrets to place its shell at the coordinates that the computer calculated the target would occupy at impact. Just as a football quarterback pedaling back in the pocket must place extra zip on his throw to
compensate for his own rearward movement, the computer removed
the imparted effect of the ship's own motion from the firing solution.
A gyroscopic stable element corrected for the pitching and rolling of
the ship. Other critical inputs included the initial muzzle velocity of
the ship's five-inch shells—adjusted for bore wear and current
weather conditions; the ship's current latitude and the relation of its
heading to true magnetic north, in order to compensate for the effect
of the earth's rotation and the "english" that it imparted to the shell's
trajectory; and the range to the target, which amplified the effects of
all the variables.

It took the computer about thirty seconds to calculate a firing solution for a new target. Running adjustments on an existing target
took only a few seconds. The computer transmitted electrical signals
to the turret motors to aim the guns accordingly. Then Bob Hagen
closed the firing key. With a flash of flame and smoke, the *Johnston*'s
main battery came barking and cracking to life. Improbably, the Battle off Samar was joined by American guns.

Through his sighting telescope, Hagen could see his target return
fire. It was the *Kumano,* the sleek 13,440-ton flagship of Admiral
Shiraishi's Cruiser Division 7. An eight-inch shell from a Japanese
cruiser struck the water off the *Johnston*'s bow and sent up a wave of
red-dyed water that washed down the entire forward superstructure.
Bob Hagen wiped his eyes clear of the redness and said to the five
men in the gun director with him, "Looks like somebody's mad at
us." But the Japanese did not prove to be the shots that Hagen's
radar-directed gun system was. Hagen's crews had lighter weaponry
but far better aim. The humans were novices to surface combat, but
the computer, like the radar and gyro that aided it, knew no fear.

The *Johnston* loosed a continuous ladder of shells over a two-
hundred-yard stretch of ocean centered on the projected path of the
heavy cruiser *Kumano.* During the five-minute sprint into torpedo
range, the destroyer's guns let fly with hundreds of fifty-four-pound
five-inch rounds. When Hagen began to see his shells hitting the
ship—flames and puffs of smoke obscuring the division flagship's upper superstructure—he tightened the ladder to a hundred yards, concentrating the barrage. He landed some forty hits on the *Kumano*

with his five-inch shells. Through his scope Hagen could see the smoky flashes tearing up the metalwork on the cruiser's decks and gun galleries. They blew out portholes and killed men in exposed positions. Although this pummeling was not enough to sink the Japanese cruiser, the waves of shock, sheets of flame, and storms of shrapnel that buffeted the *Kumano*'s superstructure played havoc with its crew's ability to return accurate fire. The Japanese gunners did not land a single hit in return on their bantamweight assailant.

With each gun mount firing seventeen to twenty rounds per minute, two mounts forward and three more aft, it didn't take long for the hot empty shell canisters, discarded through a hole in the floor of each mount, to pile up and roll and clatter across the *Johnston*'s steel decks. Jesse Cochran, leading a repair party, was grateful that he had nothing better to do at the moment than toss them over the side.

The noise of the general quarters alarm had stopped some time ago, and on the bridge no one had a whole lot to say. Only the ship really spoke: the grinding vibration of the twin propeller shafts, the rumble of the gun director rotating on its mount atop the bridge, and the shock of the five-inch guns that bucked the deck and rattled crewmen's helmets with their reports. As for the men, their emotions stayed under the skin. They were trained to deal only in facts, orders, data. The officers masked their desperation with the cool demeanor that disciplined leadership instills. The facts, the data, spoke for themselves, one more loudly perhaps than all the others combined, though it was not explicitly discussed: not one of them would get decent betting odds of surviving the gauntlet their skipper had steered them into.

The destroyer's zigzagging inbound course was not entirely random. Evans deliberately turned toward and steamed through the roiling cauldrons of the enemy's misses. Known as "chasing shell splashes," the tactic relied on the diligence of the Japanese gunners to correct their aim. Because they continuously adjusted their range and train, naval salvos were like proverbial lightning, seldom striking twice in the same place. If the Japanese had caught on to the game, they might have fired successive salvos to the same range and bearing. But they did not. They had their training too. And so the *Johnston* pressed audaciously in, closing the range.

Clint Carter's crew loaded and shot at such a brisk pace that the paint on Gun 55's barrel blistered and burned. After each shot a blast of pressured air cleared the barrel of hot gases. Even so it was dangerous to let a live round sit too long in the breech. If you cooked it too long, it would cook you right back. Carter got a scare when a sudden course change forced his loaded gun mount to pivot and strike the cam stops that kept it from discharging. It was a precaution to keep the gun, when swiveled all the way forward, from hitting its own superstructure. But for agonizing seconds the safety device imperiled its operators. The round sat cooking in the breech, waiting for the computer to release it. "I was never as scared as I was in those few seconds," Carter said.

Expecting a disastrous internal explosion at any moment, Carter raised Hagen and asked permission to fire the gun manually to prevent a detonation in the breech. But before the lieutenant could answer, the ship turned sharply again. When the director-controlled gun swung out automatically abeam to stay on target, it came off its stops and fired, ridding the breech of its time bomb.

The men assigned to train and point the gun had nothing to do as long as their weapon was on automatic director control. In Gun 54, forward of Carter's mount and above it, atop the aft deckhouse, Bobby Chastain, the trainer, was responsible for swiveling the gun mount toward its targets in the event the automatic system failed. If the mechanisms that aimed their gun were knocked out but the mount still received train and elevation data from the director or from the CIC, crews could go to "modified director control," aiming their gun manually by matching the dial pointer indicating the director's orientation.

With Bob Hagen controlling his mount, Chastain's telescope was useful only for sightseeing. Peering through the gun sight protruding through a small door positioned at eye level in front of his seat, he found that he couldn't bear the sight of the larger ships. So long as Lt. Hagen didn't need him to turn the gun, Chastain figured he'd spare himself some panic. He closed the gun sight door and pretended hard that he was safe.

Bob Hagen got information about targets from the executive officer and his radar-watchers in the CIC, or directly from the captain himself. Captain Evans was within shouting distance below, on the open-air bridge outside the pilothouse. Whenever Hagen felt the ship

182 \ THE LAST STAND OF THE TIN CAN SAILORS

taking a new course, he could yell down to Evans, "What are you up to now?" Evans would look up at him and say, "Hey, take that ship over there." After a target was chosen, Hagen slewed his director toward it, and as soon as his pointer and trainer hollered "On target!" Hagen closed his firing key, and the *Johnston*'s main battery resumed the bombardment.

Twenty

Clyde Burnett had been around the fleet long enough to know a hopeless situation when he saw one. The hourglass that measured the reasonable life expectancy of a lone destroyer charging a hostile squadron of battleships and cruisers had run out and emptied long ago. As the distance between the *Johnston* and her target closed, the chief boatswain's mate took in the sight of shell splashes from enemy battleships all around his destroyer and told the members of his repair party to lie down on deck. He felt sure they were about to take a hit.

When Bob Hagen first opened fire, the range was eighteen thousand yards. As the range closed—fifteen thousand, then twelve—with Japanese shells straddling the destroyer, Captain Evans ordered, "Stand by for torpedo attack."

The twelve-man surface search team in the fishtailing destroyer's CIC, under executive officer Lt. Elton Stirling, relayed the range, bearing, course, and speed of targets to the bridge and the torpedo crew, while the other twelve-man section, the air search team, watched and waited. Closing to ten thousand yards under a crossfire this heavy was as unlikely as a man staying dry while sprinting through a driving rain. Miraculously, the ship made it. Impossibly, she was not hit. The target cruiser was steaming forty degrees off the

Johnston's starboard bow. At ten thousand yards the *Johnston* was within the outer limit of torpedo range.

To maximize their reach, Lt. Jack Bechdel, the torpedo officer, ordered the fish set on their slowest speed setting, just twenty-seven knots. As torpedoman first class Jim O'Gorek supervised the mount crews and stood by with a wooden mallet that could be used to fire the torpedoes if their igniters failed, two torpedomen, Thomas Sullivan and John Moran, cranked mount number one to starboard and trained it to 110 degrees relative to the ship's heading, just abaft of the beam. Mount two, manned by Red Benjamin and Frank Gillis, was rotated out to 125 degrees relative. As soon as the range was good, Captain Evans shouted, "Fire torpedoes!"

With sharp rushes of compressed air, the *Johnston*'s ten torpedoes leaped from their tubes, one following the preceding at three-second intervals. They flew out over Burnett's crew huddled on deck, their motors whirring wildly as they fell toward the waves. Hitting the water, their propellers found the resistance they craved and clawed into the sea. Carrying warheads tipped with three hundred pounds of torpex explosive, the Mark 15 torpedoes were about twenty-five feet long, nearly two feet in diameter. Adjusting to their set depth of six feet, the torpedoes turned to the right per the gyro settings that Lieutenant Bechdel had given them and accelerated to twenty-seven knots, running "hot, straight, and normal" toward the leader of the four-cruiser column.

With the torpedoes away, his ship blessedly untouched, Evans ordered Lieutenant DiGardi, his officer of the deck at the helm, to bring the *Johnston* into a hard turn to port. The beauty of the maneuver was that the ship now entered her own spreading smoke screen, blotted from the view of enemy gunners. As Bechdel counted down to the torpedoes' calculated time of impact, the twin screws of the *Johnston* dug into the sea—driven by the combined sixty thousand shaft horsepower of her steam turbine engines—and drove her at top speed back toward the carriers of Taffy 3 that so desperately needed assistance.

At flank speed a *Fletcher*-class destroyer could outpace a Japanese heavy cruiser by a couple of knots. Speeding to rejoin Taffy 3 as her ten torpedoes ran the other way, the destroyer made the best possible use of that small margin, opening the range with the enemy while obscuring the interval with smoke. The flashes from the Japanese guns, and the concussion of their blast, eased only slightly as the distance opened. Whenever the squalls between the combatants thickened, the fire fell off measurably. But there was not enough rain to spare the *Johnston* entirely. It was daylight. The rising sun favored the fleet that flew its pennant from their fantails.

Destroyermen have this in common with submariners: they experience no greater suspense than while counting the seconds to their torpedoes' time of impact. Jack Bechdel's calculations were seldom wrong. Captain Evans and everyone else in the pilothouse listened to the countdown. They had shot their one spread; the ship carried ten torpedoes and no more. Bob Hagen's good work in the gun director notwithstanding, this was their best and only chance to sink an enemy ship.

At 7:24 lookouts on the *Kumano* reported three torpedo tracks close off the starboard bow. Knifing through the water at more than thirty knots, the ship was traveling too fast to evade. The *Kumano* could not make the turn.

Between squalls and smoke Ellsworth Welch saw a bright flash and the long, dark form of a ship lift out of the water slightly, as if punched from below by an enormous fist. Torpedo explosions sounded different than gun blasts. Five-inch guns stung the eardrums with their sharp, concussive bark, throwing out shock waves that patted the clothes. Torpedo explosions were deeper and heavier—basso reverberations that could be felt in the sternum as readily as heard with the ears. The men of the *Johnston* felt a deep *thrummp*—some felt a second one, and then a third. The *Johnston* whipped through thickets of smoke, emerging long enough for Lieutenant Welch and others on deck to see a tall column of water rising beside the Japanese heavy cruiser, which appeared to be burning furiously astern. One torpedo from the *Johnston* struck the *Kumano* in the bow, ripping it clear away. The crippled cruiser fell out of line, limping along at fourteen knots.

The *Kumano* could still stand and jab, but with a broken bow she could not hold her place in column in a rapid running fight. Admiral Shiraishi ordered the *Suzuya* to come alongside, and he transferred his flag to her. The *Suzuya* was not fit to resume pursuit either. Near misses from aircraft bombs had ruptured her after fuel tanks, contaminating some eight hundred tons of precious fuel with seawater, starting fires that would burn into the afternoon, and restricting the cruiser's speed to just twenty-four knots, no faster than the lumbering battleship *Nagato*. With his transfer to the crippled ship, Shiraishi took himself out of the battle. He may have had no other choice. He did not wish to hold back the two ships of Cruiser Division 7 that could still make chase. The *Tone* and the *Chikuma* sped past, joining Cruiser Division 5's *Haguro* and *Chokai* in pursuit of Sprague's carriers.

Twenty-one

The first thing Harvey Lively and Royce Hall of VC-68 saw upon breaking the surface of the cloud layer was a large formation of Avengers closing their position. As the planes drew near, Hall made out the distinctive tail markings of aircraft from another jeep, the *Gambier Bay*. Hall had flown with that ship's squadron, VC-10, before. He knew its skipper, Lt. Cdr. Edward J. Huxtable, Jr.—or knew his reputation anyway. He toggled the intercom and told Lieutenant Lively that Huxtable could be counted upon to find whatever they were going after. The lone Avenger from the *Fanshaw Bay* tagged along with its sister squadron.

Huxtable would find the targets, but there remained the question of what he would hit them with when he got there. Before taking off, VC-10's skipper had climbed into his Avenger only to find that his weapons bay was empty. He asked his plane captain to ask Buzz Borries, the air officer, for a bomb load. Huxtable watched as Borries brought the question to Capt. Walter Vieweg, standing on the *Gambier Bay*'s island superstructure. The skipper made a broad sweeping gesture with his arm as if to say, "Get these planes off my carrier." Word came back to Huxtable that he would lead his flight without a load. The absence of a heavy torpedo or bomb load meant his plane would be able to stay airborne longer. Huxtable launched immediately, turned right, climbed to two thousand feet, and joined the other Avengers from his squadron.

It took just ten to twelve minutes to find the enemy ships bearing down on their carriers. Beneath the cloud ceiling at a thousand feet, it was hard to miss them. There were clear skies to the south, but the skies over the seas where the enemy fleet lay were roofed by gray clouds. Somewhere beneath that shroud of gray were the destroyers of Taffy 3's screen. Edward Huxtable was stunned to learn that at least one American destroyer had turned to face the monstrous opponent.

Breaking through the clouds, the VC-10 skipper spotted the tin can running alone, returning to formation on a southeasterly course. He could see puffs of smoke coming from her batteries, and heavy splashes rising all around her as the Japanese fired in return. It was the *Johnston*. Transfixed by the sight, Huxtable then spied, farther to the west, the lethal slender forms of Japanese heavy cruisers giving chase. Beyond the cruisers, heading due east, he could just make out the thicker silhouettes of imperial battleships.

Huxtable decided that the heavy cruisers, faster than the battleships and better suited for pursuit, posed the most immediate threat to Taffy 3. Climbing through a cloud break to 2,500 feet, the VC-10 commander could see the cruisers firing rapidly at targets to their south. The battleships seemed not to be firing at all. Huxtable turned his formation from north to east, spreading his planes out in a wide front, and climbed to three thousand feet, above which the sky was solid overcast. Out to the east, flak dotted the skies. Apparently other planes were about. They would need all the help they could get.

The commander would have preferred more altitude. A properly planned air strike would have allowed time for pilots to locate holes in the squalls and plot their attack routes amid cloud-blinds and rain. Altitude gave a pilot options and flexibility. Over the radio came an order from the *Fanshaw Bay*'s air officer: "*Attack immediately.*" No reminder of the urgency was needed. Joined by Wildcats from VC-10, which heeled over into steep dives, strafing the enemy ships ahead of the torpedo bombers, Huxtable directed his Avengers to line up and move in behind them.

Lt. Burt Bassett watched Commander Huxtable dive left, heading for the second ship in column. Without ordnance Huxtable would make a decoy run. Its deterrent effect on the target ship would be no less pronounced; to a Japanese skipper, there was no telling what Huxtable's turkey carried in its weapons bay.

Bassett lined up on the lead cruiser. As he nosed over from 2,800 feet and emerged from the clouds, he felt the full intensity of the flak. Tracers etched burning paths in every direction. Every so often a larger shell burst nearby, releasing an invisible spray of shrapnel through a small sphere in the sky. Bassett bore in steeply and released his first bomb from 2,000 feet. Almost immediately his aircraft shuddered from a hit to his starboard horizontal stabilizer. He released the second bomb right away, while he still could, pulling out at 1,500 feet. At about 200 knots, it took about twenty endless seconds for Bassett to reach the safety of a cloud bank ahead of the cruiser.

Since he had no bombs, Ens. Robert Crocker, third in the formation, was ordered to stay out of Huxtable's first run. The fourth pilot in line, Ens. William Shroyer, went next. Angling his Avenger downward toward a battleship, Shroyer released short bursts from his two wing-mounted machine guns to sight his rockets. He fired them, and they shot ahead on coils of white smoke. Then Shroyer pulled the lever to open his bomb bay doors.

But something didn't work. The doors stayed shut, trapping two five-hundred-pound bombs in his plane's belly. Shroyer skimmed the water so low that his radioman, Louis Vilmer, Jr., looking out his small plate window in the TBM's fuselage, had to look up to see the sailors on the Japanese ship's deck. Shroyer climbed and circled for another pass, then followed a dozen Wildcats diving down to strafe. On the way in Shroyer instructed Vilmer to use the hand crank in the radio compartment to get the doors open. By the time Shroyer emerged from the clouds over a column of six large ships, Vilmer had succeeded.

Running up on a *Tone*-class cruiser from astern, Shroyer dropped his payload, and Vilmer watched the two bombs hit the water just a few feet behind the fantail, disrupting the ribbon of the cruiser's wake with their detonation. The two pilots coming in behind Shroyer, Lt. Paul Garrison from the *Kitkun Bay* and Ens. J. F. Lischer from the *Gambier Bay,* reported that the cruiser had slowed and seemed to lose steering.

When Harvey Lively nosed over to attack, he didn't say anything over the intercom. There was no "tallyho" or anything else kids heard in the movies. His first sortie against ships began without fanfare. Royce Hall just felt the plane push over into a shallow dive as flak bursts began appearing around them. When the nose of the plane pushed over, the tail swung up, the ocean dropped out of view, and Hall was left with a 180-degree view of the sky and squalls. As they approached the Japanese cruiser column from the rear, tracer bullets whizzed past him like angry fireflies to port and starboard. Lively pressed home the attack, engine at full power, the pin on the airspeed indicator trembling at 280 knots.

Lively closed on a cruiser from behind and released his four five-hundred-pound bombs. The pilot didn't have the luxury of seeing the results for himself. He leveled off fifty feet above the wave tops, having traded altitude for airspeed and aiming to preserve every bit of it for his escape. From the tiny window in his radio compartment, Willie Haskins saw the bombs hit. One landed under the fantail of the cruiser and exploded. It might have been close enough, Haskins hoped, to damage the propellers. Lively sped low along the water, parallel to a line of ships. Royce Hall had been watching the skies for enemy planes to shoot at. Nothing came. But here now were ships. He recognized the opportunity for some improvisation.

Practice, practice, practice. The answer to the question "How do you get to Carnegie Hall?" was drilled into Navy gunners from day one. In fact, the training pamphlets supplied to air gunners by the Navy's Bureau of Aeronautics played on a musical metaphor:

> *The concert violinist sets considerable store by his instrument . . . So it had better be with you and your guns. Learn to handle them naturally and firmly, with all the precision and skill of a great musician . . . At first, all good gunners looked upon their weapons as cumbersome things that crash and vibrate, feel awkward and unwieldy. They also had the inward feelings that the guns, and not they themselves, were in charge. But as they learned to give their guns close personal attention and firm handling, their guns gradually turned into useful friends and allies.*

Royce Hall had never given thought to the parallels between gunnery triangulation and the musical arts. He had devoted what few idle hours he enjoyed aboard the *Fanshaw Bay* to fleecing his squadronmates at the poker table. He had never imagined that he would have the occasion to pepper a heavy cruiser with his very own machine gun. The strikes he had flown over Leyte's jungles and cane fields involved firing rockets and dropping bombs on Japanese troop concentrations. Shooting at a by-God heavy cruiser—this was something else.

There were few things more terrifying to a sailor than strafing. Heavy machine-gun bullets could make a mess out of the exposed positions on a ship, ripping through gun shields, breaking glass, and splintering wood. They destroyed electrical connections, shattered steam pipes, and tore flesh. In that light, Hall and every other gunner in Taffy 3's six composite squadrons had a mission akin to that of the destroyer screen as a whole: to distract and delay the enemy's pursuit of the carriers. Any weapon that could be brought to bear might contribute to their escape. Only a couple hundred feet of water lay between Hall and the cream of the Imperial Japanese Navy. He cranked his turret out to port and went hunting.

Hall could see Japanese gunners depressing their guns and blazing away wildly at his plane. Shooting at an unpracticed close range and at an angle nearly perpendicular to the target's path of flight, the enemy would have needed considerable skill to knock the Avenger from the sky. It was a difficult matter of timing—like bird hunting, but with the weapons and prey inflated to giant size. As with shooting quail, the challenge was to place your lead not where the target was now, but where it would be in a second or two. Firing from the side at a fast-moving target required that the shooter lead it so that the target flew into the path of his bullets. In the panic of battle, undisciplined gunners attempting a deflection shot tended to shoot behind their targets. That was the case now with the Japanese. Lively's plane was untouched.

The same principles operated as Hall returned fire, except that his target was slow and his plane was fast. The net effect of the geometry was as if the cruiser were speeding past him, away to the rear. And the ship was so large in comparison to Hall's usual prey as to induce a sort of vertigo. Nonetheless, a target that big was hard to miss. From Pensacola Naval Air Station, where he had been a gunnery-range instructor, to the fields around Yemassee, South Carolina, where he had hunted quail and doves with his older brother, Hall was well practiced in the difficult craft of deflection shooting. Hall led the ship aft, pressing short bursts into its gray-black bulk, raking gun emplacements and gunwales. He could see the tracers spark and ricochet off the superstructure and rip through the metal shields protecting the Japanese machine-gun crews.

As Lieutenant Lively roared past the forward part of the ship, Hall raised his gun and sprayed the glass of the bridge structure. In return, originating from places tucked away throughout the steely rabbit warren of the cruiser's superstructure, tracers flew past the Avenger's wings. It was over before it had really started. The 280-knot plane overtook and passed the thirty-five-knot cruiser in just a few seconds. Lively zoomed past the last man-of-war in the column, then passed the next three cruisers ahead of her, allowing Hall a two- or three-second window in which to fire at each one. Hall emptied a two-hundred-round drum of .50-caliber ammunition, then yelled down at Haskins to send up another. Lively took his plane around for another pass while Hall changed ammo drums for the next run through the shooting gallery. Hall was beyond being scared. The poker shark of VC-68 had never felt calmer in all his life.

*   *   *

FROM TEN THOUSAND FEET, Larry Budnick picked his way through the cloud heads, looking for targets. The clouds were a nuisance to reconnaissance but ideal for stealth. Spotting a large ship below, the fighter pilot winged over into as steep a dive as possible. The roar of the FM-2 Wildcat's engine and the rushing sensation of acceleration was relief from the circling and the thinking and the worrying.

Since there was no telling how many runs he would be called upon to make, Budnick tried to conserve his ammunition. On each run he set two of his four machine guns on safe. Gone from his mind now was anything not immediately related to putting his tracers into the armored leviathan wheeling beneath him. At three thousand feet or so, he opened fire. To avoid burning out the delicate rifling of his gun barrels—the inevitable symptom of which was an erratic corkscrewing path of bullets flying everywhere except where his crosshairs were fixed—Budnick kept the bursts short, two or three seconds at a pull. Their curving bright trails disappeared into the ship's encompassing mass. The rattling he gave the ship's decks was three times as deadly as it appeared, for only one round in three had a tracer load. But really there was no telling what the effect was. It was over too quickly for fastidious observation. Budnick knew one thing. This Catholic, converted to the faith on his wedding day, considered it a miracle worthy of Mary that he was never hit. As the flak rose at him in sheets, he was glad he had made time for Lt. Chris Maino's thirty-minute services, held on the *St. Lo*'s hangar deck on most Sundays. Maino would become a priest after the war. But right now, in October 1944, he likely had in his lay ministry of aviators and airedales a flock as devout as any man of the cloth could hope to have.

Ens. Berman Dillard, a VC-10 Wildcat pilot from the *Gambier Bay*, found a hole in the clouds at 9,500 feet and began a dive on the lead cruiser. The next thing he knew he was recovering from that dive 800 feet above the sea. A large antiaircraft shell had struck his plummeting Wildcat, blowing out his glass canopy. The rushing wind carried off Dillard's helmet and goggles, and his Wildcat fell out of control through nearly two miles of sky before the ensign at last regained his senses and pulled out just a few hundred feet above the water. Suffering from a concussion and barely able to control his aircraft, Dillard headed for the Tacloban airfield on Leyte, escorted by a plane from the *Fanshaw Bay*.

*   *   *

WITHOUT A TORPEDO, ALL that VC-10 commander Edward Huxtable could do was bluff. Having done it once, now he did it again, turning back to the west above a thin cloud layer at two thousand feet. Though the skipper no longer saw any Wildcats around, he decided this wasn't the time to insist on by-the-book tactics. About two and a half miles out, the cruisers opened up a terrific barrage of antiaircraft fire. Huxtable bore in on the trailing ship's starboard bow, hoping to draw its fire from the other planes of his flight. Ensign Crocker, armed with two light rockets, followed him in. On the intercom Huxtable told the others to concentrate on the lead cruisers. Finishing his run, he pulled out to the left and patrolled ahead of the cruiser line, tracking their movements. The ships turned to the northeast, and Huxtable relayed that information to Admiral Sprague. So much smoke and rain covered the waters between the antagonists that Huxtable thought for a moment that the Japanese had lost sight of their quarry.

Commander Huxtable had lost track of his fighter escorts after the first run, but VC-10's Wildcat jocks found useful employment long after the Avengers dropped their ordnance. Starting at eight thousand feet, Ens. Joseph McGraw began a series of steep strafing runs at a battleship. He made eleven in all, then three more on a *Tone*-class heavy cruiser. Ensign Lischer and seven others from the *Gambier Bay* spotted a pair of destroyers and winged over to strafe. Lt. Richard Roby made a pair of runs on the tin cans before getting separated from the other fighters amid the squalls. Lischer and Roby made their separate ways to joining a northbound flight of Avengers and Wildcats led by the *Kitkun Bay*'s Lt. Cdr. Richard L. Fowler. Roby knew the Japanese were to the east, but Fowler evidently didn't have radio contact. Roby pulled alongside Fowler's Avenger and gestured as if to say, *They're over there.* Fowler swung off to the east and found Japanese cruisers almost immediately.

After making his runs on the destroyers, Dick Roby found that two of his four .50-caliber guns were either jammed or empty. He made several runs at the cruisers until his ammunition ran out. Thereafter he continued diving on the ships without ammunition. Roby didn't try to stay with Fowler. The *Gambier Bay* lieutenant lost him after the first pass as the planes continued their mad whirling dance over the Japanese fleet.

While making dry runs, Roby's practice was to look for an Avenger with its torpedo bay doors open. Roby would line up ahead of the TBM, hoping its pilot really had a torpedo. As often as not, the Avenger pilot was bluffing as doggedly as Roby was. Even if both planes ran in and pulled out without shooting or dropping anything, they might draw fire from other planes and force their targets into sharp turns to avoid the apparent threat. As far as Ziggy Sprague was concerned, slowing the enemy's pursuit was nearly as good as planting an actual torpedo into his ships. Owing to the frequency with which they turned to avoid air attacks both phantom and real, the cruisers' angle of chase was ajar to Taffy 3's line of retreat. The distance was not closing as fast as Kurita would have liked.

From the bridge of the *Yamato*, Admiral Ugaki was impressed by the courage of the U.S. pilots, who had been pestering and bluffing the Japanese task group since they first found them roughly twenty minutes after the fleets spotted each other. Ugaki counted airplanes taking off from the American carriers in the distance—he figured at least thirty planes attacked his battleship while he was closing with his enemy. "The rate of hits was quite good and most of the damages our cruisers sustained were due to them," he would later write.

Admiral Kurita was doubtless frustrated by the imperative his ships faced to separate and scatter when confronted with such a persistent air attack. Their flak was perhaps more effective as a spectacle than as a defense. Each time Dick Roby emerged from the clouds, he was treated to a variety show of antiaircraft ordnance. "They were shooting the craziest combinations at us you've ever seen." Star shells burst into white clouds and spat phosphorus chunks in every direction. When they peppered the wings and fuselage, the sizzling pieces made sharp snapping sounds, like the little firecrackers wrapped in white paper that kids throw on pavement. Main battery rounds were considerably more kinetic, exploding in a rainbow of colors and a blizzard of metal. Some of them left hanging in the sky snarled coils of steel mesh that radiated whipping wires at the U.S. planes. As impressed as he was by the innovation, Roby saw no planes fall to the strange killing contraption.

Like so many other Wildcat pilots, Roby lost track of how many dry runs he made before his gas tanks grew light. Without ammunition, he could still make himself useful. But without fuel, his morning was over. Roby too headed for Tacloban.

Twenty-two

The *Hoel* held her screening station on the northern edge of Taffy 3's ring, zigzagging an eastward course, making smoke to cover the flight of the carriers. The smoke she generated, and that of the destroyer escort *Raymond* ahead, off her starboard bow, was carried to the west and south by the eight- to thirteen-knot wind. Though the smoke shielded the jeep carriers like a protective shroud, no one was making smoke to cover the *Hoel*. The wind whipped it behind her, keeping her exposed to enemy sight. The ships to her south churned out their own semicumulus wall of blackness and gray. It provided a high-contrast backdrop that framed the *Hoel*'s sleek lines for Japanese gunners.

Seaman first class Sam Lucas had a clear view of Japanese ships off the stern. He could see the flashes of their big guns and the smoke billow out. Light came first, followed by horrific sound. "It seemed to take a long time before I heard the crack of the guns and the projectiles as they passed overhead. They sounded like boxcars going through the air, end over end." A salvo raised a wall of water dead ahead. There was another roar of freight trains, and three more shells struck close by to port, just thirty feet abeam the forward gun turret. Another salvo bracketed them to starboard, missing by just sixty feet.

Lieutenant Dix expected the next salvo to split the difference between the last two misses to either side and cut the air directly into the bridge. He tensed himself for it.

You stand there waiting—clutch the rail—and watch.
The bow swings back to starboard as we turn.
You're hanging on to wait—and scared to death.
And then you hear the whistling sound again.
You freeze, you flinch, you wait to hear them hit.
The seconds pass and nothing comes, no jolt.
Your hand's there on the rail—you're still alive,
But still just standing there. So then you turn
And look back aft and see the splashes leap
Well back beyond the stern—they've missed again.
The ship's still safe, but you're not quite the same.
You're moving through the motions of your job,
Yet all the time you're thinking of the odds.

The *Hoel* came through unhit, entered a squall, and enjoyed a moment's respite as rain pelted the decks. But the speeding ship passed through it in a few short minutes, entered the sunlight once again, and endured a new round of gunfire.

Standing on the bridge wing, Captain Kintberger conned his ship through the boiling whirlpools of the enemy's misses. Chasing salvos, he steered the *Hoel* through the cauldron, testing his luck, keeping his ship from falling under the arc of the shellfire. His voice was steady and sure. Dix was impressed with his skipper.

"Right full rudder. Meet her. Steady up.
"Now left full rudder. Give it all you've got."
He never once lets up. He's calm and firm.
Damn but that guy's magnificent today.

The *Hoel*'s luck held, but it was not at all clear how much longer Taffy 3's would. With every passing second the Japanese cruiser line closed with the carriers, their eight-inch salvos straddling and shaking the fragile hulls of the CVEs.

Like their fellows in the screen, Captain Kintberger and his men felt like a short-armed boxer enduring blows that couldn't be returned. Admiral Sprague's 7:16 order to make a torpedo run on the behemoths confronting them had had a bracing effect. They knew their best chance to survive required them to attack, not flee, to press within range of the enemy and take their shot. The last towering miss landed nearly close enough to pierce their tin can's hull. No one saw any point in standing there.

At 7:18, as Ernest Evans, miles to the north, was preparing to launch the *Johnston*'s torpedoes, Leon Kintberger ordered a hard turn to port. Quartermaster Clarence Hood swung the wheel and didn't bring it back until his ship was headed straight west, toward the advancing Japanese force.

* * *

TORPEDOES WERE A DESTROYER'S most powerful offensive weapon. The night before, at Surigao Strait, Jesse Oldendorf's tin cans had demonstrated their giant-slaying qualities with expert aplomb. In Taffy 3's desperate straits a torpedo attack had a purpose collateral to but no less important than actually hitting and sinking ships: forcing a superior fleet to break off its lethal pursuit. A destroyer skipper didn't need to actually hit anything, so long as he brandished the threat of doing so.

An attacking column of ships had to stay together to maximize its fighting effectiveness. Ordering Taffy 3's destroyers to attack separately from the slower destroyer escorts was the right way to do it. By staying together at flank speed and coordinating their torpedo spreads, they could make it hard for the enemy to escape their overlapping fields of fire. Speed was a destroyer's best protection. It would have been foolish to rein in the swift *Heermann* and the *Hoel* for the sake of keeping them in column with the slower DEs. So thought Captain Copeland on the *Samuel B. Roberts,* in any event. But when Commander Thomas relayed Sprague's torpedo-attack order to the screen, all Copeland heard was, *"Little fellows, make a torpedo attack."*

"He didn't designate a target or anything of that kind," Copeland would write, "and so we didn't know just exactly what was what. What did he mean by 'little fellows'?" Not fully grasping his commander's lingo, Copeland was concerned that Thomas wanted the destroyer escorts to accompany the faster destroyers. "It

just didn't seem right to me. So I got on the air and called Commander Thomas. I coined a little phraseology of my own to distinguish
DEs from the DDs, or destroyers. I said, *"Taffy 33* [denoting Commander Thomas], *this is Juggernaut. Do you want the little little fellows to go with the big little fellows?"*

Thomas replied, *"Juggernaut, this is Taffy 33. Your last transmission negative—negative. The big fellows form up for the first attack,
and the little fellows make the second attack."*

Well, that's a problem too, Copeland thought. If the screen idled
about much longer, they might well have no carriers left to protect. If
the *Roberts* was going to launch its torpedoes, there was but a small
passing window of opportunity. Certainly there was no time to form
into a column with the other three DEs ringing the wide circle of fleeing escort carriers.

Beyond questions of geometry, time, and distance was the matter
of command protocol. Because the captain of the *Dennis*, Lt. Cdr. Sig
Hansen, was the senior skipper among the destroyer escorts, and
Copeland the junior, by all rights the *Dennis* should have led the DEs
to the attack. Yet the *Roberts*, stationed astern the *Hoel* on the northwest edge of the carrier formation, was best positioned to peel off
and attack the Japanese cruiser line. In the absence of orders specify-
ing how, with whom, and when the destroyer escorts might form up,
and what targets they would engage, what was the skipper of the
Samuel B. Roberts to do?

As Copeland pondered this question, a sleek dark form slid into
view out of the smoke and squalls, swinging across the *Roberts*'s
bow. There was no mistaking a *Fletcher*'s clean lines. It was the *Heermann*, racing to form up with the *Hoel*. At the battle's outset Sprague
had ordered Amos Hathaway's destroyer to stay with the carriers,
and so the *Heermann* stayed on the far side of the formation, making
smoke. When Sprague's 7:16 order went out to prepare a torpedo
attack, Captain Hathaway had to cut clear across the middle of
Taffy 3.

At full boiler steam, Hathaway conned his ship through the thicket
of smoke and rain—right into the path of the *Samuel B. Roberts*. Faced
with a collision, Bob Copeland ordered his helm to back down, as
Hathaway steered clear. Both ships quickly rebuilt steam, but the
Heermann could not quite keep pace with the *Hoel* running in.

Copeland stood at the captain's conning station on the bridge of his ship, waiting to get his speed back, studying the evolving picture of the pursuit. Forming up with the other destroyer escorts would be impractical, if not entirely impossible. He thought, *My God, how are we going to work this?* You didn't take a destroyer escort in alone against heavy ships. But Copeland was starting to think he should just do precisely that. Why not join up with the "big boys"? He estimated the course he would need to take to put the *Roberts* in position to fire torpedoes at the approaching heavy cruisers: sixty degrees off the bow of the target ship, range five to seven thousand yards. As it happened, the Japanese men-of-war were accommodating him beautifully. With a minor course change, he would be in an optimum firing position. Waiting to link up with the other DEs would forfeit the opportunity. Copeland reached over and grabbed the handle of his squawk box, twisted it down, and threw aside his concerns about staying with the faster destroyers. "Well, Sis on you, pister. Let's go!" he said. When the order passed nearly twenty minutes later for the destroyer escorts to execute their own torpedo attack, the *Samuel B. Roberts* was long gone, already grappling with the Japanese.

Copeland called Bob Roberts, his executive officer in the CIC: "Bob, give me a course to put me sixty degrees on the bow of the leading ship in that cruiser column." The computer clicked and whirred and produced a heading just six degrees to the left of the one Copeland had figured by dead reckoning. Then Copeland grabbed the JV phone and called his chief engineering officer. In formal duty settings officers addressed each another by surname. Casually, in the wardroom, most of them trafficked in nicknames. Lt. Bill Trowbridge was known in private quarters as "Lucky." In desperate straits, Copeland opted for informality. "Lucky, this is the captain. Lucky, we are going on a torpedo attack and I have rung up full speed; we are going in at twenty knots. As soon as we fire our fish, I will ring up flank speed and I want you to hook on everything you've got. Don't worry about your reduction gears or your boilers or anything, because there's all hell being thrown at us up here, and we're just fortunate we haven't been hit yet."

Lucky pushed their good fortune a bit farther. The boilers on the *Roberts* were designed to carry 440 pounds of steam pressure. Lieutenant Trowbridge ordered water tender third class Wilfred Labbe to turn off the boilers' safety valves and build up to 660 pounds of steam. Trowbridge would need every roaring ounce of it if he aimed to live up to his nickname and get the ship through its torpedo run. The *Roberts* fell in well astern of her larger cousins the *Hoel* and the *Heermann*. In the engine room the needle on the steam gauge broke new territory.

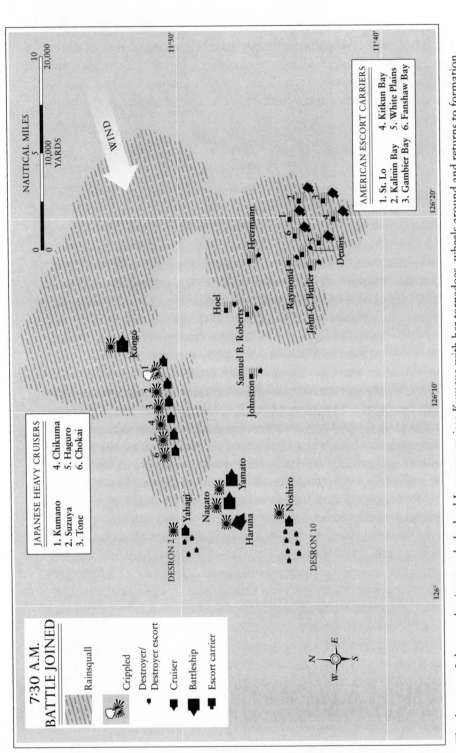

The destroyer *Johnston*, having struck the lead Japanese cruiser *Kumano* with her torpedoes, wheels around and returns to formation. The destroyer *Hoel*, already hit hard, leads the *Heermann* and the *Samuel B. Roberts* in for a torpedo attack. Hidden by rainsqualls, Ziggy Sprague gambles and turns his carriers to the south-southwest, momentarily outdistancing his pursuers.

Twenty-three

It had to be only a matter of time before Japanese shells broke not water but steel and drew men's blood. Ernest Evans and the officers of the *Johnston* had scarcely stolen a moment to celebrate their torpedo hits when the destroyer walked into a double salvo of enemy shells. Running through her own smoke to return to station with the carriers, the destroyer was rocked by a dizzying series of blasts.

Bob Hagen saw and felt the impact from the gun director. On the highest point on the ship, movements were amplified. The impact seemed to shove the destroyer sideways. All across the *Johnston*'s 376 ½-foot length, men were knocked off their feet. "It was like a puppy being smacked by a truck."

The first three rounds to hit the destroyer came from a battleship, probably the *Kongo*. The first one, a fourteen-inch shell, nearly fifteen hundred pounds, fell in a ripping arc and struck, opening a three-by-six-foot hole in the main deck, blowing out the plumbing and main drain from the ship's head, tearing up the machine shop, penetrating down into the after engine room, and exploding against the bulky iron housing of the port-side propeller shaft's main reduction gears—one of the few pieces of hardware on a destroyer substantial enough to detonate a hard-headed armor-piercing round. The second shell punched through the deck and slashed critical electrical cables and steam lines before detonating against the main steam turbine in the after engine room.

Belowdecks aft the *Johnston* was plunged into darkness. The third large shell demolished the source of the heat itself, striking a boiler in the after fireroom and extinguishing by concussion its oil-burning flames. With that hit the port-side screw stopped spinning, and the *Johnston*'s thirty-six-knot speed was cut in half. What the shell failed to do instantly, high-pressure superheated steam from shattered boiler pipes did with substantially less mercy. Not a man in the after fireroom survived the 840-degree bath that followed.

A moment later there came a sound like a whole load of sheet metal dropping onto a hard floor as the destroyer absorbed the blast of a smaller salvo. The first six-inch shell—from the *Yamato*'s secondary battery, or perhaps a light cruiser—holed the number-two exhaust stack, detonating underneath the director platform and twisting it upward on both sides of the uptake. Two other shells slammed into the port bridge wing, igniting a forty-millimeter magazine, which burned and popped smokily with the runaway bursts of antiaircraft shells.

Just seconds before impact Lieutenants DiGardi and Welch had left the bridge wing and entered the pilothouse to carry out Captain Evans's most recent course-change order. They were just in time. An explosion propelled Welch forward into a pile of the wounded and the dead. He picked himself up, dazed, and tended to the injured. Ed Block was in shock, missing a large chunk of his right shoulder. The coxswain's left shoulder was dislocated, an eardrum punctured. With small pieces of shrapnel lodged between his eyes, under his chin, and in his right eye, Block stumbled through the pilothouse hatch, past DiGardi, and crumpled against a gray metal bulkhead. Welch, standing over him, stated what was not altogether obvious—"Block is alive"—then grabbed his wrist and stuck him with a morphine syrette. As the drug permeated his bloodstream, Block regained his bearings. He made it down to the main deck on his own power, then joined the pharmacist's mates who were escorting the wounded down to Lt. Robert Browne's medical triage in the officers' ward.

The blast to the bridge all but undressed Ernest Evans. It blew the cap from his head and tore the shirt from his chest. Shrapnel lodged in his face, neck, hand, and torso. Lieutenant Browne came to his captain's aid. "Don't bother me now," Evans said. "Help some of those guys who are hurt." Evans was still in charge—coolly so, seemingly unbothered at having two fingers sliced from his left hand. He ordered the survivors to clear the bridge.

Ellsworth Welch was transfixed by the grisly sights all around him. The well-kept and orderly pilothouse had been transformed into what might be mistaken for a dirty meat locker. Body parts were strewn throughout the compartment; limbs and fingers and indeterminate remnants of flesh filled the humid air with the rich, metallic odor of blood. Fearing the sight of the carnage would hurt morale, Welch gathered up what of the mess he could and tossed it overboard.

Time seemed to stop, though events surely rushed forward. Welch found Jack Bechdel, the torpedo and assistant gunnery officer, propped up against the wheelhouse, complaining that his arms were hurt, unaware that he had lost a leg at the knee. Bechdel asked for a drink of water. Welch pulled out a syrette and gave him a shot of morphine. Something large and sharp and moving too fast for the eye had cleanly severed the head of Lt. (jg) Joe Pliska, a ship and aircraft recognition specialist who had joined the *Johnston* at Manus to train its officers. Ens. Gordon Fox died in the blast too. Signalman Joel Dixon was blown apart at his battle station.

Outside, below the bridge, at his post on the starboard forty-millimeter gun, Clarence Trader looked up and saw blood flowing like water from a hole in the steel bulkhead. Maybe it was blood. Maybe it was the residue of the crimson tower of seawater that a Japanese round had sent breaking over the *Johnston*'s superstructure. Possibly it was a swirled mixture of both. Trader heard Captain Evans ask for help removing bodies from the bridge. Clyde Burnett, the chief boatswain's mate, responded to the call, coming forward to shepherd Bechdel to the officers' ward, where the pharmacist's mates could attend to him, stick him with more morphine, and tie a tourniquet to his leg stump. Hearing someone call, "Stand by below," Bill Mercer glanced up and saw a human form being lowered from the bridge wing to the main deck. The body descended—feet, khaki trousers, torso—and stopped, seeming to hover next to him. It had no head.

It took a fraction of a second for a heavy shell to spin shrieking through the air and punch through bulkheads and decks and machinery and detonate or fail to detonate, ending lives in seconds and casting teenagers with the hard, dull look of veterans. In that time bold commissioning-day promises to sail into harm's way acquired human and material consequences. This was naval warfare in the machine age. In 1944 Annapolis was still turning out men possessed by the idea that naval service was, in the words of one historian, "clean and professional, without the complications of civilians, refugees, partisans, looting or pillage." But in fact, technology made it as brutal and hellish as anything the navy men of imperial Britain and Germany had suffered through a generation ago at Jutland.

When a heavy round from a naval rifle hits a ship and explodes, the energy released pulverizes the hardened steel of the shell and swirls up the shattered remnants of surrounding metal decks and bulkheads. All of this metal rushes outward on the edge of a wave of blast pressure that a typical shipboard compartment cannot hope to contain. The sudden and overwhelming "overpressure" turns the compartment itself into a weapon, its remains churning up into a superheated storm of fragmented or liquified metal. The blast wave's effect on people is horrific. It collapses body cavities, crushes organs, and blows flesh from bone.

The size of the killing zone—the radius within which these effects will occur—depends on the amount of explosive the shell holds. A Japanese eight-inch armor-piercing shell, three feet long and 277 pounds in weight, had a 6.9-pound bursting charge. A fourteen-inch high-explosive shell, 1,425 pounds and five feet long, contained sixty-three pounds of explosives. The *Yamato*'s giant 18.1-inch armor-piercing shells, six and a half feet long and 3,219 pounds in weight, carried a seventy-five-pound bursting charge.

The men of the *Johnston* learned in an instant that shrapnel came in many sizes, sometimes large enough to cut limbs and grind flesh, sometimes fine and particulate, filling the air with hot driving mist. They learned that shells tumbling through layers of steel filled compartments with poisonous gases, that exploding shells could kill by shock or with a cascade of flames that doused them like liquid. Gone was the mystery of why Clyde Burnett, Bob Hollenbaugh, and the other senior boatswain's mates kept them scraping paint for hours on end: it burned fiercely. The lesson had been learned in the shipboard conflagrations at Pearl Harbor and in the Solomon Islands in 1942. Now they saw it firsthand. Yet somehow ships still came off the line full of paint to scrape. This was harm, and the *Johnston* was in its way. This was what Captain Evans had promised them.

Bob Hagen had seen hell once already, from the decks of the destroyer *Aaron Ward,* damaged during the Solomons campaign. But now the absence of novelty did not diminish the horror. "I was looking out of the director at the time. Everything happened at once," Hagen wrote. The force of the hits threw him from his stool in the gun director, helmet, headphones, and binoculars torn from his head. He recovered in time to see the mainmast fracture and topple. It housed the ship's SC radar, the so-called "whirling bedspring," used for air search. The whole thing came down, seesawed over the bridge tower, and swung back and forth like an off-kilter metronome. The impact tumbled the ship's gyro stable element off its mount, tripped the internal communications circuit board for a few minutes, and cut the shearing pin that held the FD "Fox Dog" fire-control radar in its vertical position. Unable to slew his radars for elevation until the assembly was reset, Hagen climbed out of the director, grabbed the big antenna, and wrenched it into position toward the horizon.

Looking down on his ship, Hagen was dumbstruck by what had become of it. "The *Johnston* was a mess," he later recalled. "There were dead men on the deck and gaping holes from the fourteen-inch shells through which a fat man could have plummeted." Shrapnel had gashed metal bulkheads and decks like so much tinfoil.

Amid the hissing of steam and the screaming of men, Orin Vadnais peered over the side of his forty-millimeter amidships gun tub and saw chunks of solid explosives from a smashed depth charge scattered across the deck. Up out of the giant hole opened by the falling shell popped Harold Beresonsky's steel-helmeted head. A lit cigarette dangling from his lips, he started throwing chunks of the explosive overboard, casually, like a weekender cleaning up his patio.

When the big shells hit, the deck jerked up so sharply that Joseph Check rang his helmet on something hard overhead, then collapsed. Lying on the deck in the first-aid station, he could feel the thin steel growing hot to the touch as superheated boiler steam filled the engineering spaces below. Broken boiler lines were bad news for at least three reasons. The loss of steam bled the ship of engine power, slowed the turbines that ran the ship's electrical generators, and liberated superheated vapors that killed men fast. A needle-sized hole in a steam line could release a cutting spray powerful enough to sever limbs. Battleship shells were less delicate than that. Steam was gushing out of three large holes in the deck where the fourteen-inch rounds had struck.

Jesse Cochran ran to the steam-stop valves on the main deck above the after fireroom and spun the large wheel to close the lines. It did nothing to stop the lethal hissing of escaping steam, for the detonations ruptured not only the lines but the tubes inside the boilers themselves. Joseph Check saw three men climbing out of the hatch from the after engineering spaces, emerging through the thick white steam. The effort to escape sapped them of their final energies. Check watched them collapse and slump back against the bulkhead, their skin, white as ivory, covering swollen flesh. The skin fell away here and there, revealing pink patches beneath. The steam had cooked them like so many shrimp. They did not live long.

Bob Hagen was on his sound-powered phones after the first onslaught of shells, polling his gun bosses to see who was with him and who wasn't: *"All stations—Control testing!"* The replies came: *"Gun One, aye! . . . Gun Two, aye! . . . Gun Three, aye! . . . Gun Five, aye! . . . Plot, aye!"* He was relieved to hear he was not suddenly alone, but wondered after Gun 54. Bob Hollenbaugh did not respond. But the boatswain's mate first class did not keep his gun boss in the dark for long. Momentarily a messenger came on the line, calling Hagen from a forty-millimeter mount back aft. He said Gun 54 had lost power and communications, and its link to the fire-control computer was dead.

Gun 54 was worse off than the other two aft five-inch gun mounts. Guns 53 and 55 had no electrical power to rotate the mount but were still getting signals from the gun director. All they had to do to benefit from radar control was to train and elevate their guns to match the dial pointers showing the director's orientation at any moment in time. But Gun 54 was getting neither electrical power nor indicating signals for training and elevation. Hagen granted Hollenbaugh's request to fire on local control, and as Hollenbaugh would write, "Gun 54 declared its own war on the Japs."

Firing his gun the old-fashioned way—slowly and not terribly accurately—Hollenbaugh was cut off from everybody. He couldn't talk to Hagen, nor even with the men below him in the ammunition handling room. Because his shell hoist was out, the shell handlers would have to pass ammo to him by hand. Hollenbaugh jumped out of the mount's portside hatch and slid down the ladder on the aft side of the gun deck. Jumping over unrecognizable bodies, he stuck his head into the handling room, where the men were milling, unsure what to do without a working hoist to feed. He explained the problem to them and told them that their battle performance and probably also their survival would depend on keeping a steady bucket brigade of shells moving up to the gun. They would have to do it manually, the same way Hollenbaugh would be aiming.

Seated in Gun 54's trainer's brass bicycle seat to the left of the five-inch naval rifle, Bobby Chastain could only guess at the horrible extent of the carnage outside his station. The jolts and sudden movements of the ship, the sudden sickening reduction in the intensity of the engine vibrations—none of it made him optimistic. The trainer's gun sight door remained closed, for he had seen enough Japanese men-of-war for a lifetime. Now, though, with his mount partially disabled and the loud voice of his gun captain saying something about "local control," his willful ignorance had to end. Local control meant the gun crew would do its own shooting, training and elevating the gun by cranking handwheels in the mount. They had never drilled under local control before.

Back in the mount, Hollenbaugh stood on the gun captain's platform, head poking up from the turret, shouting bearings to Bobby Chastain to guide his rotation of the gun, and ranges to Samuel Moody to determine how high to elevate it. The forty-millimeter mount immediately forward of Gun 54 had its own Mark 51 director, adequate for obtaining ranges if not for a complete gyro-aided, computerized firing solution. Walt Howard, one of the crew manning that gun, passed range information to Hollenbaugh, who made do with it what he could. Chastain and Moody turned and elevated their gun by turning brass-handled wheels on either side of the mount. They cranked them furiously back and forth as the ship veered and the guns barked and Hollenbaugh relayed ranges. But for the help they received from the radar operator on the forty behind them, they might as well have been refighting the Battle of Trafalgar.

Ahead of the stricken *Johnston* loomed a large rain cloud whose gray-black mass offered sanctuary from the relentless roar and slap of the Japanese salvos. The fury of the bombardment was worthy of Neptune himself. But the rain drifting across the water inspired hope that the god of the oceans knew mercy as well as wrath. The squall's gray tendrils fell to the sea, dragged to their source by the friction of falling precipitation.

His crew might enjoy it for only a few brief minutes, for the squall appeared to be moving faster than the ship was: on a single working screw, just seventeen knots. But Evans would take what shelter he could get. Already the squalls were sheltering Ziggy Sprague and his CVEs racing south as fast as their engines could shove them. Ernest Evans steered the *Johnston* south, running for the rain.

Twenty-four

The White House staffers gathered in the Map Room were jolted from their work by the bracing immediacy of the uncoded, plain-language plea. Most of the Navy's operational communications were routinely copied to them. They scanned them for compelling news and shared it with their higher-ups as it came. As the Battle off Samar was beginning, around dinnertime on October 24, Washington time, the Map Room staff received this message meant for Admiral Halsey:

> ENEMY FORCES ATTACKING OUR FORCES COMPOSED OF FOUR BATTLESHIPS, EIGHT CRUISERS AND X OTHER SHIPS. REQUEST LEE PROCEED TOP SPEED COVER LEYTE. REQUEST IMMEDIATE STRIKE BY FAST CARRIERS.

A world removed from the fighting, at 1600 Pennsylvania Avenue, it wasn't clear who had sent it. The staffers' best guess was that it had come from the Seventh Fleet's amphibious commander, Rear Adm. Daniel Barbey, whose group seemed most prone to needing emergency assistance. No matter who it had come from, they were certain the transmission required the president's personal attention. The message was typed up in short order and submitted to Franklin D. Roosevelt as part of a briefing on the Philippines situation.

212 \ THE LAST STAND OF THE TIN CAN SAILORS

Though it is not known what he did or said upon receiving the briefing, the president was sufficiently intrigued by the unfolding events off Samar to request updates as the night progressed. The little ships were on a big stage, and now they had the president's attention.

The worldwide audience to the drama off Samar included not only the White House but James Forrestal's Navy Department, the top brass at Pacific Fleet Headquarters at Pearl Harbor, and the Japanese Combined Fleet leadership at Tokyo and Hiyoshi. At the U.S. Pacific Fleet's new advance headquarters on Guam, radio eavesdroppers manned large battery-powered receivers mounted in the cargo beds of big Marine trucks. One radioman, Albert Fishburn, defying the burning sun and the considerable distraction of nearby Japanese snipers, manned his set all day long. He was captivated by what he picked up on the circuit designated 7910J: "It just operated all day long. It was just one ship after another."

Information from the Guam radio intercepts was relayed back to Pearl Harbor, where Cdr. Jasper Holmes, deputy chief of the Navy's Joint Intelligence Center, Pacific Ocean Area (JICPOA), monitored it. When Holmes saw the report of the developing situation off Samar, he was astounded. He telephoned fleet intelligence officer Capt. Edwin T. Layton to ask about the location of Task Force 34's battleships. Holmes figured the battlewagons were already guarding San Bernardino Strait. Absent specific confirmation from Halsey, Layton was less willing to assume Lee's heavies had been detached.

As it happened, Admiral Nimitz shared Captain Layton's outlook. He did not know for sure whether TF 34 had been created per Halsey's earlier battle plan. Though it seemed sensible enough, until now he hadn't seen fit to ask. The commander in chief hated to be seen as second-guessing his theater commanders.

At 6:48 that morning Halsey had been stunned to discover that Kinkaid was assuming the actuality of a contingency—the detachment of Task Force 34. Halsey ended the mystery of his battleships' whereabouts at 7:02, when he responded to the Seventh Fleet commander's 4:12 A.M. request for confirmation that the battleships were guarding San Bernardino Strait. Halsey told him, "NEGATIVE. TASK FORCE 34 IS WITH CARRIER GROUPS ENGAGING ENEMY CARRIER FORCE." That message took the customary two-hour trip around Robin Hood's barn and the Manus receiving station before reaching Kinkaid. By the time it did, the Seventh Fleet commander had already transmitted a string of desperate messages indicating his own surprise at the impending disaster.

At 7:07 Kinkaid informed Halsey in uncoded English that Taffy 3 was taking fire from Japanese battleships and cruisers. That message reached Halsey at 8:22. At 7:27 Kinkaid radioed Halsey, *"Request Lee proceed at top speed to cover Leyte; request immediate strike by fast carriers."* The tenor of Kinkaid's pleas grew increasingly shrill. At 7:39: *"Fast battleships urgently needed immediately at Leyte Gulf."* At 8:29: *"My situation is critical. Fast battleships and support by air strike may be able to prevent enemy from destroying* [escort carriers] *and entering Leyte."* For Nimitz, that was enough. Bewildered by the evident short-circuiting of communications between the Third and Seventh Fleets, he composed a straightforward inquiry to Halsey: *"Where is TF 34?"*

A radioman on Nimitz's staff saw the implicit emphasis and repeated the interrogatory phrase, "Where is—" Then the message was passed to an ensign responsible for encoding it, a process that involved inserting nonsense phrases at the beginning and end of a dispatch, on either side of a double consonant, so as to confound unauthorized recipients.

Thus the message that the Commander in Chief, Pacific Fleet, transmitted to Halsey's radio department aboard the *New Jersey* read, "TURKEY TROTS TO WATER GG WHERE IS RPT WHERE IS TASK FORCE THIRTY-FOUR RR THE WORLD WONDERS."

To this day the world wonders whether the Third Fleet radioman who received this message aboard the *New Jersey* was scholar enough to know that the phrase "The world wonders" appears in Alfred Lord Tennyson's poem "The Charge of the Light Brigade," commemorating a battle against long odds that was fought that very day, October 25, in a different century. The world wonders too whether he gave Chester Nimitz credit for the same literary acuity, recognizing with a grin CINCPAC's historical flourish, uncannily suited to the circumstances, and assuming the reference was part of the message intended for Halsey. All the world knows for sure about the formulation and transmission of the query is that Halsey received it with the tail-end padding intact and took it as an armor-piercing broadside of sarcasm.

Reeling from the thought that his gentlemanly commander in chief had just insulted him, Halsey whipped his baseball cap from his head and chucked it to the deck, cursing bitterly. He had just ordered Ching Lee's battleships to prepare for action against Ozawa's aircraft carriers. Now he had no choice but to recall them. As Halsey raged, his chief of staff, Mick Carney, said, "Stop it! What the hell's the matter with you? Pull yourself together." Tempers cooled. Orders flew. And slowly, all too slowly, the majestic leviathans that comprised Admiral Lee's battle line pulled out of formation and swung around to a heading of 180 degrees.

It was a gesture more than anything else. Fast though they were, the battleships weren't swift enough to cover the two-hundred-mile distance in time to do Ziggy Sprague any good.

Twenty-five

Rain pelted the *Johnston*'s decks and hissed like droplets on a hot griddle, steaming on the metal above the shattered boilers in the number-two fireroom. Where it didn't completely evaporate, the rain cleaned the decks of brine and drying blood.

In Gun 54, Bob Hollenbaugh set down his sighting telescope and hopped down from the gun, allowing his crew a breather. They emerged from the illusory safety of the gun mount's thin steel walls, taking in their first unshuttered view of the killing field that the ship's decks had become. "By now the topside of the *Johnston* looked like a mess of spaghetti," recalled Robert Billie. So many men were dead, yet the ship itself continued to live, as if animated by its own force of will.

That too was an illusion. The ship was running now—maneuvering at least—principally on the sweat and pain of its sailors. The shells had knocked out not only half the ship's steam power but most of its electrical power as well. The hits had severed the cables running aft from the number-two engine room's distribution board. With the generator knocked out, the aft compartments of the destroyer were without power. The electrical pumps that might have stanched the flood of seawater into the engine rooms could not operate. Worse, there was no power to the steering engine, the motors that powered the ship's large rudder. Without electricity to move the rudder, the only way to turn the ship was via "Norwegian steam": the strong backs and shoulders of the enlisted crew.

When steering was lost, the call went out for able bodies to report aft. Men whose battle stations were redundant—gunners on light antiaircraft mounts, or survivors from crews that had been wiped out—gathered on the fantail. They took turns belowdecks, teaming up in pairs to crank the two-handled wheel attached to the hydraulic pump that turned the rudder. Facing each other and working in concert, two strong sailors could rotate the wheel reasonably well and move the rudder in accordance with orders called to them from the bridge.

The retreating destroyer was changing course so frequently that even the burliest seaman could handle just fifteen minutes at a time. And even with their best efforts, the ship was still sluggish at the helm. They never really kept up with the course-change orders that Captain Evans was calling over the JV phones from the bridge.

As leader of the number-three repair party stationed in the aft deckhouse, Lt. Jesse Cochran was in charge of restoring power to the rearmost parts of the ship. With electrician's mates Alan Cravens and Burton Hoover, gunner's mate third class Dave Lewis, chief mess cook Dusty Rhodes, and others, Cochran pulled cables from the forward engine room's distribution board to the steering motors. But struggle as they did to route casualty power aft, they could not quite complete the circuit. The juice did not flow, and there was no telling why. With masses of cables and wires twisted together like ropes and threaded through round holes in bulkheads, one was all but indistinguishable from another. Certain critical lines had been painted red. What the others did was a mystery. Combat allowed little opportunity for protracted investigation. Critical or not, each cable was responsible for some piece of machinery's proper functioning. They never sorted it out, and the rudder remained powerless.

During the twenty or thirty minutes in which Cochran and his repair party fought to restore the spark to the *Johnston*'s work stations aft, the temperature in the engineering spaces had cooled sufficiently to enable a rescue and salvage mission into the riddled bowels of the ship. Motor machinist's mate Bob Sochor, Jesse Cochran, and other rescuers put on asbestos suits and descended the ladders—slowly, blindly—to search for survivors. In the aft engine room, which was taking on water, Cochran checked the tube packing that kept ocean water from seeping in around the port propeller shaft. It was intact. He then closed the intake valve to the condenser, which turned salt water to fresh for drinking. But still the water rose.

Cochran was amazed to find several boiler room machinists crawling like oversized rats out of the bilges below the grating. To elude the killing steam, the enterprising survivors had pressed themselves against the skin of the ship's belly down in the bilges until the cauldron cooled and they could make good their escape.

Light from Sochor's battle lantern scarcely penetrated the cavernous darkness. He groped around in the stinking, steam-soaked void, found a body, tied a rope around it, and pushed upward while men on deck lifted from above. When Cochran entered the after engine room, he found warrant officer Johnny Merritt, one of the ship's best machinists and most popular "old men," lying facedown on the grates where he had fallen at his station. With a heavy wrench in hand, another warrant machinist, Marley Polk, swam beneath the grating in the dark compartment, looking for the source of the inrushing water. As he was submerged, there was a large vibration from a hit somewhere. A heavy piece of engine room machinery dislodged and splashed into the water, trapping him in the bilges. He struggled to get his head above water and ordered his rescuers to save themselves before the water again closed over his head.

Bob Sochor shimmied up the ladder to the main deck and removed his asbestos suit. He was looking down at the closed hatch leading to the after fireroom when to his amazement the round wheel started spinning, turned from below, and the hatch swung open: "Trying to climb out was a fireman by the name of West. I ran over to help him up the rest of the way. He had been down in that hot fireroom at least fifteen or twenty minutes after the boilers were hit and exploded. He stood on deck, his clothes wet and steaming, and he was shaking himself off as if to get the hot steaming clothes off his skin."

Electrical fires in the after engine room burned stubbornly but eventually succumbed to the cool gusts of rescuers' CO_2 bottles. Three feet of water covered the deck. Rescuers rigged a submersible pump, but the cord didn't reach the power supply. When a longer lead was spliced and linked to the engine room distribution board, still no power came. They would have to make do.

Sochor led West and several other wounded to the officers' wardroom, which was used as an operating room in combat. "It was an awful sight to see," Sochor said. "All those pathetic men sitting and lying on the crowded deck waiting to be treated by the doctor and pharmacists."

Joe Worling, the engineering officer, ordered Sochor and water tender third class Fielden Critz to come with him to the after fireroom. The ship was running on a single screw, the starboard propeller shaft working over capacity at 350 RPM just to maintain the limp-along speed of seventeen knots. Driven by the turbine and reduction gears in the forward engine room, the shaft was squealing loudly, a sign of possible—and doubtless fatal—engine failure. Worling gave Sochor a pail of lube oil and told him to go pour it over the shaft and the spring bearings. Wearing gas masks and holding battle lanterns, Sochor and Critz climbed down through the hatch from which West had just escaped. Experienced snipes, as engine-room and fireroom personnel were called, could descend the fifteen-foot ladders to their stations with their feet never touching the steps. Saddled with the protective suit and moving sightlessly through smoke and darkness, Sochor's progress was slower now. The fireroom was smoky, filled with steam from the shattered boilers. Cracks of sunlight shone between bent deck plates, but there was not enough light to penetrate the smoke. "With little help from our battle lantern," he recalled, "we inched our way behind the blown boiler along the narrow catwalk, up and over piping, to the top of the shaft. We poured the oil all over the shaft bearing box, which stopped the squealing sound." The ship continued creeping back to Sprague's besieged carriers.

The interlude in the squall meant that the Japanese cruisers were blind and could not fire on the Americans. A Mark 37 gun director had no such blinders—it was as sharp-eyed in the fog or the dark as it was in the clear of midday. While the ship was enshrouded by rain, the gun director's radar spied the column of Japanese cruisers closing on the escort carrier formation. As Bob Hagen and his gunners fired some 100 five-inch rounds at the nearest Japanese cruiser, the squall's only impact on the efficiency of the *Johnston*'s gunnery department was the rude manner in which it soaked Hagen's smokes. "It was the first time in my life I didn't mind having a package of cigarettes ruined," he wrote.

Time, however, was not on Taffy 3's side. Though two Japanese cruisers, the *Suzuya,* damaged by aerial attack, and the *Kumano,* hit by the *Johnston,* were out of the battle, the four others still had their legs, and their captains were determined to draw blood. Through nearly three years of war, no aircraft carrier had fallen to Japanese guns. Admiral Kurita credited heavenly intervention for the opportunity. He would soon be in position to make use of it.

*   *   *

LARGELY ON THE INDEPENDENT initiative of its different division commanders, the Japanese fleet was fanned out and advancing in roughly parallel columns: four heavy cruisers steaming southward, out to the east; the *Yamato* and the *Nagato* looming a step behind them to Taffy 3's north; the *Haruna* and the *Kongo* making independent tracks ahead of their slower heavies; and two destroyer squadrons bringing up the rear.

Against them came the *Hoel,* the *Heermann,* and the *Samuel B. Roberts,* formed into a loose semblance of a column and steaming into the open maw of the armored behemoths arrayed before them. Like the *Roberts* before her, the *Hoel* had narrowly avoided a collision with the *Heermann* as Hathaway's destroyer made its dash across the Taffy 3 formation to line up for the attack. Now the three steamed north at flank speed, while Sprague's jeep carriers ran southward. With each turn of their screws, the gulf between the destroyers and the carriers widened. Their exposure, their utter vulnerability, grew starker with every passing minute.

Destroyers were hit-and-run ships. As the Japanese had demonstrated time and time again with their own tin cans, and as Oldendorf's destroyers had shown at Surigao Strait, torpedo attacks were best executed under the cover of night. This would be no replay of Surigao Strait. Though their stacks billowed smoke amid sheltering rainsqualls, Ziggy Sprague's screening ships attacked in daylight. Their opponents had roughly three times the gun power of Nishimura's group. The Americans were unsupported by a powerful battle line whose large guns offered a sheltering canopy to hide under upon withdrawal and a devastating deterrent to enemy pursuit.

Moreover, Kurita's Center Force was not confined to a strait. Roaming free in open ocean, his ships had both room to maneuver and speed sufficient to overtake and encircle the jeep carriers and destroy them from all sides.

For the destroyer screen, the risk of encirclement was moot, for they were offering themselves for slaughter, throwing themselves willingly into it in the hope of delaying the inevitable for the carriers. Perhaps they would harry the Japanese enough to let Sprague's CVEs slip away. "I had heard all along that destroyers were expendable but never quite believed. Now I knew it was true," Everett Lindorff of the *Hoel* would write.

From the gun deck on the fantail of the *Fanshaw Bay*, situated on the northwest edge of the circular pod of fleeing escort carriers, ship's cook Harold Kight had a front-row seat from which to observe the destroyer screen forming into line for their torpedo run. His battle station was in the handling room below the ship's lone five-inch gun. When the gun was firing, he, Jack Frisch, and Warren Whitaker fed projectiles and powder cases into the hoist that supplied the crew on the open-mounted "stinger" or "peashooter." Until the enemy got closer, the crew that Kight supplied did not have anything to shoot at. But with a clear 180-degree vista off the stern, there was certainly a lot to watch.

Kight looked on awestruck as the destroyers fell into line, lit off their boilers, and left their stations by the carriers to race off toward the Japanese battle line. The little ships seemed to possess a spirit all their own. And they reminded him of something—horses. On his family's 250-acre farm in central Oklahoma, Kight worked with the Percheron draft horses that hauled his dad's plows and pulled his wagons. They were powerful animals, stalwart and dependable. He knew the habits of the big black and gray beasts. Whenever a thunderstorm loomed across the plains, the broad-shouldered workhorses became as skittish as stallions. Their eyes bulged. Their nostrils flared. Spurred by the drop in barometric pressure, they sprinted and dashed around the pasture. When they accelerated from a standstill, their hindquarters dropped down, legs jackhammering the earth, heads pulled high, manes waving in the wind.

Harold Kight thought the two destroyers and the destroyer escort, sprinting in to attack, looked like that now, like horses sprinting exuberantly across a watery pasture. At flank speed, the *Fletchers* tossed up a flaring bow wave like a mane and their sterns sat low, digging their screws into the sea, sprinting like Percherons madly energized by a low-pressure front. As the flagship of Commander Thomas's screen, the *Hoel* led the loose column, followed by the *Heermann*. Then went that determined pony, the *Samuel B. Roberts*. Kight figured this would be the last he would see of these ships and their vaguely equine nobility. He felt a lump rise in his throat at the realization that, most likely, none of them would survive to run under the thunder again.

Twenty-six

Seaman first class Sam Lucas could feel the *Hoel*'s deck vibrating from the exertions of the turbines. Their deep steam-driven hum resonated in his sternum. Lucas, a torpedoman striker, and torpedoman third class Earl Tompkins busied themselves setting the depth charges on the starboard and port-side racks on safe. There would soon likely be plenty of exploding going on. No need to contribute to the fireworks.

Painted with sharply angled camouflage patterns to confuse enemy lookouts, the *Hoel* was nevertheless inescapably framed against the veil of smoke and squalls behind her. The Japanese gunners walked splashes up and down and back along the American ship's line of advance.

Jack Creamer, the *Hoel*'s assistant gunnery officer, could see the problem the impromptu torpedo line faced: time and distance were not on their side. While the *Hoel* was laying smoke for the carriers, the Japanese had closed the range rapidly with the formation. Because Captain Kintberger's destroyer was closest to the enemy, she had the least room to maneuver to prepare her attack. The column was too long, the enemy too close, and the visibility too spotty for the U.S. ships to coordinate effectively.

The Americans and Japanese closed at a combined rate of more than fifty knots. Zigzagging to avoid shellfire and simultaneously calculating his own best approach to fire the *Hoel*'s ten torpedoes at the proper angle to the enemy ships, Kintberger was forced to seize his chance when it presented itself. The *Hoel*'s skipper elected to pass between the columns of battleships and cruisers. His ship would be exposed to fire from all sides, but at least there would be no shortage of targets. The steel decks were slick with rain. Despite the embrace of the laden tropical air, Hugh Coffelt, a gunner on one of the amidships forty-millimeter mounts, realized that he was shivering.

Fred Green, the exec, was on his game in the CIC, lining up the torpedo attack and plotting the progress of the overwhelming Japanese force.

> *Bridge, this is Combat. Range one six five double oh. Give us a sight bearing on the battleships. . . . Three four two? That checks with ours by radar. Where is the cruiser column? Three five eight? Destroyers, two nine one and three three nine. That leaves the big ships unprotected then. Captain, suggest a course of three five three.*

Then Green gave the gunnery officer, Lt. Bill Sanders, the benefit of the data flowing in from his radar.

> *Gunnery Control, this is Combat. Stand by to open fire. Range one four five double oh. Stand by. I'll give a mark on fourteen thousand yards. Stand by to open fire. Stand by . . . stand by . . . mark—one four oh double oh.*

On cue, the *Hoel*'s two forward guns opened up, crashing out at a large gray form looming off her bow. Sanders had a heavy cruiser in his sights. On the bridge, everyone's ears rang from the concussion of Guns 51 and 52. Lieutenant Dix didn't mind the roar.

> *Damn it was good to hear them speaking out. . . .*
> *The whole ship trembled with their rapid bursts*
> *And Sanders up above us grinning there*
> *Was giving out gun orders to his crews*

Making them keep a steady, even pace,
"Just like your drills—forget about the Japs."

Fourteen thousand yards was close enough for the guns. But to launch torpedoes, they needed to get a bit closer. Sanders slewed his gun director mount and trained his batteries on a battleship. The three after turrets joined in now, bucking the ship with their stiff report. The destroyer plunged ahead, fishtailing through shell splashes as the decks rattled from the exertions of her power plant. *They haven't hit us yet,* Lieutenant Dix thought as the *Hoel* closed to torpedo-launching range. *We're almost there. . . . We're all together now—let's make it good.* It all happened in the space of a hundred seconds, the events coming too fast for even the most meticulous quartermaster to record in his log.* At 7:25 A.M. the *Hoel*'s impossible luck ran out.

Leon Kintberger had been chasing salvos in a desperate bid to keep the *Hoel* alive. Battleships and cruisers had the ship's range, and so the splashes were not hard to find. The closer the ship got, however, the more futile the concept of "dodging" salvos became. It was mostly a pretense in any event, for no ship could actually *dodge* a high-velocity inbound shell. The first one that hit them was small in caliber—small at least relative to the fourteen-, sixteen-, and eighteen-inch battleship rounds that were splitting the air with palpable roars and, at the end of their twenty-mile trajectories, losing their grip on the sky and falling downward like tumbling trash cans. This one came in fast and unseen, striking the bridge high on the port side. Lieutenant Dix thought, *Oh, Jesus, this is it!*

The ship rocked and staggered. There was a flash and a *crrrump* and a whistling hail of metal that killed most of the men in the wheelhouse immediately. Lt. Earle Nason, quartermaster Herbert Dou-

---

*The sequence of events during the battle is obscured by some doubt. There is ambiguity in official documents whether the *Hoel* was hit before or after Sprague issued his order to the destroyers, the "big boys," to make their torpedo attack. The TBS logs of several Taffy 3 warships record Sprague's order going out at 7:35 or 7:40, ten to fifteen minutes after the *Hoel* was hit, on her way in to attack, at 7:25. The log of the destroyer escort *Raymond*, relied upon by Samuel Eliot Morison and John Toland, places the order at 7:16, which makes more sense, since the *Hoel* survivors consistently assert that their ship got hit on the way in and that Kintberger did not act ahead of orders. Admiral Sprague's own published account of the battle suggests that he may have issued the order even earlier. Despite the twenty-nine minutes of ambiguity—and twenty-nine minutes is an eternity in a running battle—we do know with near certainty that the *Hoel* was first hit at 7:25.

brava, fire-controlman Marcellino Dilello, and soundman Otto Kumpunen were gone in an instant. A surreal cloud of green-dyed mist settled over the carnage.

Sitting in the pilothouse lookout's chair overlooking Gun 52, seaman first class Keith McKay felt a rush of wind around his left calf, looked down, and saw that shrapnel had shredded his dungarees. Blood was running down into his shoe, so he tied a red bandanna around his ankle. He looked down at the water sloshing around the deck of the bridge and saw that it ran not green but red. The reassuring rumble and grind of Bill Sanders's rotating Mark 37 gun director stopped, leaving only ominous silence from the shattered battle station above.

The blast spattered the *Hoel*'s passageways with the remains of breakfast: pork and beans and cinnamon rolls flew out of the galley and littered the decks. The cloud of vaporized green dye dispersed and seemed to drift down the length of the ship as the *Hoel* pressed ahead. Some men who saw it wondered what new horror the Japanese now unleashed. Cries of "Gas! Gas!" could be heard from panicked crew. Thrown from his chair at the helm, Clarence Hood regained consciousness on the starboard side of the pilothouse and saw that Lieutenant Dix had taken over the wheel. Commander Thomas and Captain Kintberger were both hurt, but their injuries were minor. Hood's were too, so he took back his post.

Miles to the north, Admiral Kurita saw an American ship erupt in smoke and flame, probably the *Hoel*, and the *Yamato*'s log recorded, "Cruiser observed blowing up and sinking at 0725."

With the fire-control radar gone, control of the *Hoel*'s guns fell to the CIC team, led by Lieutenants Green and Creamer. They were able to take ranges with the much less finely tuned surface-search radar. The two officers focused on lining up the torpedo attack and relaying range and bearing information to the guns. As the ship groped its way toward the oncoming fleet, Hoyt White, a radarman in the CIC, called out ranges and bearings of the Japanese cruisers to the gunners over the sound-powered phones: 13,000 yards . . . 12,500 yards . . . The men winced at every vibration and rattle as the shells struck near the ship.

Seeing the destruction with one's own eyes evoked one kind of fear; not being able to see it was perhaps worse. The men in the CIC or the radio shack or the engine room or the gun mounts or in any of the ship's other enclosed spaces were spared the horrid beauty of the red, green, yellow, and blue waterspouts rising around the ship. Hoyt White felt the *Hoel* reel and shudder, absorbing the blows. There was no telling how serious any particular hit was, or where the next one would strike. From time to time he found himself staring at the bulkhead that stood between him and the humid, smoky air and wondering when a round might burst through it, bearing his name.

*   *   *

AS THE THREE SMALL ships pressed through the squalls on their run against the Japanese heavy ships—the staggering *Hoel* in the lead, followed by the *Heermann* and the *Samuel B. Roberts*—a sight greeted them unlike any they had seen before: a smoking gray-black wreck of metal, crawling south as they charged north. It was the *Johnston.*

Limping along on one engine, with no hydraulic steering, the ship was a ruin. And yet somehow Captain Evans was pulling her through, returning to formation. Though the destroyer remained on a fairly even keel, the battering she had taken was all too evident. The mast had toppled down around the superstructure. The metal shields and bulkheads around the bridge and the stacks were blackened, torn, riddled, and dented like a coffee can on a backyard tree stump. How a ship in that condition could still make steam was for its engineers to explain.

By any fair measure, the *Johnston* was entitled to call it a day. Her torpedo tubes were empty. At her hobbled seventeen-knot speed, she couldn't keep up with the other destroyers on the way in. Sprague's carriers needed her smoke. Everyone on the *Johnston*'s bridge had heard the admiral's order, directing the "small boys" to form up and attack. Few if any believed it applied to their ship. Surely they weren't expected to turn around and go in again.

When Captain Evans saw the *Hoel* and the *Heermann,* with the *Samuel B. Roberts* lagging behind in column, he arrived at a different view of his obligation. As long as his ship had guns that worked, the Cherokee figured he could do something in a fight. He told his dumbstruck men on the bridge, "We'll go in with the destroyers and provide fire support." Evans ordered Ed DiGardi to bring the *Johnston* around astern the *Roberts* and informed his officers of the plan. Owing to steering difficulties, the destroyer made a complete circle before steadying on course. The *Johnston* fell in line with the three other ships, plying the shell-torn waters between them and the Japanese fleet. *Oh, dear Lord, I'm in for a swim,* Bob Hagen said to himself.

Twenty-seven

On the bridge of the *Hoel,* Commander Thomas watched the other escorts in the strung-out torpedo line while Captain Kintberger steadied the ship on her own firing course. Torpedo officer Lieutenant Coleman, who had moved from the bridge to torpedo mount number two, owing to the loss of communication with his mounts, took over the helm as ranges and bearings were called out by Green and Creamer in the CIC. The *Hoel's* torpedo mounts swung out to starboard. There a battleship loomed, at a range of ten thousand yards.

Kintberger bore in closer, fishtailing in to nine thousand yards off the starboard beam of a battleship, probably the *Kongo,* whose long dark form was visible intermittently through the smoke.

"Tube One—"

"One aye!"

"Half salvo, starboard side. . . . Steady now. Match pointers."

"Ready One."

"Stand by. Fire One!"

Five torpedoes rushed over the starboard rail and smacked the sea, running hot, straight, and normal. Kintberger ordered, "Left full rudder," and the *Hoel* leaned into the helmsman's hard turn of the wheel, running away to the south.

Belowdecks, amid the roar of the boilers and the 120-degree heat, water tender third class Francis Hofstrander felt the ship shudder as a Japanese shell entered the forward fireroom on the starboard side, just above the waterline. It blasted a hole in the hull two feet in diameter, blowing a spray of red-hot shrapnel into the men working the boilers. Many were injured, but mercifully the storm of metal left the steam lines intact. The space went dark, save for the beam of daylight entering through the bulkhead's newest porthole. No one's name had been on that oversized bullet. The roar of the boilers surged on.

Seconds later another salvo struck, and one of its shells was covered with names. It entered the after fireroom, shattering lines and setting loose a holocaust of superheated steam. Those who were not immediately scalded to death were trapped by the hot steam cloud that rose to the top of the compartment and gathered by the escape hatch, blocking their exit until it cooled and condensed. Sixteen of seventeen men died. A sailor named Vern Simmons was the compartment's sole survivor.

Another shell punched through the port side into the after engine room, making a clean two-foot hole just above the waterline and exploding against the heavy steel housing of the reduction gears, freezing the *Hoel*'s port screw. The destruction of the turbine shut down half the ship's electrical generating capacity too. A cloud of wayward steam escaped topside, engulfing the crew of Gun 53 amidships in white vapor. Another shell struck below them in the gun's handling room, starting a fire that laced the white clouds through with black smoke.

Live steam swamped the forty-millimeter gun on the port side amidships. Dick Santos, a radioman striker who was the trainer on that mount, had his feet and ankles burned so severely that he could not walk. Shrapnel peppered his back and legs. Bathed in steam, the position was fast becoming untenable, but Santos couldn't move. Ship's cook third class Jim Norris, with Santos, had a clear line of sight aft. He watched the shells hit Gun 53 and the engine and fireroom: "Guys were piling out of there screaming—some were scalded and some of them were on fire. God, it was awful. I didn't count the hits. Let's say there were too damn many." Rolling masses of superheated steam finally drove Norris away from his mount. He ran toward the bow and tried to get inside Gun 52, but the crew refused him and held the hatch shut. Norris climbed down the ladder running to the main deck from Gun 52's platform and heard men praying somewhere in an interior passageway. He came upon the bodies of pharmacist's mate third class John Quinn and ship's cook first class J. R. Lindsey lying sprawled on the deck. The sight of their corpses rinsing in bloody seawater made him retch.

Across the deck from Santos and Norris, the explosion lifted the heavy tub of the starboard forty-millimeter gun right off its revolving base. From within the steam cloud Larry Morris couldn't see a thing. When the whipping wind washed it away, the seaman first class realized that several of his crew, including his gun captain, had disappeared altogether.

Three more shells from God knew where rocked the *Hoel* astern, one near the base of Gun 55, freezing the mount in train. Another one whistled overhead, slicing off a length of Gun 54's barrel as cleanly as a giant blowtorch. The six-foot tube of hardened, rifled steel clanged to the deck and began rolling to and fro with the fantail's every tilt. The final shell from this deadly salvo struck the chemical smoke generators on the fantail, spewing white phosphorus across the deck, which burned and burrowed into sailors' exposed flesh.

"Stuff just flew all over us on the forty-millimeter gun," said Hugh Coffelt, the pointer on the mount aft of Gun 53. "We had no protection at all. The Japanese kept firing at us, with great success, sometimes missing though, and when they did miss, it sounded like a freight train passing by. Then they began to use shells that would explode over us. That was when I and others on the gun got hit with shrapnel. I got hit so hard that it knocked me off my seat to the deck. I was the only pointer on that forty-millimeter gun, and I still can't figure out how I was knocked off that seat to the deck, as I was hit in my left chest, not far from my heart."

After turning on the smoke generator at the start of the battle, Sam Lucas had little else to do. He didn't relish being a spectator to the horror unfolding around him, so he lay down on the deck between the depth charge racks and the gun shield of a fantail twenty-millimeter mount. He felt no need to see what came next. Seaman first class Marvin Compomizzo and signalman second class Charles Patterson lay down beside him. They could hear the severed barrel of Gun 54 lolling heavily back and forth across the pitching deck; the sound of an aircraft engine—it sounded low, down on the water, moving in, getting louder; the chatter of machine guns out over the water—they were not American guns. They heard the screams and shouts as men ran for cover. They heard the staccato crack of the *Hoel*'s twenties firing back. They felt the ship lurch hard three times from heavy hits amidships. Then Lucas felt something burning horribly on his neck and back. He did not want to know what it was. He was too scared to give it a great deal of thought.

Dye and shrapnel and asbestos and a soaking stench of blood—it all filled the air over and around the battered after section of the *Hoel*. Somehow the destroyer did not break up and sink, although even her designers at the Bureau of Ships and her builders at Mare Island might have expected any ship to do so under such a pummeling. The three-eighths-inch steel of her hull held.

Her rudder did not. At the helm quartermaster Clarence Hood found his wheel suddenly unresponsive. The *Hoel* still carried five torpedoes that needed to get in the water. But now the ship could not maneuver to fire them. The rudder was locked in a hard turn to port, leaving the ship steaming in a circle drawn tighter because only the starboard screw was propelling them now. The *Hoel* passed through a rainsquall, but the respite was too brief to do any lasting good.

As the wounded destroyer circled against her will, the air was cut by the whoosh and roar of the concentrated enemy fusillades. The *Kongo*, which loomed off its starboard beam when the first spread of torpedoes was fired, came into view again, this time to port, as the *Hoel* wheeled around and around, out of control, helpless to evade. Shells were hitting with terrifying regularity all around the ship. The Japanese battleship's imposing fourteen-inch rifles were mounted in pairs in sleek turrets, two forward, two aft. Now somehow the battleship's dark mass seemed to be shrinking into the distance, becoming smaller as it turned away from the *Hoel*. The *Kongo*'s lookouts had spied the *Hoel*'s first spread of torpedoes. Its helmsman turned to present the smallest profile to them. Looming into view, some six thousand yards off the port beam, came the Japanese heavy cruisers. Kintberger couldn't ignore them and hope to survive. Though the ship was still locked into its sickening turn, he could not wait for his steering to come back. He and Lieutenant Coleman knew what they had to do. They would launch their last five torpedoes on the fly or they would not do so at all.

"Get set to fire," Kintberger ordered. "Lead cruiser. All remaining fish. Stand by."

"Tube Two—train out to port—curve five ahead. Quick now. We're swinging fast. All ready? Fire!"

From his forty-millimeter gun amidships, Dick Santos saw a chief standing atop the torpedo mount, hammer in hand. One by one the chief brought down the mallet on the torpedoes' manual firing pins. They leaped out in succession and hit the water as the *Hoel* continued her inexorable turn to port.

Minutes passed as the ship and her weapons ran their separate courses. The ship traveled in a counterclockwise arc as the torpedoes sped straight across the arc's base. Lynn Lowry, the bridge messenger, gasped and pointed down at the water. He could see three torpedo wakes, running along the ship's bow on the port side. Could they be from the *Hoel*? Whatever their origin, the *Hoel* was in danger of running into their path. Instinctively, before realizing the futility of it, Lieutenant Dix shouted, "Right full rudder!" But the rudder was still dead. The big undersea missiles passed several feet ahead of the bow and continued on toward the cruisers, now almost dead ahead of the stricken destroyer. Dix didn't see it. "Too much was happening to stand and watch." But others saw the torpedoes stay on course. Lieutenant Coleman announced the countdown. At about the time the *Hoel*'s second salvo was scheduled to hit, columns of water were seen rising beside the storm-gray hull of an enemy man-of-war.

With her torpedoes now spent, somehow the *Hoel* had to regain steerage and return to the carriers. Quartermaster third class Donald Ulmanek, manning the after steering room, was ordered to commence manual steering from the aft steering engine compartment. Kintberger ordered all signalmen and lookouts on the bridge to go aft, join Ulmanek, and man the wheel powering the pump that turned the rudder. Somehow the *Hoel* needed to get back on station by the carriers, laying smoke, standing by, and protecting its herd. With the gyro out, Kintberger asked Fred Green which way south was. The boss of the CIC didn't need instruments to answer that one. He responded, "Put the sun on your port beam." Kintberger told Lynn Lowry, who was leaving for the steering engine room, to get ready to steer a 180-degree base course, with ten-degree zigzags to either side.

On one good engine Kintberger would race his stricken ship

against time, against the oncoming cruisers that were relentlessly closing the distance, and against the seawater flooding his sole functioning engine room. As flames heated the decks beneath their feet, volunteers for rudder-pump duty sprinted down both sides of the 376-foot ship, under a hail of shrapnel that rained down from the explosions overhead, past dead bodies, some dismembered and others startlingly intact, through slicks of blood and pork and beans and gobs of dye-stained asbestos insulation, and through the last gasps of steam rising from the engineering spaces below. Reaching the fantail, they grabbed the hatch leading to the steering engine room, cranked it open, and pulled it up. They shimmied down the ladder, looking to restore with muscle and sweat the steam power that enabled the ship to maneuver.

Twenty-eight

The *Fanshaw Bay*'s single open-mount five-inch gun was placed on the stern as if to anticipate the likeliest circumstance of its use: fending off an assailant while beating a flank-speed retreat. As the Japanese cruiser column closed range on the jeeps, Ziggy Sprague ordered the carriers to open fire with their "peashooters."

The flagship's gun sat inside a thirty-foot-diameter turntable mounted on ball bearings. Below it, Kight, Frisch, and Whitaker loaded the hoist that brought projectiles and powder cases to the gun deck. They would do twenty or so at a time, then climb up the ladder, sit down, watch the dim forms of the Japanese ships flash at them on the horizon, and feel their teeth rattle from the blast of the *Fanny B.*'s own gun. Then they would go back below and do it again. Though an electrical elevator did all the lifting, long summers spent hoeing corn, chopping cotton, and tossing eighty-pound hay bales put Kight in good enough shape to do a lot of it himself. The gun's recoil was considerably stronger, however. Once when he was on the ladder between decks, the gun discharged and the whole ship seemed to shove forward. Kight was jarred off the ladder and dropped through space, his hands clawing through fifteen feet of air.

Watching large enemy men-of-war shoot at his ship made an indelible impression on the twenty-one-year-old Oklahoma farm boy. "The Japs would fire their big guns," Kight said, "and you'd hear it—a roar of thunder right up close—and your pants would hit your leg from the concussion of the gun. . . . And then you could see the projectile coming through the air. It wasn't blurry, it was distinct— 2,800 pounds, the size of a Volkswagen coming through the air. It was a bulge of fire with a bullet in the middle of it. It made you want to get somewhere." Usually there would be fifteen or twenty seconds to make good an escape before the shell landed.

Kight considered it "natural for any individual to want to hide or get out of harm's way." On a CVE, hiding from enemy fire was at best a psychological game. At worst, it could be downright embarrassing. "One old boy was always looking for a place to hide. He said to me, 'Here, Kight, get on top of me.' " The sailor huddled down on the deck, and Kight climbed on top of him, wondering all the while what good it would have done. "The shell would have gone through both of us."

The peashooter crews on Taffy 3's carriers fired to good effect. An old chief on the *Fanshaw Bay* watched the *St. Lo*'s gunners popping away and saltily observed, "They oughta fire that thing underwater. We could use a little jet propulsion right now." But the guns proved to be surprisingly useful in their intended application. They scored three hits on a heavy cruiser at 14,000 yards, starting a raging fire on the forecastle. Meanwhile, the *White Plains* was doing its own unlikely imitation of a fighting ship of the line. As the enemy cruisers hammered away at shrinking range, a gunnery officer shouted out, "Just hold on a little longer, boys—we're sucking them into forty-millimeter range!"

The Japanese split their four cruisers into two columns, one looking to overtake the carriers to port, the other joining a group of destroyers and advancing to Sprague's starboard quarter. Between the two columns, lagging to the rear, Sprague could see the battleships. "The Japs were now firing at us from three sides. Within this three-sided 'box,' my carriers were formed in a large circle, with the destroyers and destroyer escorts in a larger circle around them. I kept this formation on a southwesterly course, squeezing over ten to twenty degrees to one side and then to the other, according to which side was throwing the hottest fire." The ships held formation and maneuvered together, their discipline impressing even Kurita's chief of staff, Tomiji Koyanagi. "I must admit admiration for the skill of their commanders," he would write.

High above the action, it was plain enough to VC-10 skipper Edward Huxtable what the Japanese commander was trying to do. Already the cruisers, beleaguered by buzzing planes though they were, had made frightening progress outrunning Taffy 3 to the east. For Sprague, further eastward flight was futile. Huxtable advised Sprague that the best course was now south. Of course, Sprague's radar told him all of this and more. By 7:30 the Taffy 3 commander was already charging hard to the south, now and then angling toward Samar to the southwest. As the pilots pressed home their attacks, word came over the radio that Taffy 3's destroyer screen was engaging the Japanese fleet, and pilots were cautioned not to hit the inbound American ships.

Sprague's decision to turn from a southeasterly heading to the southwesterly one was risky. By turning right so sharply, he would give the Japanese a chance to turn inside him, cutting into his circular route and bearing down fast on his starboard broadside. Nevertheless, he felt the need to turn in the direction of help, toward Leyte Gulf, where Oldendorf's battleships lay. And if the Japanese didn't catch on in time, Sprague might open some distance between Taffy 3 and its pursuers.

With visibility down to half a mile and with the clouds hovering at a ceiling of 500 feet, Sprague ordered a turn to a course of 200 degrees. Kurita did not get wind of the audacious maneuver until Taffy 3 had emerged from the rainsquall. The Japanese admiral followed the escort carrier formation around in this clockwise quarter-circle, his pursuit slowed by the frequent need to evade the incessant, piecemeal attacks of the hell-for-leather American aviators. Ziggy Sprague had gambled—and, for now, won.

*   *   *

BLUE ARCHER AND THE rest of the planes from the *Kalinin Bay* needed just a few minutes to find the Japanese fleet. When Pops Keighley's radio malfunctioned, Patsy Capano took the lead. At about 7:50 they happened upon a column of destroyers. Capano, Keighley, and

Archer came out of the clouds and went right down the line, firing short bursts from their wing-mounted machine guns. The flight of Avengers climbed back into the clouds and joined with seven other Avengers and ten Wildcats hunting for bigger ships.

Within minutes an echelon of cruisers and battleships came into view. On cue from Capano, the pilots turned and plummeted. Third in line, Archer dove at two cruisers as they leaned hard into a left-ward turn. From 4,500 feet, Archer dropped all four bombs and landed two good hits. He recovered, climbed, and circled around again. Time to use the rockets. The ordnance crews on the *Kalinin Bay* aligned the rockets to follow the same path the machine-gun bullets traversed, converging a thousand feet ahead of the plane. Pushing over in a thirty-degree dive on another heavy cruiser, Archer squeezed short bursts from his wing guns to keep his aim true. Then, a thousand feet out, he pressed the button on the top of his stick and let his eight rockets fly.

Archer had become proficient using rockets at Saipan and Guam, knocking out tanks and large trucks and small houses with the weapons in support of the Marines advancing inland. Now he watched them walk up the fo'c'sle of the cruiser. Two of them hit the bridge, exploding brightly and appearing to knock loose some steel weather shields around the main superstructure.

The light bomb loads that some of the pilots carried led them to wonder what precisely they ought to be trying to accomplish. Two other pilots from the *Kalinin Bay,* whose radio call sign was "Georgia," debated whether to attack some destroyers they had found or seek out larger quarry. Tom Van Brunt, a *St. Lo* pilot returning from the aborted morning antisubmarine patrol with the other VC-65 fliers, heard a squeaky voice over his headset:

"*This is 81 Georgia. Are there any other Georgia planes in the area?*"

A low, slow southern drawl came in reply. "*This is 84 Georgia. I have you in sight. I'll join up.*"

"*This is 81 Georgia. What kind of arms do you have?*"

"*I'm loaded with hundred-pound antipersonnel bombs. What do you have?*"

"*I have the same loading. What kind of target do you think we should take, 84 Georgia?*"

"We better try one of them destroyers."

"This is 81 Georgia. I'm senior to you, and I think we ought to attack a battleship."

"This is 84 Georgia," the voice drawled. *"Won't do no good."*

Now 81 Georgia drew on a source of motivation far more powerful than mere rank: *"84 Georgia, if you're scared, go back to the carrier."*

"This is 84 Georgia. I'll go anywhere you go, God damn it!"

The Japanese cruisers endured a savage strafing attack by the fighter pilots of Taffy 3. Lt. Jim Murphy of the *Kalinin Bay's* VC-3 found the Japanese fleet almost immediately upon clearing the rainsquall that was drenching the carrier's decks.

He owed the honor of flying that day to his fleetness of foot: he had beaten his executive officer Gil Halliday by a few steps to the last plane on the flight deck. "Little Murph" was prepared to yield to superior rank, but Halliday yielded to speed. Murphy had gotten there first—"Go ahead," Halliday said, "and good luck." Murphy took off at 7:25, the last plane off the ship.

He joined Lt. Ken Hippe and Ens. George Heinmiller in strafing a heavy cruiser. Over Leyte the day before, Lieutenant Hippe had become an ace in seven minutes, shooting down five twin-engine Lily bombers that were headed for MacArthur's troops. Hippe's targets now were considerably larger, if less prone to disintegrating under his guns. Pushing over and diving down as if riding an invisible waterfall, the pilots made three runs before becoming separated. Murphy then formed up with Lt. Leonard Porterfield and dove on another cruiser. Porterfield told Murphy he was out of bullets and headed for Tacloban. Little Murph's next dance partner was Ens. Paul Hopfner, who formed up on his wing and helped him ruin a Japanese destroyer's day.

The fire that met the pilots over the fleet was considerable. "How those Japs could shoot so many guns and still not hit anyone really had me fooled," wrote Murphy. But there was little doubt as to the effectiveness of the pilots' own shooting. After his second pass on the cruisers, Murphy noted with satisfaction that the Japanese ships were maneuvering to avoid them.

*　　*　　*

THE *KALININ BAY* TOOK her first hits at 7:50, just as Blue Archer was firing his rockets at the heavy cruiser. Steaming on the windward side of the formation, exposed to view as the smoke screen was blown west, the carrier absorbed Japanese cruiser shells at the rate of about one a minute. Some skipped like rocks over her deck, gouging the wooden flight deck and showering splinters into the air. In total the fragile CVE took fifteen hits from the cruisers' eight-inch main batteries.

One shell breached the port side of the hull just above the machine shop, angled down through the machine shop, and burst in the freshwater tank and the fuel oil settling tanks. While investigating the extent of the damage to the critical oil tanks, engineering officer Lt. George H. Keeler could hear loud crashes and other novel sounds of material fracture and stress, "but above all others we could hear men screaming."

The shells' screeching impacts scrapped the innards of the *Kalinin Bay* right before the crew's horrified eyes. Armor-piercing shells penetrated the thin hull and flight deck without exploding, turning the ship into an oversized colander. Shells hitting below the waterline let torrents of ocean water rush in.

In a narrow wedge of a compartment at the very bow of the ship, seaman first class Morris Turner was up to his waist in water pouring in through two holes left by a shell that had punched clean through both sides of the hull, right at the waterline. Mattresses and large corks and pillows floated all around him as he struggled to keep the debris clear of the intake of the submersible pump he was operating. Other sailors in the compartment pressed mattresses up against the shell holes. But every time the ship moved out of a wave trough and plunged into another swell, the sudden increase in water pressure shoved aside the mattresses and forced more water in.

Standing in the rising water, Turner had trouble gaining leverage against the incoming flow. After hours of work, struggling to keep the pumps operating and the inflow down, he and the other sailors brought the water down to a manageable level. In so doing they very likely saved their ship. If the compartment had failed, the *Kalinin Bay*'s bow would have plowed under the sea, the swamped ship would have lost her speed and seaworthiness, and in all probability the Japanese would have caught her. She would have met that fate no matter the heroics of her crew. Escort carriers were not built to take fifteen major-caliber hits and survive. But the *Kalinin Bay* did just that. Shells damaged her degaussing cables and tore shelving and ruptured bulkheads and opened the hull to flooding. They ripped six holes in the flight deck and wrecked support beams below it. They punctured lube oil tanks, contaminating the ship's freshwater system, ruined radio and radar gear, sprayed compartments with metal splinters, filled passageways with noxious fumes and gases, ignited acetylene bottles, started electrical fires, and rendered bunkrooms uninhabitable. The extent of the ship's luck was truly staggering.

The day before one well-placed Japanese bomb had sunk Halsey's light carrier, the *Princeton*; a single torpedo had once filled the skies with the remains of the *Liscome Bay*. Somehow now, however, the CVE known as the *Lucky K.* took fifteen hard blows from heavy cruiser shells—at least five of which exploded—and sailed on with just five dead and fifty-five wounded. It is astounding that her losses were not far, far higher.

*   *   *

AT 7:50 ADMIRAL KURITA'S force was spread out over fifteen miles of ocean as it pursued Sprague's fleeing carriers. The crippled *Kumano*, assisted by the *Suzuya*, lagged behind as the westernmost Japanese ship as she completed the transfer of Admiral Shiraishi's flag. The light cruiser *Noshiro*, heading a column of seven destroyers, passed the two crippled heavy cruisers to their north but, forced to circle by vicious strafing attacks by Wildcat fighters, came onto a southward course that carried her away from the eastward-charging *Yamato*, the *Nagato*, and the *Haruna*. Northeast of the three other battleships, the *Kongo* was running southeast and turning a wide clockwise circle as she traced the course of the four heavy cruisers in line ahead of her. Those four ships—the *Tone*, the *Chikuma*, the *Haguro*, and the *Chokai*—on the other side of a large rainsquall from the *Yamato*, ran south by southeast, turning an arc through the compass toward the south, matching Ziggy Sprague's circular course.

As the Japanese cruisers bore down on the jeep carriers, the American pilots stepped up the tempo of their attacks, buzzing the ships with the ferocity of hornets, determined to drive them back at whatever cost. According to Ziggy Sprague:

The Wildcat pilots were given a free hand to strafe, with the hope that their strafing would kill personnel on the Japanese ships, silence automatic weapons, and, most important, draw attention from the struggling escort carriers. Sometimes two, or four, Wildcats would join up for a strafing run. Again, a Wildcat would join up and run interference for an Avenger. Then, likely as not, it would turn out that the Avenger had no torpedo or bomb and was simply making a dummy run. When their ammunition gave out, the fighters also made dry runs to turn the pursuers. Lt. Paul Garrison, of Seaside, Oregon, made twenty strafing runs, ten of them dry.

"The attack was almost incessant," Kurita's operations officer, Cdr. Tonosuke Otani, would write, "but the number of planes at any one instant was few. The bombers and torpedo planes were very aggressive and skillful, and the coordination was impressive; even in comparison with the great experience of American attack that we had already had, this was the most skillful work of your planes."

Twenty-nine

Lt. (jg) Thomas J. Lupo, an Avenger pilot from the *Fanshaw Bay*, was one of the first pilots to reach Tacloban once the initial wave of attacks by Taffy 3's pilots had crested and broken and scattered in search of a place to land. The VC-68 flier had made run after run with his squadronmates, dropping his bomb load, exhausting his ammunition, and capping off his morning by throwing assorted loose items from his cockpit at the Japanese fleet: a Coke bottle, a navigation board, and other vaguely ballistic miscellany.

He was a wild sort of kid, with a dangerous look and a reckless demeanor. His father, a New Orleans real estate developer, had tried to keep his son on a productive track, paying an architectural firm to hire him during his summers off from Tulane. But ultimately he was not optimistic about Tommy's future. The kid was given to crazy stunts: driving his convertible from the backseat with his feet on the steering wheel, drinking all night, playing pranks, chasing girls. Once his dad had tried to warn off Tommy's bride-to-be, declaring to her father, "Don't you let that girl get involved with my son. That boy will never amount to anything."

True to form, Lupo's interest in aviation seemed to grow out of defiance of his parents' will. In high school he sold enough magazine subscriptions to earn a trip by air to New York, but his parents refused to let him go. When news arrived that the Japanese had struck Pearl Harbor, Lupo was playing poker with his buddies at the house. He seized the chance for an even grander adventure. They broke up the game on the spot and ran down to the New Orleans customs house, looking to enlist. By the time he was in operational flight training at Otay Mesa, California, Tommy Lupo still hadn't kicked his inclination for derring-do. He was always happy to demonstrate his aileron control by buzzing the marshes low enough to whip up a storm of mud with his propeller wash. But he was also a proficient torpedo pilot. During the Saipan campaign he had had more than a few chances to put his dash into useful service on ground support missions against the dug-in Japanese. Such was the genius of the Navy's Bureau of Personnel to channel the rowdiness of youth toward productive ends.

Lupo eased back the throttle of his Avenger and landed on Tacloban, weaving across the muddy tarmac pocked with bomb and artillery craters and strewn with wrecked machinery. As a relatively new acquisition for its U.S. Army conquerors, the field was still pitted by the handiwork of American bombers and strewn with the remains of Japanese aircraft. Army engineers and Seabees, as the men of the Navy's construction battalion were called, were working to rehabilitate the airstrip. They were pouring truckloads of crushed coral into the muddy patches around the strip, laying a base on which to lay steel-mesh Marston runway matting. But the mud was deep, and so the coral vanished "like chunks of vanilla ice cream into a sarsaparilla soda." Lupo brought his torpedo bomber down onto a reasonably solid stretch of runway, cut his engine, and rolled to a stop.

The first person Lupo saw upon climbing out of the cockpit of the "Bayou Bomber" was an Army bulldozer operator. Knowing that any fighter planes that landed on the field would need more space than he had needed to land safely, Lupo asked the bulldozer driver to clear some more room at the end of the runway. Then, spying crates of ammunition, pyramids of 250-pound bombs, and drums of fuel stockpiled alongside the airfield, Lupo demanded to know who was in charge of the operation. The driver pointed to an Army major.

The major was already more than a little interested in who had dared park a Navy plane on his airfield, which was still in the care of the Army engineers and their bulldozers, trucks, and roller rigs and would soon be home to a Marine night fighter squadron that was setting up for operations. Lupo told him of the desperate naval battle raging over the horizon to the northeast. "We've got six jeep carriers out there under attack, and our planes have nowhere to land and rearm," Lupo said. "I'd like to get some of this fuel and those bombs and ammunition so we can bring our planes here, load them up, and get back out there."

The major took a dim view of the request. "We've got a war going on here too. I can't give you this stuff. I've got planes coming here in seven to ten days—P-51s and P-47s—and these bombs are for them."

"I have to tell you, Major, if we don't get these bombs and stop this Jap fleet, they're gonna come in here and bomb the hell out of this place and maybe recapture it. Then *their* planes will be dropping these bombs on *you*. I've gotta have these bombs, sir, or we'll have a disaster on our hands." Lupo asked who the major's superior was.

The Army officer mentioned a colonel who was stationed out toward the front. "He's out fighting a war, and I'm not going to bother him."

"Well," Lupo said, "that's just too bad."

The pilot pulled out his service revolver and pointed it at the major. Then Lupo handed the pistol to his radioman, Earl Gifford, instructing the flabbergasted aircrewman to hold the Army officer at bay. Lupo climbed into the cockpit of his plane and hailed the *Fanshaw Bay* on the radio. His fellow pilots from VC-68 and other Taffy 3 squadrons were already inbound.

Army antiaircraft gunners opened fire on a gaggle of strange planes circling the field. It took them only a few beats to recognize they were Navy aircraft. Gradually awakening to the dire circumstances of Sprague's fleet and his daring aviators, the men at Tacloban cleared the way for the pilots to land. The strip wasn't ready. The six inches of loose black sand that covered the field when Taffy 3's aviators arrived was a lousy surface to land on. Making matters worse, there were as yet no communications facilities in place to guide the planes in; no service squadrons to refuel and rearm them and take the wounded pilots to field hospitals; no airdrome or control tower to coordinate the traffic and determine how the planes would be parked. The result was going to be chaos.

The first plane from the new group touched down on a solid stretch of runway, sped forward, caught its landing gear in the soft sand, and pitched forward onto its nose. The pilot coming in behind him, seeing the wreck, pulled out of his landing approach and roared away for another pass. At that, the rest of the inbound planes dispersed "like a flight of birds at the first crack of a shotgun," an observer wrote.

Unexpectedly, a voice came on the pilots' radio circuit: *"Navy planes, Navy planes. This is Tacloban airstrip, beneath you. Can you hear me? Come in, please."* It was a young Army Air Force officer with Tacloban's fighter control group, Lt. Edward Worrad. Driving a radio-equipped jeep as the planes were circling, he was accompanied by a Navy radio liaison officer, Lt. Russell Forrester, in another radio jeep. Stranded ashore, Forrester had been champing at the bit for days as battles raged in the waters all around him. Now he was finally in a position to help. As Worrad stayed in touch with the planes in the air, Forrester made contact with the Seventh Fleet's air controller in Leyte Gulf and informed him of Tacloban's availability. A third man, Sgt. Sam Halpern from Tacloban's service squadron, joined them, checking out the planes that Worrad guided down.

Before long the three men had pieced together an out-of-pocket air control and support squad. Hastily mustering a plane-handling gang from members of the 305th Airdrome Squadron, they helped dozens of Navy Wildcats and Avengers land on the Army field as the battle raged off Samar. The Army volunteers righted flipped aircraft, extinguished fires, and loaded bombs onto the unfamiliar Navy planes. The pilots pitched in, helping to arm and service their planes before taking off again. Japanese air raids were sporadic throughout the day. And friendly planes posed hazards too. Some pilots who took off amid the fragilely managed chaos experienced harrowing and unsolicited games of chicken: an Avenger landing and taxiing down the strip south to north, while a Wildcat roared overhead, taking off north to south. It was not by-the-book airfield management, but they got the job done.

Serviced and flown off with the help of Army personnel and Navy pilots, the pilots hooked up with Navy air control through Lieutenant Forrester's jeep radio and were vectored to strike at the Japanese fleet. Fuel and oil trucks skirted around the edge of the strip, their drivers diving flat onto the black sand whenever strafing Japanese planes came in. At one point a trio of enemy fighters flew in so low that Sam Halpern mistook them for friendlies in the pattern and gave them a green light to land. Incoming planes were waved off while eight big graders and four rollers lumbered across the tarmac, flattening out the little hills and dales of sand made by taxiing aircraft. As soon as they cleared the strip, waves of Navy fliers roared in again. Only eight planes were total losses at Tacloban that day. Not a single pilot trying to land there was killed.

*　　*　　*

BLUE ARCHER, OUT OF ammo, flew wide circles over and around the Japanese fleet, dropping down to make dry runs on them before passing out of range, climbing again, and wheeling around for another run. Working from three or four thousand feet, he would dive to a few hundred feet over his targets and let his gunner and radioman take potshots at whatever targets were handy. After several such runs his gunner, in the ball turret, and his radioman, on the bilge gun below, both reported they were out of slugs. Archer was ready to call it a day and head for Tacloban. But then he heard a message from the carriers requesting a torpedo attack. This suggested desperate circumstances.

Whoever sent the message had to have known there were few torpedoes in circulation among Taffy 3's planes. Archer waved his wings, signaling two other pilots to form up on him. He passed through a squall and got down on the water, running straight for a battleship. Then it happened. The shell exploded no more than twenty yards ahead of him. "It was like running into a brick wall," he recalled. Slumped in his seat with a concussion and a back injury that made him numb, Archer fought through the pain and looked to his left. Where a second before there had been a pilot flying on his wing, now all he saw was a cloud of indeterminate aircraft parts hurtling in every direction.

Archer kept his course toward the battleship. He opened his bomb bay doors for show, hoping to persuade the dreadnought to veer from its course. Then, as he began to pull up over the ship, Archer rolled his Avenger over on its back and took his .38-caliber service revolver from its holster.

Running on anger born of pain and not a little adrenaline, he squeezed the trigger repeatedly, sending six rounds into the dark superstructure of the battleship. As he flew over the warship, Archer noticed that the Japanese gunners had stopped firing at him. The Arkansan swears he saw the faces of Japanese bridge personnel staring up at him in bewilderment. He surmised then, and believes to this day, that the Japanese saw him and, seeing his narrow facial lines, goatee, and squinting appearance, took him for a Japanese pilot flying a captured plane and mistook his pistol shots for signals of some kind.

Archer loitered over the enemy fleet for thirty more minutes, reporting their movements over the open frequency to the air officer on the *Kalinin Bay* before flying to Tacloban and landing at Lieutenant Worrad's airstrip.

Thirty

For Captain Hathaway, conning the *Heermann* through the cantering herd of CVEs amid heavy smoke, spray, and fog en route to joining the torpedo run had been no minor adventure. The *Heermann* had nearly collided with the *Roberts* and the *Hoel* on the way to attack. Now that his destroyer was clear of the carriers, navigation was the least of his troubles. The sea all around the ship boiled with enemy salvos.

When the nearest Japanese ship, a *Tone*-class heavy cruiser, was just nine thousand yards away, Hathaway ordered a half salvo of five torpedoes fired at her. With the tubes trained per executive officer Lt. Bill Carver's coordinates, chief torpedoman Arthur Owens ordered mount number one to fire her five fish. But when the command went out—*"Fire one . . . Fire two"*—the tube trainer on the second torpedo mount got excited and fired two of the five torpedoes he was supposed to be reserving for a second attack. Before the mount captain could stop him, they jumped out and ran parallel to their counterparts, leaving only three torpedoes for the second launch. The *Heermann*'s seven torpedoes left the ship cleanly, hot, straight, and normal.

Though Bill Carver reported over the sound-powered phones four large contacts, giving their range off the port bow, Harold Whitney, the *Heermann*'s chief yeoman, couldn't see them. No one could as yet: "It was an odd day—one moment the sun was shining and the sky seemed clear as a bell, and the next moment you were in a rain-squall and it was dark as night. The rain blotted out our radar, and we had no way of knowing how close we were to the battleships." Suddenly the *Heermann* emerged from a squall, and all too clearly, dead ahead, lay the four largest ships Kurita had. Lt. Bill Meadors, the gunnery officer, could see two *Kongo*-class battleships advancing in column. Beyond them, looming in the haze, were two ships that looked even bigger. Whitney figured the *Heermann* would be sunk on the spot. The bigger ships, however, seemed to be having trouble targeting the small destroyer at close range.

Lieutenant Meadors had the *Haruna* square in the sights of his director scope. He could see the battleship's four double-barrel fourteen-inch main turrets, housing rifles fifty-four feet long, turned out to starboard in a frightening array. Flashes and smoke seemed to swallow the ship each time it fired. First the front and back turrets fired, and four shells screamed overhead at mast level, hitting the ocean a thousand yards beyond the destroyer. Then the two high-mounted turrets let go. The *Heermann* madly returned fire all along. Lieutenant Meadors had the firing key closed, which caused the guns to discharge as soon as their projectile trays were rammed into the breech. Another roar came from the *Haruna*, a full broadside, and the battleship's four turrets, flashing as one, "illuminated the entire ocean on our starboard hand," Meadors wrote. The eight heavy rounds screamed overhead and missed.

Salvos from the *Haruna* and three other battleships raised walls of water all around the ship. The colorful towers blotted out the blue and gray skies. Watching the near misses bracketing his ship and cascading over his superstructure made Amos Hathaway "wish [he] had a periscope with which to see over the wall of water." "Everything looked rosy," he would write, "but only because the splashes were colored red by the dye loads."

The *Haruna*'s gunnery officer, Cdr. Masao Gondaira, saw the sleek lines of his antagonist and believed he was dueling a heavy cruiser. Harold Whitney had fewer illusions as he played a pointless game of hide-and-seek with the inbound bombardment: "The guns of the leading Jap blazed, and I could see three little dots, looking like rusty spots in the sky, coming directly at me. The little rusty spots came on, and I ducked behind the wing of the bridge, a little thin piece of metal that wouldn't stop a .45-caliber pistol slug." The first salvos missed, slapping the sea in a ladder pattern three hundred yards long. Whitney looked up and saw that the ship's signal halyards had been cut in two and the rangefinder had been lopped off. As he was looking up, something smaller hit them—a small shell or maybe some shrapnel—and wooden splinters flew, the remnants of the motor whaleboat blown from its davits.

Lieutenant Meadors's five main battery crews fired some 260 shells at the battleship. From close range, four to eight thousand yards away, Meadors watched his shells explode all along the ship's menacing form. It was anyone's guess what damage the fifty-four-pound rounds did to the armored giant. Judging by the smoke and flame that wreathed the battlewagon's towering superstructure, it was reasonable to think the destroyer was giving back a little bit of the hell that had engulfed the bridges of the *Johnston* and the *Hoel* shortly before. From what Meadors could see, the effect was considerable. About four minutes went by during which the *Haruna* lay broadside to the destroyer but did not fire at all.

While all this was happening, the *Heermann*'s seven torpedoes bubbled on their course. The last three had been fired without the aid of mechanical rangefinding. Whitney took ranges from the surface radar and relayed them to Owens, who calmly turned the dials on the torpedo mount. With a sudden release of compressed air, the torpedoes were on their way.

It took less than ten minutes for Hathaway's destroyer to fire seven torpedoes at a heavy cruiser, change course toward the battleship line, engage the lead vessel with main batteries, fire three more torpedoes, and turn to speed away. Few warships in history had ever spent ten minutes more productively. At 8:03 Hathaway returned to the pilothouse from the open-air bridge and raised Ziggy Sprague on the TBS radio. His message was remarkable for its professional nonchalance: *"My exercise is completed. Over."* Hathaway wondered at his own choice of words until he recognized his instinct that the Japanese might be eavesdropping on the circuit, in which event there was no need to inform them that his ship had fired the last of its torpedoes.

Shortly thereafter, as if to reward Amos Townsend Hathaway for his brio and dash—the only destroyer captain in history to engage directly four battleships supported by heavy cruisers and live to tell the tale—a cloud of black smoke boiled up near the stern of the *Haruna*, beneath its hindmost fourteen-inch turret. The visual evidence was followed closely by a deep blast rumbling across the water. A torpedo from the *Heermann*'s final spread of three appeared to have scored.

Ironically, however, it may have been the first fan of torpedoes, all seven of which seemed to miss, that did Ziggy Sprague the most good. They sizzled off to the north, missing their intended target, the cruiser. Continuing on, they approached the battleship *Yamato*. At 7:56 a lookout on Kurita's flagship signaled the warning, "WATCH OUT FOR TORPEDO TRACKS." Then the *Nagato* spotted three tracks approaching to starboard. Duly warned, the vessel's commander, Adm. Yuji Kobe, ordered a hard turn to port. As the wakes of the torpedoes passed alongside the *Nagato* to starboard, the battleship opened fire on a "cruiser"—probably the *Heermann*—at a close range of 9,400 yards.

All of a sudden two more torpedoes were seen approaching the *Yamato* to port. The helmsman turned her rudder hard over to port, putting the superbattleship on a northward course, away from its quarry, so as to present the smallest possible profile to the torpedoes. It was a panicked decision. Admiral Ugaki should have turned *toward* the torpedoes, combing their tracks in pursuit rather than in retreat. For ten decisive minutes—"it felt like a month to me," wrote Ugaki—the parallel spreads hemmed in the great ship, pinning her into an outbound course.

The instinct for survival demonstrated by the *Yamato*'s commander seemed to put the lie to any notion that the Center Force was on a one-way mission, driven by the "heavenly guidance" that Admiral Toyoda had invoked from Combined Fleet Headquarters. At the moment of decision the officers of the *Yamato* succumbed to the universal impulse to save their ship. They held the course north until the torpedoes' alcohol reservoirs burned dry. By the time the undersea missiles ceased their pursuit, disappearing into the four-thousand-fathom depths of the Philippine Trench, Ugaki had taken the *Yamato*'s sixty-nine-foot-long guns, and the Center Force's brain trust, clear out of the battle. In the engagement's first minute, Kurita had forfeited control of his fleet by ordering a hurried general attack. Now, having fallen back more than thirty thousand yards from the

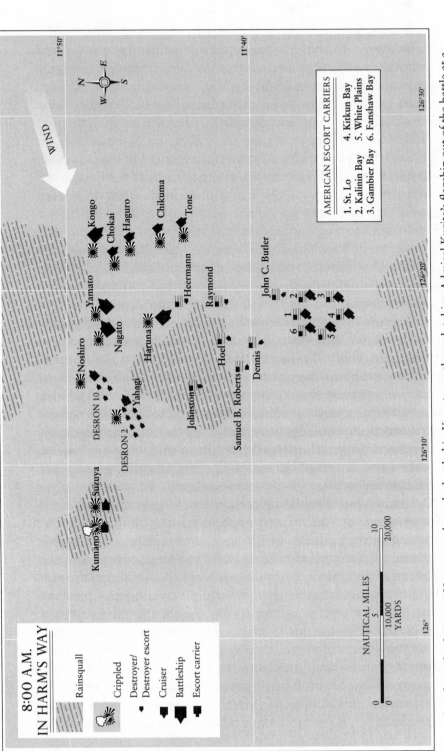

8:00 A.M.
IN HARM'S WAY

Rainsquall

Crippled

Destroyer/
Destroyer escort

Cruiser

Battleship

Escort carrier

NAUTICAL MILES
0   5   10
0   10,000   20,000
YARDS

WIND

N
W   E
S

Kongo
Chokai
Haguro
Chikuma
Tone

Yamato

Noshiro

DESRON 10

Nagato

Yahagi

DESRON 2

Haruna

Heermann

Raymond

John C. Butler

Johnston

Hoel

Samuel B. Roberts

Dennis

6 1 2 3
5 4

Suzuya

Kumano

AMERICAN ESCORT CARRIERS
1. St. Lo   4. Kitkun Bay
2. Kalinin Bay   5. White Plains
3. Gambier Bay   6. Fanshaw Bay

11°50'

11°40'

126°   126°10'   126°20'   126°30'

Torpedoes from the destroyer *Heermann* chase the battleship *Yamato* northward, taking Admiral Kurita's flagship out of the battle at a critical moment. Meanwhile, Japanese heavy cruisers, led by the *Tone* and the *Chikuma*, press down on the escort carrier formation. The *Samuel B. Roberts*, still not hit, engages enemy battleships and heavy cruisers at fleeing escort carriers, he lost what limited ability he retained to command and direct his force.

*   *   *

AT 7:50 A.M., AS Admiral Stump's Taffy 2 carriers were launching the last of their first air strike in support of Taffy 3—a raid comprising fifteen Avengers and twenty Wildcats—Admiral Sprague radioed to his destroyer escorts, *"All small boys go in and launch torpedo attack."* The *Johnston* and the *Hoel* had already passed into harm's way and launched their fish; the *Roberts* and the *Heermann* were at that moment only minutes away from releasing theirs. The new order sprang the *Dennis* and the *Raymond* into action. The *John C. Butler,* laying smoke on the far southern side of the formation, was out of position to intercept the speeding enemy cruisers.

It was preposterous to send a destroyer escort against an enemy's main surface fleet. They didn't do it on paper at the Naval War College, and it had not happened in the whole course of the war leading up to October 25. As the *Dennis* and the *Raymond* sortied, Bob Copeland's ship was fighting like a true hunter-killer, bidding to take down a heavy cruiser on the open sea. The *Hoel* had fired two salvos of five torpedoes each. The *Heermann* had fired seven, then three. If Copeland was lucky, the *Samuel B. Roberts* would soon be in position to fire her single salvo of three.

In a quieter time, in Hawaii, before the ship's departure for the far reaches of the western Pacific combat zone, the admiral who commanded U.S. destroyer forces in the Pacific had informed Copeland that he had recommended replacing the *Roberts*'s torpedo tubes with a new forty-millimeter gun mount. Copeland had surprised even himself with the tenor of his refusal: "Admiral, someday somebody is going to forget we're boys and send us over to do a man's work. If I'm ever sent to do a man's work, I want a man's weapons." Then Copeland smiled a little. "Admiral, as far as my ship is concerned, the torpedo tubes will be removed over my dead body." Due either to Copeland's persuasive skills or to lack of follow-through by the bureaucracy, the *Samuel B. Roberts* left Pearl Harbor with her one triple torpedo mount in place.

Now her captain had a chance to do what no destroyer escort had done before and actually use them against an enemy heavy.

Copeland was glad he hadn't wasted precious time trying to form up with the other DEs on the far side of Taffy 3's ring formation. Like Captains Evans, Kintberger, and Hathaway before him, Copeland knew that his first and only chance to stagger a larger foe depended on his performance now.

As the *Roberts* closed on the cruiser line, Lt. Bill Burton, Copeland's gun boss, was anxious to open fire with his two five-inch guns. Burton's two gun crews were primed and ready. But there were still about thirteen thousand yards of ocean between the *Roberts* and her target, a sleek heavy cruiser, probably the *Chokai,* steaming off the starboard bow. Every few minutes he asked, "Captain, may I open fire?" His skipper thought he had "ants in his pants." Copeland didn't want to waste valuable five-inch ammunition at extended range, where aim was dicey and hitting power diminished. He wanted to get closer, and so far, so good. He doubted the Japanese ship had yet spotted him. The sea through which the little ship charged was wreathed in smoke from the destroyers that had attacked ahead of her. Though numerous targets presented themselves, Copeland denied Burton's request to open fire. The gunnery officer kept the requests coming until finally Copeland shouted, "God damn it, Mr. Burton, I'll let you know when you may open fire!"

Through smoke that was thick but intermittent, Copeland's visibility alternated between about five miles and zero. On the radar scope's PPI screen, he could see the two green-white slivers of the American destroyers running south toward him. Aided by the scope, he had little risk of a collision, poor visibility or none. The torpedo attack was in excellent hands; Bob Roberts was lining it up. The exec wanted to close to five thousand yards and launch the three fish on a high-speed, forty-five-knot setting. At that speed, and from that range, the torpedoes would be difficult for the target cruiser to spot and avoid. Seated on the triple torpedo mount, chief torpedoman Rudy Skau had his speed-setting wrench in hand, preparing to match his aiming pointers to the coordinates relayed by the exec.

Suddenly there was a windy, ripping rush and a crash of metal as a Japanese shell passed through the *Roberts*'s rigging. The shell severed the radio antenna, and a large section of it, carrying a mass of dangling wires, fell down across the deck, whipping over Skau's hand, nearly breaking it, and knocking the wrench into the water before the adjustments could be made. The torpedoes lay in their tubes, still set on intermediate speed. A spare wrench was kept down in the torpedo shack, but Roberts and Skau both knew there was no time to fetch it.

As the *Samuel B. Roberts* closed with its target, Bob Roberts reran the firing solution in his head: the enemy's course and speed, and its range and bearing off the bow, determined the torpedo speed, deflection, and gyro setting. The variables were complex, and over the long course of a three-mile range to target, even a small error could become magnified into a gross inaccuracy. But the exec, quick with calculations, managed his best guess and shouted the tube train settings down to Chief Skau.

The *Chokai* was unleashing withering fire from her forward eight-inch batteries. But her gunners were not targeting the *Roberts*. They either did not see or did not care about the small ship with the low silhouette. No shells landed near her, though the shells arcing high overhead toward the carriers—or perhaps it was the blasts of the gun muzzles themselves—buffeted the destroyer escort with their turbulence.

Time seemed to stop, yet before Copeland knew it, the *Roberts* was just four thousand yards from the cruiser line, a little over two miles, and his three torpedoes were waterborne, racing toward the cruisers on Bob Roberts's improvised firing solution. On the broad ocean's surface four thousand yards was point-blank range.

Copeland, his ship as yet unscathed, ordered a hard left rudder, turning the *Roberts* back through her own smoke and toward the carriers. Down below, Lieutenant Trowbridge brought every pound of steam pressure on line. The deck shook from the twin turbines' whining, roaring labors. The ship ran past its rated limits, to twenty-eight and a half knots and possibly beyond. As time ran down on the torpedo run—three or four minutes—Copeland indulged himself with a peek astern. Through a gap in the smoke, he was treated to the sight of a steaming column of water and flame rising from below the after mast of what he took for an *Aoba*-class cruiser. Possibly it was the *Chokai*. As the *Samuel B. Roberts* raced back to her station to lay smoke by the carriers, Copeland heard someone yell, "We got her!" A cheer went up from all hands on deck, as if someone had hit a late-inning homer.

*   *   *

FROM HIS GUN DIRECTOR, Bob Hagen looked forward over the *John-ston*'s starboard bow and was shocked to see an American destroyer on a collision course. It was the *Heermann*. The destroyer emerged from a smoke screen heading straight at Evans's ship, just two hundred yards away. Evans shouted, "All engines back full!" Ed DiGardi ran to the pilothouse and pulled "back full" on the engine room telegraph and ordered a left full rudder. The *Johnston*'s riddled hull shuddered as its one working propeller bit into the water. The *Heermann* did the same with her twin screws.

Stationed on the depth charge racks on the *Johnston*'s fantail, Bob Deal was nearly pitched over the side from the sudden change in momentum: "Our stern dug deep into the sea, and the ocean boiled over the after deck." As water engulfed the destroyer's fantail, the *Heermann* was so close—less than ten feet—that someone could have hurdled over to the other ship's deck. Crewmen watching let out a roar of celebration as the ships backed down. Several crew on the *Johnston*'s deck at this point saw the wakes of three torpedoes passing silently below the surface, narrowly missing the ship. The two ships formed up momentarily into column—the *Heermann* would outrace the damaged *Johnston* quickly enough—and headed south astern the carriers.

At some point between 8:08 and 8:24 the *Heermann* was firing its main batteries at targets to starboard when chief yeoman Harold Whitney, Captain Hathaway's talker, heard over his headset an excited shout from a port-side lookout. Appearing unexpectedly out of the smoke and haze came a destroyer. From the starboard bridge wing, Whitney looked across his ship's narrow beam and saw the tin can steaming close alongside to port. Walking over to take a closer look, he saw the sharp rising prow, the blocky superstructure, the twin main gun mount, and the foreign dress of a sailor scurrying around pointing at the American destroyer, and he realized the ship was Japanese. "I could have thrown a potato and hit that kid running around there," Whitney said.

Whitney returned to the starboard bridge wing and called the shocking development to Amos Hathaway's attention, recommending that he order the *Heermann*'s machine-gunners to engage the intruder at point-blank range. Unfazed, the skipper said to his talker, "I can't shoot at them now. We're busy with these cruisers over here." Evidently the imperial tin can had other priorities as well. After several tense minutes the ship peeled off to port and disappeared through the smoke and squalls that had covered its arrival.

*   *   *

ZIGGY SPRAGUE'S FLATTOPS SHOULD have been run down and butchered like antelope on the steppe, but they continued to elude that seemingly predestined fate. At 8:10 A.M. Sprague's carriers were on a southwesterly heading, fleeing with the wind. The cruiser column led by the *Tone,* followed by the *Chikuma,* the *Haguro,* and the *Chokai,* was to Sprague's northeast, running south, working a clockwise circular course toward the southwest. The aggression of the screening ships and the doggedness of the pilots were making their mark. Eighty minutes into the pursuit, the Japanese still had not overtaken them for slaughter, their thirteen-knot speed advantage notwithstanding. Every time a pursuing cruiser had to veer from course to avoid a TBM approaching with torpedo bay doors open, Sprague won valuable time. Every time a Wildcat pilot rattled a cruiser's pilothouse, sending officers diving to the deck, it delayed course-change orders and frustrated the concentration of spotters peering through their binoculars.

As his carriers plodded along on a course of 205 degrees to the south-southwest, Sprague could scarcely believe his luck up to this point. At 8:14 Felix Stump heard him on the radio saying, *"We have been straddled for the last half hour. We have not been hit yet. Their shooting is very bad."*

Admiral Kurita tended to see another reason for his inability to close for the kill—his opponents were swift fleet carriers and cruisers, able to outrun him on their own. Kurita watched his ships fail to close the range and knew he could not afford to chase them forever. He had his own fuel shortages to worry about. For all Kurita knew, this was the U.S. Third Fleet. Just fifteen hours ago Halsey's and Mitscher's planes had sunk one of Japan's two greatest battleships, the *Musashi.* Aboard her sister ship, the *Yamato,* there was disagreement about where the Third Fleet was. The Japanese had heard Kinkaid's pleas for help from heavy American ships. Though Admiral Shiraishi on the *Kumano* had reason to know otherwise, having sighted "light carriers" and recorded that fact in his log, he failed to report it to superiors. And so Kurita continued to believe that his opponents were larger, faster, and more capable than they actually were. He had no idea how desperate his enemy was.

Though neither Ziggy Sprague nor his captains had any reason to know it, the best way to turn back the Japanese onslaught was for their torpedoless tin cans and their weaponless airplanes to keep the bluff going.

Thirty-one

Following its near collision with the *Heermann*, the *Johnston*'s protracted streak of astonishing luck seemed simply to run out. The ship was taking hits regularly now. Shells struck in deep syncopated rhythms, each slightly less momentous and terrifying to the crew than the one before, an undifferentiated cadence that seemed to diminish in effect as shell shock set in. An armor-piercing round passed through the thin metal of an exhaust stack without exploding. Another shell rained metal shards all over the bridge, knocked crew to the deck, and showered them with asbestos insulation. Robert Billie felt something strike his communications headset, and somehow his mouth was full of blood and broken teeth. Down in the engine room the hits jarred asbestos lagging from the steam pipes and blinked the lights. According to Charles Landreth, "the ship felt like it was shaking apart. . . . There was a noise on the earphones, and it felt like it blew my eardrums out. Then for a short time the phones were dead. . . . Then someone got on the phones and said we had been hit and everyone on the bridge had been killed."

Quartermaster Neil Dethlefs could see a large ship on the northern horizon, bright flashes leaping from its two forward turrets. The silent yellow strobes of light were followed, after a delay of several dozen seconds, by a rising, freight-train roar as the large shells ripped into the sea. He saw three hit to port and three more to starboard. "I was sure the next salvo was coming into the pilothouse," he wrote later. "I prayed that if it did, I would get the full package and not be left with an arm or leg missing."

"It didn't appear we would be alive much longer," said Charles Landreth. "Up to this time the thought of us not making it hadn't bothered me much. I still had not seen with my eyes people getting killed. But that was soon to come. Fear was written on everyone's face in the engine room." The senior engineering officer, Lt. Joe Worling, was coming and going, moving back and forth between the engine room and the fireroom that energized his turbines with steam. From the expression in their lieutenant's eyes, the men understood their chances. "I could tell by looking at him that our ship was in its first and last surface engagement," Landreth said.

*   *   *

IF SHEER HUMAN WILL could have propelled the USS *Hoel* on a southwesterly course back toward the carriers, she would have made thirty-six knots. As it was, on only one good engine, steered manually, and confronted with an unceasing rain of fire from multiple enemy ships, the destroyer had no chance to escape. As the rainsqualls began to yield to the morning sun, the Japanese had a clear view of the stricken tin can, which now paid the price for Leon Kintberger's gallant headlong run into the enemy's midst.

The wounded vessel was trapped in a savage crossfire. A cruiser was close by, so close at some four thousand yards that even the forty-millimeter guns could hit her. Their rhythmic thumping was in syncopation with the blasts of the two forward five-inchers. Targets were in oversupply, but so were Japanese shells. They came from both sides, whistling and roaring and crashing to starboard and port; exploding overhead, filling the air with candy colors and showering the decks with shrapnel, drilling straight through the hull. Lieutenant Dix:

> *You heard the whistling whine and grinding thud,*
> *The iron rumble following the blast,*
> *The rattle of the instruments and gear.*
> *You felt the shudder running through the hull.*

The shaking of the deck beneath your feet.
The quiver in your limbs as each one struck.
The masts and radars toppled down on deck,
Main Radio and Charthouse took a hit,
Boats, life rafts, stacks, were riddled with the spray
Of lead and steel from air bursts crashing high.

The decks were a killing field. Bob Prater sought refuge in the aft torpedo room, but it was full of corpses. He moved to the port side and saw steam coming out of the fireroom. "The men were coming out mortally scalded. . . . There was blood and bodies everywhere."

Around this time the skipper of the *Raymond,* Lt. Cdr. A. F. Beyer, Jr., spotted an American ship taking a terrific beating. He thought it was the *Samuel B. Roberts,* but Copeland's ship had yet to be hit—it was more likely the *Hoel.* That he apparently mistook the destroyer for a destroyer escort may have been testimony to the battering Kintberger's ship had taken. Her silhouette was scarcely even recognizable anymore. Her mast had fallen over the superstructure. She had only two working five-inch guns. Captain Beyer could see her rapid-fire salvos going out at the enemy. The bombardment that came in return was horrifying. It appeared to overwhelm her, swallowing the ship in a "curtain of flashes."

A salvo struck the *Hoel* below the waterline, bulling through the forward engine room and letting in the sea. Lt. Cdr. John Plumb got many of his men out before they were drowned at their stations and secured the boilers before they could blow. But this hit sealed the *Hoel*'s fate. Her last engine was gone. Slowly, and ever more slowly, the *Hoel* drifted, her list worsening by the minute.

Japanese heavy cruisers and battleships were firing point-blank into her hull. Bobby DeSpain took cover on the deck beside the depth charge racks. "Lying on the deck," he recalled, "I looked down at myself and thought I'd been hit. My body was covered with blood and gore that had flowed aft down the gutters onto me."

The *Hoel*'s two forward guns fired back, crudely aimed, in the absence of a working Fox Dog set and Mark 37 gun director, by the surface-search SG radar. The *Tone*-class cruiser looming just two thousand yards to port had slowed down. Whether it did so from battle damage or to steady its gun platform for a final, killing fusillade is not known. It presented an excellent target for gunners who were not ready to quit. The top hatch of Gun 52 was open, and Chester Fay, the gun captain, was standing up out of it, congratulating his crew in the mount whenever they scored a hit. On the bridge Lieutenant Dix saw him and was moved: "He looked up toward the bridge as if to say, 'We're still not licked—we've got a few rounds left. We'll sink the bastard if she stays that close.' "

Fay and his counterparts in Gun 51 swung their mounts to starboard and engaged three destroyers closing in to the point that machine guns could have opened fire to good effect had they been working. Someone on the bridge shouted the command to open fire, but power was gone and most of the men on the forties just forward of the superstructure were dead or wounded. Aft, the prospects were still worse. The light weaponry back there had been ripped to pieces and smashed, bent down and wrenched from the deck plates. Dix saw the crews of some destroyed guns hunkered behind their shields. A shell from the *Tone*-class cruiser passed through a bulkhead and through a forward magazine, starting a fire that raged below Gun 51. But its crew blasted away at one of the Japanese destroyers, which continued to press in, undaunted. Off the *Hoel*'s starboard bow, the stubby blue form of a Wildcat fighter plane appeared. The aircraft fell on a Japanese destroyer, coming in low and fast, a rain of spent shell cases cascading from its wings. The storm of .50-caliber lead rattled the Japanese destroyer so hard that the sound of the ricochets and penetrations could be heard on the decks of Kintberger's ship.

As the *Hoel* drifted, a shell struck the forward stack. Lt. (jg) Myles Barrett, the supply officer, was standing on the catwalk by the forty-millimeter remote control console, filming the battle with the ship's sixteen-millimeter movie camera. The hit set the ship's whistle shrieking. Some of the crew thought it was the abandon ship signal. From the bridge, Lieutenant Dix looked down on the decks and watched men dragging wounded to the rails and leaping into the sea. "They took no life jackets, left rafts and nets, nothing to hold them up but their arms. More than a hundred must have gone this way. They couldn't hear us yelling from the bridge."

Roy Lozano was climbing the ladder from the forward fireroom when the blast wave from the hit struck him. Whoever was above him on the ladder was blown to pieces. "The force of the explosion was so great that it ripped the seam right out of my pants," he recalled. "But we continued to climb up only to walk over dead bodies.

When we arrived topside, we went to the port side of the ship to try to get one of the lifeboats down. I don't know why we were trying to get it down, as it was shot full of holes."

The explosion in the fireroom collapsed the bulkhead that separated it from the emergency generator room, a compartment belowdecks that housed the electrical generator that kicked in if main power boards failed. Glen Foster, an interior communications electrician, was knocked to the floor as the generator toppled down on him. As hot steam poured into his space, he pushed open the hatch leading forward from his small compartment but found only smoke and fire. He tried going up to the next deck, but the escape hatch was jammed. Foster panicked when he discovered that he'd been turning the hatch the wrong way. He opened it finally, made his way through an escape hatch that led through the internal communications room, and found that it had become a charnel house, piled to a sickening depth with bodies and body parts.

One of the hits the *Hoel* took destroyed the ship's safe. As supply officer, Myles Barrett was responsible for disbursing cash to the crew on payday. With the shattering of the large iron deposit box, suddenly it was payday. "Money was fluttering everywhere. Bills came blasting out of a hole in the bulkhead," Barrett said. The fifty-dollar bills settled and stuck fast on the deck, the gruesome windfall drifting with the flow of blood down into the bilges.

*　　*　　*

THE SHIPS OF TAFFY 3's screen fired the last of their torpedoes when Captains Beyer of the *Raymond* and Sig Hansen of the *Dennis* answered Sprague's call, releasing their three torpedoes at a Japanese heavy cruiser not long after the *Roberts* did, and observing, but claiming no credit for, at least one hit. After his torpedoes were gone, Beyer wheeled the *Raymond* around to a 110-degree course, swiftly crossing four miles of sea, barking away with her main batteries until the range to the Japanese heavy cruiser was just 5,700 yards. The *Raymond* acquitted herself well enough in her ensuing gunnery duel with the *Haguro* to brag in any company. The crew in the handling room below Gun 52 worked so hard that several men collapsed from heat exhaustion. The aft repair party relieved them, with only slightly less impressive results, although some time-delay-fused antiaircraft rounds found their way into the hoist, resulting in a few shells exploding prematurely en route to the target. The *Raymond* fired 414 rounds of five-inch ammunition at the *Haguro,* landing numerous hits all across her superstructure. Then, improbably, the *Haguro* turned and headed away to the east, and Beyer checked the *Raymond*'s fire.

*   *   *

THE SMOKE FLOATING OVER the seas in the vicinity of the *Johnston* was so thick that Captain Evans ordered Bob Hagen not to fire his battery unless he could actually see what he intended to shoot. He had no idea what had become of his sister ships in the screen. No sense adding to their misery by hitting them with friendly fire.

Through the smoke, cruising seven thousand yards off the *Johnston*'s port beam, Hagen spotted the profile of the 36,000-ton British-built monster, the *Kongo.* The pagoda superstructure and mainmast seemed to crowd the shortened forecastle, where two twin fourteen-inch gun mounts lay. A third main battery mount sat just behind the after mast. Some distance farther aft, set so far astern gun number three as to accentuate her tremendous length, was her fourth main gun. Hagen took in the sight of the battleship and muttered to himself, "Well, I sure as hell can see that." Once more he slewed his director toward a new target and closed his firing key.

In just forty seconds the destroyer sent thirty shells at the leviathan, landing by Hagen's estimation fifteen hits on the superstructure tower. "As far as accomplishing anything decisive, it was like bouncing paper wads off a steel helmet," Hagen would later write, "but we did kill some Japs and knocked out a few small guns. Then we ran back into our smoke. The BB belched a few fourteen-inchers at us but, thank God, registered only clean misses."

Several miles behind the other surviving ships of Taffy 3's screen, the *Johnston* headed south at half speed. Overtaking Evans's ship to port was the cruiser line and the battleships behind them. To her right a line of enemy destroyers advanced to gunnery range. As wicked as the crossfire was, a sight now commanded everyone's attention on the *Johnston*'s bridge: an escort carrier, listing to port, dead in the water and taking heavy fire. It was the *Gambier Bay.*

Thirty-two

Given her position on the windward side of the formation, the *Gambier Bay* rode in nearly plain sight of the cruisers to her east, her own smoke screen, and that of the tailing destroyer screen blown to the west. There was no telling how many ships had drawn a bead on her now. Under fire for nearly ninety minutes, the *Gambier Bay*, steaming behind the *Kalinin Bay*, took her first hit at 8:20, when a shell penetrated her forward engine room. The sea flooded in, and even the strenuous exertions of the bilge pumps and two portable submersible pumps could not prevent the burners from being swamped. As machinists secured the flooded boilers, the speed differential between the damaged CVE and her pursuers opened widely. The tight circle of Taffy 3's six escort carriers stretched and fractured as the *Gambier Bay*, struggling along at eleven knots, dropped out of the formation and receded toward the cruisers closing in on her port quarter.

A signalman on the *Gambier Bay*'s twenty-four-inch carbon arc searchlight, Don Heric, spotted three ships to the southeast flashing a recognition signal. They were the Taffy 2 destroyers *Hailey*, *Haggard*, and *Franks*, which Admiral Stump had ordered north to intercept any Japanese ships that might pursue his CVEs. Ens. Cole Williams, the *Gambier Bay*'s signal officer, ordered Heric to acknowledge the challenge and request assistance. The signalman opened the shutters of his lamp and blinkered, "WE ARE UNDER ATTACK, PLEASE HELP." No sooner had he finished the message than a large shell ripped the air close enough to burn his forearms and knock Williams to the deck. In turn, the Taffy 2 destroyers blinkered Morse for R—standard shorthand for "message received"—then turned and withdrew to the south. Upon learning at 8:17 that Japanese battleship shells were straddling his destroyers, Taffy 2 commander Admiral Stump decided against risking his most capable escorts in a dicey offensive action. If the Japanese destroyed Taffy 3 and continued south, he would need them for his own defense. Chased by salvos of fourteen-inch shells, the *Hailey,* the *Haggard,* and the *Franks* turned and raced south after having closed, unmolested, to within fifteen thousand yards of the *Haruna* and the *Kongo.*

High above, Edward Huxtable, commander of the *Gambier Bay's* air group, VC-10, sighted the carrier taking concentrated fire from Japanese cruisers. As the FM-2 Wildcats escorting him winged over into strafing runs, Huxtable turned, descended, and leveled off in a mock torpedo attack. He made four such runs, each time keeping up the ruse, flying level with bomb bay doors open. Each time he did so, he attracted a lot of attention from Japanese antiaircraft gunners. Then Huxtable became aware of reinforcements on the way. "I heard flight leaders from the other CVE group preparing for attacks," he said, "and decided that the situation was much improved and left for Tacloban at 0915 to bomb up."

It was plain, however, that the *Gambier Bay* was in deep trouble. When the engine room was abandoned five minutes after its boilers were secured, Lt. (jg) Hank Pyzdrowski, an Avenger pilot who had been stranded when his ship turned out of the headwind in favor of its own survival, felt the intensity of the deck vibrations slacken. He looked up at the ship's tiny island superstructure and saw the battle ensign droop. With a boiler gone, the eighteen-knot ship could do only eleven knots. She began listing to port.

The volume of ordnance flying the ship's way was so great as to register on the ship's surface-search radar. In the *Gambier Bay's* CIC, Lt. (jg) Bill Cuming was watching the surface radar's A-scope, taking ranges on the Japanese ships. Every now and then a quick stray blip would appear on the graph—the echo return from an inbound Japanese shell. Cuming could do nothing with that information except appreciate how long the odds were against the ship surviving much longer.

Every minute, it seemed, a salvo landed near the ship. Usually at least one shell in each salvo inflicted some damage. The vibrations were so severe, the men had trouble staying on their feet. A shell went off behind him, and aviation machinist's mate third class Tony Potochniak was knocked to the catwalk on the port side of the ship. He stood and moved forward, preoccupied with thoughts of what the inscription on his gravestone might say: *Lost at sea, age 19 years.* Potochniak found bodies laid flat across the bloodied wooden flight deck. He entered a compartment that had been turned into a first-aid station. Lt. Cdr. Wayne Stewart, VC-10's flight surgeon, shooed him aside so he could get at a severely wounded sailor lying on a stretcher. Just then another shell hit. The blast showered shrapnel into Potochniak's hand and legs and cut down Commander Stewart as he was tending to the man. The doctor fell dead on top of his patient.

Photographer's mate second class Allen Johnson was crossing a catwalk when he came upon a sailor crumpled against a bulkhead, clutching his arms in front of him and weeping softly. "I'm ruined, I'm ruined," the kid was saying. Looking down, Johnson saw that his abdomen had been torn wide open. He walked forward, past a forty-millimeter gun mount, and encountered a crewman he had once heard griping about the boredom of life on a CVE. "When are we gonna see some *real* action?" this kid had wanted to know. Johnson looked at him now—he was glassy-eyed, gazing into the distance—and couldn't resist a dig. "Well, buddy, is this enough action for you?" No answer came from his lips but a stream of little saliva bubbles.

*   *   *

AMOS HATHAWAY HEARD HIS admiral, Ziggy Sprague, cut in on the TBS circuit at 8:26: *"Small boys on my starboard quarter, intercept enemy cruiser coming in on my port quarter."* Each carrier had its own gun, a single-mounted five-inch/38-caliber on its fantail, and its crew knew how to use it. But to fend off cruisers, Sprague would need the help of a real surface combatant.

Hathaway saw the *Johnston* limping southward, trying to comply with Sprague's order. It was quite evident, as Captain Evans's stricken ship moved to interdict, that it wasn't getting anywhere fast on one screw. A signal light blinkered the message "ONLY ONE ENGINE X NO GYRO X NO RADARS." The destroyer was in trouble. But the *Heermann* still had her legs. Hathaway swung his destroyer into a tight turn to port and tore across the rear of the carrier formation toward the enemy.

There remained the question of exactly how a destroyer bereft of torpedoes would turn away an armored ship of the line. Using double-talk on the open circuit, which he thought the enemy was surely monitoring, Hathaway tried to tell Sprague that he had no more torpedoes aboard. He heard other skippers doing the same. "As I listened," he later recounted, "it became evident that there wasn't a torpedo among us. Anything we could do from now on would have to be mostly bluff."

The *Heermann* broke from the smoke to find the squat bulk of an escort carrier bearing down on her off the port bow. It was the *Fanshaw Bay*. Hathaway backed down to a stop to avoid a collision; then, when the ship was out of the way, he had a clear view of what Sprague was anxious about. Ahead lay the *Gambier Bay*, afire amidships, listing twenty degrees to port, and taking a ceaseless battering from a *Tone*-class cruiser to her east. The wounded carrier obscured most of the Japanese ship, so Hathaway maneuvered to gain a clearer line of sight. As his viewing geometry improved, he made out the silhouettes of three more cruisers in the haze. He thought he could see two larger ships looming to the rear.

The *Heermann*'s wake boiled as Amos Hathaway's ship regained steam. Soon she was making top speed toward the Japanese cruisers. So many Japanese ships were firing on the *Heermann* that the ship was like a chameleon. Each time a new salvo landed near, she was doused in a different color. Each time the destroyer's bow bit into a wave, the water rinsed the decks and gunwales clean until a shell bearing a different hue crashed a column of seawater across her decks again. Green, yellow, red, and undyed splashes rose near the ship, one after another. Chief yeoman Harold Whitney looked at his skipper and noticed that Hathaway had been dyed red from head to foot.

The gun boss, Lieutenant Meadors, kept up a steady cadence of fire all the way in. His five gun crews kept their breech trays loaded while below them the shell hoists cycled continuously, drawing ammunition up from the handling rooms as the men down there pushed powder cases through the scuttles in the bases of the turrets. His nostrils stung by the smell of cordite and burning cork and human sweat, seaman first class Stanley Urbanski was down in Gun 52's handling room.

Round after round I take from [Ralph] Sacco, placing it in the scuttle. As the previous round is removed, I push up a new one and secure it in its seat. Forty, fifty rounds, then the violent action of the ship, a brief pause. Just enough time to bring up more shells from the lower handling room. Many times more, rapid fire, no time for thought. Keep a powder charge in the scuttle. No talk, only Sacco's orders to keep the lower hoist moving. The human machine works flawlessly. We still know nothing of the happenings around us. No feelings, no interruptions, just keep a powder in the scuttle.

James Boulton's crew in Gun 52 made good use of Sacco's and Urbanski's efficiency. Spent shell cases rattled and rolled across the deck as the *Heermann* blazed away, firing some five hundred shells in a twenty-minute duel with a *Tone*-class cruiser. Meadors counted fifty hits. The destroyer's bombardment started several fires aboard her foe. From his lookout's position on the bridge, Wallace Hock could see Japanese sailors being blown into the air from the ship's deck. There appeared to be internal explosions. A large fire raged astern, where the *Tone*-class ships had their big seaplane hangars.

The men in Gun 52, directly forward of and below the bridge, did their jobs too well. The concussion from their fire rang in Hathaway's ears, so he climbed to the fire-control platform to escape the cacophony, outside Lieutenant Meadors's gun director mount. The extra elevation improved his view of the seascape. He shouted course changes into the voice tube leading down into the pilothouse, running an eastward zigzag course, chasing roiling shell splashes to keep his ship alive. The enemy's salvos were landing closer and closer to the ship, the Japanese correcting their fire in hundred-yard steps. Hathaway could see the tight triple sets of splashes moving in his direction. The ones closest to him were red.

Destroyers did not sortie alone against columns of superior warships without paying the price. Captain Hathaway's ship had no more business surviving this approach than Captain Evans's *Johnston* had had coming through its solo run. Now a salvo found the *Heermann*. An eight-inch shot from a cruiser ripped through the ship's bow, blowing a five-foot hole in the hull and flooding the forward magazines.

Another shell struck Hathaway's destroyer amidships. It tore through an exhaust uptake leading from the boilers to the stack and exploded in a supply locker. Lt. Bob Rutter, the ship's supply officer and paymaster, was standing on a spotting platform that girdled the after stack. The explosion knocked him down against the stack, and a hot blast washed over him, covering him with a sticky substance. The new father—he had become a dad in January 1944, while the *Heermann* was at sea—prayed, "God, let me see my wife and son." He wiped a hand across his face, expecting to find blood and gore. After a terrified pause, Rutter realized he was all right, and lucky too. The mess that covered him was navy beans, cooked in storage by the blast of the shell, steamed by the sudden heat, and blown through the uptake, washing him in a blast of paste. According to Harold Whitney, Rutter "scraped the beans from his eyes and looked around with a gaze that wouldn't believe the things it saw. He was still here." Captain Hathaway later speculated that after this incident Rutter wouldn't mind if he never ate another serving of beans.

With the hits forward, Gun 52's handling room was plunged into darkness. According to Stanley Urbanski, "Suddenly all thought was lost in an explosion, total darkness, the ear-shattering hiss of a broken air ejection line. Bright red flecks scattered around our closed and dark cubicle, red-hot shrapnel. Fear sets in, I pray to my God." Urbanski heard the sounds and felt the tremors, and his imagination filled in the rest. "*Heermann* is smashing through the sea. The firing starts again. Then the most violent tremor of all, a great explosion, and our Lady is wounded. She seems to have started her way to her grave. Down, down by the bow, what seems like eternity."

As the inrushing water dragged down the bow, Hathaway momentarily thought his ship might run itself beneath the waves: "We were so far down by the head that our anchors were dragging in the bow wave, throwing torrents of water on the deck." He considered slowing the ship to reduce pressure on the critical forward bulkheads, which crewmen belowdecks had raced to buttress with odd lengths of timber. The first lieutenant, Bill Sefton, reached Harold

Whitney over the phones and pleaded with him to ask the captain to slow down. The damage to the belowdecks compartments was evident in the voluminous litter of cigarette cartons and toilet paper bobbing on the edge of the ship's bow wake. Having weighed the risks of slowing down to stem the progressive flooding, Hathaway chose to stay at speed. He was well aware of what had happened to the *Johnston* and the *Hoel* after they slowed down. Speed was his only real defense. Whitney relayed the skipper's refusal to Sefton, saying, "Just put more shoring in there and hope it holds."

Another shell, a smaller one, probably from a destroyer, struck the bridge below Hathaway, scattering shrapnel in every direction. The navigator took a spray of steel full in the face, which was left pockmarked by metal fragments, as if he had been maimed with a shotgun blast from a nonlethal distance. Its impact was dampened by the man standing beside him, who crumpled to the deck. An aviator from the *Gambier Bay* whom the *Heermann* had pulled out of the sea the previous day, Lt. (jg) Walter "Bucky" Dahlen, was cut down too. He had dodged fate the day before when he tried to land his Avenger on the carrier with his bomb load still slung aboard. Caught in a slipstream flying an overloaded plane, he was short on his approach. Mac McClendon, the *Gambier Bay*'s veteran landing signal officer, tried to wave him off, but it was too late. Dahlen's plane bounced hard, lost power, and plowed into the sea ahead of the carrier. Hathaway's ship, which had plane guard duty on October 24, picked Dahlen out of the sea. The skipper put the flier to immediate use on the bridge, assigning him to help spot and identify incoming aircraft. Dahlen was supposed to transfer back to VC-10 that morning. He never got the chance.

Harold Whitney saw the carnage in the pilothouse, saw blood running across the deck, and knew in an instant that everyone had been killed. With chief quartermaster John P. Milley lying apparently dead on deck, the wheel was abandoned, and the *Heermann* was running headlong toward the column of Japanese battleships, range point-blank—2,500 yards—and closing. Whitney seized the wheel and spun it around, away from the enemy leviathans, then called the executive officer, saying the bridge watch had been killed and he didn't know where the captain was. When Whitney suggested that the exec probably ought to be conning the ship, the officer insisted that his radar-assisted view of the battle from the CIC was probably better than what he would have on the bridge. "Continue what you're doing," the exec said. "If I want you to change course, I'll tell you."

Whitney steered the ship as he had seen the skipper do it so many times, chasing shell splashes and hoping for the best. Then he felt a hand pulling at his pant leg. It was Milley. "I'll take it," the quartermaster told Whitney. He was bleeding, barely conscious. "I'll take it," he insisted. Harold Whitney helped Milley to his feet, searching him for wounds and asking if he was all right. "I'll take it." That was all Milley would say. Satisfied that the chief was fit for his old job, Whitney went in search of Captain Hathaway, finding him on the flying bridge, shouting steering orders into the voice tube. Whitney hadn't heard a single one of them. He never let on that his captain's orders had been for naught, and Hathaway didn't seem to suspect anything was awry. Regardless of who had been doing the conning, there was no arguing with the outcome. The *Heermann* had survived her impossible run against the main Japanese strength.

*   *   *

THE STRICKEN *GAMBIER BAY* had fallen into the enveloping advance of the Japanese formation. There was nothing anyone in Taffy 3 could do about it. A heavy cruiser was blasting away at the CVE at an alarmingly close range. Observing the carrier's plight, Captain Evans of the *Johnston* issued what Bob Hagen considered "the most courageous order I've ever heard." The skipper said, "Commence firing on that cruiser, Hagen. Draw her fire on us and away from the *Gambier Bay.*" Hagen could see that all four turrets of the cruiser, with its distinctive flared prow, were swung out toward the carrier.

While the Japanese ship bracketed the carrier with its eight-inch salvos, Evans closed to six thousand yards, and Hagen loosed a fusillade that scored repeatedly. The cruiser's four turrets, however, stayed trained on the carrier. Hagen considered the Japanese captain's decision to ignore the *Johnston* foolish; he figured the Japanese ship had more than enough firepower to do in both targets.

At about 8:40, before Ernest Evans could press his attack further against the cruisers to Sprague's port quarter, a column of four destroyers appeared behind the *Johnston* to starboard, closing rapidly with the carriers. It was Rear Adm. Masafuku Kimura's Tenth Destroyer Squadron, led by the light cruiser *Yahagi*. At about eight o'clock, as the *Yamato* was running north to avoid the *Heermann's* torpedoes, strafing Wildcats had sent the *Yahagi* and her consorts into a wide circular evasive maneuver. By the time Kimura's squadron finally came around and reoriented itself on a southerly course parallel to and four miles west of the *Yamato* and about ten miles to the northwest of the heavy cruiser column, it had nearly performed, by accident, the maneuver that Ziggy Sprague had earlier feared the whole Japanese fleet would attempt: it was slicing through the arc of his retreat. As Kimura's squadron bore down on Sprague's starboard beam, the American admiral was sandwiched between it and the heavy cruisers to the east.

Had Kurita's attack been planned more deliberately, Kimura might have been joined in this attack by the Second Destroyer Squadron, which consisted of seven destroyers led by the light cruiser *Noshiro*. But that unit's progress had been delayed by relentless aerial strafing. According to Admiral Ugaki, at least twice planes from the Taffies forced the *Noshiro* and her consorts to turn away to duck eviscerating hails of .50-caliber slugs.

Ernest Evans, seeing the looming threat to the carriers, ordered Bob Hagen to check his fire against the heavy cruiser and turned westward toward the *Yahagi* and her four destroyers. Closing to within ten thousand yards of the enemy ships, Evans ordered Hagen to engage the light cruiser leading the column. Hagen scored hits practically from the first salvo. He kept up the fire until the *Johnston* was just 7,500 yards from the *Yahagi*. The American tin can took several hits from 4.7-inch shells fired by Kimura's destroyers in return. But twelve of her own shells struck the *Yahagi*.

Then, Hagen wrote, "a most amazing thing happened. The destroyer leader [the *Yahagi*] proceeded to turn ninety degrees to the right and break off the action." The lieutenant watched in astonishment as the light cruiser began withdrawing to the west. He shifted his aim to the next ship in line, a destroyer. Hagen didn't know how far the *Johnston* could push its luck: "they were sleek, streamlined *Terutsuki*-class vessels, our match in tonnage and weight of guns, but not our match in marksmanship, crippled as we were. We should have been duck soup for them."

The captain of Gun 55 on the fantail, Clint Carter, a Texan from the Sweetwater-Abilene area, was screaming down to the handling room, "More shells! More shells!" One of his gang grumbled, "I'm sure glad there ain't no Japs from Texas." Drollery in the face of mortal danger was a common sign of a disciplined combat team, and Carter had a good one. His projectileman, boatswain's mate first class Harry Longacre, was one of the best. He was strong as a bull and demanded his own space. Nothing seemed to scare him—he had had a warship blown out from under him earlier in the war, so what else was there to fear? Given to wearing gold hoop earrings, one in each ear, Longacre cut a unique profile on the crew. He was a rebel. People referred to him as "Asiatic," which meant he marched to a different drummer. By some accounts he was a lousy boatswain's mate who resisted the command hierarchy. Once he went to Captain's Mast and got busted all the way back down to seaman second for a disciplinary infraction. But at general quarters you didn't want anybody else handling the projectiles. Harry Longacre was fast, agile, and strong. Eighteen times a minute he pulled a fifty-four-pound projectile off the shell hoist and laid it into the loading tray in sequence with the powderman, who placed a powder case on the tray behind the shell. Then the hydraulic rammer assembly shoved the tray forward, socking the shell firmly into the lands and grooves of the bore. Without electrical power, on partial local control, Gun 55 had been firing almost without break from the time of the first torpedo run. Guns 51 and 52 forward kept up a steady pace throughout the fight too.

Taking a sustained battering from the *Johnston*'s five-inch gun crews, the second Japanese ship in column, a destroyer, also turned west and fled with the *Yahagi*. The next three destroyers did the same. Hagen was dumbstruck with joy at the Japanese withdrawal. Evans was too. According to Hagen, "Commander Evans, feeling like the skipper of a battleship, was so elated he could hardly talk. He strutted across his bridge and chortled, 'Now I've seen everything!' "

Evans and Hagen might have been less amazed had they known the real reason the Japanese column withdrew. It was not the *Johnston*'s gunnery that drove them off, but the fact that they had finished launching their torpedo attack at the carriers and were turning to reform.

Still, Captain Evans's audacious interception of Kimura's squadron probably encouraged the Japanese skippers to release their famed Long Lance torpedoes at extreme range and from an unfavorable angle astern their fleeing targets. Either Kimura didn't have the stomach, faced with the *Johnston*'s tireless gunnery, to close to killing range, or he, like other Japanese commanders, believed his quarry were fast fleet carriers that could not be run down in any event.

The fog of war was so thick that neither side knew exactly what was happening at any given moment. But it was only the Japanese who were moved to pure fantasy. Somehow Admiral Ugaki on the *Yamato* acquired the hyperbolic notion that the Tenth Destroyer Squadron's halfhearted attack had "accomplished the great feat of sinking three carriers, one cruiser, and one destroyer."

Thirty-three

While the *Johnston* was engaged in her shorthanded duel with the Japanese destroyer squadron, Leon Kintberger, his ship dead in the water far to the north, concluded that the *Hoel* was finished. The destroyer's graceful lines had been broken and bent beyond ready recognition. Boxed in by the enemy on three sides, the *Hoel* had no propulsive power to escape through the box's open bottom.

The *Kongo* lofted ash-can-sized fourteen-inch rounds toward her without thrift or restraint. Having passed the stricken American tin can to the south, the *Tone*, the *Chikuma*, the *Haguro*, and the *Chokai* blasted salvo after eight-inch salvo toward her. Even the *Yamato* had caught up to the fight. Recovering from her ten-minute torpedo-bracketed sprint northward, the Center Force flagship lumbered steadily south. When the *Hoel* appeared, like a sitting duck, at a range of ten thousand yards, Cdr. Toshio Nakagawa opened fire with the *Yamato*'s 6.1-inch secondary battery. The Japanese battleship's quartermaster paid the U.S. destroyer a high compliment when he noted at 8:40 A.M., "Cruiser blows up and sinks."

The Japanese observer's perception was somewhat ahead of events. The sea was only now starting to wash over the *Hoel*'s stern. Rushing into the damaged port side, the water caused a progressively worsening port-side list. The ship had taken more than forty hits of every caliber. Now Kintberger had no choice. At 8:35 he ordered the crew of the *Hoel* to prepare to abandon ship. Quartermaster Clarence Hood tried to call the order over the PA system, but the circuit was dead. Kintberger told his bridge personnel to descend to the main deck and pass the word to the men.

Willard Frenn was lucky to be alive. For most of the battle the gunner's mate first class had stayed at his station in the chief's mess, awaiting calls for gun repair. When none came, he made himself a few sandwiches, none too confident that the lack of demand for his services meant all was well topside. Having survived the blast of two armor-piercing shells that penetrated his compartment and blew him into a stack of bedding, he climbed topside and was running by the forward deckhouse below Gun 52 to find a lifeboat when he looked up and saw Lt. Bill Sanders. Though his gun director had been blasted out of action long ago, the gunnery officer was still alive, tangled up in the rigging with both of his legs shot off at the knees. Frenn asked if he could help him, and Sanders said no. "The word was to abandon ship," Frenn recalled.

Someone finally helped Dick Santos, his feet scalded beyond use, down from his amidships quad-forty mount to the port-side main deck. He saw men filing out of a hatch leading to the engineering space belowdecks. "They were burned beyond belief! God, I remember that so well because when they tried to get out of the hatch, we tried to help lift them out, and their flesh would fall off. It was a blessing that they died almost immediately," Santos wrote.

When the abandon ship order reached Gun 51's ammunition handling room, the crew exited through the chief's quarters, sloshed through the flooded mess hall, and climbed a ladder to the starboard side. Seaman Paul Miranda opened the hatch to the main deck and felt the heavy slump of a body falling against his shoulder. It was the ship's doctor, Lt. Louis Streuter. The body slid down the slippery deck and stopped against the port-side rail. Miranda stepped aside to let the crew behind him file out. Looking up, he saw Donald Heinritz, known locally as "Tiny" for his line-of-scrimmage bulk and expansive jocularity. He had given up a football scholarship to the University of Wisconsin and enlisted in the Navy, figuring he'd go help win the war and be home in six months. Now Tiny stood there, like Paul

Bunyan incarnate, balancing a load of timbers and mattresses on his lumberman's back. He was yelling at Miranda to help him shore up the hole in the port side of the hull.

A fourteen-inch battleship shell, probably from the *Kongo*, had opened a hole in the waterline big enough to drive a pair of sedans through, one beside the other. Seawater was rushing through it, filling the mess hall. Paul Miranda stood on the ladder getting ready to accompany Tiny belowdecks when another shell struck. It killed most of the men from the handling room and blew Miranda off the ladder. When he got to his feet again, Tiny was gone.

The flooding mess hall was in flames. Miranda climbed back up the ladder through the smoke and found the hatch to the main deck jammed. Fear gripped him. He pulled at the dogs on the hatch, wrenching the small steel handles until, blessedly, they turned. He walked out on the deck, and when he got there, it occurred to him that he could not swim. He had never before considered the possibility that his home might sink, leaving him alone with the ocean. An eighteen-year-old was right to wonder: on a proven ship like the *Hoel*, and with a pair of skippers like Commander Thomas and Captain Kintberger in charge, why would a man ever have to swim?

Miranda stood on the rail of the ship, working up the nerve to jump. The ship shuddered as another Japanese shell hit somewhere, knocking him to the deck. "The next thing I knew, I was lying beside gun number one, and the deck was very hot under me. In one leap I was in the water, scared as hell."

Radioman John Oracz exited the radio shack, following another radioman out the hatch. The sharp flash and blast of a shell propelled Oracz into unconsciousness. When he awoke, he was back in the radio compartment, bloody but only slightly wounded. The other radioman was gone. In the silence that followed the blast, he realized he was disoriented, lost in a labyrinth of smoke. He felt himself struggling to breathe as he rose to his feet and groped his way to the interior ladder leading from the bridge to the deck. The ladder was twisted away from the bulkhead, dangling. Looking forward, Oracz could see that the bow of the ship had risen slightly out of the water. Astern, the port side of the quarterdeck was awash. He saw the ship's doctor come out of a hatch on deck just ahead of him. "I could see that he was seriously wounded in his right side and right leg, and he was bleeding severely. He could just barely walk, and as he did, he

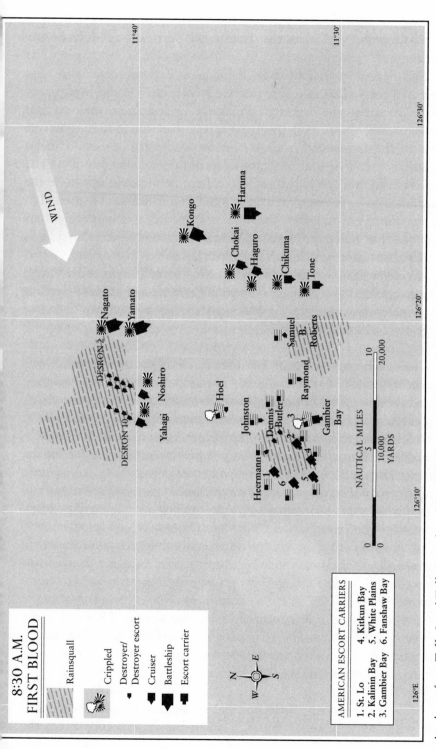

8:30 A.M.
FIRST BLOOD

Rainsquall

Crippled

Destroyer/
Destroyer escort

Cruiser

Battleship

Escort carrier

AMERICAN ESCORT CARRIERS

1. St. Lo
2. Kalinin Bay
3. Gambier Bay
4. Kitkun Bay
5. White Plains
6. Fanshaw Bay

NAUTICAL MILES

0   5   10

0   10,000   20,000

YARDS

WIND

Kongo
Haruna
Chokai
Haguro
Chikuma
Tone

Nagato
Yamato

DESRON 2
Yahagi   Noshiro
DESRON 10

Hoel

Johnston
Dennis
Butler
Raymond
Heermann
Samuel
B.
Roberts
Gambier
Bay

126°E   126°10'   126°20'   126°30'

11°40'

11°30'

As planes from Taffy 2 and Taffy 3 strafe and bomb Kurita, the end nears for the *Hoel*, dead in the water as the Japanese close in. The escort carrier *Gambier Bay* is hit too, loses steam, and drops out of formation. Sprague orders his destroyer screen to intercept cruisers looming on his port quarter. The *Haruna*, ranging out to the southeast, opens fire on Taffy 2, now steaming thirty miles to the south.

lost footing and slid down the deck to the port side. . . . I never saw him again."

Bud Walton, the chief radio technician, was vaguely aware that the crowd of sailors that had gathered with him on the bridge was gone. The men—the plotting room crew and assorted gunners and fire-controlmen and men from the CIC—were cut down and scattered by the major-caliber explosion. A large piece of metal had hit him; he felt as if he had been stomped in the chest by a mule. "The ship was listing severely to port and it became impossible, due to the accumulation of debris and dead and injured, to walk." He moved to the starboard side, where the smoke from the burning magazines was so dense that he could not see the water. "I dove over the side. It seemed to be ages before I hit the water."

Working the plotting table when the abandon ship order came, Everett Lindorff was the last man to get out of the Hoel's CIC. That meant he would live. The explosion that killed all the men ahead of him only knocked him cold.

When I woke up, I was still in the CIC trying to gather my wits as to what had happened. I remembered the ship was sinking, and I didn't know how long I was lying there. So I crawled out the hatch and down the passageway over many more bodies to the outside main deck. The first thing I saw was more bodies and smoke and fire. I saw about six men trying to lower the motor whaleboat, and I wondered why because I could see holes all the way through it. In the next minute or two there was an explosion, and the men were gone. I started aft, then a shell hit the forty-millimeter ammo and depth charges. I could hear the ammo going off, then a hatch opened and two men from the engine room came out, took a few steps, and were cut down by shrapnel. I backed up against the superstructure and looked up at the bridge. There was the captain leaning on the rail looking back, just as calm as if nothing were happening. Then a large hole opened in the superstructure just a few feet from me, and about the same time I saw someone jump over the side, so I decided it was time for me to go.

Bob Wilson's only impressions of the action derived from sound and feel: the bucking of the ship when the Hoel's guns fired, the change in inertia when the ship turned, the sickening yaw and stutter-step when hits buckled the decks. Stationed in the machine shop be-lowdecks astern, Wilson had just finished checking the starboard stuffing box, which kept seawater from leaking in around the pro-peller shaft, and was passing through the after crew's quarters back to the machine shop when the lights went out. He dogged shut the hatch behind him, and when he turned to continue through the sleep-ing quarters, there was a flash and the sound of shredding metal. Six feet from where he stood a shell pierced the starboard bulkhead and exited to port. Wilson survived only because the armor-piercing round did not explode. He was knocked flat to the deck, buried in bedding. "The compartment was filled with the smell of burnt gun-powder, and except for a little light from the hatch and some that came through the holes left by the shell, it was quite dark."

Lightly wounded by shrapnel, Wilson dug himself out from un-der the bunks and went topside, where he joined a group of men hud-dled beside the sheltering hulk of Gun 55, disabled earlier. Off both sides of the *Hoel* Wilson could see the sleek dark forms of Japanese ships flashing and roaring. Their salvos screamed in fast, ripping the humid air at flat angles to the sea. At this close range, their freight-train roar was more densely pitched than when the shells were drop-ping lazily down, fired from extended range. All around the ship Wilson saw slicks of varicolored dye spread out in the water where shells had burst. One hit the fantail, destroying a twenty-millimeter gun tub.

> *There were quite a few of us by the gun mount, which at that time was out of action. Several were wounded, and some of the gun crews who were killed when the gun was put out of action were lying on the deck by the gun mount. It seemed like I was there only a short time when someone gathered a group of us together to go forward to help out. Just as we reached the vicin-ity of the galley, some shells hit the ship in that area. I have no idea what happened to the other guys that I was with.*

His skull fractured, Wilson was dimly aware of men running past him. "Somehow I knew they were abandoning the ship and that I had to get myself over the side. I also found that I had no real control of my left arm or leg, and I couldn't get my feet to walk," he later wrote.

"I crawled forward past the passageway between the bridge structure and the deckhouse where a group of guys had been killed and many others severely wounded by a direct hit, and on up to the wardroom area, where I was finally able to get over the side."

Lt. Jack Creamer, the assistant gunnery officer, exited the plotting room with a chief petty officer named Hickman, crawling through ventilation ducts part of the way to get topside. He tried to reach the bridge, but the superstructure was such a twisted wreck of metal that there was no clear route up. He and warrant officer Louis Stillwell spent their last moments aboard the *Hoel* walking down the starboard side, helping survivors get into life jackets and over the side into the water. All around the ship clusters of heads bobbed, survivors riding the slow, rolling swells. Creamer watched numbly as a Japanese salvo struck the sea a few hundred feet to starboard, right in the middle of a big gathering of wounded survivors. "We lost many of our shipmates to that one salvo," he later recalled. "Mr. Stillwell and I went to the port side, assisted the few still there, and abandoned ship, port-side amidships."

Francis Hofstrander was the last one up the ladder out of the forward fireroom. One boiler was still working, but steam has no use when it has nowhere to go. Hofstrander and his fellow snipes were among the first to know that the ship was dead in the water. They didn't need reminding to abandon ship. Hofstrander shimmied up the ladder to the port side. He walked forward over a deck slippery with blood, through an open-air grave of mangled bodies and body parts. He saw a Japanese heavy cruiser shooting point-blank into the ship. An eight-inch shell struck at the waterline, about ten feet from where Hofstrander was standing, bringing a blinding white flash of electric light. Though the engine room was out of action, evidently a generator was still working. It had 440 volts and no place to send it. The cruiser put an end to that problem.

When Hugh Coffelt's aft forty-millimeter gun lost power, he and his crew were ordered down to the main deck to look after the wounded. He made it down from the gun tub to the port-side deck in two jumps, then went forward and bandaged a few men injured by shrapnel and the machine guns of a Japanese floatplane that had strafed the ship. Running to sick bay to get a supply of morphine, he looked aft and saw a man jogging down the deck take a direct hit and dissolve into a red mess. Shells were hitting all around Coffelt. He slipped and fell in a blood slick, recovered, turned, and ran aft down the starboard side of the ship. Surviving a running naval battle was all stupid luck anyway; a man might as well do what a man had to do.

On that side I had a chance to see so many more of the men dead, lying on the deck, some of them only half there. I went back to the fantail. There were more men dead and half dead. I stepped into the water, as it was coming over the deck already, and I swam as quickly as I could away from the ship. I stopped just for a bit, looked back, and saw shells hitting in the place where I had just been standing.

From the bridge, Captain Kintberger had a hazy view of the battle as it passed him by, running south. The escort carrier closest to the *Hoel*, the *Gambier Bay*, intermittently visible through the black and gray smoke, was listing hard to port, with shell splashes striking up the waters all around her. According to Lieutenant Dix, "That was the last we saw of friendly ships."

Friendly ships would soon see the last of Captain Kintberger's hard-charging destroyer. Through the squalls Captain Copeland spotted the *Hoel*. There wasn't much left of her. Listing severely to port, motionless in the water, the ship was a pile of wreckage. Her bridge had collapsed on itself, her mast was gone, and the amidships torpedo mounts had been blown off the ship. Fires were raging astern, and smoke and steam were pouring from unseen spaces below decks. Her stacks were cut through with holes of all sizes. Lifeboats were splintered and dangling from their davits. Guns were twisted down like crazy straws, bent in or pulled from the deck by their wire roots. From his position in Gun 41, one of the *Roberts*'s forward forties, Jack Yusen, numb from the concussion of the forward five-inch gun right next to him, couldn't even tell that the *Hoel* was a *Fletcher*-class destroyer. Its silhouette had been mangled and reformed into a grotesque approximation of a warship.

For the *Roberts*'s skipper, encountering the *Hoel* in her final minutes was "one of those disheartening things . . . that puts a lump in your throat."

We had to pass her by and leave her lying there dead in the water with a big list on her. She was on fire. We could see men scrambling around launching life rafts. We just had to steam by. In combat you have to leave the wounded behind whether they are men or ships and go on your way and fight. Nevertheless, it was something that made every man on our topside feel the same as I did, and it bothered us to leave those men at the mercy of the Japs, but there was no other choice.

Thirty-four

By 8:40 the *Samuel B. Roberts* was speeding toward the cruisers closing on the carrier formation's port quarter. When Lt. Verling Pierson on the *Fanshaw Bay* spied the destroyer escort crossing astern his CVE, racing toward the Japanese ships, he turned to an officer standing next to him and said, "Look at that little DE committing suicide."

In a loose column with the *Johnston* and the *Heermann*, the *Roberts* steamed south, the three ships cutting in and out of one another's smoke. Whenever one rode the port-side flank nearest the enemy, the other two remained concealed in the exposed ship's smoke, which was generously blown over them by the easterly wind.

In all likelihood, this apparent tactical improvision was the accidental by-product of their independent zigzag courses. None of the ships' action reports suggests a coordinated advance. Bob Copeland, however, perceived deliberate maneuvering in the haphazard dance.

Whoever was out on the advance flank was taking a terrific beating. The others would be fairly well protected in her smoke and the smoke they were laying for the protection of the carriers. So every few minutes, when it got too heavy going on the outboard flank, whoever was up there would cut in to the right,

fall in, and come down on the inside of the formation; and the
next one would push out. We . . . just played leapfrog and kept
peeling off.

Looming to port was the *Chikuma*, so close that everyone topside on the *Roberts* watched in fascination. Her eight big guns
flashed and smoked, launching eight-inch shells at the carriers.
Copeland headed toward her, closing the range between them until
the heavy cruiser was almost directly off the *Roberts*'s port beam.
The destroyer escort's torpedoes were gone. Guns were all she had
left. But in gunnery as in every other line of business aboard a destroyer escort, the *Roberts*'s crew made do with what they had. "I
came a little bit left," Copeland recalled, "and when the range was
closed down some more, I said, 'Mr. Burton, you may open fire.' "

Even as his guns blazed defiantly at the Japanese cruiser, the skipper of the *Roberts* could not help but be taken with the imperial warship's sleek lines: "It was a beautiful ship. It had quite a flare on its
bow and had four turrets all forward, a long fo'c'sle and the turrets
alternated—a low one, a high one, a low one, and a high one—right
up the fo'c'sle." As the *Roberts* approached, two of those turrets
trained slowly to starboard to engage the *Roberts,* while the other
two continued shelling the carriers.

So began the 1,250-ton destroyer escort's duel with a heavy
cruiser twelve times her weight. The necessity of the engagement did
nothing to squelch the crew's fear. Most everyone felt it. Some were
well-nigh paralyzed by it, cowering in passageways and behind bulkheads as if the ship's thin metal plate would do anything more than
block their view of the incoming projectiles. "Anybody who says that
he didn't get scared in a situation like this is either a liar or a damn
fool," Copeland wrote. "The point is, though, that you didn't stay
scared."

Naval combat offered nowhere to run, no foxholes to dive into.
You had no way to know whether the next round would fall ahead of
you, behind you, to the left or right, or come burning straight in,
right down Lucifer's pike. No degree of personal cleverness could de-
fuse or deflect a shell bound in a particular sailor's direction. Against
a faster, more powerful opponent, a sailor had neither the hope to
vanquish him nor the possibility to flee. The *Roberts* had no way out

but through this enemy cruiser. There thus remained only the duty to engage it. No one shirked from that duty. "[A]s soon as the splashes had settled back, practically everyone was over it; from then on, for the most part, we were just too busy operating and fighting the ship to think about being scared." And no one in Taffy 3 fought more resolutely than the man who led the crew of the aft gun turret on the *Samuel B. Roberts,* Paul Henry Carr.

All through the *Roberts*'s wartime service, Carr kept his aft five-inch gun—designated Gun 52 or gun number two on a destroyer escort—clean, primed, and ready for action. His skipper considered the gunner's mate third class valuable not merely for his ability to keep his weapon mechanically fit but for his leadership skills as well. "Gun number two had a crew just out of this world," Copeland wrote. "It had been outstanding from the time we shook down."

As the captain of gun number two, Carr was responsible for maintaining the delicate machinery of his mount in the midst of an inhospitable saltwater environment, and he was the catalyst to the odd mix of seamen and petty officers who manned his gun at general quarters. Carr was its full-time caretaker. "He kept that gun the way a very meticulous housewife keeps her kitchen and kitchen utensils," Copeland wrote. "It was absolutely spotless. It is not an exaggeration to say you could have eaten off the deck of that gun mount at any time."

Back home in Checotah, Oklahoma, Carr had painted a bull's-eye on the barn and practiced long-snapping a football at it for hours on end. He was no less fastidious aboard the *Roberts*. His best qualities had a way of rubbing off on his crewmen. Seaman second class Bill Stovall, a teenage enlistee, was the pointer on Carr's crew. "I doubt if [Stovall] weighed more than 115 pounds dripping wet," Copeland wrote. "He was just a little shaver, but he was cool as a cucumber." Gilbert Stansbury, the loader, and James Gregory, the trainer, were two more good men. Their counterparts on the forecastle in Gun 51 were well drilled and adept. But the gang in Gun 52 surpassed them. "It just happens that his crew on our number-two gun was the best I have ever seen and I imagine one of the best that has ever existed," Copeland wrote. "That crew was, in fact, so good that another very good gun crew, namely number one, looked more or less mediocre by comparison."

Unlike the guns on the larger destroyers, the gunnery system on the *Roberts* was relatively rudimentary, with no centralized fire-control system to direct it. A gunner on a destroyer escort could get a range from the CIC, where the exec oversaw the use of the ship's Fox Dog surface radar. In a pinch the Mark 51 director that guided the forty-millimeter antiaircraft guns could fill in. But destroyer escort gunnery was largely a nineteenth-century affair. Their pointers and trainers were busy men.

Copeland thought he might have inadvertently discovered a weakness of the vaunted Japanese ship: its inability to hit targets too close to it. The *Chikuma* was so close to the low-lying DE that her gunners seemed to have trouble depressing their guns sufficiently to take the *Roberts* under fire. At that depressed angle the gunners couldn't reload. Each time the Japanese cruiser let loose with a flaming, windy blast, the guns would rise up and the turrets would turn inboard as the crew reloaded. Silently then the guns would train out again. "We'd see the flash of fire; then we'd hear the blast, and seemingly much later but actually at about the same time—*whoosh*—they'd go right over our heads."

Copeland's two gun crews had no such trouble. Though it was debatable what damage the *Roberts*'s battery could do to a heavy cruiser, there was no doubting that Paul Carr, Bill Stovall, James Gregory, Sammy Blue, Gilbert Stansbury, and the rest of Gun 52's crew had found their groove.

> *The boys took the ammunition just the way it came up the hoist—nobody cared what it was. They just took it as it came. Five-inch blind loaded and plugged, five-inch AA, five-inch common, five-inch AP, five-inch star shells, five-inch proximity fuse: just whatever came up the ammunition hoist. It was all fodder for the guns. They threw it in as fast as they could get it. It was very odd to see those star shells banging off over there in the daylight.*

The *Roberts* couldn't match the output of Bob Hagen's teams on the *Johnston*, Bill Sanders's on the *Hoel*, or Bill Meadors's on the *Heermann*, but they did well enough. In thirty-five minutes of shooting, Carr's squad in Gun 52 popped off 324 rounds at the enemy. Gun 51 on the forecastle fired 284 more.

Five-inch guns were useless shooting at a heavily armored hull, but they made a fair mess out of an exposed position. Each hit produced sheets of flame and choking gusts of metallic and asbestos dust. The star shells unloosed furiously sizzling showers of phosphorus that ate metal and flesh alike. One such hit in the right place could be debilitating; several score of them concentrated over the compact topside decks of a heavy cruiser and delivered in a short space of time could re-create purgatory itself. From what Copeland and other observers on the *Roberts* could see, the result of their shooting was devastating to the *Chikuma:* "We had the Jap cruiser on fire from the start of her bridge superstructure, just above the main deck, clear up to the fighting tops—absolutely an inferno of flames." The cruiser's number-three gun turret was knocked out, the bridge battered repeatedly, fires set aft, underneath the secondary control tower.

But while fires raged seventy-five feet above the *Chikuma's* mainmast, the cruiser didn't falter. Capt. Saiji Norimitsu's determined gunners kept up a steady rate of fire at her two targets, the *Samuel B. Roberts* and the stricken *Gambier Bay.* Though the carrier made an easy target, amazingly, an hour and forty-five minutes into the battle the *Roberts* hadn't been touched. Now, fighting beam to beam with a ship twelve times her displacement, she seemed to be getting the better of it. As for the opposing Goliath, there was no mistaking the fact that the *Chikuma* was in some serious trouble. Her number-three gun, the third one back from the bow, was no longer firing. Her bridge was a crudely holed wreck of scorched and twisted steel. Several small fires could be seen feeding on the superstructure behind the bridge.

Thirty-five

Despite the dauntless work of its screening ships, by 8:40 the *Gambier Bay*'s fate was sealed. A salvo from a Japanese cruiser knocked out its steering hydraulics, sliced off the starboard propeller, and quenched the ship's last source of steam power, the number-three boiler. On the flight deck of the *Gambier Bay*, Lt. (jg) Hank Pyzdrowski, stranded when his ship turned out of the wind, had nothing else to do but watch the silhouettes of Japanese ships grow steadily larger. As a reader of fiction set during the age of fighting sail, he wondered whether the enemy cruisers might approach and try to board the stricken CVE. The pilot massaged his .38-caliber service revolver and the survival knife on his belt.

Pyzdrowski went down to his stateroom and discovered that his locker had been rifled and his stash of scotch raided. He sat down to collect his thoughts, and Lt. George Bisbee popped in. "Need a drink?" the pilot asked, holding forth a half-drained bottle. Pyzdrowski followed his squadronmate into the adjoining room, where mattresses taken from nearby staterooms had been gathered and stacked into a large teepee, as if the layers of foam padding could stop or even slow down the cutting arc of a shrapnel burst. From within the teepee, Pyzdrowski could hear drunken voices of some of the other VC-10 pilots who had also been stranded aboard the ship.

Empty bottles were scattered all about its base. When the after engine room was hit, the ship went dead in the water, and Capt. Walter Vieweg gave the order to abandon ship. As the emergency alarm began to sound, Pyzdrowski said to Bisbee, "Better get these guys ready to go."

*   *   *

ONE OF THE JAPANESE officers responsible for the *Gambier Bay*'s destruction, Capt. Haruo Mayuzumi, the skipper of the *Tone,* was among his nation's foremost experts on battleship gunnery. As the executive officer on the *Yamato* when that great ship was put into commission, he had overseen the installation of her massive 18.1-inch guns, whose bore size was so secret that even Admiral Kurita did not know it. As a tactical instructor at the naval gunnery school at Yokusuka in the years leading up to Pearl Harbor, Mayuzumi had studied intercepts of the radio chatter exchanged between U.S. battleship commanders and seaplane spotters during gunnery drills off the California coast. Japanese submarines and merchant ships readily eavesdropped on the plain-language play-by-play, and the Imperial Japanese Navy tallied the statistics as diligently as their counterparts did.

At a range of 22,000 yards, the Japanese learned, American battleships hit their targets just seven percent of the time. Japanese heavies scored at a rate three times that. Mayuzumi led the effort to open that performance gap still further. He knew that if the shells were fired at flat enough angles to the water, they need not actually "hit" a ship at all. A near miss that struck the water close aboard, continuing on an underwater path, could land the most devastating blow of all: a hit below the waterline. Fired from 22,000 yards, a sixteen-inch battleship shell entering the water at a seventeen-degree angle to the surface could penetrate seventy-six millimeters of face-hardened armor even if it "missed" by twenty-five meters. The shells retained a velocity of 1,650 feet per second at the time when they reached their targets. The key was making sure that the angle of entry was flat enough. If it was, the so-called "danger zone"—the surface area in which a shell might land and still cause major damage to the ship—extended 143 meters from the target's hull. Mayuzumi did not anticipate that American innovations in radar would make his work seem

292 \   THE LAST STAND OF THE TIN CAN SAILORS

primitive in comparison. But his findings influenced Japanese gunnery doctrine, which may have been why some Taffy 3 sailors witnessed shells skipping off flight decks like slices of shale across a calm pond.

As a connoisseur of gunnery but not bloodthirsty in the art of war, Mayuzumi watched a midshipman by his side meticulously guide the fire of the *Tone*'s secondary battery into the hindquarter of the *Gambier Bay*, gunning for an engine room. Suddenly he saw U.S. sailors gathering astern near some lifeboats, preparing to abandon ship. The Japanese skipper ordered, "Ceasefire," and directed his midshipman to aim at the forecastle, where no people could be seen.

At roughly that time, around nine A.M., ten minutes after the abandon ship order circulated on the *Gambier Bay*, a flight of Wildcats fell from above and rattled the gunwales around the *Tone*'s bridge with squirts from their machine guns. A round struck Mayuzumi in the thigh, ricocheting off bone and ripping away an eight-by-ten-centimeter chunk of muscle. The captain fell to the deck but never left the bridge. As the ship's surgeon tended to him, he sat there in his own blood, unable to take his eyes off the *Gambier Bay*'s crew calmly gathering and dropping rope ladders down into the water. He could not help but admire the Americans' evident bravery. His devotion to gunnery had borne fruit for the empire. He had helped sink the only U.S. carrier of the war to succumb to surface gunfire. But he and his compatriots would soon assess the cost of Taffy 3's audacious resistance, the effectiveness of which no tactician could ever have foreseen and no statistician could have measured.

Thirty-six

The *Samuel B. Roberts* was blessed with luck and a low profile to the horizon. Shells whistled by overhead as Copeland steered his ship through the effervescent whirlpools of the enemy's misses. As he conned the ship, he stayed focused on the ocean ahead of him, paying no mind to what lay behind him. Suddenly he heard a lookout shout, "Captain, there's fourteen-inch splashes coming up on our stern!" The battleship *Kongo* lay some ten thousand yards in that direction, shooting with uncanny accuracy through the haze. At 7:22 her rangefinder had been disabled by strafing Wildcats. Now it was restored. As the Cyclops fixed on the *Samuel B. Roberts*, the *Kongo*'s guns boomed salvos of 1,485-pound shells Bob Copeland's way.

Copeland turned and saw a procession of foaming columns walking up from behind. Gauging the progress of the explosions— the closest of them smacked the sea fifty yards astern—relative to the movement of his speeding ship, he knew what he had to do: hit the brakes. The normal procedure, designed to spare strain on expensive reduction gears, was to ratchet down from flank speed to standard, two-thirds, one-third, and stop. But Copeland's worries went beyond the condition of Lucky Trowbridge's precious machinery. Like a driver speeding down the freeway shifting straight into reverse, he shouted into the voice tube, "All engines back full!"

"That was the one time the old ship really shuddered and shivered and quaked," Copeland wrote. "She just kind of lay down and pretty nearly backed her stern under water." The destroyer escort's bow wave collapsed as her forward movement stopped. Almost immediately there were more sounds like runaway freight trains and an ungodly buffeting of air. Directly over the ship flew another brace of battleship shells. They smacked the ocean a hundred yards ahead, right where the *Roberts* would have been had Copeland not slammed on the brakes.

The captain had no time to congratulate himself. No sooner had he called for flank speed again than a salvo from a heavy cruiser found the mark. From the barn-door range of 5,500 yards, the cruiser spat three eight-inch shells into the *Roberts*'s low-slung broadside. The time was 8:51.

Seaman first class Bill Katsur "felt as though I were a bedsheet on a clothesline being whipped by a strong wind." The hit knocked out the electrical distribution board in the internal communications gyro room, and with the loss of auxiliary power, lights throughout many lower compartments went black. Communications throughout the ship went dead too. A second shell punctured the bulkhead of the forward handling room, penetrating without exploding and duly exiting the compartment to starboard. The third hit was the most catastrophic. It struck the main deck below the davits that held the motor whaleboat and entered the forward fireroom. Steam lines were torn, and the steam did what steam does when it is released from high-pressure lines. Amid the sudden hissing horror, all but two men died. But Jackson McCaskill, a teenage seaman second class, retained his wits. Two weeks earlier the kid had been reassigned to the black gang in the forward fireroom because he was, according to his skipper, "an absolute flop on the deck force." The eighteen-year-old outlived that reputation now. He coolly turned off the fires beneath the boilers and spun the valves that cut the flow of steam from the boilers and the supply of fuel into the burners. McCaskill pulled the headphones from the body of Chester Kupidlowsky, a fireman killed by the blast, and called the engine room to ask for help opening the escape hatch to let the live steam escape to the open air. Then, with the flesh on his feet burned down to white bone, McCaskill wedged his 130-pound frame under a deck grating, dropped down into the bilges, and lay prostrate against the last piece of cool steel on the ship, the bottom of the hull where the keel cut the sea.

In the CIC, right above the punctured number-one boiler room, Tom Stevenson, the communications officer, found himself bathed in steam and choking in a storm of asbestos that was pulverized by the explosion and blown through the ventilation ducts. The shower of insulation turned him white and filled his mouth and nostrils with thick dust. The gyro and radar were out, rendering the CIC useless. Bob Roberts, Stevenson, and the rest of the CIC gang decided to evacuate the compartment and went up to the bridge, but the small enclosure was crowded with other displaced CIC personnel looking to escape the steam. Copeland ordered the bridge cleared—with the after fireroom working and two good engines, he still had a ship that could fight. Stevenson climbed up to the signal bridge. He felt a loud blast and a hot rush of wind. Some cloth sacks full of signal flags burst into flame near him, and Stevenson noticed he had taken shrapnel in his legs, but he was so scared that he didn't feel a thing.

The battle was nearly two hours old when the *Roberts* took her first hits. With the destruction of her forward boiler, the *Roberts* slowed from nearly thirty knots to seventeen. Lieutenant Trowbridge's snipes cross-connected the number-two fireroom to both engine rooms to keep the screws turning, but the ship no longer had the power to maneuver aggressively enough to chase salvos. At the helm quartermaster third class Elbert Gentry seemed unable to process Bob Copeland's commands. "Mr. Roberts," Copeland asked, "would you please take the wheel and get this ship out on the heading that I am trying to get to?" The exec took the helm from the shell-shocked quartermaster as Copeland tried gamely to take the ship south toward the carrier formation.

The shells from the heavy cruiser cut the power to many stations on the ship—Paul Carr's five-inch gun among them. Gun 52 still fired, but with the power out, certain systems critical to the mount's safe operation no longer worked, including the automatic gas ejection system that puffed air into the breech after each shell fired, clearing it of hot gases. When that system failed, the gases stayed inside and gun number two's breech grew hotter with every salvo. George Bray, assigned to repair party number three, relieved a man in Gun 52's handling room who had dropped from the exhaustion and the heat. Bray's football prowess kept him in good shape, and he and the five other men in the compartment kept a steady supply of fifty-four-pound, twenty-one-inch-long projectiles loaded into the hoist. The men from the magazine one deck below passed ammunition up to him, and Bray dropped each shell into the hoist, nose down into its funnel-shaped housing. He'd close the hatch on the hoist, and there followed an electrohydraulic shriek as one hoist carried the live round up and the empty one cycled back down to the handling room.

Carr and his superb crew in Gun 52 were in their rhythm, grabbing powder cases out of the slot, laying them in the breech, picking the projectiles off the hoist, sliding them in ahead of the powder case, ramming shut the breech, firing the gun, kicking the spent case out the hole down onto the deck, and starting the sequence again. When the power went out, they rammed the tray into the breech by hand. When the air ejection system broke down a few minutes after that, Carr and his men got off seven or eight more shots before the inevitable happened.

In the lower handling room two decks below the gun, George Bray heard a deep, percussive *bfff*, like a big paddle smacking a mattress. There was shouting and sounds of men in pain. A shell had cooked off in the breech, detonated by contact with the overheated tray in which it sat. Burning gunpowder sprayed out of the barrel, setting part of the fantail afire. But most of the damage stayed inside the mount. The blast killed most of Carr's gun mount team immediately with a pressure wave that blew a tongue of flame down into the handling room beneath the turret.

In the gun mount itself, there were some lucky souls. When the shell cooked off, seaman second class Sam Blue had been standing by the mount's open side door, half inside and half out. The explosion propelled him, unconscious, a fair distance out into the water. He hit the surface hard enough to trigger the CO_2 cartridge on his inflatable life belt. Bill Stovall was blasted off the ship too, but not before inhaling a lungful of flames and superheated air that left him screaming in the water.

Little Sammy—the fifteen-pound, short-haired, mixed-breed mascot of the *Roberts*, the Norfolk mutt turned honorary water tender—had grown smart in the ways of ships. He could run up and down the steep ladders and find safe places to ride out the long rolls in typhoons. He was afraid of the roar down in the fireroom and had an uneasy relationship with the ship's two five-inch gun turrets. But the dog had never before seen the likes of the pulverizing rain of shellfire now smashing his ship all around him. The explosions and their bloody effects sent Sammy into a fit. "I felt sorry for him," Copeland wrote. "He was running up and down the deck with all the guns firing and the men he knew lying dead in blood and gore. He actually went off his beam."

On the bridge, Copeland felt the ship shake hard as another shell struck the heavy base of the forty-millimeter mount astern. Another tore into the deckhouse to which the mount was bolted. Looking back, the skipper caught a glimpse of the bodies of men from the gun and the Mark 51 director mount hurtling through the air. As the wind shoved aside a cloud of white smoke, which drifted heavily across the fantail, Copeland discovered that the explosion had blown away the entire machine-gun mount and with it assistant gunnery officer Lt. (jg) John LeClercq and twelve crewmen. No traces of the men or the large steel mount were ever seen again.

The deck leading forward to the ship's triple-torpedo mount lay torn away, twisted and sagging. Another concussion came as Lieutenant Trowbridge's number-one engine room took a direct hit. Normally the eight-inch armor-piercing rounds punched through the hull spaces without detonating. This one hit an I-beam supporting a large switchboard panel and exploded. The ensuing fireball left only one survivor there, a fireman named Herman Metzger.

With one screw disabled, the *Roberts* had no more speed than an escort carrier and a lot less maneuverability. Lt. Bob Roberts did his best to carry the ship through the deadly gauntlet, but its miraculous dry sprint through a driving rain had come to an end. The gunners on the *Kongo* never relented. Now they took advantage of the wounded ship's critical loss of speed. Three massive shells from the Japanese battleship screamed downward, struck aft, and exploded.

A thunderous blast knocked down everyone on the bridge except Charles Cronin, a yeoman second class who happened to be holding on to the levers of the engine order telegraph. To Copeland, "it seemed as if the whole ship went out from under us." From the force involved he guessed that the Japanese had finally wised up and loaded high-explosive rounds. Thrown from the steps leading from the open-air bridge to the pilothouse, the skipper slammed into a pile with Lieutenant Roberts and Elbert Gentry. The quartermaster lifted himself up, bleeding from the mouth, missing a tooth. As Copeland dusted himself off, he looked around and felt an insane impulse to laugh at the sight of several of his talkers sprawled across the grating of the bridge wing with their big headsets knocked askew and entangled in a ludicrous mess of wires. Amazingly, no one there was hurt. But Copeland's mood sobered when it dawned on him that his ship was no longer moving. Looking forward from the bridge, he might have wondered why.

As far as I could see, the ship was as nice as the day she left the shipyard because the damage had been down below deck, but from the stack aft she was a pretty sorry-looking sight. There were two twenty-millimeter gun tubs, number six and number eight, with parts of human bodies hanging out of them; and there was the deck of the deckhouse warped back like a piece of linoleum ripped up and from there on aft nothing but a yawning mass of blackened metal as the various thwartships and fore and aft bulkheads had been twisted together and the deck ripped off where that gun had disappeared.

There was no denying the mortal wound the *Roberts* had taken. At the waterline, about two-thirds of the way to the stern on the port side, gaped a cavernous hole seven to ten feet high and some fifty feet long. The massive opening would have neatly garaged a semitrailer parked sideways. The number-two engine room was completely demolished. When the after fuel-oil tanks ruptured, they threw flaming oil everywhere. The starboard "K-gun" depth-charge launcher was hanging over the side, and tar was oozing onto the deck from ruptured depth charges.

As if to remind the skipper that life could get worse, a torpedo wake came bubbling in to starboard. There was no way to avoid it. As the faint white wake came straight on amidships, Copeland gripped the edge of the bridge wing and screamed, his voice cracking, "Stand by for tor—!" But one last miracle remained, it seemed. The torpedo passed just under the destroyer escort's keel, missing, by the captain's estimation, by no more than a foot.

Belowdecks the men still had a chance. In the aft lower handling room, George Bray's world had gone dark. He fumbled through the void, looking for a way out. He circled back through the after steering room and heard water rushing in from somewhere. Suddenly, through an open hatch forward, water came swirling all around him. In the torrent, mattresses floated by, like rafts on the inflow, and empty shell cases too. The flow was strong enough to carry away Bray's life belt and left shoe. He hung on to some cables to steady himself.

Around this time Bob Copeland got his last look at the USS *Johnston*. When Ernest Evans's destroyer passed close by the *Roberts*, and in the midst of his own ruin, Copeland was heartbroken to see up close what had become of the proud tin can. The image of the battered ship stayed with him for the rest of his life.

> *I can see her right now. She had taken a terrific beating. Her bridge was battered and had been abandoned. Her foremast, a steel tubular mast, coming up just abaft of the bridge superstructure, had been split from shellfire and then bent down over itself. . . .*
>
> *It gave me a hurt feeling to look at it. Her searchlights had been knocked off. One torpedo mount was gone, and her number-three gun had completely disappeared. As she went by—limping along at a pretty slow speed—I saw her captain. He was a very big man with coal-black hair; his name was Evans. I had met him at some of those conferences. He was standing on the fantail conning his ship by calling down through an open scuttle hatch into the steering engine room. I can see him now. He was stripped to the waist and was covered with blood. His left hand was wrapped in a handkerchief. . . .*
>
> *As he went by—he wasn't over a hundred feet from us as he passed us on our starboard side—he turned a little and waved his hand at me. That's the last I saw of him.*

*   *   *

BOB COPELAND WAS STRUGGLING with a decision he had not wanted to make until the grotesque reality of his warship's condition thrust it upon him: should he give the order to abandon ship? He was frankly in awe of the *Sammy B.*'s ruggedness under duress. The Bureau of

Ships and the folks at Brown Shipyard really knew their trade. Lloyd Gurnett showed up on the bridge covered in the remains of shell-blasted asbestos lagging. As first lieutenant, he knew his ship's compartments and passageways and ladders and bulkheads intimately. On those raw scores, the *Samuel B. Roberts* had little left to offer the U.S. Navy. Gurnett told Copeland that the ship was settling by the stern. The starboard list was tipping the inclinometer at eleven degrees, he said. Both engine rooms were out of action, all communications and power gone. The only unanswered question pertained to the condition of the ship's main gun batteries. Could they still shoot at the enemy, and was there anything left in the magazines to shoot at them? Jack Moore was ordered forward to check on Gun 51, and Tom Stevenson was sent aft to appraise Paul Carr's group.

Stevenson didn't want to do it. He wasn't sure he could. Ever since the aft forty-millimeter gun was carried off, Tom Stevenson had been terribly shaken up. The young officer in command back there, John LeClercq, had been one of his best friends. Stevenson had spoken with him over the phones during the battle. He was impressed by LeClercq's calm as the young officer directed the firing of the after guns. He was a good kid and a good destroyerman for the same reason: he was always looking out for someone else. At one point LeClercq had had the presence of mind to train his forty-millimeter mount on a spread of torpedoes bubbling toward Sprague's carriers. Johnny LeClercq was the very picture of wholesome blond American innocence, considerate of the enlisted men, devoted to the Navy, and meticulous in his duties. He wrote home regularly to his parents in Dallas, signing the letters "Sonny." Even from a hemisphere away, he never forgot his younger brother's rites of passage—Bobby's birthdays, the first days of school. Though the twenty-three-year-old cultivated a superstitious side—he carried a carved wooden skunk for good luck—he kept a realistic attitude toward death. Informed by his mother of the passing of a friend in another theater of battle, he sat down at his desk sixteen days before the destruction of the USS *Samuel B. Roberts* and wrote this: "I am sorry to hear about H. P. Inge. He was a swell boy, and I guess that war is where brains alone won't save you, as he would still be going now if it would. . . . Tell his family—chin up and don't worry. Everything will be all right in the end."

Because he took this latter assertion as an article of faith, death never preoccupied him. He was too busy enjoying life. He seemed to walk through his days on the *Samuel B. Roberts* as if lit by a sunrise within. "The few things you saw him do and say made you want to know him better," a friend observed. Two short hours ago Tom Stevenson had shaken LeClercq's hand, wishing him luck as the general quarters gong scattered the crew to battle stations. Now Johnny, along with so many others, was gone, truly gone, the explosions so powerful as to erase them from the air. Others had died too, but their bodies remained to be counted.

The communications department boss had encountered death at sea before. Before the war his family earned their keep operating Norwegian-licensed cargo ships out of New York Harbor. The chartered Liberty and Victory ships of T. J. Stevenson & Co. took a variety of cargoes on their plodding nine-knot cruises up and down the eastern seaboard. They took lumber from St. John, New Brunswick, carried it to Jamaica, and brought sugar cane on the return leg. When he was sixteen Tom Stevenson went to sea, entering the family business as a deckboy. When he left on his first voyage, his mother stuck a big bottle of aftershave lotion in his duffel. On his first night at sea his cabinmate, a fortysomething Norwegian steward who seemed drunk all the time, stole the bottle and drank it. While Stevenson slept, the man rigged a makeshift gallows and hung himself beneath the teenager's bunk. The following morning the captain gave Stevenson one of his first shipboard duties, ordering him to gather wood from the hold and make a coffin.

It was all very unsettling, but Stevenson had stayed aboard ship and in short order become a qualified helmsman. After high school he attended Georgetown University's School of Foreign Service. One Sunday afternoon during his junior year Stevenson was watching a Redskins football game at Griffith Stadium when suddenly all of the admirals and generals in the crowd were called out of their seats. A war was on, it seemed, although nobody seemed to know exactly where this place, Pearl Harbor, was. Less than two years later, by which time Stevenson was a commissioned officer and a specialist in naval communications, the *Samuel B. Roberts* was ready for launching in Houston.

Though Tom Stevenson had joined the Navy well acquainted with death at sea, it did not prepare him for this. Nothing could have. A man hanging himself was one thing. A seagoing slaughterhouse enabled by industrial-age engines of war was quite another. Unlike the armor-piercing rounds that had penetrated earlier without exploding, the high-explosive shells that hit the *Roberts* now performed exactly as designed.

Stevenson looked down the ladder from the bridge wing to the deck at the dead whose bodies remained intact. Some of them appeared completely uninjured. There was no blood, no mess. They just lay there on the deck, unscathed, locked into poses that looked ridiculous, somehow vaguely athletic. Down at the foot of the ladder, corpses littered the deck. Stevenson decided he didn't need to go down there. There was no viable route aft in any event. He could see the deckhouse back there, blasted all apart. The passageways along the rail on either side of it were obstructed by sheets of twisted, blackened metal and bodies of a similar description. The deck was aflame with burning oil and sizzling chunks of depth charge explosives. It was plain enough that Gun 52 was no longer firing, though its barrel still glowed cherry-red.

Tom Stevenson went back as far as he could, gave an exploratory shout, and getting no encouraging response, reported the grim news to his captain. Gun 51 wasn't working either. Jack Moore came back and said there were still forty-two rounds left in the magazine, but the gun had been jarred so severely that it no longer rotated on its base.

The ship was quiet now. The guns did not fire, and the boilers no longer roared. There were no screams anymore, just a peculiar graveyard calm. The silence revealed no new horrors. If Japanese shells were still rushing by overhead, crashing in columns of colorful brine, they failed to make the same impression that they had made two hours before. They didn't matter now. The dead were so promiscuous, the damage so profound, that there was no terror left in the shells' descent.

Thirty-seven

In his final moments aboard the *Hoel,* Captain Kintberger helped Commander Thomas to the rail. The screen commander was severely wounded, with a large section of one arm torn out, from the biceps to mid-forearm. The skipper guided him overboard and jumped. The two officers hit the water and kicked out to steady themselves. Kintberger found a battered life raft whose wooden latticework had been chipped to pieces in the rain of shrapnel. He pulled several *Hoel* crew from the surrounding water into the raft's sanctuary. As he went up, over, and in, Thomas gritted his teeth and tried to grin, keeping up appearances. There was a cry from behind them, and George Driscoll was there. Someone grabbed the mortally wounded chief torpedoman by the shirt and hauled him aboard. The worst off were placed inside the raft, sheltered from the elements and stabilized so they did not have to move. Those without wounds or slightly hurt treaded water alongside, holding on to the raft's outer shell. Going overboard, Myles Barrett had lost most of his pants when they snagged on a grappling hook. Now he took off his T-shirt and used it to stop Thomas's bleeding. With his shirt turned into a tourniquet, he was left wearing only his belt, his boxers, and the back pockets of his pants, flapping in the tide.

Just minutes after the Japanese drew first blood from the *Samuel*

B. Roberts, the USS *Hoel* rolled over and sank. As her crew turned and watched, the destroyer got it over with quickly, rolling to port and going down by the stern. Her bow rising, a windy sucking sound was heard as water rushed in and forced air out of the lower compartments. Disappearing below the surface in sequence went the bridge, then Gun 52, then Gun 51, then the neatly trimmed bow. The sea swallowed her whole. Kintberger's raft moved toward the spot where the ship sank, drawn by the inward tug of seawater displaced as the ship passed into the deep. Lieutenant Dix:

> *The sound of water lapping at the raft,*
> *The voices of the others talking low,*
> *The strange unwelcome stillness of the scene,*
> *Brought home the dreadful loneliness and loss.*

Because their ship was the first to go under, the battle passed them by, the American ships disappearing over the southern horizon. Their solitude lasted only for a few minutes. Soon enough elements of the pursuing Japanese fleet appeared. John Dix heard the deep thrum of large diesel engines and saw the low form of an approaching column of destroyers. *Good God, haven't they done enough to us today?* he thought. He assumed he and his men would be butchered where they swam. The Japs would do to them precisely what the gunners and Marines aboard the *Hoel* had done to some Japanese seven months ago, at Emirau. Most everybody remembered the canoe incident at Emirau, though no one was eager to speak the name.

In March, during the drive to bypass and isolate the Japanese stronghold at Rabaul, the Fourth Marine Division had taken the island in the St. Matthias Group. The troops had met little resistance, and the *Hoel* and other destroyers patrolling the surrounding waters aimed to keep it that way. They were guarding against covert reinforcement by sea when they got their first up-close glimpse of Japanese fighting men. The destroyer came upon a native war canoe and found that it was filled with local kids, boys. It was strange, everyone thought. What were they doing in a combat zone? At least they took them for kids—until they got closer, and a man stood up in the canoe and started shooting them, one by one. They were Japanese soldiers. Their leader was not about to let them get taken prisoner.

Their audience aboard the *Hoel* didn't cotton to enemy gunfire opening up so close to them. They finished what the Japanese commander started. The forward forties were the first to open up—*poo-poom, poo-poom*. As the destroyer circled the skiff, the Marine detachment added their rifle fire to the fray. No one was left alive on that canoe.

Would the Japanese return the favor now?

Dix expected the sound of machine guns to rip the air. There was no hiding in the raft, yet there Commander Thomas and others were, crouching down inside as if they could conceal themselves. Seeing the futility of possum-playing and more than a little curious to see the men who had done in his proud ship, Dix watched the four destroyers approach. The first one struck him as absurdly huge. The *Hoel* must have looked that way to the soldiers on that canoe.

> *And see the men, how tall they seem, how clean*
> *And neatly dressed, not like we've heard they look.*
> *They're not at battle stations anymore,*
> *But khaki uniforms—must be marines.*
> *They've got a landing force aboard these ships.*
> *Look at 'em grin and point—they're wavin' now.*
> *Duck down, duck down—Okay—she's passed on by.*
> *But there's the second. Look! Her fish are gone.*
> *They fired the fish all right. Damn, here's the third.*
> *Wait, she's been hit. There, by the bridge. But she's*
> *The only one. The others all seem clean,*
> *Well-painted. Hell, these ships are smart.*

As the last enemy tin can approached, Dix feared he had pressed his luck too far with his rubbernecking. He ducked under water again and hid under the raft. Something must have told him this ship would have the killer crew. The ship steamed by, and as the raft rocked on the swells above his head, he raged at his powerlessness. Then, lungs burning, heart thumping in his chest, he went up again for air.

Myles Barrett saw them lined up by the rail. Japanese sailors, whooping it up, having a grand old time as their destroyer steamed triumphantly by. The close-up encounter with the enemy was like a throwback to another era, when sailing ships grappled and boarded one another. Even gunnery had once been conducted at such close range, yardarm to yardarm, that one ship's men could hear the other's shouts, prayers, songs, and pleas. The killing was more personal, but there also existed the possibility of surrender, capture, and mercy. By the middle of the twentieth century the reach of new weapons had made combat a cold, long-distance business. Warships didn't surrender to one another any longer. Commanders were insulated from their counterparts in closed bridges, communicating by secret codes and radio frequencies. Sea warfare became thoroughly depersonalized.

This was personal. Myles Barrett could see that the Japanese were holding objects in their hands. They were lobbing them into the water. Barrett thought he was a goner. *The Japs are throwing grenades at us.* Then the absurd reality settled in.

They were potatoes. Just potatoes.

In time, the Japanese ships were gone. No, just the *destroyers* were gone.

Captain Kintberger gave a shout, Dix turned, and a warship that made the destroyers look like bathtub toys was approaching them now. Its girth and height—all its dimensions—were on another scale altogether. Steel was piled and layered and cantilevered atop steel, capped by a wide-armed rangefinder seated atop the towering pagoda superstructure. Huge triple turrets aimed out over them at some distant point on the horizon. The sight of the battleship charging south in pursuit of Taffy 3 took Dix's breath away. They had no business being in the same ocean with this leviathan.

The sound of an airplane, a TBM Avenger, broke the spell. It bore down on that outsize superstructure's starboard side, diving like a hornet against an ox as black puffs of flak littered the sky all around it. The pilot released a bomb. As he streaked overhead and away, the weapon struck the water beside the armored hull, raising a tall column of water short of the ship. The huge ship sliced past the survivors of the *Hoel*, seeming to gloat in the pilot's failure. There went her turrets, her giant mast, her bristling secondary guns. "My God, look at that thing!" someone said. "That must be the *Yamato*."

The Japanese too watched their enemy with no small degree of interest. "Passing a fairly big dark red slick," wrote Admiral Ugaki, "we came to an area where enemy survivors were clinging to cutters and strewn all over. What did they think of the magnificent sight of our fleet in pursuit? As we were the enemies, they made no signs asking for help, though they must have wanted to."

The survivors of the *Hoel* had the first and last up-close glimpse any American sailor ever got of the IJNS *Yamato*, the largest battleship on the high seas. All across her fighting tops, crewmen stood erect at battle stations, the very image of readiness and invincibility. Dix and the others watched the superstructure and stacks loom by, the signal flags and pennants flying past, then the huge rear turret followed by an endless stretch of quarterdeck. The roaring wash of her wake seemed to cleanse the sea of her overwhelming presence.

Astern of the *Yamato*, less than a thousand feet from the bobbing American destroyermen, followed the *Nagato*, slightly less imposing, older, but no less majestic. There came the sound of another aircraft engine, then a high-pitched scream as it entered into its dive. Through the clouds appeared a Navy F6F Hellcat—the four jeeps of Taffy 1 carried a few of the late-model Grumman fighters. As the plane fell toward the Japanese ship, seaman first class Glenn Parkin could see its six wing-mounted guns winking. He was close enough to hear the rattle of the bullets hitting the battleship's metal superstructure and hardwood decks. The Japanese fired back, to no result. In about thirty seconds, the show was over. The Hellcat disappeared into the gray wash of clouds. The Japanese battleship steamed on, unperturbed.

> It made us bitter then to watch that strength,
> To feel our weakness in this awful hour,
> To see their flag so boldly flying still,
> To know we hadn't done a thing to them
> Nor held them back, nor even slowed them down.
> They've sunk the carriers, the other cans!
> Now they're re-forming, getting set to go
> To Leyte Gulf and strike our transport ships.
> What's happened? Lord, what's happened to our fleet?

Thirty-eight

By the time the *Hoel* went down, four heavy cruisers, the *Tone*, the *Chikuma*, the *Haguro*, and the *Chokai*, damaged but hungrily in pursuit, had turned the corner from a southerly to a southwesterly course, following Sprague's carriers in their clockwise evasive path. Having destroyed the *Hoel*, crippled the *Gambier Bay*, ravaged the *Johnston*, and blasted the *Samuel B. Roberts* in a mismatched duel, there was little else for the Japanese to do but polish off Sprague's resilient jeeps, then charge toward Leyte Gulf, crushing whatever else lay in the way.

Shortly before nine o'clock the tail-end Charlie in the Japanese heavy cruiser column, the *Chokai*, absorbed a hard blow. There was no telling who fired the lucky shot. It is not easy to determine whether it came from a Taffy 3 ship or a plane. Indeed, for students of the Pacific war, the exact circumstances of the *Chokai*'s demise remain largely a mystery. Sometime during the wild running fight a five-inch shell exploded near the cruiser's stern torpedo tubes. Torpedoes were foreign to U.S. heavy cruisers. While the naval treaties prohibited cruisers from carrying torpedoes in any event, American designers considered the powerful weapons too volatile and dangerous to install on ships meant to stand and fight in a battle line. In breaking the Washington Naval Treaty, Japan accepted the risks, both political and tactical. The *Chokai* now paid the price.

She had been closing on the carriers for nearly two hours now, opening fire at 7:05 and advancing implacably on Taffy 3's port quarter, chasing Sprague around a circle that she could never quite seem to close, owing to the unrelenting air attacks and the stout resistance of Taffy 3's screen. Now, running nearly due west under spirited fire from assailants hidden in smoke, the *Chokai* took a shell amidships on the starboard side. A larger blast followed it, a fiery secondary explosion likely caused by one of her own torpedoes.

At the time lookouts on the *Haguro* reported that the *Chokai* was "under concentrated shellfire from enemy main strength, receiving hits on starboard side amidships." Which American ships the *Haguro* observers considered "enemy main strength" is far from clear. Most likely it was not the *Samuel B. Roberts*. At the time Captain Copeland's ship was in the last moments of its desperate duel with a cruiser positively identified by her skipper as a *Tone*-class ship, probably the *Chikuma*. The *Heermann* too was engaged with the *Tone* or the *Chikuma* when the *Chokai* received the fateful blow before nine A.M. At that time the *Johnston* was intercepting Admiral Kimura's destroyer line; only after nine did Captain Evans's ship begin alternating fire between the Japanese destroyers and cruisers. And it couldn't have been the *Hoel* either—Captain Kintberger's destroyer was by then a ruin, her guns silent, her men leaping over the rail.

Evidence suggests that the *Chokai* was knocked out of action by the enterprising peashooter crew on the escort carrier *White Plains*. If it was the *White Plains*'s gun crew that earned the accolade "main enemy strength," it was a fine tribute to them—and not the only time during the battle that the Japanese misestimated their opponent. As likely as not, it was the *White Plains*'s marksmanship that signaled the beginning of the end for the proud imperial cruiser and a man-bites-dog shift in the momentum of the battle.

From 11,700 yards the jeep carrier's gun crew put six shells into the *Chokai*. The deadly Long Lance torpedoes that had littered the Pacific Ocean floor with the hulks of American ships now backfired on one of their own. There was a large explosion. Lookouts on the *Haguro* saw the *Chokai* signal, "ENGINE OUT OF COMMISSION." The crippled cruiser sheered out of line to port and limped away to the east, slowing and settling fast.

* * *

THROUGHOUT THE MORNING AMERICAN pilots swarmed Kurita's ships in ever greater numbers. The first planes to strike from Taffy 3's squadrons, armed for other missions, were suited only for harassment. Now the fliers from the other two Taffy groups weighed in. Taffy 1, farthest from Sprague, about fifty miles south, was largely occupied with the question of its own survival as Japanese Army bombers swarmed from bases on Luzon. Still, a number of planes from the *Natoma Bay* and other Taffy 1 carriers got into the fray off Samar. Meanwhile, mostly free of the immediate danger of air attack and surface gunfire, Taffy 2's carriers had more time in which to arm their planes for killing ships. Plane handlers and ordnancemen worked themselves to exhaustion arming and launching planes throughout the morning.

Stump's group had launched one well-armed strike at 7:45. Now its second strike—consisting of eight Wildcats and sixteen Avengers—aloft by 8:44, vectored itself into the fray. Led by Cdr. Richard L. Fowler, commander of the *Kitkun Bay*'s VC-5, these pilots had the right weapons for the job—torpedoes and five-hundred-pound semi-armor-piercing bombs. A three-plane element of TBM Avengers packed as much punch as a destroyer escort; a full squadron of the torpedo bombers matched the hitting power of a *Fletcher*-class destroyer. Their well-orchestrated arrival marked a new phase of the battle. The tin cans of Taffy 3 had held the line; now the planes were coming to turn the tide. Taffy 3 would not have to carry the hopeless fight alone any longer.

Four Avengers approached the *Chikuma* from nearly head-on, two planes coming in at a fifteen-degree angle off either side of the cruiser's bow. It was a textbook anvil attack. If the targeted ship turned to starboard, the torpedoes off the port bow would hit her. A course change to port would expose the starboard side as the proverbial broad side of the barn. Capt. Saiji Norimitsu turned his ship to starboard, giving the planes on the port side a large broadside to hit. At 8:53 a torpedo from one of these TBMs struck the *Chikuma* on the port side near the stern. According to observers on her sister ship,

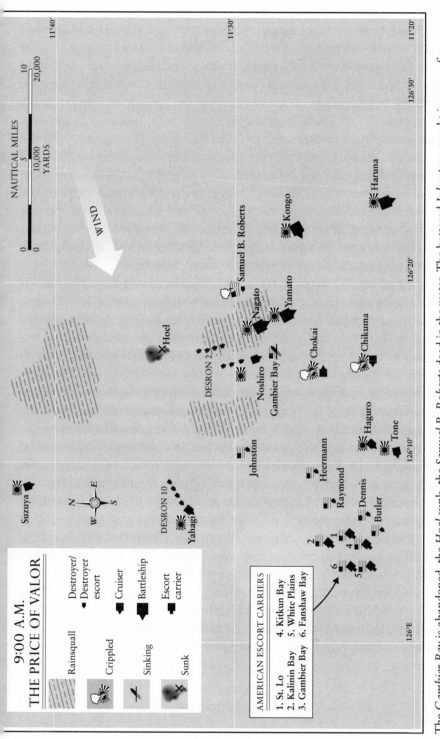

9:00 A.M.
THE PRICE OF VALOR

NAUTICAL MILES
YARDS

WIND

Rainsquall	Destroyer/ Destroyer escort
Crippled	Cruiser
Sinking	Battleship
Sunk	Escort carrier

AMERICAN ESCORT CARRIERS
1. St. Lo   4. Kitkun Bay
2. Kalinin Bay   5. White Plains
3. Gambier Bay   6. Fanshaw Bay

Suzuya

N
W   E
S

DESRON 10
Yahagi

Johnston

Heermann

Raymond

Dennis

Butler

DESRON 2

Hoel

Samuel B. Roberts

Nagato
Yamato
Noshiro
Gambier Bay
Chokai
Chikuma

Haguro
Tone

Kongo

Haruna

The *Gambier Bay* is abandoned, the *Samuel B. Roberts* dead in the water. The battered *Johnston*, caught in a crossfire between enemy destroyers and heavy cruisers, fights gamely on. The heavy cruisers *Tone* and *Haguro* bear down on Sprague's carriers. But air attacks on the Japanese pursuers intensify: the heavy cruisers *Chikuma* and *Chokai* take crippling blows.

the *Tone,* "there was a burst of flame and simultaneously a column of water almost as high as the length of the ship shot up into the air. [The *Chikuma's*] afterdeck single-mount machine gun and other gear were seen blown into the air. The after half of the afterdeck was apparently heavily damaged, and settled in the water." Indeed, the damage was very heavy. The torpedo explosion appears to have severed a sixty-foot section of the *Chikuma's* stern. Under fire from the *Samuel B. Roberts* and the peashooter crews of several CVEs, the cruiser burned fiercely. Now, with the jagged remains of her truncated quarterdeck cracked and sagging, the *Chikuma* veered to the left, running eastward on one propeller and signaling "RUDDER DISABLED" to her compeers. While his engineers struggled to restore navigability, Captain Norimitsu signaled Admiral Kurita at 9:20, "ONE PROPELLER, SPEED EIGHTEEN KNOTS, UNABLE TO STEER."

The *Chokai* too was nearing her end. Already damaged by the induced explosion of one of her own torpedoes, she took her hardest blow yet from the sky. Commander Fowler had been airborne for more than two hours guiding the improvised aerial assault on the Center Force. At 9:05 he began maneuvering in order to attack with the sun at his back to blind the enemy antiaircraft gunners. Orbiting the Japanese fleet three times before the path of his flight was aligned to his liking, he led three other Avengers and a dozen Wildcats through the clouds. Surprise was complete. No flak came his way. Already limping, the cruiser, which Fowler identified as *Mogami*-class but more than likely was the *Chokai,** didn't have a chance. In thirty-five seconds the VC-5 skipper, flying an unarmed plane, led Lieutenant Issitt, Lieutenant (junior grade) Globokar, and Lieutenant (junior grade) Turner down upon the unsuspecting ship. The blows they landed were staggering. Fowler reported that five five-hundred-pound bombs struck the *Chokai* amidships, three more blasted the bow, and another hit astern. Whether Fowler was overly optimistic or not, the cruiser was a shambles. According to Fowler, "heavy steam and black smoke rose to five hundred feet or more during a series of three heavy explosions." The pilot watched the ship reel out of control for five hundred yards or so, then shake again from an internal blast.

---

*The only two *Mogami*-class cruisers in the battle, the *Kumano* and the *Suzuya*, were huddled far to the north, out of the fight.

Capt. Kosaku Ariga, the *Chokai*'s skipper, turned his cruiser sharply to the right. At 9:18 observers on the *Yamato* logged the *Chokai* signaling, "DIRECT BOMB HIT IN FORWARD MACHINERY SPACES. ATTEMPTING TO REPAIR SAME." Although Commander Fowler claimed the ship blew up and sank within five minutes of this strike, triumphantly calling out over the radio, "*Scratch one CA,*"* it seems the foundering ship survived for the moment. Pilots from the Taffy 2 jeep *Marcus Island* reported that "the cruiser was seen to smoke heavily, stop, and then get under way slowly." Japanese records too suggest that the *Chokai* got moving again. The ship reportedly limped northward until 9:40 P.M., when, finally unnavigable and settling, she was scuttled by torpedoes from the destroyer *Fujinami*.

His lethal work done, Fowler rendezvoused with his fellow fliers and headed for Taffy 2 to land. En route, he could see two battleships headed at high speed to the southeast—the *Kongo* and the *Haruna*—firing at extreme range at Taffy 2, thirty miles to Taffy 3's south. Fowler radioed Admiral Stump on the *Natoma Bay*, informing him what was headed his way. His timing was perfect. At that moment the Taffy 2 commander was readying yet another air strike. The battleships would get some of it.

* * *

BUT THE TIDE OF battle would not turn without cost. At 9:07 the stricken *Gambier Bay*, abandoned twenty minutes before, alone and mercilessly battered by the heavy cruisers, finally sank. Captain Vieweg was among the last to leave the ship. He stayed on the bridge until he was satisfied of the crew's progress, then descended the superstructure. He couldn't see a thing. Smoke and hot gases were pouring upward from an unseen conflagration below, blinding him.

Vieweg felt his way aft, looking for the ladder down to the starboard catwalk. In the smoke and steam he missed the ladder altogether and plummeted into a void. The smoke was so black and the heat so intense that the captain, thoroughly disoriented, feared he had fallen right into the main exhaust stack. On a CVE its yawning black chasm was nearly flush with the flight deck. Panicked, Vieweg grabbed the rim of the steel enclosure he lay in and hauled himself

---

*In Navy parlance, "CA" indicates a heavy cruiser.

out of it. Then he was falling again. He broke into clear air, fell about forty feet to the water, and was nearly choked by the strap on his battle helmet when he plunged in. He surfaced to find the carrier's ten-thousand-ton bulk rolling to starboard, threatening to come down on top of him. He swam madly toward the stern and cleared the ship by the time it finally turned turtle, exhaled the last of the stale air from its compartments, and entered the formidable depths of the Philippine Sea.

From the cockpit of his Wildcat, Larry Budnick of the *St. Lo*'s VC-65 saw a carrier lying there, its keel bared to the sky. Wallowing upside down, the flat-bottomed carrier looked to the aviator like a brand-new flight deck. Strangely, the Japanese ships were still firing into the ruined ship. He had never imagined that this could happen. Carriers, no matter their size, were the queen bees of the fleet. In nearly three years of warfare all across the Pacific, not one had fallen to a hostile surface force's guns. Budnick watched the *Gambier Bay* in her final moments and wondered: *How many more are going to go? We're going to lose the whole group.*

Thirty-nine

Having apparently repelled the *Yahagi* and her four destroyer consorts only to see them double back and reengage, the *Johnston* was
surrounded by enemy ships. Evans's hobbled destroyer faced two
cruisers to port, two more straight ahead, and several destroyers loi-
tering in the smoke to starboard. Shells from Kimura's destroyers had
demolished the coding room, the chart storage compartment, and radio control. Under the renewed bombardment the forty-millimeter
ready service magazine started exploding. Then Gun 52, captained
by gunner's mate third class Donald A. Coleman, took a hit right by
the pointer's seat. Everyone in the mount was either killed or criti-
cally wounded. Fires broke out in the magazine below, filling the upper handling room with smoke and making the bridge all but
untenable. Inside Gun 55 Clint Carter didn't know what had happened, but through the sight door he could see damage-control crews
struggling to get around the rolling pile of empty brass powder casings around his gun mount.

Below the port bridge wing, empty shell casings from Gun 52 had
piled up so thickly that it could hardly turn without sending the brass
cylinders rolling and clattering all over the deck. Men on the antiaircraft guns, having nothing to shoot at, occupied themselves with this
minor hazard, slinging the spent shells, still hot to the touch, over the

side, when the shell hit. Several of the gun crew were blown out the hatch on the starboard side of the mount. Bill Mercer laid seaman first class Glenn Heriford on the deck along the bulkhead under the wing. "Merc, straighten my leg out," Heriford said. There was nothing to straighten out. His leg was practically blown off.

The smoke from the fires forward flowed upward and engulfed the gun director. "The place was full of smoke," Bob Hagen wrote, "our eyes were streaming, and we were coughing and choking as we carried out our duties. We were now in a position where all the guts and gallantry in the world couldn't save us. . . . We knew we could not survive, but we figured that help for the carriers must be on the way, and every minute's delay might count."

Where had everybody gone? Ellsworth Welch wondered as his ship drove under reddened washes of water that hissed into steam on decks made hot by fires raging below. The lieutenant returned to the bridge and found no one there. He noticed that the classified publications were gone. He jogged back to the fantail and found Captain Evans there, relaying his course changes through his talker, Joe Woolf, who shouted down a hatch to the men in the steering engine room. Evans's only problem seemed to be a shortage of rested crew to keep up with his rapid pace. The work of turning the wheel that drove the rudder pump was backbreaking. Gunners from useless gun mounts and other displaced crew gathered astern to take their turns at the pump wheel. But no sooner would they have the rudder turning one way than Evans would shout "Shift your rudder!" and they would swing it back around.

Chief boatswain's mate Clyde Burnett took turns with another big man, John Scheindele, cranking the rudder, then went back topside to help the captain pass orders. Some credit their survival to the erratic course that the manually steered destroyer made. But now the Japanese pressed in close, six to ten thousand yards away, delivering innumerable hits in the long minutes after 9:10 A.M.

For half an hour, the *Johnston* had alternated firing between the destroyers to starboard and then the cruisers to port in a futile effort to prevent both from overtaking the carriers. But now the American ship could no longer slow them. Already the *Haguro* and the *Tone*, the swiftest heavy cruisers left to the Center Force, were pinching off Taffy 3's southward flight and threatening to push Sprague's ships toward the rocky coastline of Samar. The carriers fled west with their smoke screen, helped along by the light northeasterly breeze.

*   *   *

WITH THE *JOHNSTON* OUT of the way, Kurita faced a clear path to his mission objective in Leyte Gulf. Having weathered the gallant assault by Admiral Sprague's screen—having absorbed and mostly shrugged off the thirty-nine torpedoes they had put into the water ahead of him—he was ready to make his long-planned assault on San Pedro Bay. The *Heermann* was still around somewhere but wouldn't make much trouble with its ten torpedoes gone. The destroyer escort *John C. Butler,* unable to form up with its fellow DEs when Sprague ordered them to attack at 7:50, remained on station making smoke astern the carriers. Its three fish would not have done much to stop Kurita in any event. Admiral Stump's Taffy 2, having already been the target of ranging salvos from the *Haruna,* would be next on the Center Force's list of targets: six jeep carriers with their own seven-ship screen of destroyers and destroyer escorts. With Taffy 3's carriers sunk and unable to help Taffy 2, Stump's task unit would be all the easier to brush aside.

But Kurita did not yet enjoy the clear vision of hindsight. He had seen his proudest ships battered and sunk by an American air assault. By continuing south, he would only beg for more of it. His staff had intercepted a message from Capt. Richard F. Whitehead, the Seventh Fleet's Commander of Support Aircraft, inviting all orphaned jeep carrier pilots to land at Tacloban. Kurita was worried about steaming too close to the aerial striking power that was surely now gathering ashore. His own pleas for air support had gone unanswered. The help he expected from the Imperial Army's First and Second Air Fleets on Luzon—so central to the planning of the Sho-1 plan to begin with—never came.

Beneath unguarded skies the mighty *Musashi* had become a glorified target barge. Lack of air cover had cost Kurita several valuable heavy cruisers, the fastest blades in his rack of swords. He had left Brunei with ten of them, and he was down to six before he ever turned the corner coming out of San Bernardino Strait. Now he had only two. The *Chokai,* the *Chikuma,* and the *Suzuya* had succumbed to the audacious American air attacks. The *Kumano* was unfit for pursuit after the torpedo hit from the *Johnston*. Though the morning's assaults did not come in well-organized waves like those that had struck him the previous afternoon, they were incessant and persistent, like angry hornets. He did not cherish the idea of moving closer to their hive.

Kurita wasn't sure how he would re-form and enter Leyte Gulf in any event. The Center Force was strung out and scattered across some thirty miles of ocean. Reassembling into battle formation would take time that he probably did not have. From his expansive flag quarters aboard the *Yamato,* he did not know what his cruiser skippers knew: that they opposed mere escort carriers, and that they had nearly succeeded in cutting off Sprague's flight, forcing the Americans toward shore, where they could be encircled and destroyed in passing by the rest of the Center Force. Their transmissions to him had been short and cryptic. Wisps of partial knowledge, they had offered little on which to base a well-informed decision.

Kurita was in no position to know these things for himself. The *Yamato*'s emergency turn to avoid the *Heermann*'s torpedoes had taken the flagship northward and largely out of the battle at a critical juncture. The floatplanes he had catapulted to reconnoiter the American force had never been heard from again. Since he did not know what his own task force faced, it is unsurprising that he also did not know that Ozawa's decoy force had thoroughly succeeded in fooling Halsey. For all Kurita knew, Halsey was right here under his guns. His apparent inability to overtake the American carriers owed itself, he thought, to the fact that they were none other than those of the swift Third Fleet. What other explanation could there be? He had loosed his ships into a general attack, an oceangoing foxhunt rolling over the Pacific swells. He had sought to destroy their flight decks and prevent them from launching planes. In that he had failed.

These anxieties preyed upon a mind that was thoroughly battle-fatigued. Kurita hadn't slept in three days, ever since the *Atago* had been torpedoed out from under him in the Palawan Passage on October 23. Fished from the sea and relocated to the *Yamato,* he had witnessed on the following afternoon the destruction of Japan's proudest dreadnought, the *Musashi*. He had struggled with the decision to withdraw before sunset on the twenty-fourth, then turned around again and by night threaded his large formation through the perilous San Bernardino Strait. The next morning the unexpected windfall of American aircraft carriers coming under his guns further taxed his powers of analysis and command. Now even that coveted prize threatened to elude him, though he had gotten reports claiming that several U.S. flattops, including one of the *"Enterprise* class," had been sunk along with two heavy cruisers and some destroyers. But truth was cruelly at variance with Kurita's weary senses. As an American historian would wryly note, "Outfought by pygmies, he yet thought he had conquered giants." Now Kurita had to decide whether he should press his luck, gather his scattered force, and enter Leyte Gulf.

He calculated that the transports he was to sink were, in all likelihood, empty of their valuable cargoes. On the radio he had heard Admiral Kinkaid's plain-language calls for help. The Seventh Fleet commander's 8:29 plea—*"My situation is critical. Fast battleships and support by air strike may be able prevent enemy from destroying* [escort carriers] *and entering Leyte"*—had been retransmitted by Allied radio units in the Admiralty Islands and intercepted by the Japanese on Formosa at 9:05. But Kurita did not see this as the signal of opportunity that it was. Like a defeated man, he perceived his enemy's every act as evidence of its strength and ingenuity. Nishimura's group had been destroyed. Was his next? He grew anxious, expecting powerful American reinforcements to rally to Kinkaid's call at any moment.

"Anxieties," wrote Alfred Thayer Mahan, "are the test and penalty of greatness." On the cusp of a smashing victory, a commander must keep his nerve or fail altogether. According to that great American naval strategist, who had found an attentive readership in Japan:

> *Strenuous, unrelaxing pursuit is therefore as imperative after a battle as courage is during it. Great political results often flow from correct military action; a fact which no military commander is at liberty to ignore. He may very well not know of those results; it is enough to know that they may happen, and nothing can excuse his losing a point, which by exertion he might have scored.*

But further exertion was beyond Takeo Kurita. The Japanese admiral had been pressed to his physical and emotional limits. At 9:11 on the morning of October 25, he took stock of everything he knew and did not know and issued this order to his far-flung squadron:

Rendezvous, my course north, speed 20.

The commander of Cruiser Division 7 logged the message as *"All ships reassemble."* The *Haguro's* signal department heard *"Gradually reassemble."* Semantics aside, there was no mistaking the intent to withdraw.

The *Yamato* turned to port and headed north. Admiral Kimura received the withdrawal order just as his *Yahagi* and accompanying destroyers were again bearing down on the enemy carriers. Though the *Johnston's* interdiction was gallant, it was Kurita who finally spared the jeeps. For a second time Kimura's destroyers heeled around and headed north. At 9:20 the *Tone* and the *Haguro*, nearly in position to eviscerate Taffy 3 from point-blank range, turned in column and followed suit. At 9:25 the *Kongo* stopped the hunt and took her smoking fourteen-inch guns out of the battle. Five minutes later the *Haruna* broke off her freelancing assault on Taffy 2's northernmost elements.

Rendezvous, my course north.

The mighty Center Force was going home.

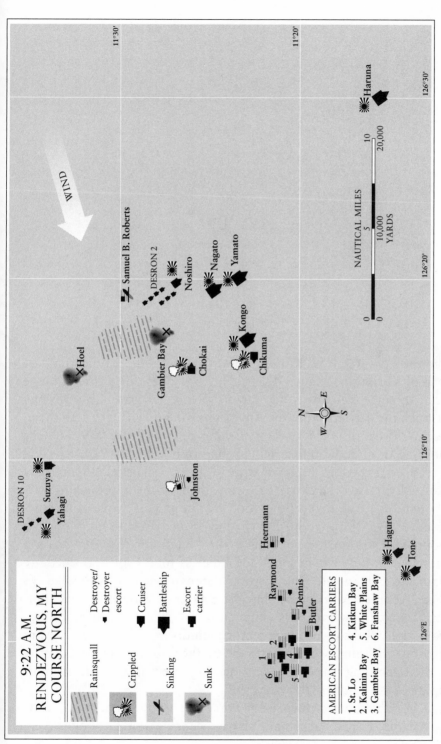

On the verge of victory, with the *Samuel B. Roberts* sinking and the *Johnston* dead in the water, Admiral Kurita loses his nerve and orders his ships to reassemble and withdraw. The threat to the U.S. beachhead in the Philippines ends.

Forty

The torpedo attack by Kimura's destroyers was the halfhearted last gasp of Kurita's beleaguered fleet. The torpedoes, fired at long range from an angle well abaft their targets' beam, had barely enough fuel to reach the carriers. Still, the Americans took no chances with them. Tex Waldrop of VC-65 was returning to his carrier after a busy morning of glide-bombing and strafing runs when he noticed a big spread of torpedoes foaming toward Taffy 3. His radioman, Roy McAnally, raised the carriers to warn them of the approaching fish. Though his plane had a three-foot hole in its port wing from Japanese flak, Waldrop swooped down and opened up with his two wing-mounted fifties on the bubbling wakes, while his eighteen-year-old gunner, aviation ordnanceman second class John Ciolek, opened fire from the ball turret. One torpedo detonated in the *Kalinin Bay*'s wake. Another exploded off the port quarter of Waldrop's own home ship, the *St. Lo,* whose peashooter crew claimed a third fish. The dramatic sight of the torpedo exploding in midocean spurred the crew to vigorous cheering. Machine-gunners on the two carriers blazed away at the remaining torpedoes, very possibly preventing a catastrophic replay of the *Liscome Bay* disaster.

The silhouettes of the Center Force ships, which had been growing steadily larger, darker, and more menacing as the minutes crept by, now began to recede. Aboard the *Fanshaw Bay*, Ziggy Sprague was occupied with avoiding the incoming Japanese torpedoes when, at 9:25, he heard a signalman shout, "God damn it, boys, they're getting away!" It was beyond comprehension. Sprague had begun the battle expecting to make history as the commander of the first carriers ever destroyed by naval gunfire. Now he made history as the victor in the most unlikely win in U.S. naval history.

"I could not believe my eyes, but it looked as if the whole Japanese fleet was indeed retiring." Sprague didn't accept the astonishing turn of events until several different pilots circling overhead confirmed it for him. Even then, Sprague wrote afterward, "I could not get the fact to soak into my battle-numbed brain. At best, I had expected to be swimming by this time."

*   *   *

AT 9:15 A.M., AS Kurita's ships were forming up to retreat, Bill Brooks, studying the sea through a hole in the cloud cover, spied a small dark speck trailing a thin wake of foam. He turned his Avenger in its direction and bore on in. The speck grew steadily larger, its boxy profile readily recognizable as an American CVE. Brooks closed range with the ship, lining up to pass alongside it with his landing gear down, indicating his request to land. A signal light flashed him a "prep Charlie," granting his request.

Wheeling around in a wide counterclockwise circle, lining up on the stern, Brooks entered the landing pattern and, with low fuel, was glad to catch an arrester wire on the first pass. The ship that took him aboard, the USS *Marcus Island,* was the adopted home of pilots from five different carriers. A mixed bag of aviators had found their way to the Taffy 2 carrier ahead of Brooks. Taken to separate debriefing rooms, they began drafting their action reports, then waited, endlessly waited, while their planes were taken down into the hangar deck for repairs and reloading. In the gathering of strangers, Brooks was happy to see a familiar face, that of his VC-65 squadronmate, Tom Van Brunt. In light of what they had seen that morning, neither man had much to say.

As the senior lieutenant in the group, Van Brunt was tapped to lead the next strike. Everyone was in a hyped-up state well before the squadron stewards served the coffee. Brooks took some deep breaths and said a few Hail Marys as he reflected on what he had been through. "I had really done some deep thinking as we were coming back. It was settling in on me what was happening. *What can I do?* I thought. I came to a realization: I didn't want to make a suicide run. A pilot was always better off alive than dead." Still, Brooks wasn't sure what could be done about the long odds facing them on the next sortie. He had no idea what the status of the Japanese fleet was. He knew only that it was big. The aviator told his crewmen, Joe Downs and Ray Travers, "I don't expect we're going to see the sunset. So if you don't care to join me on this mission, you've got my blessing. I don't think we're going to get out of this." The offer was a non-starter. The two aircrewmen wouldn't hear of it. They were all in this together.

As the plane handlers, armorers, aviation machinists, and ord-nancemen on the *Marcus Island* gassed, armed, and spotted the Avengers for launch, Tom Van Brunt diagrammed the plan of attack down in the ready room. In his whole aviation career Van Brunt had dropped just twelve torpedoes in practice. Only two of them had run true. That thought gripped him now. He was going out there for real, against real ships firing real flak that would kill him for real if his number came up and he took a hit. However slight his preparation, however, this was what he was there to do. He found a quiet place to pray for a moment and thought about his family—his older brother aboard the light cruiser *Reno;* his younger brother Bernard, whom he'd just seen at Seeadler Harbor at Manus, amid the huge gathering of Seventh Fleet ships; and his wife and first child, whose pictures adorned his desk. He prayed that somehow they would be cared for if he didn't return.

That possibility loomed large in his mind. He knew that once he was locked into a torpedo run, evasive action was out of the question. Limitations on speed and altitude and maneuverability made the chances of returning not terribly good. The men on the ships of Taffy 3 were bound to their fate. Jumping overboard was pointless—there was nowhere to go in the water—so they just went along and did their jobs. Aviators always retained the option of escape. But the impulse to escape seized few if any of the CVE pilots in action that day. The thought never entered Van Brunt's mind.

Forty-one

The *Samuel B. Roberts* was finished. Bob Copeland knew it when Lloyd Gurnett declared the ship a goner—no one would have wanted to hold on longer than the first lieutenant. "I would advise the captain to abandon ship," he called up to the bridge. Copeland then passed on the word. "Abandon ship, men. Well done." Copeland next ordered the ship destruction bill carried out. Shell-shocked and half conscious but eager to comply with the order to destroy sensitive equipment and documents that might fall into enemy hands, Elbert Gentry beat the lenses out of a pair of ordinary 7×50 binoculars, then smashed the glass face of a gyro repeater display. Howard Cayo, a soundman, was in better condition to discern what was top secret from what was not. A trained acrobat, Cayo took a sledgehammer and gave the sonar machine a few well-aimed blows. Then he took a Tommy gun and peppered the contraption liberally with .45-caliber slugs, nearly hitting his skipper, Bob Roberts, and Gentry with the ricochets. Tom Stevenson and a signalman third class named Charles Natter ran belowdecks on the steadily settling ship. The communications officer was responsible for destroying the codebooks and other sensitive publications. Stevenson did his duty, though the urgency was largely lost on him. "Under fire, you're thinking about your family. You're thinking, *This is the end*. There was nothing else to do."

Stevenson ran to the small closet adjacent to the radio shack and bagged up the metal wheels from the decoding machine, which he would throw overboard. Then he went to destroy the coding machine itself. Not finding the grenade that was supposed to be on hand for this sad contingency, Natter used a submachine gun to similar effect.

That job done, Stevenson and Natter headed below to find the safe that contained secret documents and publications, including the Leyte Gulf invasion plans. With his way lit by battery-powered battle lanterns, Stevenson climbed through a hatch scuttle and found the safe. Though the ship was shaking from hits and the list seemed to increase, he remembered the combination, and the safe door swung open. He loaded what papers he could into several weighted cloth sacks. He and Natter hauled the sacks topside and tossed them overboard. Then Stevenson went down again, alone. He fetched some more bags and ascended to the main deck.

Dick Rohde had been only too happy to hear the abandon ship order. Sitting at his desk wearing an inflatable life belt instead of a bulky kapok life vest, the radioman could feel the deck plating under his feet growing frighteningly warm. Smoke stung his nostrils. When he tried to stand, he found that his headset was still jacked into his radio console.

Rohde came out on deck and found himself standing next to his chief radioman, Tullio Serafini. "All of a sudden there was another big blast. I felt something hit me in the leg. And I looked at Serafini, and there was just blood all over the place. It was awful." He couldn't see how Serafini was ever going to make it. Half his left shoulder had been blown away, and he was bleeding severely. Rohde looked down at his own leg and saw a big hole in his dungarees. Underneath, the flesh looked like so much gristled hamburger. He had seen enough; no need to stare at that awful mess, he thought. Numb, he put it out of his mind and somehow climbed down the ladder from the radio shack to the main deck. Walking up to the rail, he removed his shoes and laid them neatly by the gunwale alongside another pair that belonged to another swimmer. Then Rohde lifted his good leg over the line and jumped in.

When he hit the water, he bobbed up and down a few times in the fuel oil and discovered that his life belt had been torn by shrapnel and did not hold him. Then, remembering his training to swim away from a sinking ship in order to avoid getting sucked under with it, he struck out. In the direction in which he swam, however, a Japanese warship loomed. Rohde was close enough to see crewmen staring at the stricken American ship. *I'm swimming the wrong way,* he thought, realizing that no one else was around him.

Floating nearby was the miniature life vest that Sam Blue had fashioned for Sammy, the ship's celebrated mascot. Rohde tucked it under his arm for a little extra buoyancy, then swam back around the stern of the ship and joined a cluster of survivors.

The dog, too, swam to momentary safety. Somehow Sammy got off the ship and, without the benefit of his custom-tailored canine flotation device, paddled out to a raft. He was there only a short time, however, when he decided that he belonged back on the *Samuel B. Roberts,* his home. The dog jumped off the raft and swam back toward the sinking ship. No one knew his fate for certain, but that was the last anyone saw of him. Sammy either drowned during the swim or went down with his ship.

Though he had commanded the *Samuel B. Roberts* barely half a year, Copeland was bonded strongly enough to his ship to view her as a living thing, a machine with its own soul and persona. Yet he understood too the reality that the source of any ship's life lay in the lives of those who crewed her. When Tom Stevenson returned with a second sackload of classified publications, Bob Copeland went in search of his wounded to make sure they got off the ship.

First the skipper ducked into his sea cabin and collected his letters and personal effects—whatever he could sweep together and carry. Then he went to the bridge, where he and Bob Roberts searched for and found the ship's muster list, watch quarter, station bill, and other administrative documents.

One of the bags Tom Stevenson had thrown overboard must not have been weighted. There it was, bobbing along on the swells. Copeland told Stevenson he had better jump in and weigh it down, lest its sensitive contents fall into the wrong hands. Still wearing his microphoned talker's helmet and realizing that this was his skipper's way of getting another man off the ship, Stevenson leaped off the amidships rail. When he hit the surface, the helmet became a drag brake, jerking his head upward while his body lurched downward. He was weighted down by a .45-caliber pistol, which he discarded. He threw away the helmet and a standard-issue bandolier of pistol ammunition around his waist too. He kept his supply of morphine syrettes. He and Lloyd Gurnett found an expiring crewman from the engine room, and they each jabbed him with a needleful of the numbing potion.

Copeland turned to his executive officer and said, "Now Bob, I want you to go down to the main deck and hustle things a little bit, and then I want you to get into the water and be out there to supervise the men."

"Captain," Roberts said, "I'm not leaving until you leave. I don't want you to be a damn fool and get heroic and go down with the ship."

Copeland seemed to appreciate the honor that underlay this particular kind of insubordination. "Now look, Bob," he said, "I'm not intending to go down with the ship. I don't know what will happen. We are still under fire. My duty is to stay here until the men are off, and I'm going to do that. As soon as everybody is off, if I'm still alive, you can rest assured that I'm getting off. I haven't any false sense of glory like those old German naval sea captains who put on their best uniforms and stood up on the bridge and went down with the ship. But I am going to wait until I get my men off."

The executive officer remained unmoved.

"Bob," the captain said, "I don't want to get tough with you; you are my exec and my good friend, but remember, this is an order. I want a responsible senior officer to be with the survivors, and I'm ordering you to leave the ship."

"If that's the way you put it, Captain, I'll go."

"That's just the way I'm putting it. I trust I'll see you in the water, but in case I don't, Bob, it's been swell being with you." Copeland stuck out his hand. "You've been a swell exec, and I want you to know that."

"It's been wonderful serving with you, Captain. I hope you make it; I'm leaving you with reluctance."

The two officers took their .45s and the bandoliers of extra ammunition from their waists and with a minor ceremonial flourish—"One, two, three"—flung their weapons into the sea from the flying bridge. At that, Roberts left his skipper to go over the side.

Copeland walked aft to the rear section of the bridge and surveyed what was left of his ship. "It gave me an awfully hurt and crushed feeling to see the men lying there wounded and dead and to see our ship, once as alive as the people on her, battered and lifeless." But even among the dead there were living. Amid a tangle of human rubble on the boat deck, Copeland saw movement. There, reclined against the ship's stack in a pool of blood, chief electrician's mate Charles Staubach was still alive.

The captain hollered for Frank Cantrell, the chief quartermaster, and a couple of radarmen to go look after him. As the men went up to check on Staubach, Copeland thought to check in on the CIC to make sure the classified radar equipment had been destroyed. The ship's interior compartments were dark. Copeland found a battle lantern, but it did not light. The nearest flashlight was equally useless. He retrieved from his pocket a cigarette lighter, and it lit, and he looked around the CIC. He was satisfied to see that the machinery had been thoroughly smashed. He found himself compelled to visit his sea cabin again. He went there and looked at the photos of his family that lay beneath a large rectangular section of Plexiglas on his desk. For forty or fifty long seconds he stood there looking at the pictures of Harriet and the kids in the flickering light.

Copeland went back to the main deck, where pharmacist's mates first class Oscar King and George Schaffer were tending to a group of wounded. Charles Staubach was there, crying, though Copeland was pretty sure the thirty-five-year-old electrician had no idea how badly he was hurt. "It really made me sick at my stomach and sick at my heart when I saw him because from his backbone clear around on his left side all was gone." From what Copeland could tell, Staubach was paralyzed. "We ripped blue chambray shirts off six or eight dead men, wadded them up, and stuck them into his lung cavity and wrapped another shirt around him and tied him, but he didn't know the difference."

Staubach didn't want to get in the water. Sobbing, he asked Copeland, "Captain, do you think I'll live?"

"Oh sure, Staubach, get off the ship, and we'll take care of you."

"I don't want to die, Captain. I've never seen my baby yet."

Copeland knew that about two weeks before Staubach had learned of the birth of his baby boy. The skipper considered him a fine man and was heartbroken that he would not live to see his newborn son. Staubach tried awfully hard. They got him into the water around 9:30.

Copeland proceeded alone to look for any remaining survivors on the ship. The passageway between the galley and wardroom section and the main deckhouse was obscured by steam rolling up from the number-one fireroom. Holding his hand over his mouth and nose to avoid the heavy stench of the steam, Copeland plowed through, making his way by memory. He reached the point where he knew a hatch to be, raised his right foot to step over it, and brought it down on top of some kind of obstruction. When he looked more closely, he found his foot planted firmly in the face of a dead radioman. His body didn't seem to have a scratch, nor did the body of the boy lying next to him, though Copeland figured these sailors had to have been blown a fair distance in order to die where they lay: "I don't think there was a whole bone in them. They were just lying there as placid and peaceful as could be."

Copeland became unhinged at the sight of those boys and the larger picture of destruction all around. So long as there had been a fight to conduct, a captain could occupy himself with any number of details that obscured the essential horror of what was happening to his ship and his men. There was the steady patter of information from the CIC team, the orders from Admiral Sprague over the TBS, sightings from lookouts, and reports from gunnery control, from damage parties, and from the engine rooms. He was freed of all that now, and despaired: "The ship had been a very live thing—the ship herself and the men on her. Now she was a battered piece of junk."

In a daze he walked the length of the deck, stopping at the motor whaleboat dangling from its davits. Its wooden bottom had been shot clean out. He stood on the deck looking straight through the whaleboat's busted hull and shuddered: "That one picture summed up the whole desolate destruction of a living ship with living men coming into an emptiness of nothing."

He was alone on that side of the ship. He moved aft, so distraught that he lost his step. His foot slipped out ahead of him, he lurched out of balance, and he found himself sitting on the deck. He put down both of his hands, and when he picked them up, they were covered with blood. It was dripping from above, right on top of him. A headless body was hanging over the edge of a gun tub overhead. The puddle beneath it was large enough that the seat of his khakis and his loafers and socks were wet with blood. He got up and continued down the deck, not really caring what he found or what he did or what would happen. "It had taken all the heart out of me," he recalled. "As I walked down toward the fantail, I was nearly drowned because when I got back to where the three fourteen-inch shells had ripped into us and taken the side out, the main deck was gone from there on, and I just barely caught myself from dropping right into the water." Lt. Cdr. Robert W. Copeland could not swim.

Finding no one in any condition to save, and doubting his ability to do it in any case, Copeland made his way back to the place where Lloyd Gurnett and the other officers had gathered. He and Gurnett used their last minutes on the ship looking for more survivors. They found a man sprawled halfway into the yeoman's office. He was still alive, though the nature of his wounds made it difficult to recognize him. "He must have had two thousand shrapnel holes in his face. When we touched him, the blood would ooze out like water from a sponge. We raised his eyelids, but he was blind in both eyes. He was unconscious. His eyeballs, his irises, and his pupils had been penetrated by fine shrapnel."

After some time they figured out he was the chief machinist's mate, Charles Smith. "How he ever got up there we'll never know. But he was still alive though barely so." Copeland ordered King and Schaffer to put Smith into a life jacket and get him over the side.

A Japanese destroyer stood nearby, lobbing the occasional shell into the *Samuel B. Roberts*'s ruined mass. The ship took four more hits while the abandon ship effort was under way. Water was lapping up over the port side of the destroyer escort's fantail when machinist's mate second class Chalmer Goheen went to check on Paul Henry Carr's gang back in Gun 52. The gun had been silent since the muffled thud of the breech explosion. Where the water hadn't yet reached, the decks were covered with burning oil. Goheen crossed the deck, peered into the gun mount's ripped hatch, and found a horrific scene. Most of the men inside had been obliterated by the blast. They had gotten off 324 rounds of the 325 the ship carried in its after magazine, firing the last seven or eight shells without a working gas ejection line to clear the breech, until one of the final rounds got them.

Looking into the mount, Goheen discovered where the magazine's last round was. It was right there before him, cradled in the arms of Paul Carr himself. The man was alive—though barely, torn from his neck to his groin. Carr was struggling to hold the shell. He begged Goheen to help him load it into the wrecked breech tray.

Goheen took the shell from Carr's arms and laid the gunner's mate on the floor of his mount. Then he took seaman first class James Gregory, whose leg had been severed near the hip, and carried him out and set him on the deck. When Goheen returned to the mount, Carr was on his feet again, shell cradled weakly in his arms. Goheen took the shell from Carr again, lifted him, and carried him out to the deck.

Paul Henry Carr of Checotah, Oklahoma, proud member of the Future Farmers of America, football and baseball letterman, brother to eight sisters, only son of Thomas and Minnie Mae Carr, died there on the deck of his battered, broken warship.

Forty-two

The *Roberts* was going down by the stern. Riding the swells, wearing a kapok life jacket and an inflated rubber belt, Bob Copeland, the skipper who couldn't swim, turned to Lloyd Gurnett and asked, "How do you go about getting out of here?" Gurnett responded, "Well, the best way, Captain, is to roll over on your back and swim on your back. Just work your arms this way and kick your legs. You'll get going." The commanding officer of the *Samuel B. Roberts* got the rhythm of it and inched his way toward a life raft they had spotted a few hundred yards away.

Where George Bray was standing on the fantail, the water was already lapping above his knees. Chalmer Goheen had asked him to help get some of the wounded overboard. Goheen brought seaman first class Willard Thurmond to Bray. Bray could tell he was a goner. He helped Thurmond to the rail, and the mortally injured man just held on there, oblivious to his wounds. Bray helped someone else off the ship, then made his way toward the fantail. By the time he reached the depth charge racks, the water was up to his waist. He just sat down and started swimming.

When they entered the water, the survivors of the *Roberts* baptized themselves in their ship's own blood. The surface of the ocean was covered with a three-inch layer of diesel fuel oil. All around the ruined ship bobbed black faces set with glaring white eyes and teeth. The substance was more a slippery kind of foam than a proper form of oil. The sea's gentle swells animated it like a slowly undulating blacktop.

Copeland had been among the last to leave—the honor of being the very last man off belonged to George Schaffer—jumping ship and joining a large group of men who had clambered over the port-side rail. Forward, where the deck sloped upward—ever more steeply, as the ship settled by the stern—there was a considerable jump to make. Off the port side, Copeland joined a small group of men on a floater net, a large web of nylon mesh woven throughout with a bunch of black rubber disks that gave it its buoyancy. Spotting a raft some distance away, some survivors formed a human chain, reached out to it, reeled it in, and tied it fast to the net. The raft, designed for twenty-five men, soon wallowed under the weight of fifty. Survivors were attracted to the group as small bits of interstellar flotsam to a star's gravitational field. They moved the raft on top of the net to increase its buoyancy.

Gathering by the life raft that kept the group together, Dick Rohde heard someone wondering whether the depth charges had been set on safe. It was Vince Goodrich's job, and God knew there had been precious little time to stick to procedure in the midst of the hellish fusillades that tore the seas around them. The question, however, was of more than procedural significance. A depth charge that burst under water produced a wave of blast pressure that could blow a man apart from the inside out. Sailors were trained to cover their buttocks, or lift them out of the water, to avoid the potentially fatal enema that an underwater explosion could give them. Once more Rohde was on the move, paddling and kicking to get away from the ship.

Wearing khaki pants and a T-shirt, drifting with a group of survivors scattered across the water on the other side of the ship, Tom Stevenson watched Japanese vessels shooting at his sinking ship from all sides. Occasionally, an errant shell would land nearby and kick up a splash, sometimes disconcertingly close. He prayed for the *Roberts* to sink quickly, if only to deprive the Japanese of the pleasure and the practice.

* * *

SEAMAN FIRST CLASS BUD Comet floated off the port quarter of the ship, right below Gun 52, where a gigantic shell from the *Kongo* had struck, gutting that side of the ship and opening its mechanical entrails to the sea. The huge cave mouth opened into an even larger void inside, a gray steel cavern whose unseen corners reached deep into the ship. From its size Comet figured the hole was the product of a Japanese shell that had detonated on contact. Nearby he saw evidence of another shell hit, much more benign: a neatly drilled hole that an armor-piercing round had made as it passed through the ship without exploding. The contrast was remarkable. Here was the difference between life and death, determined solely by the choice of ordnance on the part of a Japanese handling room crewman belowdecks on a ship many miles away. Backlit by flames licking at a far bulkhead, two objects inside that cavern commanded Comet's attention: a life raft, and the huddled form of a man inside of it.

Comet swam closer and recognized the *Roberts*'s chief boatswain's mate, Cullen Wallace. He was still conscious, kneeling inside the raft. Probably he had come down a ladder and found the raft and settled into it, hoping somehow that he could paddle his way out of the ship. But he was stuck there, evidently trapped by the inrush of seawater, arms braced on the sides of the raft. Watching Comet swim his way, the chief hollered at him a few times to come help him. The oil-soaked sailor swam back to the ship, gingerly moving past the jagged threshold of the torn hull, and grabbed the raft. Then he pulled it clear of some wreckage into the pool of water that had filled that part of the *Roberts* and that rose slowly and serenely as the ship began to sink by the stern. Comet got the impression that the chief, like his captain, could not swim. He eased the raft across the splintered opening in the hull and watched as Edward Wheaton, a radio technician, swam up and climbed in.

Comet paddled the raft around to the stern of the ship. The depth charge racks, lying over the fantail, were submerged already. The name SAMUEL B. ROBERTS, stenciled on the transom, was under water too. Blown apart like an apple on a tree stump were the remnants of the steel shell of Gun 52, Paul Carr's mount, turned defiantly out to port, its barrel still aglow. There was a tangle of metal piled into it from the side—the remains of the deckhouse beneath Johnny LeClercq's disintegrated forty-millimeter mount. From the stern Comet heard a shout. It was from an officer, hollering for help. When

Comet saw him and started paddling the raft in his direction, Wallace told him to leave him be: "Let him swim." The chief didn't want the burden of bringing anybody else aboard the raft.

But if Bud Comet remembered anything that his father had told him at the West Virginia train station six months earlier, he showed it by his actions now. *Don't dishonor your mother. . . . This country is worth dying for. . . . A coward dies a thousand times. . . .* Defying his chief's command, he paddled toward the fantail and picked up Ens. Jack Moore.

Once the crew had decided to abandon the *Roberts,* it was unbearable to watch the enemy continue to have its way with her. For all they had done, some could not escape thinking: *If only we had stayed on and fought a little longer, we might have prevented this final indignity.* "We were the proudest ship in the fleet. We really were," Tom Stevenson said. "We thought we were the cat's meow."

Shortly after ten o'clock the *Samuel B. Roberts* rolled over on her beam ends and sank by the stern. No explosion followed the ship's disappearance beneath the waves. The only reaction was a swell of sadness among the crewmen who watched her go. Floating a quarter mile away, Dick Rohde watched the *Roberts* sink. It took about an hour, but it seemed to take forever. She went down gracefully, seeming not to make a sound. Before she had fully committed herself to the deep, the *Roberts* stood nearly vertical. Stenciled with the number 413 on each side, the bow held high in the air for a moment, standing like an oblique headstone. Then the ship slowly retracted into the sea. "Boys, take off your hats. There goes a good ship," said boatswain's mate first class Red Harrington.

The sight of it moved Lloyd Gurnett to open sobbing. "As first lieutenant he knew every welded seam in her," Copeland wrote, "he knew where every fitting was attached. Love of the ship was very deep in his heart."

Once the ship was gone, the culture of cynical jocularity that had characterized the wardroom seemed to disappear. Among the men on Copeland's raft, "It seemed as if the bottom had dropped out of things. . . . Now that she was gone, everyone felt low." The whitecaps kicked up a bit now. Then Staubach, the grievously wounded chief electrician's mate, lost his mind, raving and yelling deliriously.

Scanning the oil-slicked waters for other survivors to join, Dick Rohde found his way to the raft with Jack Moore, Cullen Wallace,

Jack Yusen, Bud Comet, and others. The men had fastened together their life raft and floater net into a self-contained survival pod that kept everybody together. Wallace didn't want to do it. He said he was concerned about air attack and did not want to concentrate the men in one big vulnerable group. He also felt that such a large group would consume the raft's limited provisions too quickly. As the officer in charge of this group, Moore overrode him, feeling that the priority should be rescue rather than avoidance of air attack.

The wooden-latticed bottom of the raft had been shot up pretty well. A pharmacist's mate approached Rohde, who was sitting inside the raft, and tried to pour sulfa powder into his gaping leg wound. The radioman wondered what the point was. When he got back into the water, it would just wash the powder away.

Not considering himself too badly hurt, Rohde vaulted himself overboard. Later, looking up at a dozen or so men perched comfortably on the side of the raft, including Lieutenant West and Ensign Moore, though both officers seemed uninjured, he decided to hoist himself up and take a break from treading water. But when he tried to climb up, one of the men wound up and slugged him hard in the head, knocking him back down. Rohde was stunned at his first taste of the Darwinian imperative. With nerves running hot on a makeshift floating wagon train loaded with twice as many men as it was built to carry, Jack Moore decided, "There was going to have to be rationing with disciplinary backing. Everyone was already at each other's throat."

Forty-three

The *Hoel* had sunk first. The *Gambier Bay* went down at 9:07. The *Roberts* followed an hour later. Now came the *Johnston*'s turn. The first ship into the fight was the last to go down. Her luck had been the improbable stuff of dime novels or Hollywood fantasies: the solo charge in the battle's opening minutes, firing guns and torpedoes into the teeth of multiple enemy broadsides, wheeling under fire to escape, taking devastating hits from battleship shells, withdrawing, returning to action against the destroyer column, and fending off the last Japanese effort to sink Clifton Sprague's carriers. Her final destruction was not ensured until after the foe she had suicidally charged had turned and run for cover.

Bob Deal knew the ship was a goner. "Water columns were substantially higher and shells overhead had a distinctly different resonance. Came then an impact so severe I thought we might have struck a marine obstruction. The ship shuddered, rolled hard port and starboard, resuming course at a reduced speed. Going forward on the starboard side, I learned we had taken a hit in the engine room."

Electrician's mate first class Allen Johnson understood the fragile extent to which the *Johnston* held on to life. His battle station was the emergency generator room, tucked away on the starboard side of the ship between the forward fireroom and the galley. Before enlisting in 1942, the twenty-five-year-old petty officer had worked for four and a half years at the Birmingham Electric Company, running substations that brought steam and power into Dixie's industrial center. The *Johnston* derived its vital electrical power from generators located in the engine rooms. The generators, like the engines, were run by steam from the boiler room attached to them. With one boiler room already out and Lt. Jesse Cochran and his men struggling in vain to gain power from the other, the only source of power on the *Johnston* was the emergency generator, powered not with steam but by a diesel motor. If the engine room generators were knocked out, a pilot light went off, a relay opened, and the emergency generator kicked on automatically.

When the *Johnston* was first hit, Johnson had the terrible sensation of being lifted from the ground and shaken violently. The hit to the after engine room knocked its electrical switchboard dead. Instantly the emergency generator in the electrician's mate's cramped compartment filled the void, its three-cylinder diesel motor coughing to life. But the motor bled too. The shock of the multiple blasts belowdecks broke the lubrication pipe that ran to the motor. Oil ran down into the corner of Johnson's compartment. With motor machinist's mate second class Roger Gougeon, he scooped the oil from the floor by hand and slathered it back into the diesel motor. Johnson ran to the CIC and grabbed a roll of three-quarter-inch friction tape. It didn't stick well to the oily metal, but he used enough of it to slow if not stop the diesel motor's bleeding. His emergency station would turn out some electricity, but only for so long. The oil leaked everywhere. They were able to return only a portion of it to the engine.

From such mundane mechanical causes do gallant ships die. Without power, Bob Hollenbaugh would fire his state-of-the-art five-inch gun like a nineteenth-century artilleryman; the men in the ammunition handling room would do the work of their electro-hydraulic hoists, passing shells by hand; light would come from battle lanterns if at all; and volunteers would turn the big wheel on the rudder's steering pumps, struggling to keep up with Captain Evans's course changes, shouted down from above. They would do all these things, taking the place of their equipment, or they would die along with everyone else the next time a salvo found its mark.

The endless salvos of incoming shells passing overhead, astern, off the bow, all around the ship. Now Allen Johnson felt one land close by. When the large shell struck near his emergency generator compartment, "it felt like a freight train's coal box was dropped on top of me." The bulkhead between his compartment and the galley was blown down flat. The only source of light he had was a small sparking electrical fire that filled the compartment with flickering shadows. With a three-quarter-inch brass bolt head having ripped through his back between the shoulder blade and spine, Johnson pulled himself to his feet and called out to Gougeon. Johnson couldn't see him, and there came no answer to his call. Groping through the compartment, he felt Gougeon's head and shoulders, but his torso was pinned under something—a large mass of hot metal. It was the diesel engine. It was too heavy to move, and having run steadily for well over an hour, it was too hot even to touch. With the bolt head throbbing in his right chest cavity, Johnson was becoming numb with shock. He was sure, however, of at least two things: his friend was dead, and the time had finally come to get the hell off his dying ship.

*   *   *

AT 9:40, WHEN "AN avalanche of shells" struck the ship, inflicting her final meaningful damage, the *Johnston*'s two-and-a-half-hour sprint through hell ended. The shell that sealed the destroyer's fate struck the number-one boiler room, cutting steam to the forward turbine and stopping the starboard screw. The ship, powerless, began coasting to its final resting place. As the Pacific currents took over the work of the *Johnston*'s engines, Captain Evans passed the order to abandon ship.

She was a vehicle now suitable only for the dead. On the destroyer's main deck, on the port side amidships, lay what Jesse Cochran described as "a pile of people—bodies—half alive, half dead." Many survivors saw it, but none seemed to fathom quite how this stack of human cordwood could have formed. In part, it was the inscrutable arrangement chosen by the shock waves from heavy shells that had propelled men and parts of men out of interior compartments and into their final poses. Some sailors had been carried out and laid there by their buddies in the hope that, out in the open, they might get medical attention. Others had struggled out under

As Wildcats from VC-5 scramble on the *Kitkun Bay*, heavy shells straddle the *White Plains* astern.

In the battle's opening minutes, the destroyer *Heermann* (foreground) and the destroyer escort *John C. Butler* make smoke to conceal Taffy 3's escort carriers.

The *Gambier Bay* flees eastward into the sun while heavy salvos land nearby.

A Taffy 3 jeep carrier steams south under thunderous fire from astern.

2000 LANDING

15 SEPT. 1944

(Above) TBM Avenger pilot Lt. (jg) Earl "Blue" Archer of the *Kalinin Bay*'s VC-3, with squadron mascot Joe Kalinin.

FM-2 Wildcat pilot Lt. Richard Roby, of the *Gambier Bay*'s VC-10.

VC-10 skipper Cdr. Edward J. Huxtable (left) with his crew, turret gunner Richard S. Martin (center) and radioman Donald R. Blaney.

FM-2 Wildcat fighters from the *White Plains*.

An Avenger torpedo bomber roars skyward from the Taffy 2 jeep carrier *Marcus Island* as the catapult crew races to retrieve the cable.

(Below) Pilot's-eye sketch of the Japanese pursuit as of 7:30 a.m., by VC-10 commander Edward J. Huxtable.

SHIPS POSITIONS AS SEEN BY
LT. COMDR. E.J. HUXTABLE VC-10
AT TIME OF FIRST ATTACK
BY VC-10. (0730 APPROX)

SHEET ONE
SITUATION AT 0730 (M

JAP CA'S   →060°

RANGE TO CVE'S
≈ 20 THOUSAND YDS

VC-10 VT ATTACK

→130°

JAP BB'S   →090°

OWN FORCE ∞
130°

OWN CVE'S   →090°

REMAINDER OF
JAP FORCE
HIDDEN BY SQUALL AREA

VC-10
VT BOMBING

SQUALL AREA
(VISIBILITY 1-2 MILES)

OVERCAST
(1000-2000 FEET)

CLE

Gun camera photos from a *Kadashan Bay* Wildcat strafing a Japanese cruiser.

An Avenger overflies the *Marcus Island*.

Lt. Ken Hippe, VC-3 Wildcat pilot, became an ace in seven minutes over Leyte on October 24.

(Right) Low on fuel and ammunition, a *St. Lo* Wildcat fighter finds refuge at the Tacloban airdrome on Leyte Island.

Artist's view of *St. Lo* Wildcats strafing the battleship *Yamato*.

Lt. Burt Bassett (left), VC-10 Avenger pilot , with VC-10 skipper, Cdr. Edward J. Huxtable.

-20 ACA-1 REPORT NO. 71

Low-altitude aerial photo of a
Kongo-class battleship,
taken by a *Kadashan Bay* flier at
9:25 a.m.

25 OCT. 44 K-20 6⅜" 400° 0925

Japanese cruiser fishtails to avoid
air attack. Photo taken at about
12:30 p.m. by a *Marcus Island* flier.

The battleship *Yamato* narrowly avoiding a torpedo, bubbling by ahead.

"Rendezvous. My course north." Her main batteries aimed skyward in defiance, the battleship *Nagato* withdraws following Kurita's 9:11 a.m. order. Photo taken by a *Kadashan Bay* aviator.

At 10:50 a.m., the *Yamato* (bottom) and the heavy cruiser *Haguro* withdraw under U.S. air attack, photographed by a *Petrof Bay* airman.

The *Chikuma* circles under attack, photographed by a pilot from the *Petrof Bay* of Taffy 1.

Already withdrawing, battleships *Nagato* (center) and *Yamato* (top) maneuver under relentless air attack around 11:30 a.m. A bomb explosion is visible on the *Nagato*. Photo taken by a *Kadashan Bay* airman.

Flight deck crew on the *White Plains* brace for a kamikaze attack. It missed.

The *Gambier Bay*, listing to port, falls behind and disappears over the horizon, the first carrier ever sunk by surface gunfire.

Explosions rock the *St. Lo* following her hit by a suicide plane. She was the first U.S. warship sunk in this frightening new way.

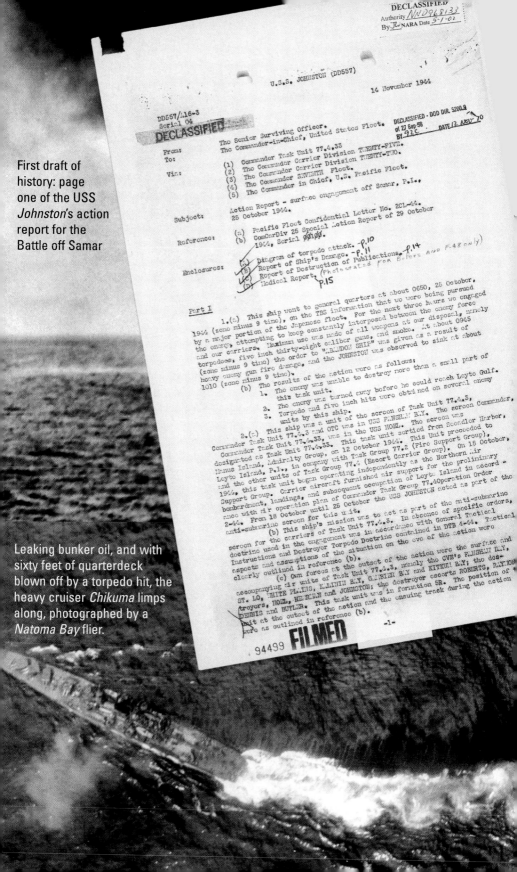

First draft of history: page one of the USS *Johnston*'s action report for the Battle off Samar

Leaking bunker oil, and with sixty feet of quarterdeck blown off by a torpedo hit, the heavy cruiser *Chikuma* limps along, photographed by a *Natoma Bay* flier.

U.S.S. JOHNSTON (DD557)

14 November 1944

DD557/A16-3
Serial 04
DECLASSIFIED

DECLASSIFIED - DOD DIR. 5200.9
of 27 Sep 58
BY 92 C   DATE 12 APY 70

From: The Senior Surviving Officer.
To: The Commander-in-Chief, United States Fleet.
Via: (1) Commander Task Unit 77.4.33.
          (2) The Commander Carrier Division TWENTY-FIVE.
          (3) The Commander Carrier Division TWENTY-TWO.
          (4) The Commander SEVENTH Fleet.
          (5) The Commander in Chief, U.S. Pacific Fleet.

Subject: Action Report - surface engagement off Samar, P.I.,
          25 October 1944.

Reference: (a) Pacific Fleet Confidential Letter No. 2CL-44.
           (b) ComCarDiv 25 Special Action Report of 29 October
               1944, Serial 00100.

Enclosures: (A) Diagram of torpedo attack. - P.10
            (B) Report of Ship's Damage. - P.11
            (C) Report of Destruction of Publications. - P.14 (Photostated FOR BuPers AND F.48 ONLY)
            (D) Medical Report. P.15

Part I

1.(a) This ship went to general quarters at about 0650, 25 October, 1944 (zone minus 9 time), on the TBS information that we were being pursued by a major portion of the Japanese fleet. For the next three hours we engaged the enemy, attempting to keep constantly interposed between the enemy force and our carriers. Maximum use was made of all weapons at our disposal, namely torpedoes, five inch thirty-eight caliber guns, and smoke. At about 0945 (zone minus 9 time) the order to "ABANDON SHIP" was given as a result of heavy enemy gun fire damage, and the JOHNSTON was observed to sink at about 1010 (zone minus 9 time).

(b) The results of the action were no more than a small part of the following:
     1. The enemy was unable to destroy more than a small part of this task unit.
     2. The enemy was turned away before he could reach Leyte Gulf.
     3. Torpedo and five inch hits were obtained on several enemy units by this ship.

2.(a) This ship was a unit of the screen of Task Unit 77.4.3. Commander Task Unit 77.4.33 and OTC was in USS HOEL. The screen Commander, designated as Task Unit 77.4.33, was in the USS HOEL. The screen was Commander Task Unit 77.4.33. This task unit sortied from Seeadler Harbor, Manus Island, Admiralty Group, on 12 October 1944. This Unit proceeded to Leyte Island, P.I., in company with Task Group 77.2 (Fire Support Group) and the other units of Task Group 77.4 (Escort Carrier Group). On 18 October, 1944, this task unit began operating independently as the Northern Air Support Group. Carrier aircraft furnished air support for the preliminary bombardment, landings, and subsequent occupation of Leyte Island in accordance with air operation plan of Commander Task Group 77.4 Operation Order 2-44. From 18 October until 25 October the USS JOHNSTON acted as part of the anti-submarine screen for this unit.

(b) This ship's mission was to act as part of the anti-submarine screen for the carriers of Task Unit 77.4.3. In absence of specific orders, anti-submarine screen for the carriers of Task Unit 77.4.3. In absence of specific orders, doctrine used in the engagement was in accordance with General Tactical Instructions and Destroyer Torpedo Doctrine contained in DTB 4-44. Tactical aspects and assumptions of the situation on the eve of the action were clearly outlined in reference (b).

(c) Own forces at the outset of the action were the surface and accompanying air units of Task Unit 77.4.3, namely the CVE's FANSHAW BAY, ST. LO, WHITE PLAINS, KALININ BAY, GAMBIER BAY and KITKUN BAY; the destroyers, HOEL, HEERMANN and JOHNSTON; the destroyer escorts ROBERTS, RAYMOND DENNIS and BUTLER. This task unit was in formation 5R. The position of each unit at the outset of the action and the ensuing track during the action were as outlined in reference (b).

-1-

94499   FILMED

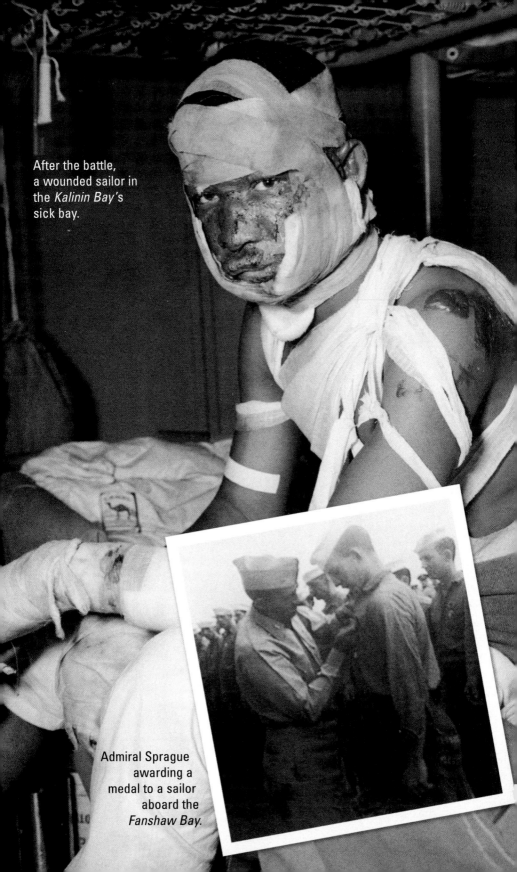

After the battle, a wounded sailor in the *Kalinin Bay*'s sick bay.

Admiral Sprague awarding a medal to a sailor aboard the *Fanshaw Bay*.

Lt. (jg) Larry Budnick of the *St. Lo*'s VC-65.

Burial at sea for a *Kalinin Bay* sailor.

Tom Stevenson (USS *Samuel B. Roberts*).

Dudley Moylan (USS *Samuel B. Roberts*).

Bill Brooks (USS *St. Lo*/VC-65).

Joe Downs (USS *St. Lo*/VC-65).

Allen Johnson (USS *Johnston*).

Larry Budnick (USS *St. Lo*/VC-65).

U.S.S. FANSHAW BAY (CVE-70)
FLAGSHIP OF FAMOUS 'TAFFY 3'
SURVIVORS OF GREATEST BATTLE
IN NAVAL HISTORY AT LEYTE GULF

Fanshaw Bay veterans are honored at the Pearl Harbor Day parade in New Orleans, December 7, 2001.

Bill Mercer (USS *Johnston*).

Paul Miranda (USS *Hoel*).

Dick Santos (USS *Hoel*).

USS HOEL

ADDINGTON, Norman T. Jr. · FC3
AKERMAN, Philip A. · S1
ALLEN, Zenie E · S2
ANSPOKER, Walter H · RM3
ANDERSON, Carl V · S1
AUSTIN, Milton H · FC1
BAKER, Marion M · LTjg
BALES, Paul E · S1
BARCLAY, Wesley J · CEM
BARNHART, Chester A · F2
BASEY, John S · S1
BASTANCHURY, John A · GM2
BELVIN, James J · CMM
BENCE, Raymond J · S2
BERRY, James O · STM1
BIENIEWICZ, Frank J · TM2
BRADFIELD, Willson B · F2
BRANNAN, Thomas J · GM3
BRANSTETTER, William C · CMM
BRASETH, George L · S1
BRETT, George M · RM1
BRILLON, Richie T · S1
BROUSSEAU, George · S2
BROUSSEAU, Hurvort D · F2
BROWN, Anderson F Jr. · F2
BROWN, Gordon N · S2
BORAZ, Jack P · FC2
BURLESON, George E · S1
BURNS, John C · S1
CALLAHAN, Fremont J Jr. · S2
CALLAWAY, Ernest S · EM3
CALVERT, Luther H · S2
CARLOCK, Ralph J

CUSTER, George H · SoM3
DALTON, Virgle A · S1
DARCY, Edward J · TM2
DAUGHERTY, Leslie R · F1
DAUM, Darius A · F1
DeSARRO, Frank P · S1
OKELLO, Macalino · FC1
DOUBREVA, Harvoll J · GM1
DOYLE, Robert J · S1
DRISCOLL, George C · CTM
DRAGER, Ervin O · CEM
DRISCOLL, George C · S1
EASTLAND, Karl S Jr · S2
ERICKSON, Carl E · GM2
EVERHART, Charles A · CMM
FAASS, Irvin L · S1
FALKNER, Ralph W · STM1
FELTON, Lewis O · TM2
FENERTY, Thomas F · S1
FISHER, George J · GM3
FORELL, Cyrus M · S1
FREY, John H · WT2
FREY, Melvin O · RM1
FROMMEYER, John G · S1
FRY, Clifford E · TM3
FULKERSON, Wallace J · MM1
FULTON, Charles M · WT1
GAFFNEY, Charles J · COX
GAISSFORD, John M · FC2
GILLES, John L · S1
GOUGH, John P · CBM
GORMAN, James F · GM2
GRAY, Lawrence O · EM3
GRIGGS, Basston D

HINES, George W · WT3
HOLCOMB, George E · SM2
HOLDER, Dowell R · RdM3
HOLMBERG, John L · SoM3
HOPKINS, Thorne L · F1
HORMAN, Paul J · F1
HORNYAK, Andrew J · F2
HUDAK, John T Jr · GM1
HUDDLESTON, Thomas L · WT3
HUDSON, Frances G · RM2
HUELSMAN, Raymond L · STM
HUFFMAN, Malcolm H · WO
HUMPHREY, Darcyl L · COX
HUTCHISON, Virgil E · S1
INGRAM, William Jr · S1
JACKIE, Gus T · S1
JAMES, Joseph · S1
JOHNSON, Charles M · S1
JOHNSON, Ernest L · S2
JONES, Herman H · MM3
JUNG, Caster R · WT2
KADLORIAN, Edmund C · S1
KANZLEITER, Merlin J · TM3
KEDERCHA, Abbott G · MM1
KENNEDY, Thomas M · WT3
KERBER, Robert E · COX
KILLOUGH, Gilbert C · S2
KIMBALL, Joe W · S1
KINGMAN, Cornell C · S1
KLEIN, Stuart A · CBM
KOEHLER, Robert L · GM2
KRUPP, James M

LEWIS, John R · WT2
LEWIS, Lloyd S · SM2
LINDSEY, J R · RdM3
LOHMAN, Aden F · S1
LYONS, Forio J Jr · S2
MADDOX, Cecil · S3
MADELL, Lawrence A · F2
MAHANEY, James F · S2
MALLORY, John R · WT3
MARTIN, Marvin F · RM2
MASLOWSKI, Henry A · S2
MAYES, Robert E · S1
McCARTY, Otis J · COX
McCLURE, Jack W · S1
McDANIEL, Leland S Jr · S1
McGOVERN, Donald J · MM1
McGRAW, Jimmy L · S2
McINTYRE, Raymond H · S1
McMILLON, Isaac B · S2
MENDOZA, Jess · MM3
MINAKO, Jimmo · MM3
MOGENSEN, Darrell E · F2
MORAN, Jesse W · MM1
MORRIS, Theodorius D · S1
MULLEN, Albert Jr · F1
MULLENS, John D · FC3
MULLENS, James E · MM1
MUNOZ, Alfred · S2
MUSHINSKI, Frank S · S1
NASON, Earle A Jr · S2

PEAK, Randolph M · EM1
PERONEY, Humbert L Jr · S1
PETERSON, Dear M · EC1
PHILLIPS, Flowd T · MM1
PITTMAN, Ernest E · WT1
PLASTERS, Everett C · S2
PLUMB, John H · EM2
POCIAS, Edward W Sr · BM2
POLLAT, Lewis A · S2
PRICE, Lloyd R · COX
PRICE, Riptond M · CWT
PUGH, Cay D · S1
QUINN, John P · F1
QUINTERO, Lee · S1
REILING, Earl L · LT
RICHARDSON, John W · TM2
RICKARDS, Clifford W · AM3
RUCKLE, Ray T · BM2
SALZSIEDER, Chester R · RdR2
SANDERS, William R · S1
SANTILLI, Roy T · S1
SCHMERER, Erwin T · TM2
SERHART, Alexis J · S1
SERDNICK, Morris H · S1
SHANNON, Leonard C · S1
SHAW, J T · S1
SHEPPARD, James E · F1
SHINE, Jesse L · S1
SHOPE, Rodney D · CMM

STILLWAGON, Douglas E · S2
STAMBERT, John W · RM2
STONE, John W · S2
STONE, Paul E · FC2
STOROST, Ray E · S1
STORY, Curtis E · S2
STOVER, Warren H · S2
STRANG, Charles L · LCDR
STRAYER, Howard T · S1
STREUTER, Louie M · S2
STUBBS, Jack W · S1
STUBBS, Kenneth G · GM2
STULTZ, Richard N · PhM3
STURROCK, Sponcen S · S2
SUDLOW, Glen G · RM2
TAYLOR, William E · S2
TERPSTRA, Robert D · WT2
THOMPSON, Robert L · S1
THORLAKSEN, Arthur M · SM2
THORNBERY, William R · SC3
THORP, Jack L · FC2
TOLFORD, Harry G · LTjg
TOPHAM, Clarkey R · RdM3
ULARNER, Donald S · OM3
WACHTER, Marvin C · MM2
WALDEN, J Lee · MM2
WALLACE, Wilbur K · S1
WARDEN, David L · FUN1
WATROWSKI, Chester J · FC3

"IN

INSCRIBE
IN THE C
OF THE
SHIPS,
USS H
SAM
FIGHTI
BATTLES
IN WHA

MAY TH
BE FOR
AND FRI

Hank Pyzdrowski
(USS *Gambier Bay*/VC-10)
at the gravesite of
Adm. Clifton A. F. Sprague.

The namesake of heroic DE-413,
the USS *Samuel B. Roberts*, FFG-58,
was nearly sunk by a mine in the
Persian Gulf in 1988.

Samuel B. Roberts survivor Jack Yusen with Capt. Paul X. Rinn, skipper of the USS *Samuel B. Roberts*, FFG-58.

(Above) The *Hoel/Johnston/Samuel B. Roberts* monument at Ft. Rosecrans National Cemetery, San Diego.

The memorial to Taffy 3 at Ft. Rosecrans
National Cemetery, San Diego. The monument
for the *St. Lo* and VC-65 stands separately.

their own power and lain down, exhausted beyond exhaustion, desperate for cooler air to breathe.

Ellsworth Welch went forward repeating the abandon ship order. Under the abandon ship plan—rehearsed many times but without much belief in its utility—Welch was supposed to report to a life raft stored on the ship's port side by the wardroom. By the time Welch got there, sailors had already released the raft and jumped into the water. Welch found coxswain Ed Block struggling in vain to put on a life jacket. The morphine Welch had given him when the bridge was first hit had made him sluggish. So the officer helped him slide into the life jacket and eased him into the water. Welch then tried to help another sailor, but the severity of his wounds made the effort moot.

Dusty Rhodes and Warren Williams climbed up on the deckhouse by Bob Hollenbaugh's Gun 54 and tossed a nylon mesh floater net into the water. "When I jumped over," Rhodes recalled, "I had two thoughts enter my mind, both silly. One, how deep is this water, I wonder if I'll hit bottom? Number two, how far is it to land?" Robert Billie dragged himself to the edge of the gunwale, crawling and rolling with his good left arm, then dropped down to the main deck amid bodies, body parts, and blood. On their way down from the gun director, Bob Hagen and several fire-controlmen passed Billie without a second look. Billie couldn't speak—he could scarcely move. He didn't blame them for consigning him to the dead. With only one good arm, he finally hauled himself to the rail. Though he wasn't able to lift himself over and into the water, the enemy obliged him. A salvo of shells struck the ship near where he lay, and the impact—the third blast he absorbed that day—propelled him overboard. He had twenty shrapnel wounds and three useless limbs. He didn't particularly like his chances in the water.

Captain Evans left the fantail and walked forward to the wardroom, where Lt. Robert Browne was busy doing what he could for the living. Evans tried to persuade the doctor to abandon ship, but Browne wouldn't hear of it. There were wounded who needed to be tended to before they were given over to Neptune's mercy in the water. The doctor could do that work better aboard ship. He would use what time he had left.

Bob Hagen, consumed with coordinating the ship's gunfire from the director mount, was slow to get the news that Evans had passed word to abandon ship.

I peered out and couldn't see a living soul on the fo'c'sle. "What the hell are we doing here?" I said. "Let's abandon ship." The last word hardly was out of my mouth when the five crewmen in the gun director with me dashed out and ran for the rail. I was so surprised that I stood stock-still a moment, then lit out myself. I made my way to the fo'c'sle—I couldn't get aft without walking over piles of bodies—and, like a man in a dream, very carefully and leisurely took off my shoes and dived in.

In the water Hagen looked back at the ship and spotted his friend, Doc Browne, carrying wounded from the wardroom to the deck. Browne had just left the rail and headed back inside when there was a whistling rush of wind and an explosion, right where Browne had entered. Hagen broke down and cried.

The enormity of the moment was lost on many of the men who had survived to this point by attending to the myriad rote details of their assigned duties. The ship was gone and their duties with it. But men still found trivialities to occupy their minds. Leaving the ship from the port side amidships, Bill Mercer swam about a hundred yards off the port quarter with another sailor. "I recall Marquard took his comb from his pocket, neatly combed his hair, and then threw his comb away saying, 'I don't guess I'll ever need that again.' " With the same habitual fastidiousness that others had exhibited, Ellsworth Welch took off his shoes and set them neatly together on deck before diving into the sea.

One of the first survivors Bob Hagen encountered in the water was torpedoman first class Jim O'Gorek. Cast afloat in four thousand fathoms of shark-infested waters, defeated in battle with friends lost forever, O'Gorek swam over to Hagen and said cheerfully, "Mr. Hagen, we got off all ten of them torpedoes, and they ran hot, straight, and normal!" Those torpedoes had made a real difference, knocking the *Kumano* out of the fight early in the battle, before it could close to effective gun range of the carriers.

Ellsworth Welch looked up and saw a Japanese cruiser firing shells into the destroyer's ruined hulk.

I would watch for belches of fire from the cruiser's guns and time the salvos so I could duck under the water before the shells hit. But wearing the life belt, I was only able to get the upper part of my body below the water. I must have looked like a duck feeding on food below.

Others saw the column of destroyers approach again. The ships that the *Johnston* had forced into premature torpedo launches were circling her like raiders hunting settlers on the prairie. They fired directly into her wrecked hull, no longer deterred by the spirited work of Bob Hollenbaugh or Lieutenant Hagen or anybody else in the gunnery department.

This was the *Johnston*'s final service to Sprague's fleeing carriers: providing a static target for frustrated Japanese gunners who doubtlessly longed to sink something, anything, with an American flag on it. Though they had straddled the carriers repeatedly, Japanese gunners had claimed only the *Gambier Bay*. The five others seemed to possess luck worthy of ancient Japan's Seven Lucky Gods themselves—the legendary *Shichifukujin*. The *Kalinin Bay* had taken fifteen hits from heavy cruiser main battery rounds and steamed on in defiance.

But the *Johnston*'s defiance was at an end. She would not get away. The decisions of her captain had ensured that she wouldn't. It was not a pointless death wish. The *Johnston*, like the *Hoel* and the *Samuel B. Roberts* before her, had fulfilled her mission so thoroughly—had parried and riposted so well—that there was nothing left for the ship to do but pay the final price.

What fate befell the *Johnston*'s legendary captain is the subject of continuing conjecture among the ship's survivors. Bob Sochor was among the last to see him. The motor machinist's mate, having gone aft to take his turn cranking the rudder pump, returned forward to fight a fire. As he walked toward the bow, "there was a terrible, blinding yellow flash" from a shell that struck the port side near the cook's galley. Knocked unconscious, Sochor regained his senses to find himself covered in blood from his own wounds and his dead shipmates surrounding him. Realizing that the abandon ship order had been passed, Sochor headed for the fantail, where the jump into the water was easier. "Everyone who was able to abandon ship had done so," he wrote. "They were in rafts and nets and swimming approximately a quarter of a mile away. I went aft as Captain Evans went forward. With neither one saying a word to the other, we passed by staring blankly at one another."

Some claim to have seen the *Johnston*'s skipper climbing into the motor whaleboat that he had ordered released. Others were less confident he ever made it into the boat. Obeying the order to release the small craft, Allen Johnson found that its pulley mechanism didn't work. The electrician's mate reached for a knife he kept in his pocket, meaning to cut the lines that kept the boat suspended from its davits, but his pants pocket had been torn away. An officer produced a blade from his boot and cut the lines. When the gig hit the water, Johnson thought it was in good condition. He saw someone wearing a khaki uniform, an officer or a chief, jump into the water, climb in, start the engine, and haul a wounded sailor aboard. Around that time, according to Johnson, Captain Evans began walking toward the fantail. As if beckoning him to safety, the gig drifted with him, down the length of the ship. But by the time Johnson abandoned ship, diving into the water under heavy fire, he, like the rest of the crew on record, had not seen whether the skipper got into the whaleboat. If he did, in all likelihood he didn't go far. The craft's bottom, badly holed in the Japanese bombardment, was not close to being seaworthy.

It has been written that so much of life is preparation, so much is routine, and so much is retrospect that the purest essence of anyone's genius contracts itself to a precious few hours. The window opened by circumstance on the genius of Cdr. Ernest E. Evans for two and a half hours on the morning of October 25, 1944, so brilliantly lit from within, was once again closed. The "Chief" of Annapolis, the Cherokee warrior unhorsed by enemy gunfire, was lost to the whirlwind, taken to a private oblivion that to this day burnishes his mystique and deepens the legend of his late, great destroyer and its magnificent crew.

Forty-four

On orders from Admiral Kinkaid, Jesse Oldendorf's old battleships had been standing by in Leyte Gulf awaiting their next move in a desperate but uncertain naval chess game. Mindful of his duty to guard MacArthur's troops ashore, Kinkaid had been keeping a wary eye on Admiral Shima all morning as the remnants of the Southern Force withdrew. Admiral Sprague's plea for help was compelling. Still, Kinkaid could not be sure that Shima would not reverse course and try again to break through into Leyte Gulf. From Kinkaid's flagship, the *Wasatch*, Sprague nevertheless received a voice message assuring him that help was on the way.

Though the Seventh Fleet battleships' magazines had spent much of their high-explosive ammunition during the shore bombardment, and a significant quantity of their armor-piercing rounds in the destruction of Nishimura's force, their armor-piercing ammunition stocks were more than sufficient to deal with another Japanese fleet. The most serious deficiency of the Seventh Fleet Bombardment and Fire Support Group was its destroyers, which had spent their torpedoes at Surigao Strait and would not be reloaded until they could tie up to a tender again. Despite Taffy 3's perilous straits, Kinkaid saw no alternative but to wait and see.

Shortly before ten A.M. the waiting ended. Satisfied that the

Southern Force wanted no further part of him and fortified by the arrival of two fresh squadrons of destroyers, Kinkaid finally ordered Oldendorf to take half his force and rally to the aid of Ziggy Sprague's beleaguered northern Taffy group. If Kurita continued charging southward, the American battle line would greet him memorably. But Kurita was already in full flight north. No sooner had Oldendorf relayed word to his commanders to prepare for a northward sprint than Kinkaid countermanded the order upon learning that Kurita's fleet was in retreat.

*   *   *

ABOARD THE *JOHNSTON*, ALL was quiet except for the flames. High above the wreckage of her silent decks, forty-eight stars still flew. Harold Beresonsky thought the ship, flying Old Glory, looked proud and defiant.

In the water, Bill Mercer and J. B. Strickland found themselves sandwiched between their beaten ship and a Japanese destroyer standing off the *Johnston*'s port quarter firing into the ship's hull. "I told Strick that I was sticking close to him because he owed me a hundred dollars. Strick said, 'If we make it, you'll sure get your hundred.' I was only joking because neither of us thought we would make it." Strickland had survived the Battle of Savo Island, a disastrous American defeat under the guns of a Japanese flotilla led by none other than the *Chokai*, late of the same day. Mercer asked Strickland how their present predicament compared to Savo Island. Strick said, "Kid, I have never seen anything like this."

At about 10:10 the *Johnston* went down. "We all watched as our home for the past year slowly slid below the surface," Mercer wrote. Orin Vadnais swam away from the ship, then turned around to see destroyers and cruisers running in their half circle around the *Johnston*, blazing away with all guns. "As I watched, she started to sink. First one end went down, and she slipped below the sea."

As the ship rolled over and went down by the bow, Neil Dethlefs wondered whether he would be home in time for Christmas. Drifting along, he came upon two seamen. One was his friend, soundman first class Wally Weigand. The other sailor was holding Weigand's head above water. Dethlefs could see that Weigand had been scalded badly. "The skin was hanging from his arms and hands like a pair of long gloves." Weigand asked Dethlefs if he was burned too. Dethlefs said no. Weigand said, "Boy, I sure am."

Checking his wounds, Bob Sochor found that much of the blood staining his skin probably belonged to other men. During his swim out to the life rafts, Sochor had met up with a young pharmacist's mate, Ken Bowers. "He was very young and religious and always carried a small Bible. He had on a life jacket," Sochor said, "so I hung on to him to rest for a few minutes. We were now about halfway between the sinking ship and the rafts and nets. He said he could not swim and he thought his life jacket would not hold the two of us. I told him I just wanted to rest a minute or so and then I would leave. We were about one-eighth of a mile from the sinking ship when I turned to him and said, 'Take your last look at the *Johnston*,' as it disappeared into the sea."

Ellsworth Welch watched the destroyer turn over slowly and settle by the bow until only the fantail was above water. "Seeing my home go down, I felt my eyes welling with tears. But I thought, *Welch, you might need the liquid*, so I ceased this unseamanly display of emotion." Bobby Chastain felt similarly. "I still remember that helpless feeling one gets while watching your home burn down."

Bowers and another pharmacist's mate, Clayton Schmuff, ministered to the wounded, injected morphine, tied tourniquets. As the survivors of the *Johnston* gathered themselves into groups, a rare sight seized their attention: the direct approach of an enemy warship. For more than three hours the ships had maneuvered under each other's fire, shooting by haphazard sight through smoke and squalls or by the blind omniscience of radar. The range between the foes had never been short enough to see the individuals who operated them. Point-blank range in a modern naval battle was anything less than three miles. Now the enemy approached so closely that men could finally look upon other men.

Clint Carter saw the ship coming before most of his shipmates did. It was bearing down on them fast. Judging by the size of the bow wake the destroyer was throwing, it was at flank speed. Then, when the ship was just half a mile or so away, it slowed, its bow fell, its wake dissipated, and it approached them slowly, warily, ominously.

The Americans weren't sure what to expect. Joseph Check, fearing the enemy gunners would spray them with bullets where they swam, took a hard breath and ducked under the surface. Clint Carter thought that for the Japanese killing the Americans with bullets would be too labor intensive when another tool stood at their disposal. His first thought was: *They're going to give us a giant enema.* A single depth charge laid into their midst would have produced a shallow underwater explosion strong enough to blow their bowels out. Watching the crew play their automatic weapons over the waters, others braced for machine-gun fire. Neil Dethlefs started to untie Wally Weigand's kapok so he could drag him under water when the murderous rain finally fell.

The destroyer edged closer and closer. It made a slight course change that left Clint Carter drifting off her starboard beam. He was taken with the ship's gold-tasseled battle pennant emblazoned with a red rising sun. Bobby Chastain, swimming no more than fifty feet from the ship's port side, could see the sailors lined up by the rail, dressed sharply in khakis and brightly polished brown boots. "They were watching us as we watched them."

It was then that Carter realized what was going on. "It appeared to me that every man on her deck was standing at attention, like a muster, giving us one big salute." As the Japanese warship slid by them, a smartly dressed officer was on the wing of the bridge, standing erect and, indeed, saluting. "As she eased by us," Carter wrote, "I'm sure of one thing . . . she appreciated a fighting lady . . . USS *Johnston*."

Another Japanese crewman was filming them with a handheld movie camera. Another flipped his thumb to his nose and delivered a raspberry. As the ship passed on by, a sailor standing on the fantail tossed an object in Carter's direction. The canister was too big to be a grenade and far too small to be a depth charge. It was a large can of tomatoes. Carter retrieved the offering, examined it, and noticed the label indicating it had been packed in Arkansas. "Three years of war and they were still eating USA canned tomatoes."

The Japanese destroyer disappeared, and the *Johnston* did too. A few minutes later the underwater hulk of the *Johnston* did to her crew what they feared its Japanese counterpart would do. There were two great explosions in the deep. Speculation flew that the ship's boilers had blown. Others doubted the shattered machinery retained enough pressure to explode and assigned blame to unsecured depth charges. Whatever the cause, the effect was breathtaking. The first sensation the men felt was a concussion to their stomach and abdomen, and a sickening thrust of pressure into their rectums. "I thought my body had been blown in half," wrote Charles Landreth. "What a wonderful feeling it was when I found out my body was still intact."

*   *   *

WITHDRAWING NORTHWARD WITH HIS harried task group, Takeo Kurita was enjoying considerably less peace of mind. He toyed with the idea of turning around again and attempting to reenter Leyte Gulf. But late in the morning he received a radio dispatch sent at 10:18 by the skipper of one of the Southern Force destroyers, the lucky *Shigure*: "*All ships except* Shigure *went down under gunfire and torpedo attack.*"

So Nishimura was dead. Kurita could see no purpose in turning around and trying again to reach Leyte Gulf. The Sho-1 plan had become a jaw with one mandible.

Forty-five

For two and a half hours Takeo Kurita had been the hunter. Now, in flight northward, he became the hunted.

Tom Van Brunt and four Avengers from the *Marcus Island* climbed above the clouds to eight thousand feet, joined with another group of Wildcats and Avengers, and turned north in pursuit of Kurita's withdrawing fleet. It was the third major strike that the Taffy 2 carrier group would marshal against the Center Force that morning.

They needed less than thirty minutes to find the withdrawing Japanese force. Against flak that reminded Van Brunt of the light-show one gets on an express subway train roaring through a local station, the *St. Lo* aviator flew to within twelve hundred feet of his target, a *Kongo*-class battleship, jerked the release lever, and felt his plane heave from the change in gravity as the torpedo plunged into the water.

As he flew over the Japanese ship, he felt the aircraft lurch again as a shell exploded near the rear of the fuselage. At once his left rudder was limp. There was nothing there. He could not turn left. The exact extent of the damage he could not yet know. His radioman, Les Frederickson, was shaken up by a nearby shell explosion that was dampened only by the TBM's thin skin. Van Brunt hugged the sea for a mile or two, testing his controls, and found that he could navigate well enough using just his right rudder. As he looped back and gained altitude for the return flight, he looked back at his target and saw a wide trail of oil issuing from astern. Van Brunt guided his riddled aircraft toward home: the friendly flight deck of the *St. Lo*.

By some impossible concatenation of independent miracles, the carrier had not taken a single hit during the battle, even though she rode the northern fringe of the circular formation of escort carriers, closest to Kurita's ships. Only three of her crew were injured with superficial wounds from shrapnel. Meanwhile, the gunners on her tail-mounted five-inch gun had acquitted themselves well. The Battle off Samar was nearly over for the *St. Lo*, as shortly it would be for Tom Van Brunt.

The naval aviator hailed the *St. Lo*'s landing signal officer and informed him that his left rudder was out. Normally landing approaches were made in a descending counterclockwise circle, a flight path that allowed planes to avoid the dangerous eddy of air trailing from the carrier's superstructure. Without a left rudder, Van Brunt could not make the usual approach. He radioed the landing signal officer that he would come in on a clockwise circle. The LSO said, "Okay, we'll try that, but let's get everyone else aboard first."

Climbing to fifteen hundred feet, he was circling the carrier at a distance, watching other planes land, when a red streak flew past his greenhouse canopy. The startling appearance of a Japanese "meatball" insignia painted on a wide white wing was Van Brunt's first indication that enemy aircraft were near. He almost collided with the Japanese plane as it descended toward the *St. Lo*.

Shortly before eleven A.M. Taffy 3 came under wholesale kamikaze attack. The Japanese Army Air Corps had debuted this horrific new mode of warfare earlier that morning, when six imperial planes took off from bases on Davao and attacked Thomas Sprague's Taffy 1 task unit. One struck the escort carrier *Santee*, starting a huge blaze that raged in the hangar deck for about ten minutes. Only the expert marksmanship of gunners aboard the *Suwannee*, the *Sangamon*, and the *Petrof Bay* let them avoid similar hits.

At 10:50 five more aircraft flying from airdromes on Luzon arrived over Taffy 3 and plummeted like osprey on ships whose day of fighting should rightly have been over. The *Kitkun Bay* was the first of Sprague's jeeps to confront the horrifying new tactic. A Zero fighter plane closed from the port side, crossed her bow, climbed, and dove at the bridge. Firing his machine guns as he came, the pilot guided his plane over the small island superstructure, glanced off a catwalk, and hit the sea.

Two more kamikazes attacked the *Fanshaw Bay*. One approaching from astern was knocked off its killing path by a five-inch shell fired by the flagship's peashooter crew. Though that explosion tore off the plane's left wing and the aircraft struck the water, where it disintegrated on impact, the bomb slung under its wing exploded fifteen feet from the hull, showering the ship with shrapnel. Van Brunt saw the carrier's gunners shoot the second plane out of the sky.

Few men aboard the *St. Lo* ever saw the plane that hit their ship. After three hours at general quarters, half the crew was still enjoying a breather. Capt. Francis J. McKenna had ordered Condition One Easy, allowing them to secure from general quarters and get a long-awaited cup of coffee. In the CIC the air-search radar's PPI scope was showing approaching aircraft. Though the planes did not transmit an Identification Friend or Foe beacon, everyone assumed they were friendly. Radio technician Holly Crawforth had other things on his mind—like how he was going to repair the *St. Lo*'s big whip antennas, shredded by the ship's own defensive bursts—when the general quarters alarm sounded. Crawforth was startled to hear the twenty-millimeter guns chattering. The crew had learned to dread the sound; whenever the twenties were shooting, it meant the enemy was close. There—they could see it. A plane was approaching from astern. A half-mile downrange, the pilot was coming in straight and level as if lining up to land.

The quartermaster told Captain McKenna, "Sir, that's a Jap." No sooner had McKenna thrown the ship into a sharp evasive turn to starboard than the Zero fighter, a bomb under each wing, rose up, nosed over, and plunged into the flight deck. In a burst of flames and smoke, the engine tore loose, bounced the length of the flight deck, and skidded off the bow. One or both bombs went off. The mangled fuselage penetrated the four-inch wooden flight deck and exploded belowdecks. Captain McKenna's first impression was that the *St. Lo* had suffered no serious damage. A few minutes passed, then the bulkheads began to collapse.

Ordnanceman John Getas was muscling a TBM off the port-side elevator and into the cavernous hangar deck when he heard a terrific crash. A ball of fire smashed down through the flight deck, fell through thirty feet of space between the underside of the flight deck and the steel decking of the hangar, and landed amid eight planes that chief petty officer Earl Roberts and his ordnance gang were arming for action. Piled around the space where their aircraft were being worked on was enough weaponry to blow a small town out of existence: eight torpedoes, six depth charges, fifteen 500-pound bombs, forty 100-pounders, and some 1,400 rounds of .50-caliber ammunition. Almost at once this orderly, carefully orchestrated world of ordnance turned into a hellish, flaming maelstrom.

Oh my God, Getas thought as the ammo went up. The first explosion shattered several planes, spilling burning aviation fuel onto the deck. It flowed into a large pool that covered a quarter of the cavernous hangar with flames two feet high. The plane that Getas was pushing jumped forward six feet from the pressure wave of the blast. Another aircraft blew up, mowing down a firefighting team and knocking the bodies of the dead and the living across the deck. Getas scrambled up a ladder and found that the flight deck had buckled horribly, black smoke pouring upward into the sky. A chief petty officer lurched by him in a daze. Everything but his shorts had been blown off. One arm hung by strips of skin. Below, at the inferno's ground zero, men shambled about, wreathed in flames. Firefighters tried to gather, dragging big hoses, only to be scattered to the sponsons and catwalks by the pops and zings of baking machine-gun rounds. In the short half hour between the enemy plane's insane plunge through the flight deck and the ship's final surrender, the crew marked time by a sequence of grievous secondary explosions that shook the ship.

The third and fourth explosions blew a hangar door from its hinges, launched a one-hundred-foot span of the flight deck high into the air, and rolled back another swath of flight deck like the top of a sardine can. The ship began listing to port.

After the fifth explosion, Tex Waldrop, the torpedo-busting TBM pilot, lit a cigar, wrapped his hands in rags to insulate them against friction, and rode a line down into the sea. In the water he broke his cigar in two and gave half to another survivor. Then the two men watched their home tear itself to pieces.

The sixth and seventh blasts followed in merciless sequence, ripping the ship apart, one fifty-foot stretch of steel at a time. Some of them sailed as high as a thousand feet into the air. John Getas saw the seventh blast from the water, some two hundred feet from the ship. As debris slapped the surface all around him, he stripped himself naked for buoyancy and backstroked away from the inferno.

Cool and collected, Captain McKenna directed the orderly abandonment from the forward part of the flight deck and the forecastle. Having seen to the evacuation of as many crew as possible, he left the ship after the seventh explosion. The skipper was the last man to ride a line down to the sea.

The eighth blast was a heavy one; McKenna thought it might have been the main bomb stowage going up. It finished the *St. Lo*, tearing her so severely below the waterline that her port list abruptly reversed itself. The ship reeled back to starboard, rolled over completely, lifted her bow from the water, and backed herself under. She stood that way for a moment, then seemed to accept her fate and went down fast. The *St. Lo*'s final protest was the detonation of her boilers, a muffled thump that created a pressure wave that hit John Getas and created the sensation of a broom handle being shoved up his rear.

* * *

HEARTSICK, TOM VAN BRUNT watched from the air as his ruined ship disappeared. He knew pilots who had landed on the ship. Now they were very possibly dead. Gone too was the air operations crew he had trusted with his life. He didn't want to try his luck landing on another carrier—you never knew how good its landing signal officer would be. Van Brunt had seen LSOs on other carriers who had to take their cues from the bridge. He didn't need that now. He turned his damaged Avenger toward Dulag, twenty miles south of Tacloban, which by all accounts was a mess of mud and wrecked airplanes.

He got there, landed, inspected his aircraft, and found, as he expected, that his left rudder cable had been severed completely. What he was less prepared to see was the condition of his elevator cable. Only three of its sixteen strands were intact. One false pull on his stick would have snapped it, plummeting him and his two crewmen into the sea. He also found that his landing hook had been shot off, without which he would have careened across a carrier flight deck right into the forward barrier, nearly as recklessly as the kamikaze that had hit the *St. Lo*.

Dulag had its own attractions. Van Brunt, along with Larry Budnick and two other pilots, spent that night with the Army. The weary pilots were given carbines, told to dig a foxhole, and instructed to watch out for the Japanese counterattack that was expected at any moment. They slept soundly in spite of everything, and the assault never came.

Part III

A VANISHING
GRAVEYARD

*When great men blunder, they count their losses in pride and
reputation and glory. The underlings count their losses in blood.*

—Theodore C. Mason, *Battleship Sailor* (1982)

Forty-six

When a ship sinks, the battlefield goes away. Currents move, thermal layers mix, and by the time the surveyors and rescuers arrive, the water that bore witness to the slaughter is nowhere to be found. The dead disappear, carried under with their ruined vehicles. No wreckage remains for tacticians to study. There are no corpses for stretcher-bearers to spirit away, no remains to shovel, bag, and bury. On the sea there is no place to anchor a memorial flagpole or a headstone. It is a vanishing graveyard.

The sudden silence was the first thing many survivors of the *Hoel*, the *Gambier Bay*, the *Samuel B. Roberts*, and the *Johnston* noticed after their ships had been smashed and swallowed. To many, the quiet was unwelcome. The noise of battle—the roar of machinery, the shrieks and blasts of shells incoming and outbound, the shouts and screams of their buddies—had anesthetized fear. Now the noise lifted like a curtain, unveiling the hidden inner vistas of their grief and shock. When their ships sank, their duties went down with them. Permanently discharged, the survivors were left without the distraction of work to do. The things they had seen could now be contemplated. The wounds they had suffered began to ache, sting, and burn.

The four groups of men were scattered over roughly thirty miles of ocean. Survivors of the *Hoel*, sunk first at 8:55, constituted the northernmost group. The Japanese had been in the heat of pursuit when the destroyer went down. The men of the *Hoel* were then treated to a full fleet review as the Center Force's leviathans paraded past them to the south. After that, the survivors had no idea what had become of the enemy—or of the rest of Taffy 3 for that matter. South of where the *Hoel*'s men swam were the survivors of the *Gambier Bay.* They had the distinction of serving on the only aircraft carrier in history ever sunk by enemy naval gunfire. Like the destroyermen, they had seen the enemy up close, had felt the heat of his muzzles firing. Finally, farther south still, floated the men from the *Johnston* and the *Samuel B. Roberts,* whose ships, having fought to the last, sank within a few minutes and a few thousand yards of each other.

Such descriptions of the groups' proximities, given with the benefit of a backward-looking bird's eye, were unavailable to the men in that terrible moment. The currents and wind took hold of them, and from their initial entry into the water, there was no telling how they moved relative to one another. A thousand men dotted the ocean's swells, cast about by the waters. For small groups and individuals alike, however, the experience of survival was one of sudden, sinking aloneness.

The lazy swells of the Philippine Sea raised and lowered the men at regular intervals. At the top of a swell, if he was inclined, a man could take in his wide surroundings and look for other survivors to merge his fortunes with. In the bottoms, surrounded by gentle slopes of seawater like the sides of a shallow bowl, he would be left to contemplate his private misery. Land was but an abstraction; though the peaks of Samar were visible where the squalls and clouds permitted, reaching up from beneath the horizon, the beaches that lay beneath them were out of sight, some thirty miles away. For a wounded, exhausted swimmer, it might as well have been a whole ocean.

For them, the world existed only in two dimensions. With their eyes at sea level, they had no vertical parallax by which to gauge distance. The physical fact of the round earth made height a telling advantage at sea. Lookouts on the ships with the tallest masts could see farthest and spot the enemy soonest. The *Yamato* was the first Japanese ship to fire not only because of her powerful guns but because her lookouts enjoyed the loftiest aerie in the flotilla. When the survivors entered the water, however, the circumference of their world shrank like a contracted camera aperture. Even on the clearest day the *Hoel*'s survivors would have been out of sight of the *Roberts*'s survivors. Any imaginary line connecting them would have arced over the face of the earth far enough that the curve of the world blocked their view.

By sweeping his arms together, George Bray gathered up a foamy pile of fuel oil and tried to splash it all away from him. But the stuff seemed to have a mind of its own. It floated back at him, sticking to everything. It would not go away. Here and there the slick was burning in the lazy manner in which oil is prone to burn.

Bud Comet paddled his raft to Bray's group and tied up fast to the small flotilla of survivors. This group was sixty-odd strong, gathered on and around a life raft whose wooden lattice bottom, suspended by ropes from the raft's hard foam ring, had been mostly shot out. Some seven feet long and four or five feet wide, the raft was more like an oversized doughnut float than a proper inflatable boat. Tied up to the raft to form a little archipelago was a floater net, a twenty-by-twenty-foot expanse of mesh netting made buoyant by hard rubber disks linked together in strings of eight. Jack Moore, Lt. Luther West, and chief Cullen Wallace were its ranking members.

Most of the men in this group were in fair health. About half of them had no injuries at all. The majority of the rest had wounds that were not immediately life threatening—holes through flesh, gashes to limbs, odd burns and scrapes, blood leaking from the ears. A few were far worse off, and these men, en route to what would probably be a slow death, were laid inside the ring of the raft. Jerry Osborne, a water tender in the *Roberts*'s demolished forward boiler room, had been scalded so severely that he had third-degree burns all over his body. He lapsed in and out of consciousness. The midocean silence was now and then cut through with his and others' long groans, at unpredictable intervals swelling into screams.

A few hundred yards away from them, on their own raft-and-floater-net assemblage, drifted another group of about fifty men, among them Bob Copeland, Bob Roberts, Bill Burton, Dudley Moylan, Tom Stevenson, Lloyd Gurnett, and two of the ship's four surviving chiefs, Rudy Skau and Frank Cantrell.

Some distance away on the current, another group of about seventeen or so *Roberts* survivors clung to a far less sturdy contraption: a pair of fourteen-foot-long wooden planks that the deck division had once used as a scaffolding for scraping and painting the side of the hull. The structure wasn't seaworthy, and a lot of the men clinging to it were in very bad shape.

It was clear to Stevenson and others that the wounded would be better off with them. Only seven could fit inside the raft, so the captain and pharmacist's mate Oscar King evaluated their wounded and decided who would gain tenancy to this prime real estate. Everyone else floated in the water around the raft, clutching the manila lines of the floater net tied up to it.

Tom Stevenson, Lloyd Gurnett, soundman third class Louis Gould, and Charles Natter, who was a particularly strong swimmer, spent a few hours on the afternoon of the twenty-fifth trying to unite the stragglers on the scaffolding with their group. They swam to it and struggled to move the bulky structure toward their own raft and net. When they tired of the impossible task of propelling the sagging mass of wood through the water, they tried to cajole the healthier survivors to swim with them. To their frustration, most of them refused to leave the scaffolding—a bird in the hand and all that. Staying put beat swimming an Olympic distance through waters well populated by large sharks. Ultimately, they settled for ferrying back to the raft men who were too weak to make it themselves and too shell-shocked to resist rescue.

Yelling deliriously, Bill Stovall, Gun 52's pointer, was among several men pulled into Copeland's raft. He had been blown from the mount's steel enclosure, his lungs scorched in the fiery blowback from the breech. He had lived long enough to see the ship sink, but as he hollered on, it was clear that the only humane thing to do was to avoid prolonging his agony. Exchanging pained, knowing glances and solemn nods, the men eased Stovall into the water and allowed it to swallow him.

*　　*　　*

WHEN THE *ROBERTS* SURVIVORS got their first glimpse of the dim gray triangles cutting the water's surface around them, the stinking oil that fouled their hair, faces, and eyes began to seem more a blessing than a curse. The high-grade American fuel—distinctive by smell from Japan's cruder Malaysian distillate—coated them completely, masking their identities from one another. Though their eyes stung from it and they couldn't see much, the oil proved to be an effective shark repellent. The men noticed the way it seemed to keep the tall fins at a distance. George Bray scooped up a handful of black foam and smeared it all over his shoeless left foot. The last thing a guy needed was a shark mistaking a white sock for an appetizer.

The oil was an efficient sunscreen too. Most of the squalls had been warmed away by the rising South Pacific sun. It baked their skin and reflected off the sea to burn their undersides as well. But the oil protected their skin. Exposure to the ocean's elements didn't seem like much of a threat at the time. They knew help was on the way.

Looking up, Tom Stevenson could see a swarm of specks against the ceiling of the blue sky—planes outbound on strike missions of some kind. The aircraft—could they be from the Taffies?—were probably too high for their pilots to spot the survivors. Optimism reigned nonetheless. Figuring on a prompt rescue, Copeland had doled out most of the raft's provisions. Each man got two malted milk tablets, a piece of Spam, and a few ounces of water.

Sure enough, a good omen soon came. Around three P.M., out of the blue, came the low-throated growl of a Wright radial engine, drowning out the sound of seawater lapping against the raft. A TBM Avenger roared by. Low over the wave tops, the pilot banked hard, circling the group and flashing a thumbs-up sign through the long greenhouse canopy. As the plane zoomed away, its engine fading with the down Doppler, everyone was jubilant. *That was it,* Stevenson thought. They were all but rescued. The pilot would call in their position, and a ship or a submarine would be sent to get them.

Forty-seven

Swimming in the bloodied waters that had swallowed their ships, none of the survivors of the late, great screening vessels of Taffy 3 were in a position to distinguish victory from defeat. The Japanese men-of-war that had sunk them had charged blithely past, presumably to sweep away the remains of Taffy 3 and to charge through Taffies 2 and 1 on the way into Leyte Gulf itself.

Who was going to tell them what had really happened? And would they even have believed it? The men of the destroyers and destroyer escorts had helped win a victory of the most impossibly resounding kind. Their dashing skippers had put themselves on the line first and started an improbable rout. Now Bill Brooks and friends, the avenging angels from the escort carrier squadrons, would help finish it.

Launching from the *Marcus Island* at 11:15 A.M., Brooks, the first Taffy 3 pilot to spot the Japanese fleet on its way south, was now among the last to watch it flee. He was in the vanguard of the Taffies' latest parting gift to the Japanese Center Force: a fifty-six-plane strike whose savagery and efficiency tended to support Kurita's decision to withdraw. Pilots from the sixteen CVEs of the three Taffies formed pickup squads on the wing. Brooks flew with Ens. William Mc-Cormick of the *Fanshaw Bay*'s VC-68 and Lt. Cdr. T. O. Murray, skipper of the *Marcus Island*'s resident squadron, VC-21. That group of fourteen Avengers and eight Wildcats merged with a group led by the *Kadashan Bay*'s skipper, Lt. Cdr. John Dale, which in turn joined planes led by Lt. Cdr. Richard Fowler, the resourceful *Kitkun Bay* air group commander who had taken a breather aboard the Taffy 2 jeep *Manila Bay* after his morning exploits. They required no navigation data to find their targets. Raging fires from the stricken *Chokai* and the *Chikuma* produced twin columns of smoke that were visible from the flight deck of Taffy 2's carriers. This gathering of planes, which rendezvoused as green-dyed shell splashes from the *Haruna* were walking the seas around Taffy 2's destroyer screen, was the fourth of six air strikes that Taffy 2 would send against Kurita that day. They found the Japanese fleet about fifteen miles east of Samar Island, off Cebu Bay.

The CVE pilots learned on the wing to do what Halsey's and Mitscher's aviators prided themselves on doing. In the days leading up to the Battle off Samar, several jeep-carrier fighter pilots had distinguished themselves in air-to-air combat against bombers swarming the Leyte invasion beachhead. Overall on the day, Wildcat pilots from the three Taffy groups downed fifty-four Japanese planes and claimed twenty more as probables. Now, with an enemy fleet within their grasp, it was the Avenger pilots' turn to work in the big leagues.

Even had the Center Force commander not recalled his ships on the brink of triumph, they still would have had to survive this angry swarm of American planes. Indeed, with such a surprising gathering of strength arrayed against him, it remains unclear what Kurita could have accomplished had he pressed south toward Leyte Gulf. First, he would have done so alone. He had learned while withdrawing that Nishimura's Southern Force had been wiped out the night before. And he strongly (and correctly) suspected that MacArthur's transports had long since unloaded the last of their troops, weapons, food, and supplies. The heavy cruisers *Tone* and *Haguro*, having gotten within five and a half miles (a short ten thousand yards) of Sprague when Kurita's order went out, might have sunk a few more CVEs, but they wouldn't have gotten far against aerial opposition such as this: fifty-six well-armed planes, and another strike arming on the Taffy 2 carriers behind them. Admiral Stump had ordered his planes to cripple as many Japanese ships as possible—there was no sense administering overkill with Halsey coming back south to clean up any messes they made. The American aviators made as many of them as they could. Kurita had more than he could handle keeping his fleet together in the face of the blue hornets from the escort carriers.

Overtaking the withdrawing ships swiftly, the pilots circled at eight thousand feet, the radio frequencies ababel with pilots excitedly reporting their contacts. If radio communication was strained, the pilots now enjoyed the relative luxury of unpressured time in which to choose their targets. As Commander Dale's section took the starboard side of the formation and Fowler's the port, Bill Brooks, Ensign McCormick, and Commander Murray passed the Japanese squadron and made a wide looping turn. When the signal went out to strike, they came in from the north, starting eight miles out and bearing down on the enemy. According to Commander Murray's afteraction report, "In a beautifully coordinated attack, strafers led glide bombers followed by torpedo planes which made their drops as the last bombs hit." The Japanese ships turned hard to port as the Americans swooped in. Murray pushed over into a steep right turn, following the ships, with McCormick behind him and Brooks bringing up the rear. When flak began to pepper the sky, the planes split formation, with Brooks and McCormick swinging to Murray's right, lining up a *Nagato*-class battleship while McCormick lined up an *Atago*-class heavy cruiser straight ahead.* "Now you're on your own," Murray said. But when McCormick opened his weapons bay doors, his torpedo fell out and plummeted to the sea.

With the battleship in view, Brooks flew down to 900 feet, lining up fifteen degrees off the ship's starboard bow and entering the critical "needle-ball and airspeed" phase of his run. If he had figured right, he would glide down to 500 feet and drop, and the battleship's counterclockwise turn, extrapolated to that point, would put it broadside to his torpedo in the last seconds of its bubbling approach. Ray Travers, hunched over his radar console's A-scope, hollered out the range to the target, first in miles, then in yards as the range closed. Joe Downs was itching for something to shoot at. He looked to starboard, and there lay a big Japanese cruiser.

"I'm gonna take on this cruiser, okay? It won't spoil your airflight, will it?" Downs asked Brooks over the intercom. Cranking the flat-sided spherical greenhouse-glass turret out to the side changed

---

*The *Chokai* was the only *Atago*-class heavy cruiser in this battle.

the plane's aerodynamics, which was not always helpful to a pilot concentrating on making a delicate torpedo run. The pilot told him not to worry about it, so Downs went hunting. The gunner cut loose, sending a hot spray of tracers, ball, and armor-piercing rounds popping and ricocheting across the ship's superstructure.

Joe Downs had nearly exhausted his ammo can when, abruptly, the plane lifted straight up with a jerk. He thought the plane had been hit. In the excitement he had all but forgotten the two-thousand-pound torpedo payload that Brooks had just released, creating quite a change in inertia.

An endless series of seconds passed—twenty or thirty of them—while the torpedo cruised the thousand-yard path to the ship. Seated rearward in the gunner's seat, Downs watched the ship shrink in the distance, then get swallowed in a flash of flame. Their torpedo struck forward of the bridge, producing a dirty geyser of water. The *Nagato*'s bulky mass heaved and shuddered, seeming to lift slightly, then drop back into the sea.

"Oh man, you got her, you got her!" Downs shouted. Mc-Cormick saw it too. Brooks circled to watch, then settled on a course that would take him back toward his adoptive home, the Taffy 3 flagship, the *Fanshaw Bay*. He was by no means unique in this regard, but it would be the third flight deck Brooks's wheels touched during that long day.

At 12:40, about twenty minutes after Murray's and Brooks's attack, the *Kitkun Bay*'s Richard Fowler led his group around a big cumulus cloud and dove down out of the sun. The loose enemy formation was looping around to the left, exposing its starboard flanks to Fowler's vengeful blue angels. The skipper dropped his bombs over a battleship, hitting it just aft of the bridge. His wingman's bombs struck near the mainmast, while two more pilots scored near-misses astern. Another Avenger pilot reported hitting the *Nagato* with a torpedo amidships. A heavy cruiser just inboard of the battleship was struck by two bombs.

Just before touching down on the *Fanshaw Bay*, Fowler picked up a transmission from the *Wasp* air group, one of Halsey's squadrons, reporting the sighting of the retiring enemy fleet. Ziggy Sprague's old ship, with the rest of Adm. John S. McCain's Task Group 38.2, was closing fast. The Third Fleet's contribution to the Battle off Samar was far too little, far too late. Because McCain's strike was launched at extended range, the pilots' fuel reserves were too low to permit deliberate target selection and preparatory maneuver. But their arrival did tend to underscore the point that had Kurita not withdrawn, he would have run smack into yet another powerful air group.

At about 2:15 P.M. the *Chikuma,* crippled earlier by *White Plains* fliers, her topside charred by salvos from the *Samuel B. Roberts,* was finished off by planes from the Taffy 2 jeep *Ommaney Bay.* Preceded by four Wildcat fighters that spat two thousand .50-caliber slugs into the cruiser, three TBM Avengers, led by the VC-75 commander, Lt. Allen W. Smith, swooped in low and lay a spread of torpedoes into her port side, just forward of amidships. Seawater rushed in, and the cruiser heeled and rocked a few times, then rolled onto its port side and sank in about fifteen minutes.

Farther to the north, Taffy 3 pilots were in hot pursuit of any other Japanese ships that could still make steam. Tommy Lupo of the *Fanshaw Bay*'s VC-68, having reholstered his pistol and reloaded with bombs commandeered from the Army, had taken off from the airfield at Tacloban sometime before. Heading north, he found a *Mogami*-class cruiser, probably the stubborn *Kumano,* limping toward San Bernardino Strait, her bow broken in the battle's early minutes. Gliding down alone, Lupo overtook the cruiser, dove on her from her starboard quarter, rode the bright rails of the ship's tracer bullets down to his bomb-release point, and walked a brace of bombs right up her back. One of his 250-pounders appeared to drop right down the ship's exhaust stack. A fountain of smoke and crud shot skyward from amidships, and as he flew away, orange tongues of flame could be seen licking through the smoke.

Intermingling orphaned pilots from Ziggy Sprague's task unit with the squadrons of his own six carriers, Taffy 2 commander Admiral Stump's carriers mustered a total of 204 sorties against Kurita, 117 by Avengers and 87 by Wildcats, dropping 49 torpedoes and 286 500-pound bombs, and firing 276 rockets and untold thousands of rounds of machine-gun ammunition. By the time the last of his pilots returned to Taffy 2 at 6:25 P.M., just before nightfall made carrier operations doubly hazardous, Kurita's force had been smashed down to size. Limping north toward San Bernardino Strait went a battered and broken Center Force, reportedly consisting of four battleships, just three heavy cruisers, two light cruisers, and seven destroyers.

Two of the battleships trailed broad slicks of oil; three destroyers and one of the light cruisers lagged behind the main group; and one heavy cruiser appeared heavily damaged. Impossible to catalog but probably significant nonetheless were the assorted lesser catastrophes inflicted by the ceaseless strafing, bombing, and battering by American five-inch shells. Twenty-four aircraft from the jeep carriers had fallen to Japanese antiaircraft fire, with forty-three pilots and aircrewmen lost or missing in action.

Some pilots survived by the slimmest of margins. Richard Roby, the *Gambier Bay* Wildcat pilot, escorted Berman Dillard back to Tacloban after a strike on the Japanese fleet. Seeing Dillard's plane swerving on an unsteady course, its pilot without a helmet and no hatch, bareheaded to the rushing wind, Roby suspected immediately that his VC-10 squadronmate was "punchier than a three-dollar bill." He couldn't keep a level heading, and if the young pilot could scarcely manage level flight, how would he handle a landing on a muddy, pitted airstrip?

Somehow Dillard reached Tacloban, made a reasonably steady approach, and eased his Wildcat onto the muddy runway. The plane taxied down the tarmac, hit a soft spot, and flipped forward, driving its propeller hub into the ground. Roby pulled around for another pass, giving the men on the ground time to push the wrecked fighter plane out of the way. Then Roby made another approach and landed. When he found Dillard, the wounded pilot had taken so much shrapnel to the face that he looked like a smallpox patient. For the pilots of VC-10, as for all the pilots of Taffy 3, the morning of October 25 had been a long one.

The aviators from the Seventh Fleet's escort carriers finished the Battle off Samar on their terms because Kurita had declined to finish it on his.

On whose terms the survivors in the water would end their ongoing struggle remained very much an open question.

Forty-eight

The impossible horror of the war's first kamikaze sinking had come upon them suddenly and without warning. Murderously effective, the attack on the *St. Lo* and the other CVEs set the lookouts on Taffy 3's remaining ships on high alert. Though Ziggy Sprague worried about the possibility of submarine attack—there had been enough odd sightings of torpedo wakes coming at his ships during the morning's fighting to alert him to the threat—he detached what remained of his screen, the *Heermann,* the *Dennis,* the *Raymond,* and the *John C. Butler,* from escort duty and ordered them to recover the survivors of the *St. Lo* dotting the sea where the carrier had gone down. Expertly conned by her skipper, Sig Hansen, her narrow hull draped in cargo nets for survivors to climb, the *Dennis* moved through the *St. Lo*'s debris field retrieving survivors. The healthiest among them clambered aboard asking, "Hey, what's for chow?" "What's the movie tonight?" or "Where the hell is haul-ass Halsey?" The worse-off were pulled from the sea and given morphine and a soft place to lie down. The *Dennis*'s rescue effort, led by first lieutenant Frank Tyrrell and chief boatswain's mate Joe Barry, saved more than four hundred survivors from the *St. Lo* and thirty-five pilots.

Retrieving the other survivors would be a much taller order. The Avenger pilot who sighted Tom Stevenson and the rest of the *Roberts* survivors, under strict radio silence, made a mental note of their coordinates to pass along to the Seventh Fleet after he landed. It seems his mission lasted longer than his memory. The coordinates that were given to Admiral Kinkaid were off by a wide margin. An attempted correction offered little more help. Admiral Stump informed the Seventh Fleet commander around 12:30 P.M. that hundreds of survivors were adrift at 11°12'N, 126°30'E, which was twenty to forty miles south of the various sites where the Taffy 3 ships had gone down.

Though Ziggy Sprague was prompt in asking Admiral Kinkaid to launch a rescue operation to save the survivors of Taffy 3, owing to the desperate nature of the fight against the continuing kamikaze attacks and the preoccupation of the PBY Catalina patrol planes with rescuing downed fliers, it wasn't until 3:30 P.M. that a serious rescue attempt was made. At that time Admiral Kinkaid ordered Tommy Sprague to detach all available screening ships and begin a search close to the original erroneous position. Because it consisted of ships unassisted by planes, the rescue mission had a margin for error much slimmer than the error itself. The destroyer escorts *Eversole* and *Richard S. Bull* steamed northeast and arrived at the specified coordinates at 11:30 P.M. Finding nothing, they returned to Taffy 1 empty-handed that night.

When Admiral Halsey finally returned from chasing Admiral Ozawa's goose, he detached several destroyers to sweep the area, looking for Japanese stragglers. Though they passed close to where some Taffy 3 survivors floated, they were looking for things considerably larger than heads bobbing on the waves. They failed to locate them as well.

*   *   *

AS THE AFTERNOON WORE on, Tom Stevenson, Charles Natter, and Lloyd Gurnett had just about given up their attempts to bring back the men floating on the planks. The survivors who clung to them, many badly hurt, were exhibiting a dangerous combination of recalcitrance and resignation. They refused to leave. The scaffolding must have been just seaworthy enough to make the reward of setting out for another precarious refuge seem dubious and theoretical, even if their captain was supposedly in charge there.

Natter did his best to help them. He was a capable swimmer,

athletic and strong. Adrenaline made up what strength he had lost from the shrapnel peppered through his shoulders. But there were limits to what the stout signalman could do. Men were not made to outswim sharks.

The predators were gathering in growing numbers. For a time the pool of fuel oil that surrounded them seemed to keep the sharks at bay. But by late afternoon enough blood had leached into the water to attract a crowd.

Charles Natter was catching a breather on the scaffolding when the sharks ended the tease and acted on their nature. One of them came up and pulled Thomas Mazura, one of his friends from the *Sammy B.*'s signal division, from his plank. Natter had little time to mourn. Like an inverted fang, another big fin glided toward him, and he was hauled under too. Seeing it all happen, John Conway was at last persuaded to take his chances swimming for Copeland's raft. The coxswain tried to talk others into joining him, but hurt and exhausted, they wanted no part of it. Conway was the only man from the scaffolding to reach Bob Copeland's raft and floater net that afternoon.

At one point Copeland counted as many as fifty shark fins cutting the surface near him. Thanks to the oil that bathed the survivors in his group, these predators were all swim and no bite. But because no one could be too confident of that, the men feared the worst whenever a fin moved closer and then disappeared under water. The captain of the *Roberts* didn't want to think about what might have happened to his signalman and the men he had gallantly tried to save.

Whether through exhaustion, wounds, or willpower, the men stayed quiet. Their stoicism impressed Bob Copeland.

> *I've read a lot of stories about how men on life rafts behave; they either curse—curse their luck and curse everybody—or they get a big shot of religion and pray and sing songs. Our men didn't do that at all. . . . They were a very quiet group. . . . They bore their suffering in almost total silence. . . . We were just beaten to a pulp, that's all.*

The only outbursts on Copeland's raft were the final thrashes of the dying. Charles Staubach, the grievously wounded chief electrician's mate, lay motionless inside the raft, tended to by healthy survivors. But around three that afternoon he went out of his head, ranting and raving deliriously before succumbing to death.

As the sun fell in the western sky, optimism about a quick rescue was turning to discouragement. Copeland noticed that Bob Roberts's stoutly girded calm was giving way to a very evident despair. "I tried to bargain with God," Roberts later wrote. "I explained to Him that my wife had just had a baby boy whom I had never seen, and that though I was ready and willing to die, if He would allow it I would take care of them as long as I lived." Copeland huddled privately with his exec until Roberts regained his composure. "He was a tower of strength from there on in," Copeland wrote.

Copeland asked Roberts, "Where do you think we are?" Roberts said, "Well, Captain, I don't know exactly where we are, but I'd say we're roughly thirty miles east of the island of Samar and about thirty miles north of its southern tip. That's as close as I can give you from the last navigational fix I had before we went into battle. That's close. We are within five miles one way or another."

Thirty miles off Samar. If they were high enough above the water, in the crow's nest of a battleship using binoculars, they might have seen its shores. But from sea level, where they floated, the line of sight to the horizon was just fourteen miles. When the clouds and rain permitted, all they could see were its peaks.

"Well," Copeland said to Roberts, "you and I are the senior officers, and we better set a good example." They each took a paddle and climbed up on the side of the raft and began stroking a course west into the setting sun.

Forty-nine

The survivors from the *Johnston* were greater in number than the *Roberts* group but were situated similarly to the other survivors from Taffy 3's sunken ships. Well over a hundred men drifted the ravaged waters on lengths of plank and timber, on floater nets and life rafts, or were held afloat only by kapok vests or life preservers. Organized and calmed by their officers and senior petty officers, they decided to let their large group disperse on the currents, each group centered on a life raft/floater net ensemble, in order to maximize their chances of detection.

The most seriously wounded were gathered inside the rafts. Howard Craven, from the electrical department, had his throat slashed clear around the neck by a large shard of shrapnel. Though few expected him to survive, he surprised them all not only by surviving but by summoning the energy and Samaritan will to tend to James Cooper and Jack Walker, who had been badly burned and lay shivering in the raft.

A large group that included Bob Hagen, Ellsworth Welch, Ed DiGardi, Jack Bechdel, Jesse Cochran, Milt Pehl, and Hank Wilson was clustered around two rafts and a pair of floater nets strung together with manila line. Wilson had gotten badly burned by boiler steam when the fireroom was hit. Pharmacist's mate Clayton Schmuff swam about making his rounds, putting sulfa powder on burns and giving morphine to the most seriously wounded. Jack Bechdel, missing most of a leg, was so benumbed by morphine that he found it within himself to sing. With a voice mellifluous and strong, he sang as if they were gathered around a campfire.

As the afternoon dragged on, Ellsworth Welch reflected on the ordeal that they had all just experienced, thinking their circumstances could only get better. "Our thoughts were, *3,000 ships, 200,000 men, thousands of airplanes. . . . It won't be long now. . . .* We were just a couple of hundred miles from the greatest naval armada ever assembled on earth." To a man they were convinced that the proximity of powerful friendly fleets all but ensured their rescue. Their admiral knew they were out there. Pilots had sighted them. Rescue would be the simple product of time, patience, and fortitude.

While they waited for America's overwhelming military power to come to their assistance, they passed the time struggling to keep their spirits up, wondering aloud about the outcome of the battle and the fates of particular shipmates, telling stories, passing cigarettes, and munching on hardtack biscuits and salty water.

By midafternoon their submerged doubts began to surface, along with the first sharks. Bill Mercer watched a particularly large one work its way toward them in a widely meandering zigzag, finally cruising by close enough that the men could extend their legs and kick at it. Faced with splashing and kicking life-forms, it elected not to harm them. The men scanned the horizon through 360 degrees, watching their hopes for a speedy rescue diminish and vanish.

*   *   *

WHEN DARKNESS FELL, THE sharks grew more assertive. In the pitch-black Pacific night, they revealed themselves by proxy. Moving through the plankton-rich waters, disturbing the photosensitive plant life, the sharks ignited an eerie phosphorescence that formed a faint glowing path toward the men in the rafts. There was splashing and cursing. Shrill voices rose and then were gone. Someone said something about spotting a ship. Someone else produced a Very pistol, and several flares lofted skyward—red, white, and green—burning arcs of colorful brilliance through the night. When there was no response in kind from the rescuer, the men feared they had alerted a Japanese ship. Their panic became quieter if no less desperate.

Drifting toward a fatal sleep, the men decided to fasten themselves together with their CO_2 inflatable life belts, assigned each
other numbers, and counted off at intervals to indicate their physical
and mental presence. Clint Carter had just finished securing himself
to Chuck Campbell when someone yelled "Shark!" and the men
started climbing atop one another toward the stars. In the zero-sum
equation of saltwater buoyancy, one man's success was another
man's sudden dunking. Something bumped Carter heavily in the
back, and he felt a wrenching force. He screamed, put both hands on
Campbell's shoulders, and lifted himself out of the water as a shark's
bear-trap jaws tore away a chunk of his kapok, along with a small
bloody piece of his side. As Carter rose up, his weight plunged Campbell under. The shark let go of Carter, Carter let go of Campbell, and
Campbell surfaced sputtering and gasping. Then the shark tasted
Carter again, and once more he dunked Campbell in his bid for the
raft. The shark let go of Carter, Campbell surfaced, and regaining his
breath, he helped lay Carter, bleeding badly, into the raft.

Chief gunner's mate Harry Henson got bitten in the thigh hard
enough to crush bone. Joe Taromino took bites in the left arm and
shoulder, Vince Scafoglio in the area of his left kidney.

In the night, despite the ministrations of their shipmate with the
slashed throat, Cooper and Walker passed away. Someone offered a
few solemn words, their life jackets and life belts were removed for
someone else's benefit, their dog tags were collected, and their bodies
were released and allowed to sink. Watching them go under, Bill
Mercer felt like "an eighteen-year-old boy going on forty."

As the night deepened, hopelessness set in for the wounded who
could no longer endure the glacial passage of time. Before Ed
Haubrich died of his severe leg wounds, he asked Dusty Rhodes, the
cook in the chief's mess, for a sandwich. A *Johnston* sailor who had
suffered a deep shark bite to the abdomen asked to be put out of his
misery. For nearly an hour he begged for his shipmates' mercy, moan-
ing, screaming, and crying. He finally received it when someone pulled
out a revolver, misfired it, then produced a knife and cut his throat.

*　　*　　*

"WHY DON'T WE ALL sing?" The survivors in Jack Moore's group
made a halfhearted attempt to render a familiar tune. "Old Mac-

Donald Had a Farm." "The Swanee River." "Deep in the Heart of Texas." "I've Been Working on the Railroad." But they had suffered too much to indulge in musical reverie. Their hearts weren't in it. "I remember a few people started singing," Dick Rohde said, "and then it just sort of died out. Nobody really wanted to sing. It didn't go over too well."

Though they stayed mostly quiet, the arrival of sharks triggered their survival instincts, and desperate spasms of fighting broke out, the men climbing one another like ladders, frantic to leave the water. They pushed one another down, clutching and grabbing with death-grip strength. They swallowed seawater, gagged, and lunged upward, coughing and swinging fists. George Bray and Chalmer Goheen tried to quell the panic, but it had a life of its own. Finally, after the men had worn themselves out, it stopped by itself.

When quiet settled in again, the men laid their heads on the sides of the raft and on the coarse rope mesh of the floater net. George Bray struggled to remain alert. He was starting to think the sharks might be toying with them. He had seen them swimming in slow circles below. Though it was hard to gauge precisely how large they were, he knew they weren't small. The last rays of daylight had revealed some big ones down there: ten, twelve feet long, he thought. There had been smaller fish present with them—hundreds of them hovering together in stationary schools. Possibly barracuda. In months past Bray and the others had occasionally seen sharks following the *Roberts* near dusk, gorging themselves as the garbage was thrown overboard. The sharks patrolling the waters off Samar on October 25, having endured the cacophony of the bloody morning, would find richer fare in the ensuing days.

Eventually George Bray stopped worrying too much about what might be in the waters beneath him. By the time the sun was dipping out of sight to the west, fear of the big predators yielded to wary acceptance. Mostly he just stopped looking down. Mostly he started worrying about what might—or might not—be coming for them from over the horizon.

Fifty

When no ship came to rescue the survivors of the *Samuel B. Roberts* during the night, Tom Stevenson feared the Japanese had won the battle. The big force of Jap cruisers and battleships, he thought, had incinerated the other ships of Taffy 3 and pressed on to the Leyte beachhead. What other conclusion could be drawn? If any of the American ships had survived, wouldn't they be combing the oceans where the *Roberts* and the others had gone down, pulling alongside and hauling them aboard to safety? The *Sammy B.*'s sacrifice, it seemed, had been in vain.

Untold hours into the deepening night, Stevenson heard a shout. The voice sounded American. With others, he called hoarsely in reply, and echoing one another, ranging by sound, the source of the shouting finally found them. It was a man, swimming alone.

Soundman Howard Cayo, the former circus acrobat, had been with the men on the scaffolding. He was one of just a few there to survive the shark attacks—saved, it seemed, by his litheness and strength. Cayo joined the group, relating the horrible story of what had happened on the scaffolding.

The fear was with them already, but now it worsened. They kicked and splashed at phantoms. Clutching the floater net hitched to Copeland's raft, kicking futilely in the direction of land while Copeland and Bob Roberts paddled from the raft, Stevenson prayed silently, *God, if you get me out of this, I'm going to become the best husband and raise a great family. That's all I'm going to ask.*

* * *

THE NIGHTTIME SKY, IMPASSIVE and immobile, betrayed no sign of the passage of time. To Jack Moore "it seemed very much like an entire week of darkness." The first indication of change that touched George Bray's senses came to him after midnight: the rich scent of land. The pure ocean air cleansed the nasal cavities so thoroughly that there was no mistaking the sweet effluvium of the Samar jungle. Its rich, warm smell came wafting over the waters, borne to them on shifting winds.

The ocean currents or tides or whatever other inscrutable forces pushed them through the waters were shifting too. When the survivors tried to swim toward shore, the currents defied them. With a man straddling the ring of the raft on each side, they paddled to exhaustion but made little apparent headway. But once the men surrendered to the current, the tides seemed to relent and even to cooperate.

When Bray heard the sound of breakers hissing on the unseen beach, he guessed that his group couldn't have been more than a mile from land. They resumed paddling. But a nagging thought made them hesitate. Samar was Japanese held. You didn't just go ashore by night without doing a little reconnoitering. The dark island was famous for danger. Discovered by Ferdinand Magellan in 1521, Samar was five thousand square miles of oozing malarial swamps fringing majestic forested mountains. The terrain was liberally soaked with the blood of insurgents, saturated with a myth of violence. From the 1901 Balangiga massacre, in which fifty-nine U.S. troops were ambushed and killed by Filipino guerrillas, provoking Brig. Gen. Jacob Smith to declare that all Filipinos over the age of ten must be killed and "the interior of Samar must be made a howling wilderness," to the nightmare campaign waged by the *pulajan* insurgency against the Manila Constabulary in 1904–05, in which rebels burned fifty-three villages in a two-month period, it had fairly earned the nickname "the bloody island." Samar had seldom known peace, even less now that its foreign occupiers were as brutal as its native insurgents.

The clouds shrouded the moon; where squalls fell to the sea, they looked like forests of trees on land. Without knowing their geographical bearings, the men could not know what to do. In the pitch dark, in the safe distance, Jack Moore spotted a patrol boat of some kind, its searchlight playing over the dark waters in their vicinity but failing to discover them.

George Bray and the others stopped paddling and lay to rest, trying to orient themselves by the position of the moon. But like the tides, that too was a shifting variable. It lay hidden behind thick clouds. They fell asleep one by one, and when they awoke again and found their bearings by the early light of daybreak, they discovered that they had drifted farther out to sea.

*   *   *

A SHIP STEAMED TOWARD them in the night, its head-on silhouette materializing tall and black against the backlighting moon. A few survivors of the *Johnston* shouted out, desperate that the ship not miss them. But when it came closer and then turned broadside to them, everyone suddenly went quiet. Its pagoda-shaped mast was all too apparent. Ellsworth Welch identified it as a *Terutsuki*-class destroyer. It was probably searching for survivors from one of the imperial cruisers sunk in the battle. The presence of a larger predator compelled men who were kicking at sharks to float motionless, loath to break the surface with an out-of-place splash that might reveal their presence. Men who were singing abruptly stopped. "What had been a very noisy group became as silent as a graveyard," Harold Beresonsky recalled. When the ship's searchlight beam swept the seas near them, the silence was broken by soft prayers.

The random strikes of the sharks terrified the men through the night. One moment a kid was there, quietly treading water. The next moment he was screaming, and seconds later he was gone. Quiet. Then screaming. Then gone. Just like that. Ellsworth Welch felt something grab the back of his life belt, rip it off, and tear his pants and shorts. "This was a situation for which I wasn't prepared," he wrote. "My contract with the Navy was to fight the enemy, not sharks." Robert Billie, wounded by the first Japanese salvo that struck the *Johnston*'s bridge, swung in and out of consciousness through much of the night. Someone tied him up to an unwounded shipmate who helped keep his face out of the water. Thanks to his shipmate's kindness, Billie would survive. Before the night was over, though, his unhurt benefactor would himself be grabbed and hauled under by a shark.

Fifty-one

At about ten A.M. on the second day at sea, the reappearance of Samar's mountain peaks boosted the spirits of Bob Copeland's men. In celebration, the skipper broke out the last of the emergency rations. Hoisting himself up to sit on the doughnut raft's ring, Copeland rubbed his fingers on his trousers to clean them of oil and ordered each man to swim up to him, whereupon he dispensed the last of the malted milk tablets, three apiece, and the last remnants of Spam and some stale fresh water.

The experience helped Copeland see a certain egalitarian nobility to his crew and officers. "On that raft we were just forty-nine very wretched human beings, entirely dependent upon ourselves and one another in an effort to sustain life. Under those conditions it made no difference to us whether a man's parents had been rich or poor; whether he was Catholic, Protestant, or Jew; whether his skin was black, brown, or white; or whether his ancestry was English, Spanish, Italian, or something else." During their second day at sea, the oil mostly dissolved and washed away from their skin, revealing those things that Copeland no longer felt mattered anymore.

Paddling gamely toward shore, Howard Cayo and Tom Stevenson straddled the overloaded raft on opposite sides. While they were laboring, straining to push the impossible weight of their craft through the low swells, a seagull began circling overhead. Seeing a potential meal, Cayo stood shakily, gathered his weight behind his paddle, and swung it upward in a wide arc. He missed the bird but caught Tom Stevenson full in the head on the follow-through, knocking the dazed lieutenant into the sea.

Around midafternoon, while Stevenson was shaking off the effects of the blow, easier pickings came their way. The men on Copeland's raft spied a wooden crate floating some distance away from them. Cayo and fireman first class John Kudelchuk took off after it and, retrieving it for their captain's inspection, discovered it to be stamped with Japanese characters. They pulled it open and discovered it was full of dried onions, more than 150 of them. They were passed around, and the men started devouring them, stopping only when they realized the extent to which the onions intensified their thirst. From that point on dehydration and exposure to sun and sea threatened the survivors' lives as surely as did the sharks.

Some of the men questioned Copeland's decision to paddle toward shore. With the possibility of rescue shrinking by the hour, they reasoned, shouldn't they be conserving their strength rather than expending it? Worn down by the multiple pressures of combat, injury, and the agony of watching so many of his crew die and his ship be smashed down around him, the skipper himself was beginning to lose his edge. There was only so much he could endure. In time Copeland started to feel, as did quite a few others, that they should risk swimming to shore under the cover of darkness and make contact with Filipino guerrillas.

But as the sun began to set, they were drifting by their best dead reckoning some four miles from the Samar coast—"too far away to make it in by night and too close to paddle very much farther in daylight without the danger of being detected in the morning," Copeland feared. While the sun set on their second day at sea, they elected to stay put and take their chances with the currents.

*   *   *

AFTER ANOTHER DAY OF riding the gentle swells, exhaustion set in, and men whose lives depended on their alertness began nodding off to sleep. At first, the problem corrected itself; when their faces hit the water, it served as a sort of self-activating wake-up call. But as their fatigue deepened, compounding the stress they had suffered in two and a half hours of battle, the comfort of the tropical waters was like morphine, a quiet way to a gentle death. The men paired off, taking turns holding each other's faces out of the water so the other could sleep.

The water's evident warmth masked its life-threatening nature. Though its temperature was worthy of the tropics, in the mid-eighty-degree Fahrenheit range, it was well below mean body temperature and thus was cold enough to sap the body of a significant amount of heat. The speed at which a body loses heat depends on the density of the medium surrounding it. Since water is denser than air, it has a correspondingly greater capacity to draw heat from a body. And so over time, the ten- to fifteen-degree differential between body temperature and the temperature of the sea sapped the survivors' energy, exposing them to hypothermia. In the quiet of the tropical night, teeth could be heard chattering. The men huddled close to gather one another's warmth.

At about ten-thirty on the second night, the *Roberts* survivors in Copeland's group spied a flashing white light on the water. Aware that other ships of Taffy 3 had gone down too, they were anxious to unite with their survivors and combine resources. But what if they were Japanese? Copeland had no weapon. There had been a .45-caliber pistol on the raft, but it had been tossed overboard owing to its weight. Their only other tools were a pair of sheath knives and two flashlights. Copeland flipped on the light in the direction of the mysterious flare and flashed Morse code for AA—Navy code for "Who are you?" He then flashed the *Samuel B. Roberts*'s call sign, VICTORY DOG 1–4–1–3, hoping his correspondent would realize who they were and why they were there. In reply, the light blinked some Morse-like signals that neither Copeland nor anyone else could make sense of. Then the lights stopped altogether. Had he been communicating with the Japanese?

Someone reported seeing a green flare like the ones the Very pistols fired. Others reported lights that none of the others could see. With the weaker among them beginning to hallucinate from fatigue and ingesting salt water, possibly the vast majority of the lights they reported were phantasms. Copeland saw more lights: a red one, a green one, several more white ones. It was hard to tell what was real, and harder to determine how far away they were. Copeland and his officers later surmised that an ocean current had carried them into a harbor, and the lights they had seen were on channel buoys and docks. It seems, however, that what they really saw were flares fired by another group of Taffy 3 survivors.

When they heard the growl of diesel engines approaching and spied the dark silhouette of a small patrol craft, perhaps half the size of the *Roberts,* Copeland began to suspect they were closer to land than he had thought before. Though they did not know it, they were probably a mere five hundred to a thousand yards from the beach. Some of Copeland's men wanted to make a ruckus and hail the ship, but the skipper dissuaded them. The ship, blacked out, passed within a hundred feet of the men.

About an hour before midnight, Copeland's exhaustion overcame him. His thoughts became vague and befuddled. He lost physical control over his hands and his head. He couldn't hold his head up out of the water, and he couldn't hold on to the tailing rope dangling from the life raft.

Copeland retained enough mental acuity to appreciate his uselessness to his men. He argued with Bob Roberts that they should just let him slip away into the deep. But the tough exec won that argument. He lifted his captain from the water, placed him on the side of the raft, and held him around the waist from midnight till dawn. Copeland quietly withdrew into himself, surrendering command of the group to his subordinate.

With the exhaustion traveled its darker twin, delirium. It was the product of fatigue and of the creeping effects of ingested salt water, a poison that tended to have a phantasmagoric effect on the brain. Though it did not seize hold of Copeland, it afflicted most of the men at one time or another during the second night.

For two days the men had had nothing to drink save the brackish water in the five-gallon water breakers that the raft carried for just this purpose. But soon enough a far preferable alternative presented itself. Tom Stevenson was delighted now to discover a freshwater source that no one had seen before—why hadn't anyone noticed it? The lieutenant became convinced that if only he could make it down to the first deck of the ship, a scuttlebutt full of cool freshwater was right there for his pleasure. Right below him: a fountain . . . Right below him: a cool, clear arch of water. Its bubbling gurgle echoed in his mind. If only he could get below, his thirst would be slaked. The ship was right down there, for chrissake, hovering there below him. *There's water down there, fellas. I'll be back in a minute.*

Fortunately for Stevenson, he had the good manners to speak his plan aloud. Hearing the young officer's suicidal brainstorm, Bob Roberts and Lloyd Gurnett grabbed hold of him and tied him fast to the floater net. As the night wore on, it was clear that the mentally sound were outnumbered and outlasted by the delirious. All of a sudden the night was filled with the siren songs of fresh drinking water, hot coffee, native girls, and warm home cooking. Bob Roberts himself was not immune. An officer swam up to the exec, saluted, and requested "permission to go below." Roberts granted it and the officer swam off. As the currents propelled the survivors westward through the night, Roberts discerned a point of land that was dotted with fine homes. A gala dinner party was in progress, tuxedoed men and gloriously begowned women enjoying a high time by the sea. The delirium was not limited to the men on Copeland's raft. Dick Rohde left Moore's group and swam around looking for a hole in the sea through which he might crawl to gain access to the freshwater scuttlebutt. Charles Cronin, a yeoman second class, retrieved him, but at the first opportunity Rohde was swimming away, looking for a hole containing lemonade. After Cronin had saved him again, the radioman realized that the Philippines weren't *all* that far from India. His older brother was over there, flying supplies over the famous "hump." Surely his brother could help him.

Through the night most of the men had dalliances with madness. On Copeland's raft, Lloyd Gurnett removed his life jacket and said he was going down to the wardroom for a cup of coffee. Though alert shipmates snapped him momentarily to his senses, he did it again every fifteen minutes, until finally they restrained him for good with a well-knotted length of manila line. At one point the strong and able Frank Cantrell declared in full basso profundo, "Object ho!" Bob Copeland lifted his head with his hands. "What is it, Cantrell?" the captain asked.

"I see a big white cottage on the beach with green shutters," his chief quartermaster said. He took no small amount of umbrage to the derisive laughter that greeted his announcement.

But there were just as many men whose derangement arrived without announcement. When they decided to leave the raft in the dark of night without any word to friends, no one knew to intervene, and they were never seen again.

Tom Stevenson, having imagined himself swimming into a Japanese-held harbor to steal a small boat, found his way back to clarity and saw that discipline was eroding. It was evident in the glazed cast of his shipmates' eyes. They reflected no visible recognition of the common predicament. The men seemed to shrink as they grew concerned with their own survival. Twelve hours before everyone had lined up in an orderly fashion and come before Captain Copeland to receive survivors' communion: a few malted milk tablets, some Spam, and a swig of brackish water. Now the men were doing whatever the hell they wanted. They argued with phantoms, ranted at the night sky. When no one was looking, some of them slipped away in search of that scuttlebutt and its bubbling arch of freshwater.

Fireman first class Eugene Wagner moaned miserably into the night, suffering mightily, possibly from ingesting seawater. As his pain and delirium escalated, Wagner went out of his head, cussing out Copeland—"Fucking captain's no good. Fucking captain's no good." Lying in the floater net, he abruptly declared that he wanted to go home and, cursing his skipper all the way, attempted to climb into the water. Copeland ordered someone to hold his arms behind his back and someone else to knock some sense into the delirious sailor. The order was executed, and Bill Katsur, next to Wagner, heard the crunch of fist on jaw. The fireman was groggy but found it within himself to continue the blue streak of obscenity. "Hit him again," Copeland ordered. Another blow fell. Wagner went silent. When morning came, he was gone from the raft.

Fifty-two

As the second day became the second night, the sea took its toll on the *Johnston*'s men, from within and without. Even those who had gone unwounded from shrapnel or sharks suffered: severe sunburn to the face, head, and shoulders, lips swollen from brine and sun, eyes bloodshot from exhaustion and exposure, skin softened by seawater and rubbed raw by wet clothing.

Ken Bowers, the pharmacist's mate, swam around doing what he could for the wounded. But a growing number of survivors were beyond the reach of his modest ministrations. What the sun had done to their skin, the salt water in their stomachs was doing to their minds. Even men who had come through the battle without a scratch surrendered to madness. Some of them gave up their struggles altogether, let go of the nets, and disappeared. Others lived rich fantasies, mingling with their shipmates as if they were back in San Francisco, guests at a cocktail party. Luther Libby, the chief machinist's mate, left his group several times, saying he was going to get a drink. Charles Landreth, Dusty Rhodes, and others looked after him, several times stopping him from swimming to oblivion.

Late during the second night Libby turned to Landreth and said, apropos of nothing, "I'll buy you a beer." Landreth said, "Chief, don't talk like that. There isn't any beer or anything else to drink except seawater, and that will kill you." Libby's eyes were glassy as he pushed off from the net. Landreth grabbed for him as he and others had done several times. But now his will to wander exceeded their ability to keep him safe. Landreth did not have the strength to hold on. Libby slipped away and was never seen again.

Machinist's mate Don Starks, who had had two ships shot out from under him, including the battleship *Arizona,* before he came aboard the *Johnston,* saw visions of land and houses and people waving at him from a distance. He waved back and on one occasion swam in their direction for a time before he realized they existed only in his head. Natives paddling out to rescue them, riding canoes laden with fruits, vegetables, freshwater, and Filipino princesses. A whaleboat, towing them to shore—*let's just get this engine started.* No, it's not a whaleboat—it's a destroyer. There: Cap'n Evans is up on that mountain over there. *I'm going to go meet him.* No, the captain just sailed by us on a ship. Said he's going to come back to pick us all up.

Most of these delirious declarations found at least a few credulous takers. "We believed it," wrote John Mostowy. "Who cared anymore?"

*   *   *

BY NIGHT GEORGE BRAY and his *Roberts* shipmates paddled, guided by the brilliant field of stars, chasing them west in their flight over the horizon. Around midnight, on the darkened horizon, they finally saw the lights. From the way they moved, the men determined the lights to be on land, not sea. They seemed to be moving to and fro, like lazy fireflies. Suspecting they might be Japanese troops, the men ceased paddling. They floated motionless and considered their options. They decided that they preferred the certainty of the dangers they knew to the unknown terrors ashore. They could make their move toward land—if such a move had to be made—by daylight, when they could better sort through the risks and the opportunities.

But after a night of fractured sleep and fragmentary dreams, the men of George Bray's group awoke to a discouraging sight. The shore was gone. The currents had toyed with the sleeping men. At first, aided by the east-by-northeasterly wind, they had flowed west, supporting the men's exhausted efforts to paddle for the beach. But then, as they slept, the currents seemed to shift, and the men drifted back out to sea so far that Bray didn't know if they would ever reach land. All they could make out were Samar's sharp mountain peaks poking up from below the horizon. Seeing no sign of rescue—no ships, no planes—the men on the raft resumed paddling.

Their kapok life vests, good only for about twenty hours, were no longer much use. Soaked through with seawater, the flotation devices had less buoyancy than the humans they were meant to save. The men took them off and got rid of them. The floater net too had its best days behind it. Its hard rubber disks had sponged up too much water to float. As a result, the net hovered beneath the ocean's surface, weighted down by its survivors. They decided to keep it, however. At least it held the group together.

The weariest and weakest of them had resigned themselves to death now. Where delirium took hold, tired minds spun fantasies of rest, recreation, and rescue. Five of the healthiest among them, George Bray, Mel Dent, Chalmer Goheen, and two others, decided to take their chances swimming to shore. There was no great send-off; the others had retreated into their private miseries. So the five men just started swimming.

They had gone west perhaps a mile or so, the rising sun behind them lighting their way, when they spotted a dark shape on the horizon. There was no gauging distance from sea level, but Bray thought the spot was getting bigger. If it was a ship, it seemed to be approaching them. And sure enough, it was a ship. It came closer and closer until the flag fluttering from its mainmast came into partial focus. It was red and white, streaked with bright red lines. The rising sun of Imperial Japan was headed their way.

*   *   *

WITH RESCUE SHIPS SEEMINGLY absent, the survivors contemplated their best alternative to rescue by American forces. Like the Japanese survivors drifting in Surigao Strait three nights before, Bob Copeland and his men would rather die than be picked up by their enemy. In view of what they had been through, a few of them—Bob Roberts, Howard Cayo, Rudy Skau, and John Kudelchuk—were in excellent shape. But for the most part, the survivors' physical and mental condition was low enough to make the prospect of capture and internment in a poorly supplied Japanese prison camp seem less desirable than a clean, quick death.

That night they had stayed quiet while a ship passed them in the dark. Now another vessel approached. Rudy Skau, the chief torpedoman, had the sharpest eyesight in the bunch. "Skau, take a good look at that ship and tell me what she is," Copeland said.

"Captain, I don't know what the hell she is. I think an American flag is flying from her. I can see red and white stripes."

Copeland pointed out that Japanese battle pennants had red and white stripes too. But after another few moments of scrutiny, Skau was convinced. "Captain, I know she's an American ship. I see a little blue corner in the flag."

Copeland asked Bob Roberts to verify the sighting. The executive officer hoisted himself up on the side of the raft and peered through the morning light. "Well, Captain," he said, "I can't be sure, but I think there's a blue corner in that flag."

They watched the ship approach them, about two miles off the coast of Samar. Some of them wanted to shout out and hail the ship. Copeland feared the worst should his trusted torpedoman prove wrong, but he also recognized the urgency to get his badly wounded men to safety. Jackson McCaskill, the deck force reject who had acquitted himself so heroically in the fireroom before the *Roberts* sank, lay helpless inside the raft, with the flesh burned from the bottom of his feet. Tullio Serafini, the old radio department chief, was in severe shock, with bones protruding through the skin of his torn legs and left shoulder.

"Okay, Skau," Copeland said, "are you dead certain?"

"Yes, Captain, I'll stake my life on it."

"All right, up you go." Copeland found the strength to help Skau hop up onto the raft. Steadying himself on the foam doughnut, Skau removed his oil-soaked khaki shirt, tied it to the end of a paddle, and began waving it back and forth.

"He hadn't waved it more than four times when, suddenly, a great blast of antiaircraft fire went up from some twenty- or forty-millimeters, and we could see the ship paying around and heading toward us," Copeland recalled.

When the ship reached the raft—it was an LCI, a landing craft from MacArthur's Navy—a crewman in green coveralls, concerned that these sailors in blackface might be Japanese, shouted down the challenge, "Who won the World Series?" Receiving the correct reply—"St. Louis, God damn it!"—the crew of the landing craft tossed a Jacob's ladder over the side. The stronger survivors climbed its wooden steps on their own power, while a stretcher was thrown over to bring up the wounded.

Tullio Serafini, delirious with pain, was too heavy for the light twenty-one-thread line they used to haul up the first three stretchers. When the ship reached him, Bob Copeland felt a wave of energy surge through his body—enough energy to wax indignant when a boatswain's mate on the landing craft asked him if he needed any help tying a bowline with the three-inch manila line he tossed down to them to secure their wounded chief radioman.

*　　　*　　　*

GEORGE BRAY AND HIS four swimming buddies looked at the ship approaching them and decided that if they were going to die, they might as well go down with the rest of their shipmates. So they turned around and swam at their best speed back toward the raft.

Back at the raft Jack Moore, watching the strange ship approach, turned to his shipmates and said, "Men, it looks as if we're going to be picked up by the Japs. We're covered with fuel oil, and they won't be able to tell we're Americans until they get right upon us. They may fire upon us. If they do, act as if you've been hit quickly." The superstructures looked all wrong for an American ship; they sloped to the rear "like an airflow Chrysler."

By the time George Bray and his entourage finally returned to Moore's group, the small ship nearly upon them, they were resigned to capture, torture, and death. Whipping smartly in the wind, the ship's flag, they could now see, was partially wrapped around its mast, its blue field of white stars invisible. Like the survivors from Copeland's group, they did not trust their eyes. It had looked to them like an Imperial Navy battle pennant. But as the ship eased up, the Old Glory flying from its mast was plain to see. The vessel coming toward them was a patrol craft from the Seventh Fleet.

From the deck of the PC, a strong voice called down the same challenge to establish their nationality that Copeland's group had received, querying them on the recent outcome of the American national pastime's championship series.

Mel Dent, who followed the major leagues with near-religious fervor, replied without hesitation, "The St. Louis Cardinals." Someone else added, "Now get me out of the water, you SOB!"

Satisfied that the oil-fouled survivors were American, the crew of PC-623 dropped a Jacob's ladder over the side and coaxed the survivors toward it. Crewmen descended to them and, arms stretched out below, hauled the survivors from the *Samuel B. Roberts* aboard its solid decks, which were already crowded with men from the *Gambier Bay,* the *Hoel,* and other weary heroes of Taffy 3.

The "hilarious happiness" Jack Moore felt as his rescuers approached did not last long. Someone hollered, "I believe Osborne's dead." Moore went to him, felt for a pulse, and thought he detected a slight murmur. Then he swam for the PC. When he reached hailing distance, he hollered to the crew that his man needed emergency help. They threw Moore a line, and the ensign tied it to the stretcher that bore Osborne aboard. Moore swam to the ship, climbed the Jacob's ladder, then went below for a shave. His skin proved to be far too raw for the task, so he sought out a place to rest. Before he could find a bunk, word reached him that barely five minutes after being hauled aboard the ship that had rescued him, Jerry Osborne had died on its deck from his wounds and exposure.

It was about nine A.M. on Navy Day, October 27.

Fifty-three

The vessels that rescued them were part of a seven-ship task group organized by the commander of the Leyte amphibious landing force, Rear Adm. Daniel E. Barbey. Under Lt. Cdr. James A. Baxter, skipper of PC-623, the group had left Leyte's San Pedro Bay at 4:06 P.M. on the day of the battle. Picking their way through the sea at ten knots, aligned in a sweeping, mile-wide search formation that Baxter led west from a designated starting point, moving with the current, toward the island of Samar, Baxter's ships had only empty oil slicks and a single Japanese survivor to show for their efforts when, at 10:29 P.M., Lt. Allison M. Levy, PC-623's officer of the deck, saw red, white, and green Very flares about twenty miles ahead to port.

Risking shelling from a nearby Japanese-held island, which was said to boast eight-inch shore batteries, Levy ordered Captain Baxter awakened and asked his skipper for permission to break formation and investigate the contact. Twice denied, Levy took matters into his own hands, turning to the helmsman and ordering "All ahead flank" and "Left full rudder." Baxter ran topside, hollered at Levy that he had disobeyed orders, and ordered the helmsman to resume the original course.

"I informed the skipper and the helmsman that I had not been properly relieved of the deck," Levy wrote, "and that I would not accept Captain Baxter's order to relieve me for another fifteen minutes so that his eyes could become adjusted to the total darkness."

As the ship continued toward the flares, Baxter's eyes adjusted, he saw the flares, and the argument became moot. Baxter set aside any issue of insubordination and agreed that the flares were probably American. Spotting a raft, he ordered the rest of his ships to investigate with him. They hit a Samaritan's jackpot. From midnight to 3:35 A.M. on October 27, the crews of the seven rescue ships busied themselves retrieving survivors of the *Gambier Bay* from the sea. Its decks crowded with almost two hundred exhausted and wounded sailors, PC-1119 was ordered back to Leyte while the others continued searching. At 7:45 A.M. another raft was found, and men from the *Roberts* were brought aboard. About forty-five minutes later they were joined in safety by survivors from the *Johnston* and the *Hoel* as well.

No one could have guessed how close to one another the four ships' survivors had drifted. The southwesterly currents and their own feeble movements over the water had swept them into the same quadrant of ocean. When James Baxter's flotilla arrived, pulling them out of the water was quick, concentrated work.

By 10:19 A.M. on the twenty-seventh, when the rescuers set course to return to Leyte, Captain Baxter's task group had saved about 1,150 survivors of the *Gambier Bay,* the *Hoel,* the *Johnston,* and the *Samuel B. Roberts.* Because of the delay in rescue, some 116 men had died at sea. The task group's flagship, PC-623, carried so many Taffy 3 survivors that Baxter had to order five thousand gallons of fuel pumped into the sea to keep his ship from foundering on the way back to Leyte.

*   *   *

CREWMEN FROM THE PATROL craft cut George Bray's blue jeans from his brine-softened legs, removed his denim jacket, and lathered his skin with rags soaked in diesel fuel to dissolve the residue of black oil that clung to him. The PC's narrow deck, covered in a brown-black ooze of blood and fuel oil, was so crowded with survivors that a man could scarcely walk across it. Bray was given a shot of whiskey, then taken to the chow hall for a few bites of oatmeal, which he promptly vomited up.

Needing a place to collapse but having seen the tight real-estate market topside, Bray walked forward from the mess hall and descended a ladder through a hatch to the crew's sleeping quarters. He poked his head into the first compartment he found and saw a sailor reclined on a bunk. The sailor asked Bray, "What are you looking for?"

"Just a place to lay down," he said.

The sailor, registering Bray's weathered condition, got up from his bunk, patted it down, and said, "Here, take mine."

The *Roberts* survivor hit the sack and was asleep for what seemed about seventeen seconds when the clatter of gunfire roused him. Several waves of Japanese planes had swooped over the small ship, strafing, drawing vigorous fire in return. The cacophony was enough to interrupt his sleep, but it did not bring him fully to his senses. He had endured forty-eight hours at sea, surrounded by sharks, barracuda, and creeping madness. No punk Jap pilot was going to come between George Bray of Montgomery, Alabama, and some hard-won rest.

*   *   *

THE OFFICERS AND TWO dozen sailors on the boat that had hauled aboard Copeland's four dozen men were overwhelmed by the work of caring for them. But they didn't mind it a bit. Most of them were already bare-chested, having given their shirts to *Gambier Bay* survivors. Weeks ago, en route to Leyte with Sixth Army troops aboard, their ship had been filled with men. Now its hull brimmed with life again, in a mission of mercy instead of assault.

Like the rest of his officers, Bob Copeland did not wear insignia on his shirt, the better to avoid torture in the event of their capture. Amid the sprawl of gaunt humanity on the ship's decks, it was all the harder to discern Copeland's rank. Covered in oil, mostly naked, he looked like any of the other half-wasted Taffy 3 survivors. The boys on the landing craft gave him a rag and a bucket of diesel oil and encouraged him to wipe himself clean. "I took about three swipes and fainted—fell right off the bench on the deck," Copeland wrote. He felt someone lift him up and plant him in a seated position. It was Earle "Pop" Stewart, a radarman third class, giving his captain a bath. Stewart had his exhausted skipper about half clean when the ship's general alarm began tolling. Japanese planes had found them too. As the LCI's crew scrambled for their machine guns, the *Gambier Bay* and *Roberts* survivors scurried for cover. The Zero fighter planes made several passes, reduced in number each time, Copeland thought, owing to the sharp aim of the crew.

A young sailor dragging a heavy canister of forty-millimeter ammunition found Bob Copeland lying across the portside passageway he needed to cross. The kid kicked the skipper in the butt, saying, "Get the hell out of the way." Copeland rolled into the scuppers and let the gunner proceed. The gunners were Dead-Eye Dicks, downing three Zeros. Miraculously, no one on the LCI was hit by the angry rain of shells spitting the other way.

When the remaining Japanese planes flew off, the survivors were taken below, forty squeezed into a compartment meant for half that number. Men who were healthy enough to hustle got a pipe berth suspended in threes from the ceiling. The rest flopped on the deck. "The place was like the Black Hole of Calcutta," Copeland wrote. "We were all stark naked and utterly exhausted. We resembled reptiles far more than human beings."

The crew stripped the *Gambier Bay* survivors to the minimum in order to accommodate the bedraggled newcomers from the *Samuel B. Roberts*. Lying on the steel deck, Copeland was given some worn khaki trousers and an old dungaree jumper without buttons. One of his men offered him a bunk, and Copeland took it. Two hours later, desperately thirsty, he awoke. Too weak to get up, he rolled over and fell sharply to the deck, landing on knees and elbows. Too exhausted to rise, he crawled over his men, getting cussed as he pressed his elbows into their stomachs and faces. He made it to a ladder, climbed upward in search of a cold drink, and found a grating to the engine room, out of which wafted comforting warm air. Beside the grating was a white porcelain bowl from the crew's mess filled with freshwater. He gulped it down, lay there for a while, then crawled back down the ladder and got back into his bunk. Twice more during the night, after stretches of fitful sleep, Copeland struggled topside, finding each time the same white bowl filled with clean water, which he eagerly guzzled. After his third long drink that night, around four A.M., Copeland was easing himself down the ladder to his sleeping quarters when he heard one of the LCI's crew enter the compartment behind him. "My God," he said, "that dog has drank a lot of water tonight."

Fifty-four

Captain Baxter's ships didn't rescue everybody.

On his second day in the water Neil Dethlefs of the *Johnston* was stung by jellyfish severely enough to scramble his mind. The quartermaster hallucinated, fading out of awareness and then back into it again. He was adrift with another sailor, radarman third class Joseph Dotson, who evidently had enough strength to keep Dethlefs from drowning, though Dotson himself did not survive. Swimming and drifting, wearing nothing but his dungarees, Dethlefs was conscious of islands nearby. He did not know how far away they were, but he had the notion to wait till dark and then try swimming for the beach. If he could make it, he might rest on dry land, then swim by morning south along the shore and be rescued in Leyte Gulf, though he could not be sure his wild plan—or the island itself—wasn't just another phantasm brought on by exhaustion, salt water, and the seeping toxins from the jellyfish.

In the afternoon Dethlefs found a standard-issue Navy peacoat drifting on the swells. He collected it and held it until nightfall, then put it on, enjoying its heavy, wet embrace. Passing in and out of consciousness, he awoke once to find that the peacoat had disappeared. And he was standing on the bridge of a vessel; the abandon ship order had been given. His perceptions cleared, and he realized he was pulling off his dungarees as if preparing to jump from the deck into the water. He saw that he was already in the water, though he couldn't remember jumping, and so he pulled them back on. When he realized that his life belt was losing its buoyancy, he removed his dungarees again, tying the legs in order to use them for flotation. But a long rip in the seat kept them from holding air. Dethlefs resumed swimming for the island. He thought he heard the distant sound of a diesel engine, like those used on PT boats.

Next he was aware of a dizzying vertigo. He was standing on his head, spinning in the water. He righted himself, felt something sharp and rough under his feet, then it was gone as another breaker twisted him back around toward the beach. He gasped for air, and water washed into his mouth again as another wave shoved him sideways and upside down. He grabbed for a hold, finding it on the sharp coral. Then blackness descended as he passed out, waking only when he perceived voices shouting at him. He sat waist deep in water, naked, disoriented. "I thought the whole Japanese Navy was coming down on me," Dethlefs recalled.

"I was sitting on a coral reef, and I could see a crowd of Filipinos on the beach yelling at me." One of the group came running across the coral, picked Dethlefs up, and headed back to shore. The American protested, "Put me down. I can walk." So his carrier obliged. Dethlefs slumped to the ground, realizing that his behind had been chopped up like hamburger from sitting on coral. Large saltwater sores covered his groin. He could not walk. So they carried him. The rest of the day was a blur of motion and voices. He was aware that people were taking him somewhere, but there was no telling where.

He perceived that he was inside a cabin in the jungle. Hands rubbed a soft substance on his sores—cocoa butter. He awoke once to drops of water falling on his face. Looking up, he saw the wide brown face of a Filipino woman, crying, the tears falling down onto his face. "Hello, Mama," he said to her. The Filipino woman had once been married to an American military man. "She adopted me on the spot," Dethlefs recalled.

They told him he was on the island of Andeau, about three miles off Samar. He did not know how long he was there. The days bled together. He was lifted and carried to the beach and placed in a dugout canoe. Men covered him with mats to conceal him, they said, from

Japanese patrolling a bridge nearby. That night Dethlefs was taken to a settlement of some kind.

"It was like a scene from *Terry and the Pirates,*" he wrote. Natives in loincloths and head-wraps, torches in hand and submachine guns strapped to their backs, took Dethlefs from the canoe and into a three-room house in the jungle. Five families seemed to be living there. They gave him a chaise longue to sleep in, fitted him with a pair of shorts, and generally treated him like a guest of honor. "The Filipino natives came from miles around to see me. Some would stand outside my window and play guitar and sing for my entertainment. I watched one man sit beside an open fire turning a pig on a spit for most of the day," Dethlefs recalled. But he couldn't eat the delectable native cuisine. Baked raw by sunburn and salt water, the skin around his mouth cracked whenever he opened it to chew, smile, or speak. His hosts fixed him a glass of warm cane-sugared water mixed with lime juice. When a large sunburn blister burst on his back, they bathed him and treated the wound. They summoned a doctor to apply tincture of pomegranate to his cuts.

As Dethlefs regained his strength, a tall figure came to the house. It was an American who went by the name Captain Smith. He was in fact an Army Air Force sergeant who had fled to the hills and joined the Filipino resistance when the Japanese had seized the airfield to which he had been stationed. Evidently he had promoted himself to captain in the reassignment. Smith berated the Filipinos for hauling Dethlefs "through every carabao wallow in the area," then asked the wounded American if he carried a gun. The sailor said no, and so Smith produced a revolver that looked to Dethlefs like a naval rifle— probably a .44 Magnum, he thought—and gave it to him.

Dethlefs's odyssey had brought him to the jungle home of Juan Bocar, a Manila attorney and former Samar national representative who became a leader in the Filipino guerrilla resistance. Bocar's guerrilla headquarters was apparently a nexus for American military personnel separated from their units in the forbidding terrain of Samar. In his care Dethlefs was introduced to a Navy dive-bomber gunner, Joe Tropp, from the Third Fleet carrier USS *Hancock.* His plane had been downed by a Japanese ship, killing his pilot.

Tropp gave Dethlefs his shoes, then the pair, escorted by a Filipino guide, embarked on a long walk through the jungle to the shore and to a sheltered cove where another American, a Texan named Colonel Davis, had a small boat. Davis told Dethlefs he would take him offshore by night, where a submarine or PT boat would come for him. For two nights they waited offshore, but neither a boat nor a sub showed itself. When a Japanese floatplane spotted them, Colonel Davis decided not to wait any longer. They would take their chances navigating the shoreline, paddling south for Leyte Gulf. The route would take them past Japanese shore batteries atop a cliff overlooking the channel they had to cross. Davis was a tough customer, but Dethlefs could sense his concern.

After dark they slipped into the boat and made their way silently past the cliffs. The enemy took no notice. The next morning they were south of Samar, approaching the island of Dinagat. They raised the American flag on their craft and navigated around the island until they spotted an American LCI, then flagged it down, using semaphore to indicate they were survivors in need of help. That night Dethlefs and Joe Tropp were embarked on a troop ship in Leyte harbor. They spent the following day watching air strikes flying out toward an enemy whose time, thanks in part to their efforts, was soon enough to come.

At least four other sailors from Taffy 3, Bill Shaw and Orin Vadnais of the *Johnston* and two survivors from the *Hoel*, made it ashore and into Juan Bocar's sanctuary. In the company of two downed fliers and another man, Shaw and Vadnais too missed two planned rendezvous with friendly ships. Like Dethlefs and Tropp, however, they found their way to safety without taking too many chances with the Japanese. An American LCI happened to be delivering supplies to the guerrillas while they were awaiting rescue. The men hopped aboard and rode to Leyte.

*   *   *

TWENTY-SEVEN HOURS AFTER GATHERING in the Taffy 3 survivors at sea, the guardian angels masquerading as the seven ships of James Baxter's task unit entered San Pedro Bay, delivering the men of the *Roberts,* the *Johnston,* the *Hoel,* and the *Gambier Bay* to the sanctuary of Leyte Gulf. In the predawn darkness of October 28, solemnly and without fanfare, their crews transferred the survivors onto hospital ships and large transports. With them went the remains of the dead and the personal effects salvaged from men buried at sea. As they finished that delicate job, the morning watch was beginning anew for the ships of the Seventh and Third Fleets.

The awful aftermath of the Battle off Samar had ended. The catastrophe had run its course. Focused on tomorrow, relieved of the tasks that constituted their daily routine, the survivors took their first steps on the uncertain journey of the rest of their young lives.

The Navy Cross

Part IV

HIGHEST TRADITIONS

I want you to know I think you wrote the most glorious page in American naval history that day.

—Fleet Adm. William F. Halsey,
comment to Rear Adm. Clifton A. F. Sprague,
at Ulithi, May 1945

Fifty-five

As the survivors of the *Samuel B. Roberts*, the *Johnston*, the *Hoel*, the *Gambier Bay*, and the *St. Lo* were being triaged at Leyte Gulf for transfer to hospital ships and transit to Hollandia in New Guinea, Brisbane, and other points east, the Battle off Samar was receding into history. It was the Battle of Leyte Gulf's penultimate chapter and the last large-scale engagement between opposing navies that the world would ever see. As it was ending around midmorning on October 25, Admiral Halsey's Third Fleet planes were falling on Admiral Ozawa's decoy Northern Force in what would become known as the Battle of Cape Engaño, Leyte's final naval action. With Leyte won, Manila would soon fall. The Navy moved on, preparing to land Marines on Japanese soil for the first time at Iwo Jima. Journalists and historians lingered behind, evaluating the battle whose true dimensions were only beginning to emerge.

The war correspondent Fletcher Pratt wrote of Leyte in 1946, "this was Trafalgar; it was Tsushima and La Hogue and Aegospotami and Salamis and all the other utterly crushing victories, after which an entire war is changed. Seldom enough in history before had an entire navy been brought to a single battle. Never before had an entire navy lost so great a proportion of its strength as the Japs had done."

The three-day series of melees around the Philippines in October

1944 was by multiple measures the most sprawling, spectacular, and horrible naval battle in history. If it was not as decisive, in the word's purest sense, as the victory at Midway, it was the greatest naval battle ever fought for the distances it spanned, for the tonnage of ships sunk, for the duration of the duels between surface ships, and for the terrible losses of human life—some 13,000 sailors, airmen, and officers, including perhaps 10,000 on the Japanese side alone, and about 850 from Taffy 3. "Our defeat at Leyte was tantamount to the loss of the Philippines," said Japan's navy minister, Adm. Mitsumasa Yonai. "When you took the Philippines, that was the end of our resources."

The Battle off Samar was a battle of firsts: the first time a U.S. aircraft carrier was destroyed by surface gunfire; the first time a ship was sunk by a suicide plane; the first time the mightiest battleship afloat fired on enemy warships. And it was a battle of lasts: the last massed ship-versus-ship action in naval history; the last time a battleship fired its main batteries at an enemy; the last time small destroyers charged an opposing battle line.

If Samar had never happened—if Halsey had left behind Task Force 34 to butcher the Center Force as it sailed through San Bernardino Strait—Leyte Gulf would probably have gone down in naval history as a major mop-up operation and a bloody one-way slaughter. As catastrophic as it was, Taffy 3's historic last stand at Samar conferred to the bloody campaign an aspect of transcendence. The victory at Leyte Gulf was the product of Allied planning, savvy, and panache, to be sure. But only Samar showed the world something else: how Americans handle having their backs pushed to the wall. As Herman Wouk wrote in *War and Remembrance,* "The vision of Sprague's three destroyers—the *Johnston,* the *Hoel,* and the *Heermann*—charging out of the smoke and the rain straight toward the main batteries of Kurita's battleships and cruisers, can endure as a picture of the way Americans fight when they don't have superiority. Our schoolchildren should know about that incident, and our enemies should ponder it."

According to Admiral Nimitz, "The history of the United States Navy records no more glorious two hours of resolution, sacrifice, and success." Though in the six months immediately ahead American troops, sailors, and airmen would suffer bloodily in the invasions of Iwo Jima and Okinawa, the Japanese, with their naval and air-power broken, would never again truly challenge the U.S. advance toward Tokyo. Accompanied by another veteran of Samar, the light cruiser *Yahagi,* the *Yamato* would make a final desperate sortie against the Americans during the Okinawa invasion. But just like her sister ship, the *Musashi,* sunk by Halsey's swarming fliers on October 24, the *Yamato* would be destroyed by American carrier planes before she reached her goal.

The judgments of historians and strategists were far removed from the immediate concerns of Taffy 3's survivors as they rode slow boats to rear areas for rest, replenishment, and recovery. Like most veterans, they would continue their lives saying that the truest heroes were the men who did not come back. Of the dead there were far too many. Among Taffy 3's ships the *Hoel* had suffered worst, with 267 dead out of a crew of 325. The *Johnston* lost 184 out of 329, the *Samuel B. Roberts* had 90 dead out of 224, and the *Gambier Bay* lost 131 men out of about 900. The *St. Lo*'s losses of 114 out of a 900-man complement seem disproportionate to the horror the ship experienced, erupting into a towering thunderhead of smoke and flame after the kamikaze hit.

The prompt rescue of the *St. Lo*'s survivors was the fruit of Ziggy Sprague's risky decision to detach the *Heermann* and his three remaining destroyer escorts from screening his carriers, even though his four jeeps had all been damaged by kamikaze attacks and stood to suffer more. None too eager to strip his CVEs of their protection, Sprague didn't mind, in his official action report, taking an indirect shot at Admiral Kinkaid for the predicament: "This desperate expedient which left the Task Unit without any screen for the next eight hours was made necessary by the absence of any rescue effort from other sources."

Sprague's gamble paid off: that afternoon nearly eight hundred men of the *St. Lo* and its air group, VC-65, were saved. The *Dennis,* the *Heermann,* the *John C. Butler,* and the *Raymond* stayed behind retrieving swimmers from the lost carrier well past dark, as Sprague retired to the southeast to rendezvous with Taffy 1 and ultimately set course for rear areas. The *Dennis* alone hauled aboard more than four hundred *St. Lo* survivors, a soaked and wounded mob nearly twice as numerous as the destroyer escort's own crew.

The ordeal of the survivors from Taffy 3's four other sunken ships was the bitterest and saddest of memories, not much less so for Sprague than for the men themselves. The mistakes of the naval high command had started the events of October 25, and the mistakes of the naval high command influenced how they ended. Though it was not his way to air dirty laundry, Sprague privately blamed the delayed rescue effort on the commander of the Seventh Fleet, Admiral Kinkaid. Sprague had a good track record of taking care of his men. Having seen to the prompt rescue of the closest victims at hand when the fighting wound down, he had relied on his fleet commander to pick up his task unit's remaining pieces. The pickup happened, but not before an estimated 116 men died during the three-day, two-night ordeal at sea. In the margins of his copy of C. Vann Woodward's 1947 book *The Battle of Leyte Gulf*, Sprague wrote, "This was a disgrace, and I blame Kinkaid who promised rescue ships upon my demand."

That Kinkaid initially received incorrect rescue coordinates might be due to the inevitability of error amid the confusion of war. That several hours passed between the Seventh Fleet commander's discovery of the inaccurate coordinates and his ordering a new search, which was based on coordinates nearly as far astray as the first ones were, seems attributable to communications breakdowns within the Seventh Fleet. Pilots had been wagging their wings at Taffy 3 survivors throughout the first afternoon. Whether they broke radio silence and called in sighting reports, and what became of the reports if they were made, is unknown.

*   *   *

AT SAN PEDRO BAY in Leyte Gulf, Bob Copeland and the survivors of the *Samuel B. Roberts* were parceled out to different ships depending on their health status. The worst off were taken to the evacuation transport *Tryon*, the moderately wounded were loaded aboard an LST, and the mostly healthy were transferred to a PC. Though the men were well cared for, mistakes happened. Somehow Tullio Serafini got loaded aboard a PC along with his skipper and other lightly injured survivors. Shortly after being taken aboard, a *Roberts* survivor crawled over to Copeland's bunk—even the uninjured were too exhausted to walk—and informed him that Serafini was dying. Lying on a cot near the fantail, the chief radioman, who even his captain said was "the kind of man I would have been proud to call my father," passed away with his tearful shipmates gathered around him.

The survivors of Taffy 3 made their meandering ways to rear areas for rest and recuperation. After attending a somber memorial for the four *Fanshaw Bay* men killed during the battle, Ziggy Sprague took his carriers to Woendi, New Guinea, for refueling, then on to Manus for six days of rest. On November 7 Sprague's carrier group set course for San Diego, arriving on November 27. The *Heermann* and the *Dennis*, flooded forward from shell hits, limped to Kossol Passage for repairs, then to Pearl Harbor.

Bob Copeland and survivors from the *Roberts* and other ships were taken aboard the hospital ship *Comfort*, which took a zigzagging course to the U.S. anchorage at Hollandia, arriving there on November 3. Copeland pulled some strings and arranged for the available *Roberts* survivors to return stateside aboard the SS *Lurline*, a passenger liner commandeered for wartime transport. In the unexpected luxury of passenger-ship staterooms, and with long hours to spend staring at the sea, the survivors had time to reflect on their experiences, to take account of the loved ones they missed, and to ponder the changes they might make to their lives now that God had entered them.

Aboard the *Heermann*, during its long trip from Kossol Passage to Pearl Harbor, Lt. Jules Steinberg engaged in a lively theological discussion with his fellows in the CIC. Someone noted that throughout the two and a half hours of battle, the twelve-man crew assigned to watch the surface radar had kept intensely busy, fixed to their scopes, plots, and voice tubes, relaying critical data to the bridge and the torpedo crew. Meanwhile, the twelve men in the air-search section, with no air attacks threatening, had nothing to do. An argument developed as to who deserved credit for the ship's excellent performance: the surface-search team and others aboard the ship for efficiently doing their jobs, or their air-search counterparts and other idlers for sitting quietly and praying with such spectacular results. "I had to admit that I didn't know the answer," Steinberg wrote. "If I were asked today, though, I'd say that God helps those who help themselves."

Ziggy Sprague had no trouble giving credit where it was due. In his official action report he wrote, "In summation, the failure of the enemy main body and encircling light forces to completely wipe out all vessels of this Task Unit can be attributed to our successful smoke screen, our torpedo counterattack, continuous harassment of enemy by bomb, torpedo, and strafing air attacks, timely maneuvers, and the definite partiality of Almighty God."

Taking the *Heermann* to rear areas for rest and replenishment after the battle, Captain Hathaway, who had been as tough on his crew as any commander ever had been, got on the PA and declared, "You are a wonderful crew, and I am happy to have served with you. By God, you all *did* something. Maybe what you did was right, and maybe it was wrong, but we came through because by God you all *did* something."

Regardless of the improbable sequence of cause and effect that brought the survivors home, their families patiently awaited news of their fate. Harriet Copeland, at home in Tacoma, knew something had gone wrong when her husband's letters abruptly stopped arriving. For three weeks the postman was empty-handed. Despite the work of Navy censors, Bob Copeland had up until then slipped enough subtle hints into his correspondence to tell Harriet roughly where the *Roberts* had been operating. When the fighting in the Philippines began to dominate the headlines, she had a fair idea he was there. "I knew there were some big battles going on, and I knew if he had his way he'd be in the middle of it," she said. Growing more apprehensive by the day—"It's the long silences that you worry about"—she heard a knock at the door one evening, well after the mailman had made his last delivery. He was back again, holding an envelope that had arrived at the station while he was on his afternoon route. He said, "I found this letter for you after I went back to the post office. I think it's from your husband. I knew you'd be anxious to have it."

The letter, probably written aboard the *Comfort,* contained a brief, matter-of-fact recounting of the battle, along with the news that he would be coming home, to San Francisco, to be hospitalized for exposure and wounds. He stayed in the naval hospital there for nearly three weeks, finally getting his release on December 19. Harriet picked him up, and the couple retreated to the St. Francis Hotel, where he had proposed to her.

"It was a sort of homecoming," Harriet said. "We just sat down together, and I said, 'Well now, what happened?' And he just started to tell me.

"He wasn't emotional about it. He was pretty pragmatic. He just told me the story in great detail. And he told me all the things that happened to them when they were hanging on to the nets—not the life raft, but the nets—and somebody would swim out and stretch the nets out and they lost some men to sharks. And Bob didn't swim a stroke. . . . It was a thrilling time and a scary time and everything. I was awfully relieved to have him back after I heard what they went through."

Bob Copeland spent Christmas in Tacoma, where he would ultimately resume his legal career, before reporting to the Naval War College in Newport, Rhode Island. Tacticians were doubtlessly eager to meet the skipper of the redoubtable *Samuel B. Roberts*. Perhaps he found it easier to share his experiences with them than with his own family. Copeland's children, Suzanne and Rob, heard stories from their mother about how the war had affected their dad. Copeland's daughter, Suzanne Hartley, said, "I know things were different when he came home from the war. I think they were for so many people. I know that [Mother] said he was just not the same person. And I don't see how you could be. I think there was a certain amount of reclusiveness. It's probably a very private thing. . . . I don't know if it's the pain of loss, or the anxiety of the stage on which they fought. It would have to change people."

Without doubt it did. Some wounds were physical. As often as not, those were borne in silence. One of the estimated forty shells that struck the USS *Hoel* peppered Myles Barrett's back with pieces of shrapnel the diameter of pencil lead. After the war, whenever one of the small wounds began to fester, his wife Elizabeth would take a pair of tweezers and extract the tiny steel fleck. Barrett never saw a doctor. It was about two years before Elizabeth picked his back clean.

Earl "Blue" Archer, the *Kalinin Bay* VC-3 Avenger pilot who suffered a serious back injury amid the brambles of flak over Kurita's fleet, went home and kept quiet about his infirmity. He soon realized he had a choice to make: he could take an eighty or ninety percent disability benefit from Uncle Sam and begin a life of inactivity, or he could take three or four aspirin twice a day and continue flying planes in the naval reserve. "I said forget it. I can make a living. I don't need your disability." Bragging about being the only pilot to get six hits on a Japanese battleship with a .38-caliber revolver was not enough for Archer. He continued flying in the reserves, got a desk job as a stockbroker, and had to forgo bowling or playing golf. His back bothers him to this day, but not much else seems to, so long as Louisiana State has a winning football team.

When Tommy Lupo, the *Fanshaw Bay* VC-68 Avenger pilot, returned home to New Orleans just before Christmas in 1944, he arrived one day behind a December 22 Western Union telegram from the chief of naval personnel informing his parents that he was missing in action. The flier had been retrieved from Tacloban after the battle and flown safely back to his carrier. But somehow the news did not reach the Bureau of Personnel. His return cured their heartache in an instant. Nothing but the passage of time, however, would heal his own scars. For months after the war, like so many other veterans, he would jump up in bed during the middle of the night, startled awake by subconscious replays of the horrible things he had seen: his roommate on the *Fanshaw Bay* running decapitated across the hangar deck during the air attack off Saipan.

Leonard Moser's postwar life began with an encouraging sign that scarred and broken combatants could be brought back whole. One day during operations off Okinawa, after the *Fanshaw Bay* had been patched up and returned to action, the aviation machinist's mate had watched as a Wildcat fighter plane came in too high on its landing approach, missed the last arrester cable, and began an uncontrolled, bouncing skid down the flight deck that ended when it hit the forward emergency barrier, flipped over, and landed with a crunch of metal and glass atop two other planes.

For the next two weeks, on orders from the engineering officer, Moser's sole duty was to set up shop on the hangar deck and try to recover at least one working aircraft out of the mess. With a hand-picked assistant, he labored around the clock. Starting with a reasonably intact fuselage, they attached the landing gear from another plane, then cannibalized instruments, guns, wing roots, control surfaces, and so on, struggling, weld by weld, to build something flightworthy. As they worked, pilots started gathering around the two airedales. Would they be able to get the work done before the next operation began? And would this Frankenstein really fly? Within ten days Moser and his helper had made a plane rise from the ashes. They declared victory.

But who would flight-test the thing? The plane *looked* flyable. Mechanics had checked her from propeller hub to rudder and found nothing wrong. Still no pilot volunteered to fly the navy blue phoenix, risen from the hangar deck to the catapult and poised to take to the air again. "I guess they didn't trust our work," Moser wrote.

Finally, a pilot stepped forward and said he would give the plane a whirl. Moser told him it was as good as any other bird the *Fanshaw Bay* had. Evidently Moser's word counted. The engine roared to life, and the reconstituted Wildcat, with the large white designation J-5 stenciled on its fuselage, roared into the air.

"He really rung it out," Moser wrote to Harold Kight. "He did dives, stalls, rolls, loops, and everything he could think of. He really put on a show for about a half an hour or so, and came in for a perfect landing." Moser jumped up onto the wing and asked if there had been any squeaks or other irregularities. The pilot told him the only problem with the plane was all the metal screws and shavings that had been left on the floor of the cockpit. When he rolled the plane, he'd gotten a face full. Otherwise it was a warbird worthy of the *Fanshaw Bay*'s battle-tested aerie.

About a year later, promoted to chief and discharged at San Francisco, Moser and his wife were reunited and driving homeward to Nebraska. Eastbound on the freeway, they noticed a freight train cruising on the railroad tracks alongside them. It appeared to have a military cargo. Looking closer, Moser saw that several of the train's flatcars carried aircraft, Wildcats among them. Moser scanned the line of planes bumping along on their own ride home, and damned if he didn't see a fuselage stenciled with J-5 and a familiar squadron insignia. It was the same aircraft he had rebuilt aboard the *Fanshaw Bay* a year or so before. "We drove along beside it for several miles. It sort of gave me a funny but wonderful feeling to tell my wife that there was the plane we rebuilt. She remembers that day. I guess the wonderful feeling was the fact that I wasn't in the Navy anymore."

Not in the Navy anymore. The war was over. The job had been done. And so the reservists went back to their families, searching for new ways to define themselves as citizens of a nation at peace. Leonard Moser's roadside encounter with Wildcat J-5 seemed to open up the hope that if scarred and broken machines could be patched up and brought home, scarred and broken men could be too.

Fifty-six

Rear Adm. Clifton Sprague, the unconquered hero, returned to Philadelphia to rejoin his family after the war. His daughter Patricia was shocked when she saw him get out of the car. He stood there in his khaki-green uniform, looking as if he had come straight from a street fight. In a manner of speaking, of course, he had. "He had two black eyes. He looked as tired as I've ever seen him," she said. "Remarkably enough, he did not talk much about the battle. It was just his duty, he did it, and that was all he expected."

With his retirement in 1951, Ziggy Sprague ended his thirty-seven-year career in naval aviation. With the exception of an article he wrote for the April 1945 issue of *American* magazine and a few scribbled marginal notes in his copy of C. Vann Woodward's book on Leyte Gulf, Clifton Sprague never wrote about the events off Samar; nor did he ever share with his wife, Annabel, or their two girls his memories of the fateful battle. "The Navy years were over for the Sprague daughters as well," Patricia wrote, "and busy with growing families, we did not think to ask him to reminisce." The retired admiral threw himself into home improvement projects, followed the stock market, and watched boxing matches and baseball games on TV. From the time World War II ended until his death from heart failure on April 11, 1955, Clifton A. F. Sprague, pioneer of naval aviation, never flew in an airplane again.

Like their commander, the ships of Taffy 3 did not seem to meet the challenge of ending life as dramatically as they had lived it. Most of the escort carriers were decommissioned, placed in reserve status, and sold as scrap metal after the war. Although their veterans like to joke today that their ships were cut to pieces, sent to the smelter, and reincarnated as Toyotas, that seems unlikely, insofar as Sprague's four surviving carriers were sold, in the late forties and fifties, to U.S.-based machinery and steel concerns. Of all the Taffy 3 ships, only the *Heermann* met the ironic end of steaming under a foreign flag. After serving with distinction through the end of the Pacific war, Amos Hathaway's patched-up tin can was decommissioned in 1946, mothballed in the reserves, and sold to the Argentine navy in 1961, where it served as the *Brown.*

That a gaudily decorated ship such as the *Heermann* could be traded away to a foreign fleet may suggest the degree of institutional amnesia or ennui that gripped the Navy as memories of the war dulled and gathered dust. For years afterward the veterans of Taffy 3 were content to leave those memories buried. Many survivors seethed in quiet rage at the way they or others were treated during their time stranded on the rafts. Some blamed Admiral Sprague for failing to rescue them. Most were angry at Admiral Halsey for leaving them vulnerable in the first place. They generally kept such emotions pent up, seldom if ever speaking of them with their spouses or children.

They corresponded with shipmates they had grown closest to. Johnny LeClercq's mother was the recipient, at her home on Live Oak Street in Dallas, of a series of moving letters from *Samuel B. Roberts* survivors. Dudley Moylan, Tom Stevenson, and others wrote to her, at first to give personal testimony to the circumstances of Johnny's death, and later to assure her that his memory was still with them. "No one suffered pain, nor were there any mangled bodies; they were all killed by the terrible blast," Stevenson wrote her on December 1, 1944. "John died a hero's death. . . . Yes, you can rightly be proud of your son. I know that I am proud to have had him as a friend."

The details must have been hard to take. But with John's official status as missing in action, most likely Mrs. LeClercq was glad to have the uncertainty of his fate dispelled. It must have brought a degree of closure to be informed by shipmate J. M. Reid, "I hold no hope that he is alive, none at all."

On the tenth anniversary of the battle, on October 25, 1954, long after the shock of the Western Union telegram had subsided, Dudley Moylan wrote Mrs. LeClercq to say:

> *It is very easy for me to think of the* Roberts *and her men as still sailing somewhere, only I am rudely not with them. I miss them both, the living and the dead, and sometimes I can't remember in which group a friend belongs. They stay alive and they stay young while I grow old. Young and carefree, young all over, young and smiling like Johnny. It is a good way to remember them.*

* * *

MOSTLY THEY GOT ON with their lives. The fleet commanders had been quick to send words of congratulations and praise, and official citations and awards came their way too. Chester Nimitz greeted the four surviving Taffy 3 carriers on their return to Pearl Harbor with a message that read in part, "Your successful fight against great odds will live as one of the most stirring tales of naval history. . . . As long as our country has men with your heart, courage, skill, and strength, she need not fear for her future." Ziggy Sprague lobbied successfully to get all thirteen ships of Task Unit 77.4.3 awarded a Presidential Unit Citation. Ernest Evans was Taffy 3's sole recipient of the Congressional Medal of Honor. Sprague received the Navy Cross, as did Bob Copeland, Leon Kintberger, Amos Hathaway, and several pilots, including Bill Brooks, Tom Van Brunt, Tex Waldrop, Richard Fowler, and Edward Huxtable. Sprague's Navy Cross citation read like the rest of them, in part:

> *For distinguishing himself by extraordinary heroism in action against an enemy of the United States. . . . Admiral Sprague's personal courage and determination in the face of overwhelming enemy surface gunfire and air attack were in keeping with the highest traditions of the Navy of the United States.*

But strangely, for all the honors handed out, the Battle off Samar was for a time the victory whose name the Navy dared not speak. To celebrate it too vigorously, Admiral Nimitz felt, would unavoidably be to criticize the Navy's most spectacular old lion. After the war Nimitz tried to quash official criticism of Admiral Halsey, fearing the public relations damage it might do to the Navy. The wartime public was in the thrall of Bull Halsey's spark-plug persona and quotable wit. With budget battles to be fought in the postwar period, it risked too much to allow his reputation to suffer. Though Nimitz believed Halsey had blundered at Leyte—"It never occurred to me that Halsey, knowing the composition of the ships in the Sibuyan Sea, would leave San Bernardino Strait unguarded," he wrote in a personal letter to Adm. Ernest J. King, who was himself outraged by Halsey's decision—he suppressed open criticism of Halsey.

When one of Nimitz's staffers included a pointed rebuke of Halsey in a draft of the Commander in Chief, Pacific Fleet's official report on Leyte, Nimitz ordered a rewrite, scrawling on the report, "What are you trying to do . . . start another Sampson-Schley controversy? Tone this down." Evoking the memory of the morale-shattering feud between two admirals during the Spanish-American War, Nimitz held true to an early career vow he'd made, never to let public controversy cloud the Navy's achievements again.

Halsey himself seemed less sheepish, maneuvering to receive credit for as much of the Leyte victory as possible while deflecting fallout from the near disaster at Samar. As Taffy 3's survivors were hunkering down for their first night at sea, Halsey radioed Nimitz, *"It can be announced with assurance that the Japanese Navy has been beaten, routed, and broken by the Third and Seventh fleets."* As Halsey must have anticipated, President Roosevelt read the dispatch to the Washington press corps, at six P.M. EST on October 25. A naval historian observed, "Though he participated in only portions of the far-flung battle, Halsey upstaged his fellow commanders and announced the victorious news as though his had been the directing hand." In his 1947 autobiography Halsey sustained his defensive stance, torpedoing his close friendship with Kinkaid with a single sentence: "I wondered how Kinkaid had let 'Ziggy' Sprague get caught like this."

For his part, Ziggy Sprague had faith that Taffy 3's exploits would one day receive their due. "Our Navy, for reasons that are clear to me and possibly to you too, has never played up this action to any extent," he wrote in a personal letter to the superintendent of

Annapolis, Vice Adm. Aubrey Fitch, in 1947, "but I am convinced that history will accord the proper place for it in the decisive actions of the war, probably a half a century or more after I have passed on."

After the Leyte contretemps Halsey dulled his five stars still further when he chose to steam his fleet through major typhoons in December 1944 and July 1945, with significant loss of life. Halsey became a polarizing figure. Most sailors loved him, as did the public. But by the end of the war a powerful undercurrent of disenchantment began to emerge. As a possible indicator of the Navy's ambivalence about Halsey's legacy, no class of ship was named for him. A class of supercarriers was named for Admiral Nimitz. A sleek new breed of destroyer honored Halsey's less-famous contemporary, Adm. Raymond Spruance. Halsey's name would grace only individual ships. The guided missile cruiser USS *Halsey* (CG-23) was commissioned in 1963 and deactivated in 1994. A new *Arleigh Burke*–class destroyer of the same name (DDG-97) will be completed in 2005.

The rank and file of Taffy 3 would content themselves with quieter accolades. When Bud Comet, discharged in Seattle, arrived back at his parents' coal company–owned house in West Virginia, an envelope awaited him. Bearing a return address to the White House, it contained a letter from Harry Truman, a Presidential Unit Citation, a Bronze Star, and a letter of commendation for meritorious conduct. His dad asked Bud what the decorations meant. All the *Samuel B. Roberts* survivor could say in reply was they meant that he had not dishonored his mother. The elder Comet looked at him intently and nodded his head, then asked whether the awards had any monetary value. Bud said no, he didn't think so. His father said that if they didn't have any monetary value, then what Bud had done was for his own satisfaction. "You've done well. But don't dwell on it. You can throw this stuff in the fireplace and burn it. It has no value from this point on. Knowing in your heart that you did well is all the satisfaction that you need."

"His logic was good," Bud said. "But my wife didn't throw nothing in the fireplace. She kept it."

Over the years Bud Comet has kept quiet about a lot of things. There are certain aspects of his ship's final hours and their horrible aftermath that he just does not want to discuss. But for others the ice began to break, and the memories began to thaw, when the survivors' reunions began in the 1970s. Though Ziggy Sprague, Cdr. William

Thomas, and a gathering of men from individual ships had held small "Taffy 3 reunions" for several years beginning in October 1946, the survivors of the *Gambier Bay* were the first to organize, in 1969. Eight years later the group sponsored a "Philippines pilgrimage" that would enable them to keep their vow to honor their dead, to acknowledge and dignify their sacrifice with a proper burial ceremony at the site of the sinking. Led by their onetime executive officer, Rear Adm. Richard Ballinger, and their chaplain, Rev. Verner Carlsen, the *Gambier Bay* group set out on an adventure of remembrance.

They took a Philippines Airlines flight to Honolulu, leapfrogged to Guam, then flew over Saipan and Tinian and through a rainsquall that told them it was October in the southwestern Pacific again. They landed in Manila, greeted by VIPs from the U.S. and Philippine navies; visited the U.S. naval base at Subic Bay; stood by the shrine to Douglas MacArthur at Red Beach on Leyte; and toured the sacred ground where GIs fell at Bataan and Corregidor.

On October 24, 1977, they boarded a Philippine navy ship out of Manila. Screened by leaping porpoises, the RPS *Mt. Samat* navigated San Bernardino Strait and steamed into the waters off Samar where the *Gambier Bay* had gone down. A typhoon loomed somewhere over the horizon, raising whitecaps and long, rolling swells. "They're telling us that they know we're here," a shipmate said. "They're kicking up the sea from below."

As Chaplain Carlsen began reading the eulogy, their voices hushed, and all that could be heard was the slap of swells against the ship's cold hull. The historian of the *Gambier Bay*/VC-10 Association, Tony Potochniak, tossed overboard a cylindrical capsule stenciled with the name of the ship and containing the personal effects of the dead and American and Philippine flags. "We now commit this capsule to the deep, in loving memory of you, our killed in action and deceased shipmates," he said. As the names of the dead were called out, wives of the survivors took turns tossing a red carnation into the sea as the Filipino honor guard fired a single rifle shot.

*   *   *

A TREMENDOUS AMOUNT OF unwritten and untranslated history remains to be unearthed on the Japanese side. One wonders how or whether their veterans commemorate the battle. Certainly not many of them remain. The Japanese losses during the Sho-1 operation can only be guessed at, but they are sure to have been disastrous. Of the ten heavy cruisers that left Brunei, only three, the *Tone,* the *Haguro,* and the *Kumano,* made it back through San Bernardino Strait. Total Japanese losses are estimated to be around eleven thousand men.

Admiral Kurita's reputation lay in tatters following his timid performance on the brink of victory off Samar. Owing in part to the endless inscrutability of his motives—he was exhausted and confused in his thinking; he was unclear that his objective could be achieved; he feared too many U.S. planes were gathering at Tacloban; Kinkaid's pleas had spooked him into believing powerful reinforcements were on the way; he was low on fuel; he was regrouping to attack another American fleet—he has never been given the benefit of the doubt. In the novel *War and Remembrance,* which features an extensive and vivid narration of the Battle off Samar, Herman Wouk put a particularly harsh assessment in the mouth of one of his characters: "Kurita's role at Leyte had elements of the noble and the pathetic, before his collapse into imbecility."

A problem that plagued the Japanese side throughout the battle was fundamental confusion about the nature of the enemy who opposed them. In no small part due to the smoke roiling from the stacks and sterns of the U.S. ships, the Japanese were nearly unanimous in mistaking Ziggy Sprague's task unit for something considerably more powerful than it really was. Kurita would describe Taffy 3 in his own action report as a "gigantic enemy task force including six or seven carriers accompanied by many cruisers and destroyers."

Watching his first salvos roar off just before seven A.M.—the first time the mighty *Yamato* had ever fired on an enemy ship—Battleship Division 1's Admiral Ugaki saw an American vessel smoking and believed the battleship's opening broadside had sunk her. After the air raids started, the Japanese perceived "salvos of medium-caliber guns" hitting near the *Yamato.* That no ship in Sprague's fleet boasted medium-caliber weaponry—as the six- or eight-inch guns of cruisers were generally called—revealed the extent of Kurita's bewilderment. In a landscape of tropical squalls and enemy smoke, he was not at all certain what to make of the fleet that had materialized unexpectedly on the southern horizon.

Clearly by late 1944, however, hard experience had equipped both the Americans and the Japanese to appreciate the new rules of naval combat in the aircraft-carrier age. By the time the jeep carriers of Taffy 2 mustered their air groups and began launching big strikes against the Center Force after eight A.M., and once Tacloban's airstrip had been organized as a makeshift staging ground, Kurita was facing air assaults from more than a dozen escort carriers, or the rough equivalent of four or five fleet carriers. No matter how overmatched the Americans were at Samar, no matter how dashing their screening ships were in intercepting the superior force during the critical first ninety minutes of the unlikely battle, the strength of the U.S. forces that Kurita confronted was more formidable than many analysts have allowed. It does nothing to diminish the valor of the tin can sailors aboard Taffy 3's destroyers and destroyer escorts, or of the gallant aviators and airedales who flew on that day, to say that Kurita's ultimate victory was by no means assured, and that withdrawing in the face of continuous and savage air assault was perhaps the prudent thing to do.

An assessment offered by Ziggy Sprague has the beauty and inescapable merit of simplicity: of Kurita's decision to withdraw, he wrote to Admiral Fitch in 1947, "I . . . stated [to Admiral Nimitz] that the main reason they turned north was that they were receiving too much damage to continue and I am still of that opinion and cold analysis will eventually confirm it."

After postwar interviews with Japanese commanders were completed by the U.S. Strategic Bombing Survey and by the historian Samuel Eliot Morison and his staff, and after the accounts of Admirals Ugaki, Koyanagi, and others were published, Japanese voices were seldom heard in the history books. In 1984 Hank Pyzdrowski, the VC-10 Avenger pilot and executive director of the *Gambier Bay*'s Heritage Foundation, received a letter with a Japanese postmark. "Dear Sirs," it began,

I have the honor to write the Men of the Gambier Bay *as the ex-Commanding Officer of the* Tone, *heavy cruiser of the Imperial Japanese Navy, who fought against bravest shipmates of the* Gambier Bay *in the United States Navy, off Samar island in the morning of October 25, 1944.*

The correspondent, Capt. Haruo Mayuzumi, in neat cursive script blocked off on graph paper, recited his naval curriculum vitae, then, rather than discuss the battle from a personal standpoint, launched into a technical discussion of Japanese naval gunnery. It seemed strange, a chilly disquisition that would warm only a gunner's mate's heart: after explaining, complete with charts, graphs, and diagrams, how the caps of Japanese shells were engineered to break away so as to maximize their killing effect while traveling under water, he wrote, "I am very grateful when I read *The Men of the Gambier Bay* [by Edwin P. Hoyt] and knew some effect of 8" 91-A.P. of my ship."

But Mayuzumi was more than a technician. He showed flashes of mercy and humanity too. He recalled that while firing on the sinking *Gambier Bay*,

> *my fire control officer did never direct his gun fire to the spot in which many men were waiting to come down by Jacob's ladders. My young midshipman . . . was whole-heartedly sending fire to the outside of the engine room. Suddenly many crew and passengers gathered near life boats near engine room. I immediately ordered "Ceasefire." The midshipman soon ordered to aim [at] the forecastle where no person could be seen. . . . I saw you brave men, under gunfire and the flame, calmly waited the turn to go down by Jacob's ladders. . . . I now eagerly pray good luck to all brave men of the* Gambier Bay.

The survivors' groups took it upon themselves to remember their dead and celebrate their victory, in part because no one else would do it for them, least of all, for a time, the U.S. Navy. But ultimately it was the Navy's decision to commission a ship in their own skipper's honor that brought the *Samuel B. Roberts* survivors together and catalyzed their first efforts to hold a reunion. For thirty-eight years they had tried to suppress the painful memories of the war. But in 1982 the christening of an *Oliver Hazard Perry*–class frigate in Bob Copeland's name helped show them the benefits of remembrance.

The son of *Roberts* survivor Jack Yusen, an attorney in Washington state, saw it announced in the bar association newsletter that Bob Copeland, the Tacoma attorney and naval reserve rear admiral who had passed away in August 1973 at the age of sixty-three, would be honored with a namesake warship. The younger Yusen called his father and said, "Dad, wait till you see what I've got to show you!"

Jack Yusen, a charismatic organizer and leader, and others began collecting names and addresses and tracking down *Samuel B. Roberts* survivors, as the men of the *Gambier Bay* and other ships had been doing for years. The USS *Copeland* (FFG-25) was commissioned on August 7, 1982. The *Samuel B. Roberts* Survivors Association's first formal reunion was that same year, thirty-eight years since they had last gathered as a crew. The year before, unknown to them, another *Perry*-class frigate, the USS *Clifton Sprague* (FFG-16), had been commissioned. But that ceremony had been attended only by Sprague's family. Three years later, in 1985, more official recognition followed when a frigate, the USS *Carr* (FFG-52), was named for the *Roberts*'s heroic gunner's mate.

The Taffy 3 reunions take place annually now, many of them in late October to coincide with the battle's anniversary, others in May, over the Memorial Day holiday. The survivors from the destroyers, destroyer escorts, jeep carriers, and composite squadrons are proud of what they did. When *Fanshaw Bay* survivor Harold Kight undertook to gather an oral history of his wartime home, a shipmate wrote to him, "I think the more of us that get together, the more history may come to remembrance. A lot of history ain't set down yet."

They're a generation of optimists. The newsletter of the Roberts Association features a regular section titled, "Our family keeps on growing!" It is filled with news from shipmates and their families, from long-lost survivors found six decades after the battle. Of course, the family's first generation is not growing. It is shrinking, as it must. The Taffy 3 associations will not be around forever. Though they are formidable negotiators, their reunion coordinators exert slowly diminishing bargaining power over hotel and conference center managers every year. The escort carrier associations get a robust turnout owing to the larger complement of their ships. The *Samuel B. Roberts* Survivors Association, on the other hand, now holds its reunions jointly with the *Johnston* survivors and the tiny group from the *Hoel*. Perhaps the children and grandchildren who appear in growing numbers at the annual events will sustain the reunions beyond the passing of the last survivor. One hopes that they will.

To see the three groups of tin can sailors together at their joint reunion is like watching three tightly knit fraternities mingle, each with its own traditions, full of pride, but vaguely uncertain about the other groups. Though they have absolutely everything in common, they don't seem to mix very much. While they show a cautious curiosity and no shortage of collegiality, there is not a lot of mingling and sharing of experiences. Maybe everything that can be said has been said. Maybe they've heard all the stories already. Or maybe the experiences are too painful still. If so, clearly they always will be.

The *Hoel* guys, mindful that their ship was the first to sink and with the heaviest loss of life, seem leery of all the attention the *Johnston* has gotten. Historians have been understandably drawn to Ernest Evans's dashing sortie against the Japanese fleet, to Bob Hagen's vivid and detailed official action report, and to his gripping personal account published in the May 26, 1945, issue of *The Saturday Evening Post*. None of that ever kept the old skipper Amos Hathaway from griping at reunions, often in mixed ships' company, that Ernest Evans had run off ahead of orders and fought his own war.

To men from the other ships, a lot of the talk has sounded like bragging. Of course, there is a fine line between bragging and pride. The *Roberts* guys appear to walk it well. Just as Bob Copeland used to insist, they dress sharply. There's a measure of solemnity and seriousness to them, but they have an unmistakable spark—the irreducible pluck of the destroyer escort sailor. Nevertheless, in the hospitality room, when all three groups are together, there is a palpable feeling that people are afraid to say the wrong thing, to inadvertently put down the contribution of another ship.

The men bonded with each other at an age when bonds harden like epoxy, in their late teenage years and early twenties. Tested by traumatic experience, the bonds became all the more enduring. Through the years the dynamics have stayed largely the same. Joe Downs, in his seventies, still seems to regard Bill Brooks, in his eighties, the way a seventeen-year-old enlisted aircrewman regards a twenty-four-year-old commissioned pilot who holds the younger boy's life in his hands, which is to say, as nearly a superhero. "Oh man, I like that guy," he said. "A hell of a hunk of a man." They see each other as they did six decades ago. Picture a black-and-white photo of young Jack Kennedy, skipper of PT-109, having cheated death and with his whole life in front of him. This is how they see each other, but in living color. Brooks's VC-65 squadronmate Tom Van Brunt joked, "At this time in my life, one of my greatest pleasures is finding my glasses before I forget why I'm looking for them." But they see each other just fine. This time-travel magic does not seem to work outside the immediate naval fraternity. When a survivor meets someone from another ship, it's understandable that the natural bond isn't always there: he sees not an eighteen-year-old but an old man.

At the 2001 joint reunion of the *Samuel B. Roberts, Johnston,* and *Hoel* associations in Albuquerque, the banquet speaker told a story that punched a sizable hole in this barrier of time. Capt. Paul X. Rinn, a fifty-five-year-old New Yorker who prickles with smarts, was the skipper of the third ship to bear the name *Samuel B. Roberts*, a *Perry*-class guided-missile frigate, FFG-58. On April 14, 1988, escorting Kuwaiti oil tankers through the Persian Gulf in the midst of the Iran-Iraq war, the *Roberts* entered a minefield. Captain Rinn backed her down gingerly, but the ship struck a mine nonetheless, reeling from a monstrous blast that lifted the ship so high that when she fell back to sea her bow plunged under water. The explosion fractured the ship's keel, blew eight-thousand-pound gas turbine engines from their mounts, and opened a twenty-eight-foot hole in her side. The volume of inrushing water was so great that in less than a minute, according to Rinn, the *Roberts* "went from being a 4,000-ton ship to a 6,000-ton ship." She was sinking at a rate of a foot every fifteen minutes. Flames were rising 150 feet above her, nicely silhouetting the frigate for the missile-armed Iranian patrol plane and fast attack boat that were closing in.

"We took care of the Iranians, and they went away," Rinn told the Albuquerque reunion gathering, "but there was no doubt it was not going to be a good night. And at one point about an hour and a half into this, after I've thought, *I'm not sure we can save this ship, but we've got to try our damnedest*—do you remember the film *Titanic*, when the lights start to flicker, then go out?—well, we had our *Titanic* moment. The lights flickered—and then they went *on*. And I remember standing on the bridge thinking, *I don't know how that happened, but God is good. Let's see what we can do to save this ship.*"

Captain Rinn then told his elder tin can sailors the reason his ship survived. It had to do with the teamwork and courage of an entire 214-man crew—and in particular the enterprise of two enlisted men, a fireman named Jim Tilley and a third class petty officer named George Carr. Tilley was not the most shipshape sailor. He had been a regular defendant at Captain's Mast, where Rinn, against the repeated advice of his senior chief, always ended up giving the kid another chance. When the *Roberts* hit the mine, Tilley was manning auxiliary machinery room number one, a belowdecks compartment that was supposed to have been evacuated owing to the threat of mines in the area. Something told Tilley that the ship might need emergency power, and so he dogged down the hatch and stayed at his station.

Trapped belowdecks by ladders and bulkheads that had collapsed on top of his station, Tilley brought the auxiliary diesel on line with the generator, a job that usually required three people, tripped in the gear connection using an emergency technique known as a "suicide start" for the possibly destructive consequences of a malfunction, and restarted the flow of electricity that powered the lights and the pumps fighting the flooding. Tilley singlehandedly kept the *Roberts* from succumbing to its "*Titanic* moment."

From that point on, petty officer George Carr—who shares a surname but no family heritage with petty officer Paul Henry Carr, insofar as George is black—kept the pumps running in a critical aft compartment for about thirty-six hours straight. Aware that operating a finicky pump even for just an hour was no minor feat, Rinn was amazed—and puzzled. He couldn't remember Carr ever having gone to P-250 school, where the Navy taught the kind of advanced pump maintenance that Carr would have needed to know to do what he did. When Rinn asked, the thirty-one-year-old petty officer said no, he never went to P-250 school. "Captain, you've gotta understand something about me: I can't swim a lick. I saw those sharks and I saw those snakes in the waters around here, and I decided there was *no way* those pumps were stopping."

Captain Rinn had made a large bronze plaque displaying the image of old DE-413 and the names of all her crew, mounting it on the bulkhead in the amidships passageway leading to the quarterdeck. The plaque was always a focal point during the initiation of new crew members. Now it found another use. "It sent a chill through me on the night of the mining, as we were fighting to save the ship, to see crew members passing the plaque and reaching out and touching it, not just one or two guys but seemingly everyone who passed it. Clearly they were bonding with the heroism of the past."

Here, then, beyond citations and medals and newspaper articles and unexercised bragging rights, is the true legacy of the Battle off Samar. It gave substance to a living tradition. The story, the history, of Navy men in extremis animates the idea that Americans can do anything when it is necessary and when it counts. As Captain Rinn put it:

Legend, tradition, history can drive a commitment to excellence that raises people and has them perform at a level above anything they ever dreamed they could do. And it makes all of us realize the potential that everybody has who serves for you and goes to sea on ships.

The veterans should be celebrated for the distinguished citizens they have become. But they should be remembered too as they remember themselves: as kids, frozen in time.

"I'm still trying to impress my dad," Bud Comet said. "I'm still trying to tell him, 'Hey, I've been a good son. I've honored you and I've honored Mom, and I hope that you're pleased. I hope, if you've been watching over me all these years, that you're pleased with the way I've conducted myself.' "

ACKNOWLEDGMENTS

I am proud to acknowledge the cooperation and friendship that so many veterans of the Battle off Samar offered to me during the several years of research and writing that produced this book. Unfailingly gracious and generous, they made it possible to breathe life into events nearly sixty years old. Without their support, this book couldn't have been written.

I owe a particular debt to Royce Hall, Bill Hewson, Harold Kight, Thomas Lupo, Elden McClintock, and Bill Murry of the USS *Fanshaw Bay*/VC-68 Survivors Association; to Hank Pyzdrowski of the Heritage Foundation of the USS *Gambier Bay*/VC-10 Association; to Edwin Bebb and Harold Whitney of the USS *Heermann* Survivors Association; to Myles Barrett and Paul Miranda of the USS *Hoel* Association; to Bob Chastain, Bob Hagen, and Bill Mercer of the USS *Johnston* Association; to Tom Glenn and Owen Hilton of the USS *Kalinin Bay*/VC-3 Survivors Association; to Dean Baughman of the USS *Kitkun Bay* Survivors Association; to George Bray, Dick Rohde, Tom Stevenson, and Jack Yusen of the USS *Samuel B. Roberts* Survivors Association; and to Bill Brooks, Larry Budnick, Holly Crawforth, Joe Downs, John Ibe, and Les Shodo of the USS *St. Lo*/VC-65 Association.

In addition to the many survivors who allowed me to interview them (they are listed in the Bibliography), many veterans and family members sent me valuable written records, accounts, and other documents as word spread of my project. Thanks to Myles Barrett, Michelle Bedard, Marvin Cave, Jackie Weaver Dennison, Bob DeSpain, Ed DiGardi, John Downs, Bob Heflin, Don Heric, Owen Hilton, John N. Hines, Bob Hollenbaugh, John Kaiser, William Katsur, John Land, Robert LeClercq, Bill Long, Donald E. Mackay, Mike McKenna, Vernon Miller, James Murphy, Sam Palermo, Sr.,

Tony Potochniak, Paul Rinn, Brad Scholz, Art, A.J., and JoAnn Sosa, Ron Vaughn, Ellsworth Welch, David C. Wright, and Zachary Zink.

Because Bantam Books senior editor Tracy Devine was my friend before she became my editor, I know her better than to think that the careful attention she gave to this book was anything other than her professional order of the day. In ways large and small, Tracy's smarts and good sense touched and improved almost every page of the manuscript.

I am grateful to Bantam publisher and president Irwyn Applebaum and deputy publisher Nita Taublib for their belief in and faithful sponsorship of this project; to assistant editor Micahlyn Whitt for professionally and creatively overseeing maps and illustrations; to copy editor Janet Biehl for her many good saves and suggestions; and to designer Glen Edelstein for his fine visual aesthetic. Frank Weimann, my literary agent, creates opportunities for writers every working day. I am glad he helped create this one for me. John F. Wukovits deserves thanks for his generosity with his research materials on Taffy 3. Ron Powers offered valuable comments on portions of early drafts.

For assistance with research, thanks to Ellen Holzman at Traditions Military Video, Jane Yates, Director of the Citadel Archives & Museum, Charles Kahler and Cynthia Nunez at Ft. Rosecrans National Cemetery, Mike and Cyndy Gilley and Ray Gourlay at Do You Graphics, Shelley Shelstad at History on CD-ROM, Janea Milburn at the Naval Historical Center, and Patrick R. Osborne at the National Archives and Records Administration. Special thanks to Elsa Hornfischer for help in transcribing interviews with survivors.

And last and foremost of all, thanks to Sharon Hornfischer, for the vital and many-faceted support that only a spouse can provide.

MEN OF TASK UNIT 77.4.3 KILLED
IN ACTION, OCTOBER 25–28, 1944

KEY

OFFICERS RANKS

ENS—Ensign
LT JG—Lieutenant (junior grade)
LT—Lieutenant
LCDR—Lieutenant Commander
CDR—Commander
CAPT—Captain
RADM—Rear Admiral

ENLISTED RATINGS
Numerals indicate a 1st, 2nd, or 3rd class rating. A "C" denotes a chief, e.g., CMM for Chief Machinist's Mate or ACM for Aviation Chief Metalsmith.

AEM—Aviation Electrician's Mate
AM—Aviation Metalsmith
AMM—Aviation Machinist's Mate
AOM—Aviation Ordnanceman
AR—Airship Rigger
ARM—Aviation Radioman
ART—Aviation Radio Technician
B—Boilermaker
BkR—Baker
BM—Boatswain's Mate
CK—Cook
CM—Carpenter's Mate

COX—Coxswain
EM—Electrician's Mate
F—Fireman
FA—Fireman Apprentice
FC—Fire Controlman
GM—Gunner's Mate
HA—Hospital Apprentice
IC—Interior Communications Electrician
M—Metalsmith
MaM—Mailman
ML—Molder
MM—Machinist's Mate
MoMM—Motor Machinist's Mate
PhM—Pharmacist's Mate
PhoM—Photographer's Mate
PR—Parachute Rigger
QM—Quartermaster
RdM—Radarman
RM—Radioman
RT—Radio Technician
S—Seaman
SC—Ship's Cook
SF—Shipfitter
SK—Storekeeper
SM—Signalman
SoM—Sonarman (or Soundman)
StM—Steward's Mate
TM—Torpedoman's Mate
WO—Warrant Officer
WT—Water Tender
Y (or YN)—Yeoman

USS *HEERMANN* (DD-532)

Name	Rank/Rate	Name	Rank/Rate
Doan, Howard F.	QM3	Rousum, Althon	MM2
Evanowski, Thomas P.	SoM2	Warren, Chester E.	RM2

USS *HOEL* (DD-533)

Name	Rank/Rate	Name	Rank/Rate
Addington, Norman E., Jr.	FC3	Childers, Samuel A.	WT3
Akerman, Phillip A.	S1	Compomizzo, Marvin L.	S1
Allen, Charles T.	Y2	Cook, Norman G.	GM2
Allen, Zollie E.	S2	Cowgill, Donald F.	F2
Amspoker, Walter H.	SM3	Croddy, John J.	FC3
Anderson, Carl V.	S1	Cruickshank, James	SoM2
Austin, Milton H.	FC1	Custer, George H.	SoM2
Baker, Marion W.	LT JG	Dalton, Virgle R.	TM3
Bales, Paul E.	S2	Darcy, Edward J.	TM2
Barclay, Warren J.	CEM	Daugherty, Lester R.	F1
Barnhart, Chester A.	CGM	Daum, Dallas A.	S1
Basey, John S.	F2	Desarro, Frank P.	F1
Bastanchury, Jean A.	GM2	Dilello, Marcellino	FC1
Belvin, James J.	CMM	Doubrava, Herbert J.	QM2
Bence, Raymon J.	MM2	Doyle, Robert J.	S1
Berry, James D.	StM1	Drager, Ervin O.	GM3
Bieniewicz, Frank J.	TM2	Driscoll, George C.	CTM
Bradfield, William B.	S2	Eastland, Van L., Jr.	EM1
Brannan, Thomas A.	MM2	Erickson, Carl E.	S2
Branstetter, William C.	GM3	Everhart, Charles A.	RdM3
Braseth, George L.	LT JG	Faass, Irvin L.	S1
Brett, George H.	BM1	Falkner, Ralph W.	S1
Brillon, Alcide E.	MM3	Felton, Lewis D.	S1
Brousseau, George	S1	Fenerty, Thomas F.	S1
Brousseau, Herbert D.	S2	Fisher, George J.	S1
Brown, Anderson F., Jr.	S2	Forell, Cyrus M.	LT
Brown, Gordon N.	S1	Frey, John H.	WT3
Burke, John P.	FC2	Frey, Melvin G.	S1
Burleson, George E.	S1	Frommeyer, John H.	TM3
Burns, John L.	S1	Fry, Clifford E.	S1
Callanan, Howard J., Jr.	ENS	Fulkerson, Wallace J.	WT1
Callaway, Enoch E.	EM3	Fulton, Charles M.	CCS
Calvert, Luther H.	RM3	Gaffney, Charles J.	COX
Carlock, Ralph J.	SC2	Gaisford, John M.	S2
Chapman, Eugene R.	WT3	Gilles, John L.	S1
Chelakis, Forrest F.	EM3	Goggin, John P.	CBM

Name	Rank/Rate	Name	Rank/Rate
Gorman, James F.	GM2	Killough, Gilbert C.	FC3
Gray, Lawrence G.	QM3	Kimball, Joe W.	MM1
Griggs, Bennie G.	S2	Kingman, Carroll C.	S1
Grohman, Alois E.	BkR2	Klein, Stuart A.	S2
Gross, Willie M.	StM1	Koehler, Robert A.	S2
Grumbine, Roy J.	ENS	Krupp, James H.	GM3
Gurley, Thomas R.	QM3	Kumpunen, Otto E., Jr.	SoM3
Haight, Donald H.	RdM2	Lack, John D.	F1
Hallgren, Lloyd A.	F1	Lake, Ronda, Jr.	B1
Harper, Oswald H., Jr.	S2	Landers, Rexford Q.	S1
Hayse, Harold T.	WT1	Landrum, Donald R.	S1
Hendricks, Marion L.	S1	Landsperger, James C.	S1
Hines, George W.	WT3	Laney, James B.	MM1
Holcomb, George E.	SM2	Lattanzi, Querino L.	S1
Holder, Dowell B.	RdM3	Lavin, Thomas F.	S1
Holmberg, John L.	SoM3	Lawrence, James O.	SK1
Hopkins, Thaine L.	S2	Lewis, John B.	EM3
Horman, Paul J.	B3	Lewis, Lloyd S.	S1
Hornyak, Andrew J.	F2	Lindsey, J. R.	SC1
Hudak, John T., Jr.	TM2	Lohman, Allen F.	M3
Huddleston, Thomas L.	WT3	Lyons, Felix J., Jr.	M3
Hudson, Francis G.	RdM2	Maddox, Cecil	S2
Huelsman, Raymond L.	MM3	Madely, Lawrence A.	EM2
Huffman, Malcolm H.	WO	Mahaney, James F.	BM1
Humphrey, Derryl I.	COX	Malory, John R.	S2
Hutchison, Virgil E.	S1	Martin, Marvin E.	COX
Ingram, William, Jr.	S1	Maslowski, Henry A.	CWT
Jackie, Gus T.	MM1	Mayes, Robert E.	S1
James, Ausbin	S1	McCarty, Ollie J.	S2
Johnson, Charles R.	S1	McClure, Jack W.	S1
Johnson, Ernest L.	S2	McDaniel, Leland S., Jr.	LT
Jones, Herman H.	MM1	McGovern, Donald J.	TM2
Jung, Cletus E.	MM3	McGraw, Jimmy L.	S1
Kadlubiak, Edmund C.	MM2	McIntyre, Raymond K.	RM3
Kanzleiter, Merrill J.	F2	McMillon, Isaac B.	BM2
Kedersha, Albert G.	MM1	Mears, Allen G.	BkR2
Kennedy, Thomas M.	S2	Mendoza, Jess	S1
Kerben, Robert E.	S1	Minard, Jimmie	S1

Name	Rank/Rate	Name	Rank/Rate
Mogensen, Darrell E.	TM2	Ruckle, Ben T.	S1
Moran, Jesse W.	S1	Salzsieder, Chester R.	MM1
Morris, Theophilus D.	S1	Sanders, William R.	LT JG
Mullens, James E.	F1	Santilli, Ray T.	RdM2
Mullens, John D.	S1	Schmierer, Ervin T.	F1
Mullins, Albert, Jr.	S1	Senart, Aloys J.	S1
Munoz, Alfred	S1	Seronick, Morris H.	S1
Mushinski, Frank S.	CMM	Shannon, Leonard C.	MM2
Nason, Earle A., Jr.	LT JG	Shaw, J. T.	MM2
Nolen, Wyley P.	S2	Sheppard, Joe E.	S1
Oberg, Gordon F.	RdM3	Shine, Jesse L.	FC3
Odegaard, Wallace E.	S1	Shope, Rodney D.	WT3
O'Hearn, William F.	GM2	Simpson, Robert W.	RM3
Olson, Robert H.	F1	Smith, Lionell E.	S2
Orr, John W.	FC3	Smith, Walter A.	F2
Ostern, Hans E.	WT2	Snow, Johnnie M.	StM1
Palmer, Clifford E.	FC2	Spannare, Charles D.	SoM3
Palmer, William E.	S2	Spitzberg, Samuel	S1
Panawash, Willard R.	S1	Stallings, Cecil	S1
Patten, Ray	MM2	Stamper, David R.	S2
Peak, Randolph M.	F2	Stanislaus, James	S1
Peroney, Humbert L., Jr.	BM2	Stashinsky, Joseph	S2
Peterson, Dean W.	F1	Steuber, Lawrence H.	S2
Phillips, Floyd T.	FC2	Stewart, Lee C.	S1
Pittman, Ernest E.	S2	Stillwagon, Douglas E.	S2
Plasters, Everett C.	S2	Stimbert, John W.	S2
Plumb, John H.	LCDR	Stone, John W.	S2
Pocias, Edward W., Sr.	S2	Stone, Paul E.	S2
Pollat, Lavern A.	H	Storost, Roy E.	S1
Price, Lloyd R.	S1	Story, Curtis E.	S2
Price, Richard H.	RM2	Stover, Warren H.	S2
Pugh, Coy D.	GM2	Strang, Charles L.	S2
Quinn, John P.	PhM3	Strayer, Howard T.	S2
Quintero, Lee	F1	Streuter, Louis W.	LT
Reiling, Earl L.	RM2	Stubbs, Jack W.	S2
Richardson, John W.	S2	Stubbs, Kenneth G.	S2
Rickards, Clifford M.	F1	Stultz, Richard N.	S2
Roberts, Percy T.	SK3	Sturrock, Spurgeon S.	S2

Name	Rank/Rate	Name	Rank/Rate
Sudlow, Glen G.	S2	Watrobski, Chester J.	WT1
Taylor, William E.	WT2	Weidman, Arthur W.	MM2
Terpstra, Robert D.	S1	Welch, Eugene	GM3
Thompson, Robert L.	StM2	Wells, William A.	EM2
Thorlaksen, Arthur M.	SC2	Wesemann, Kenneth R.	QM2
Thornbery, William R.	FC2	West, Billy E.	F1
Thorp, Jack L.	S2	Westerberg, Gordon G.	MM3
Tolford, Harry C.	LT JG	White, Edward B.	S2
Topham, Stanley R.	RdM2	Wickstrom, Gustof A.	WT3
Ulmanek, Donald S.	QM3	Wilburn, Ralph O.	S1
Wachter, Marvin C.	MM2	Wilson, Marion E.	BM2
Walden, J. Lee	S1	Wright, William V.	S1
Wallace, William R.	PhM1	Zaverack, Nelson	S2
Warren, David L.	S2	Zuccari, Francis J.	S1

USS *JOHNSTON* (DD-557)

Name	Rank/Rate	Name	Rank/Rate
Adams, Warren G.	F1	Brooks, Francis L.	S2
Adcock, Henry K.	TM3	Broom, Ralph W.	S2
Akey, Samuel J.	COX	Brown, Arthur D.	S2
Alamanza, Eulalio J.	S2	Brown, Elbert L.	S2
Andrada, Jack	S2	Browne, Robert T., M.D.	LT JG
Andrill, Edward L.	S2	Bruce, Charles A.	CPhM
Arabie, Jasper	S2	Buchanan, Roy E.	RM3
Austin, Orion W.	S1	Burgess, William E.	MM1
Barber, Ursel	MM2	Burnett, William G.	RM3
Bayich, Joseph J.	S1	Butler, Justin J.	SF1
Bayless, Merrill J.	WT1	Cagle, Terry D.	RdM3
Bechdel, John K.	LT JG	Cannon, Abhrum H.	RdM3
Benjamin, Richard P.	TM3	Cannon, Vance H.	F1
Bergman, Reynold M.	S1	Carden, Clarence	COX
Boehm, Fred W.	COX	Carroll, Alvie R.	S1
Borneman, Howard C.	EM2	Castro, Salvatore	MM1
Bowman, George M.	GM2	Centola, Victor L.	CSK
Boyer, Hubert F.	COX	Charles, Virgil W.	F1
Brodie, George S.	EM2	Clark, Jerry L.	QM3

Name	Rank/Rate	Name	Rank/Rate
Clark, Kenneth P.	F1	Haltom, William E.	GM2
Coleman, Donald A.	GM3	Hanke, Kenneth E.	F1
Conway, Jack T.	QM3	Harrison, Edward N.	EM3
Cooper, James W.	FC3	Haskell, Charles O.	F1
Cote, Real J.	F1	Hattan, Joseph F.	S2
Cowart, Lee	S1	Haubrich, Edward U.	S1
Cramer, Robert C.	QM2	Havanas, George W., Sr.	S2
Cribbs, Ernest B.	GM3	Helfer, Johnnie A.	ML2
Critz, Fielden W.	WT3	Heriford, Glenn E.	S1
Dale, Fritz E.	F2	Herr, Eugene L.	RM2
Delong, Ralph W.	SC1	Hill, John E.	SK1
Deutsch, Walter P.	LT	Hirshell, John E., Jr.	S1
Dittrich, Charles J.	S1	Hodges, Grant M.	WT1
Dixon, Joel H.	SM3	Hofmann, Walter N.	FC1
Dobrowolski, Edward E.	S2	Holt, Clifford D.	RdM3
Dotson, Joseph C.	RdM3	Hongola, Stanley G.	TM3
Duke, Clarence C.	S2	Honnold, Harry E.	F1
Dykes, Dennis W., Jr.	WT3	Horne, Robert P.	CRM
Dzinbak, Richard P.	S1	Huber, Vernon K.	Y3
Eaton, Iris W.	S1	Huebscher, Otto F.	MM3
Edminster, Earl E.	SoM3	Jaeger, Harry A.	F1
Elliott, George L.	S1	Jiminez, Luis	BkR2
Ellis, William N.	WT3	Kawalec, Frank	WT2
Evans, Ernest E.	CDR	Kelley, Robert C.	TM2
Farris, Harold D.	S1	Killgard, Earl E.	S1
Felix, Alfredo R.	CK2	Kilpatrick, Charles H.	ENS
Finley, Billy G.	S1	Klemm, Philip M., Jr.	S1
Fitzwater, Hurley	WT2	Langford, Orbie	WT3
Fleming, George H.	S1	Lasure, Samuel A., Jr.	RT3
Fortney, Samuel O., Jr.	SC3	Legay, Percy H., Jr.	MM1
Fox, Gordon W.	ENS	Lewis, George T., III	EM1
George, Robert C.	RdM3	Libby, Luther R.	CMM
Gillette, Leigh	EM3	Little, Harlan A.	RdM2
Gillis, Frank G.	TM2	Lucero, Lee J.	F1
Gosslin, Duane J.	S1	Lytton, Verle J.	GM2
Gougeon, Roger P.	MM2	Massari, Joseph F.	GM2
Grahek, Edward J.	SK3	Merritt, John A.	ENS
Gray, James N.	StM1	Mirsky, Solomon	RdM3

Name	Rank/Rate	Name	Rank/Rate
Moran, John R.	TM2	Sperring, Charles E.	WT2
Moran, Lewis R.	WT1	Stambough, Archie F.	F2
Neubrand, Stanley L.	RdM3	Stangl, Reinhardt J.	F1
Nodell, Leonard M.	MM3	Steburg, Frank A.	CMM
Olson, Elmer B.	RdM3	Sternberg, Reinhardt H.	MM3
Page, Gilbert	RdM3	Stirling, Elton B.	LT
Parks, Archie P.	RM1	Taromino, Joe A.	S1
Peden, William N.	MM3	Taylor, James B.	FC1
Pendro, Joseph F.	SK3	Tessendorf, Sheldon E.	F2
Perkins, Thomas E.	FC3	Thompson, Carlton T.	FC1
Pettinato, Joe	BkR2	Tolman, Milton A.	F1
Pickett, George R.	F1	Towle, Russell	COX
Pliska, Joseph B.*	LT JG	Trottman, Warren E., Jr.	MM2
Polk, Marley O.	WO	Trudel, Fredrick C.	MM2
Pompei, David A.	SF1	Tuttle, Stephen M.	MM2
Rash, Oscar S.	CWT	Underbakke, Bevis A.	RdM3
Ratliff, William T.	S2	Urbanski, Elmer L.	MM2
Reed, Thomas E.	MM2	Virden, Calvin C.	F2
Reisinger, Joseph W.	MM2	Walker, Jack D.	BM2
Ricks, Melvin C.	MM1	Walker, Leo D.	S1
Riley, William F.	WT3	Watt, Robert N.	F1
Robinson, Virgil D.	RM3	Weaver, Albert A.	S1
Robinson, William A.	StM1	Weddle, Henry F.	MM2
Robles, Joseph R.	MM1	Weeks, Chester S.	WT2
Rock, Joseph M.	SK3	Weigand, Walter R.	SoM1
Sandberg, Stanley B.	LT JG	Weiler, Valentine	FC2
Sauvola, Roy H.	F1	West, Philip L.	F1
Savage, Gilbert	StM1	White, Walter E.	F1
Scafoglio, Vincent S.	WT3	Wiant, Thomas S.	MM2
Sheeley, John M.	F1	Willard, Glenn R.	S1
Short, Keith L.	S1	Williams, William K.	RM3
Simmons, Paul H.	WT2	Wilson, Henry M.	LT JG
Smoyer, Ralph E.	GM2	Worling, Joseph L.	LT
Snyder, Royal	LT JG	Wright, James E.	StM1
Sorensen, James F.	EM3		

* Squadron recognition officer, reported for temporary duty, September 3, 1944.

USS *DENNIS* (DE-405)

Name	Rank/Rate	Name	Rank/Rate
Curtis, William A.	FC3	Grater, George W.	S1
Davis, Charles B.	F1	Sambo, John A.	F1
Emery, Maynard W.	F1		

USS *SAMUEL B. ROBERTS* (DE-413)

Name	Rank/Rate	Name	Rank/Rate
Abair, Russell, Jr.	S1	Gregory, James A.	S1
Abramson, Albert L.	S2	Groller, John J.	GM3
Anderton, Wilber E.	RM3	Grove, Frederick A.	CWT
Bard, Francis P.	WT3	Haag, Justin C.	MM2
Barrett, Harold	S2	Harris, Woodrow W.	S1
Bartlett, Ray E.	F1	Hausman, Donald R.	GM3
Bates, Fred W.	S2	Hawkins, Hubert B.	S2
Bingaman, Richard A.	F1	Hodges, Troy T.	MM3
Brady, Norbert F.	MM3	Hood, Enoch	S1
Braun, Lloyd G.	MM2	Kensler, Jacob D.	F1
Butler, Vernon R.	SK3	Kilbum, Fred	S1
Butterworth, William F., Jr.	F2	Knisley, Charles E.	S1
Caddarette, Joseph W., Jr.	BM2	Kupidlowski, Chester P.	F1
Carr, Paul Henry	GM3	Kyger, Lewis C.	F2
Cummings, Robert P.	MM3	Lecci, Joseph	F1
Davis, John K.	S2	LeClercq, John S.	LT JG
Debellis, John B.	F1	Levitan, Herman J.	F1
Decubellis, Ralph	F1	Locke, John, Jr.	S1
Downes, Elroy	S2	Longo, Louis V.	F1
Fickett, Robert W.	S2	Macon, Shirley R.	CGM
First, Cecil	StM1	Maher, Edward M.	RM3
Freye, Albert H.	MM3	Mazura, Thomas J.	SM3
Gallerini, Leonard N.	MM3	Merritt, George H.	FC3
Goggins, J. C.	BM	Meyer, Herman E.	F1
Goldstein, Leonard S.	S2	Miller, Mike	GM2
Gonyea, Martin C.	PhM3	Moran, John J.	MM1
Gray, John R.	EM2	Mort, William C.	WT3
Green, Joseph F.	SK2	Mudre, Steve	S1

Name	Rank/Rate	Name	Rank/Rate
Natter, Charles W.	SM3	Spears, Melvin L.	F1
Newmiller, John J.	S2	Stansberry, Gilbert J.	S2
O'Connor, Dudley B., Jr.	WT2	Staubach, Charles	CEM
Oliver, Clarence E.	MM3	Stovall, William E.	S2
Orlowski, Joseph	S2	Strehle, Fred A.	SC1
Osborne, Jerry G.	WT1	Sullivan, John J., Jr.	EM3
Paone, John J.	S2	Thurmond, Willard A.	S1
Pierson, Hilan R.	CMM	Trowbridge, Herbert W.	LT
Riebenbauer, Leopold R.	ENS	Ulickas, George P.	MM2
Ross, Charles A.	S2	Wagner, Eugene	F1
Rozzelle, John T.	S1	Wallace, Percy H.	S1
Saylor, Arthur E., Jr.	F1	Weaver, James K.	EM2
Schafer, Darl H.	CM2	Wetherald, Thomas R.	MM1
Scott, Harold K.	S1	Wethington, Cloy W.	MM2
Serafini, Tullio J.	CRM	Wilson, Charles J.	S2
Shaffer, Russell W.	S2	Zaleski, Frank M.	S2
Smith, Charles N.	CMM	Zunac, John R.	F1

USS *ST. LO* (CVE-63)

Name	Rank/Rate	Name	Rank/Rate
Ancona, Anthony	S1	Cameron, Bruce	S2
Armstrong, Marvin M.	F1	Cragin, Marleau J.	PhoM1
Arnoldy, Theodore F.	S2	Daily, Joe F.	WT2
Banks, Herman W.	EM2	Deere, Troy O.	TM2
Barber, Milton M.	F2	Dexter, Warren E.	CEM
Bartlett, Willie E.	LT3	Doerr, Paul J.	S2
Baucom, John B.	S2	Donor, Joseph J.	CTM
Bettinger, William A.	F2	Durrance, William	S2
Blair, Ernie B.	S2	Eppler, Chris G.	S1
Blair, Roland F.	CMM	Estle, Robert C.	GM3
Brower, William A.	S1	Faulkenberry, Mack A.	LT JG
Brown, Warren W.	F1	Fox, Louis W.	LT
Bruce, Robert W.	MM2	Garay, John	AMM3
Bryant, James	CK2	Gargis, Dalton	CMM
Bugajsky, Edward J.	S2	Glazer, Albert	AMM2
Buschur, Paul A.	S2	Glover, James G., Jr.	F2

Name	Rank/Rate	Name	Rank/Rate
Gourley, Lawrence W.	S2	Olah, Alex S.	AOM3
Greaves, William B.	ACM	Palmer, John A.	LT
Groth, Gordon W.	S2	Pasamonte, Norberto	CCK
Hancock, Stanley T.	B3	Pinion, John O., Jr.	EM3
Harmon, Clayton H.	SC3	Radke, Edward E.	AMM3
Harris, Thomas W.	S2	Rathgeb, Robert L.	S2
Hayes, John S.	S1	Rawdon, Glenn D.	F1
Heath, James M.	StM1	Reed, Homer H.	SF2
Hemmerling, Leonard R.	PR1	Refco, Emil	AOM3
Holmes, William A.	MM1	Robinson, Pedro	F1
Horn, Eugene K.	AMM1	Rosenbaum, Merrill K.	CEM
Jett, Melvin S.	SF3	Rozmarynowski, Arthur A.	EM3
Johnston, Lawrence C.	LT JG	Schmidt, Stanley L.	COX
Jones, Thomas L.	F2	Silverstein, Leon	S1
Kelly, Thomas A.	LT	Simms, Warren C.	F2
Krause, Walter P.	S1	Skotzke, Frank R.	S1
Lawler, Orville E.	CGM	Sonnier, Ulysses	AMM2
Leonhardt, Eugene C.	F1	Staples, Clinton V.	MM3
Lewandowski, Edmund P.	S1	Steele, Lynn E.	AMM2
Lind, Farris R.	AMM3	Sullivan, Calvin C.	S1
Lovelady, Obed L.	S1	Thornton, Brown M., Jr.	AMM2
Lyle, Robert P.	AEM2	Tobin, Harry R.	SC3
Mallory, Charles H.	LT JG	Upchurch, Thomas M.	F2
Mann, Maybern C.	WT1	Weiss, Lester H.	MM1
Maye, Fred L.	F2	Welch, Grant D.	S2
McGee, John R.	S1	Wenthe, Claude L.	MM3
McKenna, Francis X.	F1	West, Bryce L.	S2
McMakin, William C.	WT1	Wojciechowski, Joseph W.	S2
McMillon, Ben	S2	Wonacott, Porter L.	F1
Mendenhall, Gordon C.	SF3	Woolman, Alan D.	LT JG
Muehe, William V. W. F.	EM3	York, Max L.	QM3
Nelson, Albert L.	AOM1		

COMPOSITE SQUADRON 65 (VC-65, USS *ST. LO*)

Name	Rank/Rate	Name	Rank/Rate
Armstrong, James W.	ARM2	Peterson, Clarence H.	AMM2
Aycock, Elmer O.	AMM1	Riley, Joseph T.	LT
Bristol, Frank G.	ARM2	Schell, Artemus J.	CAPT, Army
Cole, George H.	ACMM	Shepler, Jack L.	AMM2
Crittenden, Arthur G.	S2	Short, Millage L.	ACOM
Davis, Larry L.	StM1	Taber, Victor C.	AMM3
Heinrich, William, Jr.	AOM3	Taylor, Robert P.	AMM2
Jones, Ralph M.	LCDR	Welch, Roy B.	AMM3
McClary, Charles A.	AMM3	Wrinch, Robert W.	LT JG
Moore, Mason H.	S1		

USS *WHITE PLAINS* (CVE-66)

Name	Rank/Rate	Name	Rank/Rate
Hensley, Gale	AMM3	Lancaster, James M.	AMM3
Johnson, Meredith B.	PhoM1	Wilson, Bill	S2

COMPOSITE SQUADRON 4 (VC-4, USS *WHITE PLAINS*)

Name	Rank/Rate	Name	Rank/Rate
Albright, Roger R.	AMM3	Reams, Clyde F.	ENS
Carson, Harold H.	LT JG	Richardson, Clifford C.	AOM3
Conners, James R., Jr.	ENS	Stewart, Leonard L.	ENS
Dyer, Lance C.	ENS	Wood, Karl M.	ARM3
Evins, Robert C.	LCDR		

USS *KALININ BAY* (CVE-68)

Name	Rank/Rate	Name	Rank/Rate
Choin, Robert E.	RdM2	Moran, Charles R.	RM2
Demetrescu, Aur	S1	Wilson, Charles A.	RT1
Gunter, Berchard K.	RM2		

COMPOSITE SQUADRON 3 (VC-3, USS *KALININ BAY*)

Name	Rank/Rate	Name	Rank/Rate
Brown, Robert T.	LT	Henderson, Raymond W.	AMM3
Burton, Leland S.	ARM3	Hopfner, Paul	ENS
Capano, Patsy	LT	Mooney, Pierce D.	LT
Carlson, Kenneth V.	ARM3	Simpson, William E.	LT
Galloway, Gordon E.	AMM3	Stein, John H.	ARM2
Gordon, Malcolm J.	ARM2	Yarashes, Vincent	ENS

USS *FANSHAW BAY* (CVE-70)

Name	Rank/Rate	Name	Rank/Rate
Doenges, Gerald G.	YN2	Nester, Howard W., Jr.	LCDR
Ledford, Charles A.	S1	Thrasher, Edward G.	AMM2

COMPOSITE SQUADRON 68 (VC-68, USS *FANSHAW BAY*)

Name	Rank/Rate	Name	Rank/Rate
Kostyal, Phillip L.	ENS	Peterson, Leonard D.	LT

USS *KITKUN BAY* (CVE-71)

Name	Rank/Rate	Name	Rank/Rate
Hatfield, Graham C.	AMM2		

COMPOSITE SQUADRON 5 (VC-5, USS *KITKUN BAY*)

Name	Rank/Rate	Name	Rank/Rate
Latimier, William S.	ARM3	Orutt, Frank L.	AOM2
Lucas, James	ENS	Pollard, Allen	ENS

USS *GAMBIER BAY* (CVE-73)

Name	Rank/Rate	Name	Rank/Rate
Allen, Robin E.	PhM2	Foran, Harvey L.	PTR2
Alm, Frederick E.	S2	Forsythe, John A.	F1
Altiman, Charles M.	S2	Franklin, Edmond T.	WT2
Arpin, Louis W.	S1	Geppelt, Robert G.	CRM
Averill, Donald E.	S1	Gibson, Maurice D.	S1
Bailey, Rollie D.	S2	Gilman, Clinton	S1
Barnett, Mearl L.	S2	Gray, Frank W.	S1
Barrett, Marshall C.	S2	Hanna, John M.	S1
Berdahl, Alfred R.	MM2	Harrell, Rossie	StM1
Berning, Leslie E.	S2	Hartsoc, James L.	MM3
Berry, John M.	MM3	Hatheway, Ivan E.	AOM3
Bishop, Floyd E.	S2	Henderson, James D.	SC2
Blake, Glenn E.	MM3	Henry, Wilfred	RM3
Bowers, John W., Jr.	SF3	Herterstein, Arthur E.	S2
Brown, Kenneth V.	S1	Holland, James L.	S1
Brown, McLain R.	FC3	Holt, Leo W.	EM2
Brown, Scott	S2	Hooks, Carson L.	COX
Buderus, William H.	LT	Horn, William D.	F1
Buford, John D., Jr.	CWO	Jackson, John M.	StM1
Buttry, Robert H.	HA1	Jarrell, Harvey, Jr.	S2
Cambra, Edward	S1	Johns, Otto J., Jr.	S2
Case, Leonard P.	RM2	Johnson, William	StM1
Choate, Edward A.	COX	Jordan, Robert L.	MM2
Christensen, Julius K.	S2	Kalbe, Walter H.	CMM
Cole, Norman L.	S2	Kamats, Mike T.	F1
Conklin, John L.	S1	Keenan, John F.	S1
Cowles, Marion D.	MM3	Kimball, Sidney C.	LT
Crawford, George A.	ACMM	Kirk, Bob	S2
Crawford, William E.	S2	Klotkowski, Henry S.	S2
Davis, J. C.	StM1	Knight, Robert W.	SK2
Deery, Robert J.	S2	Kozlowski, George J.	S2
Devine, Harold P.	WT3	Larkin, Joseph B.	AOM2
Edmondson, Joseph C.	LT JG	Laurn, Alvin E.	WT1
Faust, Anthony S.	RM3	Le Maire, John R.	S2
Finch, George G.	CWO	Lewis, Angelo P.	S2
Fish, Joe S.	SK2	Lucchesi, Louis L.	S2

444 \ *Men of Task Unit 77.4.3*

Name	Rank/Rate	Name	Rank/Rate
Marshall, Walter F.	SC3	Shipley, Roger E.	FC1
Martin, Leonard G.	SC1	Short, Edward B.	S1
Mayes, Morrison W.	S1	Shriver, Warren F.	F1
McDonough, Thomas E.	GM3	Sicherman, Burton H.	PhM2
McLaughlin, Henry A.	S2	Skaggs, Ralph L.	SK2
Miller, George	PhoM2	Smehyl, Charles	MoMM1
Mudd, Raymond L.	S1	Smith, Ernest J.	GM2
Muntz, Eugene	WT2	Smith, William F.	F2
Murray, Eugene T.	S1	Smurda, John R.	AMM2
Naslund, Lage T.	F1	Stone, Harold R.	M1
Parmantje, John J.	S1	Stoner, Lyle T.	SK3
Pilgrim, Edward F.	CWT	Straiton, James L.	F1
Pittman, Everett	EM2	Sturdy, Billy G.	S2
Pribisko, Mike J.	F1	Tellier, Leslie W.	MM2
Prokop, Edward J.	AMM3	Thomas, Harrell A.	SC3
Pruitt, Forest W.	BM1	Treece, Otis A.	S2
Rawlings, Cecil A.	S1	Wall, Theodore	S2
Raymond, Ralph N.	BM2	Weiss, Freddie E.	AOM2
Reynolds, Homer R.	S2	White, Edgar	S2
Richardson, Hubert L.	StM1	Whitted, Raymond C.	AOM3
Rizzo, Charles V.	SC3	Wilder, Paul	WT1
Ruffin, Reginald F.	SC3	Williams, Junior R.	S2
Sabovik, John D.	AMM3	Worland, Manuel F.	S1
Schniederjans, Daniel J.	S2		

COMPOSITE SQUADRON 10 (VC-10, USS *GAMBIER BAY*)

Name	Rank/Rate	Name	Rank/Rate
Bell, Vereen M.	LT	Mentlick, William E.	ART1
Dahlen, Walter A.	LT JG	Phipps, John S.	ENS
Gallagher, William	LT JG	Saint, George M.	ARM2
Gardner, Rudolph S.	ARM3	Stewart, Wayne H.	LCDR
Holly, Leonard	AMM3		

Bibliography

Books

Astor, Gerald. *Crisis in the Pacific: The Battles of the Philippine Islands by the Men Who Fought Them.* Donald I. Fine, 1996.

Battle Stations!: Your Navy in Action. Unattributed compilation. William H. Wise & Co., 1946.

Blair, Clay, Jr. *MacArthur.* Pocket Books, 1977.

Cox, Robert Jon. *The Battle off Samar: Taffy III at Leyte Gulf,* 2d ed. Ivy Alba Press, 2001. Available on the author's website, www.bosamar.com.

Cutler, Thomas J. *The Battle of Leyte Gulf: 23–26 October 1944.* HarperCollins, 1994.

Doscher, J. Henry, Jr. *Little Wolf at Leyte: The Story of the Heroic USS Samuel B. Roberts, DE 413, in the Battle of Leyte Gulf during World War II.* Eakin Press, 1996.

Dull, Paul S. *A Battle History of the Imperial Japanese Navy (1941–45).* Naval Institute Press, 1978.

Dunnigan, James F., and Albert A. Nofi. *Victory at Sea: World War II in the Pacific.* William Morrow, 1995.

———. *The Pacific War Encyclopedia.* Facts On File, 1998.

Fahey, James J. *Pacific War Diary, 1942–45.* Houghton Mifflin, 1963.

Falk, Stanley L. *Decision at Leyte.* W. W. Norton, 1966.

Field, James A., Jr. *The Japanese at Leyte Gulf: The Sho Operation.* Princeton University Press, 1947.

Friedman, Norman. *U.S. Destroyers: An Illustrated Design History.* Naval Institute Press, 1982.

Halsey, William F., and J. Bryan III. *Admiral Halsey's Story.* McGraw-Hill, 1947.

Hara, Tameichi. *Japanese Destroyer Captain*. Ballantine, 1961.

Hopper, E. B. Foreword to *Ships of the United States Navy: Christening, Launching and Commissioning*. Navy Department, Naval History Division, 1975.

Howarth, Stephen. *To Shining Sea: A History of the United States Navy, 1775–1991*. Random House, 1991.

Hoyt, Edwin P. *The Battle of Leyte Gulf*. David McKay Co., 1972.

———. *The Men of the* Gambier Bay. Paul S. Eriksson, 1979.

Hurley, Vic. *Jungle Patrol: The Story of the Philippine Constabulary*. E. P. Dutton, 1938. www.bakbakan.com; last viewed by author Nov. 22, 2002.

Ito, Masanori, with Roger Pineau. *The End of the Imperial Japanese Navy*. Translated by Andrew Y. Kuroda and Roger Pineau. W. W. Norton, 1962.

Jernigan, Emory J. *Tin Can Man*. Vandamere Press, 1993.

Kernan, Alvin. *Crossing the Line: A Bluejacket's World War II Odyssey*. Naval Institute Press, 1994.

Lawson, Robert, and Barrett Tillman. *Carrier Air War: U.S. Navy Air Combat, 1939–46*. MBI Publishing Co., 1996.

Layton, Rear Adm. Edwin T., USN (Ret.). *"And I Was There": Pearl Harbor and Midway—Breaking the Secrets*. William Morrow, 1985.

Love, Robert W., Jr. *History of the U.S. Navy*, vol. 2: *1942–1991*. Stackpole, 1992.

Macintyre, Donald. *Leyte Gulf: Armada in the Pacific (Ballantine's Illustrated History of World War II, no. 11)*. Ballantine, 1969.

Mahan, Alfred Thayer. *Mahan on Naval Warfare*. Little, Brown, 1941.

Manchester, William. *American Caesar: Douglas MacArthur, 1880–1964*. Little, Brown, 1978.

Mason, Theodore C. *Battleship Sailor*. Naval Institute Press, 1982.

Miller, Nathan. *War at Sea: A Naval History of World War II*. Scribner, 1995.

Morison, Samuel Eliot. *History of United States Naval Operations in World War II*, vol. 3: *The Rising Sun in the Pacific, 1931–April 1942*. Little, Brown, 1948.

———. *History of United States Naval Operations in World War II*, vol. 8: *New Guinea and the Marianas, March 1944–August 1944*. Little, Brown, 1953.

————. *History of United States Naval Operations in World War II*, vol. 12: *Leyte: June 1944–January 1945*. Little, Brown, 1958.

————. *History of United States Naval Operations in World War II*, vol. 13: *The Liberation of the Philippines: Luzon, Mindanao, the Visayas, 1944–45*. Little, Brown, 1959.

————. *The Two-Ocean War: A Short History of the United States Navy in the Second World War*. Little, Brown, 1963.

Naylor, Roger C. *The Rangefinder: Tarawa to Tokyo, Destroyer Squadron 47*. Privately published, 2002.

Nichols, David, ed. *Ernie's War: The Best of Ernie Pyle's World War II Dispatches*. Random House, 1986.

O'Connor, Raymond, ed. *The Japanese Navy in World War II*. Naval Institute, 1969.

Potter, E. B. *Nimitz*. Naval Institute Press, 1976.

————. *Bull Halsey*. Naval Institute Press, 1985.

Prados, John. *Combined Fleet Decoded: The Secret History of American Intelligence and the Japanese Navy in World War II*. Random House, 1995.

Pratt, Fletcher. *Fleet Against Japan*. Harper & Bros., 1946.

Reneau, Patricia Sprague, and Courtney Sprague Vaughan. *Remembered and Honored, Clifton A. F. "Ziggy" Sprague, Vice Admiral, USN, 1896–1955*. Privately published, 1992.

Roscoe, Theodore. *United States Destroyer Operations in World War II*. United States Naval Institute, 1953. Abridged and released as *Tin Cans: The True Story of the Fighting Destroyers of World War II*. Bantam Books, 1960.

Schofield, William G. *Destroyers—60 Years*. Bonanza Books, 1962.

Spector, Ronald H. *Eagle Against the Sun: The American War with Japan*. Vintage, 1985.

————. *At War at Sea: Sailors and Naval Combat in the 20th Century*. Viking, 2001.

Spurr, Russell. *A Glorious Way to Die: The Kamikaze Mission of the Battleship Yamato, April 1945*. Newmarket Press, 1981.

Stafford, Edward P. *Little Ship, Big War: The Saga of DE 343*. William Morrow, 1984.

Stewart, Adrian. *The Battle of Leyte Gulf*. Charles Scribner's Sons, 1980.

Taylor, Theodore. *The Magnificent Mitscher.* W. W. Norton, 1954.

Toland, John. *The Rising Sun: The Decline and Fall of the Japanese Empire, 1936–45.* 2 vols. Random House, 1970.

Ugaki, Matome. *Fading Victory: The Diary of Admiral Matome Ugaki, 1941–45.* Edited by Donald M. Goldstein and Katherine V. Dillon. Translated by Masataka Chihaya. University of Pittsburgh Press, 1991.

Van der Vat, Dan. *The Pacific Campaign: The U.S.–Japanese Naval War, 1941–45.* Simon & Schuster, 1991.

Woodward, C. Vann. *The Battle for Leyte Gulf.* Macmillan, 1947.

Wooldridge, E. T., ed. *Carrier Warfare in the Pacific: An Oral History Collection.* Smithsonian History of Aviation Series. Smithsonian Institution Press, 1993.

Wouk, Herman. *War and Remembrance.* Little, Brown, 1985.

Wukovits, John F. *Devotion to Duty: A Biography of Clifton A. F. Sprague.* Naval Institute Press, 1995.

Y'Blood, William T. *Red Sun Setting: The Battle of the Philippine Sea.* Naval Institute Press, 1981.

———. *The Little Giants: U.S. Escort Carriers Against Japan.* Naval Institute Press, 1987.

Yoshida, Mitsuru. *Requiem for Battleship* Yamato. University of Washington Press, 1985.

Official Reports and Government Documents

Commander in Chief, United States Fleet. Top Secret—Ultra, Summary of Radio Intelligence, Oct. 21–26, 1944. National Archives and Records Administration, College Park, Md.

Commander in Chief, Pacific Fleet. Top Secret—Ultra Intercepts, Oct. 24, 1944 (242029), Oct. 25, 1944 (250739), Oct. 25, 1944 (252034). National Archives and Records Administration, College Park, Md.

Commander Task Unit 77.4.2 (Commander Carrier Division 24). "Reoccupation of Leyte Island in the Central Philippines, during the period from 18 October 1944 to 29 October 1944, including the air-surface engagement with major units of the Japanese Fleet on 25 October 1944." Serial 00114, Nov. 2, 1944.

———. "Addenda to Action Report." Serial 00121, Nov. 8, 1944.

Commander Task Unit 77.4.3 (Commander Carrier Division 25). "Action Against the Japanese Main Body off Samar Island, 25 October 1944, Special Report of." Serial 00100, Oct. 29, 1944.

———. "Action Report—Leyte Operations—12 October through 27 October 1944." Serial 00110, Nov. 6, 1944.

Commander Task Unit 77.4.32 (Commander Carrier Division 26). "Action off Samar Island, 25 October 1944—Special Report." Serial 00014, Oct. 28, 1944.

———. "Support of Leyte Operations, 12 October–1 November 1944; Comments and Conclusions." Serial 0030A, Nov. 14, 1944.

Composite Squadron Three (VC-3), USS *Kalinin Bay.* Aircraft Action Report No. 113, Oct. 25, 1944.

Composite Squadron Four (VC-4), USS *White Plains.* Aircraft Action Reports Nos. 60, 61, 62, 62-A, 63, covering action on Oct. 25, 1944.

Composite Squadron Five (VC-5), USS *Kitkun Bay.* "Action with Enemy Surface Fleet on 25 October 1944—Observations and Comments of." Serial 008, Oct. 31, 1944; Aircraft Action Reports [Enclosures H and I to USS *Kitkun Bay* Action Report, Oct. 28, 1944].

Composite Squadron Ten (VC-10), USS *Gambier Bay.* Aircraft Action Reports Nos. 2-B, 3-B, 4-B, 5-B, and 6-B, Oct. 25, 1944 (included with CTU 77.4.32 Action Report, Serial 0157, Nov. 18, 1944).

Composite Squadron Twenty (VC-20), USS *Kadashan Bay.* "Squadron Commander's Report." Serial 003, Oct. 31, 1944; Aircraft Action Reports Nos. 69 (Oct. 26, 1944), 70, 71 (Oct. 27), 72 (Oct. 31), 73, 74, 75 (Oct. 26).

Composite Squadron Twenty-One (VC-21), USS *Marcus Island.* Aircraft Action Reports Nos. 64, 65, 66, 67, all covering attacks against the Japanese Center Force on Oct. 25, 1944.

Composite Squadron Sixty-Five (VC-65), USS *St. Lo.* Aircraft Action Reports Nos. 30–44, 31–44 (Nov. 1, 1944), 32–44 (Nov. 6, 1944), 33–44, covering action on Oct. 25, 1944.

Composite Squadron Sixty-Eight (VC-68), USS *Fanshaw Bay.* "Combat Report of Action with Units of Jap Fleet from 0650 to 1015, 25 October 1944, made by Lt. Comdr. R. S. Rogers, USN." Oct. 25, 1944; Aircraft Action Reports Nos. 30–35.

———. "Composite Squadron Sixty-Eight, history and accomplishments of." Serial 012, Nov. 11, 1944.

———. "War Record of Composite Squadron 68." Dec. 26, 1944.

Composite Squadron Seventy-Five (VC-75), USS *Ommaney Bay.* "Squadron Commander's Action Report, 22 October to 30 October inclusive." Nov. 3, 1944; Aircraft Action Reports Nos. 48, 49, 50, 51, Oct. 25, 1944.

Composite Squadron Seventy-Six (VC-76), USS *Petrof Bay.* Aircraft Action Reports Nos. 70, 71, Oct. 25, 1944.

———. "Supplement to ACA Report No. 70" and "Supplement to ACA Report 71," Nov. 28, 1944.

Composite Squadron Eighty (VC-80, USS *Manila Bay*). "War Diary— Period 1 September 1944–31 October 1944." Nov. 1, 1944.

Department of the Army, Office of the Chief of Military History. *The United States Army in World War II (The War in the Pacific), Leyte: The Return to the Philippines.* Edited by M. Hamlin Cannon. 1954.

DesDiv 94 (destroyers of the Taffy 2 screen, Task Unit 77.4.23), "Combined TBS Log, USS *Haggard,* USS *Hailey,* USS *Franks,* 0600 to 1200 Item, 25 October 1944," in Serial 0105, USS *Haggard* Action Report, Enclosure A.

Navy Department. *The Bluejacket's Manual.* U.S. Naval Institute, 1943.

Navy Department. Communiqué No. 554, "Teamwork, Gallantry Aboard Carriers Lauded by Sprague." Nov. 17, 1944. Published in *Honolulu Advertiser,* Nov. 17, 1944.

Navy Department, Bureau of Aeronautics. *Pilot's Handbook of Flight Operating Instructions, Navy Model FM-2, British Model Wildcat VI Airplanes.* AN 01-190FB-1, Jun. 15, 1945.

Navy Department, Bureau of Aeronautics, Training Division. *Gunnery Sense: Some Hints for Air Gunners.* May 1943.

Navy Department, Bureau of Naval Personnel, Standards and Curriculum Division, Navy Training Courses. *Gunner's Mate 2c.* 2 vols. Government Printing Office, 1945.

Navy Department, Bureau of Ships and Bureau of Aeronautics. *Radar System Fundamentals.* Navships 900,017, Apr. 1944.

Navy Department, Office of the Chief of Naval Operations, Naval History Division, *Dictionary of American Fighting Ships,* vol. 3. 1968.

Navy Department, U.S. Pacific Fleet. Press release No. 641, Nov. 19, 1944.

USS *Albert W. Grant* (DD-649). "Action Report—Operations Against Central Philippines, Leyte Area, and Night Surface Action of 24–25 October against Japanese Task Force in Surigao Strait." Serial 0106, Nov. 11, 1944.

USS *Boise* (CL-47). "Action in Surigao Strait on Morning of 25 October 1944, Report of." Serial 069, Oct. 30, 1944.

USS *Daly* (DD-519). "Battle of Surigao Strait, October 25, 1944—Action Report." Serial 078, Oct. 30, 1944.

USS *Dennis* (DE-405). Deck Log. Oct. 20–27, 1944.

USS *Fanshaw Bay* (CVE-70). "Action Report on Leyte—Philippine Islands Operation." Serial 0160, Nov. 2, 1944.

———. "Action Report on Leyte—Philippine Islands Operation, supplemental report on." Serial 0173, undated.

———. Ship's Log, Oct. 25, 1944.

USS *Gambier Bay* (CVE-73). "Report of Action of U.S.S. *Gambier Bay* (CVE-73), culminating in its loss 25 October 1944." Serial 002, Nov. 27, 1944.

———. "Narrative by Captain W. V. R. Vieweg, USN, Commanding Officer," Dec. 18, 1944.

USS *Haggard* (DD-555). "Combined TBS Log, DesDiv 94" (USS *Haggard,* USS *Hailey,* USS *Franks*), 0600–1200." Serial 0105, Oct. 25, 1944.

USS *Hoel* (DD-533). "Combined Action Report and Report of Loss of USS *Hoel* (DD-533) on 25 October 1944." Serial 0050, Nov. 15, 1944.

USS *John C. Butler* (DE-339). "Action of 25 October 1944 off Samar Island—Report of." Serial 003, Nov. 9, 1944.

USS *Johnston* (DD-557). "Action Report, Kwajalein Atoll." Serial 03, Feb. 3, 1944.

———. "Action Report—Island of Guam." Serial 024, Aug. 12, 1944.

———. "Action Report—Surface Engagement off Samar, P.I., 25 October 1944." Serial 04, Nov. 14, 1944.

USS *Kadashan Bay* (CVE-76). "Action Report—Leyte Island, Philippine Islands." Serial 066, Oct. 31, 1944.

USS *Kalinin Bay* (CVE-68). "Action Report of 25 October 1944—Engagement with Enemy Units East of Leyte, P.I." Serial 094, Oct. 30, 1944.

USS *Kitkun Bay* (CVE-71). "Surface Action Report—Submission of." Serial 005, Oct. 28, 1944.

USS LCI(G)-340. Deck Log. Oct. 1944.

USS LCI(G)-341. Deck Log. Oct. 1944.

USS LCI(L)-337. "Report on Rescue Search Mission of 25 October through 27 October." Nov. 2, 1944. www.bosamar.com/lci337.html; last viewed by author Jan. 19, 2001.

USS *Ommaney Bay* (CVE-79). "Action Report—Period 14–31 October 1944—Leyte Island Landing and Sea Action off Samar Island (25 October 1944)." Serial 0018, Nov. 3, 1944.

USS PC-623, Deck Log. Oct. 25–28, 1944.

USS PC-623 (Task Group 78.12). War Diary. Oct. 25–27, 1944.

USS *Petrof Bay* (CVE-80). "Action Report covering the period from 20–30 October 1944 during which the *Petrof Bay*, as part of TU 77.4.1, furnished Direct Air Support for the landings at Leyte Island in the Central Philippines and participated in the Battle with the Jap Surface Forces off Samar on 25 October 1944." Serial 052, Nov. 2, 1944.

USS *Raymond* (DE-341). "Action Report—Leyte Gulf Operation and Samar Battle." Serial 142, Nov. 2, 1944.

USS *St. Lo* (CVE-63, formerly USS *Midway*). "Action Report, Battle of Samar." Nov. 23, 1944.

USS *Samuel B. Roberts* (DE-413). "Combined Action Report, Surface Engagement off Samar, Philippine Islands, and Report of Loss of USS *Samuel B. Roberts*, DE-413, on 25 October 1944." Nov. 20, 1944.

———. Amplifying Report of Lt. William S. Burton, USNR. Prepared at the request of the Office of Naval Records and Library, Film No. 313, recorded Dec. 16, 1944.

USS *West Virginia* (BB-48). "Action in Battle of Surigao Strait, 25 October 1944, Report of." Serial 0538, Nov. 1, 1944.

USS *White Plains* (CVE-66). "USS *White Plains* (CVE-66), Action Report of: Attack on Central Philippine Islands, 17 October–25 October 1944." Serial 0011, Oct. 27, 1944.

United States Strategic Bombing Survey. Interrogation of Vice Adm. Takeo Kurita [commander of Center Force], USSBS No. 47, Tokyo, Oct. 16–17, 1945.

———. Interrogation of Cdr. Kokichi Mori [torpedo officer, Southern Force (Vice Adm. Shima)], USSBS No. 233, Tokyo, Nov. 3, 1945.

———. Interrogation of Cdr. Tonosuke Otani [Center Force staff operations officer], USSBS No. 437, Tokyo, Nov. 24, 1945.

Newspaper, Magazine, and Internet Articles

Arnold, O. Carroll, "Come on Boys, Let's Get 'Em." *Yankee*, Dec. 1984, p. 78.

Ash, Leonard D., and Martin Hill. "In Harm's Way." *Retired Officer*, Oct. 1994: www.bosamar.com/harms.html; last visited by author Jan. 19, 2001.

Associated Press. "Tiny U.S. Carrier Force Routs Jap Squadron." Nov. 30, 1944.

Baker, A. D. "Battlefleets and Diplomacy: Naval Disarmament Between the Two World Wars." *Warship International*, no. 3, 1989: www.warships1.com/W-INRO/INRO_Battlefleet.htm; last visited by author Feb. 12, 2003.

Baldwin, Hanson W. "4 Small U.S. Ships, Lost, Averted a Possible Philippines Disaster." *New York Times*, Nov. 15, 1944, p. 1.

Brown Shipbuilding Company [Houston, Tex.]. "*Samuel B. Roberts*, Built at Brownship, Meets Death of Hero in Philippines." *Brown Victory Dispatch*, Nov. 25, 1944, p. 1.

———. "He Saw *Roberts* Help Save Day Off Samar." *Brown Victory Dispatch*, Dec. 16, 1944, p. 1.

———. "*Samuel B. Roberts* Hit Jap Cruiser in Torpedo Attack." *Brown Victory Dispatch*, Jan. 13, 1945, p. 2.

Cutler, Thomas J. "Greatest of All Sea Battles." *Naval History*, Sept./Oct. 1994, p. 10.

Czarnecki, Joseph. "Were the Best Good Enough?: The Performance of Japanese Surface Forces in Torpedo Attack versus the Expectations of the Decisive Battle Strategy." www.warships1.com/W-Tech/tech-067.htm, Apr. 16, 2000; last visited by author Feb. 12, 2003.

———. "Performance of U.S. Battleships at Surigao Strait." www.warships1.com/W-Tech/tech-079.htm, Jul. 16, 2001; last visited by author July 21, 2001.

Deac, Wilfred P. "The Battle off Samar." *American Heritage*, Dec. 1966, p. 20.

Dickinson, Cdr. C. E., with Boyden Sparkes. "Plug That Last Rat Hole." *Saturday Evening Post*, Jan. 27, 1945, p. 12.

DiGiulian, Tony. "Definitions and Information about Naval Guns." www.warships1.com/Weapons/Gun_Data.htm, Jun. 7, 2001; last visited by author July 21, 2001.

DiGiulian, Tony, and Lloyd D. Morris. "Distance to the Horizon." www.warships1.com/W-Tech/tech-011.htm, Apr. 18, 2001; last visited by author Jul. 21, 2001.

Farris, James W. "Tacloban." *Friends Journal,* vol. 20, no. 1, Spring 1997; reprinted in *USS* St. Lo *(CVE-63)/VC-65 Newsletter,* vol. 35, Feb. 1998, p. 25.

Forrester, C. S. "The Great Naval Battle of the Philippines." *Saturday Evening Post,* Jan. 20, 1945, p. 18.

Hackett, Bob. "Senkan!: IJN *Kongo:* Tabular Record of Movement." www.combinedfleet.com/kongo.htm; last visited by author Feb. 13, 2003.

———. "Senkan!: IJN *Haruna:* Tabular Record of Movement." www.combinedfleet.com/haruna.htm; last visited by author Feb. 13, 2003.

Hagen, Robert C., as told to Sidney Shalett. "We Asked for the Jap Fleet— and Got It!" *Saturday Evening Post,* May 26, 1945, p. 9.

Hall, M. Royce. Letter to the editor, *CVE Piper* (newsletter of the Escort Carrier Sailors & Airmen Association, Inc.), Dec./Jan. 1999, p. 1.

Hathaway, Cdr. Amos T., USN. "The Battle as I Saw It," *American,* Apr. 1945, p. 41.

Hayostek, Cindy. "Valor off Samar" (about Lt. Cdr. Edward Huxtable, VC-10), *World War II,* Sept. 1998. www.thehistorynet.com/WorldWarII/ articles/1998/09982_text.htm; last visited by author May 23, 2001.

———. "Edward J. Huxtable." www.ussgambierbay-vc10.com/ officerbackground/hux.htm; last visited by author Oct. 3, 2001.

Hemingway, Al. "The Real MacArthur" (interview with Roger Olaf Egeberg, M.D., Douglas MacArthur's personal physician). *World War II,* Sept. 2000. www.thehistorynet.com/WorldWarII/articles/2000/ 09002_1text.htm; last visited by author May 23, 2001.

Honolulu Advertiser, "Teamwork, Gallantry Aboard Carriers Lauded by Sprague." Nov. 17, 1944.

Hubbard, Lucien. "Scrub Team at Tacloban." *Reader's Digest,* Feb. 1945, p. 8; originally published in *Liberty* magazine.

Jennings, Ed. "Crosley's Secret War Effort: The Proximity Fuze." www.warships1.com/W-Tech/tech-075.htm, Feb. 1, 2001; last visited by author Feb. 12, 2003.

Jurens, William J. "The Evolution of Battleship Gunnery in the U.S. Navy, 1920–1945," pts. 1–2. *Warship International,* no. 3, 1991. www.warships1.com/W-INRO/INRO_BB-Gunnery_p1.htm; last visited by author Feb. 13, 2003.

Koyanagi, Tomiji. "The Battle of Leyte Gulf," in *The Japanese Navy in World War II*, Raymond O'Connor, ed. U.S. Naval Institute Press, 1969.

Levy, Allison M. "USS PC 623 Crewmen Recall Taffy 3 Rescue." *Patrol Craft Sailors Association Newsletter*, no. 34, Oct./Dec. 1996. www.bosamar.com/pc623.html; last visited by author Jan. 19, 2001.

MacDonald, Scot. "Small Boys off Samar: '. . . Survival Could Not Be Expected.' " *Surface Warfare*, Feb. 1980, p. 13.

———. "In the Footsteps of Brave Men: USS *Samuel B. Roberts* Commissioned." *Surface Warfare*, Mar./Apr. 1986, p. 2.

McAvoy, John. "Hathaway Leaves the Citadel." *Brigadier* (newspaper of The Citadel), Jan. 19, 1979. Courtesy of the Citadel Archives & Museum, Charleston, S.C.

McKenna, Michael F. (son of Capt. Francis McKenna, USS *St. Lo*). "A Brief Summary of the Battle off Samar and Tribute to Clifton A. F. Sprague." Address delivered at memorial ceremony, Ft. Rosecrans National Cemetery, Pt. Loma, San Diego, Calif., Oct. 25, 1994. Courtesy of Courtney Sprague Vaughan.

McMurtry, Charles H. "Battle of Philippines: Trapped U.S. Fleet Stands Off Japs." Associated Press, Nov. 24, 1944.

Mitchell, John. "Remembering the Battle of Leyte Gulf." *Thousand Oaks* (Calif.) *News Chronicle*, Oct. 25, 1987, p. 13.

Mullener, Elizabeth. "Remembrances of World War II: The Battle for Leyte Gulf." *New Orleans Times-Picayune*, Oct. 26, 1994, p. 1.

Okun, Nathan. "Underwater Projectile Hits." Sept. 7, 1999. www.warships1.com/W-Tech/tech-041.htm; last visited by author Feb. 13, 2003.

Ottenheimer, Eldon. "Why Powerful Jap Fleet Failed to Sink Small U.S. Force Remains Mystery," *Dallas Times*, Nov. 1, 1944.

Pasadena Star-News, "Pasadena Flyer Sighted Strong Jap Task Force, Aided in Historic Battle." Jan. 1, 1945.

Reynolds, Quentin, George E. Jones, Frank D. Morris, and Ralph Teatsorth. "America's Greatest Naval Battle." *Collier's*, three-part series, Jan. 13, 1945, p. 11; Jan. 20, 1945, p. 18; Jan. 27, 1945, p. 18.

Roby, Richard. "Stories of Two Taffy III Airmen." *USS St. Lo (CVE-63) VC-65 Newsletter*, vol. 34, Sept. 1997. Originally published in *Old Shipmates*, newsletter of the USS Gambier Bay Survivors Association, May/Aug. 1995.

Slover, Gene. "The Mark 1 Fire Control Computer." www.warships1.com/ W-Tech/tech-056.htm, May 29, 2000; last visited by author Feb. 12, 2003.

———. "Roll, Pitch and Yaw: Fire Control Problems and Mark 1/1A Solutions." www.warships1.com/W-Tech/tech-074.htm, July 6, 2000; last visited by author Feb. 12, 2003.

Sprague, Rear Adm. C.A.F., as told to Lt. Philip H. Gustafson. "The Japs Had Us on the Ropes." *American*, Apr. 1945, p. 40.

Tully, Anthony P. "Shell Game at Surigao: The Entangled Fates of Battleships *Fuso* and *Yamashiro*." www.combinedfleet.com/atully06.htm. Posted Jun. 15, 1999; last visited by author Apr. 24, 2003.

———. "Solving Some Mysteries of Leyte Gulf: Fate of the *Chikuma* and *Chokai*." *Warship International*, no. 3, 2000, p. 248.

USS *St. Lo*/VC-65 Association. "History of Composite Squadron 65 (VC-65)." www.stlomidway6365.org/squadron/history.html; last visited by author May 6, 2001.

Welch, Stuart. "1200 Survivors of U.S. Carrier 'Gambier Bay,' Sunk in Philippines, Arrive in S.F." *San Francisco Chronicle*, Dec. 2, 1944, p. 3. Courtesy of George Bray.

Whitney, Harold E. "The Battle of Samar." *Our Navy*, Nov. 1, 1946, p. 12.

"World Battlefronts" (news summary on the Leyte campaign). *Time*, Nov. 6, 1944, p. 26.

Wright, David Curtis. "Ensigns H. L. Jensen, W. C. Brooks, and the Beginning of the Battle off Samar, 25 October 1944." Unpublished manuscript. Courtesy of David Curtis Wright, University of Calgary, March 2003.

Eyewitness Accounts—Unpublished or Privately Published

[Individuals are identified by their rank or rating as of Oct. 25, 1944.]

Bedard, C. K. [AMM3, USS *Kitkun Bay*]. Excerpt from journal, Oct. 14–31, 1944. Courtesy of Michelle Bedard.

Brown, Joseph [USS *Gambier Bay*]. "Account of Joseph Brown." www.ussgambierbay-vc10.com/leytegulf_reports/survivors.htm; last visited by author Dec. 30, 2001.

Budnick, Larry, and Wayne Hammett [Lts. (jg), VC-65, USS *St. Lo*]. "S-Q-U-A-D-R-O-N" [narrative history of pilot training and VC-65]. Undated. Courtesy of William C. Brooks, Jr.

Carlsen, Verner [Chaplain, USS *Gambier Bay*]. "Account of Verner Carlsen." www.ussgambierbay-vc10.com/leytegulf_reports/survivors.htm; last visited by author Dec. 30, 2001.

Ciolek, John S. [AOM2, VC-65, USS *St. Lo*]. "What Did You Do During the War, Daddy?" Undated narrative. Courtesy of Les Shodo.

Copeland, Robert W., Rear Adm., USNR [Lt. Cdr., USS *Samuel B. Roberts*], with Jack E. O'Neill and Richard K. Rohde, eds. *The Spirit of the* Sammy B. 1950. USS Samuel B. Roberts Survivors Association, 2000.

Cordner, William F. [Lt. (jg), USS *Gambier Bay*]. www.ussgambierbay-vc10.com/leytegulf_reports/survivors.htm; last visited by author Dec. 30, 2001.

DeSpain, Bob [S1, USS *Hoel*]. Personal narrative. Undated.

Dix, John C. W. [Lt., USS *Hoel*]. *Missing off Samar.* 1949, reissued by Pocahontas Press, 2000.

Farris, James W. "The *St. Lo*—A Story of Survival." Undated. Courtesy of William C. Brooks, Jr.

Fetridge, Arthur E. [Lt. Cdr., USS *Kalinin Bay*]. "To the Men on the *Kalinin Bay.*" Oct. 30, 1944.

Fluke, R. W. [AOM3, USS *Fanshaw Bay*], rewritten by C. L. Wright. "The Fighting *Fanny Bee*" [prose poem]. Courtesy of M. Royce Hall.

Frenn, Willard [GM1, USS *Hoel*]. Personal narrative. Undated.

Gibson, W. R. "VC-65 Personnel History, Before and After October 25, 1944." Undated. Courtesy of William C. Brooks, Jr.

Goheen, Leo Carl [S1, USS *St. Lo*]. "The Sinking of the USS *St. Lo*, CVE-63." Undated. Courtesy of William C. Brooks, Jr.

Green, Maurice Fred [Lt., USS *Hoel*]. "Fred Green Report." www.ussjohnston-hoel.bigstep.com/generic.html?pid=31; last visited by author Feb. 16, 2003.

Harrington, Joe. [USS *Fanshaw Bay*]. "Turn On the Lights," personal narrative. Undated. From the collection of Elden L. McClintock.

Hobbs, Bishop [Air Dept., USS *Gambier Bay*]. "Account of Bishop Hobbs." www.ussgambierbay-vc10.com/leytegulf_reports/survivors.htm; last visited by author Dec. 30, 2001.

Holloway, James L., III [Lt., USS *Bennion*]. "The Battle of Surigao Straits." Address to the Naval Historical Foundation's Leyte Gulf Symposium, Oct. 22, 1999. www.navyhistory.org/whats_new/holloway.htm; last visited by author Mar. 4, 2003.

Kanaskie, Adam [Electrical Dept., USS *Gambier Bay*]. "Account of Adam Kanaskie." www.ussgambierbay-vc10.com/leytegulf_reports/ survivors.htm; last visited by author Dec. 30, 2001.

Katsur, William [F1, USS *Samuel B. Roberts*]. Untitled narrative. Undated (c. 1994).

Keeler, George H., Jr. [Lt., USS *Kalinin Bay*]. "Memories of the USS *Kalinin Bay* (CVE 68)." Jun. 17, 1988. www.bosamar.com/keeler.html; last visited by author Jan. 19, 2001.

Lamar, Hal. *I Saw Stars: Some Memories of Commander Hal Lamar, Fleet Admiral Nimitz's Flag Lieutenant, 1941–45*. Admiral Nimitz Foundation, 1985.

Lewis, David A. "Life in the Navy During World War II, 1942 through 1945." Undated. Courtesy of David A. Lewis.

Lewis, David A. "Rest in Peace, Eddie" [on the death of Eddie Thrasher, AMM2, USS *Fanshaw Bay*]. Nov. 12, 2001. Courtesy of David A. Lewis.

Mackay, Donald E. [Lt. (jg), USS *St. Lo*]. Letter to Michael F. McKenna. May 20, 1982. Courtesy of Donald E. Mackay.

Mallgrave, Fred J. [Ens., USS *Gambier Bay*]. "Account of F. J. Mallgrave." www.ussgambierbay-vc10.com/leytegulf_reports/survivors.htm; last visited by author Dec. 30, 2001.

McClintock, Elden L. [Ship's Historian, USS *Fanshaw Bay*]. "Turn on the Lights." Undated narrative. Courtesy of Elden L. McClintock.

McKay, Keith, ed. *At Rest 4,000 Fathoms Under the Waves, USS* Hoel, *DD 533* [collecting many survivors' narratives]. USS Johnston/Hoel Association, 1990.

McKenna, Capt. Francis J., USN [Capt., USS *St. Lo*]. "Narrative of Events Concerning Loss of USS *St. Lo* (CVE 63)." www.bosamar.com/slloss.html; last visited by author Feb. 16, 2003.

Mercer, Bill [S1, USS *Johnston*]. "GQ Johnny: A Very Short Story." Undated narrative. Courtesy of Bill Mercer.

Mercer, Bill, and Bob Chastain, eds. *The Fighting and Sinking of the USS* Johnston *(DD-557) as Told by Her Crew* [collecting many survivors' narratives]. USS Johnston/Hoel Association, 1991.

Moore, Jack [Ens., USS *Samuel B. Roberts*]. "A Japanese Admiral's Dream Come True." Nov. 1944.

Murphy, James [Lt. j.g., VC-3, USS Kalinin Bay]. "I Remember," *Spinning a Yarn* (USS Kalinin Bay/VC-3 Association newsletter). March 1999, p. 14.

Nickless, F. P. [QM, USS *St. Lo*]. "The Battle off Samar Four Days Later—One Man's Story." Oct. 29, 1944. Courtesy of William C. Brooks, Jr.

Parkin, Glenn H. [S1, USS *Hoel*]. "Historical Account of Glenn H. Parkin." www.ussjohnston-hoel.bigstep.com/generic.html?pid=48; last visited by author Feb. 15, 2003.

Phillips, D. H. [Chaplain, USS *Heermann*]. *God Rode Destroyer 'X.'* Privately published, 1956.

Pierson, Verling W. [Lt., USS *Fanshaw Bay*]. "Fighting Fanny Bee." Oct. 27, 1944. Courtesy of Robert C. Hagen.

Rabenstein, Maynard [RM2, USS *Dennis*]. "Invasion of the Philippine Islands (Leyte)." www.bosamar.com/rabenstein.html; last visited by author Feb. 17, 2003.

Raynor, Gilbert S. [AGM2, VC-5, USS *Kitkun Bay*]. "Notes on Battle off Samar." www.bosamar.com/account.html; last visited by author Jan. 19, 2001.

Roberts, Everett E. [Lt., USS *Samuel B. Roberts*]. Autobiographical narrative (unabbreviated version). Feb. 15, 1995. Courtesy of William Katsur.

Shodo, Leslie [AMM2, VC-65, USS *St. Lo*]. "Diary of Leslie Shodo." Oct. 1–Nov. 29, 1944. Courtesy of Les Shodo.

Short, Winston B. [SM3, USS *St. Lo*] "*St. Lo* Experience—Memories of Oct. 25, 1944." Undated narrative (ca. June 2003). Courtesy of Winston B. Short.

Sisul, Joe [GM1, USS *Fanshaw Bay*]. "Navy Days." 2001. Courtesy of Elden L. McClintock.

Sochor, Bob [S1, USS *Johnston*]. "Come Hell and High Water." Apr. 14, 1991. www.bosamar.com/sochor.html; last visited by author Jan. 19, 2001.

Sprague, Clifton A. F. [Rear Adm., Task Unit 77.4.3 (Taffy 3)]. Handwritten marginalia in his copy of *The Battle for Leyte Gulf* by C. Vann Woodward. Courtesy of John F. Wukovits.

Urbanski, Stanley R., ed. [S1, USS *Heermann*]. *History of USS* Heermann, *1943–46, 'Destroyer X'* [collecting many survivors' narratives]. USS Heermann Survivors Association, 1988.

USS *Gambier Bay* & VC-10 survivors' accounts. www.ussgambierbay-vc10.com/leytegulf_reports/survivors.htm. Includes accounts by Earl Bagley, James Ball, Joseph Brown, Verner Carlsen, William Cordner, Wayne Galey, Charles Heinl, Bishop Hobbs, Andy Judd, Adam Kanaskie,

William Kroger, W. E. Lynch, William McClendon, F. J. Mallgrave, Marshall L. Mitchell, Donald Topczewski, Michael Towstick, Louis Vilmer. Last visited by author Feb. 16, 2003.

USS St. Lo Association. *Attack on the* St. Lo [featuring the artwork of John M. Downs]. USS St. Lo CVE-63/VC-65 Association.

Van Brunt, Thomas B. [Lt., VC-65, USS *St. Lo*]. "October 25, 1944: A Day to Remember." Undated. Courtesy of William C. Brooks, Jr.

———. "A Bird's-Eye View of History's Greatest Naval Battle: The Battle for Leyte Gulf, October 24 and 25, 1944." Speech given to the Rotary Club of Tallahassee, Florida, Aug. 30, 1995. Courtesy of Thomas B. Van Brunt.

Welch, Ellsworth [Lt. (jg), USS *Johnston*]. Untitled Memorial Day address. May 30, 1994. Courtesy of Ellsworth Welch.

Whitney, Harold [CY, USS *Heermann*]. Untitled narrative. Jan. 7, 2003. Courtesy of Harold Whitney.

Wood, Russell [Lt. (jg), VC-4, USS *White Plains*]. "Memoir of Battle." www.bosamar.com/vc4bat.html; last visited by author Feb. 21, 2003.

Videotapes

"Destroyer Escorts of the 1940s and 1950s." Traditions Military Video.

"Great Lakes Naval Training Center: Navy Boot Camp in the 1940s." Traditions Military Video.

"Leyte Gulf Battle—Veterans." Courtesy of Hank Pyzdrowski, USS Gambier Bay Survivors Association, 1977.

"Navy Man in the 1940s." Traditions Military Video.

"Showdown at Leyte Gulf" [documentary]. A&E Home Video, 1993.

"Taffy 3 Remembered" [footage of the dedication of the Taffy 3 Memorial in San Diego, with cut-ins of battle footage]. Traditions Military Video.

"USS *Kalinin Bay* CVE-68/VC-3 Pilots & More" [interviews with personnel from Composite Squadron Three]. Courtesy of Elmer T. Glenn, USS Kalinin Bay Survivors Association.

Interviews

Archer, Earl "Blue," Lt. (jg), VC-3, USS *Kalinin Bay,* Nov. 10, 2001.

Barrett, Myles, Lt. (jg), USS *Hoel,* Jan. 30, 2002.

Bassett, Burt, Lt., VC-10, USS *Gambier Bay,* Mar. 16, 2001.

Bebb, Edwin, Lt., USS *Heermann,* May 27, 2002.

Branham, Bill, S1, USS *Samuel B. Roberts,* Mar. 16, 2001.

Bray, George, S1, USS *Samuel B. Roberts,* Apr. 13–14, 2001.

Breeding, Ed, Ens., VC-65, USS *St. Lo,* Apr. 16, 2001.

Brooks, Bill, Ens., VC-65, USS *St. Lo,* Mar. 18, 27–28, 2001; Mar. 11, 2002.

Budnick, Larry, Lt. (jg), VC-65, USS *St. Lo,* Apr. 4, 2001.

Carter, Clint, GM2, USS *Johnston,* Sept. 18, 2001.

Chastain, Bob, S1, USS *Johnston,* Oct. 1, 2001.

Chastain, Bob, interview by Ronald E. Marcello, University of North Texas Oral History Collection, Aug. 2, 1994. Transcript courtesy of Bob Chastain.

Cochran, Jesse, Lt. (jg), USS *Johnston,* Nov. 6, 2001.

Comet, Bud, S1, USS *Samuel B. Roberts,* Jan. 15, 2002.

Copeland, Harriet, widow of Lt. Cdr. Robert W. Copeland, USS *Samuel B. Roberts,* Feb. 12, 2001.

Correll, Jim, GM1, USS *Johnston,* Oct. 25, 2001.

Crawforth, Holly, RT2, USS *St. Lo,* Mar. 27, 2001.

Cuming, Bill, Ens., USS *Gambier Bay,* Dec. 30, 2001.

DiGardi, Ed, Lt. (jg), USS *Johnston,* Apr. 17–18, 2001.

Dodd, Peggy Carr, sister of Paul Henry Carr, GM3, USS *Samuel B. Roberts,* Apr. 10, 2002.

Downs, Joe, AOM3, VC-65, USS *St. Lo,* Apr. 27, 2001.

Durfee, Bud, USS *Kalinin Bay,* May 24, 2001.

Getas, John, AOM3, USS *St. Lo,* Apr. 18, 2001.

Gifford, Earl, ARM1, VC-68, USS *Fanshaw Bay,* Jul. 13, 2002.

Goodrich, Vince, SOM3, USS *Samuel B. Roberts,* Jan. 29, 2002.

Hagen, Robert C., Lt., USS *Johnston,* May 22, 2001.

Hall, M. Royce, AOM1, VC-68, USS *Fanshaw Bay,* May 2, 2002.

Hammett, Wayne, Lt. (jg), VC-65, USS *St. Lo,* Apr. 11, 2001.

Hartley, Suzanne, daughter of Lt. Cdr. Robert W. Copeland, USS *Samuel B. Roberts,* Feb. 12, 2002.

Heric, E. Don, SM2, USS *Gambier Bay,* Sept. 14, 2001.

Hippe, Kenneth, Lt. (jg), VC-3, USS *Kalinin Bay,* May 26, 2001.

Hollenbaugh, Robert, BM1, USS *Johnston,* Oct. 14, 2001.

Hood, Clarence, QM3, USS *Hoel,* Jan. 21, 2002.

Johnson, Allen, EM1, USS *Johnston,* Oct. 31, 2001.

Katsur, William, F1, USS *Samuel B. Roberts,* Mar. 11, 2003.

Kight, Harold L., SC3, USS *Fanshaw Bay,* May 26, 2001.

Lewis, Steve, son of Dave Lewis, GM2, USS *Johnston,* Sept. 12, 2001.

Lucas, Sam, S1, USS *Hoel,* Jan. 31, 2002.

Lupo, Thomas J., Lt (jg), VC-68, USS *Fanshaw Bay,* Sept. 29, 2001.

Mercer, William, S1, USS *Johnston,* Apr. 1, 2001.

Mostowy, John, Cox, USS *Johnston,* Sept. 12, 2001.

Moylan, Dudley, Ens., USS *Samuel B. Roberts,* Jul. 25, 2002.

Murry, William, MaM3, USS *Fanshaw Bay,* Oct. 8, 2001.

Pace, John E., Lt. Cdr., USS *John C. Butler,* interview by John F. Wukovits. Nov. 15, 1993. Transcript courtesy of John F. Wukovits.

Pehl, Milt, USS *Johnston,* Oct. 8, 2001.

Randles, Dale, MM1, USS *Johnston,* Sept. 6, 2001.

Reneau, Patricia Sprague, daughter of Rear Adm. Clifton A. F. Sprague, interviewed in "Taffy 3 Remembered" videotape, Oct. 24, 1996.

Rhodes, Harold "Dusty," S1, USS *Johnston,* Oct. 30, 2001.

Roby, Richard, Lt., VC-10, USS *Gambier Bay,* Feb. 28, 2002.

Rogers, Richard S., Lt. Cdr., VC-68, interview by John F. Wukovits. 1993. Transcript courtesy of John F. Wukovits.

Rohde, Richard, RM2, USS *Samuel B. Roberts,* Mar. 15, 2001.

Steinberg, Julius, Lt. (jg), USS *Heermann,* Apr. 16, 2001.

Stevenson, Thomas, Lt. (jg), USS *Samuel B. Roberts,* Mar. 16, 2001.

Thompson, Derrill, CRM, USS *Hoel,* Feb. 2, 2002.

Turner, Morris, S1, USS *Kalinin Bay,* May 24, 2001.

Van Brunt, Thomas B., Lt., VC-65, USS *St. Lo,* Mar. 15, 2001.

Welch, Ellsworth, Lt. (jg), USS *Johnston,* Oct. 31, 2001.

Whitney, Harold, CY, USS *Heermann,* Jan. 31, 2003.

Yusen, Jack, S2, USS *Samuel B. Roberts,* Jan. 13–15, 2002.

Correspondence

Archer, E. L. ("Blue") [Lt. (jg), VC-3, USS *Kalinin Bay*]. Letter to William Long, USS Kalinin Bay Survivors Association, April 2001. Courtesy of Blue Archer.

Bacon, Betty [widow of Robert Bacon, USS *Johnston*]. Letter to author, Sept. 15, 2001.

Beagle, Clayton [USS *John C. Butler*]. Letter to author, Mar. 18, 2001.

Bray, George [S2, USS *Samuel B. Roberts*]. Correspondence with shipmates, responses to Battle off Samar questionnaire, various dates, 1984.

Brooks, William C., Jr. [VC-65, USS *St. Lo*]. Letters and e-mails to author, various dates.

Budnick, Larry [Lt. (jg), VC-65, USS *St. Lo*]. E-mails to author, various dates.

Canter, Shelton Carl. Letter to Mrs. John S. LeClercq, Dec. 22, 1945. From the collection of Robert LeClercq.

Carew, Robert E. [SM1 (flag), USS *Fanshaw Bay*]. Letter to Harold Kight, Mar. 14, 1986. Courtesy of Harold Kight.

Chambers, Ray [USS *Samuel B. Roberts*]. Letter to Geroge Bray, undated (probably 1984). See Bray Correspondence with shipmates above. Courtesy of George Bray.

Copeland, Robert W. [Lt. Cdr., USS *Samuel B. Roberts*]. Letters to William Katsur, Apr. 24, 1945, and Dec. 27, 1945.

Downs, Joseph A. [AOM3, VC-65, USS *St. Lo*]. Letter to author, Apr. 20, 2001.

Follmer, Frank [CM1, USS *Fanshaw Bay*]. Letters to Harold Kight, Mar. 11, 1986, and Apr. 10, 1986.

Getas, John [AOM3, USS *St. Lo*]. Letter to author, Apr. 23, 2001.

Glenn, Elmer T. [USS *Kalinin Bay*]. Letter to author, Apr. 23, 2001.

Glocheski, Virgil [Lt. (jg), USS *Fanshaw Bay*]. Letters to Harold Kight, Jun. 14, 1986, and Sept. 6, 1986. Courtesy of Harold Kight.

Hagen, Robert C. [Lt., USS *Johnston*]. Letter to author, May 1, 2001.

———. Letter to *Naval History* magazine, Dec. 28, 1999.

Hall, M. Royce [AOM1, VC-68, USS *Fanshaw Bay*]. Letters and e-mails to author, various dates.

———. Letter to Henry A. Pyzdrowski, Jan. 14, 1988; published in *Heritage*, newsletter of the Heritage Foundation of the USS *Gambier Bay* and VC-10, Oct. 1988, p. 17.

———. Letter to James H. Flatley, Jul. 1997. Courtesy of Royce Hall.

Harrington, Joe C. [USS *Fanshaw Bay*]. Letter to Harold Kight, Mar. 10, 1986. Courtesy of Harold Kight.

Harrington, Red [BM1, USS *Samuel B. Roberts*]. Letter to George Bray, received May 22, 1984. Courtesy of George Bray.

Jacobs, Vice Adm. Randall, Western Union Telegram to Mr. and Mrs. John S. LeClercq. Nov. 19, 1944.

Kight, Harold [SC3, USS *Fanshaw Bay*]. Correspondence with shipmates, in response to Battle off Samar questionnaire, various dates, Mar.–Dec. 1986. From the collection of Harold Kight.

LeClercq, John S., II [Lt. (jg), USS *Samuel B. Roberts*]. Letters home. Various dates, Aug.–Oct. 1944. From the collection of Robert LeClercq.

Lupo, Thomas J. [Lt. (jg), VC-68, USS *Fanshaw Bay*]. Letter to author, May 17, 2002.

Mackay, Donald E. [Lt. (jg), USS *St. Lo*]. Letter to author, Nov. 7, 2001.

Mayuzumi, Haruo [Capt., IJN *Tone*]. Letter to Henry A. Pyzdrowski, July 23, 1984. Courtesy of Henry A. Pyzdrowski.

McClintock, Elden L. [Ship's Historian, USS *Fanshaw Bay*]. Correspondence with various shipmates.

Mercer, Bill [S1, USS *Johnston*]. Letters and e-mails to author, various dates.

Michiels, Larry [shipmate of Cox. Samuel Booker Roberts]. Letter to Lloyd Gurnett, Sept. 7, 1984. Courtesy of George Bray.

Miller, Vernon [WT1, USS *Fanshaw Bay*]. Letters to Harold Kight, Mar. 14, 1986, and Apr. 12, 1986. Courtesy of Harold Kight.

Mittendorff, William. Letter to Mrs. John S. LeClercq and narrative titled "Johnny Was Like That." Undated, circa Mar. 1947. From the collection of Robert LeClercq.

Moser, Leonard [AMM1, USS *Fanshaw Bay*]. Letter to Harold Kight, Apr. 25, 1986. Courtesy of Harold Kight.

Moylan, J. Dudley [Ens., USS *Samuel B. Roberts*]. Letter to Mr. and Mrs. John S. LeClercq, Oct. 25, 1954. From the collection of Robert LeClercq.

———. Letter to George Bray, May 27, 1984. Courtesy of George Bray.

Orgill, Dale V. [AMM3, USS *St. Lo*]. Letter to author, Feb. 9, 2002.

Philipps, Ernest [AOM, USS *Fanshaw Bay*]. Letters to Harold Kight, Jun. 1986 and Aug. 18, 1986. Courtesy of Harold Kight.

Pyzdrowski, Henry A. [Lt. (jg), VC-10, USS *Gambier Bay*]. Letter to author, Mar. 15, 2001.

Reid, J. M. [USS *Samuel B. Roberts*]. Letter to Mrs. John S. LeClercq, Sr., Jan. 16, 1945. From the collection of Robert LeClercq.

Rhodes, Dusty [S1, USS *Johnston*]. Letters to author, Sept. 13, 2001, and Nov. 6, 2001.

Rinn, Paul X. [Capt., USS *Samuel B. Roberts, FFG-58*]. E-mail to author, Dec. 3, 2002.

Roberts, Everett E. [Lt., USS *Samuel B. Roberts*]. Letters to William Katsur, Feb. 15, 1995, and Feb. 16, 1996.

Rohde, Dick [RM3, USS *Samuel B. Roberts*]. Letters and e-mails to author, various dates.

Rutter, Robert [Lt. (jg), USS *Heermann*]. Letter to author, June 22, 2002.

Saunders, Gene [VOC-2 (observation composite squadron), USS *Fanshaw Bay*]. Letter to Harold Kight, Dec. 12, 1986. From the collection of Harold Kight.

Skau, Rudolph H. [CTM, USS *Samuel B. Roberts*]. Letter to George Bray, undated (probably May 1984). Courtesy of George Bray.

Steinberg, Julius [Lt. (jg), USS *Heermann*]. Letter to author, Apr. 5, 2001.

Stevenson, Tom [Lt. (jg), USS *Samuel B. Roberts*]. Letter to Mrs. John S. LeClercq, Sr., Dec. 1, 1944. From the collection of Robert LeClercq.

——. Letter to author, Mar. 30, 2001.

——. Letter to Mark G. Pond, Oct. 25, 1982. Courtesy of Tom Stevenson.

Turner, Bob [AMM1, USS *Fanshaw Bay*]. Letter to Harold Kight, Dec. 1986. Courtesy of Harold Kight.

Van Brunt, Tom [Lt. VC-65, USS *St. Lo*]. Letter to author, Mar. 17, 2001.

Vaughan, Courtney Sprague [daughter of Rear Adm. Clifton A. F. Sprague]. Letter to author, Oct. 15, 2001.

Welch, Ellsworth. [Lt. (jg), USS *Johnston*]. Letter to author, Nov. 7, 2001.

Internet Sites

USS Gambier Bay/VC-10 Survivors Association website: www.ussgambierbay-vc10.com

USS Johnston/USS Hoel Survivors Association website: www.ussjohnston-hoel.bigstep.com

USS St. Lo (CVE-63)/VC-65 Association website: www.stlomidway6365.org

USS Samuel B. Roberts Survivors Association website: www.de413.org

Battle off Samar website (by Robert Jon Cox): www.bosamar.com

Source Notes

The account of Admiral Kurita's passage that begins and ends the opening section draws from Cutler, *Battle of Leyte Gulf*, 219–21; Field, *Japanese*, 76, 86–87, 98; Prados, *Combined Fleet*, 662–67; Toland, *Rising Sun*, 682, 702; Ugaki, *Fading Victory*, 492; and Woodward, *Battle*, 87–88. The depiction of midwatch aboard the *Samuel B. Roberts* is based on Copeland, *Spirit*, and George Bray and Tom Stevenson interviews. "Douglas, where do we go from here?" . . . "Leyte, Mr. President . . . ," Morison, *History*, vol. 12, 7. "The President . . . I shall return," Manchester, *American Caesar*, 292–311; Potter, *Nimitz*, 385. MacArthur Returns to Philippines . . . [headline], *Dallas Morning News*, Oct. 20, 1944, 1; MacArthur on the beach, Toland, *Rising Sun*, 676–77; Morison, vol. 12, 136–37; Prados, 401. "*Skunk 184 Degrees* . . ." and other TBS transmissions presumably overheard on the *Roberts* during midwatch are taken from the radio logs and action reports of the *Daly*, *Boise*, and *West Virginia*. The ship had rolled so sharply . . . , Vince Goodrich interview. As ever, sailors learned . . . , Ernie Pyle, unpublished dispatch, www.de220.com/Life%20on%20a%20DE/DE–Life.htm. "Hey, Captain . . ." "That's not a storm . . . ," Bray interview.

Chapter 1
"May she be a sound ship . . . ," *Brown Victory Dispatch*, Nov. 25, 1944, 1. Train ride to Houston, George Bray, Vince Goodrich, Dudley Moylan, Richard Rohde, and Jack Yusen interviews. "I know what it's like for you guys . . . ," Rohde interview.

Chapter 2
Construction and commissioning of the *Samuel B. Roberts*, Copeland, *Spirit*, Tom Stevenson and Richard Rohde interviews. Bob Copeland's childhood, Harriet Copeland interview. "He stood on his own . . . ," Copeland, 3. "Lloyd knew his navy . . . ," Copeland, 3. Samuel Booker Roberts on Guadalcanal, *Gismo* [*Roberts* ship's newsletter], Aug. 4, 1944; Program, Dedication of the Taffy 3 Memorial Monument, Oct. 23, 1996; Copeland, *Spirit*, 5. "If launching may be likened to birth . . . ," E. B. Hopper, foreword to *Ships of the United States Navy* (Dept. of the Navy, Naval History Division, 1975). Commissioning ceremony, www.history.navy.mil/faqs/faq108.htm. "I think I overdid it . . ." and "There's an old saying . . . ," Copeland, 17; Harriet Copeland interview. "Jack Roberts had made his own way . . . ," Copeland, 9. *What a ship!* and "What are you guys looking at?" Jack Yusen interview. In a stained-glass window, Dudley Moylan interview. "We were short of destroyers," Copeland, 29. "They are rough and tumble little ships . . . ," Ernie Pyle, www.de220.com/Life%20on%20a%20DE/DE–Life.htm. Destroyers escorts (DEs) were every bit the equal of destroyers . . . , see data in

Friedman, *Destroyers*, 412, 421. *Roberts*'s collision with a whale, Stevenson, Rohde, and Yusen interviews; Copeland, 11. "I was belowdecks when there was a great shock . . . ," Gene Wallace quoted in *Brown Victory Dispatch*, Jan. 13, 1945, 2. "It is legendary in the Navy . . . ," Copeland, 11. "My dad figured . . ." and "I want to talk to you . . . ," Bud Comet interview. Background on Everett E. Roberts, Everett E. Roberts, autobiographical narrative. "As fast as a slide rule . . . ," Copeland, 6. "As long as I have the confidence and trust . . . ," John LeClercq, letter to his mother, Aug. 31, 1944, 4. Bringing the dog Sammy aboard: In *Spirit* (12) Copeland credited himself and Lloyd Gurnett for bringing Sammy aboard ship; George Bray said some enlisted men did it. Speculation flew in *The Gismo* . . . , *Gismo*, Aug. 4, 1944.

Chapter 3
This account of the *Roberts*'s crossing-the-line ceremony is from Copeland, *Spirit*, 19–26, and Vince Goodrich and Richard Rohde interviews.

Chapter 4
History of the destroyer, Friedman, *Destroyers*, 7, 11, 111, 167–68. "The hunting dogs of the fleet," Urbanski, *Heermann, 1943–46*, n.p. The USS *Hoel*'s wardroom, Myles Barrett and Clarence Hood interviews. "Nelson touch," in Mahan, *Mahan on Naval Warfare*, 201–2. Amos Hathaway's photographic memory, Harold Whitney interview. "He was a son of a bitch," Julius Steinberg interview. Bebb feared his skipper would resent . . . , Edwin Bebb interview. A handful of marbles . . . , Steinberg interview. "This is going to be a fighting ship . . . ," Hagen, "We asked for the Jap Fleet," 9–10. Account of the *Johnston* during the Marshalls invasion, Jesse Cochran, Robert Hagen, Robert Hollenbaugh, and Ellsworth Welch interviews; accounts by Edward Block, Milt Pehl, and others in Mercer and Chastain, *The Fighting and Sinking of the USS Johnston*. "Damn it, they need fire support," Cochran interview. "The captain put the make on him . . . ," Hagen interview. "The gun boss could fire a hundred shots . . ." and "We were all so green . . . ," Hagen interview. An average rate of fire for a five-inch/38-caliber crew, Roscoe, *Destroyer Operations*, 18. "You may now bring on the Japanese fleet," Hagen, "We asked for the Jap Fleet," 10. "Mr. Hagen, that was very good shooting," Jim Correll interview.

Chapter 5
Ziggy Sprague, "tousled hair swinging fore and aft," "clever in nearly every sport," *Lucky Bag* in Reneau, *Remembered*, following p. 152; Wukovits, *Devotion*, 14. Sprague in Rockport, Massachusetts, Reneau, 7; Wukovits, 3. "Fleet aviation must be developed . . ." and "the advantage will lie . . . ," Spector, *At War at Sea*, 138. "Instrument face," Reneau, 36; Wukovits, 29. Pensacola aviation fatalities, Wukovits, 25. "Aviation is essentially and fundamentally . . . ," Spector, 146. "Just a lot of noise," Wukovits, 26. Sprague and Annabel Fitzgerald, Wukovits, 39–41. "We're not prepared . . . ," Wukovits, 48. The *Tangier* at Pearl Harbor, Reneau, 87–88. "I was eating, drinking, and breathing aviation," Halsey and Bryan, *Admiral*, 52. Sprague "came in quietly . . . ," Wukovits, 83; "took a very green crew," Wukovits, 86. "The air group is the only reason . . . ," Wukovits, 84. "You can train a pilot for $50,000 . . . ," Taylor, *Magnificent*, 236; Reneau, 130; Arleigh A. Burke in Wooldridge, *Carrier*, 169. "When he was promoted from Captain to Admiral," Reneau, 118. Capt. Douglass P. Johnson of the *Fanshaw Bay*, William Murry interview. "Piss on them then," *Fantails* [USS *Fanshaw Bay* newsletter], Jul. 25, 1986, 3. "The commanders of all fleets . . . patriotism, and subordination," www.history.navy.mil/faqs/faq59-7.htm. Bogan was a "first-class horse's rear end," Joe Harrington, "Turn On the Lights." "The entire crew [of the *Fanshaw Bay*] was in-

competent" and "the worst ship I'd ever seen . . . ," Y'Blood, *Little Giants*, 171; Wukovits, 113. "For the first time . . . hadn't received an *Essex*-class command," Christopher W. M. Carson, undated letter to Clifton Sprague, quoted in Reneau, 200. "A conglomeration of farmers . . . ," Leonard Moser, supplement to letter to Harold Kight, Apr. 25, 1986, 2. "Active men need . . . ," "Planning the menu . . . ," *Cook Book of the United States Navy*, 1944, 3. "Hey, we had good chow . . . ," Harold Kight interview. *[A] large mess serving 1,000 men . . . , Cook Book*, 13. Sinking of the *Liscome Bay*, Y'Blood, 1–9; Dix, *Missing*, 11. "A jeep carrier bears the same relation . . . not wholly successful results," Fletcher Pratt, "Jeep Carrier at Best a Makeshift Affair," *Boston Globe* and Overseas Press Service, 1944. History of CVE development, www.usmm.org/peary.html; Y'Blood, 34–35; Vice Adm. Fitzhugh Lee, in Wooldridge, *Carrier*, 204; www.aws.org/about/blockbuster.html. "Boy, I thought we'd bought the farm . . . ," Vernon Miller, letter to Harold Kight, Apr. 12, 1986, 10–11. *Fanshaw Bay* damaged off Saipan, Joe Sisul, "Navy Days"; Leonard Moser, letter to Harold Kight; Thomas Lupo interview and letter to author.

Chapter 6

Background on World War II–era pilot training: Bill Brooks, Larry Budnick, Joe Downs, Earl Gifford, Royce Hall, Wayne Hammett, Thomas Lupo, and Thomas B. Van Brunt interviews. "Damn Navy . . . ," Van Brunt, "A Bird's-Eye View." In some divisions on the *St. Lo*, as many as 90 percent of the men requested transfers, Donald E. Mackay, letter to Michael F. McKenna, May 20, 1982, 17. "We respected their view . . . ," Brooks interview. Pilots could see submarine silhouettes, Downs interview. Sinking of USS *Seawolf*, Brooks and Downs interviews; Morison, *History*, vol. 12, 27–28; Wukovits, *Devotion*, 113–14; Y'Blood, *Little Giants*, 107–8. Aircraft production and pilot recruitment, Spector, *At War at Sea*, 148; Vice Adm. Herbert D. Riley, "Filling the Pipeline," in Wooldridge, *Carrier*, 102; Lawson and Tillman, *Carrier Air War*, 152–57. "Like getting into a shoebox," Brooks interview. Like "a Hollywood premiere, Chinese New Year's and Fourth of July rolled into one," Morison, vol. 8, 302; "I heard pilots express the opinion . . . ," Rear Adm. James D. Ramage, "Turn On the Lights," in Wooldridge, 180–81. Lt. Cdr. Ralph Jones's "big glom," Brooks interview. "We razzed the torpedo pilots a lot . . . ," Budnick interview. Background on aerial ops over Leyte, Earl Archer, Bill Brooks, Joe Downs, Earl Gifford, Thomas Lupo, Richard Roby, and Thomas B. Van Brunt interviews. "Hey coxswain . . . ," Van Brunt interview. "Landing on half a block of Main Street . . . ," Ernie Pyle, in David Nichols, ed., *Ernie's War*, 395. "They came out like sausages . . . ," Rear Adm. Herbert D. Riley, in Wooldridge, 102.

Chapter 7

Discussion of the Sho plan is based on Prados, *Combined*, 586–87, 606, 608. Halsey's strikes on Formosa, Morison, *History*, vol. 12, 92–95; Prados, 608–9. ". . . nothing but so many eggs thrown . . . ," Morison, vol. 12, 93. Activation of Sho-1 plan, Morison, vol. 12, 91; Prados, 621; Field, *Japanese*, 23–39. Ozawa's force composition is based on Prados, 644–47; Morison, vol. 12, 320–23. Halsey's orders to "cover and support" MacArthur "in order to assist in the seizure . . . of the Central Philippines," Morison, vol. 12, 58. ". . . large scale logistic preparations . . . " Prados, 615.

Chapter 8

"Like elaborate religious scrolls" and "These battleships will be as useful . . . as a samurai sword," Prados, *Combined Fleet*, 126–27. Japanese dissent to the Sho plan, Koyanagi, "The Battle of Leyte Gulf," in O'Connor, *The Japanese Navy*, 109;

Prados, 588. "To intercept and destroy . . . in a Decisive Battle," Prados, 587. "Please give the Combined Fleet the chance . . . ," Cutler, *Battle of Leyte Gulf*, 67. U.S. air strikes on Nishimura, Morison, *History*, vol. 12, 190; Prados, 629; Tully, 2. *"Skunk 184 degrees, 18 miles,"* TBS radio log, in USS *West Virginia* action report; Morison, vol. 12, 213. The wording varies slightly in USS *Boise's* TBS Log Sheet.

Chapter 9

Morison's chapter in *History*, vol. 12, 198–241, is the most gripping and authoritative account of the Battle of Surigao Strait to date. Toland's account in *Rising Sun*, 697–703, is based on many Japanese sources. In his valuable article, "Shell Game at Surigao," Tully traces the discrepancies and dispels much of the confusion surrounding the action. As he explains, some authors, including Cutler, Field, and Woodward, relied on an errant Japanese source and in so doing transposed the identities of the *Fuso* and *Yamashiro*. "Too beautiful to serve our purpose," USS *Daly* action report, 2. The ships up the strait heard a tremendous racket and "I've got a big one in sight . . . ," Holloway, "Battle of Surigao Straits." Like "animals in a cage," Morison, *History*, vol. 12, 215. A "huge, red-hot iron plunged into the water," Shigeru Nishino, skipper of *Shigure*, quoted in Toland, 699. "Notify your maximum speed," Tully. "Each explosion was a round ball . . ." and "The ship which was hit . . . ," USS *Daly* action report, 4. "Two faint [explosions] and a loud snap" and "Flames reaching above the mastheads," Tully. The *West Virginia's* gunnery officer laughed aloud . . . , Woodward, *Battle*, 114. The devastating accuracy of this gunfire . . . , Morison, vol. 12, 228. "It seemed as if every ship . . . ," Oldendorf quoted in Astor, *Crisis*, 385–86. It seems that the *Shigure's* skipper mistook Nishimura's own ship for the *Fuso*, Tully, citing the Naval War College analysis of the battle. A projectile-man . . . broke his left hand . . . : USS *Boise* action report, Executive Officer's Report, 2, identifies this man as S1 Clayton M. Boone. *"We have arrived at battle site,"* Shima quoted in Toland, 701. "Burning like a city block," Morison, vol. 12, 236. "I HAVE RUDDER DIFFICULTIES," Falk, *Decision*, 163. "If we continued dashing," Falk, 164. "In the pale pre-dawn twilight . . . ," Holloway. At daylight seven heavy pillars . . . , USS *Daly* action report, 6. "All survivors in water are Nips . . ." and "Let them sink," USS *Daly* action report, Enclosure C, Voice Radio Log, 5.

Chapter 10

"The fact that I survived . . . ," Hara, *Japanese*, 4. "Large target . . . ," USS *Denver* to Oldendorf at 0421 hours, per USS *West Virginia* action report, TBS Log Sheet. *"Keep track of enemy . . . ,"* Berkey to McManes at 0333 hours, in USS *Boise* action report, 7. "We have one dead in the water . . . ," McManes to Berkey at 0348, in USS *Boise* action report, 8. "We have quite a few survivors in the water," Cdr. M. H. Hubbard to Oldendorf at 0557, USS *Daly* action report, Enclosure C, Voice Radio Log, 5. *"Pick them up . . . ,"* Capt. T. F. Conley to skippers of DesDiv 112 at 0611, USS *Daly*, Enclosure C, 5. "Take three destroyers . . . ," Oldendorf to Hayler at 0636, USS *Boise* action report, 12. "By God, I think we finally got 'em," Tom Stevenson interview.

Chapter 11

"We do not mind death," Ito, *End*, 100. "I know that many of you are strongly opposed . . . ," Prados, *Combined Fleet*, 631; Ito, 100. "After the spray and smoke had disappeared . . . ," Morison, *History*, vol. 12, 172. "The giants of Japan's Navy . . . ," Ito, 11. The construction of the *Yamato* is discussed in Spurr, *Glorious*, 24–27; Japan's overall shipbuilding strategy is discussed in Ito, 11, 12, 15–18. *"Strike! Repeat: Strike! . . . ,"* Halsey and Bryan, *Admiral*, 214. The destruction of the *Musashi* is from Cutler, *Battle of Leyte Gulf,* 146–53; Field, *Japanese,* 66–69; Lawson and Tillman, *Carrier Air War,* 131–33; Prados, 639–42; Toland, *Rising Sun,* 686–94; and Ugaki, *Fading,* 488–91. "Damn fool! My responsibility is so great . . . ," Toland, 691–92. "PROBABILITY IS GREAT . . . ," Ito, 108.

Chapter 12

"IF WE CONTINUE WITH OUR PRESENT COURSE . . . ," Ito, *End,* 108. "WITH CONFIDENCE IN HEAVENLY GUIDANCE . . . ," Prados, *Combined,* 641; a slightly different translation appears in Morison, *History,* vol. 12, 189. Background on Vice Adm. Willis Lee is from Halsey and Bryan, *Admiral,* 257. Discussion of Halsey's mission orders is from Potter, *Nimitz,* 416. Halsey's decision to attack Ozawa's decoy force is discussed in Potter, *Halsey,* 417, and in Morison, vol. 12, 193–96. The reports that the carriers *Amagi* and *Katsuragi* had joined Ozawa, erroneously circulated by JICPOA, are discussed in Prados, 649. "Before we're through with 'em . . . ," Morison, vol. 3, 212.

Chapter 13

This account of **Taffy 3's morning activities** is taken from Bill Brooks and Joe Downs interviews; the action reports of CTU 77.4.3 (Rear Admiral Sprague) and CTU 77.4.2 (Rear Admiral Stump); action reports of the *St. Lo* and VC-65; Sprague, "The Japs Had Us on the Ropes"; and Thomas Van Brunt, "Bird's-Eye View." *We're never going to see daylight,* Brooks interview. "*Enemy surface force of four battleships . . . ,*" *St Lo* action report, 2; Sprague, "The Japs," quotes this sighting report slightly differently. *Now there's some screwy young aviator . . . ,* Sprague, 40. "Air plot, tell him to check his identification," Sprague, 40. "*I can see the pagoda masts . . . ,*" Van Brunt, "A Bird's-Eye View," 3. "*Question: Is TF 34 guarding San Bernardino Strait?*" Cox, *Battle,* 48; Falk, *Decision,* 172; Cutler, *Battle of Leyte Gulf,* 216; Potter, *Bull Halsey,* 300–1. In discussing the system for routing communiqués between the Third and Seventh Fleets through Manus, Potter (in *Bull Halsey,* 290, 300) points out that Kinkaid had the means to broadcast his query directly to Halsey aboard the *New Jersey,* had Halsey's flagship been assigned the right frequency. "My gut feeling was . . . ," Brooks interview. It is unclear in official records which of the two gallant ensigns spotted Kurita first, Bill Brooks of VC-65 or Hans Jensen of VC-20. Morison is unhelpful, having apparently confused Jensen and Brooks (see vol. 12, 246; see also Sprague, "The Japs"). David C. Wright has used the weight of circumstantial evidence to conclude in an as-yet-unpublished study that Jensen was first. The Taffy 2 flier's Navy Cross citation credits him with being the first pilot to detect, sight, report, and attack Kurita's force off Samar. Toland and Y'Blood agree, though the action report of Jensen's own squadron doesn't support the conclusion. It's abundantly evident in any case that the professionalism and enterprise of both pilots were instrumental to the timely recognition of the Japanese force. "Anybody hurt back there?" and "a live pilot rather than a dead hero," Brooks interview.

Part II

In no engagement in its entire history . . . , Morison, *History,* vol. 12, 275.

The battle narrative in Part II is drawn almost exclusively from eyewitness accounts of participants. This has been a blessing, for the rich lode of personal narratives found, among other places, in the valuable crew memory books of the destroyers *Hoel, Johnston,* and *Heermann,* and the vivid memoir of Captain Copeland of the *Samuel B. Roberts,* has not been thoroughly mined by previous authors. But it has also been a curse, for some of the eyewitness accounts, written and oral alike, have been compromised by the passage of years. Though memories are long, they are vulnerable to influence by things one has read or heard secondhand. Generally I used only what the witnesses saw and experienced. I have tried to steer clear of hearsay and secondhand observation.

Citations of the crew memory books are abbreviated as follows:

- *"Hoel"* = Keith McKay, ed., *At Rest 4,000 Fathoms Under the Waves; USS Hoel, DD-533*, USS *Johnston/Hoel* Association, 1990.
- *"Johnston"* = Bill Mercer and Bob Chastain, eds., *The Fighting and Sinking of the USS* Johnston, *DD-557, as Told by Her Crew*, USS *Johnston/Hoel* Association, 1991.
- *"Heermann"* = Stanley R. Urbanski, ed., *History of USS* Heermann, *1943–46, 'Destroyer X,'* USS *Heermann* Survivors Association, 1998.

Chapter 14

"How about some bacon . . . ?" Mercer, "GQ Johnny," 23, and in *Johnston*, 128. "I thought someone was joking . . . ," Burnett, in *Johnston*, 27. "Our Combat Air Patrol . . . ," and *"I'm drawing fire. . . . The bastards . . . ,"* Dix, *Missing Off Samar*, 14. *"Where the hell is Halsey?"* Robert Rutter, letter to author; Ed DiGardi interview. "Designed to jar the brain . . . ," and *Maybe it's just a false alarm . . . ,* Dix, 16. "Surface radar reports . . . ," "Well, there's a storm . . . ," and "Object on the horizon . . . ," Copeland, *Spirit*, 35–36. "If you're interested . . . ," Tom Stevenson interview. LeClercq and Stevenson, Tom Stevenson, letter to Mrs. LeClercq. "A large Japanese fleet . . . ," Moore, "A Japanese Admiral's," 2. "This will be a fight against overwhelming odds . . . ," USS *Samuel B. Roberts* action report, Part VI. Tullio Serafini background, Copeland, 8, 69; Moore, 1–2. "Be a good, stout boy . . . ," "Serafini's entrance . . . ," and "What are the odds . . . ?" Moore, 2.

Chapter 15

The Center Force's opening moves are from Prados, *Combined Fleet*, 670–71 and Field, *Japanese*, 98–101. "Each unit seemed very slow . . . ," Ugaki, *Fading Victory*, 492. "I feared the spirit of all-out attack . . . ," Ugaki, 493. *"Cruiser divisions attack!"* Prados, 672. "WE ARE ENGAGING ENEMY . . . ," Prados, 671. "BY HEAVEN-SENT OPPORTUNITY . . . ," Cox, *Battle off Samar*, 63.

Chapter 16

This is an impossible situation . . . , Robert Hagen interview. *All hands to general quarters . . . ,* and *Why didn't I think of that?* Ellsworth Welch, in *Johnston*, 181. "That was the only time . . . ," Robert Billie, in *Johnston*, 12. "Please, sir, let us not go down . . . ," Hagen interview. "A captain who could strike . . ." and "I can see him now . . . ," Hagen, "We Asked for the Jap Fleet," 10. "But we are not making smoke" and *"I want a smoke screen . . . ,"* Charles Landreth, in *Johnston*, 120; Jesse Cochran interview; Cochran, in *Johnston*, 63. "We were making smoke . . . ," John Mostowy, in *Johnston*, 137. "This is fun," Bill Mercer, in *Johnston*, 128. Evans's "heart grinning," Hagen 10.

Chapter 17

"I wouldn't say it was like . . . ," and "Neither could such dream stuff . . . ," Sprague, "The Japs Had Us on the Ropes," 41. Development of the *Yamato's* guns was so secret, Kurita, USSBS interrogation, 5. "I thought, we might as well give them . . . ," Sprague, 112. "I wanted to pull the enemy out . . . ," and "If we were going to expend ourselves . . . ," Sprague, 114. *"Signal execute on receipt . . ."* and other TBS commands are from CTU 77.4.3 (C.A.F. Sprague) action report, TBS Log Sheet, Enclosure G, 2, and USS *White Plains* action report, Radio Log, Enclosure B, 1. "*Come in please* . . . ," CTU 77.4.3 action report, Enclosure G, 2. "*To any or all* . . . ," CTU 77.4.2 action report, 14. "*Don't be alarmed, Ziggy* . . . ," Morison, *History,* vol. 12, 252. "**Go after them** . . . ," CTU 77.4.2 (Stump) action report, 14. "**. . . no orders were received . . .**" and "**using the initiative . . . ,**" CTU 77.4.2 action report, 30. **Sprague played golf in a hurry,** Wukovits, *Devotion,* 38.

Chapter 18

"**Sir, what's that?**" and "**Well, it looks like somebody's shooting . . . ,**" Ed Breeding interview. "**Tell us what the hell . . . ,**" Holly Crawforth interview. *Let me the hell off this thing* and "*I'm over here* . . . ," Larry Budnick interview. "**Hey, Guns, what's going on?**" and "**Oh hell, some SOB . . . ,**" Royce Hall interview. "**My first thought was . . . ,**" Royce Hall, letter to *The CVE Piper.* "**He was not inclined to exert himself . . .**" Lewis, "Life in the Navy during World War II," 15. "**A futile gesture . . . ,**" Verling Pierson, "Fighting Fanny Bee." "**What are you doing . . . ,**" "**I am going to check . . . ,**" and "**He got in, started it up . . . ,**" Leonard Moser, letter to Harold Kight, 8, and addendum, 3; per the VC-68 action report, this pilot may have been Lt. W. J. "Lucky" Slone. *Lord, please don't let me die sitting here* . . . and background on Archer, Earl Archer interview.

Chapter 19

"**This salvo measured the carrier** . . . , USS *White Plains* action report, Enclosure A, 2; see also engineering report, Enclosure J. **Japanese recognition books,** Prados, *Combined Fleet,* 676. **Lookouts on the** *Kumano,* Prados, 672. "**At this point it did not appear . . . ,**" CTU 77.4.3 (Rear Adm. C.A.F. Sprague) action report, Enclosure C, 1. "*Stand by to form two torpedo groups* . . . ," CTU 77.4.32 (Rear Admiral Ofstie), Enclosure F (*Kitkun Bay* Log Sheet), 1; the 7:16 A.M. time is per the USS *Raymond* action report and Morison, *History,* vol. 12. However, the CTU 77.4.32 action report puts this order later, at 7:35. This later time is questionable, insofar as the *Hoel* for one was already inbound and had been severely hit on the way in at about 7:25. "**Admiral Halsey is shooting at us,**" Clint Carter interview. "**All this time I had been completely, sickeningly impotent,**" Hagen, "We Asked for the Jap Fleet," 72. **Mark 1A fire-control computer,** Navy Department, *Gunners Mate 2c Training Course,* vol. 2, 184, 191; Robert Hagen interview. "**Looks like somebody's mad at us,**" Hagen, "We Asked for the Jap Fleet," 72. *Johnston's* **pummeling of** *Kumano,* USS *Johnston* action report, 3; Hagen and Bob Chastain interviews. "**I was never as scared . . .**" Clint Carter, in *Johnston,* 41. "**What are you up to now?**" and "**Hey, take that ship over there,**" Hagen interview.

Chapter 20

"**Fire torpedoes!**" Hagen, "We Asked for the Jap Fleet," 72. *Johnston's* **torpedo attack,** USS *Johnston* action report, diagram of torpedo attack; Thomas Sullivan, in *Johnston,* 172; Robert Hagen interview. **Torpedo hits on** *Kumano,* Kurita, USSBS interrogation, 5; USS *Johnston* action report, 3; Ellsworth Welch, in *Johnston,* 182; Morison, *History,* vol. 12, 256. Welch described seeing "one of the [torpedoes] hit the fantail" (182); Prados (*Combined Fleet,* 675) wrote that the *Kumano* was hit "forward of the number ten frame," which blew away her bow.

Chapter 21

This chapter is based on eyewitness accounts of the VC-10, VC-65, and VC-68 pilots and aircrew, including accounts by Edward Huxtable, Burt Bassett, Berman Dillard,

J. F. Lischer, and William Shroyer in VC-10 action report No. 2-B; Louis Vilmer's personal narrative at www.ussgambierbay-vc10.com; Larry Budnick and Royce Hall interviews; and Y'Blood, *Little Giants,* 164–66. *The concert violinist sets considerable store* . . . , Navy Department, *Gunnery Sense,* 8–9; Royce Hall interview; Royce Hall, letter to *CVE Piper,* 3. **Roby pulled alongside Fowler's Avenger** . . . , Richard Roby interview. "**The rate of hits was quite good** . . . ," Ugaki, *Fading Victory,* 495. **Kurita was doubtless frustrated** . . . , Kurita, USSBS interrogation, 5. "**They were shooting the craziest combinations** . . . ," Roby interview.

Chapter 22

"**It seemed to take a long time** . . . ," Sam Lucas, in *Hoel,* 44. *You stand there waiting* . . . and "*Right full rudder. Meet her* . . . ," Dix, 24–25. "**He didn't designate a target** . . . ," "**It just didn't seem right to me** . . . ," and "*Taffy 33, this is Juggernaut* . . ." Copeland, *Spirit,* 39. "**Well, Sis on you, pister. Let's go!**" Copeland, 40–41.

Chapter 23

"**It was like a puppy being smacked by a truck,**" Hagen, "We Asked for the Jap Fleet," 72. *Johnston's* damage, USS *Johnston* action report, "Damage to the USS *Johnston,*" 1–2. **Just seconds before impact** . . . , Ellsworth Welch, in *Johnston,* 182. "**Block is alive,**" Edward Block, in *Johnston,* 19. "**Don't bother me now,**" Hagen, "We Asked for the Jap Fleet," 74. *Johnston's* bridge casualties: to Bechdel per Welch, in *Johnston,* 182; to Pliska per Mercer, in *Johnston,* 129; to Fox and Evans per Hagen, "We Asked for the Jap Fleet," 74; to Dixon per Edward DiGardi, in *Johnston,* 86. "**Stand by below** . . . ," Mercer, in *Johnston,* 129. "**. . . clean and professional, without the complications** . . . ," Spector, *At War at Sea,* 24. Data on Japanese ordnance is from "Japanese Naval Guns," www.warships1.com/Weapons/WNJAP_main.htm, updated Sept. 10, 2002. "**I was looking out of the director** . . . ," Hagen, "We Asked for the Jap Fleet," 72; USS *Johnston* action report, 6. "*The Johnston* **was a mess** . . . ," Hagen, 72. "*All stations—Control testing!*" Hagen, 74. "**Gun 54 declared its own war** . . . ," Bob Hollenbaugh, in *Johnston,* 105.

Chapter 24

ENEMY FORCES ATTACKING OUR FORCES . . . Prados, *Combined Fleet,* 679–80. "**It just operated all day long** . . . ," Prados, 678. "NEGATIVE. TASK FORCE 34 IS WITH CARRIER GROUPS . . . ," Potter, *Bull Halsey,* 301. "*Request Lee proceed at top speed* . . . ," Morison, *History,* vol. 12, 294. "*Fast battleships urgently needed* . . . ," and "*My situation is critical* . . . ," Prados, 682. "TURKEY TROTS TO WATER GG WHERE IS . . . ," Falk, *Decision,* 202–3; Cutler, *Battle of Leyte Gulf,* 251; Wukovits, *Devotion,* 177. "**Stop it! What the hell's the matter** . . . ," Halsey and Bryan, *Admiral,* 220.

Chapter 25

"**By now the topside of the** *Johnston* . . . ," Robert Billie, in *Johnston,* 13. **Damage control efforts aboard the** *Johnston,* USS *Johnston* action report, "Damage to the USS *Johnston,*" 1–2; Jesse Cochran and Dusty Rhodes interviews; Jesse Cochran, in *Johnston,* 64. **Death of Marley Polk,** Hagen, "We Asked for the Jap Fleet," 74. "**Trying to climb out was a fireman by the name of West** . . ." "**It was an awful sight to see** . . . ," and "**With little help from our battle lantern** . . . ," Bob Sochor, in *Johnston,* 163–64. "**It was the first time in my life** . . . ," Hagen, "We Asked for the Jap Fleet," 74. "**I had heard all along that destroyers were expendable** . . . ," Everett Lindorff, in *Hoel,* 38. **Kight looked on awestruck as the destroyers fell into line** . . . , Harold Kight interview.

Chapter 26

This chapter and the next, covering the *Hoel*'s torpedo sortie and devastating first hits, are drawn mostly from the written accounts of survivors in the *Hoel*'s crew memory book, the ship's action report, Lieutenant Dix's *Missing Off Samar*, and interviews with Myles Barrett, Clarence Hood, Sam Lucas, and Derrill Thompson. *Bridge, this is Combat . . . Gunnery Control, this is Combat . . .*, and *Damn it was good to hear them . . .*, Dix, 27. *They haven't hit us yet*, Dix, 28. *Oh, Jesus, this is it!* Dix, 28. The blast spattered the *Hoel*'s passageways . . . ," Bob DeSpain, personal narrative. "Cruiser observed blowing up and sinking," Morison, *History*, vol. 12, 258; Field, *Japanese*, 102. "We'll go in with the destroyers . . . ," Hagen, "We Asked for the Jap Fleet," 74. Owing to steering difficulties, the destroyer made a complete circle . . . , Robert Hagen interview. *Oh, dear Lord, I'm in for a swim*, Hagen, 74.

Chapter 27

"Tube One—" "One aye!" Dix, 29. "Guys were piling out of there screaming," Jim Norris, in *Hoel*, 56–56. "Stuff just flew all over us . . . ," Hugh Coffelt, in *Hoel*, 7. Per Dix, 31, the *Hoel* was locked into a port turn; the ship's action report states that it was a starboard turn, but that paragraph has been hand-annotated, "Delete." "Get set to fire . . ." and "Tube Two—train out to port . . . ," Dix, 31. "Too much was happening to stand . . . ," Dix, 31. Morison identifies the target of the *Hoel*'s second torpedo spread as the *Haguro*. Though one disagrees with a grand master only at his grave peril, I have departed here from Morison's narrative, which has the *Haguro* leading the Japanese cruiser column and thus being the *Hoel*'s victim. The *Hoel*'s action report states that the torpedoes struck the lead heavy cruiser, but makes no claim as to its class. Field's account (*Japanese*, 103–7) has the *Tone* in the lead and the *Haguro* third in a column of four. However, there is no evidence that either the *Haguro* or the *Tone* took a torpedo hit in this action—see Prados, *Combined Fleet*, 673–76. At 7:57 *Haguro* lookouts spotted two torpedo tracks passing astern; Prados, 676. One of the photo sections of this book features a handsome shot of the *Haguro* withdrawing at flank speed, unimpeded, at about 10:50. The authors of the action report of the *Hoel*—and of the *Johnston*, *Samuel B. Roberts*, and other lost ships—may be excused for any ambiguity: They wrote them several days after the battle, after extended trauma, and without the aid of logs or other records cast adrift in the Philippine Sea. As with many other particulars of this action, the truth may lie beyond our reach. "Put the sun on your port beam," Fred Green, in *Hoel*, 24.

Chapter 28

"The Japs would fire their big guns . . ." Harold Kight interview. "They oughta fire that thing underwater . . . ," "Just hold on a little longer . . . ," and "The Japs were now firing at us from three sides . . . ," Sprague, "The Japs Had Us on the Ropes," 114. "I must admit admiration . . . ," Koyanagi, in O'Connor, 114. Pilots were cautioned not to hit the inbound American ships, VC-10 action report, No. 2-B, Lt. J. R. Jackson narrative. VC-3's exploits are per Y'Blood, *Little Giants*, 170; the VC-3 action report; Murphy, "I Remember," and Earl Archer interview. "This is 81 Georgia . . ." Thomas Van Brunt, "A Bird's-Eye View." "How those Japs could shoot so many guns . . . ," Murphy, 15. Damage to *Kalinin Bay* is from the USS *Kalinin Bay* action report; Keeler, "Memories"; CTU 77.4.3 action report; and Morris Turner interview. "But above all others we could hear men screaming," Keeler. *The Wildcat pilots were given a free hand to strafe . . .*, Sprague, "The Japs Had Us on the Ropes," 116. "The attack was almost incessant . . . ," Field, *Japanese*, 102.

Chapter 29

Lt. (j.g.) **Thomas Lupo background and narrative** are from Thomas Lupo interview. His account of the Tacloban incident was confirmed by his gunner in an Earl Gifford interview. **"Like chunks of vanilla ice cream in a sarsaparilla soda,"** Falk, *Decision,* 185 (unattributed). **"Like a flight of birds at the first crack of a shotgun,"** *"Navy planes, Navy planes...,"* Hubbard, "Scrub Team at Tacloban," 10–11. See also Farris, "Tacloban."

Chapter 30

The *Heermann*'s **7:54 A.M. torpedo attack** was directed at a *Tone*-class cruiser, "the leading ship in a column of four large ships," USS *Heermann* action report, 9. Morison asserts that it was the *Haguro*—see *History*, vol. 12, 259—but more likely it was the *Tone*. The USS *Heermann* action report later states, "We . . . fired at one heavy cruiser positively identified as the *Tone* class. Seven torpedoes were fired at this cruiser with unknown results" (17). **"It was an odd day—one moment the sun was shining . . . ,"** Whitney, "Battle of Samar," 13. **". . . illuminated the entire ocean . . . ,"** USS *Heermann* action report, Enclosure B, gunnery officer's report, 2. Hathaway **"wish [he] had a periscope"** and **"Everything looked rosy . . . ,"** USS *Heermann* action report, 5. **"The guns of the leading Jap blazed . . . ,"** Whitney, "Battle of Samar," 13. **"My exercise is completed. Over,"** CTU 77.4.3 (C.A.F. Sprague) action report, Enclosure G, TBS Log Sheet, 4. **"WATCH OUT FOR TORPEDO TRACKS!"** Prados, *Combined Fleet,* 676. **". . . it felt like a month to me,"** Ugaki, *Fading Victory,* 493. **"All small boys go in and launch torpedo attack,"** CTU 77.4.3 action report, TBS Log Sheet, 3. **"Admiral, someday somebody is going to forget we're boys . . . ,"** Copeland, *Spirit,* 30. **"Captain, may I open fire?"** and **"God damn it, Mr. Burton . . . ,"** Copeland, 41. **"We got her!"** Copeland, 42. Cox (*Battle off Samar*) states the *Roberts*'s victim was the *Chokai*. The USS *Samuel B. Roberts* action report indicates an *Aoba* class cruiser, though no such ships were with Kurita off Samar. **"All engines back full,"** Ed DiGardi, in *Johnston,* 86. **"Our stern dug deep . . . ,"** Bob Deal, in *Johnston,* 70. **"I could have thrown a potato and hit that kid . . . ,"** Harold Whitney interview. **"We have been straddled for the last half hour . . . ,"** CTU 77.4.2 (Stump) action report, 15.

Chapter 31

"The ship felt like it was shaking apart," Charles Landreth, in *Johnston,* 120–21. **"I was sure the next salvo was coming into the pilothouse,"** Neil Dethlefs, in *Johnston,* 75. **"It didn't appear we would be alive much longer"** and **"I could tell by looking at him . . . ,"** Landreth, 120–21. *You heard the whistling whine . . .* Dix, *Missing Off Samar,* 32. **"The men were coming out mortally scalded . . . ,"** Robert Prater, in *Hoel,* 69–70. Cdr. A. F. Beyer, Jr., **spotted an American ship taking a terrific beating . . . a "curtain of flashes,"** USS *Raymond* action report, Enclosure A, 2; Beyer's sighting occurred between 7:56 and 8:14, as the *Hoel* was being hit repeatedly. The *Dennis* spotted a U.S. destroyer being hit at 8:02; USS *Dennis*, Deck Log, 409. **"Lying on the deck, I looked down at myself . . . ,"** Bob DeSpain, personal narrative. **"He looked up toward the bridge as if to say . . . ,"** Dix, 33–34. **"They took no life jackets, left rafts and nets . . . ,"** Dix, 35. **"The force of the explosion was so great . . . ,"** Roy Lozano, in *Hoel,* 42. **"Money was fluttering everywhere . . . ,"** Myles Barrett interview. **"Well, I sure as hell can see that"** and **"As far as accomplishing anything decisive . . . ,"** Hagen, "We Asked for the Jap Fleet," 74.

Chapter 32

Gambier Bay's plight, USS Gambier Bay action report; contact with Taffy 2 destroyers, E. Don Heric interview; CTU 77.4.2 action report, 15; Naylor, Rangefinder, 172; DesDiv 94, Combined TBS Log, Oct. 25, 1944. "I heard flight leaders from the other CVE group . . . ," VC-10 air action report No. 2-B. Huxtable narrative. The volume of ordnance flying the ship's way . . . , Bill Cuming interview. Lost at sea, age 19 years, Hoyt, 201–2. "I'm ruined, I'm ruined," "When are we gonna see some real action?" and "Well, buddy, is this enough action for you?" Hoyt, Men of the Gambier Bay, 203. "Small boys on my starboard quarter, intercept . . . ," CTU 77.4.3 action report, TBS Log Sheet, Enclosure G, 4. "ONLY ONE ENGINE X NO GYRO X NO RADARS," USS Heermann action report, 9. "As I listened, it became evident . . . ," Hathaway, "The Battle as I Saw It," 41. Each time a new salvo landed near, she was doused in a different color, Harold Whitney, "Battle of Samar"; USS Heermann action report, 22. Round after round I take from [Ralph] Sacco . . . , Urbanski, in Heermann, n.p. "God, let me see my wife and son . . . ," Robert Rutter letter to the author, June 22, 2003; Whitney, "Battle of Samar," 14; Hathaway, 116. "Suddenly all thought was lost . . ." and "Heermann is smashing through the sea . . . ," Urbanski, in Heermann. "We were so far down by the head . . . ," Hathaway, 116. Litter of cigarette cartons and toilet paper . . . , Rutter, letter. "Just put more shoring in there . . . ," Whitney, 3. The navigator . . . as if he had been maimed with a shotgun blast, Phillips, God Rode Destroyer 'X,' 35. "Continue what you're doing . . . ," Whitney, 2. "I'll take it," Whitney interview; Whitney, "Battle of Samar," 14. "The most courageous order I've ever heard," and "Commerce firing on that cruiser, Hagen." Hagen, "We Asked for the Jap Fleet," 74. "A most amazing thing happened . . . ," USS Johnston action report, 4. "They were sleek, streamlined . . . ," Hagen, 74. "More shells! More shells!" and "I'm sure glad there ain't no Japs from Texas," Hagen, 74; Clint Carter, in Johnston, 41. "Commander Evans, feeling like the skipper of a battleship . . . ," Hagen, 74. DesRon 10 had "accomplished the great feat of sinking . . . ," Ugaki, Fading Victory, 495.

Chapter 33

"Cruiser blows up and sinks," Field, Japanese, 107. Lieutenant Sanders caught up in the rigging, and "The word was to abandon ship," Willard Frenn, personal narrative. 2. "They were burned beyond belief!" Richard Santos, in Hoel, 75. "The next thing I knew, I was lying . . . ," Paul Miranda, in Hoel, 52. "I could see that he was seriously wounded . . . ," John Oracz, in Hoel, 60; Oracz remembers Lieutenant Streuter's body going overboard, but Miranda recalls it resting against the portside rail. "The ship was listing severely to port . . . ," L. E. Walton, in Hoel, 82. When I woke up I was still in the CIC . . . , Everett Lindorff, in Hoel, 38–39. "The compartment was filled with the smell of burnt gunpowder . . . ," There were quite a few of us by the gun mount . . . , and "Somehow I knew they were abandoning the ship . . . ," Bob Wilson, in Hoel, 88–89. "We lost many of our shipmates to that one salvo . . . ," Jack Creamer, in Hoel, 15. On that side I had a chance to see so many more of the men dead . . . , Hugh Coffelt, in Hoel, 7–8. "That was the last we saw of friendly ships," Dix, Missing off Samar, 33. Hoel's final minutes . . . , "one of those disheartening things . . ." We had to pass her by . . . , Copeland, Spirit, 44.

Chapter 34

"Look at that little DE committing suicide," Pierson, "Fighting Fanny Bee." Whoever was out on the advance flank . . . , Copeland, Spirit, 45. "I came a little bit left, and when the range was closed . . . ," Copeland, 43. The account of the Roberts's duel with the *Chikuma* and the exploits of Gun 52 is from Copeland, 43–50. Carr's squad in Gun 52 popped off 324 rounds, USS *Samuel B. Roberts* action report; the ship fired a total of 608 rounds during the battle. "We had the Jap cruiser on fire from the start of her bridge . . . ," Copeland, 45; USS *Samuel B. Roberts* action report; Burton amplifying report, 2.

Chapter 35

Pyzdrowski wondered whether the Japanese might try to board, Hoyt, *Men of the Gambier Bay*, 206. "Need a drink?" and "Better get these guys ready to go," Hoyt, 207. Background on Japanese battleship gunnery and *Tone's* firing on *Gambier Bay*, Haruo Mayuzumi, letter to Henry A. Pyzdrowski.

Chapter 36

"Captain, there's fourteen-inch splashes . . . ," Copeland, *Spirit*, 45. "All engines back full!" "That was the one time . . . ," and "She just kind of lay down . . . ," Copeland, 46. Katsur "felt as though I were a bedsheet on a clothesline . . ." Bill Katsur, untitled narrative, 5. "An absolute flop on the deck force," Copeland, 48; George Bray and Tom Stevenson interviews. "Mr. Roberts, would you please take the wheel . . . ," Copeland, 49–50. Destruction of Gun 52, Bray interview; Bray disagrees with Copeland's account of these events, which the captain did not witness. "I felt sorry for him. He was running . . . ," Copeland, 56; Bray interview. "It seemed as if the whole ship . . . ," Copeland, 50. "As far as I could see, the ship was as nice . . . ," Copeland, 51; Bray interview and correspondence. "Stand by for tor—!" Dudley Moylan interview. *I can see her right now. She had taken a terrific beating . . .* , Copeland, 51. "I am sorry to hear about H. P. Inge . . . ," John LeClercq, letter to his mother, Oct. 9, 1944. "The few things you saw him do and say . . . ," Mittendorff, letter to Mrs. LeClercq. Tom Stevenson background, Stevenson interview.

Chapter 37

Hoel's final moments, Myles Barrett, Clarence Hood, Sam Lucas, and Derrill Thompson interviews; Dix, *Missing Off Samar*. The sound of water lapping at the raft . . . and *Good God, haven't they done enough to us today?* Dix, 38. *Hoel's* Emirau incident, Hood interview; Dix, 39. And see the men, how tall they seem . . . , Dix, 39. The Japs are throwing grenades at us, Barrett interview. "My God, look at that thing!" Glenn Parkin, "Historical Account." "Passing a fairly big dark red slick . . . ," Ugaki, *Fading Victory*, 495. Hellcat attacks, Parkin. It made us bitter then to watch that strength, Dix, 41.

Chapter 38

Triangulating from the source material to determine who was shooting at whom at any given point during this battle has been one of the challenges of writing this narrative. Taking the next step and drawing causal links between hits claimed and damage suffered is doubly difficult. In untangling the thicket of evidence concerning the cruisers *Chokai* and *Chikuma*, Tully's analysis in "Solving Some Mysteries of Leyte Gulf" has been helpful. "ENGINE OUT OF COMMISSION," Tully, citing *Haguro* action report; Morison, *History*, vol. 12, 266, 284; Ugaki, *Fading Victory*, 494–95. The account of the U.S. air attacks is from USS *Kitkun Bay* action report, Enclosure I (VC-5 action report) and CTU 77.4.2 action report, 15. "There was a burst of flame and simultaneously a column of water . . . ," CruDiv 7 War Diary, as quoted in Tully, "Solving," 249–50. "ONE PROPELLER, SPEED EIGHTEEN KNOTS, UNABLE TO STEER," Prados, *Combined Fleet*, 675. "Heavy steam and black smoke rose to five hundred feet . . . ," *Kitkun Bay* action report, Enclosure I, 3. "DIRECT BOMB HIT IN FORWARD MACHINERY SPACES . . . ," Tully, "Solving," 255. "*Scratch one CA,*" VC-21 action report No. 66. "The cruiser was seen to smoke heavily . . . ," VC-21 action report No. 66; Tully, "Solving," 255. Sinking of the *Gambier Bay,* USS *Gambier Bay* action report; Vieweg narrative. *How many more are going to go?* Larry Budnick interview.

Chapter 39

"Merc, straighten my leg out," Bill Mercer, in *Johnston,* 129. "The place was full of smoke . . . ," Hagen, "We Asked for the Jap Fleet," 74. Kurita's state of mind and evaluation of circumstances is from Kurita, USSBS interrogation; Field, *Japanese,* 109, 116, 123–26; Morison, *History,* vol. 12, 296–300; and Ugaki, *Fading Victory,* 497. Herman Wouk's well-researched analysis in his novel *War and Remembrance* is also of note. "Outfought by pygmies . . . ," Field, 126. "*My situation is critical . . .*" Prados, *Combined Fleet,* 682. "Anxieties are the test and penalty of greatness . . ." and *Strenuous, unrelaxing pursuit . . . ,* Mahan, *Mahan on Naval Warfare,* 80. *Rendezvous, my course north, speed 20, Yamato* action report, per Morison, vol. 12, 297. "*All ships reassemble*" and "*Gradually reassemble,*" Morison, vol. 12, 297 n. 15.

Chapter 40

Tex Waldrop intercepting torpedoes, Ciolek, "What Did You Do," 11; USS *St. Lo* action report, 4. "Goddamn it, boys, they're getting away!" and "I could not believe my eyes . . . ," Sprague, "The Japs Had Us on the Ropes," 116. "I had really done some deep thinking . . ." and "I don't expect we're going to see the sunset . . . ," Bill Brooks interview. He found a quiet place to pray . . . , Van Brunt, "A Bird's-Eye View," 4.

Chapter 41

"I would advise the captain to abandon ship," Moore, "A Japanese Admiral's narrative," 4. "Abandon ship, men. Well done." Moore, 5. "Under fire, you're thinking about your family . . . ," Tom Stevenson interview. In *Spirit* Bob Copeland has Stevenson going belowdecks with George Schaffer to carry out the ship destruction bill; Stevenson remembers that it was Charles Natter. "All of a sudden there was another big blast . . . ," Richard Rohde interview. Sammy's disappearance is from Copeland, 56, and George Bray interview. "Now, Bob, I want you to go down . . . ," and "Captain, I'm not leaving until you leave," Copeland, 53. "It gave me an awfully hurt and crushed feeling . . . ," Copeland, 53. "It really made me sick at my stomach . . ." and "We ripped blue chambray shirts . . . ," Copeland, 53–54. "Captain, do you think I'll live?" Copeland, 54. "I don't think there was a whole bone in them," "The ship had been a very live thing . . . ," and "That one picture . . . ," Copeland, 54. "It had taken all the heart out of me," Copeland, 55. The death of Paul Henry Carr is per Copeland, 55, and George Bray interview.

Chapter 42

"How do you go about getting out of here?" Copeland, *Spirit,* 57. The rest of the account of the *Samuel B. Roberts* is from George Bray, Bud Comet, Vince Goodrich, Dudley Moylan, Richard Rohde, Tom Stevenson, and Jack Yusen interviews. "We were the proudest ship in the fleet," Stevenson interview. "Boys, take off your hats . . . ," Ray Chambless, letter to Geroge Bray. "As first lieutenant he knew . . ." and "It seemed as if the bottom had dropped out . . . ," Copeland, 58. "There was going to have to be rationing . . . ," Moore, "A Japanese Admiral's narrative," 6.

Chapter 43

"Water columns were substantially higher . . . ," Bob Deal, in *Johnston*, 70. "It felt like a freight train's coal box . . . ," Allen Johnson, in *Johnston*, 115. "An avalanche of shells," USS *Johnston* action report, 4. "When I jumped over, I had two thoughts . . . ," Dusty Rhodes, in *Johnston*, 155. *I peered out and couldn't see a living soul* . . . , Hagen, "We Asked for the Jap Fleet," 74. "I recall Marquard took his comb . . . ," Bill Mercer, in *Johnston*, 130. "Mr. Hagen, we got off all ten . . . ," Hagen, 74. *I would watch for belches of fire* . . . , Ellsworth Welch, in *Johnston*, 183. "There was a terrible, blinding yellow flash" and "Everyone who was able to abandon ship . . . ," Bob Sochor, in *Johnston*, 165. In his essay "Experience" Ralph Waldo Emerson wrote, "So much of our time is preparation, so much is routine, and so much retrospect that the pith of each man's genius contracts itself to very few hours."

Chapter 44

Sprague received a voice message assuring him help was on the way is from Sprague's marginalia in his copy of Woodward, *Battle for Leyte Gulf,* 171. See also Morison, *History,* vol. 12, 294–96. "I told Strick that I was sticking close . . ." and "Kid, I have never seen anything like this," Bill Mercer, in *Johnston*, 130. "As I watched, she started to sink . . . ," Orin Vadnais, in *Johnston*, 179. "The skin was hanging from his arms and hands . . ." and "Boy, I sure am," Neil Dethlefs, in *Johnston*, 77. "He was very young and religious" and 'Take your last look at the *Johnston*,' Bob Sochor, in *Johnston*, 165. "Seeing my home go down . . . ," Ellsworth Welch, in *Johnston*, 184. "I still remember that helpless feeling . . . ," Bob Chastain, in *Johnston*, 48. *A giant enema,* Clint Carter, in *Johnston*, 42. "They were watching us . . . ," Chastain, 48. "It appeared to me that every man on her deck . . . ," Carter, 42. Japanese saluting, Dethlefs, 77. "As she eased by us . . ." and "Three years of war and they were still eating . . . ," Carter, 42. "I thought my body had been blown in half," Charles Landreth, in *Johnston*, 122. *All ships except* Shigure *went down* . . . , Morison, vol. 12, 238.

Chapter 45

"Okay, we'll try that . . . ," Van Brunt interview. "Sir, that's a Jap," Crawforth interview. Kamikaze hit on *St. Lo,* McKenna, "Narrative of Events"; USS *St. Lo* action report; Morison, *History,* vol. 12, 302; Reynolds et al., "America's Greatest Naval Battle," Jan. 27, 1945, 70, 72; and Larry Budnick, Holly Crawforth, John Getas, and Thomas B. Van Brunt interviews.

Part III

Chapter 46

This account of the *Roberts* survivors in the water is based on Copeland, *Spirit,* and on George Bray, Bud Comet, Richard Rohde, Tom Stevenson, and Jack Yusen interviews.

Chapter 47

This narrative of the air attack on the departing Center Force is drawn from the action reports of CTU 77.4.2, VC-5 (Enclosures H and I in the USS *Kitkun Bay* action report), VC-20, VC-21, VC-65, VC-68, and VC-75, as well as from Y'Blood, *Little Giants,* 237–41, and William Brooks, Joseph Downs, Thomas Lupo, Richard Roby, and Thomas B. Van Brunt interviews. "Oh man, you got her, you got her!" Downs interview.

Chapter 48

"Hey, what's for chow?" Arnold, "Come On Boys," 123–24. **It seems his mission lasted longer than his memory:** Tom Stevenson told me that he met this pilot at a Taffy 3 reunion in Charleston several years ago. The pilot, unable to land on his CVE after the battle, had been diverted to an airfield on Leyte. By the time he landed, he had forgotten the coordinates of the survivors. "I was trying to survive too," the flier said to Stevenson at the time. **Death of Charles Natter:** Bob Copeland learned the details of Natter's demise from John Conway after the war (Copeland, *Spirit*, 59). **Fifty shark fins cutting the surface, and** *I've read a lot of stories* . . . , Copeland, 59. **Copeland's conversation with Bob Roberts** is from Copeland, 60.

Chapter 49

"Our thoughts were, *3,000 ships . . . It won't be long now*," Ellsworth Welch, in *Johnston*, 184. Like "an eighteen-year-old boy going on forty," Bill Mercer, in *Johnston*, 131. **A** *Johnston* **sailor . . . asked to be put out of his misery . . .** , Milt Pehl interview; see also Pehl, in *Johnston*, 149, which does not describe a mercy killing but states only that the sailor "succumbed and was finally at peace." **"Why don't we all sing? . . . I remember a few people started singing . . ."** Richard Rohde interview.

Chapter 50

God, if you get me out of this . . . , Tom Stevenson interview. "It seemed very much like an entire week of darkness," Moore, "A Japanese Admiral's narrative," 7. "The interior of Samar must be made a howling wilderness," "Remembering Balangiga," in Jim Zwick, ed., *Sentanaryo/Centennial: The Philippine Revolution and Philippine-American War*, www.boondocksnet.com/centennial/balangiga.html. The *pulajan* insurgency . . . "the bloody island," Hurley, *Jungle Patrol*. "What had been a very noisy group . . . ," Harold Beresonsky, in *Johnston*, 9. "My contract with the Navy was to fight the enemy, not sharks," Ellsworth Welch, in *Johnston*, 184.

Chapter 51

"On that raft we were just forty-nine very wretched human beings . . . ," Copeland, *Spirit*, 61. "Too far away to make it in by night," Copeland, 62. Requested "permission to go below," Everett Roberts, autobiographical narrative, 2. "Object ho! . . . What is it, Cantrell? . . . I see a big white cottage . . . ," Copeland, 63. "Fucking captain's no good . . . ," William Katsur interview; Katsur narrative, 9; Copeland refers to this incident obliquely (59).

Chapter 52

"I'll buy you a beer," Charles Landreth, in *Johnston*, 123. **Other incidents of madness among the** *Johnston*'s **crew** are from the accounts of Clyde Burnett, Jesse Cochran, John Mostowy, and Don Starks in *Johnston*. "Skau, take a good look at that ship," Copeland, *Spirit*, 63. "Who won the World Series? . . . St. Louis, God damn it!" Wukovits, *Devotion*, 186; Levy, "USS PC 623 Crewman," Yusen interview. "Men, it looks as if we're going to be picked up by the Japs . . . ," Moore, 10. "Hilarious happiness," Moore, 10.

Chapter 53

Rescue mission of PC-623: Levy, "USS PC 623 Crewman," PC 623 War Diary and Deck Log; Morison, *History*, vol. 12, 313–16. "I informed the skipper and the helmsman that I had not been properly relieved of the deck and that I would not accept Captain Baxter's order . . . ," Levy. "What are you looking for?" "Just a place to lay down," George Bray interview. "I took about three swipes and fainted,"

Copeland, *Spirit*, 67. "Get the hell out of the way," Copeland, 67–68. "The place was like the Black Hole of Calcutta" and "My God, that dog has drank a lot of water . . . ," Copeland, 68.

Chapter 54

This account of Neil Dethlefs swimming ashore is from Dethlefs's own account in *Johnston*, 73–82. The ordeal of Bill Shaw and Orin Vadnais is recounted in Vadnais, *Johnston*, 178–80, and in "Bronx Youth and 3 Rescued After Epic Escape off Samar," *New York World Telegram*, Nov. 17, 1944.

Part IV

I want you to know I think you wrote the most glorious page . . . ," Halsey's words are from Sprague's letter to his wife, May 1945, quoted in Reneau, *Remembered*, 171. In that letter Sprague referred to Halsey as "The gentleman who failed to keep his appointment last October." He continued: "He [Halsey] then went on and was so flattering it was embarrassing. All I could mumble was 'I hope your praise is deserved.' " Reneau, 171.

Chapter 55

"This was Trafalgar; it was Tsushima . . ." Pratt, *Fleet Against Japan*, 242. "Our defeat at Leyte was tantamount . . . ," Morison, *History*, vol. 12, 338. "The vision of Sprague's three destroyers . . . ," Wouk, *War and Remembrance*, 1285. "The history of the United States Navy records . . . ," Cox, *Battle off Samar*, 165. "This desperate expedient . . . ," CTU 77.4.3 action report, Enclosure C, 3. "This was a disgrace, and I blame Kinkaid . . . ," Sprague, marginalia in his copy of Woodward, *Battle for Leyte Gulf*, 216. "The kind of man I would have been proud to call my father," Copeland, *Spirit*, 69. "I had to admit that I didn't know the answer . . . ," Julius Steinberg, *Heermann*, n.p. "In summation, the failure of the enemy main body . . ." CTU 77.4.3 action report, Enclosure B, 2. "You are a wonderful crew . . . ," Hathaway as quoted in Harold Whitney, Jan. 7, 2003 narrative, 3. "I knew there were some big battles going on . . . ," "It was a sort of homecoming . . . ," Harriet Copeland interview. "I know things were different when he came home . . . ," Suzanne Hartley interview. "I said forget it. I can make a living. I don't need your disability," Earl Archer interview. "He really rung it out . . . ," Leonard Moser, letter to Harold Kight, Apr. 25, 1986, 13–16.

Chapter 56

"He had two black eyes . . . ," Patricia Sprague Reneau interview in "Taffy 3 Remembered" videotape. "The Navy years were over for the Sprague daughters . . . ," Reneau, *Remembered*, 221. Most of the escort carriers were decommissioned . . . and sold as scrap: ships' histories are from *Dictionary of American Naval Fighting Ships*, www.hazegray.org/danfs. "I hold no hope that he is alive . . . ," J. M. Reid, letter to Mrs. LeClercq, Jan. 16, 1945. "Your successful fight against great odds . . . ," Nimitz's letter to the survivors is quoted in Ciolek, "What Did You Do." *For distinguishing himself by extraordinary heroism,* Reneau, 237. "It never occurred to me that Halsey . . ." and "What are you trying to do . . . ?" Wukovits, *Devotion*, 190. *"It can be announced with assurance that the Japanese Navy has been beaten . . ."* and "Though he participated in only portions . . . ," Wukovits, 189. "I wondered how Kinkaid had let 'Ziggy' Sprague get caught like this," Halsey and Bryan, *Admiral*, 219. "Our Navy, for reasons that are clear to me . . . ," Sprague, letter to Fitch, Sept. 26, 1947, quoted in Reneau, 185. "You've done well. But don't dwell on it," Bud Comet interview. **Taffy 3 reunions began in 1946:** Thanks to Myles

Barrett for a copy of these early "Taffy Three Reunion Notes." *Gambier Bay* veterans' 1977 Philippines pilgrimage, videotape courtesy of Hank Pyzdrowski. "**They're telling us that they know we're here,**" quoted in *Old Shipmates,* newsletter of the USS *Gambier Bay*/VC-10 Survivors Association. (First Quarter 1978), 35. "**We now commit this capsule to the deep,**" *Old Shipmates* (First Quarter 1978), 36. "**Kurita's role at Leyte . . . ,**" Wouk, *War and Remembrance,* 1280. A "**gigantic enemy task force . . . ,**" Field, *Japanese,* 100. *I have the honor to write the Men of the* Gambier Bay . . . , Haruo Mayuzumi, letter to Henry A. Pyzdrowski, 10, 11, 14. "**Dad, wait till you see what I've got . . . ,**" Jack Yusen interview. "**I think the more of us that get together . . . ,**" Gene Saunders, letter to Harold Kight, 1. "**Oh man, I like that guy,**" Joe Downs interview. "**At this time in my life, one of my greatest pleasures . . . ,**" Van Brunt, "A Bird's-Eye View," Paul Rinn told of FFG-58's ordeal in a speech at the 2001 joint reunion of the *Samuel B. Roberts* and *Johnston/Hoel* survivors associations in Albuquerque. Rinn, now retired from the Navy, is a vice president at Whitney, Bradley and Brown. "**I'm still trying to impress my dad. . . . the way I've conducted myself,**" Bud Comet interview.

Photo and Art Credits

TITLE PAGE
Wildcats from VC-5 scramble on the *Kitkun Bay* (National Archives)

ENDPAPERS
The destroyer *Heermann* (foreground) and the destroyer escort *John C. Butler* making smoke (National Archives)

PART OPENERS
Part I: National Archives
Part II: National Archives
Part III: © John Downs
Part IV: U.S. Navy

PORTRAIT PHOTOGRAPHS OF *HOEL* AND *JOHNSTON* CREW MEMBERS APPEARING THROUGHOUT
© Bill Mercer, *The Fighting and Sinking of the USS Johnston DD-557 As Told by Her Crew*, Johnston/Hoel Association, Sept. 1991; and Keith McKay, *At Rest 4,000 Fathoms Under the Waves, USS Hoel DD-553: The Story of a Valiant Ship's Last Hours and the Survivors Who Manned Her to the End*, Johnston/Hoel Association, 1990.

PHOTO AND ART INSERT I

Page One
Background poster of Fleet Adm. William F. Halsey (Naval Historical Center)
Inset photograph of Fleet Adm. William F. Halsey (National Archives)
Inset photograph of Gen. Douglas MacArthur and Vice Adm. Thomas C. Kinkaid (National Archives)

Pages Two and Three
Background photograph of the Center Force battleship *Kongo* (Naval Historical Center)
Background photograph of the Center Force flagship *Yamato* (Naval Historical Center)
Inset photograph of Vice Adm. Takeo Kurita (Naval Historical Center)

Pages Four and Five
Background photograph of escort-class carrier riding heavy seas (U.S. Navy)
Inset photograph of escort-class carrier riding heavy seas (U.S. Navy)
Inset photograph of Rear Adm. Clifton A. F. ("Ziggy") Sprague (National Archives)
Photograph of Ens. John S. LeClercq (courtesy of Robert LeClercq)

Pages Six and Seven
Annapolis portrait photograph of Cdr. Ernest E. Evans (U.S. Naval Academy)
Background photograph of the *Johnston's* commissioning ceremony (Naval Historical Center)
Inset photographs of Cmdr. Ernest E. Evans (Naval Historical Center)
Inset photograph of the USS *Johnston* (Naval Historical Center)

Pages Eight and Nine
Background photograph of the USS *Hoel* (National Archives)
Inset photographs of Cdr. Leon Kintberger (courtesy of Mrs. Dora Kintberger Schleider)
Inset photographs of Paul Henry Carr (courtesy of Peggy Carr Dodd)

Pages Ten and Eleven
Background photograph of the USS *Samuel B. Roberts* (Naval Historical Center)
Inset photograph of Lt. Cmdr. Robert W. Copeland (Naval Historical Center)
Inset photograph of sailors on the *Fanshaw Bay* (collection of Harold Knight)

Pages Twelve and Thirteen
Background art of FM-2 Wildcat strafing the battleship *Yamato* (watercolor by John Downs)
Inset photograph of Ens. William C. Brooks (courtesy of Bill Brooks)
Inset photograph of Jack Yusen (courtesy of Jack Yusen)
Inset photograph of Dick Rohde (courtesy of Dick Rohde)

Pages Fourteen and Fifteen
Background photograph of the USS *Heermann* (National Archives)
Inset photographs of Cdr. Amos T. Hathaway (U.S. Navy)
Inset photograph of Gun Captain Clint Carter aboard the USS *Johnston* (collection of Will Carter)
Inset photograph of Lt. Tom Stevenson (courtesy of Tom Stevenson)
Inset photograph of Lt. Robert C. Hagen (courtesy of Bob Hagen)

Page Sixteen
Background photograph of the *Gambier Bay* under fire (National Archives)

PHOTO AND ART INSERT II

Page One
Photograph of Wildcats on the *Kitkun Bay* (National Archives)
Photograph of the destroyer *Heermann* and destroyer escort *John C. Butler* making smoke (National Archives)
Photograph of the *Gambier Bay* fleeing eastward (National Archives)
Photograph of Taffy 3 jeep carrier (collection of David C. Wright)

Pages Two and Three
Inset photograph of TBM Avenger pilot Lt. Earl "Blue" Archer (courtesy of Blue Archer)
Background photograph of Wildcat pilot Lt. Richard Roby (National Archives)
Inset photograph of Cdr. Edward J. Huxtable with his crew (National Archives)
Photograph of FM-2 Wildcat fighters from the *White Plains* (National Archives)
Background photograph of an Avenger torpedo bomber taking off from the *Marcus Island* (U.S. Navy)
Pilot's-eye sketch of the Japanese pursuit (National Archives)

Pages Four and Five
Background photograph of an Avenger torpedo bomber flying over the *Marcus Island* (U.S. Navy)
Inset photograph of gun camera photos (National Archives)
Inset photograph of Lt. Ken Hippe (National Archives)
Inset artist's rendering of *St. Lo* Wildcats strafing the *Yamato* (watercolor © John Downs)
Inset photograph of Lt. Burt Bassett amd Cdr. Edward Huxtable (National Archives)
Inset photograph of a *St. Lo* Wildcat at the Tacloban airdrome on Leyte Island (National Archives)

Pages Six and Seven
Background photograph of the *Nagato* withdrawing following Kurita's order (U.S. Navy)
Inset photograph of a *Kongo*-class battleship taken by a *Kadashan Bay* flier (National Archives)
Inset photograph of the *Yamato* narrowly avoiding a torpedo (National Archives)
Bottom left photograph of Japanese cruiser fishtailing (National Archives)

Pages Eight and Nine
Background photograph of the *Gambier Bay* listing to port (National Archives)
Inset photograph of the battleships *Nagato* and *Yamato* taken by *Kadashan Bay* airman (National Archives)
Inset photograph of the *Chikuma* as photographed by a *Petrof Bay* pilot (National Archives)
Inset photograph of the flight deck crew of the *White Plains* (National Archives)
Photograph of explosions aboard the *St. Lo* (bottom left) (National Archives)
Inset of official declassified action report for the Battle off Samar (National Archives)
Photograph of the *Chikuma* as photographed by a *Natoma Bay* flier (National Archives)

Pages Ten and Eleven
Background photograph of a wounded sailor (National Archives)
Inset photograph of Admiral Sprague awarding a medal to a sailor (National Archives)
Photograph of Lt. Larry Budnick (U.S. Navy, collection of Larry Budnick)
Photograph of a burial at sea on the *Kalinin Bay* (National Archives)

Pages Twelve and Thirteen
Present day photographs of Tom Stevenson, Dudley Moylan, Bill Brooks, Joe Downs, Allen Johnson, Larry Budnick, Bill Mercer, Paul Miranda and Dick Santos (the author)
Photograph of *Fanshaw Bay* veterans (Sharon Hornfischer)

Pages Fourteen and Fifteen
Background photograph of the *Hoel/Roberts/Johnston* monument at Ft. Rosencrans National Cemetery (courtesy of the USS *St. Lo* CVE-63/VC-65 Survivors Association)
Inset photograph of Hank Pyzdrowski (courtesy of Hank Pyzdrowski)
Inset photograph of Jack Yusen with Capt. Paul X. Rinn (collection of Jack Yusen)

Page Sixteen
Photograph of the Taffy 3 memorial at Ft. Rosencrans National Cemetery (courtesy of the USS *St. Lo* CVE-63/VC-65 Survivors Association)

Index

Archer, Earl "Blue," 173–74, 236–37, 239, 246–47, 411–12
Avenger (TBM) torpedo bombers, 74–76, 77–78, 80–81, 83–88, 127, 191, 310, 365

Ballinger, Richard, 419
Ban, Masami, 108–9, 111
Barbey, Daniel E., 211, 393
Barrett, Myles, 262, 263, 303, 305–6, 411
Barry, Joe, 370
Bassett, Burt, 188–89
Baxter, James A., 393–94, 397, 400
Bebb, Edwin, 47
Bechdel, Jack, 55, 184–85, 205, 374, 375
Benjamin, Red, 184
Benson, William S., 59
Beresonsky, Harold, 207, 346, 380
Berkey, Russell S., 103, 110
Bertelli, Angelo, 21
Beyer, A. F., Jr., 261, 263–64
Billie, Robert, 145, 215, 259, 341, 380
Bisbee, George, 290–91
Block, Edward, 50, 204, 341
Blue, Sam, 36, 288, 296, 327
Bocar, Juan, 399–400
Bogan, Gerald F., 63–64, 122, 127, 129
Borries, Buzz, 187
Boulton, James, 269
Bowers, Ken, 347, 387
Bray, George, 10–12, 20–21, 149
and enemy attacks, 295–96, 298–99
and rescue, 391, 394–95
in the water, 333, 361, 363, 377, 379–80, 388–89
Breeding, Ed, 169, 170

Brooks, William C., 76, 78–81, 323–24, 424
background of, 84
before battle, 82–89, 91, 132–34
and enemy ships, 134–41, 159, 324, 364–65, 366–67
Navy Cross to, 416
Brown, R. W. (PT 493), 107
Browne, Robert, 204, 341, 342
Budnick, Larry, 84, 170–71, 192–93, 314, 355
Burke, Arleigh, 129, 418
Burnett, Clyde, 51–52, 55, 146, 183–84, 205, 206, 316
Burton, Harold, 24
Burton, Lee, 146
Burton, William S., 24–25, 149, 254, 286, 361
Buzbee, James, 53, 178

Campbell, Chuck, 376
Cantrell, Frank, 329, 361, 385
Capano, Patsy, 173, 236–37
Carlsen, Verner, 419
Carney, Robert B. "Mick," 129, 214
Carr, George, 425–26
Carr, Paul Henry, 287, 288, 295–96, 300, 331–32, 335, 423, 426
Carter, Clint, 178, 180–81, 273–74, 315, 347–48, 376
Carver, Bill, 248
Cassidy, William F., 110
Cayo, Howard, 325, 378, 381–82, 389
Chastain, Bob, 181, 209, 347, 348
Check, Joseph, 207–8, 347
Ciolek, John S., 322
Claggett, Bladen D., 120
Clark, J. J. "Jocko," 61

Cochran, Jesse, 162, 180, 208, 216–17, 339, 340, 374
Coffelt, Hugh, 223, 230, 282–83
Coleman, Donald A. (*Johnston*), 315
Coleman, Lieutenant (*Hoel*), 228, 231–32
Comet, Bud, 31–33, 335–37, 361, 418–19, 427
Compomizzo, Marvin, 230
Congressional Medal of Honor, 416
Conway, John, 372
Cooper, James, 374, 376
Copeland, Harriet, 26, 410
Copeland, Robert W., 424
  abandoning ship, 299–302, 325–31, 333–34
  after the war, 410–11
  before battle, 4, 8, 9, 11, 24–26, 28, 29–31, 34, 35–36, 116, 134
  crossing the equator, 39–42
  death of, 422–23
  and enemy attacks, 283–84, 285–88, 293–300
  and enemy ships, 148–51, 198–200, 253–55, 289
  enlistment of, 22–24
  family of, 26
  and his ship, 45, 327, 328–30, 336; *see also* USS *Samuel B. Roberts*
  Navy Cross to, 416
  and rescue, 390–91, 395–96, 408, 409
  ship named for, 422
  in the water, 361, 363, 372–73, 378, 381–86, 389–91, 411
Coward, Jesse G., 107–8, 113
Craven, Howard, 374
Cravens, Alan, 216
Crawforth, Holly, 170, 352
Creamer, Jack, 222, 225, 228, 282
Critz, Fielden, 218
Crocker, Robert, 189, 193
Cronin, Charles, 297, 385
Cuming, Bill, 266–67

Dahlen, Walter "Bucky," 271
Dale, John, 365, 366
Davis, Colonel, 400
Davison, Ralph E., 127, 129
Deal, Bob, 256, 338
Dent, Mel, 389, 392
DeSpain, Bobby, 261

Dethlefs, Neil:
  and enemy attacks, 259–60
  and enemy ships, 162–63, 348
  and rescue, 398–400
  in the water, 346–47, 348, 397–98
DiGardi, Ed, 163, 184, 204, 226, 256, 374
Dilello, Marcellino, 225
Dillard, Berman, 193, 369
Dix, John C. W., 67, 146–48
  and enemy attacks, 225, 232, 262, 283
  in the water, 305, 306, 307
  writings of, 197, 223–25, 260–61, 304, 305, 307
Dixon, Joel, 205
Doolittle, Jimmy, 2
Dotson, Joseph, 397
Doubrava, Herbert, 147, 224–25
Downs, Joe, 85, 87, 88, 89, 132, 134–36, 139–41, 324, 366–67, 424

Emirau, canoe incident, 304–5
Erwin, Doctor, 31, 36
Evans, Ernest E.:
  abandoning ship, 340, 341, 343–44
  and enemy attacks, 203–10, 216, 226–27, 267–68, 272, 273, 299, 309, 315–16, 339
  and enemy ships, 159–63, 178, 180, 181–82, 183–85, 198, 254, 264, 270, 274–75, 424
  at Guam, 50–51
  and his men, 49, 51–52, 54–56
  Medal of Honor to, 416
  naval career of, 48–49, 344

Fay, Chester, 262
Fields, Gerald E., 133
Fishburn, Albert, 212
Fitch, Aubrey, 418, 421
Fitzgerald, F. Scott, 60
Forrestal, James, 212
Forrester, Russell, 245
Foster, Glen, 263
Fowler, Richard L., 194, 310, 312–13, 365, 366, 367, 416
Fox, Gordon, 205
Frederickson, Les, 350
Frenn, Willard, 277
Frisch, Jack, 220, 234
Fukudome, Shigeru, 93–94

Garrison, Paul, 189, 241
Gentry, Elbert, 295, 297, 325
Getas, John, 89, 352–54
Gifford, Earl, 244
Gillis, Frank, 184
Goheen, Chalmer, 331–32, 333, 377, 389
Gondaira, Masao, 249
Goodrich, Vince, 334
Gougeon, Roger, 339–40
Gould, Louis, 362
Green, Fred, 146, 223, 225, 228, 232
Gregory, James, 287, 288, 332
Gringheri, Tony, 178
Gurnett, Lloyd, 24, 25, 33, 35–37, 39
    abandoning ship, 325, 328, 331, 333, 336
    and enemy attacks, 300
    in the water, 336, 361, 362, 371, 385

Hagen, Robert C., 49–56, 256
    abandoning ship, 341–42
    after the war, 424
    and enemy attacks, 203, 207, 208, 227, 272, 273, 288, 316
    and enemy ships, 159–61, 163, 178–82, 183, 185, 218–19, 264, 343
    and shakedown cruise, 54–55
    in the water, 342, 374
Hall, Royce, 171–72, 187, 190–92
Halliday, Gil, 238
Halpern, Sam, 245
Halsey, William F., Jr. "Bull," 5, 61, 85, 119
    errors in judgment of, 417–18
    Ozawa's ships as decoy for, 128–31, 132, 214, 318, 371, 405
    and Sibuyan Sea battle, 121–23, 126, 132
    and Taffy 3's predicament, 138–39, 149, 211, 212–14, 365, 406, 415, 417–18
    and Third Fleet, 6, 93, 94–96, 97–98, 100, 102, 120, 121–22, 126–31, 134, 405
Hansen, Sig, 199, 370
Hara, Tameichi, 116
Harrington, Red, 34, 336
Haskins, Willie, 171, 190, 192
Hathaway, Amos T., 46–49, 199, 219,

248–52, 254, 256, 267–72, 410, 416, 424
Heinmiller, George, 238
Heinritz, Donald, 277–78
Hellcat (F6F) fighter planes, 127
Helldiver (SB2C) dive-bombers, 127
Henson, Harry, 376
Heric, Don, 265–66
Heriford, Glenn, 316
Himelright, George, 53, 178
Hippe, Ken, 238
HMAS *Arunta,* 107
HMAS *Perth,* 12
Hock, Wallace, 269
Hofstrander, Francis, 229, 282
Hollenbaugh, Bob, 50, 51–52, 55, 206, 208–9, 215, 339, 341, 343
Holloway, James L. III, 113
Holmes, Jasper, 212
Hood, Clarence, 147, 198, 225, 231, 277
Hoover, Burton, 216
Hopfner, Paul, 238
Howard, Walt, 209
Huxtable, Edward J., Jr., 187–89, 193–94, 236, 266, 416

IJN *Amagi,* 130
IJN *Asagumo,* 108, 113–14
IJN *Asashio-Kagero* class destroyers, 154
IJN *Atago,* 98, 119–20, 318
IJN *Chikuma,* 153, 156, 186, 202, 240, 252, 257, 276, 279, 286–89, 308, 309, 310–12, 317–18, 321, 365, 368
IJN *Chitose,* 95
IJN *Chiyoda,* 95
IJN *Chokai,* 153, 155, 156, 186, 202, 240, 252, 254–55, 257, 276, 279, 308–13, 317–18, 321, 365, 366
IJN *Fuso,* 94, 100, 102, 108–10, 111, 113–14, 117, 124
IJN *Haguro,* 153, 156, 186, 202, 240, 252, 257, 263–64, 276, 279, 308, 309, 311, 316, 320, 321, 365, 420
IJN *Haruna,* 94, 96, 118, 125, 153, 156, 157, 165, 202, 219, 240, 249–52, 279, 311, 317, 320, 365
IJN *Hyuga,* 96
IJN *Ise,* 95
IJN *Katsuragi,* 130
IJN *Kirishima,* 127

IJN *Kongo*, 13, 94, 96, 118, 125, 137, 153, 156, 157, 165, 202, 203, 219, 228, 231, 240, 252, 264, 276, 279, 293, 297, 311, 320, 321, 335
IJN *Kumano*, 153, 156, 177, 179–80, 185, 202, 219, 240, 252, 312n, 318, 342, 368, 420
IJN *Maya*, 98, 120, 122
IJN *Michishio*, 108
IJN *Mikuma*, 12
IJN *Mogami*, 99, 102, 109, 112–13
IJN *Musashi*, 12, 94, 96, 98, 118, 120, 121–24, 125, 126, 130, 131, 132, 257, 317, 318, 407
IJN *Myoko*, 122, 130
IJN *Nachi*, 112–13
IJN *Nagato*, 94, 96, 118, 124, 125, 153, 155–57, 165, 186, 202, 219, 240, 251, 252, 279, 307, 311, 321, 366–67
IJN *Noshiro*, 154, 155–58, 165, 202, 240, 252, 273, 279, 311, 321
IJN *Shigure*, 102, 107, 108, 111, 113, 116, 349
IJN *Suzuya*, 153, 156, 185, 202, 219, 240, 252, 311, 312n, 317–18, 321
IJN *Takao*, 98, 120, 124
IJN *Tone*, 153, 156, 186, 202, 240, 252, 257, 276, 279, 291, 292, 308, 311, 312, 316, 320, 321, 365, 420, 421
IJN *Yahagi*, 124, 154, 156, 158, 165, 202, 252, 273–74, 279, 311, 320, 321, 407
IJN *Yamagumo*, 108
IJN *Yamashiro*, 94, 99–100, 108, 110, 111–12, 117, 124
IJN *Yamato*, 94, 96, 117, 118, 120, 121–22, 122, 125, 132, 138, 153, 155–57, 165, 177, 194, 202, 204, 206, 219, 225, 240, 251, 252, 257, 273, 275, 276, 279, 291, 306–7, 311, 318, 320, 360, 407, 420
IJN *Zuiho*, 95
IJN *Zuikaku*, 92, 95, 130
Inoguchi, Toshihira, 122, 123, 126
Ito, Masanori, 118, 121

James, Duke of York, 105
Japan:
   Doctrine of Decisive Battle, 101, 119
   historians' views of, 419–22
   ships, *see* IJN entries

Japanese Army Air Corps, kamikaze attacks by, 351–54, 370, 371, 406, 407
Japanese Center Force:
   air attacks on, 365–69
   before battle, 117, 118–20, 128, 129
   capability of, 118, 165–66, 206, 219–20, 291
   maps, viii, 156, 202, 252, 279, 311, 321
   off Samar, *see* Samar
   ships, 153–54
   in Sho-1 plan, 96, 100, 118–19, 317
   at Sibuyan Sea, 121–24, 132
   withdrawal of, 264, 273, 274, 320, 321, 323, 346, 349, 350, 364, 367–68, 369
   see also Kurita, Takeo; *specific ships*
Japanese Northern Force:
   as decoy for Halsey, 128–31, 318, 371, 405
   map, viii
   in Sho-1 plan, 95–96
   see also Ozawa, Jisaburo
Japanese Southern Force:
   map, viii
   in Sho-1 plan, 96, 97
   at Surigao Strait, 98, 99–104, 106–14, 118, 120, 130, 132, 148, 168, 349, 365
   see also Nishimura, Shoji
Jensen, Hans, 134
Johnson, Allen, 267, 338–40, 344
Johnson, Douglass P., 63, 70
Jones, Ralph M., 83, 91, 169–71

Kaiser, Henry J., 68–69, 76, 177
Kato, Kenkichi, 123
Katsur, Bill, 294, 386
Keeler, George H., 239
Keighley, Bill "Pops," 173, 236–37
Kennedy, Jack, 424
Kenny, Bob, 172
Kight, Harold L., 65, 66, 220–21, 234–35, 413, 423
Kimura, Masafaku, 272–73, 274–75, 309, 315, 320
King, Ernest J., 417
King, Oscar, 329, 331, 362
Kinkaid, Thomas C., 6, 99
   and rescue attempts, 371, 407–8
   and Seventh Fleet, 98, 128, 132–33, 134, 345, 408

and Taffy 3's predicament, 138–39,
    168, 212–13, 257, 319, 345–46,
    408, 417, 420
Kintberger, Leon S., 45–46, 48, 254
    and abandoning ship, 277–78, 280,
        283, 303–4, 309
    and enemy attacks, 222–25, 231–33,
        260–62, 276–78, 280, 283
    and enemy ships, 197–98, 228
    Navy Cross to, 416
    in the water, 304, 306
Kobe, Yuji, 251
Koepp, George, 70
Koyanagi, Tomiji, 100, 118, 155, 236,
    421
Krueger, Walter, 7
Kudelchuk, John, 382, 389
Kumpunen, Otto, 225
Kupidlowsky, Chester, 294
Kurita, Takeo:
    attack by, 169, 177, 194–95, 225
    before battle, 1, 3, 12, 13, 117,
        118–20, 125–26, 128, 129, 130,
        131, 155–58, 165
    career of, 12–13
    loss of control, 251–53, 257, 273,
        291, 317–20, 366
    off Samar, 139–41, 149, 152, 219,
        236, 240–41
    in Sho-1 plan, 94, 96, 98, 100,
        118–19, 124, 125–26, 317
    at Sibuyan Sea, 121–24, 130, 132,
        177
    withdrawal of, 320, 321, 346, 349,
        350, 365–66, 368, 369, 420–21
    see also Japanese Center Force
Kusaka, Ryunosuke, 94

Labbe, Wilfred, 200
Landreth, Charles, 259, 349, 387–88
Lawler, Joseph T., 122–23
Layton, Edwin T., 212
LeClercq, John, 18, 30, 33, 35, 150,
    297, 300–301, 335, 415–16
Lee, Willis "Ching," 127, 128, 129,
    130, 134, 136, 139, 212–14
Leeson, Robert A., 106–7
Levy, Allison, 393–94
Lewis, David A., 172, 216
Leyte campaign:
    battles of, viii, ix; *see also specific*
        sites
    personnel, ix–xi

significance of, 405–8, 420
start of, 105–14
    see also specific IJN and USS ships
Libby, Luther, 387–88
Liberty ships, 68–69
Lindorff, Everett, 220, 280
Lindsey, J. R., 230
Lischer, J. F., 189, 194
Lively, Harvey, 171, 187, 189–92
Longacre, Harry, 51–52, 274
Lowestoft, Battle of, 105
Lowry, Lynn, 232
Lozano, Roy, 262–63
Lucas, Sam, 196, 222, 230–31
Lupo, Thomas J., 71, 242–44, 368, 412

MacArthur, Douglas, 2, 3, 4–8, 10, 85,
    96, 97, 98, 100, 101, 104, 127–28,
    130, 131, 134, 138–39, 345, 365,
    419
MacBride, George H., 133
Magellan, Ferdinand, 379
Mahan, Alfred Thayer, 46, 319
Maino, Chris, 193
Mayuzumi, Haruo, 291–92, 421–22
McAnally, Roy, 322
McCain, John S., 127, 367–68
McCaskill, Jackson, 294, 390
McClendon, Mac, 271
McClintock, David H., 120
McCormick, William, 364, 366, 367
McGraw, Joseph, 194
McKay, Keith, 225
McKenna, Francis J., 170, 352, 354
McManes, K. M., 107
Meadors, Bill, 249, 250, 268–69, 288
Mercer, Bill, 146, 162, 205, 316, 342,
    346, 375, 376
Merritt, Johnny, 217
Metzger, Herman, 297
Miller, Vernon, 70
Milley, John P., 271, 272
Miranda, Paul, 277–78
Mitscher, Marc A., 62, 81–82, 93, 97,
    121, 127, 129, 257
Moody, Samuel, 209
Moore, Jack:
    and enemy attacks, 300, 302
    and enemy ships, 150–52, 160
    and rescue, 392
    in the water, 336–37, 361, 376–77,
        379, 380, 391
Moran, John, 184

Morison, Samuel Eliot, 82, 129, 224n, 421
Morris, Larry, 230
Moser, Leonard, 70–71, 172–73, 412–13
Mostowy, John, 162, 388
Moylan, Dudley, 18, 33, 35, 148–49, 361, 415, 416
Mullenix, Henry M., 68
Murphy, Jim, 238
Murray, T. O., 364–65, 366, 367

Naito, Masanao, 122
Nakagawa, Toshio, 276
Nakazawa, Tasuku, 101
Nason, Earle, 224
Natter, Charles, 325–26, 362, 371–72
Navy, U.S.:
    air squadrons of, 73–76
    battle line of, 105
    burial at sea, 88–89
    as carrier-based fleet, 59–60, 420–21
    Cook Book of, 65–66
    gunfire of, 115, 206, 289, 310
    Liberty ships, 68–69
    mistakes of high command in, 407–8, 416–18
    names of ships, 73, 418, 422
    personnel, ix–xi
    pilots of, 62–63, 79–89, 91, 194–95, 241, 310, 364–69
    PT boats of, 106–7
    Seventh Fleet, viii, ix, 42, 43, 98, 107–8, 128, 134, 345, 408
    Third Fleet, viii, 6, 93, 94–96, 97–98, 100, 102, 120, 121–22, 124, 126–31, 132, 134, 257, 405
    tin cans of, 43–44
    see also specific ships (USS)
Navy Cross, 416
Nelson touch, 46
Nimitz, Chester W., 5, 6, 97, 127–28, 152, 212–13, 406, 416, 417, 418, 421
Nishimura, Shoji, 13, 345
    death of, 112, 113, 349
    in Sho-1 plan, 94, 96, 124, 125
    in Surigao Strait, 99–104, 106–7, 108, 110–12, 118, 130, 132, 148, 319, 365
Nishimura, Teiji, 99

Norden, Carl, 58, 60
Norimitsu, Saiji, 289, 310, 312
Norris, Jim, 229–30

Oberlin, Joseph W., 70
O'Gorek, Jim, 162, 184, 342
Oldendorf, Jesse B., 8, 42, 119, 134, 139
    in Leyte Gulf, 168, 236, 345–46
    at Surigao Strait, 98, 99, 100, 101, 102–4, 105, 107, 109, 111, 112, 113, 114, 117, 122, 132, 133, 148, 198, 219
    and Taffy 3's predicament, 149, 345–46
Oracz, John, 278
Osborne, Jerry, 361, 392
Osmeña, Sergio, 7
Otani, Tonosuke, 155, 241
Owen, Julian, 55
Owens, Arthur, 248, 250
Ozawa, Jisaburo, 13, 123, 124
    as decoy for Halsey, 128–31, 132, 214, 318, 371, 405
    in Sho-1 plan, 2–3, 94, 95–96
    see also Japanese Northern Force

Parkin, Glenn, 307
Patterson, Charles, 230
Pehl, Milt, 50, 374
Pierson, Verling, 172, 285
Pliska, Joe, 205
Plumb, John, 147, 261
Polk, Marley, 217
Porterfield, Leonard, 238
Potochniak, Tony, 267, 419
Prater, Bob, 261
Pratt, Fletcher, 405
Presidential Unit Citation, 416, 418
Pyle, Ernie, 29, 91
Pyzdrowski, Hank, 266, 290–91, 421

Quinn, John, 230

Reid, J. M., 416
Rhodes, Dusty, 216, 341, 376, 387
Rinn, Paul X., 425–26, 427
Roberts, Earl, 353
Roberts, Everett E. "Bob," 27, 32, 33, 34–35
    abandoning ship, 325, 327–28
    before battle, 4, 25, 31, 116

crossing the equator, 38
and enemy attacks, 295, 297
and enemy ships, 149, 200, 254–55
in the water, 361, 373, 378, 384, 385, 389–90
Roberts, Jack, 25, 27, 150
Roberts, Samuel Booker, Jr., 25, 27
Roby, Richard, 194–95, 369
Rogers, Richard S., 73
Rohde, Dick, 11, 18–20, 21, 326–27, 334, 336–37, 377, 385
Roosevelt, Franklin D., 5, 6, 63, 97, 211–12
Roosevelt, John, 62, 63
Roosevelt, Theodore, 43
Rutter, Bob, 270

Sacco, Ralph, 269
Samar, battle off:
  battle joined, 169–75, 176–82, 183–86, 187–95, 196–201, 202, 203–10, 211–14, 215–27, 228–33, 248–58, 259–64, 265–75, 276–83, 285–89, 308–14, 315–17
  before battle, 117, 145–52, 155, 157–58
  dramatis personae, ix–xi
  maps, viii, 156, 202, 252, 279, 311, 321
  men killed in action, 431–44
  official silence on, 416–17, 422
  ships in, 153–54; see also specific IJN and USS ships
  significance of, 405–6, 426–27
Sammy (mascot), 35–37, 296–97, 327
Sampson, Chuck, 147
Sampson-Schley controversy, 417
Sanders, Bill, 223–25, 277, 288
Santos, Dick, 229, 230, 232, 277
Scafoglio, Vince, 376
Schafer, Dari, 39
Schaffer, George, 329, 331, 334
Scheindele, John, 316
Schmuff, Clayton, 347, 374
Sefton, Bill, 270–71
Serafini, Tullio, 34, 39, 150–51, 326, 390, 391, 408
Shaw, Bill, 400
Sherman, Forrest, 61, 62, 151
Sherman, Frederick C., 127, 129
Shima, Kiyohide, 94, 96, 99, 107, 111, 112, 113, 345

Shinoda, Katsukiyo, 108, 112
Shiraishi, Kazutaka, 157, 177, 179, 185–86, 257
Sho-Go (Victory Operation) plan, 93, 94
Sho-1 plan, 1–3, 12, 94–97, 98, 100–101, 111, 118–19, 124, 125–26, 317, 349, 420
Shroyer, William, 189
Sibuyan Sea, 121–24, 126, 130, 132
Simmons, Vern, 229
Skau, Rudy, 254–55, 361, 389, 390
Smith, Allen W., 368
Smith, "Captain," 399–400
Smith, Charles, 331
Smith, Jacob, 379
Smoot, Roland, 107, 111, 112, 115
Sochor, Bob, 216–18, 343, 347
Sprague, Annabel Fitzgerald, 60
Sprague, Clifton A. F. "Ziggy," 57–65, 119
  after the war, 414–15, 421
  and aviation pioneers, 58–60, 79
  before battle, 132, 133, 134, 136, 137–38, 141
  credit given by, 409–10, 417–18
  death of, 414–15
  and enemy attacks, 210, 214, 220, 236, 250, 273, 323
  and enemy ships, 149, 159, 164, 177, 194, 198, 199, 219, 234, 235–36, 240–41, 420
  on Fanshaw Bay, 63–65, 72, 141, 149, 164
  marriage and family of, 60
  Navy Cross to, 416
  at Pearl Harbor, 60–61
  and rescue attempts, 371, 407–8
  and reunions, 418–19
  as Taffy 3 commander, 63–67, 70, 132, 133, 154, 165–68, 224n, 253, 257, 267–68, 317, 345, 346, 370, 409
  and Wasp, 62–63, 82
Sprague, Thomas L., 61, 133, 167, 371
Spruance, Raymond, 119, 418
Stadler, H., 114
Stansbury, Gilbert, 287, 288
Starks, Don, 388
Staubach, Charles, 329, 336, 372–73
Steinberg, Jules, 409

Stevenson, Tom, 4, 10, 25, 33, 415
abandoning ship, 325–28, 334
and enemy attacks, 295, 300–302
and enemy ships, 149–50
in the water, 334, 336, 361–62, 363,
370, 371, 378–79, 381–82,
384–86
Stewart, Earle "Pop," 395–96
Stewart, Wayne, 267
Stillwell, Louis, 282
Stirling, Elton, 183
Stovall, Bill, 287, 288, 296, 362
Streuter, Louis, 277, 278
Strickland, J. B., 346
Stump, Felix, 167–68, 253, 257,
265–66, 310, 313, 317, 365, 371
Sullivan, Thomas, 146, 184
Surigao Strait, 98, 99–104, 105–14,
117, 118, 120, 122, 130, 132, 133,
148, 168, 198, 219, 365

Tacloban airstrip, 242–46, 317, 369
Taffy 1:
kamikaze attack on, 351
map, viii
and Taffy 3 support, 310, 371
Taffy 2:
map, viii
and Taffy 3 support, 141, 167, 253,
265–66, 310, 313, 317, 365, 421
Taffy 3:
abandoning ships, 277–84, 291–92,
299–302, 303–7, 309, 325–32,
333–36
after the war, 415–19, 422–27
awards and citations to, 416, 418
before battle, 8, 57, 63, 67, 68,
132–34, 137–38
capability of, 28–29, 43–44, 70, 85,
137–38, 154, 165–66, 220–21,
257–58, 291–92, 409–10, 417–18,
421
commander of, see Sprague, Clifton
A. F. "Ziggy"
and enemy attacks, 203–10, 211–14,
215–27, 228–33, 248–58, 259–64,
265–75, 276–83, 285–89,
293–302, 308–14, 315–17
and enemy ships, 139, 149, 159,
162, 164–68, 175, 198, 253
kamikaze attacks on, 351–54, 371
maps, viii, 156, 202, 252, 279, 311,
321

men killed in action, 431–44
off Samar, 148
personnel, x
and rescue, 370–71, 390–92,
393–96, 397–400, 407–8, 415
reunions of, 418–19, 422–27
and sharks, 362–63, 372, 375–76,
377, 378, 380
ships of, 154; see also specific ships
(USS)
significant contribution of, 406
survivors, 359–63, 364, 370–73,
374–77, 378–80, 381–86, 387–92,
401, 408–13
Taromino, Joe, 376
Task Force 34, 128, 134, 136, 138–39,
212–13, 406
Task Force 38, 97, 127
Thomas, William Dow, 46, 47, 48, 278
abandoning ship, 303
and enemy attacks, 225, 228
and enemy ships, 159, 177, 198–99
and life raft, 305
and reunions, 418–19
Thurmond, Willard, 333
Tilley, Jim, 425–26
Tokyo Rose, 83
Toland, John, 224n
Tompkins, Earl, 222
Toyoda, Soemu, 94, 95, 100, 126, 251
Trader, Clarence, 205
Travers, Ray, 32, 78, 85, 88, 135, 137,
139–41, 324, 366
Tropp, Joe, 399–400
Trowbridge, Herbert W. "Bill";
"Lucky," 38–39, 40, 200,
200–201, 255, 293, 295, 297
Truman, Harry S, 418
Turner, Morris, 239
Tyrrell, Frank, 370

Ugaki, Matome, 120, 125–26, 157,
194, 251, 273, 275, 306, 420, 421
Ulmanek, Donald, 232
Urbanski, Stanley, 269, 270
USS Alabama, 128, 149
USS Albert W. Grant, 108, 111, 112,
115
USS Arizona, 126
USS Bache, 107
USS Beale, 107
USS Bennion, 108, 113
USS Birmingham, 130

USS *Boise*, 110, 112
USS *Bryant*, 107
USS *Cabot*, 122, 129
USS *California*, 8, 105, 110
USS *Carr*, 423
USS *Casablanca*-class escort carriers,
  68–69, 76
USS *Clifton Sprague*, 423
USS *Columbia*, 110, 114
USS *Copeland*, 423
USS *Dace*, 98, 120, 122
USS *Daly*, 107, 109, 114
USS *Darter*, 98, 120
USS *Dennis*, 154, 409
  and enemy ships, 199, 253, 263
  maps, 156, 202, 252, 279, 311, 321
  men killed in action, 438
  survivors rescued by, 370, 407
USS *Denver*, 110, 111, 113, 114
USS *Enterprise*, 82, 95, 97, 102, 122,
  130, 149
USS *Essex*, 127
USS *Essex*-class fleet carriers, 70, 155,
  177
USS *Fanshaw Bay*, 122, 154, 412
  before battle, 63–65, 67, 68, 72,
    132, 133, 136, 141
  and enemy ships, 149, 159, 164,
    171–73, 234–36, 323
  first mission of, 69–72
  kamikaze attack on, 352
  maps, 156, 202, 252, 279, 311, 321
  men killed in action, 442
  name of, 73
USS *Fletcher*-class destroyers, 43–44, 52,
  165, 177, 184, 199, 220–21, 310
USS *Franklin*, 102, 127, 149
USS *Franks*, 265, 266
USS *Gambier Bay*, 154
  abandon ship, 291–92, 313–14
  before battle, 68, 133
  dead and injured from, 407, 419,
    443–44
  and enemy attacks, 264, 265–67,
    268, 272, 289, 290–92, 308
  and enemy ships, 159, 187–89
  maps, 156, 202, 252, 279, 311
  off Samar, 146
  sinking, 313–14, 338, 360, 419, 422
  survivors, 359, 360, 394, 396,
    400–401, 405, 419, 423
USS *Haggard*, 265, 266
USS *Hailey*, 265, 266

USS *Halford*, 107
USS *Heermann*, 28, 43, 46–48, 154,
  165, 409
  after the war, 415
  and enemy attacks, 248–53, 268–72,
    309, 407
  and enemy ships, 198, 199, 201,
    219, 221, 226–27, 253, 256–57,
    317, 318, 406
  maps, 156, 202, 252, 279, 311, 321
  men killed in action, 431
  survivors rescued by, 370, 407
USS *Heywood L. Edwards*, 108
USS *Hoel*, 28, 43, 45–46, 47, 48, 67,
  154, 165
  abandon ship, 277–84, 303–7, 309
  dead and injured from, 407, 432–35
  and enemy attacks, 222–27, 229–33,
    250, 260–63, 271, 276–83, 308
  and enemy ships, 146–48, 159,
    177–78, 196–97, 198, 199, 201,
    219, 221, 228, 253, 343, 406
  maps, 156, 202, 252, 279, 311, 321
  sinking, 304, 338, 343, 424
  survivors of, 304–7, 359–60, 394,
    400–401, 405, 423–24
USS *Hornet*, 95
USS *Houston*, 12
USS *Hutchins*, 107, 109
USS *Independence*, 129, 131
USS *Intrepid*, 61, 97, 121–22, 127, 129
USS *Iowa*, 128
USS *John C. Butler*, 154, 370, 407
  and enemy ships, 253, 317
  maps, 156, 202, 252, 279, 311, 321
USS *Johnston*, 154, 165, 256
  abandon ship, 340–44
  before battle, 28, 43, 48–56, 145
  dead and injured from, 407, 435–37
  enemy attacks on, 203–10, 215–19,
    226–27, 250, 259–60, 267–68,
    271, 272, 299, 308, 309, 315–17,
    339–40, 343
  and enemy ships, 145–46, 159–63,
    178–82, 183–85, 188, 198, 253,
    270, 273–75, 276, 318, 320, 343,
    348, 406
  maps, 156, 202, 252, 279, 311, 321
  shakedown cruise of, 54–55
  sinking, 338–44, 346–47, 348, 360
  survivors of, 343, 346–49, 359–60,
    374–76, 380, 387–88, 394,
    400–401, 405, 423–24

USS *Kadashan Bay*, 134, 365
USS *Kalinin Bay*, 154
  before battle, 63, 68
  enemy attacks on, 239–40, 322
  and enemy ships, 159, 173–74,
    236–38
  maps, 156, 202, 252, 279, 311, 321
  men killed in action, 441–42
USS *Killen*, 107
USS *Kitkun Bay*, 154
  before battle, 68
  and enemy ships, 159, 310
  kamikaze attack on, 351–52
  maps, 156, 202, 252, 279, 311, 321
  men killed in action, 442
USS *Leutze*, 108
USS *Lexington*, 59, 60–61, 68, 76, 127
USS *Liscome Bay*, 67–68, 70, 72, 240,
  322
USS *Louisville*, 112, 113
USS *Marcus Island*, 323–24, 350,
  364–65
USS *Maryland*, 7, 8, 105, 110
USS *McDermut*, 107, 108
USS *McGowan*, 104, 107, 108
USS *Melvin*, 107, 108, 109
USS *Midway*, 63, 76–77, 83, 89–90; *see
  also* USS *St. Lo*
USS *Mississippi*, 7, 103, 105, 109
USS *Missouri*, 28
USS *Monssen*, 107, 108
USS *Newcomb*, 108
USS *New Jersey*, 128, 138, 213
USS *Oklahoma*, 126
USS *Pennsylvania*, 8, 105
USS *Phoenix*, 110
USS *Portland*, 113
USS *Princeton*, 130, 240
USS *Raymond*, 154, 196
  and enemy attacks, 224n
  and enemy ships, 253, 263–64
  maps, 156, 202, 252, 279, 311, 321
  survivors rescued by, 370, 407
USS *Remey*, 107, 108
USS *Richard P. Leary*, 108
USS *Robinson*, 107
USS *Rowell*, 78–79
USS *Samuel B. Roberts*, 154
  abandon ship, 299–302, 325–32,
    333–36
  before battle, 3–4, 8–12, 22–35, 37,
    67, 116, 134
  building of, 17–18

  commissioning of, 21, 26
  crossing the equator, 38–42
  dead and injured from, 407, 438–39
  and enemy attacks, 254, 285–89,
    293–302, 308, 309
  and enemy ships, 148–52, 198–201,
    219, 221, 226–27, 253–55, 312,
    343, 368
  maps, 156, 202, 252, 279, 311, 321
  name of, 25, 425
  in Persian Gulf (III), 425–26
  shakedown cruise of, 26–27, 30–31
  sinking, 333–36, 338, 343, 360
  survivors of, 333–37, 359, 360–63,
    370–73, 378–80, 381–86, 388–92,
    394, 396, 400–401, 405, 408–13,
    422–24
USS *Saratoga*, 59, 68, 76
USS *Seawolf*, 79
USS *Shelton*, 78
USS *St. Lo*, 154
  abandon ship, 354
  before battle, 68, 76–78, 89–90,
    132–33, 135
  dead and injured from, 407, 439–41
  and enemy ships, 159, 169–71, 177,
    235, 322, 350–54
  kamikaze attack on, 351–54, 370,
    407
  maps, 156, 202, 252, 279, 311, 321
  pilots from, 132–33, 135, 169–71,
    354
  sinking, 354
  survivors of, 354, 370, 405, 407–8
USS *Tangier*, 61, 168
USS *Tennessee*, 8, 105, 110
USS *Wachapreague*, 107
USS *Wasatch*, 98, 345
USS *Washington*, 127, 128, 149
USS *Wasp*, 61, 62, 63, 82, 127, 367
USS *West Virginia*, 7, 8, 105, 110
USS *White Plains*, 154
  before battle, 63, 68
  and enemy ships, 159, 164, 176,
    235, 309, 368
  maps, 156, 202, 252, 279, 311, 321
  men killed in action, 441
USS *Wolverine*, 84
USS *Yorktown*, 61
U.S. Strategic Bombing Survey, 421

Vadnais, Orin, 346, 400
Van Brunt, Bernard, 89–90, 324

Van Brunt, Tom, 323, 352, 424
  before battle, 84, 87, 89–90, 91, 133
  at Dulag, 354–55
  and enemy ships, 237, 324, 350–54
  Navy Cross to, 416
VC-65 air squadron, 83–85, 91, 135,
  169–71, 322, 407, 441
VC-68 air squadron, 73–76, 187, 242,
  244–46, 442
Vieweg, Walter V. R., 187, 291, 313–14
Vilmer, Louis, Jr., 189

Waldrop, Leonard "Tex," 84, 91, 322,
  353, 416
Walker, Jack, 374, 376
Wallace, Cullen, 335–36, 337, 361
Wallace, Gene, 30
Walton, Bud, 280
War and Remembrance (Wouk), 406,
  420
Washington Naval Treaty, 59, 101, 121,
  309
Weigand, Wally, 346–47, 348
Welch, Ellsworth, 49, 56, 146
  abandoning ship, 341, 342
  and enemy attacks, 204, 205, 316
  and enemy ships, 160, 185
  in the water, 342–43, 347, 374, 375,
  380

West, Luther, 337, 361
West, Philip L., 217–18
Weyler, George L., 103, 105, 110
Wheaton, Edward, 148, 335–36
Whitaker, Warren, 220, 234
White, Hoyt, 225–26
Whitehead, Richard F., 317
Whitney, Harold, 47, 248–50, 256,
  268, 270–72
Wildcat (FM-2) fighter plane, 86, 133,
  194, 240–41, 365
Williams, Cole, 265–66
Williams, Ted, 44
Williams, Warren, 341
Wilson, Bob, 280–82
Wilson, Hank, 374
Wiltsie, Irving D., 67–68
Woolf, Joe, 316
Worling, Joe, 163, 218, 260
Worrad, Edward, 245, 247
Wouk, Herman, 406, 420

Yamamoto, Isoroku, 2, 100, 103, 104,
  118
Yoakum, Don, 70
Yonai, Mitsumasa, 406
Yusen, Jack, 27–28, 283, 337, 422–23

ABOUT THE AUTHOR

JAMES D. HORNFISCHER is a writer, literary agent, and former book editor. A Phi Beta Kappa graduate of Colgate University, he has graduate business and law degrees from the University of Texas at Austin. He lives in Austin, Texas, with his wife and their three children.

Contact the author at jim@hornfischerlit.com and visit the author's website at www.tincansailorsbook.com.